HISTORY, METAPHORS, FABLES

signale | TRANSFER
german thought in translation

Series editor: Peter Uwe Hohendahl, Cornell University

Signale|*TRANSFER* provides a unique channel for the transmission of critical German-language texts, newly translated into English, through to current debates on theory, philosophy, and social and cultural criticism. *Signale*|*TRANSFER* is a component of the series *Signale: Modern German Letters, Culture and Thought,* which publishes books in literary studies, cultural criticism, and intellectual history. *Signale* books are published under the joint imprint of Cornell University Press and Cornell University Library. Please see http://signale.cornell.edu/.

HISTORY, METAPHORS, FABLES

A Hans Blumenberg Reader

HANS BLUMENBERG

Edited, translated, and with an
introduction by Hannes Bajohr,
Florian Fuchs, and Joe Paul Kroll

A Signale Book

CORNELL UNIVERSITY PRESS AND CORNELL UNIVERSITY LIBRARY
ITHACA AND LONDON

Published by arrangement with Suhrkamp Verlag Berlin.

Original German-language articles and essays © Suhrkamp Verlag Berlin.

Introduction and English-language translations © Cornell University Press except:

Chapter 6: Levin, David Michael, ed., *Modernity and the Hegemony of Vision*, © 1993 by the Regents of the University of California. Published by the University of California Press.

Chapter 8: Baynes, Kenneth, James Bohman, and Thomas McCarthy, eds., *After Philosophy: End or Transformation?*, pp. 428–457, © 1986 Massachusetts Institute of Technology, by permission of The MIT Press.

Chapter 13: Blumenberg, Hans, and Anna Werz, trans., "'Imitation of Nature': Toward a Prehistory of the Idea of the Creative Being," in *Qui Parle* 12, no. 1 (2000): 17–54. © 2000, Editorial Board, *Qui Parle*. All rights reserved. Republished by permission of the copyright holder and the present publisher, Duke University Press (www.dukeupress.edu).

Chapter 20: "The Concept of Reality and the Possibility of the Novel," from *New Perspectives in German Literary Criticism: A Collection of Essays*, Amacher, Richard E., and Victor Lange, eds., David Henry Wilson and others, trans. © 1979, Princeton University Press.

Chapter 21: Blumenberg, Hans, and David Adams, trans., "Pensiveness," *Caliban* 6 (1989): 51–55. © 1989, Presses universitaires du Midi.

All used by permission.

Chapter 12 first appeared as: Blumenberg, Hans, and Joe Paul Kroll, "The Relationship between Nature and Technology as a Philosophical Problem," *Graduate Faculty Philosophy Journal* 40, no. 1 (2019): 19–30, DOI: 10.5840/gfpj20194012

Cornell University Press and Cornell University Library gratefully acknowledge the College of Arts & Sciences, Cornell University, for support of the Signale series.

First published 2020 by Cornell University Press and Cornell University Library

Library of Congress Cataloging-in-Publication Data
Names: Blumenberg, Hans, author. | Bajohr, Hannes, editor, translator. |
    Fuchs, Florian, 1987– editor, translator. | Kroll, Joe Paul,
    1979– editor, translator.
Title: History, metaphors, fables : a Hans Blumenberg reader / Hans
    Blumenberg ; edited, translated, and with an introduction by Hannes
    Bajohr, Florian Fuchs, and Joe Paul Kroll.
Description: Ithaca : Cornell University Press : Cornell University
    Library, 2020. | Series: Signale transfer : German theory in translation |
    Includes bibliographical references and index.
Identifiers: LCCN 2019032673 (print) | LCCN 2019032674 (ebook) |
    ISBN 9781501732829 (hardcover) | ISBN 9781501747984
    (paperback) | ISBN 9781501747991 (epub) | ISBN 9781501748004 (pdf)
Subjects: LCSH: Blumenberg, Hans—Translations into English. |
    Philosophy, German—20th century.
Classification: LCC B3209.B832 E5 2020 (print) |
    LCC B3209.B832 (ebook) | DDC 193—dc23
LC record available at https://lccn.loc.gov/2019032673
LC ebook record available at https://lccn.loc.gov/2019032674

CONTENTS

HISTORY, METAPHORS, FABLES

Hans Blumenberg: An Introduction

HANNES BAJOHR, FLORIAN FUCHS, AND JOE PAUL KROLL

The philosopher Hans Blumenberg (1920–1996) has, in the quarter-century since his death, become a modern classic in his native Germany, making him one of the most important philosophers of the postwar period. His reception in the English-speaking world has been slower: even though the three major volumes *The Legitimacy of the Modern Age*, *Genesis of the Copernican World*, and *Work on Myth* have been available in translation since the 1980s,[1] it was only during the previous decade that the life and work of Blumenberg began to move past the realms of academic rumor or a secret reserved for the initiated. Through a host of more recent translations—among them such central texts as *Paradigms for a*

---

1. Hans Blumenberg, *The Legitimacy of the Modern Age*, trans. Robert M. Wallace (Cambridge, MA: MIT Press, 1983); Hans Blumenberg, *The Genesis of the Copernican World*, trans. Robert M. Wallace (Cambridge, MA: MIT Press, 1987); Hans Blumenberg, *Work on Myth*, trans. Robert M. Wallace (Cambridge, MA: MIT Press, 1985).

Metaphorology or *Care Crosses the River*—Blumenberg's versatility, in substance and style, has become ever clearer.[2] All these works are milestones on an intellectual path that is nevertheless still hard to see as a whole for an anglophone audience. *History, Metaphors, Fables: A Hans Blumenberg Reader* offers a guide along this path: it contains his most important philosophical essays, many of which provide explicit discussions of what in the large tomes often remain only tacit presuppositions and often act as précis for them, as well as selections of his nonacademic writings (which were frequently more literary and took the form of essay-like shorter pieces published in newspapers and literary magazines). By presenting its principal themes, the *Reader* thus provides an overview of Hans Blumenberg's work, which spans almost twenty books published during his lifetime and a steady flow of further volumes from his extensive archive. It also offers at least a glimpse of the richness and originality of the thought he brought to bear on a staggering variety of topics in smaller forms.

Moreover, any introduction to Blumenberg has to grapple not only with the unwieldiness of his work but with the additional problem that he cannot be reduced to one overarching concept, method, or field of study, which partly explains why his work has not founded a particular school of thought. Blumenberg was, in Isaiah Berlin's terms, a "fox," and as such eludes easy categorization. The topics he covered include but are not limited to modernity and secularization, the philosophy of history, the history of science and technology, language philosophy and rhetoricity, aesthetics and literary theory, philosophical anthropology, theology, and mythical thought, to name just a few. Instead of providing an exhaustive interpretation of Blumenberg's oeuvre, which must be reserved for detailed

---

2. Hans Blumenberg, *Paradigms for a Metaphorology*, trans. Robert Savage (Ithaca, NY: Cornell University Press, 2010); Hans Blumenberg, *Care Crosses the River*, trans. Paul Fleming (Stanford, CA: Stanford University Press, 2010). See also Hans Blumenberg, *The Laughter of the Thracian Woman: A Protohistory of Theory*, trans. Spencer Hawkins (New York: Bloomsbury, 2015); Hans Blumenberg, *Lions*, trans. Kári Driscoll (London: Seagull, 2018); Hans Blumenberg, *St. Matthew Passion*, trans. Paul Fleming and Helmut Müller-Sievers (Ithaca, NY: Cornell University Press, 2020).

studies, we shall give only a compact summary of his life and work, and clarify the selection and makeup of this *Reader*. With this volume in hand as a guide, we hope that new audiences can begin to discover Blumenberg's extraordinary intellectual path and his versatility, erudition, and inquisitiveness. Readers already acquainted with Blumenberg will find new light shed on familiar questions, often from surprising angles.

Biographical Background

Hans Blumenberg was born on July 13, 1920, in Lübeck on the Baltic coast of northern Germany into a well-to-do Catholic household.[3] His father dealt in devotional prints and art objects, and supported his only son's intellectual curiosity. Blumenberg attended a humanistic *Gymnasium* in his hometown and appears to have been a gifted pupil with interests ranging from languages and philosophy to the natural sciences. He was twelve years old when the National Socialists took power in 1933 and the school's liberal principal was replaced with a party member. In the following years, Blumenberg became increasingly marginalized: His mother was of Jewish origin (she had converted to Catholicism) and after the Nuremberg Laws of 1935 went into effect, Blumenberg was classified and harassed as "*Mischling* [mongrel] of the first degree" and a "half Jew." After his graduation in 1939, he was barred from studying at a public university and instead attended Catholic institutions of higher education: first the theological seminary in Paderborn and

---

3. See the most recent biographical summaries: Kurt Flasch, *Hans Blumenberg: Philosoph in Deutschland. Die Jahre 1945–1966* (Frankfurt am Main: Klostermann, 2017); Angus Nicholls, *Myth and the Human Sciences: Hans Blumenberg's Theory of Myth* (New York: Routledge, 2015), 11–14; Ada Kadelbach, "'Mißachtung' und 'Versöhnungsversuch': Hans Blumenberg und Lübeck," in *Hans Blumenberg beobachtet: Wissenschaft, Technik und Philosophie*, ed. Cornelius Borck (Freiburg: Alber, 2013), 254–271. See also Blumenberg's only explicitly autobiographical text about his youth in Lübeck: Hans Blumenberg, "An Georg Rosenthal erinnernd," in *Katharineum zu Lübeck: Festschrift zum 450jährigen Bestehen, 19. März 1981*, ed. Bund der Freunde des Katharineums (Lübeck: Bund der Freunde des Katharineums, 1981), 55–57.

then the Jesuit college St. Georgen in Frankfurt. While focused on scholastic and neo-Thomist philosophy, St. Georgen also offered a varied philosophical curriculum that included German idealism as well as contemporary existential philosophy. With regulations for *Mischlinge* becoming stricter, Blumenberg had to quit for good by the end of 1940.

After first trying to continue his studies privately while helping in his father's business, he was forced to work in a sector essential to the war effort. In 1943, he entered the Dräger factory, which, among other things, produced gas masks and equipment for submarines. Heinrich Dräger helped *Mischlinge* by employing them in different posts in his business, and intervened several times when the Gestapo tried to apprehend them at his factories.[4] However, even Dräger could not prevent Blumenberg's seizure during "Aktion Hase" in February 1945, an operation by the Nazi engineering group Organisation Todt to draft forced laborers, and his deportation to the labor camp at Zerbst near Dessau. When the camp was dissolved by Soviet troops on April 6, 1945, Blumenberg managed to flee and went into hiding with the family of his future wife, waiting out the rest of the war.

In the fall of 1945, trying to make up for lost time, Blumenberg enrolled at the University of Hamburg to study philosophy, Greek philology, and German literature. His teacher was Ludwig Landgrebe (1902–1991), a former assistant to Edmund Husserl. Blumenberg followed him to the University of Kiel to write, under Landgrebe's supervision, his first and second dissertations (the latter being the *Habilitation* allowing access to a professorship) in rapid succession in 1947 and 1950. During this period, Blumenberg had already begun to write shorter articles for newspapers and academic journals. His very first philosophical publication, "**The Linguistic**

---

4. Angus Nicholls has shown that Dräger was nonetheless "a deeply ambivalent figure," employing forced laborers as well as profiting directly from the war production while helping certain members of his staff, and even giving "6,000 Reichsmarks to Blumenberg immediately following the war, which then enabled Blumenberg to finance the writing of his doctoral dissertation." See Nicholls, *Myth and the Human Sciences*, 12.

Reality of Philosophy" (1946/47),[5] written before Heidegger's "Letter on Humanism" was published, stands out both in the thematic focus that would remain central for his work—the necessary intertwinement of language and history—and in setting the stage for Blumenberg's coming to terms with the two dominant figures of phenomenology, Heidegger and Husserl.

The Qualifying Theses

Heidegger and Husserl also inform Blumenberg's theses, which until 1960 remained his only book-length works. The dissertation, "Contributions to the Problem of Primordiality of Medieval Scholastic Ontology,"[6] brings Blumenberg's early neo-Scholastic education to bear on Martin Heidegger's critical history of Western ontological thought. Already in *Being and Time*, Heidegger had lamented what he later came to call a "forgetfulness of being," expressed in the claim that the Middle Ages had not developed a "primordial" concept of being,[7] which he had famously found in the Pre-Socratics. Against this notion, Blumenberg pits the divine "illumination" of the high-medieval Augustinian tradition as an alternative but nonetheless genuine expression of a primordial experience of being. Although the dissertation criticizes a detail of Heidegger's historical interpretation, it is nevertheless articulated wholly in the language of his fundamental ontology. This is true of the *Habilitation* as well. "The Ontological Distance: An Investigation into the Crisis of Husserl's Phenomenology" widens the scope and confronts Heidegger's project with Husserlian transcendental phenomenology as rival

---

5. Originally published as Hans Blumenberg, "Die sprachliche Wirklichkeit der Philosophie," *Hamburger Akademische Rundschau* 1, no. 10 (1946/47): 428–431. In this introduction, texts that appear in this *Reader* are set in boldface, followed by the publication date.

6. Hans Blumenberg, "Beiträge zum Problem der Ursprünglichkeit der mittelalterlich-scholastischen Ontologie" (PhD diss., University of Kiel, 1947). In this introduction, the titles of untranslated works are provided in English in the text with their original title given in a footnote.

7. Martin Heidegger, *Being and Time*, trans. John Macquarrie and Edward Robinson (Oxford: Blackwell, 1962), 43 (German, p. 22).

ways of grasping the world.[8] The two extremes of the "ontological distance"—Husserl's ontology of essence (*Wesensontologie*), which stands for the distanced attitude of the sciences, and Heidegger's ontology of existence (*Existenzontologie*), which articulates a vision of *Dasein*'s absolute immediacy to the world—ultimately appear deficient to Blumenberg, though his sympathies still appear to lie with Heidegger. But instead of offering a third position, Blumenberg takes a step back. For him, the oscillation between these poles of world-relation are contingent historical possibilities that can be traced throughout the course of philosophy.[9]

Soon after Blumenberg's *Habilitation*, these critical undertones become more apparent and he begins to distance himself from Heidegger. Between the mid-1950s until the mid-1970s, there is no mention of Heidegger in virtually any of Blumenberg's texts. This shift of interest and philosophical alignments is a probable reason he published neither his dissertation nor his *Habilitation*.[10] With this farewell to Heidegger, Blumenberg turned toward a non-ontological view of history. In his interrogation of the Western intellectual tradition, he increasingly confronted the questions, already hinted at in "The Linguistic Reality of Philosophy," of how history manifests itself in language and how these manifestations allow an inference to past realities. That reality itself has a history is an assumption Blumenberg first formulated in these theses. While the Heideggerian "history of being" may be one of its inspirations, a more frequently cited source can be found in Husserl's concept of the "life-world" as the unreflected "pre-givenness" of the world, which is explicated in his *The Crisis of European Sciences and Transcendental Phenom-*

---

8.   Hans Blumenberg, "Die ontologische Distanz: Eine Untersuchung über die Krisis der Phänomenologie Husserls" (*Habilitation* diss., University of Kiel, 1950).

9.   The most detailed discussion of the qualifying theses to date can be found in Flasch, *Blumenberg*, chaps. 5 and 6. See also Felix Heidenreich, *Mensch und Moderne bei Hans Blumenberg* (Munich: Fink, 2005), chap. 2; Oliver Müller, *Sorge um die Vernunft: Hans Blumenbergs phänomenologische Anthropologie* (Paderborn: Mentis, 2005), chap. B1; Philipp Stoellger, *Metapher und Lebenswelt: Hans Blumenbergs Metaphorologie als Lebensweltthermeneutik und ihr religionsphänomenologischer Horizont* (Tübingen: Mohr Siebeck, 2000), chap. IIA.

10.   According to Blumenberg's publisher, Suhrkamp, the theses are scheduled to appear as books in the coming years.

enology.[11] Blumenberg adapts the concept of life-world in many, and not always necessarily compatible, ways, but one of its outgrowths is what he calls the "concept of reality" (*Wirklichkeitsbegriff*), which he theorized repeatedly during the course of his career. One could characterize the concept of reality as the historicized version of Husserl's life-world: concepts of reality prescribe what, within a given historical period, can be thought of as real. Often present only beneath the surface of Blumenberg's major works, the concept of reality is a tool of enduring importance for his thought, making appearances not just in his explicitly historical writings but also in his political theory, his aesthetics, and his literary theory.

Branching Out

Having received his *venia legendi* ("permission to read"; that is, to lecture as a professor) with his second thesis, Blumenberg remained in Kiel as an assistant professor (*wissenschaftlicher Mitarbeiter*) until 1958. The 1950s mark an exploratory period in his oeuvre. He worked on a broad range of topics and in a broad range of styles and genres, and laid out numerous threads that he, sometimes with significant delay, would take up again in the course of his career. One of them was his increasing interest in the history of science for his conception of intellectual history. "Cosmos and System: On the Genesis of the Copernican World" (1957),[12] to give only one example of the persistence of questions and concerns in Blumenberg's oeuvre, focuses on the epochal break marked by Copernicus and takes up the issue of historical ruptures and epistemic changes. The

---

11. Edmund Husserl, *The Crisis of European Sciences and Transcendental Phenomenology: An Introduction to Phenomenological Philosophy*, trans. David Carr (Evanston, IL: Northwestern University Press, 1970). Because of Landgrebe's intimate knowledge of Husserl's papers (he spent time in the archive in Leuven during the war), Blumenberg was acquainted with Husserl's discussion of the life-world from the last part of *Crisis*, even though it was not published until 1954.

12. Hans Blumenberg, "Kosmos und System: Aus der Genesis der kopernikanischen Welt," *Studium Generale* 10, no. 2 (1957): 61–80.

topic is expanded on in the 1965 collection *The Copernican Turn*,[13] and went on to find its grandest formulation in *The Genesis of the Copernican World* of 1975.[14]

The project that may have been the most coherently pursued by Blumenberg in the 1950s was an ambitious philosophy of technology. It was given programmatic status in the text **"The Relation between Nature and Technology as a Philosophical Problem"** (1951),[15] Blumenberg's first lecture as an assistant professor in Kiel. Still tinged with the Heideggerian vocabulary of being but skeptical of his negative view of technology, Blumenberg interleaves the historical status of technology with changes in the interpretation of reality. In human creative power he finds a mark of the Modern Age, and in this discussion a strain of thought emerges that soon leads him to the associated question of aesthetics. In **"'Imitation of Nature': Toward a Prehistory of the Idea of the Creative Being"** (1957),[16] Blumenberg traces how the conceptual history of *technē*, referring both to technology and art, only at the end of the Middle Ages allows for a human capacity to bring something radically new into the world. Although this epochal schema prefigures that of *The Legitimacy of the Modern Age* and points to the engagement with human self-assertion and curiosity in the next decade, Blumenberg's interest in technology reaches an analytical high point in the 1963 essay **"Phenomenological Aspects on Life-World and Technization."**[17] Here, Blumenberg articulates his reception of Husserl's "life-world" most succinctly and applies it in the service of a phenomenology

---

13. Hans Blumenberg, *Die kopernikanische Wende* (Frankfurt am Main: Suhrkamp, 1965).

14. Blumenberg, *Genesis of the Copernican World*.

15. Originally published as Hans Blumenberg, "Das Verhältnis von Natur und Technik als philosophisches Problem," *Studium Generale* 4, no. 8 (1951): 461–467.

16. Originally published as Hans Blumenberg, "'Nachahmung der Natur': Zur Vorgeschichte der Idee des schöpferischen Menschen," *Studium Generale* 10, no. 5 (1957): 266–283; republished in *Wirklichkeiten in denen wir leben: Aufsätze und eine Rede* (Stuttgart: Reclam, 1981), 55–103. This book is Blumenberg's only self-edited volume of essays.

17. Originally published as Hans Blumenberg, "Lebenswelt und Technisierung unter Aspekten der Phänomenologie," *Filosofia* 14, no. 4 (1963): 855–884; republished in *Wirklichkeiten in denen wir leben*, 7–54.

of technology. Yet before this project could come to fruition in the form of a monograph, Blumenberg appears to have abandoned his philosophy of technology. Only recently have these texts been published in collected form.[18]

The connection between language and epochal formation also remained on Blumenberg's mind, but it was not until 1957 that he explicitly devoted an essay to it. With "**Light as a Metaphor for Truth,**" Blumenberg formulated the seed of the project for which he is, at least in Germany, best known: his "metaphorology."[19] While metaphorology initially seemed to be an extension of conceptual history—a research project aimed at investigating the semantic changes to central concepts of philosophy that is most closely associated with Erich Rothacker, Joachim Ritter, and Reinhart Koselleck[20]—it at the same time called into question the very centrality of concepts and terminologies as the only and authentic bearers of philosophical thought. Instead, it makes the case for studying the role pre- and nonconceptual speech plays in the language of philosophy. Where traditionally theories of truth would be interpreted in terms of their propositional content or logical validity, Blumenberg's article instead looks at the metaphors with which truth is described and which operate, as he puts it in the subtitle, "At the Preliminary Stage of Concept Formation."

Two years later, now a full professor in Hamburg, Blumenberg gave this approach its manifesto with *Paradigms for a Metaphorology* (1960).[21] The "**Introduction**" outlines possible theoretical foundations

---

18. Hans Blumenberg, *Geistesgeschichte der Technik: Mit einem Radiovortrag auf CD*, ed. Alexander Schmitz and Bernd Stiegler (Frankfurt am Main: Suhrkamp, 2009); Hans Blumenberg, *Schriften zur Technik*, ed. Alexander Schmitz and Bernd Stiegler (Berlin: Suhrkamp, 2015).

19. Originally published as "Licht als Metapher der Wahrheit: Im Vorfeld der philosophischen Begriffsbildung," *Studium Generale* 10, no. 7 (1957): 432–447.

20. On Blumenberg's relation to conceptual history, see Elías José Palti, "From Ideas to Concepts to Metaphors: The German Tradition of Intellectual History and the Complex Fabric of Language," *History and Theory* 49, no. 2 (May 2010): 194–211; Christopher D. Johnson, "Blumenberg's 'Huge Field': Metaphorology and Intellectual History," *Intellectual History Review* 22, no. 2 (2012): 289–292.

21. Hans Blumenberg, *Paradigms for a Metaphorology*, trans. Robert Savage (Ithaca: Cornell University Press, 2010). It originally appeared as a special issue of the *Archive for the History of Concepts* (*Archiv für Begriffsgeschichte*) and was

for a metaphorology—most importantly Kant—while its remaining chapters consist of nine fairly distinct studies of specific metaphorological complexes, such as the "mighty" truth, the difference between organic and mechanical background metaphorics, or the metaphorics of geometric symbolism. Their semantic historical behavior permits or resists their transformation into concepts; hence, Blumenberg proposes them as "paradigms" that might help found a systematic metaphorology. By investigating the nonconceptual, yet-to-be-settled semantic layers of emerging terminologies, Blumenberg's metaphorology is concerned less with the truth of metaphysics than with analyzing philosophy's own unthought and shifting foundations. While he concedes that ornamental metaphors may indeed only provide rhetorical flourishes, Blumenberg draws attention to what he calls "absolute metaphors," of which "truth as light" would be an example, which cannot simply be converted back into conceptuality. On the one hand, whole unarticulated world interpretations can be inferred from the use of absolute metaphors; on the other, they provide themselves guidance and have a pragmatic function.

The early 1960s also mark the end of Blumenberg's first career as a writer outside of academia. Only in the 1980s would he return to his role as a feuilletonist and essayist that he played at this time, and then it would be in a different, more idiosyncratic vein. While covering topics as diverse as the dawn of the nuclear age, the introduction of paperback books, or political polling—often published under his pen name, "Axel Colly"[22]— it is his writings on literature that account for the largest share of these texts. His essays, devoted to, among others, Jean-Paul Sartre, Ernst Jünger, Evelyn Waugh, Hans Fallada, Jules Verne, Aldous Huxley, and T. S. Eliot, have only recently been collected in an edited volume.[23] Of particular note is

---

strictly speaking not a separate book, even though it was listed as such in Blumenberg's publications: Hans Blumenberg, "Paradigmen zu einer Metaphorologie," *Archiv für Begriffsgeschichte* 6 (1960): 7–142.

22. *Hans Blumenberg alias Axel Colly: Frühe Feuilletons (1952–1955)*, ed. Alexander Schmitz and Bernd Stiegler, *Neue Rundschau* 129, no. 4 (2018): 5–123.

23. Hans Blumenberg, *Schriften zur Literatur 1945–1958*, ed. Alexander Schmitz and Bernd Stiegler (Berlin: Suhrkamp, 2017).

"The Absolute Father" (1952/53), an essay on Franz Kafka's "Letter to My Father," in which he interprets the overbearing father figure as a "reoccupation" of the absent medieval God, employing a concept that would figure prominently in *Legitimacy*.[24] "The *Mythos and Ethos* of America in the Work of William Faulkner" (1958) anticipates the themes of *Work on Myth* and testifies to Blumenberg's interest in the structure of the novel as a literary genre.[25]

Defending the Modern Age

That Blumenberg should write in the more populist mode of mass media—newspaper articles and radio essays—when developing this unusually large thematic oeuvre suggests a conception of philosophy as a discursive, not always strictly academic, endeavor. It shows how his interest lies in a cultural philosophy in its double sense: as a philosophy that not only addresses cultural issues but also locates its academic and strictly philosophical side within its own cultural environment, which is that of a postmetaphysical modernity. This philosophical ethos also comes to the fore in the speech "World Pictures and World Models" (1961), which Blumenberg gave after he was appointed full professor at the University of Gießen in 1960.[26] In the modern age, the scientific world model and the cultural self-understanding (which in an ironic inversion of Heidegger's use of the term he calls "world picture") are no longer congruent. Philosophy's task is not just to explicate this divergence but also to dismantle remaining monist and exclusive world pictures. Blumenberg, then, locates philosophy's critical function in reducing total expectations

---

24. Originally published as Hans Blumenberg, "Der absolute Vater," *Hochland* 45 (1952/53): 282–284.

25. Originally published as Hans Blumenberg, "Mythos und Ethos Amerikas im Werk William Faulkners," *Hochland* 50 (1958): 234–250. Blumenberg's longer early writings on literature appeared in *Hochland*, a Catholic cultural journal, while he published his shorter pieces mostly in the newspapers *Bremer Nachrichten* and *Düsseldorfer Nachrichten*.

26. Originally published as Hans Blumenberg, "Weltbilder und Weltmodelle," *Nachrichten der Gießener Hochschulgesellschaft* 30 (1961): 67–75.

of meaning—even if, as is true for his later works, modernity's loss of meaning may itself be mourned.

His interpretation of the modern age is thrown into sharper relief in a text that would become the basis for his most famous book, *The Legitimacy of the Modern Age*. Presented in 1962 at the seventh German congress of philosophy, next to talks by luminaries such as Theodor W. Adorno, Eric Voegelin, and Karl Löwith, "**'Secularization': Critique of a Category of Historical Illegitimacy**" (1964) challenges the notion of modernity as the illegitimate appropriation of medieval theological patterns, concepts, and institutions.[27] Against such a substantialist view of history, Blumenberg presents a functional model in which "positions" of past thought systems become vacant and are "reoccupied" with new but unrelated concepts. Eschatology, to give an example, is not secularized into the concept of progress, as Löwith had argued in *Meaning in History* (1949).[28] Instead, once it loses its status as an explanation for the course of history, this function is taken up by the entirely distinct concept of scientific progress.

The Legitimacy of the Modern Age (1st ed., 1966) is built on this core argument but expands it into a far-reaching model for Western history. Taking up many of the themes Blumenberg developed in the preceding decades, it deals with the success of human self-affirmation and creativity against the absolutism of medieval theology, the ban on and the rehabilitation of curiosity from Socrates to Freud, and the impossibility of a clear identification of epochal thresholds—all the while operating with the "concept of reality" without mentioning it in so many words. As in "World Pictures and World Models," *Legitimacy* argues for philosophy's task as making explicit these processes of reception, and thus dismantling inherited but overcome positions—chief among them that history indeed has an identifiable course—instead of reoccupying them

---

27. Originally published as Hans Blumenberg, "'Säkularisation': Kritik einer Kategorie historischer Illegitimität," in *Die Philosophie und die Frage nach dem Fortschritt: Verhandlungen des Siebten Deutschen Kongresses für Philosophie, Münster 1962*, ed. Helmut Kuhn and Franz Wiedmann (Munich: Pustet, 1964), 240–265.
28. Karl Löwith, *Meaning in History* (Chicago: University of Chicago Press, 1949).

anew. *Legitimacy* was a widely discussed and controversial book. Probably the most famous opposition was voiced by Carl Schmitt in *Political Theology II*, who accused Blumenberg of confusing legitimacy with legality, misunderstanding his writing, and propagating the nihilistic hubris of modernity.[29] Both entered into an exchange of letters and their dispute continued in their published work.[30] Taking this and other discussions into account, Blumenberg published a radically rewritten and enlarged version of the book in three parts between 1973 and 1976, which were finally collected in one volume in 1988.[31] It was this expanded version, a palimpsest of numerous reactions, rebuttals, and revisions, and not the original from 1966 that served as the basis of the English translation—a fact that may explain the relative hermeticism of the book.

"Poetics and Hermeneutics" and the "Theory Series"

While *Legitimacy* was certainly Blumenberg's most important publication in the 1960s, he also made an institutional impact on the German intellectual scene. In Gießen, he met the philologists Hans Robert Jauß and Clemens Heselhaus, and together with Wolfgang Iser, they founded Poetics and Hermeneutics (Poetik und Hermeneutik).[32] This interdisciplinary group of humanities scholars

29. Carl Schmitt, *Political Theology II: The Myth of the Closure of any Political Theology*, trans. Michael Hoelzl and Graham Ward (Cambridge: Polity, 2008), 116–130.

30. Hans Blumenberg and Carl Schmitt, *Briefwechsel 1971–1978 und weitere Materialien*, ed. Alexander Schmitz and Marcel Lepper (Frankfurt am Main: Suhrkamp, 2007).

31. As part 3: Hans Blumenberg, *Der Prozess der theoretischen Neugierde* (Frankfurt am Main: Suhrkamp, 1973); as parts 1 and 2: Hans Blumenberg, *Säkularisierung und Selbstbehauptung* (Frankfurt am Main: Suhrkamp, 1974); as part 4: Hans Blumenberg, *Aspekte der Epochenschwelle: Cusaner und Nolaner* (Frankfurt am Main: Suhrkamp, 1976); as a single volume: Hans Blumenberg, *Die Legitimität der Neuzeit: Erneuerte Ausgabe* (Frankfurt am Main: Suhrkamp, 1988).

32. See Anselm Haverkamp, "Nothing Fails Like Success: Poetics and Hermeneutics—A Postwar Initiative by Hans Blumenberg," *MLN* 130, no. 5 (2015): 1221–1241; Julia Amslinger, *Eine neue Form von Akademie: Poetik und Hermeneutik—die Anfänge* (Paderborn: Fink, 2017).

held biannual thematic conferences to discuss, among other things, aesthetic theory, art history, and literary studies, often branching out into the philosophy of history and, later, philosophical anthropology. From the first conference in 1963, Blumenberg occupied a special position in the group and was mainly responsible for its programmatic orientation. Although first presented outside the group's context, "**Socrates and the *objet ambigu***" (1964), a formulation of Blumenberg's ontology of art through an interpretation of Paul Valéry's, served as a lasting reference point for Poetics and Hermeneutics, in which he describes the aesthetic attitude as the result of tolerating an ambiguity the scientific attitude would not allow for.[33] Likewise, the text that opened the first meeting, "**Concept of Reality and the Possibility of the Novel**" (1964), took on an almost programmatic role. In the first public formulation of the concepts of reality, Blumenberg tests their heuristic yield by applying them to the case of the novel as a literary form that is only possible in a world whose reality is neither, as in the Middle Ages, guaranteed by God, nor, as in antiquity, immediately self-evident. "**Speech Situation and Immanent Poetics**" (1966), from the second meeting of Poetics and Hermeneutics, updated Blumenberg's view on language theory. He explicitly aligns himself with hermeneutics and takes a stance against both the ideal language theories of Husserl (and, implicitly, the Vienna Circle) and the language relativism of Benjamin Lee Whorf and ordinary language philosophy.[34] Despite its apparent productivity for him, as the papers Blumenberg presented at the group meetings often were the seed from which his later books sprang, Blumenberg soon retreated from Poetics and Hermeneutics. "Wirklichkeitsbegriff und Wirkungspotential des Mythos" ("The

---

33. Originally published as Hans Blumenberg, "Sokrates und das *objet ambigu*: Paul Valerys Auseinandersetzung mit der Ontologie des ästhetischen Gegenstandes," in *EPIMELEIA: Die Sorge der Philosophie um den Menschen*, ed. Franz Wiedemann (Munich: Pustet, 1964), 285–323.

34. Originally published as Hans Blumenberg, "Sprachsituation und immanente Poetik," in *Immanente Ästhetik—Ästhetische Reflexion: Lyrik als Paradigma der Moderne*, ed. Wolfgang Iser, Poetik und Hermeneutik II (Munich: Fink, 1966), 145–155.

Concept of Reality and the Effective Potential of Myth," 1971),[35] a wide-ranging exploration of myth and anthropology, became the basis for his *Work on Myth*, and from his contribution to the seventh meeting in 1974, where he made a last appearance after a considerable absence, grew *The Laughter of the Thracian Woman* (1987) more than a decade later, which contains his critique of the wide interdisciplinary approach the group had taken in the 1970s.[36]

Blumenberg also exerted influence on the German academic scene in other ways. In 1965, the year he became professor of philosophy at the newly founded University of Bochum, he joined the philosophers Jürgen Habermas and Dieter Henrich and the religious scholar Jacob Taubes as coeditor of the *Theorie* series at his publisher, Suhrkamp. The two-pronged series' aim was to introduce both contemporary theory and classic philosophical texts to a German audience: Thomas S. Kuhn's *The Structure of Scientific Revolutions* was as much part of *Theorie* as a new translation of the writings of Sextus Empiricus.[37] Blumenberg's own impetus seems to have been the promotion of first-time translations of historic texts. At different times and for different publishers, he had edited works by Nicholas of Cusa, Galileo Galilei, and Giordano Bruno—thinkers close to his heart—while also adding extensive introductions.[38] As with

---

35. Hans Blumenberg, "Wirklichkeitsbegriff und Wirkungspotential des Mythos," in *Terror und Spiel: Probleme der Mythenrezeption*, ed. Manfred Fuhrmann, Poetik und Hermeneutik IV (Munich: Fink, 1971), 11–66.

36. Hans Blumenberg, *The Laughter of the Thracian Woman: A Protohistory of Theory*, trans. Spencer Hawkins (London: Bloomsbury, 2015).

37. These books are only given as examples for the two series, *Theorie 1* (the classics) and *Theorie 2* (contemporary philosophy): Thomas Kuhn, *Die Struktur wissenschaftlicher Revolutionen*, trans. Kurt Simon (Frankfurt am Main: Suhrkamp, 1967); Sextus Empiricus, *Pyrrhoniae hypotyposes: Grundriss der pyrrhonischen Skepsis*, trans. and ed. Malte Hossenfelder (Frankfurt am Main: Suhrkamp, 1968).

38. Hans Blumenberg, "Einleitung," in Nikolaus von Cues, *Die Kunst der Vermutung. Auswahl aus den Schriften*, ed. Hans Blumenberg (Bremen: Schünemann, 1957), 7–69; Hans Blumenberg, "Das Fernrohr und die Ohnmacht der Wahrheit," in Galileo Galilei, *Sidereus Nuncius: Nachricht von neuen Sternen*, ed. Hans Blumenberg (Frankfurt am Main: Insel, 1965), 5–73; Hans Blumenberg, "Das Universum eines Ketzers," in Giordano Bruno, *Das Aschermittwochsmahl*, ed. Hans Blumenberg (Frankfurt am Main: Insel, 1969), 7–51.

Poetics and Hermeneutics, his engagement at *Theorie* was short lived, and he left the board of editors in 1970.[39] By the late 1960s, Blumenberg had also grown disillusioned with the toll his administrative duties took on his time and he withdrew increasingly from public life, the lecture circuit, and academic engagements. All of this, as well as the discursive shift toward the Left around 1968, may have played a role in Blumenberg's decision to take up an offer at the University of Münster in 1970. He remained at this comparatively remote and sedate institution until his retirement in 1985.

Philosophical Anthropology

In the 1970s, Blumenberg turned toward a new research interest: philosophical anthropology. Usually traced back to its three main figures, Max Scheler, Helmuth Plessner, and Arnold Gehlen, this specifically German current of thought had considerable academic heft in postwar Germany. A radically diverse school, many of its proponents saw their task in formulating an often scientifically informed, unified philosophy of human beings and their capabilities.[40] Philosophical anthropology's main opponents at the time were adherents of fundamental ontology and critical theory. For once sharing an adversary, both Heidegger and Adorno formulated attacks on its thought.

Blumenberg's first tentative reflection on the topic was "**An Anthropological Approach to the Contemporary Significance of Rhetoric**" (1971), originally published in Italian, with its German version not appearing for another ten years.[41] Here, Blumenberg extends

39. See the discussion in Hans Blumenberg and Jacob Taubes, *Briefwechsel 1961–1981*, ed. Herbert Kopp-Oberstebrink and Martin Treml (Berlin: Suhrkamp, 2013), 328.

40. For a history of this current of thought in Germany, see Joachim Fischer, *Philosophische Anthropologie: Eine Denkrichtung des 20. Jahrhunderts* (Freiburg: Alber, 2009). A brief English overview is given in Joachim Fischer, "Exploring the Core Identity of Philosophical Anthropology through the Works of Max Scheler, Helmuth Plessner, and Arnold Gehlen," *Iris* 1, no. 1 (2009): 153–170.

41. Originally published in Italian as Hans Blumenberg, "Approccio antropologico all'attualità della retorica," trans. Vincenzo Orlando, *Il Verri. Rivista di Let-*

his preoccupation with language by turning toward its role not just in historical systems of thought but in human behavior as such. Focusing in particular on rhetoric, that is, speech that aims to persuade rather than to express the truth, he understands it as one vital tool of existence among others for a being to whom any final truths are unavailable and whose mortality presses it to act. Two years earlier, Blumenberg had already devoted a detailed study—similarly rehabilitating "Sophism" against "Platonism"—to the ability of rhetoric to stand in for action, a quality that gives it a quintessentially political character. But while **"The Concept of Reality and the Theory of the State"** (1968/69) was still much more concerned with historical shifts in reality concepts, "Anthropological Approach" seeks to outline a "deep history" of rhetoric.[42]

This growing interest in philosophical anthropology also seeps into historical works, palpably so in *The Genesis of the Copernican World* (1975),[43] the continuation and crowning achievement of Blumenberg's engagement with the history of science and of astronomy in particular. Again taking up the rise of the modern age, this time from the standpoint of the Copernican revolution, Blumenberg approaches it by tracing the effect that the lost central position in the world and the universe had on the philosophical and scientific self-conception of humanity. At the center of the argument, however, is the question about the relationship between finite humans and an infinite cosmos, and Blumenberg follows the different, and not always equally possible, historical responses to what now appears as an anthropological constant from antiquity through the Renaissance and to the twentieth century, from the ancient contemplation of the stars, via the invention of the telescope, to the success of astronautics.

Around the same time, Blumenberg slowly begins to integrate the notion of the "life-world," which earlier was brought to bear

---

teratura no. 35/36 (1971): 49–72; republished in German as Hans Blumenberg, "Anthropologische Annäherung an die Aktualität der Rhetorik," in *Wirklichkeiten in denen wir leben*, 104–136.

42.   Originally published as Hans Blumenberg, "Wirklichkeitsbegriff und Staatstheorie," *Schweizer Monatshefte* 48, no. 2 (1968/69): 121–146.

43.   Blumenberg, *Genesis of the Copernican World*.

for historical understanding, into his general anthropological re-orientation. The first signs of this appear in **"Observations Drawn from Metaphors"** (1971), an attempt to update the metaphorological project by extending research matter from the tropes of strictly phil-osophical texts to contemporary discourse in the form of journalis-tic debates, political strategies, scientific projects, and quotidian speech.[44] But Blumenberg also expands the explanatory scope of metaphorology from an instrument to sketch the genesis of concept formation to one that traces its extratextual motivations in the life-world. That this life-world is now conceived of in anthropological terms becomes clear from the progressive transformation of meta-phorology into a "theory of nonconceptuality." The 1979 essay **"Prospect for a Theory of Nonconceptuality"**[45] and the only recently published lecture manuscript **"Theory of Nonconceptuality"** (circa 1975)[46] are the furthest developed articulations of this expanded project, which construes humans as relying on the *actio per distans* (action at a distance), no less exemplified by the trap of the prehis-toric hunter-gatherer than by the philosophical concept. However, it is to its practical execution, rather than the theory itself, that Blu-menberg dedicates most of his work. *Shipwreck with Spectator* (1979),[47] devoted to seafaring as existential metaphor, and *The Readability of the World* (1981),[48] pursuing the metaphor of the book of the world, are demonstrations of nonconceptuality at work following very specific examples.

---

44. Originally published as Hans Blumenberg, "Beobachtungen an Met-aphern," *Archiv für Begriffsgeschichte* 15, no. 2 (1971): 161–214. Blumenberg de-cided to reprint only a segment ("Paradigm, Grammatically") as an independent text later: Hans Blumenberg, "Paradigma, grammatisch," in *Wirklichkeiten in denen wir leben*, 157–162.

45. Originally published as Hans Blumenberg, "Ausblick auf eine Theorie der Unbegrifflichkeit," in *Schiffbruch mit Zuschauer: Paradigma einer Daseins-metapher* (Frankfurt am Main: Suhrkamp, 1979), 75–93.

46. Originally published as Hans Blumenberg, *Theorie der Unbegrifflichkeit*, ed. Anselm Haverkamp (Frankfurt am Main: Suhrkamp, 2007).

47. Hans Blumenberg, *Shipwreck with Spectator: Paradigm of a Metaphor for Existence*, trans. Steven Rendall (Cambridge, MA: MIT Press, 1997); originally published as Hans Blumenberg, *Schiffbruch mit Zuschauer*.

48. Hans Blumenberg, *Die Lesbarkeit der Welt* (Frankfurt am Main: Suhrkamp, 1981).

That not only metaphors but also other forms of nonconceptual expression can be explained by an anthropological model is apparent in the massive *Work on Myth* (1979). In the first few pages, Blumenberg sketches an anthropology that conceives of humans as struggling with the "absolutism of reality," the overbearing presence of an outside world for which they are biologically unfit.[49] While on the one hand it acts as an anthropological model that explains the need for distance from and representation of the world through figures of cultural "significance" such as myths or metaphors, the absolutism of reality is also that which is always already overcome in the myths that have been handed down to us. Having passed through an age-old reception history, myths are significances in their most foundational forms. And while they were initially tools against terror, they are now elements of play, supplying the source material for aesthetic variations. In the second part of the book, Blumenberg gives a detailed case study of the work on the Prometheus myth, with a particular focus on Goethe, a writer he especially cherished.[50]

For a long time, *Work on Myth* was Blumenberg's most explicit theoretization of anthropology, which remain scarce in his published work. He now and then hinted at his interest in unifying phenomenology and philosophical anthropology, such as in *Life-Time and World-Time* (1986),[51] a book that again takes up the disproportion between humans and the world, now from a temporal angle. But only ten years after his death, with the posthumous publication of *Description of the Human* (2006), and to a certain extent in *Theory of the Life-World* (2010) and other late *Phenomenological Writings* (2018), it became clear that Blumenberg had worked on the ambitious project of a "phenomenological anthropology."[52] Based

---

49. Blumenberg, *Work on Myth*, chap. 1.

50. "Prefiguration: Work on Political Myth," a chapter with reflections on myth and politics Blumenberg decided to exclude from *Work on Myth*, has only recently been published: Hans Blumenberg, *Präfiguration: Arbeit am politischen Mythos*, ed. Felix Heidenreich and Angus Nicholls (Berlin: Suhrkamp, 2014).

51. Hans Blumenberg, *Lebenszeit und Weltzeit* (Frankfurt am Main: Suhrkamp, 1986).

52. Hans Blumenberg, *Beschreibung des Menschen*, ed. Manfred Sommer (Frankfurt am Main: Suhrkamp, 2006); Hans Blumenberg, *Theorie der Lebenswelt*, ed. Manfred Sommer (Berlin: Suhrkamp, 2010); Hans Blumenberg, *Phän-*

on lecture notes and essays from the latter half of the 1970s, *Description* aimed at supplying phenomenology with an anthropological foundation by developing a speculative account of the evolutionary pressure leading to the emergence of consciousness.

New Genres

Toward the end of the 1970s and at the beginning of the 1980s, Blumenberg's productivity, doubtlessly aided by his retreat from the public, reached new heights, shifting away from contemporary academic debates toward the activity of writing itself. He completed and published numerous books in quick succession, whose initial impulses can often be traced back, sometimes several decades, to observations regarding a particular metaphor or philosophical notion. This is the case in *The Readability of the World* and *Shipwreck with Spectator*, but it also goes for *St. Matthew Passion* (1988),[53] which looks at how the "Death of God" can be traced through imaginings of the death of Christ through centuries of seeming profanization. In Blumenberg's final book publication, *Cave Exits* (1989), the reception history of the cave allegory from Plato onward, first investigated in an essay from 1960, is combined with an anthropological contemplation on the primal scene of human cave dwelling.[54]

Although Blumenberg's scholarly books seem like holistically designed studies, they are the product of a compilatory spirit that testifies to a stunning thematic perseverance administered by his *Zettelkasten*.[55] This slip box system of organizing summaries, ex-

---

omenologische Schriften 1981–1988, ed. Nicola Zambon (Berlin: Suhrkamp, 2018).

53. Hans Blumenberg, *St. Matthew Passion*, trans. Paul Fleming and Helmut Müller-Sievers (Ithaca, NY: Cornell University Press, 2020).

54. Hans Blumenberg, *Höhlenausgänge* (Frankfurt am Main: Suhrkamp, 1989); Hans Blumenberg, "Das dritte Höhlengleichnis," *Filosofia* 11 (1960): 705–722.

55. On Blumenberg's *Zettelkasten*, see Ulrich von Bülow and Dorit Krusche, "Nachrichten an sich selbst: Der Zettelkasten von Hans Blumenberg," in *Zettelkästen: Maschinen der Phantasie* (Marbach am Neckar: Deutsche Schillergesellschaft, 2013), 113–129; Karin Krauthausen, "Hans Blumenbergs präparierter Valéry,"

cerpts, and thought notes for later compilation is the basis of all of Blumenberg's writings, counting more than thirty thousand index cards and going back as early as 1942, when, during a bombing raid on his hometown, the first version of the *Zettelkasten* was destroyed. As his characteristic working method, it has by now acquired a certain mystique of its own, particularly in conjunction with another feature of Blumenberg's composition process: from the 1960s onward, he only rarely wrote but instead dictated his texts, which were then typed up by his secretary and again revised several times until the final text was done.[56] Since this writing method allowed him to work on several books simultaneously, a large number of manuscripts—most unfinished but many completed—remained unpublished at the time of Blumenberg's death. Today, they can be found, together with his *Zettelkasten*, among his papers housed at the German Literary Archive in Marbach, Germany.

Even if the *Zettelkasten* was a tool from the start, its compilatory method had a palpable impact on Blumenberg's writing style only during the 1980s. This shift suggests Blumenberg's interest had moved from the systematic to the casuistic and serial, from the all-encompassing groundwork to the anecdotal observation. A considerable part of these later books can be seen as results of the erudite synthesis of miscellanea, many of which were published in journals or newspaper feuilletons before they reappeared in books or were earmarked for posthumous publication. Indeed, the 1980s saw Blumenberg's second phase of nonacademic writing, this time settling for smaller and more literary forms, such as a series of glosses, essays on concepts, commentaries on anecdotes, or fable interpretations, which appeared in newspapers, such as *Frankfurter Allgemeine Zeitung* and *Neue Zürcher Zeitung*, or literary journals, such as *Akzente*. The turn toward a more narrative philosophy is already

Zeitschrift für Kulturphilosophie 6, no. 1 (2012): 211–224. Rich visual material can be found in Ulrich von Bülow and Dorit Krusche, "Vorläufiges zum Nachlass von Hans Blumenberg," in *Hans Blumenberg beobachtet: Wissenschaft, Technik und Philosophie*, ed. Cornelius Borck (Freiburg: Alber, 2013), 273–287.

56. Odo Marquard, "Entlastung vom Absoluten: In memoriam," in *Die Kunst des Überlebens: Nachdenken über Hans Blumenberg*, ed. Franz Josef Wetz and Hermann Timm (Frankfurt am Main: Suhrkamp, 1999), 18.

prefigured in *Shipwreck with Spectator* (1979), which was published not in Suhrkamp's academic series, but in the *Bibliothek Suhrkamp*, dedicated to essays and world literature. While in *The Laughter of the Thracian Woman: A Protohistory of Theory* (1987) the fabulatory origin of philosophy itself becomes a topic, a practical high point of the more aphoristic and literary experiments is the book *Care Crosses the River* (1987), which unfolds by way of narrative the implications of a fable in a less academically philosophical and more meditative manner.[57]

"Pensiveness," the title of his 1980 speech in acceptance of the Sigmund Freud Prize for scholarly prose, now became Blumenberg's declared mode of philosophizing.[58] This noninstrumental thinking intends to relieve philosophy from its scientifizing tendencies and to rehabilitate its foundation in questions of the life-world.[59] Fables, as much as anecdotes, allow for pensiveness, and the texts "**Moments of Goethe**" (1982),[60] "**Beyond the Edge of Reality: Three Short Essays**" (1983),[61] and "**Of Nonunderstanding: Glosses on Three Fables**" (1984)[62] may represent this style of thought as much as "**Unknown Aesopica: From Newly Found Fables**" (1985), Blumenberg's own literary attempt to pose philosophical problems in the form of fables.[63] They are not an accidental byproduct of unwritten larger monographs, but have become a genre unto themselves. Even the last essay included in this volume, "**Advancing into**

---

57. Hans Blumenberg, *Care Crosses the River*, trans. Paul Fleming (Stanford, CA: Stanford University Press, 2010); originally published as Hans Blumenberg, *Die Sorge geht über den Fluß* (Frankfurt am Main: Suhrkamp, 1987).

58. Originally published as Hans Blumenberg, "Nachdenklichkeit," *Neue Zürcher Zeitung*, November 22, 1980, 65–66.

59. See Paul Fleming, "On the Edge of Non-Contingency: Anecdotes and the Lifeworld," *Telos* 158, no. 1 (2012): 21–35.

60. Originally published as Hans Blumenberg, "Momente Goethes," *Akzente* 29, no. 1 (1982): 43–55.

61. Originally published as Hans Blumenberg, "Über den Rand der Wirklichkeit hinaus: Drei Kurzessays," *Akzente* 30, no. 1 (1983): 16–27.

62. Originally published as Hans Blumenberg, "Vom Unverstand: Glossen zu drei Fabeln," *Neue Zürcher Zeitung*, March 24, 1984, 67.

63. Originally published as Hans Blumenberg, "Unbekanntes von Äsop: Aus neuen Fabelfunden," *Neue Zürcher Zeitung*, October 5/6, 1985, 69–70.

Eternal Silence: A Century after the Sailing of the *Fram*" (1993),[64] written three years before Blumenberg's death, offers not just the philosophical reading of an episode in the history of polar expeditions ripe with significance, but draws on an anecdote to muse on the relationship between media-archaeology and nihilism.

Afterlife

Hans Blumenberg's death on March 28, 1996, in his home in Altenberge near Münster, did not spell the end of his publication record. His *Nachlass* (estate) contained numerous completed manuscripts, the first two of which were already published the following year, and to this day the stream of books is uninterrupted. A first wave of posthumous volumes predominantly contained the literary short forms of Blumenberg's late phase,[65] but after the turn of the millennium the more strictly philosophical work once again returned into focus. The 1998 republication of *Paradigms*, previously available only as a special volume of a journal and long out of print, had already drawn attention to the metaphorological project that was known only to a few, while the invaluable volume *Aesthetic and Metaphorological Writings* (2001)[66] made accessible a number of

---

64. Originally published as Hans Blumenberg, "Vorstoss ins ewige Schweigen: Ein Jahrhundert nach der Ausfahrt der 'Fram,'" *Neue Zürcher Zeitung*, December 24, 1993, 53–54.

65. Hans Blumenberg, *Ein mögliches Selbstverständnis* (Stuttgart: Reclam, 1997); Hans Blumenberg, *Die Vollzähligkeit der Sterne* (Frankfurt am Main: Suhrkamp, 1997). These were soon followed by *Lebensthemen: Aus dem Nachlaß* (Stuttgart: Reclam, 1998) and *Begriffe in Geschichten* (Frankfurt am Main: Suhrkamp, 1998); *Gerade noch Klassiker: Glossen zu Fontane* (Munich: Hanser, 1998); *Goethe zum Beispiel* (Frankfurt am Main: Insel, 1999); *Die Verführbarkeit des Philosophen* (Frankfurt am Main: Suhrkamp, 2000); *Löwen* (Frankfurt am Main: Suhrkamp, 2001) (published in English as *Lions*, trans. Kári Driscoll [London: Seagull, 2018]). One could group the later publication *Sources, Streams, Icebergs: Observations Drawn from Metaphors* (*Quellen, Ströme, Eisberge: Beobachtungen an Metaphern*, ed. Dorit Krusche and Ulrich von Bülow [Berlin: Suhrkamp, 2012]), originally from the 1980s, into this category.

66. *Ästhetische und metaphorologische Schriften*, ed. Anselm Haverkamp (Frankfurt am Main: Suhrkamp, 2001).

earlier and hard-to-find essays, many of which are included in this *Reader*. With *Description of the Human, Theory of Nonconceptuality*, and *Theory of the Life-World*, pieces of Blumenberg's philosophy were published that, despite what his late work may seem to suggest, share a surprising commitment to systematicity in the service of bringing together the phenomenological and anthropological tradition, while his *Writings on Literature 1945–1958*, *Writings on Technology*, and the *Phenomenological Writings 1981–1988* collected published and unpublished material by topic. Apart from several smaller books such as *Prefiguration* on political myth, *The Naked Truth* on this particular metaphor, and *Rigorism of Truth* on Sigmund Freud and Hannah Arendt,[67] the correspondences with Carl Schmitt and with the religious scholar Jacob Taubes deserve to be mentioned, as they allow insight into Blumenberg's direct engagement with his contemporaries, and indeed with his adversaries.[68] (At the end of this volume, we have compiled a bibliography that lists all of Blumenberg's publications to have appeared by the time of this writing.)

If Blumenberg was well known during his lifetime, his reputation has grown just as the number of his publications has increased, as has the variety of interpretations, which would be expected for a philosopher with such a varied body of work. Readings of Blumenberg depend on which of his different bodies of work is chosen to be central, to which tradition he is ascribed, and in which context he is received.[69] Read as a theorist of modernity—for instance,

---

67. Blumenberg, *Präfiguration*; Hans Blumenberg, *Die nackte Wahrheit*, ed. Rüdiger Zill (Berlin: Suhrkamp, 2019); Hans Blumenberg, *Rigorism of Truth: "Moses the Egyptian" and Other Writings on Freud and Arendt*, trans. Joe Paul Kroll (Ithaca: Cornell University Press, 2018). On the relationship between Blumenberg and Arendt, see Hannes Bajohr, "The Unity of the World: Arendt and Blumenberg on the Anthropology of Metaphor," *Germanic Review* 90, no. 1 (2015): 42–59, and Martin Jay, "Against Rigor: Hans Blumenberg on Freud and Arendt," *New German Critique* 44, no. 3 (2017): 123–144.

68. Blumenberg and Schmitt, *Briefwechsel 1971–1978 und weitere Materialien*; Blumenberg and Taubes, *Briefwechsel 1961–1981*.

69. For the American reception of Blumenberg, see Paul Fleming, "*Verfehlungen*: Hans Blumenberg and the United States," *New German Critique* 44, no. 3 (2017): 105–121; for the early French reception, see Denis Trierweiler, "Un au-

by Richard Rorty, Martin Jay, and Alasdair MacIntyre—*Legitimacy* becomes the main text;[70] subsumed under the school of philosophical anthropology, *Work on Myth* but also the later *Description of the Human* are the central works;[71] if Blumenberg is understood as a conceptual historian, *Paradigms*, the texts on metaphorology and nonconceptuality, make up the corpus, adding the essays for Poetics and Hermeneutics once he is conceived of as a theorist of language;[72] if one chooses to read him as a historian of science, *Genesis of the Copernican World* may become the main work to rely on;[73] and interpreted as literary theorist or even as a poet-scholar himself, then beside his early criticism, it is particularly the late glosses, feuilletons, and anecdotes that take center stage.[74]

tisme de la réception: À propos de la traduction de la 'Légitimité des temps modernes' de Hans Blumenberg en France," *Esprit* (July 2000): 51–62.

70.   Richard Rorty, "Against Belatedness," *London Review of Books* 5, no. 11 (1983): 3–5; Martin Jay, review of *The Legitimacy of the Modern Age*, by Hans Blumenberg, *History and Theory* 24, no. 2 (1985): 183–196; Alasdair MacIntyre, review of *The Legitimacy of the Modern Age*, by Hans Blumenberg, *American Journal of Sociology* 90, no. 4 (1985): 924–926. See also Elizabeth Brient, *The Immanence of the Infinite: Hans Blumenberg and the Threshold to Modernity* (Washington, DC: Catholic University of America Press, 2002); Jean-Claude Monod, *La querelle de la sécularisation: Théologie politique et philosophies de l'histoire de Hegel à Blumenberg* (Paris: J. Vrin, 2002); Heidenreich, *Mensch und Moderne*.

71.   Angus Nicholls, *Myth and the Human Sciences*; Denis Trierweiler, ed., *Hans Blumenberg: Anthropologie philosophique* (Paris: Presses Universitaire de France, 2010); Vida Pavesich, "Hans Blumenberg's Philosophical Anthropology: After Heidegger and Cassirer," *Journal of the History of Philosophy* 46, no. 3 (2008): 421–448.

72.   Ernst Müller and Falko Schmieder, *Begriffsgeschichte und historische Semantik: Ein kritisches Kompendium* (Berlin: Suhrkamp, 2016); Johnson, "Blumenberg's 'Huge Field' "; Dirk Mende, "Histories of Technicization: On the Relation of Conceptual History and Metaphorology in Hans Blumenberg," *Telos*, no. 158 (March 26, 2012): 59–79; Frank Beck Lassen, "'Metaphorically Speaking': *Begriffsgeschichte* and Hans Blumenberg's *Metaphorologie*," *Archiv für Begriffsgeschichte. Sonderheft* 7 (2010): 53–70.

73.   David Ingram, "The Copernican Revolution Revisited: Paradigm, Metaphor and Incommensurability in the History of Science: Blumenberg's Response to Kuhn and Davidson," *History of the Human Sciences* 6, no. 4 (November 1, 1993): 11–35; Pini Ifergan, "On Hans Blumenberg's *Genesis of the Copernican World*," in *Hans Blumenberg beobachtet: Wissenschaft, Technik und Philosophie*, ed. Cornelius Borck (Freiburg: Alber, 2013), 149–167.

74.   Fleming, "On the Edge of Non-Contingency"; Joseph Leo Koerner, "Ideas about the Thing, not the Thing Itself: Hans Blumenberg's Style," *History of the*

It lies beyond the scope of this introduction to delve into these different interpretations, let alone evaluate them. Suffice it to say that despite some attempts to boil down all these fields into a single project or even gesture,[75] it seems less reductive simply to acknowledge Blumenberg's versatility—a versatility whose further exploration we hope this *Reader* will encourage.

About This Reader

Already in this overview of Blumenberg's life and work, we have mentioned all of the texts collected in this volume. As noted at the beginning, we had two criteria for selection: the centrality of the texts for Blumenberg's oeuvre as such—the core canon, as contestable as this notion is—and their illustrative value for the genres, topics, or types of question he was engaged in but for which no such canon has yet crystallized. Since we have already given a chronological overview of Blumenberg's life and work, and since many of the topics were, as he put it, *Lebensthemen* (life themes),[76] the *Reader* is divided into four thematic sections; however, since these *Lebensthemen* reemerged, often under different guises or from new perspectives, throughout his career, the sections themselves follow a chronological order. All editorial additions, such as translations of Latin or Greek sources and missing references, are enclosed within square brackets.

The first part, titled "History, Secularization, and Reality," begins with Blumenberg's very first philosophical publication, "The Linguistic Reality of Philosophy," and includes not only his speech on "World Pictures and World Models" and his first public argument against the "secularization" thesis ("'Secularization': Critique of a Category of Historical Illegitimacy"), but also two texts on the concept of reality that have never been reprinted in German: "Prelimi-

---

Human Sciences 6, no. 4 (1993): 1–10.

75. Odo Marquard famously tried to summarize Blumenberg's main motivation to "gain distance from the absolute"; see Marquard, "Entlastung vom Absoluten."

76. Blumenberg, *Lebensthemen*.

nary Remarks on the Concept of Reality," which, notwithstanding its title, provides a résumé of its motivating questions, and "The Concept of Reality and the Theory of the State," which applies the concept of reality to political theory.

"Metaphors, Rhetoric, and Nonconceptuality," the second part, traces the development from Blumenberg's "Light as a Metaphor of Truth: At the Preliminary Stage of Philosophical Concept Formation" and his stated program in the introduction to *Paradigms for a Metaphorology* to his turn toward an anthropological theory of rhetoric in "An Anthropological Approach to the Contemporary Significance of Rhetoric." Providing the main sections of the often overlooked "Observations Drawn from Metaphors," this section follows Blumenberg's reformulation of metaphorology as a theory of nonconceptuality up until "Prospect for a Theory of Nonconceptuality." It includes an extensive excerpt from his posthumously published lecture "Theory of Nonconceptuality," which also gives a good introduction to his anthropological thought.

The third part, "Nature, Technology, and Aesthetics," concentrates less on historical realities as such and more on their specific application. Changes in the concept of nature come most readily to the fore in "The Relationship between Nature and Technology as a Philosophical Problem," a reception history of *technē*, and Blumenberg traces its consequences for technology and art through the historical reevaluation of the concept of mimesis in "'Imitation of Nature': Toward a Prehistory of the Idea of the Creative Being." This section includes his first extensive discussion of the concept of the life-world, "Phenomenological Aspects on Life-World and Technization," and his writings produced in the context of Poetics and Hermeneutics, on aesthetics in "Socrates and the *objet ambigu*: Paul Valéry's Discussion of the Ontology of the Aesthetic Object and Its Tradition" and "The Essential Ambiguity of the Aesthetic Object" as well as on poetic language in "Speech Situation and Immanent Poetics."

The final part, "Fables, Anecdotes, and the Novel," gives a sample of Blumenberg's writings on literature, from the early interpretation of Kafka in "The Absolute Father" and the study on "The *Mythos* and *Ethos* of America in the Work of William Faulkner" to the theorization of the novel as a genuinely modern genre in "The Concept of Reality and the Possibility of the Novel." Furthermore, it shows Blumenberg's own stylistic versatility and mode of literary thought in the analyses in "Pensiveness" and "Of Nonunderstanding: Glosses on Three Fables," and indeed the production of fables in "Unknown Aesopica: From Newly Found Fables," but also his interest in the significance of anecdotes, apocryphal stories, and historical vignettes, as in "Beyond the Edge of Reality: Three Short Essays," "Moments of Goethe," and "Advancing into Eternal Silence: A Century after the Sailing of the *Fram*."

We are, of course, aware that our selection can be challenged; many will miss texts that would have had an excellent claim to being included. Although we have reproduced some previously translated essays, for considerations of length we have done so only for the most important ones. Not part of the *Reader* but easily accessible are "Self-Preservation and Inertia: On the Constitution of Modern Rationality" (1969),[77] "The Life-World and the Concept of Reality" (1972),[78] "On a Lineage of the Idea of Progress" (1974),[79] "Money or Life: Metaphors of Georg Simmel's Philosophy" (1976),[80]

77. Hans Blumenberg, "Self-Preservation and Inertia: On the Constitution of Modern Rationality," in *Contemporary German Philosophy*, vol. 3, ed. Darrell E. Christensen et al. (University Park: Pennsylvania State University Press, 1983), 209–256; originally published as Hans Blumenberg, "Selbsterhaltung und Beharrung: Zur Konstitution der neuzeitlichen Rationalität," *Akademie der Wissenschaften und Literatur in Mainz: Abhandlungen der geistes- und sozialwissenschaftlichen Klasse* 19, no. 11 (1969): 335–383.

78. Hans Blumenberg, "The Life-World and the Concept of Reality," trans. Theodore Kisiel, in *Life-World and Consciousness: Essays for Aron Gurwitsch*, ed. Lester E. Embree (Evanston, IL: Northwestern University Press, 1972), 425–444; posthumously reprinted in German as Hans Blumenberg, "Lebenswelt und Wirklichkeitsbegriff," in *Theorie der Lebenswelt*, 157–180.

79. Hans Blumenberg, "On a Lineage of the Idea of Progress," trans. E. B. Ashton, *Social Research* 41, no. 1 (1974): 5–27; not translated into German.

80. Hans Blumenberg, "Money or Life: Metaphors of Georg Simmel's Philosophy," trans. Robert Savage, *Theory, Culture and Society* 29, no. 7/8 (2013): 249–262; originally published as Hans Blumenberg, "Geld oder Leben: Eine metaphorologische Studie zur Konsistenz der Philosophie Georg Simmels," in *Ästhetik und Soziologie um die Jahrhundertwende: Georg Simmel*, ed. Hannes Böhringer and Karlfried Gründer (Frankfurt am Main: Klostermann, 1976), 121–134.

"Being—A MacGuffin: How to Preserve the Desire to Think" (1987),[81] and "Does It Matter When? On Time Indifference" (1987).[82] Constraints of space have likewise kept us from collecting all the texts we would have liked to include, among which the most notable omission is the overly long treatise "The Concept of Reality and the Effective Potential of Myth."[83] With the exception of "Theory of Nonconceptuality" and the introduction from *Paradigms*, we have also refrained from including any excerpts from Blumenberg's books. Although chapters from qualifying theses or, for instance, *Life-Time and World-Time, The Readability of the World*, or *Description of the Human* would have given valuable insights into Blumenberg's thought,[84] we wanted to present only self-contained texts, while hoping that these books will one day be rendered into English in full. We are convinced that these stand-alone, and often shorter, pointed, or even playful texts present a multiperspectival Blumenberg not yet easily accessible to non-German readers, and hence may offer an invitation to delve further into Blumenberg's work where the sturdier monographs might be seen to raise the bar. To give Blumenberg a new and expanded readership beyond a German audience is, after all, the intention of this *Reader*, and with it we hope to make a case for and a contribution to this goal.

---

81.   Hans Blumenberg, "Being—A MacGuffin: How to Preserve the Desire to Think," trans. David Adams, *Salmagundi* no. 90/91 (1991): 191–193; originally published as Hans Blumenberg, "Das Sein—ein MacGuffin: Wie man sich Lust am Denken erhält," *Frankfurter Allgemeine Zeitung*, May 27, 1987, 35.

82.   Hans Blumenberg, "Does It Matter When? On Time Indifference," trans. David Adams, *Philosophy and Literature* 22, no. 1 (1998): 212–218; originally published as Hans Blumenberg, "Gleichgültig wann? Über Zeitindifferenz," *Frankfurter Allgemeine Zeitung*, December 30, 1987, 3.

83.   Blumenberg, "Wirklichkeitsbegriff und Wirkungspotential des Mythos."

84.   Blumenberg, *Lebenszeit und Weltzeit*; Blumenberg, *Die Lesbarkeit der Welt*; Blumenberg, *Beschreibung des Menschen*.

PART I

HISTORY, SECULARIZATION, AND REALITY

1

THE LINGUISTIC REALITY
OF PHILOSOPHY

(1946/1947)

Both in gaining and expanding knowledge of one's field, the questions of the primary and universal foundation of our cognition and
our relationship to the world cannot be passed over like an unhewn
and unheeded rock. Whoever today turns with an alert and responsible awareness of this fact toward the efforts of philosophical
clarification and engagement with the work that has been done on
these problems is to be confronted with an often discouraging resistance, a recalcitrance of philosophical ideas, which the disheart-
ened all too often interpret as exclusivity or esotericism on behalf
of philosophical thought. This resistance emanates essentially from
the linguistic reality into which the philosophical body of ideas has
entered. In discussing it, we can leave aside a difficulty that appears
in other realms of knowledge and in poetry: that some, and often

Originally published as "Die sprachliche Wirklichkeit der Philosophie" in *Hamburger Akademische Rundschau* 1, no. 10 (1946/47): 428–431.

the, basic achievements offer themselves only through the medium of a foreign language, and that no translation [Über*setzung*] can replace [er*setzen*] the encounter with the original document. The basic problems of the linguistic reality of philosophy, however, will arise in every linguistic guise.

These problems make themselves known, to articulate it provisionally, in that the philosophical reality of language shatters and transgresses the terminology not only of everyday life but also of that with which the scholar is intimately familiar. To this we have to add an aspect that causes frustration, and indeed fundamental concern, in anyone familiar with the complex terminology of the natural sciences: that philosophy as a science appears to possess nothing resembling a uniform terminology and by that fact alone largely stands out against the other spheres of the exact analysis of reality. Even where the consistent use of concepts seems to suggest such uniformity, a closer look soon reveals contradictions and differentiations of meaning.

Language as articulation of thought appears to have two basic possibilities at its disposal: one monological and the other dialogical. Mere vocalization, relieving oneself of the burden of thought, being confronted with oneself by means of language, and presenting thought to oneself with the goal of clarifying and shaping it— all this describes the monological mode. The dialogical mode contains communication, the creative transmission [*Hinüberzeugen*] of a thought, coperforming [*Mitvollzug*] it and objectifying it into commonality, and confronting objections, while what is said must be something definite held in common. There is no doubt and no denying that the language of philosophical thought is bound to the claim of objective validity and dialogical communication. A philosopher's monologue cannot oblige us to heed and engage with it. In monologue, a thinker retreats from the sphere in which a matter is regarded jointly and in which one asserts valid claims about it; this is a retreat from the sphere of science in its very form.

Does the linguistic reality of philosophy mentioned above not prove the failure of this basic demand for dialogical statements? Should not philosophy, as the science of the most universally valid norms, structures, and attitudes, by necessity and by its essence also arrive at a valid linguistic form? Does the failure of linguistic objectivity therefore not in effect mean a verdict against philosophy's claim to being scientific? In our situation, in which so much depends on a positive encounter with the philosophical spirit, these questions are worth examining. In this enterprise, we should be led not by premature programmatic demands but only by the will to understand the deeper sources of the problem touched upon, and to propose it as a topic of discussion and reflection in the first place.

To begin with, the linguistic reality of philosophizing is rooted in the human mind's millennia-long process of attaining consciousness. The Greeks coined many lasting concepts by taking on the most decisive basic problems. It is both highly appealing and relevant for understanding the whole problematic of philosophical language to pursue these conceptual origins with the help of the documents still available to us. Characteristic of these origins is that they stem from quotidian or poetic speech about the world. For example, at the beginning of pre-Socratic thought, reflection on the basic form of assertion—the existential proposition [*Seinsaussage*]—leads to the central concept of "being." This primordial [*ursprünglich*] thought conceives of human speech as a vessel of truth; truth is only comprehensible as judgment where one element (the subject) is determined through another (the predicate). Already in Heraclitus, this basic form stands in opposition to the disorder of isolated words; it is the logos, in which the agonal structure of reality, the world-law, announces itself. With the exception of the development that leads from Sophism to skepticism, Greek thought orients itself by the form of language, all the way through to Aristotle's development of the doctrine of the categories. It is precisely through close contact with the most universal elements of language use that concepts are coined. In Aristotle's categories, to give just one example, the status of concept is still recognizable in that strange intermediate position between isolation from the living context of dialogical speech and independence gained through substantivization. The notion that language immediately springs from the understanding of being keeps Greek terminology, in its main lineage, within the validity of living language use. Only the increasing specialization of the scientific disciplines in late antiquity, in the formation of grammar and dialectics, for instance, tends to obscure this cohesion.

Yet only after the reception of Greek thought in the realm of the Latin language, by patristics and medieval thought, are we confronted with the first moment that detached philosophical language critically from its primordial rootedness in general validity: the translation of philosophical terminology into Latin. This translation—and this is significant—occurred by empathically reenacting the primordial linguistic sense, but from the petrified, in effect technical, meaning that stemmed from its use within the Scholastic traditions. To this should be added the shifts in meaning that important concepts underwent within the Arabic-Islamic or Jewish intellectual sphere. The conceptual artistry of the Middle Ages, dialectical and tradition-bound, did its part to prevent any recourse to the primordial linguistic content, let alone the creation of new concepts from new motives of thought.

This does not yet reveal the full genetic burden of the linguistic reality of philosophy. The extent of this burden is unique compared to all other sciences and is founded in the unrepeatable continuity of questioning and researching. Thus, the general and exemplary validity of the concrete issues reveals itself to be the true source of the linguistic problematic, and it instructs us to catch sight of the problem of the things themselves in it. The most cumbersome part of the genetic burden that rests on language is the fact that the concepts that were adopted and translated from Greek entered Western philosophy's bifurcating lineages of thought as fixed ciphers, so that despite being based on diametrically opposed world pictures [*Weltbilder*] and understandings of being [*Seinsverständnisse*], they appeared in identical linguistic shape. Be it the naturalism of the Averroists or the personalist metaphysics of the Thomists, the realism of transcendentals or medieval nominalism—they all use the same conceptual apparatus. The modern age, too—no matter whether one understands it to be a revolt against Scholasticism or its successor—adopts the preformed and preburdened language of philosophy. The consequence is an immense relativization of concepts. Traditional terminology serves the intellectual achievements of the realist systems no less than those of the critique of knowledge and of idealist metaphysics. One need only think of the protean change in meaning undergone by concepts such as the transcendental, substance, or indeed matter itself!

It is astonishing, despite fundamental upheavals in thought, how few innovations and primordial approaches the conceptual language of philosophy has accomplished since the reception of its ancient foundations. In the present, however, this seems to have changed in one fell swoop. Certain prominent works by contemporary thinkers constitute a downright attack on the ossified and overburdened conceptual edifice of tradition that has become so ambiguous. Since the call "to the things themselves!" rang out, providing a new impulse to philosophical investigation, we have seen a downright eruption of conceptual innovations. Between this new understanding of things and the old one of traditional terminology, there seem to be no correspondences whatsoever. But nor can we recognize many interconnections to our commonplace understanding; quotidian terms in particular are called into question as distorting and obscuring. Generally valid language, it is said, is too heavily predetermined by traditional interpretations to be an organ suitable to a primordial approach to the facts. Some thinkers try to establish a novel philosophical idiom by constantly and repeatedly regarding these things anew. But here the dilemma of our understanding is no less severe than in traditional language, albeit of a different nature. Admittedly, at times it seems to us as if the commonality of a primordial understanding shines through in a new conceptual coinage, but on the whole we are obliged to determine the meaning of concepts through laborious textual interpretation so that we can handle them like formulae.

How can we explain this linguistic eruption in contemporary philosophy? What is the relationship between its intentions and our basic problem of communication [*Verständigung*]?

Edmund Husserl, whose phenomenological method was the key factor that launched these conceptual innovations, grappled with these questions in his 1910 essay "Philosophy as Rigorous Science."[1] That a thought directed at the things themselves might begin with deductions from concepts, as Scholasticism still contended, is out of the question today. Husserl, however, stresses that language has an important initial function even for phenomenological analysis in that it points out phenomena in the first place and encourages the explanation of things through the formation of words. Indeed, the phenomenon finds its clarification in the, as it were, "fully intuitional realization of experiential concepts."[2] But in all these "stimulations" and "indications" we can already see that the phenomenon's full intuitiveness exceeds the scope of the "stimulating" or "indicating" word or sentence; if the phenomenon is to be described, that is, linguistically captured, then it is impossible to simply fall back on the original concept. Instead, the expressions that suffice for designating the phenomenon at the beginning of the investigation become, in its course, "fluid and ambiguous."[3] What is characteristic for the progress of such an analysis is that a multitude of "equivocations" [*Äquivokationen*], both coarse and fine, emerge and become visible. Should they be captured conceptually, then neologisms are inevitable. It is obvious, however, that such an analytic method is bound to progressively multiply the number of neologisms in accordance with the progressive discovery of equivocations, so that the stock of language that is available to the commonly valid understanding cannot be enough to include the results of these ever-expanding clarifications.

But we must ask ourselves: Is there a rigorous methodology that allows us to fix the found elements of intuition in language? And is it even possible to complete this task, or would we one day find ourselves stuck and discouraged in a plethora of uncovered equivocations too immense to oversee? On this question, Husserl himself may be quoted and his assertion offered up for consideration: "A definitive fixation of scientific language presupposes the complete

---

1. [Edmund Husserl, "Philosophy as Rigorous Science," in *Phenomenology and the Crisis of Philosophy*, trans. Quentin Lauer (New York: Harper and Row, 1965), 71–148.]

2. [Husserl, "Philosophy as Rigorous Science," 96; translation altered.]

3. [Husserl, 96.]

analysis of phenomena—a goal that lies in the dim distance—and so long as this has not been accomplished, the progress of the investigation, too, looked at from the outside, moves to a great extent in the form of demonstrating new ambiguities, distinguishable now for the first time, ambiguities in the very concepts that presumably were already fixed in the preceding investigations. That is obviously inevitable, because it is rooted in the nature of things."[4]

The impressiveness of this passage, which it remains for us only to acknowledge, lies in the assurance that although we are only at the beginning, we have at our disposal a method that is qualified ultimately to accomplish the exact fixation of conceptuality that hitherto has eluded philosophy—even if it may lie in the "dim distance." In our effort to confront the resistance of philosophical language today, we will have to keep this approach in view and make it the measure of our achievements.

Translated by Hannes Bajohr

---

4. [Husserl, 96.]

2

WORLD PICTURES AND WORLD MODELS

(1961)

If the University of Gießen is able to rebuild its philosophical faculty, as we may now confidently hope, then this appears to us as a process of normalization, as a step toward a full restitution of its status as a university.[1]

But also beyond that, there is something unique and symptomatic about this process, if we see it against the backdrop of our intellectual and institutional history. From the bosom of the predecessor of our philosophical faculty, namely, the old Faculty of the

Originally published as "Weltbilder und Weltmodelle," *Nachrichten der Gießener Hochschulgesellschaft* 30: 67–75; from Hans Blumenberg, *Schriften zur Technik*, ed. Alexander Schmitz and Bernd Stiegler (Berlin: Suhrkamp, 2015), 126–137.

1. [In 1960, Blumenberg became professor of philosophy in Gießen. The University of Gießen, founded in 1607, was reduced to the status of a polytechnic after World War II. It did not become a full university again until 1957, and this process of reconstitution is what Blumenberg refers to here.]

Arts, the natural sciences have developed since the end of the Middle Ages. The ceaseless desire of philosophy to ask questions had nourished them and made their first major achievements possible through its logical and methical foundation. Yet at the end of this path stands the full independence of the scientific disciplines, and even, in positivism, their brusque turning away from all philosophical premises and conclusions. What is unique about the restitution process at Gießen, which we hope to be witnessing, is that this genetic procedure appears in reverse: this university that was dominated mostly by the natural sciences because of its almost deadly *capitis damnatio* [capital punishment] is restoring itself from the autonomy of its own will and despite the pressure to expand within existing faculties by resurrecting the philosophical faculty. I think I am able to see very well that here a necessity has imposed itself that arose out of the particular situation at Gießen. A university is no conglomerate of disciplines and faculties but has its own vibrant economy of specialization and interdependence, of the solitude within and the exchange between its areas.

I have tried to prepare some thoughts on what the university can expect from the constitution of its philosophical faculty, or, more specifically, what it can expect from philosophy.

The task that falls to philosophy within the association of academic fields can be traced back to its function in the spiritual economy of humans in general. The countless definitions that have been given for philosophy's achievements in its history have a basic formula at their core: philosophy is the emerging consciousness of humans about themselves. This may sound highly abstract and speculative, but it gets at something elemental. Humans try to conceive of themselves through the incentives, conditionalities, and possibilities that are "vital" and active in their lives. They become aware of what they are by bringing to language their own case before themselves. Whether philosophy is essentially practiced as intellectual history, as epistemology, as anthropology or ontology, as ethics, or as formal logic—in the end, each is just a variation of a homogeneous teleology: what is human is impelled toward language and what has not yet become, or could not yet become language, is dark, unresolved, compulsive, or automatic. The emergence of language is a process of humanization, which is true as well and in particular for the sciences and their theoretical behavior.

Only in language is the fateful incongruence of action and consciousness reconciled, which becomes more and more decisive for our current situation. Machines can help us to skip levels of consciousness, and we often have to respond to the overexertion of objective demand by automatizing ourselves—for example, by using formulas that we do not fully grasp. Thus, our consciousness is "bypassed" by a set of behaviors and actions that result from the inherent laws of our areas of life, which are objectivized and have become autonomous, and are constantly forcing themselves on us. From the conditions and necessities of circumstances immediately result achievements to master the physical world. In itself this is not yet a moral problem, but rather the prelude to any moral problem. We have to know what we are doing to be able to ask ourselves whether it is also what we ought to be doing. The connection between what we know and what we ought to do has become more complicated than Socrates was originally able to see.

We constantly adopt forms of action, obvious ways of behaving, or allegedly plausible things, all of which announce themselves to us as mere "demands of the day." That we have a "history" means, after all, that we do not have to repeatedly and in all matters begin afresh, if that were even possible. However, our desire to understand our history and ourselves in that history also means that we should not submit to what is given and blindly accept our conditionalities but, rather, we must bring them to language. The sciences too employ "devices" [*Vorrichtungen*] of behavior, namely, in the form of their methods. When a scientist sets to work, he adopts a whole stock of methods from his discipline, and his pursuit of knowledge always already precedes his understanding of them: he is capable of doing more than he knows and is able to account for. This is likely a fundamental experience of any scientific career. However, it means that science is technology for a large part, even before it becomes applied science and goes on to yield more technology.

It is, after all, not as Descartes had imagined when he wrote his *Discourse on Method*, which gained him the reputation as the founder of the modern age and its scientific spirit. Descartes wanted a comprehensible method that was in principle transparent to any-body and that was meant to precede and standardize any practice of knowledge. This method was supposed to establish and secure science not only as the mastery of things but also as man's com-plete self-possession; in the end, theory and morality were supposed to merge into one, and through this unity, vouchsafe human self-fulfillment and existential happiness. Even though for Descartes and his time humans were no longer at home in the middle of the uni-verse or at nature's core of meaning, they were postulated all the more vehemently as the meaningful basis for understanding nature and the entirety of the sciences. Here, we find a difference between the total notion of nature on the one hand and the purpose assigned to the totality of understanding nature on the other—a distinction that would later turn out to be highly significant. It is here that "world picture" [*Weltbild*] and "world model" [*Weltmodell*] were separated for the first time, or more precisely, it is here that their fundamental difference becomes visible at all.

I should clarify the two concepts. As "world model" I define the total notion of empirical reality, which depends on the current state of the natural sciences and takes the entirety of their statements into account. I call "world picture" that embodiment of reality through which and in which humans recognize themselves, orient their judg-ments and the goals of their actions, measure their possibilities and necessities, and devise their essential needs. The world picture has "practical power," as Kant would have put it.[2]

Within the world model designed by Descartes, it had to be de-nied that the mechanism of all world processes had anything to do with the purpose of human existence. The body-automaton, which had been synchronized with the *ego cogito* [thinking I] in an enig-matic way that would go on to torment the modern age, had noth-ing to do with human self-consciousness. In this world mechanism, the human could only discover itself as a decoy, though still remain-ing at the center of Descartes's "world picture." Only recent schol-arship has learned to see that the founder of the modern world

---

2. [Immanuel Kant, *Critique of Pure Reason*, ed. Paul Guyer and Allen W. Wood (Cambridge: Cambridge University Press, 1998), A 569/B 597.]

model, which maintained its validity up to Kant and Laplace and beyond, had retained a medieval, humanistic, and anthropocentric world picture. It directly determined what science could mean for Descartes and what ends he had to assign it in the scheme of his method. Science had the function of serving humans. Yet it delivered inhumane models, ideas of nature that ruthlessly alienated humans and estranged them from themselves. All inconsistencies of Cartesian and modern philosophy have their origin in this ambivalence. Yet still, humans, random products of vortices of matter in the world model, found in the world picture expressions of and clues to a meaning exceeding the physical realm. For that reason, the knowledge of nature had to turn directly into human fulfillments and salubrities. Therefore, the final products of all theoretical knowledge were medicine and morality. One could also say the world model was an "organ" of the world picture, if this expression is permitted. Since its humane function had already implied the human place in nature, the world model did not have to state anything about it and could only go on to confirm it through its expected achievements. The world picture contained the interpretation and, as it were, the "instruction manual" for all world models imaginable. But at the same time, this meant that within this world model no sufficient insight could ever be gained into what human cognitive abilities implied for the human being itself. Freed from this justificatory context, science was not able to know on its own terms what it was doing. It was an easy task to assign philosophy its place and power in this framework: it steadily nourished and supplied scientific activity with a conscious sense of purpose, which was contained in the world picture.

Up to now, however, I have merely been evoking a historical circumstance.

Does its "doctrine" also apply to the contemporary or any status of the sciences? If that were true, philosophical questions would have only to return to the origins in history—would have only to regain the initial meaning of this intellectual process—to fulfill their task of bringing to consciousness the meaning that is alive, albeit hidden, in our scientific conduct.

But as regrettable as it may be for the self-evaluation of philosophy in our present, the diagnosis does not allow for this type of tried and tested therapy. Philosophy cannot simply function as the "good memory" of the sciences, as their *memoria*, storing their original meaning ready for retrieval. We must instead accept that history essentially has its reality in separating the functions from their origins and innervations. "History" means that causes effective in the origin do not govern what is in the process of becoming and what has already become. Meaning is no constant in history. The sphere of our actions separates itself from our motivations to act, and a change of purpose exists that autonomously regulates itself and cannot be mastered by merely conserving or restoring original senses of purpose. History is an irreversible nexus of events. Exactly for this reason, everything hinges on the fact that we comprehend and bring to language what we are factually doing.

It is a bald observation that in our current reality the function of the sciences no longer has anything in common with the motivations of their early modern origins. Science has become autonomous. It generates the necessities and principles of its own progress. And if science is indeed something like a meaningful whole—the university as an institution rests on this conviction—then it does not receive this meaning from a sphere of meaning behind or above it, but continuously creates, awakens, and maintains this meaning from within the vitality of its own actions.

These considerations allow me now to define this issue more accurately: the "autonomy" of science means that the correlation of world model and world picture is ruptured. This sounds like a "historical accident"—like a fracture brought about from the outside. But in fact, it was the "world model" that occupied the position of the "world picture" and it is still in the process of consuming the remaining substance of the world picture's stock. That something like a faith in science can exist at all is a result of science no longer being conditioned by any belief in a world picture.

This issue becomes tangible for the first time in the manner in which the Copernican system (while having only a very limited scope as a world model) took on the role of a world picture determining consciousness. As a theoretical statement presented by Copernicus in 1543, it did not contain anything about humans and their position in the world. That humans still looked to this model to find pictorial orientation for their self-assurance in the cosmos reveals the change in meaning of this mainly theoretical construct.

Newton's universe of mechanical gravitation soon became the guiding schema for those who in fact had reason neither to find nor to seek anything there, namely, for the moralists and moral philosophers. One has only to think of Voltaire. All of this helps to frame the historically momentous phenomenon of philosophers starting to glance over the shoulders of naturalists so that the former might glean basic metaphysical principles from the models of the latter. It is curious that philosophy begins to project the role slipping from its grasp onto the natural sciences. Here, one may quickly conclude that *this* was the failure of philosophy: that it no longer coined world pictures that were originally and recognizably its own, nor resolutely resisted the draining of the existing inventory of world pictures. Instead, one might suppose, philosophy was fascinated by the exact sciences and, though in a different form of language, withdrew from the realm of intuitiveness and thus from any eidetically concise conceivability, leaving vacant the "position" governing the power of world pictures. It is only to be expected, then, that philosophy has been constantly called to convey to us once again a world picture of a striking and compelling bindingness. The way in which our current intellectual situation might be called susceptible to worldviews and dogmatisms is undoubtedly a result of the vacant function of the world picture. Speculating on the frustration felt at the loss of meaning, an abundance of substitutes has realized that this potential can be occupied almost at random and has begun to exploit it.

At this point, I might be stating an unsettling point: philosophy will not put forth a new world picture in the future, or any such attempt is bound to fail. This may sadden us, because it is a tremendous loss of meaning for a great tradition. But would it be exactly "philosophical" to evade a truth for that reason?

This thesis demands justification. First of all, the circumstances of how the world picture was lost require a more accurate description. When I said above that in the modern age the world model had taken the position of the world picture, this sounds like an illegitimate claim of rights, or a usurpation. And indeed, it has been stated more than once that the natural sciences of the modern age have destroyed the status and the bindingness of world pictures.

This, however, is wrong. The predicative capability of the world model entered into the continuing loss of the power of the world picture, only furthering what it was itself too impotent to engender. What disempowered the world pictures was the acute new experience of their plurality, an experience that was immediately transformed into historical reflection and critique. The idea that what is valid "beyond the mountains" must be the opposite of what seems certain and obvious on this side, as Montaigne first expressed it, illustrates the fundamental experience from which the historicization of the world picture emerged.[3] This experience caused its powerlessness, which ultimately became bearable only in its aesthetic version. I need only remind you of the implications that the genres of the travel report and the utopian travel novel had for the spirit of the Enlightenment. No element of the obvious remained untouched and was not turned into a contingent historical and geographical fact if seen from a world picture's differently real or fictitious perspective. The historical knowledge about the power of world pictures that accumulated here already meant their disempowerment and is an undeniable reason for the futility of any attempt at their rehabilitation. Taking the ground of validity from under the world pictures was therefore the very specific achievement of the attitude we today call that of the "humanities" [*geisteswissenschaftlich*].

The disintegration of the world picture's function by way of critique and its reoccupation through the world model demonstrate an intimate collaboration between the historical and the scientific attitude. But might this be the type of commonality we could recommend for the *universitas litterarum* [comprehensive university] of today? I would like to answer such a question firmly in the negative.

---

3. [Michel de Montaigne, "Apology for Raymond Sebond," in *The Complete Essays* (Stanford, CA: Stanford University Press, 1958), 437.]

And I would like to go even further by saying that the rehabilitation of the world picture is a demand that philosophy should forgo at all costs and neither should the natural sciences give in to the temptation of replacing the world picture by world models.

Of course, it is correct that world pictures have had a very positive function in the history of human consciousness. It was necessary that humans were not constantly and directly confronted with their eccentric place in nature whose meaning was always precarious. In this regard, imaginative horizons could have a shielding effect and keep internal matters protected. One only has to think of what the world picture of magic, the cosmos picture in antiquity, or the *ordo* idea in the Middle Ages meant in this regard. It is, however, not at all surprising that world pictures with very different contents, such as that of magic and that of the stoic *pronoia* [care; forethought], could have equivalent meaning for consciousness.

Yet we must understand the positivity of world pictures as being subject to certain conditions. The most important one can be formulated by saying that the function of the world picture is essentially monistic. A "world picture" does not accept any other world pictures besides itself; already the plural formulation "worlds" or "world pictures" is a language artifact from the age of historical reflection, a piece of a philosophy of philosophy. Only the unchallenged validity of a world picture within a homogeneous intellectual sphere contains both the ideality and the tolerance that allows one to be humane in it, keeping intact at the same time the innervating balance between comprehensibility and strangeness, between giving reasons and giving norms.

In contrast, the simultaneity of a pluralism of world pictures that has now become tangible causes this tension to subside into historical reflection and relativization. The humanities, in the widest sense, are the presentation and externalization of the world pictures' pluralism. They make worlds accessible and comprehensible for us, but at the same time take away our ability to adopt one of these worlds obviously and unquestionably as our own. In the fading away of world pictures—in the perfection of their verbal and hermeneutical transmission—only one faceless world remains as a formal horizon of all translatability, which despite its unity can no longer be enhanced to the monism of a single world picture. History makes no returns.

It is on the level of a dualism of world pictures that the world pictures' function becomes negative. Here, their tension reverts into the opposite extreme and increases to the point of terror and to the intolerance of codified dogmatisms. At the same time, the exclusivity and animosity of the competing world pictures is all the more charged with affect, the smaller and subtler the differences between them are. The mortal enmity between early Christianity and Gnosticism may serve as an example. Equally, in the present day, the increased tensions between East and West are closely related to the fading of real structural differences. Here, however, another important factor comes into play: beneath the competing world pictures, interests stemming from rather less rarefied spheres interpose themselves imperceptibly. World pictures are becoming pretexts under which interests are advanced. This type of substitution is implied when one speaks of world pictures as ideologies. Discovering the possibility of the abuse of world pictures as ideological instruments— even when what is at stake is not the historically primal idea but its secondary instrumentalization—has ultimately discredited the pictorialization [*Verbildlichung*] of the world and made it an impossible philosophical task.

At the same time, this impossibility passes judgment on those world models that have taken on the status of world pictures and are fulfilling their function pseudomorphically. Their dubiousness lies in the fact that transforming theoretical conceptions of totality into pragmatic principles will remain indifferent against idealization or ideologization, that is, against the capacity to lead or the potential of being tempted. In a world like ours, any intellectual substance has to be saved from being manipulated.

Darwin's theoretical model of the kingdom of organisms and the place of humans in its developmental mechanics was only a partial continuation and elaboration of the mechanistic world model as such. Seen as a theoretical statement, it contained nothing about how humans have to understand themselves, what they were allowed to do, and what they ought to do. Yet once translated into a "world picture," from which it seemed the answers to these questions could be read, it turned into a blatant biologism with truly fateful consequences.

Something similar is true for the history of materialism. According to its origin and inner logic, it is a statement of an epistemological economy. It makes statements about the conditions of the possibility of scientific objects, namely, that exact research can only reach as far as it can be furnished with quantifiable substrates. This is a world model that has to exactly define what it is supposed to achieve and cannot achieve anything beyond its so defined explanatory value. This world model is dogmatized by materialism: it is a hypostatized theory of science of a specific historical stage. Yet out of this solidification, it attempts to represent a theory of humans and their actions, to reduce—in a word—the law of nature and the law of history to one and the same root, and to be a "world picture," in all its bindingness, for general human behavior. No doubt the "mind" [*Geist*] can exercise rule inside forms such as these and need not bemoan its impotence.

What I meant when I cautioned against the return of world pictures as a dangerous illusion has perhaps become clearer now. Definite consequences may now be drawn for the problem of the commonality of the sciences within the *universitas litterarum* that I pointed to at the beginning. Such commonality of the sciences cannot be realized by blurring their borders, or by encroaching on or borrowing from each other. The university does not present itself as a potpourri of its disciplines but rather through the full presence of the guiding idea of science, which shines through the vitality and awareness of each discipline's knowledge practice. And yet philosophy cannot and must not be the schoolmaster of other disciplines. Nor can it be their rear guard, reveling in syntheses. For philosophy does not transcend science outwardly but inwardly. It does not invent the idea of scientific rigor but rather brings this idea to language in each stage of its self-development. The danger inherent in the closed technical terminologies of the sciences is that they seem to have already fulfilled their exactitude in their formal structure and therefore also pretend to have solved the task of their "scientificity." However, the true rigor of a science lies in the congruence between the definition of its expected achievements and the results it produces. Not to state more than we can know—this is much more difficult to realize than the enthusiastic observer of science might at first imagine. Scientific insights are provisional statements to which the reservation of having to prove themselves is constantly applied; if they stabilize into pictures, this reservation is endangered, weakened, made latent, and soon to be forgotten.

It is not the essential and primary point of science to be in command of the matters and powers of the world, and to take possession of them (in fact, this is the point of technology, which is both applied science and the source of scientific problems), but rather to keep our notion of the world at the disposal and under the command of theoretical responsibility. If historical subject matters are at the center when philosophy is taught at universities, if students are laboriously introduced to long-abandoned systemic constructions, the goal is not to convey to them just another bit of knowledge, but to make transparent the critical approach to systems in general. Whoever has learned to find their way into the labyrinth of a system—whoever truly has studied it—can also find his way out of every system, however he might have gotten into it. This person, in other words, has become resistant to seduction.

Today, we may be lacking a positively articulated notion of education, but one thing can nonetheless be maintained: education consists quite essentially of such resistance to temptation. After our own historical experience, it appears to me that this is quite a lot and very positive indeed, and that we should be doing a great deal to fulfill it.

Certainly the loss of world pictures is a painful amputation, as humans have the ineradicable need to demand answers to their ultimate and all-enveloping questions. But especially if this is the case, philosophy has to radically deny humans any obedience to their needs through the coming-to-language of scientific consciousness. Here, a point seems to have been reached at which the much-lamented schism between the natural sciences and the humanities no longer exists. On the day of its anniversary celebration, I would sincerely like to wish the Justus Liebig University that in its further development this may be and remain the Archimedean point of a deeply rooted commonality between its faculties and disciplines, between their work in research and in teaching.

Translated by Florian Fuchs

3

"SECULARIZATION"

Critique of a Category of Historical Illegitimacy

(1964)

That the world has become ever more *worldly* and continues to do so is a complaint that has not ceased since the early days of Christianity. But such a statement has a comprehensible meaning only in *theological* terms, and its assessment likewise depends on theological principles. From the perspective of a dialectical theology, this claim may even meet with a positive assessment, in that growing worldliness is read as the formula for a spiritual cleansing of *this world*, which reveals itself as what it is precisely as a consequence of becoming more worldly. Secularization would thus portend that judgment of final separation which is anticipated as the eschatological event. This *spiritual* usage of the word has nothing to do with secularization as a *historical* category, though it appears in a most

Originally published as Hans Blumenberg, "'Säkularisation': Kritik einer Kategorie historischer Illegitimität," in *Die Philosophie und die Frage nach dem Fortschritt: Verhandlungen des Siebten Deutschen Kongresses für Philosophie, Münster 1962*, ed. Helmut Kuhn and Franz Wiedmann (Munich: Pustet, 1964), 240–265.

modern form, that of the *wave of secularization*, thus dressing itself in the cloak of a natural phenomenon.

When it is claimed that (to list a number of examples chosen at random)

... the final state promised by the *Communist Manifesto* was a secularization of the biblical paradise;

... the modern work ethos was a secularization of the ideal of holiness and its method, asceticism;

... the notion of guilt found in our criminal law was a secularization of the sacred guilt relation in which the sinner stood before God;

... the notion of theoretical certainty, which has become doubtful in modern epistemology, was the secularized form of the fundamental theological problem of certainty of salvation;

... the ideas of the unity of mankind and its political organization in a League of Nations or the United Nations were secularizations of the unity of redeemed mankind in the last days;

... Laplace's demon was the secularization of divine omniscience in the form of a mechanistic ideal of knowledge;

... the democratic idea of the equality of all before the law was a secularization of the Christian equality of all men before God

—when these and countless similar claims are made,[1] the aim is very much not to reach spiritual conclusions, a pre-eschatological *judgment*, but to *understand* certain historical processes.

What emerges here is a *precise* usage of the term secularization, one that goes back to its original *legal* meaning and content, that

---

1. Hermann Lübbe's lecture, which directly preceded my own at this congress, releases me from the task of supplying instances of the term's use, thus allowing me to avoid appearing to engage in polemics [Hermann Lübbe, "Säkularisierung als geschichtsphilosophische Kategorie," in *Die Philosophie und die Frage nach dem Fortschritt: Verhandlungen des Siebten Deutschen Kongresses für Philosophie, Münster 1962*, ed. Helmut Kuhn and Franz Wiedmann (Munich: Pustet, 1964), 221–239]. For the purposes of the critical analysis to be undertaken here, it is furthermore immaterial that this category of historical understanding is already in heavy use, rather than being a concept to be newly proposed or constructed on a purely hypothetical basis. Of course, the term's actual use has a significance of its own, one that provides an additional clue to the intellectual situation in which we find ourselves.

is, the *expropriation* of ecclesiastical possessions as it has been practiced and referred to since the Peace of Westphalia.[2] It is easy to see that there is an *analogy* between the usages of the term secularization recounted here and these processes of expropriation—an analogy that makes the idea of secularization liable to be used as a basic concept of historical understanding. The transference taking place here draws its assumptions from the *features* of the process of expropriation, which are as follows:

a)   the ability of the expropriated goods to be identified;
b)   the legitimacy of primary ownership;
c)   the seizure being unilateral.

So far as modern authors find it necessary to define the terms they use at all, the specimens gathered here display the above features. "Becoming worldly [*Verweltlichung*], that is, the release of spiritual or ecclesiastical ideas and notions, likewise the release of spiritual (consecrated) objects and persons from their ties to the divine."[3] Furthermore: "Today, it is customary to speak of secularization where ideas and knowledge are untied from their original source in revelation and made accessible to human reason by its own power. Hence, secularization concerns operations of the mind that were originally enabled by faith but are subsequently performed by man

---

2.   This is to say that the full range of meanings in the conceptual history unfolded by Hermann Lübbe has not been absorbed into or *transferred* to its usage as it is relevant to historical examination. In particular, the programmatic elements and immediate value judgments entailed by *secularization* [*Verweltlichung*] as a kind of transfer of power or change of rule within a realm imagined and constant have been omitted. This is not to exclude the possibility of *secularization* [*Säkularisation*] occasionally appearing as the historical statement of a quantitative distribution of shares between spiritual and temporal instances, a shifting of competences between transcendent and immanent allegiances. Such proportions, distributions, and demarcations may perhaps be *identified* from case to case and compared to preceding and subsequent situations, but this does not suffice as a foundation of an understanding. The boundary drawn here aims to delineate a basic concept of understanding, which takes its bearings from a model process and the necessity of which is in need of further scrutiny.

3.   Siegfried Reicke, "Säkularisation," in *Die Religion in Geschichte und Gegenwart* (Tübingen: Mohr, 1961), 5:1280.

with the abilities at his disposal."[4] Finally: "By exposing and creating awareness of the process of secularization, the continuity between the present and the past is preserved. . . . There is a continuity of the historic even in the negative relation of the past to the present. . . . The reality in which we actually live is obscured by misleading notions."[5] This is clear only inasmuch as it implies that we find in our relationship with the past a discontinuity that does not actually exist, and we do so, it would seem, because of a reluctance to acknowledge a debt to the past on the part of the present. The historical interpretation that works with the category of secularization uncovers the concealed facts of the matter, and in doing so, calls attention to an *objective cultural debt*—no shorter formula for the implications of *secularization* is conceivable.[6]

For the time being, it should be quite coolly noted that a historical interpretation seeking to avail itself of the expression *secularization* bears, from a methodical perspective, the *burden of proving* that the *features* of the seizure are in evidence in the thematic process. Failing that, what emerges may well be a statement that sounds profound and creates the illusion of having understood something, but its grasp for a historical structure misses the mark.

I shall now move on to the *thesis* of my remarks, which maintains that the use of the category of secularization, particularly in its most commonplace formulas, is neither equal to nor even aware of this methodical burden of proof. An impressive and well-known

---

4. Martin Stallmann, *Was ist Säkularisierung?* (Tübingen: Mohr, 1960), 33. The scheme of expropriation is only just discernible in the background, making itself felt in the cautious phrasing ("untied . . . made accessible"), but the author is completely aware of the transfer implied here: "The term 'secularization' first appeared in the study of history, where it denoted the transfer of ecclesiastical and spiritual rights to jurisdiction or property to secular powers. The word then came to be applied to a process in intellectual history, whereby ideas and behaviors untied themselves from the religious context within which they were originally founded and were henceforth deduced from general reason. This transfer from one sphere to another is usually stated without asking how this word's apparently multiple meanings were made possible." Stallmann, *Was ist Säkularisierung?*, 5; note the reflexive use of *untie*!

5. Friedrich Delekat, *Über den Begriff der Säkularisation* (Heidelberg: Quelle & Meyer, 1958), 55f.

6. Delekat, *Über den Begriff der Säkularisation*, 60.

book can thus simply assume the origin of the historical idea of progress from theological eschatology as *known*, but none of the above features has yet been cited in support of the claim that the idea of progress was a secularized form of eschatology.[7]

There is nothing to substantiate the claim of a transposition of eschatology into the idea of progress. The crucial *formal* difference is this: eschatology speaks of an event irrupting into history, in relation to which it is transcendent and heterogeneous; the idea of progress extrapolates into the future from a structure immanent to history and forming part of any present.[8]

More important still, however, is a *genetic* difference: in its late form, though historically antecedent to the modern age, eschatology is an answer to the question concerning the meaning and course of history as a whole; the idea of progress is originally a structural formula for *theoretical* processes and as such was applied in the *aesthetic* realm as a formula of protest against the binding claims for constant exemplars made on behalf of humanism.[9] There is thus

---

7. [Blumenberg refers here to Karl Löwith, *Meaning in History: The Theological Implications of the Philosophy of History* (Chicago: Chicago University Press, 1957).]

8. Progress claims that subsequent history is foretold not in the register of metaphysical insights, but as laws of a history that has already been grasped rationally and that one always believes already to have *experienced* to an extent sufficient to justify induction. To this effect, Kant speaks of "a possible representation a priori of events which are supposed to happen then," "a divinatory narrative of things imminent in future time," by dint of the theoretical subject simultaneously being his object's principle: "But how is a history a priori possible? Answer: if the diviner himself creates and contrives the events which he announces in advance." Immanuel Kant, *Conflict of the Faculties*, trans. Mary J. Gregor (Lincoln: University of Nebraska Press, 1979), 141, 143. The truth of total historical conceptions would thus be founded in an ideal case of the axiom *verum et factum convertuntur* [the true and the made are convertible], which has been formulated since the days of Vico. A neat example of how this immanence could be misunderstood and how *soothsaying* [*Wahrsagen*] in the sense of that axiom could come to be misunderstood as divination [*Weissagung*] is to be found in Friedrich Nicolai's reaction to Kant, whom he calls the "inventor of a soothsaying narration of history"—in doing so missing the point in a manner that was to prove influential linguistically. Friedrich Nicolai, *Über meine gelehrte Bildung* (Berlin: Nicolai, 1799), 94–99.

9. The relative contributions of the theories of science and art to the emergence of the new historical consciousness have been brought closer to a functional classification in Hans Robert Jauß's lecture at this congress, adding to the case for

little to be said in favor of the claim that the *factual* historical succession of an eschatological interpretation of history by the idea of progress represents the endurance of a notion whose substance has become alienated from its origin.

No less questionable is the historical applicability of the category of *secularization* according to the *second criterion*, which demands that an idea belong originally and singularly to the theological realm if we are to speak of secularization. The prerequisite is that it should be at all possible *methodically* to elucidate the question of *property rights* to the supposedly secularized notions. In the first instance, the legality of the acquisition and ownership of ideas is but an analogy to property rights to objects. If this analogy is taken too far, such as by imagining a sale or purchase in good faith, historical understanding is left empty-handed. By contrast, it manifestly makes more sense and is easiest, methodically speaking, to admit talk of secularization only where a genuine and authentically theological subject matter is at issue. We would then be faced with a kind of property in the sense of *copyright law* [*urheberrechtlich*], in which the act of seizure takes a particularly drastic form.[10] There can be no doubt that historical hypotheses of the kind discussed here assume the original and primal *un*worldliness[11] of a notion to be self-

---

the immanent authenticity of the idea of progress [Hans Robert Jauß, "Ursprung und Bedeutung der Fortschrittsidee in der 'Querelle des Anciens et des Modernes,'" in *Die Philosophie und die Frage nach dem Fortschritt*, 51–72].

10. Of course, this methodical maxim cannot deny its position within the modern age's frame of reference: as far as theology is concerned, it cannot sensu stricto claim property rights to its contents based on copyright, but only by gift of Revelation. I might have chosen a more neutral phrasing and spoken of a "relation of primary property." If I chose to adhere to the version I presented at Münster, I did so not from a quasi-historical respect for something that was said once, but specifically to underscore the peculiarity and conditionality of the historical attitude as distinct from the ahistorical *participation* in immanent self-interpretations.

11. To speak of *unworldliness* in a purely historical context can only mean that statements that can be deduced or verified neither *by the world* (i.e., empirically) nor by pure rationality are espoused and accepted as binding by virtue of faith in their origin and legitimation. From a purely formal perspective, the possibility of *secularization* rests in consciousness of the motive of espousal and bindingness diminishing, i.e., it is explicitly denied or implicitly *annulled* by the assertion that such claims must admit of an empirical or a priori foundation. A transformation of a material kind need not yet follow from this.

evident, to detect in their *becoming* worldly a process that is irreversible, possible in this direction only.

This feature of authenticity seems to be provable for the claim that, in the modern age, theological eschatology recurred in various secular transformations, for example as utopias of earthly paradise, as the essence of revolutionary programs, or as the notion of history as the final court of appeal. But before the possibility of the historic succession of such notions is considered, the questionable origins of biblical-Christian eschatology itself must be brought to bear. With regard to the status of the unclear methodic issue pertaining to this question, it is striking that one of the first authorities for the historical applicability of the category of secularization does not grant eschatological notions any heterogeneity vis-à-vis the cosmological-cyclical speculations emanating from the world of the Hellenistic mind: Rudolf Bultmann derives biblical eschatology from a basic myth of a kind of constant regeneration of the world, such as we may encounter in Stoic cosmology, but the cyclical process had been shortened to just *one* period. There is no need for me to discuss the substance of this thesis here;[12] suffice it to point out that this deduction of eschatology leads us back to a thoroughly profane interest in knowledge [*Wissensinteresse*]. Human curiosity seeks to explain the course of the world as a whole, but this explanation has no direct bearing on the life of the individual. Shortening unlimited cyclical recurrence to a single cycle alters nothing about the *theoretical* nature of this perception of the world. The radical shift in the meaning of such notions takes place only once the anticipated great and ultimate cosmic events are moved into the lifetime of the individual or a generation.

We find this *immediate expectation* of the imminent apocalypse, so completely different in nature, in the sphere from which the New Testament originates. In terms of content, little has changed from Jewish apocalyptic thought, but by shortening the space of the anticipation to a time frame that renders it acute for the present moment gives it a completely heterogeneous function: the immediate

---

12. Rudolf Bultmann, *History and Eschatology* (Edinburgh: Edinburgh University Press, 1957), chap. 3. See my review of this book in *Gnomon* 31 (1959): 163–166.

expectation no longer epitomizes the fulfillment of disappointed expectations in history and postponed secular hopes; following the Babylonian exile, compensations for a destroyed national existence developed whose consoling effect was counterbalanced by their highly *indefinite* nature; their purpose was to make history tolerable, to bestow on it a surrogate of meaning. Immediate expectation, on the other hand, destroys the significance of history by directly confronting the individual with the care for his salvation, demands that he abandon all earthly ties, and renders all attempts at self-assertion and providing for the future objectless. It is something radically different on the one hand to impose on history a framework of boundary notions, with creation at the beginning and judgment and apocalypse at the end, and on the other to do away with any meaning that an image of history might have by rendering what happens *in* the world insignificant against what happens *to* it.

If one takes these two different forms of eschatology—one a speculation framing and justifying history, the other an immediate expectation exploding history and stripping it of any relevance—to be entirely heterogeneous in their meaning and assignable to a common category only with regard to some nonessential overlap in their imagery, the immediate expectation emerges as the authentic and genuinely theological point of departure for a process in intellectual history that might, at first sight, lend itself to being interpreted as secularization. For because the immediate expectation was directly and perceptibly *disappointed* by the continuation of history and the life of the individual, and by the continued existence of the world, it finds itself compelled to perform artful modifications to its content and to its acute threat. By permitting the return and the acceptance of history, eschatology *historicizes* itself and becomes secular. Sources still allow us to trace how the earliest Christians' eschatological mood of *hope* in the last days shifted to an eschatological mood of *fear* throughout the subsequent epoch. Soon, the community is no longer praying for the Lord's second coming, but asking *pro mora finis*, for a postponement of the end and a stay of execution.[13] The

---

13. See Karl Georg Kuhn, "Maranathâ," in *Theologisches Wörterbuch zum Neuen Testament*, ed. Gerhard Kittel (Stuttgart: Kohlhammer, 1942), 4:470–475

last judgment becomes God's secret reserve in history, which does not so much confront human consciousness with its acute crisis as it serves to justify God for not sparing the Christians from the expressions of His wrath against the pagans, thus making them pay the price for the longed-for continuation of the history of the not-as-yet separated *genus humanum* [human race].[14]

The seed of the *philosophy of history* is sown the moment that the biblical claims about the end of the world can no longer withstand a literal reading but must instead be interpreted more or less as *allegories*. A speculative eschatology founded chiefly on Daniel and the Revelation of St. John the Divine was in no further need of being secularized, for the theological elements it uses are already primarily attempts to answer the meaning of history itself. What was more, the unity of eschatology was torn apart: in the Middle

---

(on 1. Cor. 16:22); Didache 10:6; Rev. 22:20; Tertullian, *Apologeticum*, 32:1, 39:2. On the process by which acute eschatology retrogresses, see Martin Werner, *Die Entstehung des christlichen Dogmas*, 2nd ed. (Berne: Haupt, 1941) (on which see Hans Blumenberg, "Epochenschwelle und Rezeption," *Philosophische Rundschau* 6 [1958]: 102–107).

14. Tertullian, *Apologeticum*, 41:3: "For He who has once for all ordained an everlasting judgment after the end of the world, does not hasten the separation, which is a circumstance of the judgment, before the end of the world. Meanwhile he deals impartially with the whole human race, both as indulging and reproving; he wished that good and evil should be shared alike by his own servants and by the wicked, so that, by an equal partnership, all might have experience both of his gentleness and of his sternness." Franz Oehler and John E.B. Mayor, eds., *Q. Septimi Florentis Tertulliani Apologeticus: The Text of Oehler, Annotated, with an Introduction*, trans. Alexander Souter (Cambridge: Cambridge University Press, 2012), 212. Into what untold distance the events of the end of days are remythologized here is most plainly visible in the necessity of making jurisdiction at the community level ("this violence is pleasing to God"), which was won by prayers "for the state of the world" (Oehler and Mayor, *Q. Septimi Florentis Tertulliani Apologeticus*, 111), plausible as a provisional substitute for doomsday postponed: "For our judgment too is delivered with great weight, as among those who are sure that they are acting under the eye of God, and there is the greatest anticipation of the future judgment" (Oehler and Mayor, 113). This, if anything, is eschatology secularized: it serves to explain the unchanged course of the world and to sanction discipline within the *factio Christiana*. And Tertullian is no outlier: to his treatise "Tertullian als Schriftsteller" [Tertullian as a writer] Karl Holl added a handwritten note that nearly sounds disappointed: "No apologist seems to hope for the Lord's imminent return!" Karl Holl, *Gesammelte Aufsätze zur Kirchengeschichte* (Tübingen: Mohr, 1928), 3:11n.

Ages, there was a *cosmic* eschatology and an *individual* one, and it was inevitable that man should have become preoccupied with questions concerning his own last things. The late doctrine of an individual judgment for each deceased person relegated the general judgment of the last days to a remote position with little effect on the individual mind. The question concerning history's meaning and form was thus uncoupled from the original care for salvation, an attitude that was neither at home in the world nor directed toward it, and integrated into the system of a dogmatic explanation of the world.

We would thus find a piece of real *secularization* in the question concerning history if it were possible to find evidence of the third feature given earlier: the *unilateral* nature of the seizure, the expropriation, and thus the distortion to an inauthentic condition, alienated from its origins. But this feature is absent, and it is absent not just on account of our failure to prove it methodically, but for a reason to which I already alluded when I said that eschatology has *historicized itself*. It is not that much-derided *autonomous thought* had seized, speculatively usurped, and violently remade the question concerning the end and goal of history; it is instead the inner consequence of the original eschatological idea itself and its ineluctable fate that forced its secularization. The excessive stress placed on the ethical demands in the acute situation of the imminent anticipation, the inevitable refutability of the apocalyptic prophecies, the necessary disappointment of a renunciation that would have triumphed only in the world's undoing—these factors force answers to questions that had not previously posed themselves and to answer which theology could not attempt an infinite number of times. The elasticity in answering this question, of which theology had a sudden need, the studied indeterminacy and ambiguity of allegorical speculations, the distinct contrast with subtle dogmatic exactitude in other theological articles—all suggested the possibility that this might, after all, be a question not of revelation but rather of secular responsibility.

To speak of secularization as an act of expropriation assumes a quite natural state of competition to obtain between a spiritual instance and a temporal one. Secularization would accordingly be of the historic forms of an infringement of the temporal instance on the spiritual, in this case the form of the appropriation of its ideational substance. From the perspective of intellectual history, however, this assumption is a fiction, or a stock piece of theology's traditional self-interpretation. A province of secularity or, more accurately, one beyond the remit of theology, was delimited and stabilized only in the course of the all-encompassing process in which an unworldly, eschatological anticipation was disappointed and banished to speculative indeterminacy. Man now found himself, alone and left to his own devices, with the burden of newly arisen big questions, the inscrutability of a history of which he had only just become aware as such. *Worldliness—secularity—*could not exist until there was *unworldliness:* that which claimed to be *not of this world* called this *world* into question, while at the same time logically opening up the possibility to it to prove itself *qua* world, as permanent and reliable, and for its continued existence to be desired—for example, worthy of being prayed for. In this case, secularization is anything but expropriation as a unilateral, unlawful act, but instead the constitution of a previously unknown worldliness from its religious disavowal and unrealization [*Entwirklichung*]. Primary secularization is not a transformation of something given but the original inception, the primary crystallization of that secularism which by the term secularization could first be accused of unlawfully infringing on areas beyond its remit. There is nothing primordial about the duality of the two instances; instead, it is a secondary product of processes internal to a mode of thinking itself—one that is, in the broadest sense, eschatologically dominated.

To summarize the foregoing with regard to the example of the theory of progress: it is not the case that the modern idea of progress was made possible only by the precedence of theological eschatology or that it had appropriated and transformed the latter's claims contrary to its original intention. What is true, however, is that the idea of progress was forced to extend the scope of its claims, which were originally circumscribed and specific to certain objects, thereby "*overstretching*" them to the generality of a philosophy of history. It had to do so to answer a question that, as it were, remained at large, abandoned and unsaturated, after theology had made it *virulent*. As one possible answer to the question concerning history in its entirety, one might say that the idea of progress was *drawn into* eschatology's function for consciousness. In the process, it was enlisted for an explanatory performance that overtaxed its rationality. An originally theological imaginative content was not subjected to a violent transposition, but rather, what was in itself already a secular, not secularized, notion was reinterpreted and overinterpreted, burdening it with, if you will permit the phrase, the responsibility for theology's failure and self-denial [*Versagen und Sich-Versagen*]. The emergence of the idea of progress and its stepping in for the religious interpretation of history are thus two completely different processes. I do not wish to overstate the argument for the sake of inverting it, but the violence of the transposition—the reinterpretation and overinterpretation to the point of inauthenticity—was not visited upon eschatology, by the worldly upon the unworldly instance. Instead, it was the idea of progress, which emerged independently and in different contexts, that was now required for a *task* that exceeded and distended its original rationality, driving it to make a metaphysical claim about the totality of history.

These considerations have thus not only sought to clarify the methodical burden of proof for applying the category of secularization, but at the same time have come across the reason secularization could appear as an elementary form of explaining historical processes: the historical identity and methodical identifiability of supposedly *secularized* notions is an illusion created by the identity of the *function* that altogether heterogeneous contents can assume in certain *positions* within man's system of understanding the world and himself. In our intellectual history, Christian theology has played the eminent part of the expander of this system by creating such *positions* that could no longer be undone or, within the theoretical economy, remain unoccupied. To theology, no question need remain unanswerable, and thereupon is founded the ease with which it inserts titles into the economy of human needs for knowledge. One might call this a charge and compare it to the charge brought by Leibniz against Descartes for having, in the radicalism of his doubt, demanded evidence of a kind that neither he nor anyone else would ever be able to provide.

The willingness to take on such a liability and to deal with it as one's own continues largely to define the intellectual history of the modern age. That this desperate effort to come to terms with the legacy of theology should lead to the more or less open insinuation that the legacy had been obtained by disreputable means has a tragic aspect. What actually occurs in the process thought of as secularization is not the *transposition* [*Umsetzung (Transposition)*] of an authentically theological content into its secular self-alienation, but the *reoccupation* [*Umbesetzung*] of a position that had become vacant yet could not be eliminated as such.

The example to which I have hitherto devoted the most attention, the thesis regarding the origin of the idea of progress, which has become a truism, cannot, however, be applied as a paradigm by which to understand all cases of supposed secularization. There are cases in which early Christianity was under a similar *problem pressure* raised by alien questions as has just been explained with regard to modern rationality. We shall have to rid ourselves of the assumption that there is such a thing as a fixed canon of *great questions* that, throughout history, have continuously stimulated human curiosity, and that this canon had its counterparts in the changing mythological, theological, and metaphysical systems. The questions do not always precede the answers. There is such a thing as the spontaneous, primal generation of great claims of acute effect. When their credibility and validity dwindles, they leave behind equally great questions, to which new answers are then needed. I need only remind you to what extent the dwindling *mythos* of the Greeks *prescribed* the questions philosophy would have to answer. The history of philosophy is taken up with the effort to live up to this supposed measure of its powers, and with the disappointments that were inevitable in the process. It would appear, then, that there are problems that are posed only by their supposed solutions being proffered, or by what might appear as a solution after the fact. Questions that have thus become established and stabilized are difficult to banish, and amidst the competition between manifold forms of intellectually coping with the problems of human existence, the presence of these big questions offers a criterion that must be satisfied.

This is not, however, a phenomenon that first appears in the post-Christian era—early Christianity itself had to address it. The early Christians too were asked questions that Christianity did not come equipped to solve, or at least not to the degree of precision demanded of it in the Hellenistic world. If, for instance, one considers how strongly our tradition has been affected by the problem of immortality, it will keep on coming as a surprise to find that this question does not exist in biblical sources dating from before the exile. And even in the New Testament, there is palpable uncertainty in formulating the goal of salvation, an uncertainty that was removed only by the precise demands of Greek metaphysics. For a number of reasons, Greek philosophy was able to know more precisely which conditions had to be met in a promise of *happiness*, and it, in turn, prescribed its own obligatory program to Christian patristics. This is to say that Christianity, as it entered into the Hellenistic world, was already assigned a *role*; a scope for action, a matrix to be filled, and a claim to being heard could be justified only by taking on this role. For the first time, a system of assertions appeared under the guise of the *final* shape of *philosophy*. Theology created this peculiar claim by cloaking itself in the language of ancient metaphysics and claiming to answer the universal questions that had confounded it. Patristic authors repeatedly assert that Jesus had answered all the ancient philosophers' questions. I draw attention to this phenomenon because it shows that the modern syndrome known as secularization is not unique. The Christian reception of classical antiquity and the so-called modern secularization of Christianity are, both structurally and functionally, to a great extent analogous historical phenomena: patristic Christianity appears in the role of ancient philosophy; modern philosophy largely *stands in* for the function of theology.

A more important observation still is this: already in the polemics and apologetics accompanying the reception of Christianity in the ancient world, the language of notions of *property* is in evidence, as are the attendant accusations of *unlawfulness*. To acquire and to assert legitimacy is, in history, the basic aspiration of that which is new or claims to be; to contest or to dash this legitimacy and the self-confidence resulting from it is the technique by which the existing order asserts itself. Early Christianity not only claimed legiti-

macy for its possession of the truth by virtue of revelation but also
denied paganism the legitimate ownership even of those notions
held in common, or indeed that Christianity had taken from it.[15]
The ploy to have the philosophers secretly learn from the Bible so
as to pass off the reception of their dictums as the restitution of
alienated property occurs again and again in patristic literature. Of
the much-quoted Stoic doctrine, according to which the cosmos existed for man's benefit, St. Ambrose writes: "Unde hoc, nisi de nostris
scripturis, dicendum adsumpserunt?" [From what source have they
claimed that this must be said, if not from our scriptures?][16] Tertullian, as radical as ever, grabs this problem by the root. Regarding the
nature of the soul, he says (in *De amima* I, 6) that what mattered
was not the truth of a statement as such, but rather its origins—
and it was better to remain ignorant, if God had not wanted to
reveal something, than to learn of it through men who had presumed to gain an understanding of it had thus succeeded in acquir-
ing this truth. This is a case of Tertullian's famous technique of *prae-
scriptio* [legal objection]—of his devising—whereby the opponent in

---

15. Augustine feels free to put this in general terms: "Moreover, if those who
are called philosophers, and especially the Platonists, have said aught that is true
and in harmony with our faith, we are not only not to shrink from it, but to claim
it for our own use from those who have unlawful possession of it." St. Augustine,
On Christian Doctrine, trans. J. F. Shaw (Mineola, NY: Dover, 2009), 75. Note
how the claim is backed with legal sanction—how is such language possible? It
seems to me that a form of Platonism is at work in the background here, according
to which truth obtains by virtue of a relation of origin—as of an image to an
original a truth identified with God, and already in Plato this dependency of the
image is something that cannot be exempted and ignored but must always be *im-
plemented* as a factor essential to its content. The patristic authors thus claim not
only to integrate such elements of truth as they *find* in the ancient philosophers
into their system and to make use of it as that which is available to all—in modern
terms, that which is objective [*das Objektive*]—but also in fact to be the first to
restitute its full *truth* by restoring its genetic relationship of dependency. Such a
Platonic trace can be identified even in the theologically grounded accusation that
is contained within the concept of *secularization*: just as an image not only represents an original but also and indeed rather conceals it and causes it to be forgotten (Plotinus, Third Ennead, Seventh Tractate: "Time and Eternity"), the supposedly secularized notion takes the place of the original, authentic claim not as a
reminder but to make it dispensable—and to expose this genetic nexus by means
of history already is restitution enough.

16. *De officiis ministrorum* I, 28.

a dispute is put at a disadvantage by the formal legal conditions before the matter at hand can even be argued. Accordingly, he forbids heretics to cite scripture in their arguments, for a thing could be used only by its lawful owner, and lawful ownership comes into being by being acquired from the hand able to dispose of it.[17]

These few allusions are intended to show that it was not only with the application of the concept of secularization to the context of intellectual history that the basic notion of property in ideas and its legitimacy was awakened and became effective for historical understanding. Instead, this basic notion is indissolubly tied to the problem of epochs in our tradition and the specific interpretation given to it by theology. But finding it to be historically conditioned does not yet suffice to prepare a critique of the concept of secularization. What must be added is to note the thoroughgoing historical change in the relationship between the concept of truth and the basic notion of property. The modern age truly begins when the legitimacy of property in ideas as stemming from their authentic inception alone becomes the norm, and with the concomitant radical rejection of property being founded in anything like a *gift* [*Schenkung*]. In theology, the moment of grace was taken to such a pitch that it elicited the objection of the theoretical self-assertion of reason: only a truth that is self-produced is a truth that can be truly owned. But this capacity for self-producing truth applies, in principle, to every rational subject; it is an *objective* given. The principle of the interchangeability of the predicates *verum* [what is true] and *factum* [what is made], which is of such foundational significance for the modern age, deprives the notion of property in ideas that can be passed down, or of their unlawful appropriation, of any basis. Truth can no longer be a heritable fief, a distinction claimed by a few or a particular group.[18]

---

17. I refer to my earlier studies on the problem of reception: "Kritik und Rezeption antiker Philosophie in der Patristik," *Studium Generale* 12, no. 8 (1959): 485–497; "Das dritte Höhlengleichnis," *Studi e Ricerche di Storia della Filosofia* 39 (1961); "Augustins Anteil an der Geschichte des Begriffs der theoretischen Neugierde," *Revue des Etudes Augustiniennes* 7 (1961): 35–70; "'Curiositas' und 'Veritas': Zur Ideengeschichte von Augustinus, Confessiones X 35," *Studia Patristica* 6 (1962): 294–302.

18. Against Descartes's voluntarism in the foundation of rational truths, Leibniz is able to make the objection—which, though simple, was considered to be

It is also connected with the change in the historical preconditions of the notion of intellectual property that we—quite independently of examining the applicability of the concept of secularization as a historical category—must conclude that at least this concept, too, is itself the result of secularization. Although the historian may not concur in the value judgment implicit in this notion—neither in regretting the loss of spiritual property nor in satisfaction at its cleansing for the benefit of the temporal realm—by using the category, he nonetheless enters into Christianity's self-interpretation. From the theological self-definition, the historian adopts the assumption, which is a necessary corollary of the idea of revelation, of a *beginning* that cannot be deduced from the history preceding it and has no preconditions, and with which begins a historical formation that is not merely new, but *final*. Any historical self-confidence that afterward thought it could once more define a new beginning or thought it had done so was bound to come into conflict with the Christian era's claim to finality.

The *modern age*—no matter what it might have made its program—would merely by dint of its self-confidence as being new and beginning from the ground up have been un-Christian, which is to say, in theological terms, *secular*. From the theological position in this conflict followed the necessity of putting this new claim to finality in the wrong, and *secularization* is the term by which this need could be met. There is no fault to be found with the internal consistency of this connection. But this does not yet make secularization a category of historical understanding, but first a concept of theological self-interpretation and self-assertion.

But this does not yet explain the fact that this notion could nonetheless make so much sense to historical thinking as a means to understanding intellectual-historical configurations; indeed, it was fascinating to many. Even if continuing the critique for which approaches

---

compelling—that the properties of a geometrical object would then apply only *velut privilegium* [by privilege], which is to say, with sly ambiguity, that they belonged to neither the object nor the knowing subject by their own virtue. See Gottfried Wilhelm Leibniz, *Philosophische Schriften*, ed. Carl Immanuel Gerhardt (Berlin: Weidmann, 1880), 4:274. See Hans Blumenberg, *Paradigms for a Metaphorology*, trans. Robert Savage (Ithaca, NY: Cornell University Press, 2010), 32.

and examples are given here should lead to most supposed diagnoses of secularization to fall short of the standard of proof, the question still remains whether the appearance in all these phenomena cannot be objectively grounded. I believe that it is possible to get to the root of this appearance. The modern age was not only content to let the positions that were occupied within the system to be passed down to it; it even did all it could to conceal the *competition* into which it had entered by claiming that after the *final* epoch in history, there should be another epoch, a turn in history, and that it was once again to be final and unsurpassable. I need only to remind you of the astonishing fact that only in the seventeenth century did the chronology symmetrically focused on the birth of Christ as its zero hour become firmly established.[19]

---

19. See Adalbert Klempt, *Die Säkularisierung der universalhistorischen Auffassung. Zum Wandel des Geschichtsdenkens im 16. und 17. Jahrhundert* (Göttingen: Musterschmidt, 1960). Although Klempt defines his concept of the "secularization of the European life of the mind" in the sense at issue here as the "critical transformation of notions and habits of thought that were originally framed in terms of theology and the Christian faith in salvation into such as could be contemplated in worldly terms" (Klempt, *Die Säkularisierung der universalhistorischen Auffassung*, 7), he does not follow through on the program he has thus set himself. The manner in which political history becomes untied from the history of the Church is a process of dissociation, of the separation of competences, not of the *transformation* of an identical substance. The doctrine of the two kingdoms permits Melanchthon systematically to categorize and make obligatory also the extrabiblical historical literature republished in the age of humanism but also to admit its standing in its own right, which consisted in the objective-quantitative fact that, against this corpus, biblical events appeared as a minute and provincial excerpt from the *series historiarum mundi* [sequence of world history]. Moreover, the corpus of profane history kept growing against the horizon of a world that was itself expanding, whereas that of the Bible remained constant. The separation of subject matters leads to a separation of methods: Jean Bodin makes a pithy semantic distinction between *intueri* [being regarded], with which *historia divina* [divine history] is to be approached, and *explicare* [explaining], which is proper to *historia humana* [human history]. See Jean Bodin, "Methodus ad facilem historiarum cognitionem," chap. 1 in *Œuvres philosophiques de Jean Bodin*, ed. Mesnard, "Corpus général des philosophes français" (Paris: Presses Universitaires de France, 1951), 3:101–475. But in fact, such systematizations offer protection against encroachments looking to transform either *genus historiae* [class of history]. Of course, this opens up new opportunities for profane history to structure its matter and consider it as a whole, such as a negative forerunner of the idea of progress in the rejection of the scheme of the four metals and their descending order of value con-

The modern age did not seek to demonstrate its constitutive *secularity* but rather shied away from doing so: the first centuries of the modern age are of a forced *spiritual* attitude that phenomenally overshadows anything medieval. During these centuries, the world of sacred language was fearfully preserved, drawn into the philosophical and political spheres, drawn over as the preferred *cover*. It is far from being the case that the modern age possessed that cheerful confidence in itself and its right which Burckhardt bestowed on his Renaissance and of which Nietzsche believed all post-Christianity to be capable. The modern age let itself be put in the wrong and has become questionable to itself in its historical legitimacy. It no longer wished to be the epoch of theology, yet it could not escape the fate of the heir: being unable to disentangle itself from theological interpretation. This epoch begins with the explosive problem of *justification* not only in relation to the history of *dogma*—justification, in the broadest sense, remains its innermost problem.

That an epoch's legitimacy should become questionable to those living in it is a phenomenon that had never existed before and outside the modern age. Nor could it have, for an understanding of oneself as belonging to an epoch had previously not even been possible. It was only by giving itself its name that the modern age was even able to bring forth the structural concept of an epoch and, along with it, all the problems associated with situating caesuras in history. But the idea of history taking a radical turn from damnation to salvation, from the inauthentic to the authentic, developed within Christianity—albeit as a secondary guise under which appears the interpretation of the primal event of redemption, which after all was supposed not to turn history around, but to terminate it. Of course, the possibility thus experienced and the language coined from it helped the modern age articulate its self-perception as an epoch making a break with previous history—and after all, signs even appeared in the heavens to prove it. But evidence that

---

tained in the Book of Daniel, with reference to signs pointing to the reverse. Yet this is not *secularization* in the sense of the transformation of a notion originally developed in theological terms, nor can it be, for the allegoresis of Daniel is itself of palpable *worldliness* in being a posteschatological historical speculation.

the epochal turn was interpreted or stylized as an imitation of Christianity's theological founding event is sought in vain. It must be granted, however, that the sources do not always present us with what it was possible to think, but only what was felt not to exceed the capacity of the times.

Secularization as a category of historical understanding is *one* symptom (among many) of how uncertain the modern age feels of its legitimacy; it is a theologically determined category of wrong [*Unrecht*]. Not, I should make clear, a "theological" category of wrong, for as such it would possess criteria sui generis that cannot even be discussed here. It is, after all, a *secularized* category, which is not to say, however, that as a basic concept of service to the historian it was exempt from the interest of theologians. On the contrary, as a category of wrong, there is a potential for it to be invoked, the implication of a writ of execution, and therein lies the notion's *ideological* moment. What I intend *ideological* to mean here is the extratheoretical interest that is latently perceived and always able to be activated in the context of theoretical objectification. It is not by chance that the secularization syndrome is so well suited to the activities of cultural criticism, which, in its search for suitably remote responsibilities for the unease felt toward the present, today consist largely of standing in judgment over the foundation of the modern age and the factors involved in it. After all, what else are we to make of all the gratuitous profundity associated with the term *secularization*? What can it mean for the ideal of a terrestrial, political realization of happiness to have been able to be formed only as a transposition of the promise of otherworldly beatitude? It should be noted that the theological depiction of eternal bliss as a *visio beatifica* [beatific vision] no longer has anything in common with the biblical illustration of the *kingdom of heaven* but everything to do with the blissful *theōria* [contemplation] of ancient philosophy. Furthermore, what can it mean to say that the Marxist idea of revolution was *an idea of the final judgment transposed into a secular register* and that its imagined goal, the state of communism, was the *earthly paradise*, secularized messianism? Indeed, there is simply no need for anything to be transformed or distorted here; instead, the elementary, primal longing for universal justice keeps imagining ever new satisfactions—especially when the usual ones have proved ineffective and worn out.

It is remarkable how many things can emerge from *secularization*. The same original substance appears in manifold metamorphoses, which are quite dissimilar to each other. The same origin is supposed for the communist *final state* as for *eternal progress*, and thus for a finite notion of history as well as an infinite one. The deeper antitheses are ignored for superficial resemblances: it is of no consequence whether a paradise is terrestrial-messianic or heavenly; the crucial difference is whether this final state transcends human efforts or is immanent to them, that is, whether man can attain it by his own exertions or depends for it on grace, which cannot be earned. To get caught up in appearances is, of course, facilitated by language, which properly constitutes the illusion of secularization.

The durability of theologically conditioned elements of language in particular is not something I regard as a quasi-mechanical phenomenon but as a meaningful fact that is open to interpretation. What I earlier called the *reoccupation* of a system's functions in the process of historical epochs changing requires *constancy* of language, particularly where content is being replaced and this replacement is in need of concealment. Just as the content of the ideas that genuinely underpin an activity can get lost amid its *ritualization*, with a new meaning taking over the form of that activity to secure the sanction of its tradition and unquestionability, so the enduring semantic element merely denotes a position that must not be touched and, at the same time, is familiar and sanctified to consciousness.

Accordingly, Proudhon, the "theologian of progress" (Karl Löwith), purposely availed himself of theologically tinged language and rhetoric, though he did so not in a continuity of substance but only in the continuity of the claims associated with them. In Proudhon, such linguistic mimesis is actually connected to a theory, according to which history weighs on us so irrevocably that we cannot make the inherited and deeply infected language bend to our will, can give voice to the *revolution*'s boldness only in the cloak of *tradition*, and can never be sure that the meaning carried along from history does not in fact overlie the present meaning actually intended. In his *The System of Economic Contradictions, or The Philosophy of Poverty* (1846, preface), Proudhon clearly saw what we are still at pains to understand: that it is only *tradition* that creates the possibility for the revolution to formulate itself in the first place, in a manner comparable to that in which sensory perception is the precondition for the metaphorical articulation of intellectual concepts. Ultimately, this also applies to the *worldliness* or *secularity* meant by secularization: the "world" constantly invoked in sacred language only learned to understand and formulate itself in terms of the *un*worldly, and it never again escaped the language in which it had done so.

The case of the supposedly secularized paradise provides a fine opportunity to study this configuration. It goes without saying that theology, once spurred by the Greeks to frame its ideal of beatitude in more precise terms, did much to expand the linguistic capacity of human ideas of fulfillment; mysticism and religious poetry took inspiration from any abstraction and tried to render it more palpable. In nothing is language as powerful as in formulating claims in the realm of the intangible and unprovable. Hobbes phrased this in striking terms: "Even the most insubstantial arguments are sufficient for hope. Yea, even what the mind cannot truly conceive can be hoped for, if it can be expressed."[20]

That more should be uttered than the mind can perform is a fact—a logically vexing fact—that we must take into account as a history-making factor of the first order. It is thus that emotional intensities are created, and there is no escaping that even a radically changed idea of the fulfillment of individual and social existence should express not its contents but the urgency of its claims in the very same language in which this claim was first accumulated. If, for instance, an ultimate, unsurpassable claim is to be made for the position of art and the irrevocable, absolute self-responsibility of the artistic act—what a difference of affective significance between the abstract formula whereby the artist had made of his work a

---

20. Thomas Hobbes, *Man and Citizen: De Homine and De Cive*, ed. Bernard Gert (Garden City, NY: Anchor Books, 1972), 57.

piece of highest reality, and the archetypally familiar one that he made art the true judgment day![21] But it would be patently non-sensical to say that the idea of art, its seriousness and existential relevance, had at some point sprung from the transformation of the eschatological notion of judgment day or even of only one of its elements.

I can thus only attempt to formulate my thesis by saying: the constancy of language indicates a constant *function* for consciousness, but not a genetic nexus of *content*. There is no denying that, for instance, the resonance of an appeal of the kind of the *Communist Manifesto* to modern consciousness was prepared by expectations that became articulable in the language of theology; yet this resonance is founded not on the *Manifesto* containing supposedly secularized—that is to say, unlawfully expropriated—theology, but on the neediness of a consciousness overextended and then disappointed by the great questions and great hopes of its history. Faced with such a text, the question to ask first, from a methodical perspective, is not how it came to be, how the elements of its content fell together. Attention should rather be directed toward the needs, to serve and to relate to which a proclamatory text will never forgo.

---

21. Marcel Proust: "Excuses have no place in art and intentions count for nothing: at every moment the artist has to listen to his instinct, and it is this that makes art the most real of all things, the most austere school of life, the true last judgment." Proust, *Time Regained*, trans. Andreas Mayor and Terence Kilmartin (New York: Modern Library, 1993), 275. *Judgment Day* also has a share in the richest *secularized* artistic self-testimony of which we know, the aesthetics of Jean Paul, where the judgment is decisive idealization by the poet according to good and evil: "But the poet—even the comic poet—cannot take any real character from nature without transforming it, as the day of judgment does the living, for hell or heaven." Jean Paul Richter, *Horn of Oberon: Jean Paul Richter's School for Aesthetics*, trans. Margaret R. Hale (Detroit, MI: Wayne State University Press, 1973), 19. Humor, too, appears in the potency of Judgment Day (99), as does wit (144). Jean Paul draws on the language of the Christian tradition for all it is worth, from using it as a purely rhetorical ornament to playing with blasphemous frivolity; he uncovers its ironic disposition to lay bare the finite fact against its own infinite ideality. Creation and incarnation are his favorite metaphors for the poetic process, but they serve not just its metaphysical exaltation but also to lay open its insuperable conundrum. A functional analysis of these linguistic elements in Jean Paul that went beyond mere cataloging would be able to designate paradigms for our problem.

(Note that the needs I speak of here are not of an economic kind, for they explain little, lacking as they do historical specificity.) What is more, any demand of an immanent human ideal of fulfillment could, in this historical situation, appear only as an antithesis to the transcendent ideal of fulfillment; yet an antithesis can articulate itself only with permanent reference to and in explicit competition with the thesis to which it opposes itself. This is true even of Heine's naively stylized verses: "On earth we fain would happy be."[22]

The field of linguistic phenomena that might indicate processes of secularization is broad indeed, but in each case such diagnoses require methodical securing by means of an analysis of function. In the deepest Middle Ages, we can observe the interweaving of mysticism and courtly love, and with them of the rules and the language of love both heavenly and profane. It should be noted here that the audacious sleight of language is one of the forms by which love proves itself—the pretense of something that had hitherto not been dared but would nonetheless be risked in this one and absolute case. Mysticism thus becomes erotic, and eroticism avails itself of the store of untouchably hallowed notions. Remember that the Middle Ages found all substances to be worthy of spiritualization, that in its lapidaries and bestiaries it subjected everything physical to religious allegoresis and, in doing so, opened up a trove of expressive possibilities that could now be applied secondarily to things that were to participate not only in consecration by spiritualization but also in the absolute bond of the religious. The discovery of the interchangeability of religious and profane notions was initially a rhetorical technique by means of which a wealth of parallels and associations was established to which any intellectual intent could subsequently help itself.[23] Contrary to the presumption of clandestine substitution and concealment evoked by the charge of a wrong

---

22. [Heinrich Heine, "Germany, A Winter Tale," *The Poems of Heine*, trans. E. A. Bowring (London: Bell & Daldy, 1866), 329.]

23. Gerhard Hess (*Pierre Gassend. Der französische Späthumanismus und das Problem von Wissen und Glauben* [Berliner Beiträge zur Romanischen Philologie, 9:3/4] [Jena: Gronau, 1939], 30) provides revealing instances from La Mothe le Vayer and Gassendi, particularly what is a highly characteristic passage from Gassendi (*Opera Omnia* [Lyon: Anisson, 1658], I, 231B) in which God's incarna-

that is coupled with the concept of secularization, these linguistic diagnoses not only appear openly but quite emphasize the marks of their origin, because only by doing so can they discharge their function of suggesting the obviousness of the exchange, the equivalence.

In the modern literature of self-presentation, we encounter a further sphere in which consciously *secularized* linguistic forms function. As a stylistic device for the sincerity of laying oneself bare, a linguistic form has developed that is designed to perform as a literary equivalent of the pitilessness with which religious thought would have man be recognized and seen through by God. Imitation of St. Augustine's *Confessions* alone does not suffice to explain this phenomenon, for Augustine still believed that God knew more about the human soul than it could ever know about itself. The particular disrespect with which, for instance, Rousseau consciously imitates Augustine's confessions, far from being a kind of legitimation by means of a literary authority, is the stylistic device by which such uncompromising exposure is made believable. Rousseau not only refers to the Last Judgment as the tribunal that one day will rule in his favor; in revealing himself, he anticipated man's transcendental state of being revealed before God. Humanity, before which he confesses, does not just temporarily fill the judge's position. Rather, its judgment replaces the appeal to the final judgment, which is rendered irrelevant by being, as it were, anticipated experimentally. Indeed, Rousseau makes it perfectly explicit that he has grown indifferent to the moment of Judgment Day—let the trumpet sound when it will. Self-knowledge has become the only form of knowledge adequate to divine knowledge. From an iconological perspective, it is telling that the book has changed its place in the courtroom: whereas all of apocalyptic literature features a ledger of humanity kept beside God's throne, to be opened before the assembly of humankind on doomsday, Rousseau writes the book for his case himself and intends to step before the tribunal with it in hand, speaking the

---

tion is adduced in support of the Epicurean concept of reality, with Christ and Lucretius each testifying in the other's favor.

proud words, themselves revealing in their sequence of objects: "Here is what I have done, what I have thought, what I was."[24]

This instance of linguistic, stylistic secularization acts as a prop for a literary sensation, the shock of such unflinching self-presentation. By referring to the image's sacred background, this literary genre's new claim simultaneously legitimizes and heightens itself. Yet what we have before us here surely is more than an occurrence at the level of linguistic expression. Instead, there can barely be any doubt that this is a real secularization of God's transcendent judgment to a literary self-judgment—though this could be verified only in the context of a comprehensive interpretation.

It would appear, in any case, that even by strict methodical criteria something like secularization exists in the history of the modern mind. I wish to point to an entire category of historical evidence that might be summarized under the heading "Man Compares Himself to God." The anthropology of the modern age largely developed by picking up the thread of theological notions of God as a subject, and this fact can in no way be glossed over by pointing out that such theological notions can themselves be traced to man's self-understanding as a subject. Over the course of centuries, infinite work has been done on the concepts of the person and the subject according to the program of *via eminentiae* [way of eminence] and *via negationis* [way of negation], the development of which goes back to antiquity. Yet what was brought down to earth at the end of this work is not what had previously been projected into the heavens. To say, "God is the 'infinitely distant man'"[25] is a perspectival illusion from a historical vantage point at which philosophy, in its concept of the human subject, has worked through the attainments of the entire theological tradition. I need only call to mind what it meant for the modern age, in the moments when its self-confidence was at its boldest, to say that man was a *creative being*. That was an act of conscious secularization, one that, in the

---

24. [Jean-Jacques Rousseau, *Confessions*, trans. Angela Scholar (Oxford: Oxford University Press, 2000), 5.]

25. Edmund Husserl, *The Crisis of European Sciences and Transcendental Phenomenology: An Introduction to Phenomenological Philosophy*, trans. David Carr (Evanston, IL: Northwestern University Press, 1970), 66.

aesthetic realm in particular, aimed to ascribe to man the realization of a possibility that had before been the preserve of God.[26]

The transition lies in the term *alter deus* [another god], the *deus in terris* [god on earth], which at first was used with pious intent and was but a hyperbolic rephrasing of man's creation in the divine image. The palpable wrongfulness, the identifiability, the original authenticity, indeed the violence of unilateral expropriation—that is to say, the required features of an act of secularization—permeate the very style of this language. In epistemological considerations, comparisons with the mode of knowledge ascribed by theology to God can be found from Galileo to Husserl. I hope to retrace that path of modern self-articulation on another occasion.

These methodical caveats and objective distinctions have, I hope, taken us some distance away from so-called *Toposforschung* [the study of literary topoi], whose problem is its assumption of *constants* in intellectual history and thus ultimately its substantialist ontology of history. But it was in the very act of remarking that linguistic secularization could consciously be developed into a stylistic device for intellectual sensation and provocation that we hit on a discontinuity of *substance* that was overlaid by the transfer of form. As a historical category, the explanatory value of secularization depends crucially on the preservation of a substantial element. The simultaneous appearance of *Toposforschung* and the secularization thesis can thus be recognized as being not coincidental but founded in a shared historical *metaphysics of substance*. Establishing constants, however, invariably entails the renunciation of some knowledge [*Erkenntnisverzicht*]; they are contingent facts that can be examined or resolved no further. That the possibility of discovering constants should evoke such fascination in the natural sciences is due not to their ability to render the processes of nature more intelligible but merely to the enhanced reliability they impart to our calculations thereof.

---

26. Of course this is merely the side of the process that recalls Prometheus's theft; the other aspect is the ontological opening of the possibility of creative man by means of the voluntaristic theologoumenon of uncreated world (see my treatise "'Imitation of Nature': Toward a Prehistory of the Idea of the Creative Being" [in this volume]).

Only in the natural sciences, however, is there an equivalent to such renunciation of knowledge (and one that is at heart technical rather than theoretical); to introduce constants in the humanities [*geisteswissenschaftlich*] can only be understood as an act of renunciation with no corresponding gain. Here, factual presence, insofar as it can be philologically ascertained, is but a transitional point that understanding is always pushing to surpass. One need only consider how premature and superficial it would be to conclude the existence of a living substance of tradition from the extensive and manifold use and remaking of elements of classical mythology in contemporary literature, long inventories of which might be produced; what preserves us from deluding ourselves that we are in the midst of a new Renaissance is the healthy dose of historicism with which every act of relating to our tradition is admixed. But the manner in which mythical dimensions continue to this day to encircle this tradition as a horizon of perpetual reference is a good example of a nonsubstantialist system of *positions* that, in history, can be repeatedly occupied, filled, newly substantiated—named hollow molds to which particular functional values are ascribed. I am afraid that many of the expectations tied to the syndrome of secularization will turn out to be groundless when the supposed continuity of a disavowed substance emerges as a complex of the kind of the mythical appeal, the repetition of something of archaic familiarity to better assimilate what is still unfamiliar and uncanny.

For all the fully developed parallel in form and content with the biblical Passion story, its unmistakable signatures from the betrayal by Judas to the empty tomb, the thirty-three-year-old French corporal in William Faulkner's *A Fable* (1954) is in fact not a secularized Christ. Instead, in its figurative realization he represents a problem that could be experienced only in consequence of the great World Wars: the biblical Passion becoming unreal and fading into a mythical horizon.

This is the moment to return to the notion of secularization as an *objective cultural debt*. A more balanced appraisal of the phenomena to be considered under this rubric will reveal not only the debts that can be deduced from the idea of a historical substance that was once formed and enriched, or even revealed, but also accounts of what debts history continues to owe any present. This ambiguity is part of the essence of the historical: the idea of history as the judgment on the world is not only the denial of an objective debt to the theological idea of an eschatological Judgment Day but also the statement of and additional claim to that which has been withheld from our history by that act of transcending those dues internal to history.

We must be aware that we are discussing a term that, already in the second and third generation, has been used with such lack of clarity with regard to its methodical conditions and so unquestioningly with regard to its implications that it is overripe for critical analysis. The unquestioning nature of its use is best recognized in the fact that we can already encounter remoter descendants of the term *secularization*, the metaphorical levels of meaning, as it were, of a metaphor. Only in passing shall I quote some examples culled from my reading, notably "the Platonic idea, secularized by Aristotle"; Marx's secularization of philosophy to a theory of political action; the idea that the glass and steel architecture of the World's Fairs "may be looked upon as a secularization of the Gothic"; the characterization of the "conditions under which modern medical institutions function" as "secularized and 'corporate [*großbetrieblich*]'" when compared to traditional conceptions of the medical profession; or finally, the description of a well-known screen actor in an equally well-known newspaper, according to which his allure, dash, and arrogance "look like secularized Hapsburg."[27] But in more remote scholarly fields, too, the success of some theses seems to depend, probably even in method, on the success of the secularization theory, such as the hypothesis situating the origin of the Hellenistic novel in the history of religion.

At the background of this entire question lay the broader problem, the key to describing which is the clue of *secularization* as a category of historical *illegitimacy*. I call this problem that of the legitimacy of

---

27. [Only the first two quotations could be traced: Klaus Oehler, *Ein Mensch zeugt einen Menschen: Über den Missbrauch der Sprachanalyse in der Aristotelesforschung* (Frankfurt am Main: Klostermann, 1963), 183; Hans Sedlmayr, *Art in Crisis: The Lost Center* (London: Hollis and Carter, 1957), 50.]

the modern age. This problem results—as do all problems of historical legitimacy—from an epoch's claim to bring about and to be able to bring about a radical break with all tradition, and the discrepancy between this claim and the reality of history, which is never able to start completely afresh. But the crucial difference is whether I can say that the modern age was to be understood as the *result* of what was indeed the theologically conditioned era that preceded it, tied also in contradiction and self-assertion to the givenness of that against which they rise up—or whether I am compelled to say that the modern age was but a *metamorphosis* of that very medieval era's theological substance and thus nothing more than its *derivation,* known by the title of *secularization,* and thus in sum "*a Christian heresy.*"[28] If the substance of the modern age were indeed a secularized one, it would then have to conceive of itself as the epitome of "that which 'in actual fact [*der Sache nach*]' ought not to be."[29] In that case, something like an "objective cultural debt" would indeed exist, and it would follow from the applied category to look for recognition of this debt [*Schuld*] and its restitution, or even to demand them. In this respect, it may be accurate to speak of secularization as the *ultimate theologoumenon,* which intends to burden theology's heirs with a sense of guilt for the testator's demise.

Translated by Joe Paul Kroll

---

28. Carl Friedrich von Weizsäcker, "Ethische und politische Probleme des Atomzeitalters," *Außenpolitik,* May 1958, 305.

29. Carl-Heinz Ratschow, "Säkularismus," in *Die Religion und Geschichte und Gegenwart,* 3rd ed. (Tübingen: Mohr Siebeck, 1961), 5:1288.

4

THE CONCEPT OF REALITY AND THE THEORY OF THE STATE

(1968/1969)

The relationship of the state to the norm of peace is conditioned by its reference to reality in a twofold sense: first, to that reality the state claims for itself and manifests in political actions, and second, to that reality it grants to *that* which it itself is *not*. The concept of reality is a contrastive concept; it evades definition, for "only that which has no history is definable."[1] The more compelling claim in a particular case; what can be neither overlooked nor ignored; what we expect and what places burdens on us; what we fight for and what we rebel against; what is able to mobilize emotions and sacrifices—all this and this at least is of the rank of reality. How reality is understood is part of "what is involved in the notion of a

---

Originally published as "Wirklichkeitsbegriff und Staatstheorie" in *Schweizer Monatshefte* 48, no. 2 (1968/69): 121–146.

1. Friedrich Nietzsche, *On the Genealogy of Morals*, trans. Walter Kaufmann (New York: Vintage, 1967), 80.

form of life,"[2] from which can be understood the complex of actions of an individual or a society—beyond the assumption that there are only responses to stimuli—as the unity of a behavior toward reality that gives itself rules or at least can be reduced to rules. It is the concept of reality toward which theoretical and practical attitudes converge.

By way of comparative and competing presence it can be understood what it means to say the state claims reality and grants it to that which exists "beside, above, and beyond the state, and often enough even against it."[3] As if it were a prepared specimen, the extreme situation shows this fact: it is in war that the state sees an upswing of its own reality as the most extreme and exclusive bindingness, of the self-evidence of its necessity and its right, which tends toward absolutism; this occurs not only in war but also on the brink of war, also in the simulation that anticipates war as a "cold" one. Only the crisis essentializes the state's existence; the state of emergency is the textbook case of its vindication. Whoever campaigns for the state as a "higher reality" and whoever identifies himself with the state thinks it as a subject of crises—and is easily inclined to think it into crises. There is little that is surprising about the insistence with which politicians in power muse about the perfect coordination of a possible "state of emergency." The external, manipulated crisis as a tool for inner stabilization is another common part of the political trade. Given, however, a technological state in which real wars endanger the state itself and as such, and in which they can destroy its identity even as a subject of crises, the hypothetical war—the "phantom war"—becomes a medium that promises to push states to crystalline solidity. Thus, there is a correlation between the threat to peace and the evidence of the state, and it suggests to infer an analogous correlation that a weakened state would strengthen peace. This correlation, however, does not mean that the disempowerment of the state would be a causality of a peaceful evo-

---

2. Peter Winch, *The Idea of a Social Science and Its Relation to Philosophy*, 2nd ed. (London: Routledge, 1990), 41.

3. Thomas Mann, *Reflections of a Nonpolitical Man* (New York: Ungar, 1983), 107.

lution, even if it is true that since time immemorial the state has been the subject of peace only in a state of exhaustion: such peace as it has enjoyed has only ever been "cold." There is no need specifically to conclude this type of peace; it is the inertial state of the political world, which exists as long as there are no acting forces disturbing it. Only the virulent state is potentially such a disturbing factor. And virulence here means reality, tending toward the comparative of reality.

It is an elementary Aristotelian train of thought that lets us assume that the state, given it is something "existing by nature," acts toward the perfection of its condition, as do all things in nature, that is, toward the display of its necessity at every place and in every moment, and not merely toward ensuring the preconditions of its naked existence but toward preemption vis-à-vis any possibility of its destabilization. Its entelechy is the densest presence and inescapable potency, which can, after all, only be verified in the medium of crisis. However useful the Hobbesian model has turned out to be, in which the individual's state of nature is rationally neutralized as the surrender of everyone to everyone into the convention of absolute dominion—the individual simply enters another, albeit mediate, "state of nature," in which he, powerless, is turned over to "history" as the autonomous execution of this convention, that is, to the self-actualization of the state, which detaches itself from the zero point of the rationality that founded it and transitions into a second naturalness, which—like everything that is "natural"—implies the strictest prohibition against doubting what is and how it is.

However: Is there no other connection between the norm of peace and the reality of the state than that of peacefulness by virtue of exhaustion, from the calculus of power that, just at this very moment, is insufficient, and sees no opportunity to seize? Is the relationship of the state to reality—and thus, its relationship to the norm of peace—a *constant* in history and thus for political theory? To pursue this question, one is forced to take a detour.

I.

The theory of the sovereign state is a result of the declining Middle Ages. It would be romanticism to hold that against it.[4] This theory of the state had found its systematic formulation in the reception of Aristotle's *Politics* since the thirteenth century and sharpened it in the exacerbation of the struggle between imperial and papal power in the Middle Ages. What Aristotle had delivered was, in contradistinction to Plato's *Republic*, not so much a theory of the perfect state as one of the perfection of the state *insofar as* it fulfills the nature of humans as "political beings." From this prerequisite followed two conclusions: first, that of the "naturalness" of the state by virtue of its anthropological foundation; second, the impossibility of the theory of the state being surpassed by a transcending theory of the ordered relations among states or the rationality of their self-abandonment for the constitution of higher structures.

At the beginning of the sixteenth century—and this is not the place to discuss the details of the reception and reshaping of Aristotelian premises in the fourteenth and fifteenth centuries—this was already a well-known part of the tradition. But now this traditional theory of the state found itself, as it were, caught between two opposing positions: one appealed to the *realism* of political situations and a theory of acting according to them; the other was the formation of the rational fiction in the shape of a *utopia*. The first is represented by Machiavelli's *Prince*; the second by Thomas More's *Utopia*.

---

4. "Sovereignty" here does not mean a boundary concept [*Grenzbegriff*] in the sense of Carl Schmitt's definition: "Sovereign is he who decides on the exception." Carl Schmitt, *Political Theology: Four Chapters on the Concept of Sovereignty* (Cambridge, MA: MIT Press, 1985), 5. But the political quality, which is able to present itself "purely" only in the extreme state, has a tendency toward being independent from the question of whether this condition is actually met, and instead takes the right of definition for what is extreme into its own hands. This *conceptus terminator* [boundary concept] is not essential to the political, but it is essentially attractive to it. Herein lies the connection between the claim to reality and the problem of peace. The question of the competency for what lies beyond ordered competences is no longer a problem within political reality but concerns the competition of a heterogeneous reality with the political one. It is here that every resistance against comparativization has to start.

Both works—it is worth keeping this in mind—emerged almost at the same moment in history. The tract on the prince was finished in its first draft at the end of 1513, although it was published only posthumously in Rome in 1532. The tract *Of a Republic's Best State and of the New Island Utopia* was printed in 1516 in its Latin version in Louvain; the first English edition appeared in 1551 in London. What does the simultaneous occurrence of these two extreme manifestations of political theory mean?

It was Ernst Cassirer who first compared Machiavelli's *Prince* to Galileo's *Discourses* in terms of their meaning and their historical function, even though more than a century lay between the two works. This comparison is still exciting because it seems so palpably justified and yet evades systematic explication. What is decisive is the separation of politics from the systematic field of analogies of physics and ethics, just as Galileo had to separate physics from metaphysics and, initially, also from cosmology in the vein of Aristotle, or just as Hugo Grotius had looked for an autonomous ground of legal theory this side of metaphysics and theology. Machiavelli was not so much the founder of a new science, the theory of the state, as Galileo was for physics; rather, he was the one who made visible a new object for a possible science by overilluminating the specimen and bringing to light a new reality as such. For Machiavelli was a theoretician despite himself: a man thrown from the trajectory of political success, he found himself forced merely to *speak* of a thing he deemed relevant only to *do*. Theory for him was a surrogate, not a requirement of action. But what this literal rethinking forced him to do was itself only a type of being affected by just that absolute reality that cannot be regarded "from the outside." Even where the amorality of this new political realism met its theoretical resistance in the anti-Machiavellism of the Enlightenment, it could not be the return to an alleged unity of morality and politics; in this respect, Machiavelli's autonomization of politics has been irreversible.[5]

---

5. On Machiavelli and Galilei, see Ernst Cassirer, *The Myth of the State* (New Haven, CT: Yale University Press, 1946), 116–128; on Galilei and Grotius, see

By showing the reality of politics in its specimen form, Machiavelli broke with the traditional understanding of reality as nature in the same way that the new physics of the *Discourses* came about because Galileo went to the *arsenali* [arsenals] of Venice to fathom the achievements of human ingenuity. Contemplating phenomena, the classical ideal of the theory of the starry sky, was insufficient in both fields. Technology, the principle of "violent motion" in the sense of the Aristotelian tradition, revealed the nature of such things. The principle of the new physics, which Galileo had just touched upon, designates a state of affairs that is not encountered in nature as a phenomenon: the inertia of bodies. Analogously, Machiavelli had forgone the Aristotelian derivation of the state from human nature. What excited him was the state in its, as it were, experimental situation, as if he wanted to represent as well as apprehend "the inborn ineptitude of men to rule or be ruled"[6] in contradistinction to the ancient canon of the "political animal." Thus, he is not interested in the old, historically or spiritually legitimized state structures, whose history looks like growth and which have assumed something like naturalness; he is interested in the emergence and preservation of new dominions and exercises of power. The art of the state, the *arte dello stato*, has its equivalent in the artificiality of power as the normal case of the political structure—a power whose preservation is always problematic, such that its boundary case is the statics of that historical inertia of survival. The private man who, through his own skill (*virtù*) or favored by chance (*fortuna*), has ascended to rulership, is the paradigm of the political artifact; for him, everything given (*occasione*) becomes mere matter onto which he imprints the form of his decisions.[7] Machiavelli uses the model of the Aristotelian hylemorphism to assign political actions to the

---

Ernst Cassirer, *The Philosophy of the Enlightenment* (Princeton, NJ: Princeton University Press, 1951), 241–242.

6. This is how Goethe puts it in "Flüchtige Schilderung florentinischer Zustände," the addendum to his translation of Benvenuto Cellini, in Johann Wolfgang von Goethe, *Gedenkausgabe der Werke, Briefe und Gespräche* (Zurich: Artemis, 1948), 15:883.

7. Niccolò Machiavelli, *The Prince*, trans. David Wooton (Indianapolis: Hackett, 1995), 18–19.

categories of the *artes mechanicae* [mechanical arts]. Here, a basic trait of the modern age becomes apparent: the materialization of that which had previously looked like nature—and could thus claim the sanction of all that is obvious—into the substrate of demiurgical processes. Even before the Ptolemaic cosmos had been shattered, the state had lost its peculiar, medieval shell-like character [*Gehäusecharaker*]. It is no longer the framework in which the scenes of history unfold before a hidden spectator but it is the actor itself. The task of theory is to grasp its actions, not its construction.

With the realist's new pathos, Machiavelli invokes the factual (*verità effetuale della cosa*) against the imaginary republic of the Platonic tradition (*immaginati repubbliche*), which had just enjoyed a renaissance in that very city of Florence in which Machiavelli was trying to ingratiate himself with his treatise.[8] Plato had derived his *Republic* from the three-tiered structure of the human soul; at the center of the work stood the theory of ideas,[9] and the famous cave allegory illustrated the necessity of binding the state to the knowledge of absolute reality. Political action was to be founded on the self-evidence of the relation to reality: this self-evidence could be reached at the end of the ascent from the shadows of the cave to the cosmos of the ideas. Plato himself had felt the need to add a *genetic* presentation to the *static* construction of his *Republic*; this was supposed to happen in a trilogy of which only the first dialogue was completed. The *Timaios* covers cosmology and suggests that this time Plato wanted to derive the state not from the structure of the human soul but from that of the cosmos. If nature could become cosmos, so the state can, in the same way, be cosmos as well—this, at least, might have been the goal of the late trilogy's argument. In any case, nature and state could be assigned to one homogeneous concept of reality, to which corresponded a similarly homogeneous ideal of "theory."

Machiavelli's realist disillusionment was aimed against the *Republic* and not yet the *Utopia*. It was only to eighteenth-century

---

8. Machiavelli, *The Prince*, 47.

9. [*Ideenlehre*, often also translated as the theory of forms; here and in the following, "form" is reserved for the German *Form*.]

readers, who rediscovered the *Prince*, that the utopia of Enlightenment must have seemed close to the gist of Machiavelli's argument. But this rested on the misunderstanding—still unresolved today— that regards utopias as belonging exclusively to the Platonic tradition. This ignores that already Thomas More's *Utopia* shares an aspect with Machiavelli's *Prince* that separates both from the prerequisites of the Platonic as well as the Aristotelian theory of the state: they no longer refer to the natural cosmos—neither to the cosmos of the ideas nor to its likeness in the phenomena nor to the teleology of a human nature that fulfills itself in the state. The political reality, as it looks to both of these sixteenth-century authors, is not the continuation of physical reality "by other means."

Utopia—its name says as much—has no place. Unlike the cave allegory, no topography can be given for it through which a path leads to the self-evidence of ideas. Its function is of a different kind. It is aimed critically against the facticity of what is. But it does not define what *ought* to take its place, although it does hint at what could do so: it mobilizes possibility against reality, even if only in order to throw the latter into sharper relief. It is a part of materialization as a basic trait of the modern age that it plays off as enlightenment the *scientia possibilium* [science of the possible] against what has become and what is extant. "The man of intelligence sees far into the immense ocean of possibilities, the fool scarcely sees anything possible but the actual."[10] But at the same time, this is the weakness of utopia—while it expands the horizon of the possible, it does not find self-evidence for surpassing it. "According to modality, rationalism quits reality without arriving at necessity. *Possibility* is its immense field."[11] This is what Kierkegaard, in *The Sickness unto Death*, called "the despair of possibility . . .

---

10. Diderot, "Philosophical Thoughts," in *Diderot's Early Philosophical Works*, trans. Margaret Jourdain (Chicago: Open Court, 1916), 46. Translation altered.

11. Friedrich Schiller to Johann Wolfgang von Goethe, January 19, 1798, in *Correspondence Between Schiller and Goethe from 1794 to 1805*, ed. L. Dora Schmitz (London: Bell, 1890), 2:17.

due to the lack of necessity."[12] This still contains a residue of Platonic needs, which unmistakably remains in the modern age's theory of the state.

The difference between the utopian and the Platonic tradition becomes immediately evident in the prototype of the genre, Thomas More's *Utopia*. The text explicitly negates the evidence of the model it demonstrates. Toward the end of the report on the island of Utopia, the rite of its inhabitants is described, which comes to an end with a great prayer in which priests and people together give thanks for living in the *best* of states. But at once they qualify the certainty of this state-mindedness by adding the request that the deity let them know should there be a *better* political system. This caveat is a gesture of humility, but one that not by accident stands at the end of a political-theoretical demonstration that claims to be a challenger to Plato's *Republic* and which indeed has been received as such.

Any Platonism must exclude such a qualification. The beholder of the ideas, who at the same time is imagined as the competent politician, not only learns that the ideal cosmos is the true model of a world but also that it is the only truth. Granted, to abide by the image of the cave, humans had once been able to mistake the shades for the true reality, but it is unthinkable that this illusion could be repeated in the one who has already found the way to knowledge. Ideas are not of the kind that they allowed for a *mallon on*, an increase in reality. They indubitably let one know the finality of what has been reached. The claim to such certitude of final evidence is, throughout the tradition, part of Platonism, even if, eventually, beyond contemplation a higher stage of unsurpassable certitude is found in "touching" the One. Political philosophy's trust in evidence always had a "coercive streak" [*Zug der Gewalttätigkeit*], which Jacob Burckhardt already perceives in Plato.[13]

---

12. [Soren Kierkegaard, "The Sickness unto Death," in *Fear and Trembling and The Sickness unto Death*, trans. Walter Lowrie (Princeton, NJ: Princeton University Press, 1941), 306.]

13. [Jacob Burckhardt, *History of Greek Culture* (Mineola, NY: Dover, 2002), 101.]

Plato's state in its moderated late form, as it is presented in the *Laws*, prohibits its citizens from traveling, and commands those who nonetheless had reason to do so to depict circumstances outside as inferior to those within one's own state. Thomas More's Utopians, on the contrary, specifically ask for enlightenment, that is, to be told if there is a state anywhere better than theirs. This difference from Platonism is significant for the function of utopia in the modern age. That the fictional state is set in the future—which originally was not part of utopia—is not essential; it can just as well seek the binding force of a historical formation, as continued by Montesquieu's romanticization of the medieval Frankish legislature, or the exotic imagination of the prototypical travel novel. Even though Hythloday, the narrator of *Utopia*, claims that the state he depicts was capable of permanent existence, he himself calls this statement a *humana coniectura*, a human conjecture. It seems more of a hypothesis than an eternal idea.[14]

In view of the contemporaneity of *The Prince* and *Utopia*, another aspect from the prehistory of the utopian state demands consideration: the island of the Utopians is no natural structure but came into being by artificial separation from the mainland. The isolation from the common realities of contemporary political life seemed possible only at a cost that must have reeked of hubris to the humanistically educated reader. The Greeks, as Burckhardt repeatedly proves, deemed "great enterprises, through which the shape

---

14. Recent philological analysis has removed *Utopia* from its designation as being part of the Platonic tradition and reception. See Hans Süßmuth, *Studien zur Utopia des Thomas Morus* (Münster: Aschendorff, 1967); Karl-Heinz Gerschmann, "Nicht-platonische Quellen zur Utopia des Thomas Morus," *Der Staat: Zeitschrift für Staatslehre und Verfassungsgeschichte, deutsches und europäisches öffentliches Recht*, no. 7 (1968): 471–486. What testifies a Platonic influence and dependence in More falls into the work's last formation phase and is already a piece of self-interpretation toward the thought of "competition" with Plato's *Republic*. This self-stylization quickly fixated the readers of the soon successful book onto the impression of Platonic succession. But the assumption of a tradition only serves to highlight the idea of competition: already the first edition begins with a Latin poem in which the utopian is praised as the possible victor over the Platonic state, and the following introductory letter by Petrus Ægidius [Peter Giles] recommends *Utopia* as a more important possession for every man than Plato's work.

of whole landscapes was altered, always as sacrilegious,"[15] and the sanction of the *inviolata terra* [unplowed earth] is indeed present in More's utopia when the report, which begins with a drastic alteration of nature, closes with the lamentation about the pretensions of man.[16] Utopia, the state, thus does not rest on the fundament of eternally valid ideas and their physical replication but on an act of determined disengagement from nature's givenness. The horizon of the concept of reality, within which Machiavelli and Thomas More draft theories that are antipodal in their content, proves to be homogeneous in pushing for a break with the classic sanctions of the "pre-given." The aspect of violence and power, which stands at the beginning wherever statehood comes into being, is the common axiom, as is something else: the impossibility of distinguishing appearance and reality [*Schein und Sein*], the lack of that clear structure of an increase of evidence in the Platonic cave allegory as the result of the political process. In *Utopia*, this was the invocation of the absolute witness, who alone was capable of revealing the relativity of the supposedly best state over against that which perhaps was better. In Machiavelli, it was, much harsher, the appearance of unbroken continuity and unquestioned naturalness that was to be given, after the fact, to the power won by struggle.

At this beginning of modern philosophical thought about the state it is confirmed that "reality" is always understood in a relation of contrast. Realities are quantified as such precisely by their ability to be defended against the charge of irreality. *Platonism* meant: the idea as an authority against what was "merely appearance." *Machiavellism* meant: appearance as an authority against what was "merely idea." *Utopia* meant: the fiction of the possibility

---

15. [Jakob Burckhardt, *Griechische Culturgeschichte*, 3 vols., ed. Leonhard Burckhardt et al. (Munich: C. H. Beck, 2002), 2:99; this section is not included in the English translation.]

16. "Isthmum perfodere" [to dig through the Isthmus] was among the proverbs on which Erasmus—since 1499 part of More's circle of friends—commented in his *Adages* (Desiderius Erasmus, *Adages IV iii 1 to V ii 51*, ed. John N. Grant [Toronto: University of Toronto Press, 2006], 76). For the formula of the *inviolata terra*, see the Dicaearchus quote recorded by Varro (*Greek Philosophy: A Collection of Texts with Notes and Explanations*, ed. C. J. de Vogel [Leiden: Brill, 1953], 2:243).

as an authority against what was "merely contingent fact" and thus less than its rational surpassing.

But these antitheses have not yet revealed anew the elementary antagonism that was contained in the making of the metaphysical tradition: Plato's demonization of Sophism, his turn away from rhetoric by means of philosophy. The concept of reality that this metaphysical tradition would have to work through and with whose consequences it would have to come to terms could ultimately be reduced to the fundamental opposition between "words" and "things." Platonism is a philosophy against the rule of the word, the postulate of visual perception against listening, of self-evidence against persuasion, of *res* [things] against *verba* [words]. "Only words" is the pervasive topos denoting the irreality of that which is unimportant. The disrepute in which political rhetoric stands is, already in Plato, based on the precondition that truth had its own potency and would prevail if the weaker logos was not, by a perversion of proportions, made into the stronger. The technical conception of politics, which gave rhetoric its enduring ambivalence, was supposed to be put in the wrong by appealing to an ultimate and actual reality of a type like that of the ideas. That in modern-age "realism" this problematic was latent and pressed toward becoming explicit again belongs to the late perceptions of the epoch; to let it come into its own and to analyze it without prejudice is still hampered by the power of tradition.

II.

We begin to hesitate to dismiss verbal demonstrations of politics by calling them "mere rhetoric," a designation that has long spelled anathema. Occasionally, perhaps even increasingly, we may take comfort in a politics of "mere words" being conducted. Have we not all too often dared to demand that the state should, after all those words, finally follow up with actions? An analysis of our most recent history demonstrates how preferable, particularly with regard to global structures, is the substitution of words for facts and actions, proclamations for decisions. Everything can depend on leaving it at words, to—as one has become accustomed to saying—"settle for declarations." What, since Bernard Baruch's coinage during the discussion of the Truman doctrine in 1947, has been called the "Cold War" has become a behavioral pattern on the part of the superpowers, in which words are increasingly passed off as realities—and no one would say that we would have preferred to see the realities themselves instead. As a behavior in a world in which the risk of acting is apt to disqualify all the possible achievements of acting, the "big words" begin to sound reassuringly sweet. I see little sense in abstracting from this situation to get to morality more quickly. "From a higher point of view," this may seem far from satisfactory. But is this point of view obvious and rationally compelling, and does it not share in the contempt for Sophism with its metaphysical implications? The disdain of the pragmatic in favor of what is supposed to be above all reason comes under scrutiny from a skepticism that rejects being told what the "actually real" [*eigentlich Wirkliche*] is.

We do not know how stable such a situation is and can be. Thus, one probably should not accept as obvious and final the thesis that "the technical world does not stabilize itself."[17] It is, in any case, a threshold notion of all technicity that its functionality has to follow from objective immanence [*aus der sachlichen Immanenz*]. Let us suppose we were able to approximate this threshold value of immanent regulation, in which case the axiom would gain validity whereby political action best fulfills its purpose by only simulating the classical quality of "decisiveness" [*Entscheidungsfreudigkeit*], and perhaps only to assuage cravings for functionality and endogenous dissatisfactions. This is an irritatingly exaggerated formulation, but it seems useful to me as an antidote against overestimating the traditional scope of political "reality."

One needs to understand how little is done and can be done where the great political alternatives are at stake, and that not only in foreign but also in domestic politics. It is, of course, itself a political need to uphold the understanding that much could be done if only this or that—especially people—were different. Occasionally,

---

17. Carl Friedrich von Weizsäcker, "Friede und Wahrheit," *Die Zeit* 26 (1967).

there are reckless demonstrations that the reserves of the completely different are exhaustible. The widespread disappointment with the Grand Coalition in the Federal Republic[18] is based on the fact that something was realized too hastily and arose from superficial necessities, which, as the last resort for producing the capacity for political agency, had been a pragmatic myth and needed to be well guarded as such. It is comparable only to the last great reserve of the general strike: the strong arm that makes all wheels stop remains a *fascinosum* and a *tremendum* only if it remains on this side of the disenchantment of its application.[19] With respect to what could be decided, what can be decided is ever more reduced; if this does not become tangible in the phenotype of what happens, it is due to the need of the modern news services for "events," which corresponds more to its capacities than to the realities. Ultimately, even the possibility of war will pass over into "verbal modality." This does not mean that one will not be able to think of war as a means anymore, but it means that this notion can no longer be thought through to the end. Such a state would be a bad peace but not the worst—not that kind of peace that stems from an insight and a conviction, from a great human effort, and that to expect and to demand man cannot stop, and on whose conditions to meditate he cannot cease, but the kind of peace resulting from the certainty of disappointment and the inevitable catastrophe should its opposite be attempted. It has been said often enough that the extreme sensitivity of modern structures in terms of supply, administration, and production renders any notion of violence, even of the most conventional kind, risky in the extreme. The reason that today this statement still needs to be qualified is that this sensitivity of the organization of daily life has not been attained everywhere in the world; at a lower degree of

---

18. [The term "Grand Coalition" refers to a governing coalition between the two largest parties. In the Federal Republic of Germany, this was the case when, under chancellor Kurt Georg Kiesinger, the Christian Democrats and the Social Democrats first formed a coalition (1966–1969).]

19. [Blumenberg refers here to the concept of the *mysterium tremendum et fascinans*—the religious experience of terror and rapture—that religious scholar Rudolf Otto described in his 1917 book *The Idea of the Holy* (New York: Oxford University Press, 1923).]

sensitivity, the risk of the "little adventures" remains liable to be underestimated.

Carl Friedrich von Weizsäcker has put forward the thesis that world peace is inevitable but by no means certain.[20] According to him, this lack of certainty is not *only* a weakness in the theoretical calculation but also has an immanently rational function: it secures the constant necessity for the great effort that the goal of world peace demands. This argument is, in its logical structure, reminiscent of Kant's postulate of the existence of God, which had to remain theoretically unproven not only because it cannot be proven but also because of the practical results the theoretical certainty of divine judgment over all action would yield for moral autonomy: freedom would become calculation. Whether, because of its inevitability, world peace is also certain is thus not only what no one *can* know but also what no one *may* know. But this paradox needs to be stated more radically. A state that concluded its certainty from the inevitability of peace would neglect its own armament and would, through the vulnerability of its internal structures, offer the opportunity for extortion to anyone ready to attack; by so doing, it would make possible the subcutaneous shift in power structures that always entails the risk of greater conflict. Even the uncertainty of the reaction to an act of aggression must be preserved and remain relevant.

The consequences for the "peace morality" of the individual citizen are most peculiar. The obligation to perform military service has become more compelling, for it alone sustains the uncertainty of the reaction to a violation of peace. But should this risk not be enough to uphold the self-evidence of the inevitability of peace, then a conclusion follows that cannot be anticipated politically but is essentially private. If the only definable aim for armed power and the alliances it makes possible—to render war pointless by making it more dangerous—has manifestly failed, then military service ceases to be bound by that aim. Whatever comes next does not compensate

---

20. Carl Friedrich von Weizsäcker, *Ist der Weltfriede unvermeidlich? Bergedorfer Gespräche zu Fragen der freien industriellen Gesellschaft* 24 (Hamburg: Decker, 1967), 7.

for the aims that might have made it bearable. What is politically almost unthinkable would be logically inevitable: the armed forces would have to be dissolved and all alliances declared unrealizable. No state could or would be permitted to announce this beforehand; each would have to do so at point X and most likely would do it. When considering the antinomies of this situation, one must expect the charge of a new Machiavellianism and its attendant gestures of revulsion. To give the determined, self-avowed, or recognizable violator of the peace what he wants after no demonstration of the risks could deter him and to surrender before the showdown—that is a thought which is hard to bear even when expressed in terms such as these. But especially over against any resistance the classical political mentality might put up, here too the premise must be upheld that no victory can any longer be accounted as a gain, that the loser may trust in the aggressor soon being confronted with the complexity of the problems of a world that is only possible by virtue of technology, and that the illusion of his gain must soon become clear to him. Can one count on the aggressor thus being forcibly turned toward rationality?

To answer this question, another paradox of our political reality needs to be thought through: the paradox of the powerless power. The instruments of power have increased in today's world by a tremendous measure. It is possible to think that they accumulate to an almost absolute degree by a cartel of the superpowers. But this conventional view of power ignores the question of what equivalent of the exercise of power is adequate to the dimensions of which we are speaking here. Doubtless there always have been ends that could not be achieved by mere power. But the question that is relevant here is, What share in all that can be or ever has been the object and aim of political power do those things have that can *no longer* be achieved by power, and of what dignity are they in relation to classical conceptions of power? And furthermore, In which direction is the proportion of this share developing?

One must begin with the most primitive form of the exercise of power to answer this question, with the identification of humans with their physical capabilities and the command over them. In this elementary view, the capacity for work and battle can be calculated from the number of people in a political structure's orbit of force. But this very type of power in the classical sense has become as uninteresting as it is irrelevant. To control industrial and military capacities today means to rule over "heads" in the strict and strictest sense, and thus no longer in the sense of a *pars pro toto*. The failure of colonial rule as well as the formation of blocs are connected to this process. The expansion of borders, disposition over territories and their populations have become ineffective, because one loses the aforementioned heads by ruling them against their will. While the force of human power and dexterity that needs to be coerced can be replaced by technology almost at will, spontaneous intelligence and the capacity for invention continue to elude the grasp of force. Whatever one may wish to call the powers and qualities that might at this moment be the objective of an expansive political will to subdue, they can no longer be separated from the free consent to this will as were pure work and armed service, the skills of artisans, and the minds of officials. This explains the inevitable late and belated attempts to pursue imperial politics as ideological politics.

That power should lose its terror at the moment it is represented, as it were, in its pure state, is due less than some believe to the terror that can be brought to bear against it, but rather to the fact that its exercise has, to an almost laughable degree, become futile, and its debasement must proceed quickly as a political goal. Though it may seem as if the paradox of powerless power consisted above all in the unwieldy and outsized weapons on which it rests and with which it is not allowed to do anything, this superficial phenomenon conceals the, if I may say so, humane surprise that the substance of what can be neither won nor ruled by power has become crucial, in modern reality, to the continued existence of that very reality. The point in the technological-cultural development of a state from which on its political sphere can no longer afford conflicts with the intellectual one is revealing in this regard. We live in a world in which exercising power must become onerous, and the allure of power is out of all proportion to the risks that have to be taken for its sake. This need not mean that political behaviors as phenomena change radically. But such immutability can be mere appearance. In other spheres, too, for instance in labor struggles, we can observe that the classical repertoire of historically acquired behaviors is retained as a ritual. The verbal modality of which I spoke can be understood as atrophied, purely phenomenal constancy. The *res–verba* antithesis would have become the *verba pro rebus* [words in place of things] thesis—and this in turn would be something like the return of Sophism from its Platonic exile, of course under a new aspect that the tradition could not have imagined.

Anybody rethinking the present from the vantage point of that tradition and by its means will be disappointed or even horrified by this analysis. Should the state no longer be the true and actual realization of the *zōon politikon* [political animal] but the bearer of a "role"—a mere speaking role at that—in the economy of human history? And should what in its dignity was once to be grasped by contemplating the cosmos now be assigned to the sphere of institutionalized rhetoric? If disappointment and horror are to be expected here, then the very obviousness of this reaction requires investigation. Insights might be gained here by referring back to the concept of reality.

Just as over the course of the history of European culture nature lost its fatedness to politics, politics in turn seems liable to be surpassed by the relevance of other structures. What animates life and determines its vagaries is real in the highest degree: the weather can be the epitome of all realities, and the weather god the absolutely supreme being. For a long time, the political medium of human life has surpassed the physical in its implacability. Science and technology have led to a neutralization of nature, and thus to the peculiar irreality for humans that it has adopted in its reserves within modern civilization. The difficulty of this state of affairs is that the central strand of the history of science in the modern age is the science of nature, but the very success of this natural science has dimmed and leveled nature as the epitome of fateful pre-givenness for humans. Only hesitantly did philosophical thought follow this change in the primacy of realities against the paradigms set by tradition. How hard it was to follow in thought the primacy of the political is expressed in a letter by Marx dated March 13, 1843, in which he discusses Feuerbach's *Preliminary Theses for the Reformation of Philosophy* [1842]: "Feuerbach's aphorisms seem to me incorrect only in one respect, that he refers too much to nature and too little to politics. That, however, is the only alliance by which present day philosophy can become truth."[21] Is it possible that this phase, too, in which politics is the epitome of fateful reality for humans, is already of the past or on its way there? A sober appreciation of the facts that matter here seems hidden from our sight by the sleight of hand by which new and heterogeneous factors are simply subsumed under the heading of the political, because the institutional schemata of the classical political portfolios have been applied to them. It has become almost self-evident for us that there is something like economic politics that no longer is exclusively, or even is at all, trade politics in the classical sense. And as soon as science as a basis of the modern possibilities of life had become acute enough, "science politics" was dignified by being made capable of constituting a department, and thereby integrated into the corpus of politics. "Educational politics," too, only looks as if it were the continuation of the classical *cultus* department.[22]

To declare everything "politics" obfuscates the change in the real circumstances. If the exercise of power at home and abroad became the definition of the political, then this was based on the idea of the self-preservation of the state as the epitome of its being an end in itself. And self-preservation was one of those categories of the political derived from the concept of nature. It may be that in the supersession of these categories rests the humane potential of the process outlined here. What speaks in favor of this chance is that the traditional repertoire of political substance has been dislodged, those "grand" concepts of natural borders, legitimate claims, sovereignty, *Lebensraum*, of independently securing one's existence and being master of one's domain—the displacement of all these notions that so often have been examined and abused, on which life and death have been staked, by a new scale of regulatives and possibilities of thought. Rousseau was still able to express the result of his experience

---

21. *Collected Works of Karl Marx and Friedrich Engels* (New York: International Publishers, 1975), 1:400.
22. [The German term for ministries of science, education, and the arts; it descended from the ministries of religion that were once also responsible for schooling.]

of his stay in Venice as one of the "great truths, useful to the happiness of the human race": "I had seen that everything depends radically on politics, and that, from whatever aspect one considers it, no people ever would be anything other than what it was made into by the nature of its Government."[23] But would he have allowed this "substantial" concept of politics to be applied to what today, as economic politics, is not only called politics "as well," but politics above all else?

It is undoubtedly a fact that elections, crises, formations of governments increasingly occur under the influence of economic factors and situations. Not to mention that the interests of economic existence are behind the enforceability of almost all demands of different provenance, for instance science and education politics. But above all: where only a few years or decades ago a government would have been toppled by a lapse in foreign policy, it survives these situations easily today, while a minute decrease in the growth rate of production or an increase in unemployment plunges it into a desperate situation. Economic policy is not only a portfolio in the cabinet that has existed in Germany for fifty years (namely, since October 21, 1917). Although this portfolio—for the greatest part of its short history as part of the cabinet—existed in the shape of a dull management politics, it has increasingly become the substance of politics, or, what is essentially the same, the desubstantialization of its historically sanctioned form. And it seems that the shift of political quality toward the economics department is advancing: the "Freiburg imperative" Walter Eucken formulated, which limited economic policy to "creating the forms by which the economy is ordered,"[24] will retreat in favor of the postulate that growth needs to be steered since the automatism of self-controlling systems has evinced alarming fluctuations.

It is in this context that the changed significance of financial policies belongs. In the form of the parliament's right to permit and

---

23. Jean-Jacques Rousseau, *The Confessions and Correspondences*, ed. Christopher Kelly et al., trans. Christopher Kelly (Hanover, NH: University Press of New England, 1995), 340.

24. [Walter Eucken, *Grundsätze der Wirtschaftspolitik* (Tübingen: Mohr Siebeck, 1960), 336.]

reject budgets, it used to be the classical instrument of exercising power in the state, that is, of politics in the most precise sense. For some time now it has been degenerating visibly to the status of a dependent variable in economic politics. The reason is that economic politics is responsible for the growth of state revenue, which alone remains to limit the latitude of governmental action. Parliamentary budget debates—once among the greatest moments of controlling the executive—now have taken on the character of a fictitious re-enactment of a formerly great role.

It is surprising how disproportionate, by traditional measures, the fatedness of economic politics is to the fact that its instrument is essentially the word in public discourse: the trustworthy piece of information, the call to nonintervention by others, guiding principles, planning projections, and encouragements to consume. However much economic politics gives itself the appearance of an embodiment of "measures"—everyone knows how little can be done with such things once the winds turn against them, when elementary trust fades and an indefinable reticence emerges. Instead of the levers that power might pull, there is talk of "discussing" an economic boom "to death," of exuding confidence, of verbally anticipating the intended turnaround, of the effect the prognosis might have on its object, of the investment climate (which, like the "working climate," is always in need of attention), and of the "impetus of fine words." Such verbal politics is, whatever else it may be, certainly also a demonstration of the powerlessness of power, that is, of nonpolitical politics, if one were to imply that politics is an ahistorical constant. But it is precisely in a field that has not always had the dignity of the political that rhetoric is most likely to lose the disrepute whereby its indispensable function resides in the falsification of truth, the manipulation of an otherwise free faculty of decision making, and confounding appearance and reality. Indignation at separating words from realities, of course, always lies ready at the heart of a tradition that claimed to concern itself with what really is and with the things themselves. "[H]e who is solicitous about truth ought not to frame his language with artfulness and care, but only to try to express his meaning as he best can. For those who are particular about words, and devote their time to them, miss the things."[25] That misunderstanding should be nearly inevitable if this sentiment is not taken to the most obvious norm is due to the elementary "complex" of our intellectual heritage, which seeks to render Sophism impossible and accept as real only that last reality itself, which *after* Socrates has always been a reality beyond and above man. The state has been ontologically weakened as the "actuality of the ethical Idea," while "the individual himself has objectivity, truth, and ethical life" only by virtue of his membership thereof.[26] This weakening is, to be sure, a rule for a reorientation in thought that has yet to be enacted. But it is not such a reorientation that would draft a new concept of reality and, as it were, prescribe the course of events; rather, it is simply one that *r*eenacts [nach*vollzieht*] the aporia of the disempowerment of power and saves it from *false* disappointment.

One might object that all this resembles, by consequence or infelicitous approximation, the thesis of the withering away of the state in the communist final state Marx described. Alas, I dare not comment on final states. My concern is with an analysis of tendencies. In this matter, one should not be deterred by the reproach of working with a prepared specimen, for specimens render the invisible visible. The expression of the "withering away of the state" turns out to be itself realistic, that is, bound to a specific concept of reality, one that would hold the state to be nonexistent at the moment when, in the schema of the *res–verba* antithesis, it had shifted completely to the side of the "mere words." But the transformation of internal and external conflicts, disturbances, threats, and aggressions onto the plane of the word is, anthropologically speaking, a familiar fact already, and we are beginning to get used to the idea that the often vilified "endless discussion" can very well replace and transpose the momentary discharge of a conflict. In Plato's critique of Sophism, it was considered the epitome of rhetorical-demagogical depravity to try to turn the weaker logos into the stronger. That this

25. Clement of Alexandria, "The Stromata," in *The Ante-Nicene Fathers*, ed. Alexander Roberts, James Donaldson, and Arthur Cleveland Coxe (New York: Scribner's, 1900), 2:347.

26. Hegel, *Elements of the Philosophy of Right*, trans. Allen W. Wood (Cambridge: Cambridge University Press, 1991), 275–276.

critique, during the whole of our tradition, was met with approval was due to the polyvalence of the Greek term "logos." The precondition for the discriminatory formula was that the weaker logos was weaker because it lacked truth and reason; left to their own devices and their inner strength, the truer logoi would be the stronger. Rhetorical artifice falsifies this natural relationship. The modern equivalent to this position is the superstition that without resorting to propagandistic arts, political parties would prevail by virtue of the political truth contents of their platforms. However, an effective democracy's schema of succession essentially excludes this assumption. Rather, it implies that whoever is in power is likely to gamble away the right to remain there, because the burden of proof for what before had only been an argument is now on him, while the opposition has alternative arguments up its sleeve for exactly this case. Here, power neither resides in truth, nor truth in power. Power means *potentia*—and it must remain so: possibility is its reality. Equally wrong is the assumption that possibilities would "push" for their realization, truth for being recognized, the tool for its use, the weapons for the battle. It may not yet be moral progress to persuade someone who is about to strike because he believes that conflict is inevitable to stop in his tracks and talk it over. But where morality never could be realized, it may not be the only and best way simply to keep demanding it, or, under the heading of "reethicization,"[27] to suggest with deceptive romanticism that it had once existed; instead, it might be better to question that reality itself, from which something was for so long demanded in vain.

The cynical maxims contained in his mirror of princes have made Machiavelli's separation of ethics and politics suspect. It seems intolerable to us indeed that he should give the prince, newly risen to power, counsels so fundamentally different as, on the one hand, not to let any member of the ancestral dynasty live, and, on the other, to change nothing about laws and taxes. But this type of political technique is not only aimed at the free use of poison and dagger; it also hints at the unfolding of a rationality content to refrain from, prevent, or simulate certain actions. As paradoxical as it may sound,

---

27. [Von Weizsäcker, *Bergedorfer Gespräche*, 12.]

Machiavelli's separation of ethics and politics is consistent with a theory of the political minimum. To make the transition into the verbal modality presupposes that actions in this realm can no longer be too sacred not to be "reoccupied" by means of quasi-actions. Only somebody prepared to risk praising the blessings of *realism* could shy from the resulting political *nominalism*.

Of course, demagoguery and propaganda—a technique availing itself of big words, not words alone—are also located on this lineage. But what has been become equally apparent for a long time is that there is a solid technique of at least placing speeches ahead of actions, and information ahead of intervention, of replacing the latter by the former. It has become the epitome of political strategy to prevent mistakes and misjudgments with regard to intentions and potentials, and thus the irreversible actions of a potential opponent, to treat him as long as possible as a competitor within the field of rationally planning thought, to establish a set of signals regarding shared structures of thinking and to let him know what and how one thinks oneself. It has become a strategy that can no longer permit politics by any means other than those of the word. The meaning of immense technical and economic efforts consists to a good part in rendering this information—these words and signals— credible and maintaining this credibility. Of course, it is itself a play on words to say that here words have become actions and not "mere" words. *How to Do Things with Words* is the title of an important book by J. L. Austin—maybe another one still needs to be written: *How to Do Nothing with Words.*[28]

The idea of an "open world" can prevail—in fact, it is in all likelihood already doing so—and not only because the defeats of secrecy have become evident, the instruments of technical reconnaissance omnipresent, and the inner logic of scientific and technical processes in isolated systems has resulted in a virtual equivalent of the disabled communication. It is doing so also and above all because the availability of information has proved to be the most important factor in avoiding crises. One of the key reasons for major crises

---

28. [J. L. Austin, *How to Do Things with Words* (Oxford: Oxford University Press, 1962).]

has been the difficulty of estimating risks. In a world that has been made more transparent and permeable, the poker player will come to seem an anachronistic type of politician. In this game, rules have developed for securing mutual understanding—without there being an understanding to that effect. Powers that, in the style of classical enemies, demonize, deride, and threaten each other maintain, below the surface of official rhetoric, constant contact, like the United States and China in Warsaw. Even the great cases of espionage have been reevaluated as a type of economy of involuntary information, at least if one notices how despite upholding draconian penalties its consequences are neutralized by exchanging agents. While in the past even one's own man in the other camp was barely considered an honorable subject, today, after his work is done, he can be presented and decorated as a hero of preempted information. Not only does one want to be safe from surprises but one also wants to let the other side know that one is. The unlikelihood of great secrets being kept must be demonstrated, the synchronicity in the expansion of potentials must be verified. The great world powers failed to reach an agreement on "open skies,"[29] but only few years later, reconnaissance satellites began to do the very same work, and it is astounding that there has never been a reaction comparable to the U-2 incident,[30] or even a clear protest. The press, too, does similar things, straddling the "abyss of treason" [*Abgrund von Landesverrat*]:[31] it impedes governmental attempts to wield the forces of fate and to pursue foreign policy in secret, under unverifiable conditions. The uncertainty about what in the future can still

---

29.   [In 1955, the United States put forward a proposal for a treaty with the Soviet Union that would allow reconnaissance flights over each other's territory; while not adopted, it is regarded as a significant moment of détente politics in the Cold War.]

30.   [In May 1960, an American U-2 spy plane was shot down over Soviet territory. The incident caused the collapse of the "Four Powers" summit and a deterioration of relations between the United States and the Soviet Union.]

31.   [This is a reference to the so called "Spiegel affair" of 1962, a political scandal in which Defense Secretary Franz Josef Strauß accused news magazine *Der Spiegel*'s reporting on the state of the defense forces to be treasonous. In the wake of a police raid at the *Spiegel*'s offices and the imprisonment of its editor in chief, Strauß had to resign.]

be placed under the heavy interdict of treason is symptomatic of the fact that the aggregate state of political reality is changing.

The reality one refers to when claiming to be a political "realist" acquires its gravity and authority only once the state, in its own claim to reality, ceases to compete with it and no longer pretends to *be* the necessity it only has to *satisfy*. This becomes clear when decisions that have become possible today can no longer be made as political ones. This is what is called a loss of substance, but whether it is rightly called a *loss* ought to be questioned, and whether a loss of *substance* remains bound to the assumptions of the concept of reality and its permanence that are at issue here.

III.

When it becomes impossible to demonstrate under what conditions world peace might be attainable as the result of comprehensible processes, the sense of resignation regarding its enforceability moves this indispensable norm close to the realm of eschatological hopes, which always imply that only the end of the world renders a new world possible. Once its religious trust has been exorcised from this schema, it can be rethought as the magical formula whereby the quality of that which is yet to come is vouchsafed by the destruction of that which is. Yet one must not lose sight of the fact that *all* that the weakening of the state can make possible is a peace of, as it were, a technical quality. Its imperative would be hypothetical, not categorical. It would be desired as the precondition for something else. But what would this something else be?

The idea that once people are made *happy* they become *peaceful* all by themselves is deeply rooted in the utopian tradition. But it presupposes that the reality of the state is not of such autonomous density that it could evade its citizens' will to peace. That this precondition is not given forces us to treat the problem of peace as a matter of technical reason, as a question *preliminary* to a more fundamental (though not, it would appear, more pressing) topic: that of *how* humanity would live in peace, *what* it might make of the opportunity that came to them by means of technology. The inevitability of peace is not its certainty, but nor does it explain why it should be attractive to human imaginations of happiness. Utopia does not imply rationality; it must outdo it without destroying it. There are reasons to recall these attributions. To a lofty imagining of human possibilities, it must seem a betrayal of utopia to entertain the possibility that what ought only to be realized as a human effort, with the emphatic gesture heralding great change, might be but a rational consequence.[32] The two problems need to be disentangled. Utopia cannot promise peace, because peace is the precondition of utopia. Global peace does not, as such, entail the global happiness of humanity. The former is only the first step, to avoid

---

32. [In an earlier draft of this text, Blumenberg at this point added a passage that he later worked into the essay "Dogmatische und rationale Analyse von Motivationen des technischen Fortschritts" (*Dogmatic and Rational Analysis of Motivations for Technological Progress*, 1970), posthumously published in Hans Blumenberg, *Schriften zur Technik*, ed. Alexander Schmitz and Bernd Stiegler (Berlin: Suhrkamp, 2015), 258–276:

> In a certain way, Walter Benjamin's phrase is correct that realizing the idea of technology [*Technik*] would constitute *treason against utopia*. For utopia idealizes a target value beyond the line of progress; a state whose essential property is unsurpassability, that is, static finality. Progress does not lead toward unsurpassable states and this is what it means to call it "infinite." *Utopia*, and in this lies its significance, calls into question any *factual* state that *progress* is capable of reaching by confronting it with the qualitatively wholly other. Yet at the same time, *progress* renders every *utopia* problematic because it *demonstrates* the practice of surpassing factual states while utopia always remains silent on the question of how the *transition* into its state comes to pass. The most consistent form of utopia is the refusal of what Adorno has called the "brushed-in portrait of utopia" [Theodor W. Adorno, "Progress," in *Critical Models: Interventions and Catchwords* (New York: Columbia University Press, 2005), 151]—any positive determination is withheld, for it can only be developed under the very circumstances that have to be overcome, that is, under those of an extrapolation of progress. Here, we are asked to trust in the absolutely unknown, which only by virtue of a sleight of hand, the double negation, can be passed off as positive. The *antithesis of utopia and progress* rests upon a very elemental *suspicion* inherent to all critiques of progress: progress never brings qualitative change, which means that it does not have a direction that could be qualitatively specified. What is meant here could be put thus: the changes effected by this progress leave man unchanged, and have, above all, no moral correlate. (Blumenberg, "Dogmatische und rationale Analyse von Motivationen des technischen Fortschritts," 261.)]

despairing of the latter. It is alarming to see how few human problems are solved by world peace; nevertheless, it is the problem of problems. Yet enthusiasm and kindling constructive powers can only affect what might come *after* peace is achieved. Such a future will call into question any present, but that must not mean to deny it the indulgence of the minimum of rational expectations for which it can take credit.

Even if one insists that the norm of peace cannot be part of a utopia—because as the condition of the possibility of any projects about happy states of affairs it possesses the evidence that must elude all such projects—there is nevertheless an important connection between utopia and the problem of peace after, in the modern age, utopian thought became the essential factor for the contingency of the state, that is, against the Platonic element in the theory of the state. But the historical function utopia assumes in support of the possibility of world peace cannot obscure the difference that the problem of peace must be regarded under the condition of consistency with circumstances as they exist at present, because approaching this necessary state requires "that each intermediate form, each transitional phase must be able to exist independently."[33] It may be possible to demand a mutation of man so that all men would be happy, but one cannot begin with the demand for a radical change of human attitudes to reach the inevitable, namely, humanity preserving its own bare existence.

Utopia confronts any reality with the possibilities it has spurned, and in so doing it renders the conditions and institutions objectionable by way of the *contingency* of everything merely actual. Reality does not admit its own contingency, but rather conceals it by obtaining for itself the proof of necessary *consistency*. Because the modern age attempted to define itself through a concept of its own history's consistency—namely, progress—it resisted being called into question not only by theological transcendence but also by the tran-

---

33. Von Weizsäcker, *Bergedorfer Gespräche*, 12. This important principle of any discussion of the problem of peace is described by von Weizsäcker as "a special case of the very general proposition of Darwin's theory of evolution . . . that only those living beings can exist today whose ancestors were all viable at every moment of past history." Von Weizsäcker, 9.

scendence of utopia. As the permanent realization of possibilities, progress makes us forget that it is always only the extension of the possibilities inherent in a present reality. Utopia as a literary genre is displaced from its original function as soon as it is made to serve progress: its transcendence is interpreted as the apparent omission of a period of time and is thus retrieved into the immanence of the one time. The utopia situated in the future as an extrapolation of what must come to pass anyhow is capable of generating optimism or resignation, but both attitudes tend to leave history to its own devices. In light of this, the displacement of the exotic utopia by the utopia about the future, of the social by the technical utopia, is a loss of function, because in this process, the concept of reality of consistency is adopted along with the category of progress. That the province of utopia has, by its very name, no place signifies exactly that it is located outside the context of realities.

It is for this reason that utopias remain unaffected by Hegel's dictum in the preface to the *Philosophy of Right* rejecting all attempts to develop the ideal state: "issuing instructions on how the world ought to be: philosophy, at any rate, always comes too late to perform this function."[34] Utopia, of course, cannot issue instructions on how the world or a state ought to be, but it can at least teach that they do not have to be as they are, that the consciousness of their self-evidence is contestable. The contingency following from utopia is the antithesis to the self-evidence of the ideal from which metaphysics had deduced the cosmos. This inevitable order that occupied the space of all possibilities could be tyrannical, as already the Gnostics had felt, and could inspire the sense of imprisonment and the yearning for deliverance, or point to the resort of escaping into private mysticism. The threat of this lapse into coercion applied to no less a degree to the state, which sought to evoke its cosmic dignity: it was impossible to deny it the right to make claims of a fundamental nature on the life of its citizens. Chaos was the only alternative the cosmos held in store, and this is at the root of the inevitability of resigning to the given order. As late as Hobbes, this

---

34. [G. W. F. Hegel, *Elements of the Philosophy of Right*, ed. Allen W. Wood, trans. H. B. Nisbet (Cambridge: Cambridge University Press, 1991), 23.]

is the structure of the argument demonstrating the indissolubility of the state contract and the absolutism he deduced from it as the epitome of reason itself: the self-preservation of the state as the elementary definition of all political acts is the delegated self-preservation of the individuals. The individual enters into the mythically preexisting contract as he does into original sin. He is always supposed to have already surrendered himself as a legal entity and yet legitimizes the pure coercion directed against himself as the consistency of a legal condition that he is responsible for. In this way, reason submits to the "surplus" it finds in the factual state, instead of calling it into question from the perspective of the economy of the inevitable. However, it is not the rationality of this model of the state's founding as such that is doubtful, but the contradiction between the motive for entering into the contract and the surrender of being a legal entity that supposedly follows from it: one cannot be forced to surrender oneself to preserve oneself.

Any rational argument for how the norm of peace may be served will have a formal similarity to the conception of the state contract: just as the state represents the rationality of the individuals for whom the state of nature would be their demise, the protection of peace represents the rationality of the states to whose demise an international "state of nature" must lead today. If the political theory of the modern age makes the self-preservation of the state the highest political principle, it must be measured not only according to whether it *serves* this principle with every one of its theoretical steps; it must also prove that it is *satisfying* it. This criterion holds especially for the "state of nature," recurring on the international level, of the right of everyone to everything and thus the absolute conflict of the conditions of everyone's self-preservation. Was not the same rationality that had motivated the individual to enter into the *pactum subiectionis* [pact of subjection] as the abandonment of their absolute natural right also bound to assert itself on the level of the absolute right of states? That can only mean that as a consequence of the idea of giving up rights through contracts, a treaty between states was necessary if the force of reason emanating from the principle of self-preservation was to be served. Yet the classical theory of treaties had not advanced into this opening of its consistency, for it advocated not the abstract principle of the preservation of the state but rather the concrete principle of the preservation of specific states and state forms that had arisen historically from the given physical entities of peoples and their territories. It was with according explicitness, and as a consequence of the theory of treaties, that the demand for a "treaty between states" was voiced by Destutt de Tracy in his commentary on Montesquieu from 1819.

"Nations, as they respect each other, stand in precisely the same relations as savages, who, belonging to no nation, and being bound by no social obligations among themselves, have no tribunal to which they can apply for redress, no public power of which to claim protection, and consequently, each, so circumstanced, must submit or make use of his individual strength in self-defense."[35] What the states lacked to reach a condition of a "society which is organized and perfected"[36] was the founding of a common court of law and a superordinate coercive power. This aim had admittedly always been taken for a pipe dream, but seen from the perspective of the treaty, this second step for overcoming the "state of nature" was probably even less difficult than the first must have been. Here, utopia is drawn into the consistency of progress. But could logic alone be trusted? Probably not as long as the "state of nature" between the states did not yet entail the threat to everyone by everyone that Hobbes had assumed to obtain between individuals. At least the subjects of history, the fictitious entities of the states, could still be thought of as able to survive any war and any crisis; this prevented the idea of repeating the state contract on a higher level from being self-evident. But it was not for this reason alone that it seemed unthinkable that the act of the second and final overcoming of the "state of nature" could be analogous to the first; rather, the element of surrender to a superordinate power was what absolutely contradicted the final reality of the state.

---

35. [Antoine Destutt de Tracy, *A Commentary and Review of Montesquieu's Spirit of Laws* (Philadelphia: Duane, 1811), 86.]

36. [Destutt de Tracy, *A Commentary and Review of Montesquieu's Spirit of Laws*, 88. Translation altered.]

Thus, even Kant, in his philosophical sketch *Perpetual Peace* of 1795, could not go beyond the construction of a "pacific federation"[37] of sovereign states that would create international law, although he expressly writes that in their relationship among themselves they must be treated as if in a "state of nature." He does not infringe upon the unquestionability of hypostatizing the state since he demands this *foedus pacificum* [pacific federation] to come into being without states having "to submit to public laws and to a coercive power which enforces them, as do men in a state of nature." The future of the great peace in the "idea of federalism" as the "substitute for the union of civil society" lies *between*, not *above* the states.[38] The positive rational idea of a "world republic" he deems to be logical but not historically inevitable, because it would, given the existing pluralism of states, presuppose the self-contradiction of going against the will to self-preservation inherent to each state. From this, Hegel deduces in his *Elements of the Philosophy of Right* that the state is "[i]ndividuality, as exclusive being-for-itself."[39] States are not only factually "in a state of nature in relation to one another" but this state remains unsurpassable, for "their rights have their reality not in a universal will with constitutional powers over them, but in their own particular wills."[40] Those who wish for a superordinate totality, be it even of the type of a federation of states, "know little of the nature of a totality and of the self-awareness which an autonomous nation possesses."[41] If it manifests the "march of God in the world"[42] that the state is, then this absolutism of the reality of the state is at the very least the dead end for the norm of peace, and then it follows that "conflicts between states can be settled only by war."[43] To see the state as "some-

---

37. [Immanuel Kant, "Perpetual Peace: A Philosophical Sketch," in *Political Writings*, ed. Hans Reiss, trans. H. B. Nisbet (Cambridge: Cambridge University Press, 1991), 104.]

38. [Kant, "Perpetual Peace," 104.]

39. Hegel, *Elements*, 359 (§322).

40. Hegel, 368 (§333). [Translation altered.]

41. Hegel, 360 (§322).

42. Hegel, 279 (§258).

43. Hegel, 369 (§334).

thing technical more than something spiritual,"[44] that is, something that according to Hegel "will not be deemed to deserve the emphatic designation of being real,"[45] at least opens up the latitude of that which "has no greater value than something that is possible."[46] Once again it becomes clear what it means to address the concept of reality as the foundation of the theory of the state and to subject it to critical inquiry with regard to its implications for the norm of peace. The consistency of the theory of the state contract, which is, as it were, truncated, is merely an illustrative model for this.

Classical theories of the state suffer from the weakness that the process of constituting the state is supposed to lead to a self-contained structure in a single decisive step. This unspoken normative requirement even caused the reception of Montesquieu's theory of the state to ossify into the dogmatism of the separation of powers, and caused it to join the ranks of other "blueprints." But a reading of the *Spirit of the Laws* reveals that it is not about describing the emergence of the state from the precivil condition; instead, it aims at reducing the always already historically extant state to the measure of human tolerability. Montesquieu's aversion to the theory of the state contract rests upon his not aiming to provide a foundation for the state and "building" it, but to absorb and inhibit the genuine dynamic of power. The urge to exercise power seemed to him a given energy that had been introduced into history as nature, and nothing was too insignificant or small if it might counteract this energy. Even the despot might occasionally be swayed by human sentiment—just as the beach's most minute obstacles, its pebbles and grasses, can offer resistance to the sea, which appears

---

44. Thomas Mann, *Reflections of a Nonpolitical Man*, trans. Walter D. Morris (New York: Ungar, 1987) 107.

45. [Hegel, *Encyclopedia of the Philosophical Sciences in Basic Outline. Part 1: Science of Logic*, trans. and ed. Klaus Brinkmann and Daniel O. Dahlstrom (Cambridge: Cambridge University Press, 2010), 33 (§6). Translation altered.]

46. [Hegel, *Encyclopedia of the Philosophical Sciences in Basic Outline*, 34 (§6). Emphasis removed.]

to want to flood the whole world.[47] Voltaire crushed this simile with ridicule. Laconically, he remarks that it is the laws of gravitation that make the sea recede, not the grasses and pebbles.

Such collision of elementary metaphors makes one feel with terror how the constructive weakness of the idea provokes the critic to the most severe vividness: once something is typified as a natural occurrence, it excludes even the smallest latitude of the word and of human affect. Correcting the image by referring it to the laws of nature makes the notion of moderating the state appear unreal. Almost as an illustration of this clash of metaphors, the first trace of the problem of peace appears in Kant, forty years before he wrote his tract on perpetual peace. In November 1755, news of the Lisbon earthquake with thirty thousand dead shook Europe; Kant thrice picked up his pen to explain the event to his fellow citizens and to reconcile it with the theodicy of German Enlightenment once more. But as Kant finished his "History and Natural Description of the Earthquake," the conflict that would become the Seven Years' War had begun. The book's last sentence is addressed to the Prussian king, to whom Kant had recently dedicated his *Universal Natural History and Theory of the Heavens*: "A prince who, activated by a noble heart, allows himself to be moved by these hardships of the human race to avert the miseries of war from those who are threatened on all sides by serious misfortune, is a beneficent tool in the gracious hand of God, and a divine gift to the peoples of the earth who can never assess its worth in keeping with its magnitude." Kant throws his pebble against the flood, appealing with the natural against the political catastrophe; his argument, however, is in the phrase "hardships of the human race."[48]

Translated by Hannes Bajohr

---

47. Charles de Montesquieu, "L'Esprit de Lois," in *Oeuvres complètes de Montesquieu* (Paris: Didot, 1846), 198 (II,4), with Voltaire's note.

48. [Immanuel Kant, "History and Natural Description of the Most Noteworthy Occurrences of the Earthquake That Struck a Large Part of the Earth at the End of the Year 1755," in *Natural Science*, ed. Eric Watkins (Cambridge: Cambridge University Press, 2012), 364.]

Preliminary Remarks on the Concept of Reality

(1974)

Real is what is not unreal. I am aware that this sentence must strike a logician as disastrous. But as a tautology, it is not supposed to be a definition but rather serves the function of a methodical rule. After all, for the concept of reality [*Wirklichkeitsbegriff*], we cannot use the etymology of the words "real" and "reality" as a guiding thread for its conceptual history. Only by heeding this fact can we avoid the fate that befell the "concept of being" [*Seinsbegriff*]. From the hypostatization of a grammatical element—the copula—and with the help of the possibilities language afforded to the participle and the infinitive with an article, "being" set itself up to gain a special position in metaphysics that

---

Originally published as "Vorbemerkungen zum Wirklichkeitsbegriff," in *Akademie der Wissenschaften und Literatur in Mainz. Abhandlungen der geistes- und sozialwissenschaftlichen Klasse* 4 (1974): 3–10.

thrives on this element's ambiguities, which Aristotle was the first to point out.[1]

The concept of reality does not permit us to choose any linguistic equivalents from the lexical arsenal as easily as we could if, for instance, we were to write the conceptual history of the "urge for knowledge," where we could be on the lookout for terms like "curiosity," "striving for wisdom," "natural disposition for truth," "wanting to know," or "knowledge drive." The concept of reality is an "implicative predicate." The reason for this is its predominantly pragmatic function. The guiding thread toward the concept of reality is any form of "realism," albeit not chiefly that realism, which calls itself so. The rule that real is what is not unreal urges us to take a detour via that which in each case is deemed unreal and is rejected as such. The concept of reality's indeterminacy and historicity is based on the very fact that the ways of being unreal prove to be inexhaustible. To expose what is illusionary never guarantees that the "remainder" of what is not exposed in this way is the permanently and reliably real. Put theoretically, falsification is the nonattainable par excellence.

This explains why every realism can itself be instrumentalized. The label "reality," attached to what is to be designated as authoritative, authenticates the positive proposition as that which is meant to be thought of as possible. This implies that the concept of reality becomes ambiguous exactly at that point where its implicative function can be studied in the greatest detail—in aesthetics.

The more general the object we discuss, the less we can discuss it by trying to grasp the object itself and keep it fixed in our regard. Quite the contrary: one can speak best of the most general by "disregarding" it, by regarding something else or that which is completely different. It is not only the Platonic and mystic tradition that has spoken of the highest principle by consistently looking at what it is not, and then according a negative value to all it found. Already in the didactic poem of Parmenides, philosophy begins by declaring its topic to be what is [*das Seiende*] but having almost nothing to say about it, while a lot more could probably have been

---

1. [Aristotle, *Posterior Analytics* 92b14, *Metaphysics* B.3, 998b22.]

said about the sphere of appearances, understood as that which is not [*das Nichtseiende*]. If we want to state a minimally meaningful proposition about such general things as the "world" or "life," we likewise can do so only by disregarding the overwhelming topic and choosing a guiding schema. There may be something arbitrary about this choice unless we can show that we dare to approach the discussion of such generalities only because we already possess our orientation. Metaphor is not the retrospective illustration of the overly abstract but the initial encouragement to engage with it in the first place. It opens up access to the highest degrees of abstraction. Let me mention an instructive example of this method. In 1900, Georg Simmel published his *Philosophy of Money*.[2] The very topic served him as a detour by which to speak of the more abstract topic of "value." But not until two decades later, at the end of his path, did it become clear to what degree of abstraction he was able to raise the insights of this early investigation into the concept of "life as transcendence."[3] Money, it turns out, is the primary metaphor for the expression "life," which otherwise seems completely lacking in content. With a view to the problem of time, "life" is the contrasting concept for a whole register of cultural criticism with its stigmata of petrification, overinstitutionalization, anachronistic vestiges, and ritualized immobility. Life is the epitome of the very counterdynamic to the liquidity of all values that Simmel had discovered in his earlier *Philosophy of Money*.

It is imperative to clear the path toward such primary intuitiveness in a methodical way, if discussion of the implicative concept of reality is not to lapse into the same sterility that, despite all the efforts of Heidegger's successors, we must ascribe to the history of the concept of being—and, in its wake, even to the supposed "history of being" itself. Intuitiveness has the reputation of being merely

---

2. [Georg Simmel, *The Philosophy of Money*, ed. David Frisby (London: Routledge, 1990). Blumenberg elaborates on his reading of Simmel's work in "Money or Life: Metaphors of Georg Simmel's Philosophy," *Theory, Culture & Society* 29, no. 7–8 (2013): 249–62.]

3. [Georg Simmel, *The View of Life: Four Metaphysical Essays with Journal Aphorisms*, ed. John A. Y. Andrews (Chicago: University of Chicago Press, 2010), chap. 1.]

illustrative and elaborative only because, by virtue of its belonging to the discipline of rhetoric—for instance, in the form of metaphor and simile—it seems as though it was added after the fact and is thus genetically dispensable. This is a false appearance that the author unavoidably creates by reversing the sequence of his presentation.

Reality is not only, in the traditional sense, the actualization of a thing in relation to its pure possibility, but, additionally, its actuality in consciousness. This can mean reliability as well as urgency, depending on what seems to be at risk or what is demanded. From the direction of given reality, the alternative to reliability and meaning also intrudes into the theoretical attitude and engulfs it in a dilemma that only the entire process of modern science has completely brought to the surface: if the need for reliability becomes absolute, our receptiveness to meaning, relevance, and urgency tends toward zero.

Descartes intensified his doubt about the existence of the world as it appears to us to the point of considering it a deception by a *genius malignus* [evil spirit]. He turned the reliability of the great metaphysical guarantee for human life in the world—"to go forward with confidence in this life"[4]—into the thorn in the side of modern philosophy; admittedly, it soon exchanged transcendent for transcendental presuppositions. What is crucial, however, is that the medieval guarantee had replaced the loss of the ancient assumption that you can tell simply by looking that reality is not unreal, provided that one is not only confronted with unreality, like the prisoners in Plato's cave facing their shadows.[5] In search of a guarantee for reality, Descartes is still wholly entangled in the Middle Ages, although he can no longer share its trust in the indubitability of this guarantee.

The great deception, which Descartes introduces only as the boundary value of his doubt, presupposes two things: first, the implication of the real's claim to be what it appears to be; and sec-

---

4. [René Descartes, *Discourse on Method* (Indianapolis: Hackett, 1998), 6.]

5. [Blumenberg discusses Plato's cave with regard to the concept of reality in "The Life-World and the Concept of Reality," in *Life-World and Consciousness: Essays for Aron Gurwitsch*, ed. Lester E. Embree (Evanston, IL: Northwestern University Press, 1972), 425–444.]

ond, the possibility that all features of the real may be imitated or simulated, without the production of these features yielding the objective equivalent of reality.

It was only Leibniz who saw, against Descartes, that the complete simulation of reality would no longer be a deception, since it would lack both the implied claim about the nonexisting as well as the harm of disappointment for whoever is affected by it.[6] Put differently: the great Baroque idea of life as a dream is, for Leibniz, not only without any horrors but the expression of a new concept of reality in which the internal consistency of everything given is identical to the possible solidity of reality. Reality is no longer like an assertion whose credibility depends on the quality of the speaker.

On the other hand: unreality now menaces any reality as an irrevocable reservation, just as even the longest chain of inductive verification is theoretically exposed to the ever-present possibility of falsification. We understand what we mean by the expression "real" not in regard to a disjunction that is available at any given moment but in relation to the possibilities that lie within this process.

The belief that there is such a thing as a stigma of "noninventability" constitutes, if I may say so, the anachronism that haunts modern aesthetic realisms. We need only think of the ambiguous relationship it has to probability [*Wahrscheinlichkeit*]: for an event to appear realistic, it must be improbable to the extent that no one could have possibly invented it—and so one may take a piece of information from a newspaper. Another case: the protagonist of a modern novel "reads a novel in which too much happens" and confirms the realism of the author who created him with the words: "In reality, it is not like this at all."[7] The result is the inversion of the argument: because little happens in reality, it is enough to write a novel in which nothing much transpires to give it the mark of noninventedness.

---

6. [Gottfried Wilhelm Leibniz, "Critical Thoughts on the General Part of the Principles of Descartes," *Philosophical Papers and Letters*, ed. Leroy E. Loemker (Dordrecht: Kluwer), 383–412.]

7. [Walter Helmut Fritz, *Die Beschaffenheit solcher Tage* (Hamburg: Hoffmann und Campe, 1972), 127.]

The difference to antiquity's concept of reality is that in modernity there is nothing for us that could dispel all illusions and prove itself to be the definitely real. On this assumption rested the faith common to both Greeks and Hebrews that a god, if he were to appear, would remove any doubt in the reality of his presence precisely because such an ideal value of indubitability incarnate was possible. Modernity's attack on miracles elucidates the concept of reality based on immanent consistency not so much by uncovering its contradictions, but, more radically, by establishing that there can be no such thing as the instantaneous self-evidence of reality. To sidestep a thing so as not to collide with it is the most elementary form of deeming it real. But to trace this detour around the thing—a pragmatic and completed gesture—does nothing to indicate whether it was in fact real; it only makes what had been important in this process appear indifferent now. The presupposition of antiquity was that one would stop in front of the thing if one could rely on standing before the pure and final reality, not leaving open a comparison of realities—put Platonically: if one had arrived at the idea itself.

The traditional concept of being is not something like the abstract remainder of a more complete concept of reality; it is an utterly different construction. This can be illustrated by way of the "modalities." As regards the concept of being, the necessary (*ens necessarium*) is the exemplary, and in fact, exhaustive "case." The real is only its dependent and contingent residual state. The possible belongs to its character insofar as it allows the factual to be determined a "case" of the possible: because different things and different ways would be possible, it is not the necessary.

For the concept of reality, the same approach leads to a completely different set of characters. The *ens necessarium*, if it existed among us, would be that which is indifferent, autarkic, and thus ineffective. This showpiece of the metaphysical tradition would not be able to sustain itself in our consciousness; our attention would lose it the same way one drops a pebble when one no longer knows why one picked it up in the first place. Metaphysicians of all stripes had to discover with horror that their proofs of an *ens necessarium*, which they often thought successful, were unable to affect the presence of what had thus been proved in consciousness. And it was not by chance that the very same tradition has had the greatest difficulties to ascribe any effectiveness to the found *ens necessarium*—and why should it? Why should we care about it, and why it about us? Pascal rightly noted in his famous *Mémorial* that his god had nothing in common with the "god of the philosophers."[8]

Likewise, the factual affects us only insofar as it offers possibilities. For this reason, matter—this futile substrate for idea and form, the *hyle* [matter] of antiquity—becomes for the modern concept of reality the point of convergence of the theoretical and the practical attitude. It is therefore only consistent that it ultimately reveals itself to be the equivalent of energy.

This can be shown even more distinctly in the transformation of the concept of space. For antiquity, space—the pure possibility of the simultaneous—is not a reality. It becomes reality as soon as the fact enters into consciousness that space is the great consumer of time, that even light itself does not traverse it instantly. As soon as the finite speed of light was not only discovered but had also turned out to be a value that was small in relation to the size of the world, space could become a determining, powerful, consciousness-worrying reality. The man of the modern age who tries to increase the natural speed of movement for himself to gain the time that is his definitely finite potential discovers the reality of space by realizing that to conquer it, he has to exert the greatest part of his own energy and the energy he has at his disposal.

For the modern age, it is highly significant that reality discovers itself only in the moment in which it steps out of the sheer unavailability of mere resistance—without becoming pure availability, however. What is effortlessly and automatically available sinks back into the obviousness of something that is nothing at all, as does the necessary, as soon as it exists. What is or becomes unreal is that which does not imply any possibilities.

It is, however, not enough to trace back the changes in the concept of reality—from antiquity to the Middle Ages and to the modern age—to certain historical causalities, events, or discoveries, such

---

8. [Blaise Pascal, "Memorial," *Great Shorter Works of Pascal*, trans. Emile Cailliet and John C. Blankenagel (Philadelphia: Westminster Press, 1948), 117.]

as the discovery of the finite speed of light. There is a logic to this change that is much more elemental. Embedded in antiquity's concept of reality was that the world corresponds to man's capacity for understanding. Aristotle's dictum that, in a way, the soul is everything, was the maximally reduced formula that was still prevalent in the Middle Ages and the Renaissance. To this formula corresponds the expectation that experience is, in principle, finite and can be reduced to a catalog of distinct *Gestalten*, each of which communicates its reality in the instantaneous self-evidence of a confirmed ought-to-be. The Platonic theory of ideas and the notion of *anamnesis* [recollection] are merely consistent interpretations of the basic fact that such instantaneous self-evidence, such confirmation in propria persona [*Leibhaftigkeit*], might exist. Even Husserl tried to rediscover this self-evidence in his phenomenology by choosing the metaphor of an experience in propria persona for the original impression.[9]

It is easy to see that an excess of the given—a genuine disproportion between world and consciousness, against which the latter, as it were, has to defend and shield itself—has remained unknown to this concept of reality. Even the all-ruling randomness of the atomists kept on producing the same worlds.

Only the Middle Ages destroyed the "fit" between world and consciousness in favor of the omnipotence of the creation principle and at the expense of human confidence in the world, of course without quite permitting the ultimate conclusion: the suspicion that without any regard for man, the world could be the epitome of an infinite manifold of phenomena never to be fully grasped by experience. The finite typicality of always already achieved experiences is not a reliable arsenal for the experiences that are still to come. The consciousness of reality depends on an economy that might be its own but is not that of the given. Man in the modern age is the inundated creature; his concept of reality aims at avoiding the unexpected, at containment, at producing consistency against the case

---

9. [Edmund Husserl, *Logical Investigations*, trans. J. N. Findlay (London: Routledge, 2001), 2:86. Findlay translates Husserl's *leibhaftig* (bodily, personified) as "in propria persona," which I have adopted here.]

of inconsistency. His experience is reduced to categories whose scope, on the one hand, a priori excludes the boundary case of the perfectly irregular, and on the other, has to set a very high threshold for allowing the purely singular.

Here, an ambiguity becomes possible that could perhaps express itself in the anxious question of whether the real in the strict sense might be precisely that which could break through the consistency of the consciousness of reality. The theoretical attitude of the scientist cannot make much of this ambiguity, because it is the methodically developed expression of that effort of economy and its capacity. It is the aesthetic attitude that works with this ambiguity. The fiction of the classical realisms consists in the assumption that in the compression of descriptive means—in the precision of unlocking what before had already become commonplace and thus unreal—reality can be grasped. Against this realism, there is another that breaks open the immunization of consciousness through consistency by means of paradox, contradiction, and the absurd. "Real reality is always unrealistic," as Kafka put it;[10] and this conception is directed against the disappointment that finds in successful consistency only the dull "and so on" of the always already given. From this perspective, the aesthetic sensibility does not tolerate the successful performance of the theoretical attitude. To the pragmatic concept of reality as an actuality in consciousness, only that is valid which cannot be rejected, suppressed, and leveled to the status of a theoretical object. The quotidian—which cannot be of interest to the theoretician, because it is already incorporated into the consistency of the ordinary—must seem like the enormity that does not require any distracting events to be restored to that kind of reality with which man is engaged in such a way that he has always already retracted his attention from it. This turn of the aesthetic interest can only be understood if one conceives of it as running counter to the capacity of theory, which long ago successfully took on what is out of the ordinary.

---

10. [Gustav Janouch, *Gespräche mit Kafka: Aufzeichnungen und Erinnerungen* (Frankfurt am Main: Fischer, 1981), 91.]

One last remark must address the claim that modern age's concept of reality as immanent consistency has a high affinity to simulation. It is to be expected that in a crowded world, authentic dealings with reality must be replaced more and more by simulators. Already a decade ago, an intelligent misprint turned an "outer-space simulator" [*Weltraumsimulator*] into a "world simulator" [*Weltsimulator*]; this last is the boundary idea of the convergence of reality and unreality. Similar to Leibniz's defense of the ideal dream against the radical doubt of Descartes, we cannot even say that putting an end to the conflict between everybody's claim to reality by the inexhaustibility of simulation would be lacking a human perspective.

Translated by Hannes Bajohr

PART II

METAPHORS, RHETORIC, AND NONCONCEPTUALITY

6

LIGHT AS A METAPHOR FOR TRUTH

At the Preliminary Stage of Philosophical Concept Formation

(1957)

If indications are not misleading, a revival of philosophical research into the history of concepts is imminent. Several factors are behind this trend, including a recognition of the futility of the conceptual neoproduction that has erupted during the last decades, increasing embarrassment about the difficulties of mutual understanding in philosophy, and paradigmatic accomplishments in theology with regard to research on concepts.

If this long-neglected work is profitably to be taken up again, one will, above all, have to revise the scope of the term *philosophical concept*, as compared with earlier approaches. Because of the

Originally published as "Licht als Metapher der Wahrheit: Im Vorfeld der philosophischen Begriffsbildung," *Studium Generale* 10, no. 7 (1957): 432–447; from Hans Blumenberg, *Ästhetische und metaphorologische Schriften*, ed. Anselm Haverkamp (Frankfurt am Main: Suhrkamp, 2001), 139–171. English-language version published in *Modernity and the Hegemony of Vision*, ed. David Michael Levin (Berkeley: University of California Press, 1993), 30–86.

peculiarity and history of philosophical statements, *terminology* has a much broader meaning here than in other disciplines, which have either drawn their concepts from philosophy itself or been able to construct their own conceptual apparatus by establishing unambiguous definitions. In constantly having to confront the un-conceptualized and the preconceptualized, philosophy encounters the means of articulation found in this nonconceptualizing and preconceptualizing, adopts them, and develops them further in separation from their origin. The notion that the philosophical logos has "overcome" prephilosophical mythos has narrowed our view of the scope of philosophical terminology; besides concepts in the strict sense, which are offset by definition and fulfilled intuition [*Anschauung*],[1] there is a broad range of mythical transformations, bordering on metaphysical conjectures, which find expression in a metaphorics with diverse forms.

This preliminary stage of a concept is, in its "aggregate state," more vivid, more sensitive to the ineffable, and less dominated by fixed traditional forms. Often, what could not find a medium within the rigid architectonics of systems found expression here. Careful research in this area should be able to unearth a wealth of resources. The hope is that the present study of metaphors of light and their accompanying milieu will contribute, in both content and method, to a philosophical "metaphorology."[2]

In their expressive power and subtle capacity to change, meta-phors of light are incomparable. From its beginnings, the history of metaphysics has made use of these characteristics in order to give an appropriate reference to its ultimate subject matter, which can no longer be grasped in material terms. Again and again, this cipher has been used in attempting to show that there is more to the con-

---

1. [In philosophical texts, "intuition" is the standard rendering of *Anschauung* but it should be understood not in its contemporary sense of nonrational perception but rather in its older sense, stemming from the Latin *intueri* (to gaze upon), where the visual dimension found in the German (*schauen*, to look) is implicit. See Robert M. Wallace, "Translator's Notes," in *The Genesis of the Copernican World* (Cambridge, MA: MIT Press, 1987), 692.]

2. [See Hans Blumenberg, *Paradigms for a Metaphorology*, trans. Robert Savage (Ithaca, NY: Cornell University Press, 2010) and the texts in part II of this volume.]

cept of being [*des Seins*] than an empty abstraction which one could extract from beings [*dem Seienden*] as their most general real predicate.[3] The relation of unity to plurality, of the absolute to the conditional, of origin to descent—all found a "model" of sorts here.

Light can be a directed beam, a guiding beacon in the dark, an advancing dethronement of darkness [*Finsternis*],[4] but also a dazzling superabundance, as well as an indefinite, omnipresent brightness containing all: the "letting appear" that does not itself appear, the inaccessible accessibility of things. Light and darkness can represent the absolute metaphysical counterforces that exclude each other and yet bring the world-constellation into existence. Or, light is the absolute power of being, which reveals the paltriness [*Nichtigkeit*] of the dark, which can no longer exist once light has come into existence. Light is intrusive; in its abundance, it creates the overwhelming, conspicuous clarity with which the true "comes forth"; it forcibly acquires the irrevocability of Spirit's consent. Light remains what it is while letting the infinite participate in it; it is consumption without loss. Light produces space, distance, orientation, calm contemplation; it is the gift that makes no demands, the illumination capable of conquering without force.

The intent here is not to fill in the details of this short and doubtless fully incomplete outline of the expressive potential of metaphors of light but rather to show the way in which transformations of the basic metaphor indicate changes in world-understanding and self-understanding. What we call "history" in a fundamental sense is of course always in conflict with the essential inertia of the materials providing the evidence in which a basic change in the conception of reality not only can become manifest but can actually, for the first

---

3. [This distinction is notoriously difficult to translate. Here, *das Sein* has been translated as "being," while *das Seiende* has been rendered either (in the plural) as "beings" or (less commonly) as "what is"; in the latter case, the German is always given in brackets.]

4. [In German, there are several words for darkness: *Finsternis*, which has connotations of utter and foreboding darkness; *Dunkelheit*, which connotes an obscuration of vision; and *das Dunkel*, which generally corresponds to the English "the dark." In this essay, *Finsternis* is the most common term. Whenever "darkness" has been used to translate either of the other terms, the original German will be given in brackets.]

time, achieve articulation. Here, however, it is precisely traditional philosophical terminology, as it populates indices and specialist dictionaries, that is capable of only the slowest shifts of meaning. In the history of ideas, settled definitions that emerge from the reshuffling of concepts tend to be genuinely "slow on the uptake," just as, in philosophy, by the time a "system" comes together, the underlying substructure is usually already in motion again. These conditions explain the significance of immature, groping, tentative modes of expression, among which metaphors of light have a privileged position. Outstanding achievements have already been made in research on individual periods,[5] but only a more comprehensive periodicization can make apparent the real "achievement" of these metaphors.

In all likelihood, the concept of light originally belonged to a dualistic conception of the world, as the second part of Parmenides's poem [*The Way of Opinion*][6] documents for us (and for the Pythagorians, according to Aristotle's report).[7] Light and darkness are, like fire and earth, fundamental primordial principles. Their enmity leads to the awareness that being is nothing assured, that

---

5. The work that must be mentioned first of all remains Clemens Baeumker's "Witelo, ein Philosoph und Naturforscher des XIII. Jahrhundert," *Beiträge zur Geschichte der Philosophie des Mittelalters* 3, no. 2 (1908): 1–71, incomparable in its collection of material. Concerning antiquity, see Rudolf Bultmann, "Zur Geschichte der Lichtsymbolik im Altertum," *Philologus* 97, no. 1/2 (1948): 1–36; Julius Stenzel, "Der Begriff der Erleuchtung bei Platon," *Die Antike* 2 (1926): 235–257. On the Middle Ages, see Jakob Gessner, "Die Abstraktionslehre in der Scholastik bis Thomas von Aquin mit besonderer Berücksichtigung des Lichtbegriffs," *Philosophisches Jahrbuch* 44, no. 3 (1931): 362–371; 44, no. 4 (1932): 457–475; and 45 no. 1 (1932): 65–82; Martin Honecker, "Der Lichtbegriff in der Abstraktionslehre des Thomas von Aquin," *Philosophisches Jahrbuch* 48 (1935): 268–288; Ludwig Baur, "Die Philosophie des Robert Grosseteste," *Beiträge zur Geschichte der Philosophie des Mittelalters* 18 no. 4–6 (1917); Pierre Garin, *Le théorie de l'idée suivant l'école thomiste* (Paris: Desclèe, 1930); and Raoul Carton, *L'expérience mystique de l'illumination intérieure chez Roger Bacon* (Paris: Vrin, 1926). With regard to St. Augustine, Bonaventure, mysticism, and Nicholas of Cusa, the relevant literature contains a wealth of material, of which insufficient use has been made. With regard to the modern age, it evidently still needs to be proven that the history of metaphors of light continues at all.

6. Hermann Diels, *Die Fragmente der Vorsokratiker*, 3 vols. (Berlin: Weidmann, 1939), 28 B 9; in this connection, see also Simplicius's commentary on fragment 8, 53–59.

7. Aristotle, *Metaphysics* 1.5.986a25.

truth is nothing self-evident. But the fact that Parmenides situates this dualism in the *second* part of the poem already points toward its being overcome; it belongs to the sphere of *doxa*. At the beginning of the poem, the path to the truth leads *eis phaos*.[8] In the center of his work, Parmenides uproots the dualism of being and not-being, truth and appearance, light and darkness: being does not exist *because* it is not not-being (since not-being would then be *necessary* for its being),[9] and light is not *essentially* the opposite of darkness; rather, in the essence of light, darkness is destroyed and overcome. Thus, Plato was not the first to release the concepts of being, truth, and light from a dualistic reliance on their opposite. Plato was, however, the first to demonstrate, by means of metaphors of light, that this splitting-in-two implies what can be termed the *naturalness* of the connection between being and truth.

What this means is that being *is*, as "nature," *of its own accord* (not in virtue of its opposite), and that, in exactly the same way, it is true, i.e., it is true of its own accord and not in virtue of a subsequent process of thought discovered in a situation of untruth. Truth is light upon being itself, being as light, i.e., being as the *self-presentation* of beings. That is why cognition in its highest form bursts out of the inactive, calm contemplation of *theōria*. That is why, in Platonic *anamnēsis*, the truth that has already been seen penetrates, again and again, into that which is forgetful of its origin. That is why, in the *Republic*'s allegory of the cave, an original situation is constructed with a perfectly artificial and forcible screening off of "natural" light, a situation that no longer has anything dualistic about it and which only later must be bent back into a dualistic schema. The drama of truth is not a cosmic agon between light and darkness but rather only a process of man's withdrawing himself or handing himself over—a matter, thus, of paideia.[10] Truth is not only present; it is insistent.

---

8. Diels, *Die Fragmente der Vorsokratiker*, 28 B 1, 10.

9. Diels, 28 B 2, 5.

10. Martin Heidegger, "Plato's Doctrine of Truth," trans. John Barlow, in *Philosophy in the Twentieth Century: An Anthology*, ed. William Barrett and Henry D. Aiken (New York: Random House, 1962), 3:257–258. [Original German edition of 1947, 25–26.]

In the Platonic allegory of the cave, it is said of the Idea of the Good—which figures there as the sun that puts everything in the light of being—that (as the origin of knowability, being, and essence) it is not itself a being, but rather something that stands out, in virtue of its dignity and strength, above beings.[11] This statement is not at all metaphysically laden: that which gives everything else visibility and "objecthood" cannot, in the same way, itself have the character of an object. Light is only seen in what it lets become visible. The "naturalness" of light consists precisely in this, that it only "dawns," in its own sense, with the visibility of things, and thus is itself not of the same nature as that which it evokes. But already in Plato, this *difference* is tinged with *transcendence*; the *metaphorics* of light already has a *metaphysics* of light implicit in it. A way of expressing the naturalness of truth turns into its opposite: truth becomes "localized" in transcendency.

Despite an abundance of gods of nature, Greek religion did not have a deity of light,[12] precisely because light was too comprehensive to be grasped: it is the *wherein* of nature, not its component part, "daylight as the brightness in which one moves, in which the world articulates itself, in which it becomes surveyable and understandable, in which the distinction between here and there, between this and that, is possible . . . and which, at the same time, thereby makes existence [*Dasein*] understandable to itself."[13] Spirit and material things are equally in this brightness. "Illumination" is not an inner as opposed to an outer occurrence; rather, ontic and ontological elucidation [*Erhellung*] are identical. There is no *mysticism* of light in Plato; light is not a peculiar, special dimension of experience.[14] Aristotle formulated the same point in more sober terms when he said that that which sees becomes colored itself, so to speak,

---

11. Plato, *The Statesman* 509B.

12. Ulrich von Wilamowitz-Moellendorff, *Der Glaube der Hellenen*, 2nd ed. (Darmstadt: Wissenschaftliche Buchgesellschaft, 1955), 10:135.

13. Rudolf Bultmann, "Zur Geschichte der Lichtsymbolik im Altertum," 13.

14. Julius Stenzel, "Der Begriff der Erleuchtung bei Platon," 256.

and that the reality of the perceived and the reality of the perceiving are identical.[15]

Therein lies the radical difference between light and darkness: darkness is unable to bring about this identity; it is ontically and ontologically impotent. From this perspective, it is easy to grasp the full difference that exists with regard to the meaning of "light" and "darkness" in the Neoplatonism of late antiquity. There, they become antagonistic forces that dispute with each other over the soul; they exercise, seize, and "incorporate" force.

Thus, in order to see what precisely "light" meant at the time, one must pay attention to how "the dark" is to be understood as well. There is an autonomous, "romantic" darkness [*Dunkelheit*] of the dark, and there is a darkness [*Dunkel*] that lies under the light and in the light. Corresponding to the perspective of classical Greek philosophy developed here, the following can be said of Greek tragedy: "Classical tragedy indeed shows the dark underground of human existence, but not as something that is to be sensed dimly. On the contrary, it elucidates this dark underground with a ruthlessly bright light."[16]

The transcendency of light implied in the Platonic allegory of the sun becomes dominant in Hellenistic thought. The brightness that fills the cosmos like a medium is withdrawn, concentrated, objectified as a metaphysical pole. Radiance comes to mean a decline, a loss of darkness [*Dunkel*], and consumption comes to signify loss. The "unnatural" protection of the cave is extended to the cavernous nature of the entire cosmos, which seizes light, swallows it, and exhausts it. The previously translucent surfaces of the spheres thicken into cave walls. Light, now otherworldly and pure, does not allow for theoretical lingering in joyful contemplation; it demands extraordinary, ecstatic attention, in which

15. Aristotle, *De Anima* 3.2.425b20–27. See Walter Bröcker, *Aristoteles* (Frankfurt am Main: Klostermann, 1935), 148: "Aristotle takes seeing to be not primarily some occurrence in the subject, but rather the visible's showing itself."

16. Kurt von Fritz, "Tragische Schuld und poetische Gerechtigkeit in der griechischen Tragödie," *Studium Generale* 8, no. 4 (1955): 228.

fulfilling contact and repellent dazzling[17] become one. Few are equal to this task. The deadly light must be made available to mortals in the more cautious dosages of the *phōtismos* of mysteries. Thus, light becomes a metaphor for "salvation," for immortality.

The cosmic *flight of light* is the precondition for the concept of "revelation," which announces a return of light as an eschatological event and bids man to prepare himself for it. By holding the transcendent in reserve, light demands a purer condition of humanity than now happens to be the case.[18] It is no longer being *in* the light and seeing that offers man fulfillment; instead, what drives him on is the idea of looking *into* the light itself and letting everything else that is visible be extinguished. Light's flight from the world results in man's urge to enter the light. This leads directly to the Neoplatonism of late antiquity and to gnosis. Here, the classical conception of *theōria* has lost its footing: being is no longer the self-presentation of beings; it has become something "formless that cannot be glimpsed";[19] it does not open eyes but shuts them. Absolute light and absolute darkness collapse into each other. Consistent with this, the Areopagite will coin for every coming mysticism the phrase *theion skotos*.

Until now, this particular dimension (the "de-lumination" of the world) has been given more attention than the unanimity of other dimensions of Hellenistic and late Classical thought. What has been

---

17. [The German here (*Blendung*) has a range of meaning, extending from "confusion" and "deception" to "the act of blinding a person." It has been rendered throughout as "dazzling" in order to capture the broad sense of a (painful) bewilderment caused by light.]

18. Seneca, *Epist. Mor.* 102:

Cum venerit dies ille, qui mixtum hoc divini humanique secernat, corpus hie, ubi inveni, relinquam, ipse me diis reddam (22) . . . Alia origo nos expectat, alius rerum status. Nondum caelum nisi ex intervallo pati possumus. (23 sq.) . . . aliquando naturae tibi arcana retegentur, discutietur ista caligo te lux undique clara percutiet. Imaginare tecum, quantus ille sit fulgor tot sideribus inter se lumen miscentibus. Nulla serenum umbra turbabit: aequaliter splendebit omne caeli latus: dies et nox aeris infimi vices sunt. Tunc in tenebris vixisse te dices, cum totam lucem et totus aspexeris, quam nunc per angustissimas oculorum vias obscure intueris, et tarnen admiraris illam iam procul: quid tibi videbitur divina lux, cum illam suo loco videris? (28)

19. Plotinus, *Enneads* 6.7.17: "amorphos kai aneideos."

overlooked above all is that skepticism, too, represents a reply to the cosmic flight of light. Indeed, it is not at all an elementary "accident" (of the school) that skepticism breaks out in the middle of the Platonic Academy. Here, too, a position is being taken with regard to the fundamental ontological event of light's transcendency, and it is an attitude of flight, of shutting out the world, of rejecting *theōria* for *epochē*. One needs only to remind oneself that Socrates, in the *Phaedo*, has to experience the way turning toward reality itself dazzles the eye, and that the conclusion he draws from this is to escape to logoi and to observe in them the truth of beings.[20] Vision wants to defend itself from this dazzling immediacy; it does not want to look into the sun and is content with the stand-in mediacy of logos.

Skepticism can situate itself in this tradition; it simply takes the next step, following the proven failure of logos in the dispute among the schools. It does not concern itself with the experience of light and dark at all. But before this step can be taken, the classical connection between *eudaimonia* and *theōria* had to be broken. A completely happy existence is presupposed for man as an *inner* possibility. But in skepticism, this interior is peculiarly *empty*; it is the sheer difference that remains after the subtraction of any connection to the world. *That* something remains in *epochē*, and *what* it could be never came into question for skepticism; like Epicureanism, it took for granted the assumption that happiness was guaranteed simply by protection against unhappiness, confusion, and pain. The skeptic is the negative version of the mystic: he too closes his eyes, not against the dazzling abundance of absolute light, but against the questioning and confusing urgency of *obscuritas rerum*. In shutting off the *outer* dark, however, the *inner* light has still not yet been won. This is the point on which the Stoics brought their moral absolutism to bear. Consistent with this, they sought a *positive* definition of the concept of happiness and connected it with the inner self-evidence of ethical life.

This engagement of the various Hellenistic schools of thought with one another on the basis of their mutual ontological implication

---

20. *Phaedo* 99E-100A.

becomes clear in Cicero. He coined the concept of "natural light" for the tradition.[21] And he linked the metaphor of light with inner moral self- evidence. For Cicero, light is no longer the universal brilliance in which all beings are found equally; rather, a sort of anthropocentric *economy* is attached to light. Human life finds itself in a clearing [*Lichtung*] appropriate to its necessities. In the theoretical sphere, the gleam of probability, to which the "naturalness" of truth is reduced, "suffices." In the practice of methodically playing theses off each other, as the Academic skeptics engaged in it, *probabile* "shines" forth.[22] Wanting to go further is *arrogantia*, upon which the teleological economy of truth does not look highly. Outside the clearing that is economically appropriate to man, the dark is given its due. Among the *vitia* that violate the norm of *sapi-*

---

21. Wilhelm Dilthey, *Gesammelte Schriften* (Leipzig: Teubner, 1923), 2:177.

22. *De officiis* 2.2.8: "Contra autem omnia disputantur a nostris (sc. academicis), quod hoc ipsum probabile elucere non possit, nisi ex utraque parte causarum esset facta contentio." Typical of the unclarity of the meaning of metaphors of light is the transitive rendering that Karl Atzert gives *elucere* in his translation (Limburg: Steffen, 1951): "Das geschieht deshalb, weil sich das Wahrscheinliche erst *ins rechte Licht rücken* läßt, wenn man . . ." ["This happens because the apparently true lets itself *be put in the proper light* only when one . . ."]. Karl Büchner (Zürich: Artemis und Winkler, 1953), by contrast, renders it adequately: "weil eben *dieses Einleuchtende* nicht *aufstrahlen* könnte, wenn nicht . . ." ["because just *this plausibility* cannot *shine forth*, when not . . ."]. Atzert basically brings the modern transformation of metaphors of light into Cicero, while Büchner does well to leave the skeptic with the remainder of Platonic presuppositions at which he hints. The Academic skepticism is generally "more Platonic" than it wants to know. Not only does it "break out" institutionally in Plato's school but it is moreover a result of Platonism itself, of Platonism's transcendency of Ideas. The rumor about Arcesilas passing on Platonic orthodoxy to an esoteric circle of pupils (Sextus Empiricus, *Pyrrh. Hyp.* 1.33.234) while pretending to be a skeptic fits perfectly in this regard. Above all, however, the Platonic remainder is in the meaning of the apparently true. In this concept, the difference between Idea and appearance is transferred to "truth" itself. Cicero translates the Skeptics' *pithanon* as *verisimile* and initially retains the metaphorical character of this with a *quasi* (*Luc.* 53), only then to terminologize it. The apparently true not only "appears" (in the sense of deception) to be the true but is the "showing through" [*Durchscheinen*] of the true, the appearance of the true that is sufficient for man. In his dispute with Academic skepticism (*Contra Academ.* 2.27), Augustine draws a connection to the presupposition of *verum* in *verisimile*.

entia, he mentions not only carelessness in giving approval, but also an orientation toward *res obscurae* and *non necessariae.*[23]

This sort of exclusion would have been unthinkable earlier, given the ontological assumptions of classical ancient philosophy. The natural striving for knowledge, as Aristotle formulates it at the beginning of the *Metaphysics,* moves in a sphere of *universal* theoretical brightness and visibility, and *theōria* represents the comprehension (via imaginative reenactment) of an absolutely divine act. Cicero sees knowledge in the context of human specificity and neediness; theoretical activity comes to have moral premises. Under the title of *curiositas,* the Middle Ages will continue this trial in terms of theoretical hubris.[24]

For Cicero, it is in accordance with practical principles that light and dark are divided in the theoretical domain. The claim upon beings that is open to man is not primarily *scire* but *uti.*[25] Thus, light's center of intensity must lie in the principles of human action; only in these *res necessariae* are full light and compelling self-evidence assured. Plato's self-luminous *agathon,* which gives light to everything else, is not extended into transcendency but rather internalized in the most intimate immanence of moral consciousness— which *also* means, however, that it is theoretically hidden. Cicero accepts the Stoic principle that if one has any doubt whatsoever as to the rightness or wrongness of an act, one should refrain from

---

23. *De officiis* 1.6.18.

24. In his paraphrase of *De officiis,* St. Ambrose already goes beyond Cicero in polemicizing against his making an exception for geometry and astronomy. For Ambrose, that which is set aside is a "matter of salvation" (*De officiis ministorum* 1.26.122) and not, as with Cicero, of *societas.* The idea of leaving *res obscurae* alone is already suggested to the Christian in the belief in a judge, "whose notice the hidden does not escape" (1.26.124). It is easy to see how the stage is already set here for the medieval identification of *curiositas* with natural science.

25. *De divinatione* 1.35: "Latet fortasse (sc. causa) obscuritate involuta naturae. Non enim me deus ista scire, sed his tantum modo uti voluit." The importance of this view for Cicero has been pointed out by Günter Gawlick in studying the phrase *Perdifficilis et perobscura quaestio* in his dissertation, "Untersuchungen zu Ciceros philosophischer Methode" (University of Kiel, 1956). See there the extensive further evidence documenting the "natural" darkness [*Dunkelheit*] of things outside the "economic" clearing of being [*Seinslichtung*] centered around human beings.

performing it at all.[26] But the acceptance of this presupposition lands him in an unnoticed contradiction with his own Platonic "residuum of light." For can there be any doubt about right or wrong at all if what is stated in the next sentence is true? *Aequitas lucet ipsa per se, dubitatio cogitationem significat iniuriae.* The good is so authentically in-the-light that it rules out doubt.[27] Corresponding to the internalization of pure light are the inward forms of its obscuration by the passions.[28] But at the same time, internalized light also pushes its way out again: Cicero treats *gloria* as the "emanation" of *virtus* that has been taken up and confirmed by the *communitas*; virtue shines forth and commands the respect of the human community.[29] Moral quality is still related to aesthetic quality and, at its highest level, can turn into it—a Platonic inheritance!

Excursus: The Cave

Darkness, as the power dualistically opposed to light, as a vanquished emptiness, as the natural background zone of the economic clearing of the humanly knowable, as a dazzling envelope of pure and absolute light—these are the correlates of the metaphorics of light considered thus far. In this field of signification, metaphors of the cave gain a special position. The

---

26. *De officiis* 1.9.30: "Quocirca bene praecipiunt, qui vetant quicquam agere, quod dubites acquum sit an iniquum."

27. Several editions have wanted to polish away the inconsistency here by placing an *enim* after *aequitas*. Atzert, for example, corrects (without any justification in the apparatus criticus) his own edition of 1939 in the revised edition of 1949, but does not properly consider the unmotivated *enim* in his 1951 translation. This can also be said of Büchner and Gigon.

28. *Tusc.* 3.2: "Nunc parvulos nobis dedit (sc. natura) igniculos, quos celeriter malis moribus opionibusque depravati sic restinguimus, ut nusquam naturae lumen appareat."

29. *De officiis* 2.9.32: "Etenim illud ipsum, quod honestum decorumque dicimus, quia per se nobis placet animosque omnium natura et specie sua commovet maximeque quasi perlucet ex iis, quas commemoravi, virtutibus, idcirco illos, in quibus illas virtutes esse remur, a natura ipsa diligere cogimur." In Kant's concept of "respect," the accent is shifted almost entirely to *cogimur*: "Respect is a tribute we cannot refuse to pay to merit whether we will or not." Immanuel Kant, *Critique of Practical Reason*, trans. Lewis White Beck (New York: Macmillan, 1956), 80. Here, metaphors of light are no longer of use.

cave is not simply the world opposed to light in the way that darkness is the "natural" opposite of brightness. The world of the cave is an "artificial," indeed perfectly violent underworld, relative to the sphere of natural light and natural dark: a region of screening off and forgetting, a surrogate and derivative of being. It is appropriate to address metaphors of the cave at this point, since it is Cicero who, in his discussion of a cave allegory found in an early Aristotelian dialogue, exemplifies most pronouncedly the just-mentioned features of cave metaphors.[30]

In this connection, the Stoic Balbus attempts to show that the *admirabilitas* of the world have paled for us as a result of our becoming accustomed to them, and that people who had always lived under the earth would, upon surfacing and beholding the cosmos, instantly believe in the existence and effectiveness of gods. The most important difference from the allegory of the cave in Book 7 of Plato's *Republic* is that in Cicero the situation in the cave is merely a thought experiment for hypothetically reducing the factor of being accustomed. The normal situation (*haec loca, quae nos incolimus*) is outside the cave, within sight of the cosmos in a constant and thus experientially flattened way. In Plato, the space outside the cave is the extraordinary residing place of the wise, whereas the situation in the cave represents our "normal" condition; the people in the cave are precisely not *atopoi*, as Glaucon asserts, but rather *homoioi hēmin*, as Socrates declares in rebuke.

---

30. *De natura deorum* 2.37.95. Valentin Rose (1886), Richard Walzer (1934), and William David Ross (1955) have no doubts with regard to this quote. Without further consideration, Werner Jaeger (*Aristoteles* [Berlin: Weidmann, 1923], 167) sees it as providing evidence for the proximity to Plato, as well as the young Aristotle's reconstruction of Plato. A comment of Erich Burck's led me to wonder about the authenticity of the text under discussion: there is, indeed, too much Stoicism in it. But that can still be laid at the doorstep of Cicero's understanding of "translation." Günter Gawlick, "Untersuchungen zu Ciceros philosophischer Methode," has produced important new evidence in support of this. The whole question probably cannot yet be answered definitively. We are on firm ground, however, when we utilize the text only for the context in which, for us, the question occurs.

Already, in Plato, the artificiality of the cave world of objects is implied: the shadows that appear on the cave wall are generated by artificial equipment, artistic forms, and all sorts of productions by human hands.

Nonetheless, the Platonic cave is impoverished compared to that of Cicero. There, the emphasis is on brilliance and splendor to prevent the slightest feeling of dissatisfaction or malcontent. Everything is there, *quibus abundant ii, qui beati putantur.* Cicero's cave world is one of "urban" luxury, a dazzlingly appointed sphere of culture, which captivates in virtue of its sheer attractiveness. In the Platonic cave, by contrast, man is chained and is in a situation of constraint which, although it is presupposed, virtually forces the question—which is not stressed until Neoplatonism—of what caused this. For Cicero, it is crucial that the cave world seem able to "compete" with the upper world, since the ascent out of this sphere is conceived as a matter of pure coincidence and is only considered in terms of the surprise that it effects.

In Plato, by contrast, the release from the chains, the painful reorientation, and the climb up the steps of disillusionment make up the crucial notion of paideia, which is meant to create an awareness, in retrospect, of the cave world as a sphere in which being and truth were lacking. In Cicero, in spite of all the brilliance with which the actual cosmos is portrayed, the realm of artificial light has nothing horrifying about it. Cicero has become familiar with the economy of the dark. One might almost say that he might have had a certain affinity for his conception of the cave, in which nature has been turned completely into *res obscura* and all certainty continues to be allocated to the *inner* light.

The expressive power of Cicero's cave metaphor lies precisely in the fact that the cave has lost its (forgive the expression) "existential seriousness"; it has become a hypothesis, a mental exercise. The contrasting background of *obscuritas rerum*, along with the internalization of *lumen naturae* corresponding to it, have undermined the assumptions behind the image of the cave.[31] From here on, radical reinterpretations of "cave" become possible. The entire cosmos had been equated with a cave once before by the pre-Socratics;[32] but it is Neo-platonism that, for the first time, really makes something of this identity.

Partly as a result of vivid allegorical readings of Homer, the grotto of the nymphs in the *Odyssey* gets cosmologically extended in meaning, as in the *De antro nympharum* of Ploti-nus's student Porphyry, where cosmos and cave stand for each other. The one is the *symbolon* of the other, and man is the *tertium*, who is prevented by temptation and gentle force from reaching his cave-transcending destiny. Here, the cave, identi-fied with the cosmos, issues in a scenario of the incarnation characteristic of Eastern Christian symbolism: Christ is born in a cave instead of a stable, and Justinian insists that the cave cult of Mithras is a diabolical usurpation of this symbolic lo-cus.[33] The topos of "the light in the cave" has become possi-ble only as a result of this constellation.[34] The paideutic path no longer leads out of the cave; the gaze is directed into the dark, because in it the unbelievable—that light could appear *here*—has become believable. The Platonic opposition of the cave fire to the sun of the Good has been eliminated: the light

---

31.   See Heidegger, "Plato's Doctrine of Truth," 261 [German, 53]: "Where the truth is of another essence and is not unhiddenness or at least where unhiddenness is not a component of this definition, an 'allegory of the cave' has no basis from which it can be clarified." The depth and "exactness" with which Plato's metaphor of the cave is supported can, in fact, be seen in its rehearsal at *Phaedo* 109E, where the mistaking of being [*Seinsverwechslung*] and the ascent out of the deceiving depths are already implicit.

32.   Pherecydes of Syros, Diels, 7 B 6.

33.   *Dialogus cum Tryphone Judaeo* 78.5–6 (possibly in response to *Protev. Jacobi* 18.1). On this, see Carl Schneider, *Geistesgeschichte des antiken Christen-tums I* (Munich: Beck, 1954), 250, where (Ps.) Basilius, *Hom. in nativ. Christi* is again referred to. See also Ernst Benz, "Die heilige Höhle in der alten Christenheit und in der östlichen orthodoxen Kirche," *Eranos-Jahrbuch* 22 (1953).

34.   A most recent reflection of this is in Ezra Pound's "Canto XLVII": "The light has entered the cave. Io! Io! / The light has gone down into the cave, / Splen-dour on splendour!"

in the cave is of one essence with its origin; it is its steward and guarantor, and not a deceitful source of shadows. The inside of the cave has been reassessed positively.

As individualized caves, the small room and the monastic cell become, in the Middle Ages, places where the truth is openly present, an indication that now everything can be expected *from within*. *Intra in cubiculum mentis tuae, exclude omnia praeter Deum* is a new motto that generates caves and chambers in which one can *wait* for the light, as the belief in *grace* implies. But this conception immediately turns into a metaphor for the "inner space of self-possession," as Montaigne understands "cave" (*tanière*).[35] The cave remains in use as a contrasting metaphor vis-à-vis the new and emergent. Francis Bacon formulates the awkwardness of the individual within its subjective world under the title *idola specus*;[36] disposition, education, and experience represent each person's own particular cave, which breaks and weakens the "natural light" for each. The "cave" denotes the facticity of the subject, the world of its own in which the subject always already finds itself. Significantly, Bacon renders *idia phronēsis*, the phrase used by Heraclitus, to whom he refers by name, as "own little world." And leaving the cave is now no longer the paideutic path of the wise individual into full light but rather a *method*, a "technique" for the production of a "greater common world" for all.

Leaving the cave becomes a metaphor within the philosophy of history; it denotes a *new epoch* of humanity. This is how Descartes used the metaphor. He compares the Scholastics' fight against the new science to the ways of "a blind man, who, to fight without a handicap against someone who is sighted, makes his opponent go into the depths of a very dark

---

35. Cf. Hugo Friedrich, *Montaigne* (Bern: Francke, 1949), 307.
36. *Novum Organum* 1.42: "Idola specus sunt idola hominis individui: Habet enim unusquisque (praeter aberrationes naturae humanae in genere) specum sive cavernam quandam individuam, quae lumen naturae frangit et corrumpit . . . ut plane spiritus humanus (prout disponitur in hominibus singulis) sit res varia, et omnino perturbata, et quasi fortuita: unde bene Heraclitus, homines scientias, quaerere in minoribus mundis, et non in maiore sive communi."

cave"; in publishing his method, by contrast, he "would be doing almost the same as if [he] were to open some windows and make some light of day enter into that cave where they have descended to fight."[37] This is a significant new image in place of the paideutic path out of the cave, for here the space itself is transformed. It does something not only to man but *to the world*, something that no longer depends on the individual's education and will. This is not, however, a momentary act, but rather a historically continuous path of discovering the truth, *qui ne se découvre que peu à peu*. The window metaphor takes this into account with its implication of light gradually gaining access. Recall the significance of the closed, medieval chamber in Descartes's portrayal of the turning point in his thinking: "I remained for a whole day by myself in a small stove-heated room."[38] Here the relation of the room to the world is still completely medieval: the "direction" is from the outside to the inside.

Nicholas of Cusa illustrated this with the image of a cosmographer (*Compendium* 8). To produce a map of the world, the cosmographer first collected all the empirical data, *clauditque portas et ad conditorem mundi internum transfert intuitum*. This internal "ground" of the world is the immediate relationship between man's mind and God's, the *signum conditoris, in quo vis creativa . . . relucet*. In the medieval chamber's screening off of the world, the creative potency of man lights up for the first time. Only through asceticism does man take hold of the world.

From this point on, the cave becomes the accepted metaphor in the philosophy of history for the point from which "progress" must begin. The problems of human socialization are exemplified by the hypothetical situation of leaving the primordial cave (where, quite fittingly, the relics of primordial man are also sought and found). The topos of the history-initiating departure

---

37. Descartes, *Discourse on Method*, trans. Donald A. Cress (Indianapolis: Hackett, 1980), 38; first French edition, 71.
38. Descartes, *Discourse on Method*, 34; French edition, 11.

from the cave was already given an initial form in antiquity. In Vitruvius, for example, it is the flames of a forest fire that lure people out of the cave and socialize them for the first time;[39] in Cicero, it is rhetoric that manages to "convince" them to come out of an isolated cave existence and enter into community.[40]

This ambiguity between an automatic instinctual process and a primordial intellectual accomplishment runs through the entire history of the motif of leaving the cave. The return to the cave, by contrast, is a matter of deviant curiosity, as in Don Quixote's descent into a cave (*Don Quixote de la Mancha*, vol. 2, chaps. 22 and 23) or in the remarkable imitation of Cicero's allegory of the cave in Jean Paul,[41] where the hero, Gustav, in accordance with a condition of his parents' marriage contract, spends the first eight years of his life underground "for heaven" (in the Stoic sense!), with the paideutic idea of keeping the child from "being hardened to both the beauty of nature and the distortions of humans"; and it is expressly confirmed later that the plan worked, for "the beauty of nature was the only thing he could talk about enthusiastically with other (viz. female) beauties—and he could condense, in the most lively way, all the world's charms into *one* morning, when he described his entrance up out of earth into the great hall of the world."[42] But the return to the cave, whence humanity stepped forth into its "progress," can also signify a distancing from this progress: the cave thus becomes a locus of aristocratic seclusion, of withdrawal from the lowly spheres of the commonly human, of the desire for a reorientation of movement in history. Zarathustra's cave is of this type. [*End of excursus.*]

Returning to the point where this digression began, we can say that the transcendency of light, on the one hand, and its internalization on the other, characterize the transition from the metaphorical

---

39. *De architectura* 2, prooemium.
40. *De inventione* 1, prooemium.
41. *Die unsichtbare Loge: eine Biographie* (1793), section 3.
42. *Die unsichtbare Loge*, section 30.

to the metaphysical usage of the notion. Both correlates of this development are linked by a crucially new idea: light acquires a *history*.

The inner light of the mind [*Geist*] is descended from transcendent light—not, however, by means of "illumination" but by means of "dispersal"; not because of a message but due to an "accident" of theft, of illegitimate cosmic implication. The drama of the diaspora and reunification of absolute light is the fundamental conception of gnosis. Light no longer shines into the world to wake it into being; instead, it gets lost in an alien and enemy sphere; it must be liberated and led back to its origin. The paideutic history of *man*, who comes out of the dark into the light, has been transformed into a history of *light*, which loses itself to the dark and returns to itself. Man is only a "vehicle" for this history, which is not a human but a cosmic drama. With this, the concept of "world" lands in an irresolvable ambiguity: without the descent [*Herabkunft*] of divine light, there would be no visibly formed cosmos, no origin of the material world; at the same time, however, this creation of the world represents the metaphysical ruin of pure light, the contamination and distortion of the absolute.

Plotinus, too, in his discussion of the origin of *kakon*, describes the emergence of the cosmos and the origin of evil *at the same time*.[43] For Plotinus, the pure light of the Good and the pure dark of matter are each *mē on*. The drama of intermingling, from which *to on* emerges, is played out between these two poles; from the perspective of this origin, what is [*das Seiende*] has a negative value. This negativity of what is corresponds to that of logos. Whereas Socrates, in the *Phaedo*, sought refuge in logoi, now the mind must be awakened from its state of laboring under logoi and redirected to the ineffable and nonconceptual contemplation of pure light.[44] Likenesses no longer refer back to the original, as in Plato, but rather deceitfully seduce one away from it; only those who look, know.[45] There is only one "object" of true knowledge: light itself and in itself. *Descent is,*

---

43. *Enneads* 1.8.
44. *Enneads* 6.9.4.
45. *Enneads* 6.9.9.

by itself, decline. Therein lies an irrevocable immanent conclusion of the metaphysics of light: light, as the Good, represents self-squandering and self-emanation; precisely thereby, however, light also represents distancing from itself, loss of self, and self-humiliation. This will be the main difficulty in the Christian reception of the metaphorics of light: *kakon* cannot emerge as a result of God's self-emanating, luminous essence. This is the central problem in Augustine's metaphysics, which he sets out to solve in his argument with Manichean gnosis. The cosmos, as God's "creation," can no longer represent light's mésalliance.

The starting point for the *Christian reception* of the metaphorics and metaphysics of light is the peculiar separation that the biblical report of Creation makes between the origin of "light" (on the first day) and that of "lights" (on the fourth day). This provided an easy entrance, which could hardly be missed, for the idea of a light that cannot be localized in the cosmos and that precedes all beings. The Christian tradition's extremely rich "language of light" took its point of departure from this approach.

We are not concerned here with an inventory; instead, our attention is directed, once more, to transformations of meaning occurring in the transition to and reception of this language of light. Central themes of this transformation can already be found in Genesis: the light of the first day represents *created* light. It has its source in a divine command; its opposition to darkness is not a primordial dualism but is based on God's positing and dividing. God Himself is beyond this opposition and has it at His disposal. This requires a reversal of the initial, dualistic cast that late antiquity gave to metaphors of light.

Far more important, however, is the unavoidable collision that occurs between the implications of that conception of light, on the one hand, and the fundamental assertion of the *willful* positing of beings on the other. If the connection between phenomenal beings and the "ground" of being is understood in terms of the "model" of light, then the implication of a "natural" overflowing of light onto the lit, of the emanative transformation of "ground" into "grounded" cannot be ruled out. This is indeed what metaphors of light have a tendency, immanently, to assert: that the entirety of a "ground" squanders and expresses itself, yet without diminishing. Implicit in metaphors of light is, further, the idea that they presuppose, if not a dualistic counterprinciple, then certainly a reflecting and passive underlying "ground": the substratum entailed by the classical concept of *hylē*, which appears in the light. This is where differences emerge between the language that has been handed down and what it now has to say.

With his attempt to transform biblical statements into Greek metaphysics, the Alexandrian Jew Philo had already decided how the image of light would be received. In his allegorical reading of Genesis, *De opificio mundi*, Philo succumbs almost completely to his "guiding image" of light. Just as he puts the light of the first day and the lights of the fourth day in the *genetic* context of aesthetic light emerging out of noetic light, he understands *noēton phōs* as "emission" rather than "creation."[46] The introduction of the concept of will was not able to stave off the "naturalism" of this image, because the concept of will is synonymous, for Philo, with that of the Platonic Ideas, which the Academic Antiochus had already dynamized.[47] Attempts have repeatedly been made since then to apply metaphors of light to an effective form of divine will, viewed as "emanation."[48] There is, however, an insurmountable heterogeneity here between metaphysical fact and metaphorical category. In Philo, the accent is suddenly shifted, in the Platonic sense: light is not the worldly first-created but is rather the otherworldly creator; as Creator, God is *phōs*,[49] is Himself *noētos hēlios*,[50] the original

---

46. *De opificio mundi* c.8 (ed. Cohn, 1889, 9).

47. Willy Theiler, *Die Vorbereitung des Neuplatonismus* (Berlin: Weidmann, 1930), 50.

48. An illustrative example is found in Salomon ibn Gabirol (Avicebron), *Fons vitae* 4.31 (ed. Baeumker, in *Beiträge zur Geschichte der Philosophie des Mittelalters* 1, no. 2 [1895], 254): "Dubitas quod lumen infusum in materia [!] sit defluxum ab alio lumine, quod est super materiam, scilicet lumine, quod est in essentia virtutis agentis? Et hoc est voluntas, quae eduxit formam de potentia ad effectum." In Moses Maimonides (*Dux neutrorum* 1.72), the metaphor of light is applied to the motor force emanating from the first sphere of heaven.

49. *De somniis* 1.13.75 (ed. Cohn-Wendland).

50. *De virtutibus* 22.164.

source of the light of being.[51] This "naturalization" of the biblical idea of creation remains the essential indication of how metaphors of light are used until the High Scholastic Middle Ages.

The association of metaphors of light with Gnostic dualism slowed their Christian reception but did not prevent it. By developing a concept of freedom, and by strictly formulating the ex nihilo of creation thinking, Augustine undermined dualism and prepared the way for the final Christian legitimation of *illuminatio*. Never before and never since has the language of light been handled in such a subtle and richly nuanced way. The predominantly epistemological interest in *illuminatio* has not yet been able to generate a suitably encompassing study; for that reason, we will neglect this (epistemological) dimension here, in order to draw attention to what has usually been neglected. Most important is the way in which Augustine distances himself from the Gnostic usage of metaphors of light. He accuses the Manicheans of not distinguishing *inter lucem quod est ipse Deus* and *lucent quam fecit Deus*. God *is* not simply light; He is *lucifica lux*.[52]

Augustine renounces the idea of the emanative homogeneity of the light of being (from absolute light to noetic light to aesthetic light), and thereby renounces the idea of a magnificently unified conception as well. He calls for metaphysical divisions: as between uncreated and created, so too between light *qua cernimus* and light *qua intelligimus*.[53] In our terminology, he *traces the metaphysics of light back to the metaphorics of light*! He argues with rhetorical vehemence against the Manichean *fabella* of light's primordial struggle with darkness, against the entire dramatic mythology of defeat, consumption, and degradation by darkness and light's reliberation, purification, and elevation—all with the help of man.[54] Not only is Augustine's God beyond the reach of such an attempt to grasp Him, but light, which God gives to humans, is not *tale lumen, quod ab aliquo possit obtenebrari*.[55] This is not only a matter of the in-

51. *De Cherubim* 28.97.
52. *Contra Faustum Manichaeum* 22.8.
53. *Contra Faustum Manichaeum* 20.7.
54. *Contra Faustum Manichaeum* 13.18.
55. *Enarratio in Psalmum* 26.2.3.

contestability of His saving Will but also of the illuminative under-
pinnings of the truth that is accessible to man. Man himself cannot
be light: *Lumen tibi esse non potes; non potes, non potes.* Man is
not light [*Licht*] but only a lamp [*Leuchte*] that has been lit by light:
*Lucerna et accendi potest, et exstingui potest; lumen verum accen-
dere potest, exstingui non potest.*[56] This talk of *lumen illuminatum*
and of *participando illuminari* is meant not only to set out a strict
distinction of *being* but also to signify the absolute character of the
truth available to man.[57]

Augustine made this discovery against the background of Academic skepticism. In contrast to the Neoplatonists' ecstatic concept
of truth, in which the highest level of the disclosure of truth is seeing-
into-the-light, Augustine returns to the classical form of the metaphor of seeing-in-the-light: we can recognize the light only by the
certainty that it grants us in elucidated beings.[58] Light is always,
so to speak, "behind us," and that is true precisely for *lux interior*,
which is responsible for things being laid plain to us—*qua res quaeque manifesta est.*[59] In itself, this hiddenness of revealing light is
indicated, in the same place, by the paradoxical and (in spite of being analogous to Neoplatonic formulations) completely autoch-
thonous talk of *insensibilias tenebrae huius lucis.*[60] Notwithstanding the oft-desired terminological harmonization with Plotinus—for
example, in the case of *attingere* and *amplecti*—the sheer inwardness

---

56. *Sermo* 182.5.
57. *Epist.* 140.7.
58. *Epist.* 120.10: "sed invisibiliter et ineffabiliter, et tamen intelligibiliter lucet, tamque nobis certum est, quam nobis efficit certa quae secundum ipsum (sc.
lumen) cuncta conspicimus." Deviating from his stance on Manichaeism, Augustine attempted to harmonize his relation to the Neoplatonists and thus did not
stress the distinctions in the metaphysics of light sharply enough. (*De civitate Dei*
10.2). Even in the phrases that sound Neoplatonic and esoteric—such as, "sed
paucissimis (sc. conceditur) videre quod verum est" (*De div. quaest.* q. 46)—what is
meant, in fact, is only reflection upon the origins [*Herkunft*] of certainty, not ecstatic, mystical contemplation of its source [*Quelle*].
59. *De genesi ad litteram imperfectus liber* 5.24: "Convenienter autem lucem
hanc dici concedit, quisquis concedit recte dici lucem, qua res quaeque manifesta
est. . . . haec lux qua ista manifesta sunt, utique intus in anima est, quamvis per
corpus inferantur quae ita sentiuntur."
60. *De genesi ad litteram imperfectus liber* 5.24.

of *illuminatio* rules out an interpretation in terms of ecstasy.[61] In Augustine, the "locus" of *illuminatio* is the "depths" of the soul, especially *memoria*'s "ground" of inwardness.[62] What the ecstatic act would have to have missed is precisely the "direction" from which *illuminatio* comes.

Instead, the paideutic moment associated with the metaphorics of light becomes prominent again: the crucial drama is not the history of light but human *conversio*. To put it in the language of Plato's allegory of the cave, the accent is on turning away from the shadows, or more narrowly and precisely, on breaking the chains that forced the gaze toward the shadows. Everything depends on something that, in Plato, the prisoners in the cave were not able to accomplish by themselves, although this is treated as incidental there and is given no importance in comparison with the path of paideia. At the start of the path of paideia, there is now an all-important condition, namely, the act of *gratia*, which can be grasped in the experience of *conversio*. Augustine's doctrine is a "metaphysics of conversion."[63]

Finally, it should be noted that Augustine's aversion to the implication of "flow" in the language of light represents an essential difference from the Neoplatonist metaphysics of light. He sets the emanantistic *fluere* in strict opposition to one of his favorite terms, the substantialist *manere*: *nihil est enim omne quod fluit . . . est autem aliquid, si manet, si constat, si semper tale est.*[64] The development of the idea of *creatio ex nihilo* implies a sharper outline of what is [*des Seienden*] than the Neoplatonic overflow of light onto the dark "ground" of primordial matter; against the background of nothingness, the moment of keeping oneself in being, of *custodire se velle* (as an intensification of the Stoics' *suum esse conservare*), establishes itself as a basic characterization of all that is [*alles Sei-*

---

61. *Pace* Jakob Barion, *Plotin und Augustinus* (Berlin: Junker und Dünnhaupt, 1935), 152.

62. *De Trinitate* 14.6.8–7.10; see also *Confessiones* 10.20.29–21.30.

63. Etienne Gilson, *Introduction à l'étude de St. Augustine* (Paris: Vrin, 1929). German edition (Hellerau: Hegner, 1930), 399.

64. *De beata vita* 2.8.

enden] (after *existentia* and *essentia*), for which Augustine coins the term *manentia*.[65]

The light of the Neoplatonists, which flows out in stages and which hypostatically multiplies and forms itself, is also the target of the Augustinian creation terminology, with its emphasis on the momentary totality of the creative act. This is evinced most succinctly in the *ictus condendi*, in the "push" that "grounds" being, which expressly exceeds the "flow" of *gradibus attingere* and *gressibus pervenire*.[66] Augustine cannot accept the "naturalness" (in the sense of *natura non facit saltus*) implied by the metaphorics of light, as long as he holds onto the idea of the radical originating "leap" (*Seinsur-"sprung"*) of being via the *mandavit* (viz. *Deus*) *et creata sunt*. In the medieval tradition, these boundaries of the metaphorics of light have all too often become blurred. The figurative as well as phonetic affinity between *lumen* and *flumen* comes to assert itself once again, in spite of Augustinian reservations.

Excursus: The Eye and the Ear

In the language of the metaphorics of light, the eye (as the *organ* associated with light) does not become explicitly significant until the correspondence between elucidation and vision has partly or even completely ceased to be obvious. Such a process (of ceasing to be a matter of course) can mean a return either to a dazzling, extreme brightness that hurts the eye, blinds it, and forces it to shut itself, or to a dulling of the eye itself, due to everything from the impurity of those who see, to the willful and culpable shutting of the eye against what is, by nature, its to see.

In Plato's allegory of the cave, the relativity of the disruption of sight is seen in terms of the starting situations relative to different paths: both the one who comes out of the light into the darkness and the one who steps out of the dark into the light cannot see at first, because the organ cannot immediately make

---

65. *Epist.* 11.3.
66. *De genesi ad litteram* 4.33.51.

the transition.[67] Becoming accustomed to the light diminishes its dazzling effects. At the same time, however, it is also an essential source of deception about one's own standpoint vis-à-vis being, since it functions ambivalently: after a while, one sees as well in the half light of the cave as in daylight.

The absolutely dazzling, to which no one can ever become accustomed, first emerges in Neoplatonism. But here it comes to mean something positive: the coincidence of seeing and not-seeing found in the dazzling effect of pure light is the fundamental confirming experience of all mysticism, in which the presence of the absolute attests itself, in which all thinking and speaking is surpassed, and which represents the uniquely adequate way of encountering transcendency.[68]

At the same time, by way of painful presence of the eye-penetrating violence of that which is seen, the sense of sight passes into a perception by the sense of touch, a "contact." The distance involved in vision is lost; in its place, the highest grade of evidence for the reality of the "object" comes to be that of the tactile faculty. With the loss of the distance and standpoint involved in sight, the one who previously had been "only" someone who saw has simultaneously become another; he is

---

67. *Republic* 518A.

68. It is perhaps Nicholas of Cusa who has best expressed this mystical, methodological function of darkness [*Dunkelheit*] as the criterion of the correct path, in order, significantly, to justify the obscurity [*Dunkelheit*] of his own metaphysics: "It is just as in the case of someone who seeks the sun and approaches it in the correct manner: as a result of the overpowering light of the sun, darkness emerges in his weak eye; and for him, who seeks the sun, this fog is a sign that he is on the right path, and were the dark not to appear, then he would not be on the path to that brilliant light." (Letter to the Abbot of the Tegernsee Cloister, September 14, 1453 [Vansteenberghe, ed., *Autour de la docte ignorance* (Münster: Aschendorff, 1915), 113n5].) This fits perfectly with Nicholas's metaphysics of *coincidentia oppositorum*. In a single sentence, he effortlessly carries out the objectification of subjective mystical experience: "Deus est maxime lux, quod est minime lux." (*De docta ignorantia* 1.4). The pseudohermetic *Liber XXIV philosophorum* (prop. 21) of medieval mysticism had already given this a protoformulation: "Deus est tenebra in anima post omnem lucem relicta." And Bonaventure says: "Excaecatio est summa illuminatio" (*In Hexaem.* 22.11). In Nicholas of Cusa's *docta ignorantia*, this entire tradition is given its densest wording.

no longer this self and no longer himself; he *belongs* to the Other, which cannot be regarded purely theoretically. To want (and to be able) to do that, would be an illusion.[69] With this moment of nonvisual "belonging" [*Gehören*],[70] however, the language moves into another sensory realm: from seeing to hearing, from metaphors of light to those of the word, from the eye to the ear as the relevant organ. This is a transition that always bears on the possibility of *freedom* as well.

In addition to the meaning it has in the context of imperative dazzling, the shutting of the eyes can also represent the introduction of introversion, of inner contemplation, the free act of turning one's gaze inward. This is the characteristic attitude in Augustinian soliloquies, sustained by the emphasis on the inner *illuminatio* in contrast to the ecstatic encounter with the absolute. But Plotinus, too, was familiar with this screening off of the gaze directed outward at the tempting and self-alienated world, which must be traversed, either into transcendency or into inwardness, if one is not to succumb to it.[71] From this point on, the entire mystical tradition is situated in this ambiguity of shutting one's eyes.

Augustine gives the metaphor of shutting one's eyes yet another meaning: it is useless to open one's eyes in the darkness, but it is also useless to "be in the light" and to keep one's eyes shut.[72] The first image illustrates the situation of the "good heathen," the impotence of a subjective desire to see, in the absence of grace, the objective condition for vision. The second image illustrates the situation of the "bad Christian," who subjectively spoils the objectively given possibility of vision. This opposition could not have been articulated within the classical approach to metaphors of light, for it presupposes the involvement of the eye.

---

69. Plotinus, *Enneads* 6.9.10: "hoion allos genomenos kai ouk autos oud'antou."
70. [Blumenberg is making use here of an untranslatable German homophony between *Gehör* (the sense of hearing) and *gehören* (to belong to).]
71. *Enneads* 1.6.9; 5.5.7.
72. *Enarratio in Psalmum* 25.2.14.

There is yet another, extreme form that this metaphor can take, one that can be asserted only after "darkness" [*Dunkelheit*] has gained a positive value, as in the Romantic concept of night and darkness [*Dunkelheit*]. Novalis will speak, in his first "Hymn," of the "infinite eye, which opens the night to us." Here, the light of the diurnal world signifies limitation and unfreedom through its association with the finitude of a gaze that is bound to and determined by material things, whereas the dark of the night signifies the diminishment of material determination, which makes it possible for the horizonless entirety of being to be affectively present as a unity.

For Greek thought, all certainty was based on visibility. What logoi referred back to was a sight of form [*gestalthafter Anblick*], i.e., *eidos*. Even etymologically, "knowledge" [*Wissen*] and "essence" [*Wesen*] (as *eidos*) are extremely closely related to "seeing" [*Sehen*]. Logos is a collection of what has been seen. For Heraclitus, eyes are "more exact witnesses than ears."[73] This is a formulation that deeply shaped the Occidental tradition precisely when it found itself faced with a conception of a completely different type, namely, the conception found in the biblical intellectual world's concept of certainty. For the Greeks, "hearing" is of no significance for truth and is initially nonbinding. As an imparting of *doxa*, it represents an assertion that must always be confirmed visually.

For the Old Testament literature, however, and for the consciousness of truth it documents, seeing is always predetermined, put into question, or surpassed by hearing. The created is based on the Word, and in terms of its binding claim, the Word always precedes the created. The real reveals itself within a horizon of its signification, a horizon allocated by hearing. Just how inaccessible the biblical meaning of "hearing" must have been for those thinking within the Greek tradition is brought out in the first fundamental confrontation of these two intellectual worlds, which we find documented

---

73. Diels, *Die Fragmente der Vorsokratiker*, 22 B 101a. See the parallels quoted by Diels.

in Philo Judaeus, who tried to make the meaning of the Old Testament intelligible within the Greek cultural horizon. What is remarkable there is that he must *translate* at precisely the point where the moment of "hearing" is involved. In this way, as has already been shown, the Creation image of the Word calling out of the void is transposed into an image of light emanating into the darkness [*Dunkel*] of matter, and his explicit view is that the only seeing that does not deceive is that through which beings are presented in their being.[74] Consistent with this, Philo's personified "logos" must first of all prepare the organs that will receive its revelation, which it does by *transforming* human ears into eyes. It is then to these that logos manifests, as light, its nonverbal essence.[75] And Philo reinterprets the fundamental event of the Old Testament—the giving of the law on Sinai—as an experience of "illumination."[76]

In the New Testament, hearing the Word is the source of faithfulness. Not wanting to hear means rejecting an offer of salvation.[77] But this already anticipates the form of the harmonization with Greek *theōria*, which then takes place in the work of the Church Fathers and the Scholastics, where vision comes to represent a mode of eschatological finality. The history-ending Second Coming (which has been held in reserve) consists in God, who until this point has been hidden, becoming visible. From this, the allocation of the classically ideal *theōria* to *status gloriae* develops. Thereafter, questions of human knowledge are interpreted in terms of a deficiency vis-à-vis *status viae*, which needs hearing as a guiding anticipation of conclusive *visio*.

This is a complete transformation of the Old Testament account, where the impossibility of beholding God is absolute

---

74. *De fuga et inventione* 208: "apseudes d'horasis, hēi ta onta ontōs katanoeitai."

75. See Hans Leisegang, *Der heilige Geist* (Leipzig: Teubner, 1919), 1:215.

76. Leisegang, *Der heilige Geist*, 216ff.

77. Gerhard Kittel, *akouō*, in *Theologisches Wörterbuch zum Neuen Testament* (Stuttgart: Kohlhammer, 1933), 1:216–225. See there all the evidence for the following.

and not merely temporary. The provisionality of hearing in the New Testament is further confirmed by the primacy of seeing in John, who represents most powerfully the arrived presence of the *eschaton*. In exactly the same way, the eschatologically significant Easter event shows the moment of the has-been-seen to its best advantage in comparison with mere hearing. There are plenty of approaches here for *theōria* (which has been eschatologically held in reserve) to stream back into worldly existence. "Hearing" restricts itself again: hearing [*Vernehmen*] the Word gets reduced to "heeding" [*Gehorchen*].

In Augustine, this meaning component forges links with the Roman idea of obligation found in *auctoritas*: following the Skeptics' undermining of "seeing," an equivalence of the instances of *ratio* and *auctoritas* becomes possible.[78] "Truth" becomes the integration of "hearing" and "seeing." But even within Augustine's thought, this equilibrium between the two "witnesses" to truth is fleeting: in the late writings, "hearing" the Word about divine predestination displaces vision's aspiration to seek *insight* into the reasons of the divine will. Once again, we see that the metaphorics of the *eye* is crucially connected to the concept of *freedom*, whereas the metaphorics of the *ear* indicates the limits, or even suspension, of freedom.

The "qualities" of the "eye" and the "ear" that let them say something metaphorically imply an entire phenomenology of the senses.[79] For example, the attitude of not wanting to hear is marked, even if only metaphorically, as more serious than the attitude of not wanting to see, since the ear is, by nature, always open and cannot be shut. Thus, not hearing presupposes a greater degree of contrariness and of intervention in nature than does not seeing. Compared to the language of "illumination," the Gnostic metaphor of the "call" found in the

---

78. *De ordine* 9.29: "Ad discendum necessario dupliciter ducimur auctoritate atque ratione."

79. See Hans Jonas, "The Nobility of Sight: A Study in the Phenomenology of the Senses," *Philosophy and Phenomenological Research* 14, no. 4 (1954): 507–519. See further the analyses by Hans Lipps, *Die menschliche Natur* (Frankfurt am Main: Klostermann, 1941), 25–28, 76–88.

Mandean and Manichean doctrines points toward a more compelling, more powerfully "gripping" phenomenon, that of the absolute claim to *metanoia*. Luther's language in *De servo arbitrio* plays metaphors of the ear against those of the eye: the merciful Lord's offer allows none of the distance for free consideration that two parties have when they catch sight of each other.[80] That which is not expected and has not been prepared for, the character of "grace" as a pure event, comes through in the language of "hearing."

The eye wanders, selects, approaches things, presses after them, while the ear, for its part, is affected and accosted. The eye can *seek*, the ear can only *wait*. Seeing "apprehends" things; hearing is apprehended. The term "listener" [*Zuhörer*] lacks the sense of disengagement implied by "onlooker" [*Zuschauer*]. Correspondingly, the "Word" does not have the cosmic universality of "light." The Word is essentially "directed at" something; one can obey it and submit oneself to it, but one cannot stand "in" the Word, in the sense of *in luce esse*. That which demands unconditionally is encountered in "hearing." Conscience has a "voice," not light. For Kant, the moral ought is *given* as an unavoidable "fact of reason" before it can be deduced—that is, before insight into it can be achieved—from its premise of freedom. Accordingly, Kant speaks of the "voice of reason," which is "with respect to the will . . . so distinct, so irrepressible, and so clearly audible to even the commonest man."[81] Here, the structures of "hearing" can still be found beyond all transcendental metaphysics.

Finally, metaphors of "hearing" are also significant for grasping the phenomenon of *tradition*. "Seeing" is oriented

---

80. The way the humanist Melanchthon returns from the language of hearing back to that of seeing is characteristic: "Lux quid sit, cerni rectius potest, quam dici, estque illa ipsa claritas quae cernitur, quae omnia ostendit, sic et in corde nostro, clara ostensio, lux est" (*Commentarius in Genesin* c.1 [*Corp. Reform.* 13, 767]).

81. Immanuel Kant, *Critique of Practical Reason*, trans. Lewis White Beck (New York: Macmillan, 1956), 36. See Hans Blumenberg, "Ist eine philosophische Ethik gegenwärtig möglich?," *Studium Generale* 6, no. 3 (1953): 179.

toward the *repetition* of eyewitness experience, most clearly
in the restoration of the phenomenon itself in all experimental methodology. The demand for the *presence* of the object
under study is the point of departure for the modern idea of
science, and in Bacon and Descartes, this demand is formulated in opposition to the validity of *auctoritas*. Here, needing
to rely on tradition appears as a lack of knowledge that can,
in principle, be remedied. Implicit in this reproach is the assumption that reason does not need to "hear," because it can,
at any time, make the objects under study accessible to sight
(experimentation) and insight (deduction). Ontologically, this
means that every condition is *iterable*; there is no unique and
actual experience. Or rather, such experience has no significance for the human fund of knowledge. Only if the actual-
and-unique is essential for man does "hearing" a tradition have
binding force. Only then must man allow something to be
"handed down" to him without being able to expect to see it
himself.

In judging the value of tradition, a teleological moment is
always implied, namely, that "truth" is *intended for man* and
that it is for that reason that it *reaches* him via the precarious
stream of cultural transference. The denial of vision that is entailed in listening to tradition always includes an element of
teleological trust that "theoretically" cannot be justified. For
this reason, in the attitude of "hearing" (i.e., in being dependent on tradition), there is often a hidden insufficiency, which
presses for a shift from *veritas asserentis* to *evidentia obiecti*,
to put it Scholastically. The metaphorical language indicates
this insufficiency primarily where the facts of tradition—of
auctoritas, and thus of "hearing"—appear in metaphors of
light.

Cicero seems, once again, to have been at the start of this.
Thus, in connection with his "translation" of Greek philosophy into the Latin medium, he speaks of *lumen litterarum Lati-
narum* (*Tusc.* 1. 5), of *lux auctoris* (1.5.11). Rhetoric becomes
the primordial form of this light. In *Scienza Nuova*, Vico portrays the history of jurisprudence as light spreading over the

obscurity [*Dunkelheit*] of facts (4.14.2). And at the end of *Démocratie en Amérique*, Tocqueville says, negatively, that ever since the past stopped shedding its light on the future, the human spirit has been lying in darkness. [*End of excursus.*]

The path of metaphors of light in the Middle Ages needs to be sketched only briefly here, not only because comprehensive studies of it are already available but also because its course has already been decided in the transition from antiquity to the Middle Ages. Arabic and Jewish Prescholasticism amalgamated Neoplatonism and Aristotelianism in that "light" was equated with "form": *forma est lumen purum.*[82] Albertus Magnus passed this amalgam on to Latin Scholasticism in *De causis et processu universitatis*, in which there is a striking ease in the way he adopts the metaphor of "flux" (*influentia constitutionis ad esse*) or adopts *diffusio intellectus agentis* as *lumen luminis rei*.[83]

Thomas Aquinas is completely hostile to the "language of light," because, in his view, it blurs the distinction between metaphysics and metaphorics. For him, light is a *qualitas per se sensibilis et species quaedam determinata in sensibilibus*, and, in this respect, "light" may be spoken of, in intellectual contexts, only *aequivoce vel metaphorice*, where the *ratio manifestationis* of what is [*des Seienden*] (i.e., its ontological truth) is concerned.[84]

His contemporary Bonaventure, by contrast, handles the metaphorics of light with a mastery comparable only to that of Augustine. Light is the *natura communis* of what is [*des Seienden*],[85] a fundamental state and underlying determination of all things, even before their differentiation. In Bonaventure, however, dawn breaks primarily in the inwardness of man, whose light is a *possession*—not a gradually elucidating *acquisition*—which precedes and makes possible all cognition, just as all truths are based on "truth." Light changes and becomes one with the "ground" of identity of the subject

---

82. Ibn Gabirol, *Fons vitae* 4.14.
83. *De causis et processu universitatis* 1.1, c.1.
84. *Sententiarum* 2, dist. 13, q.1, a.2.
85. *Sententiarum* 2, dist. 12, a.2, q.1, arg. 4.

itself. Thus, God is *secundum veritatem in anima*—not, however, as its object or idea, but rather as its capacity for truth and, in this respect, *intimior animae quam ipsa sibi*.[86] What this very bold wording of the internalization of *illuminatio* means is this: the subject can always become objective to itself in reflection, and to the extent to which it can do so, a light is required that must thus be "more internal" to the subject than the subject is to itself. This provides a formulation for the discovery of the idea, already suggested in Augustine, that inner light has to be "behind" the self, so that looking into the light becomes impossible here. The *lux veritatis, in qua cuncta relucent*,[87] is "given" only in the self-certainty of the subject's capacity for truth: not in *cognitio* (for that, Bonaventure allows for the possibility of an Aristotelian tabula rasa) but in *notitia*, as being's radical prefamiliarity with the subject.[88]

Thus we find formulated in the metaphorics of light something that in terms of cognition is *more* than mere receptivity. The mystical emotion of *amor* (which is the vehicle of all relations of being) and the sustaining pretheoretical *notitia* are but two aspects of *one* fundamental relation: *Amor et notitia animae connaturales sunt*.[89] Here it becomes possible to grasp the philosophical "achievement" of illuminative representations: they point to a radical *unity* of the mind, beyond the psychological plurality of its "faculties." And they point, in the same way, to the ultimate unity of the horizon, in which all that is becomes phenomenal [*in dem alles Seiende zur Gegebenheit kommt*].

---

86. *Sententiarum* 1, dist. 1, a.3, q.2, concl. Characteristically, just this wording returns, extracted from the metaphorics of light, in Luther, in reference to the *verbum dei* (*Werke* 9 [Weimar]: 103), that is, as the absolute intimacy of "hearing."

87. *Itinerarium mentis* 2.9.

88. *Sent.* 2, dist. 39, a.1, q.2, concl.

89. Bonaventure *Sent.* 1, dist. 3, p. 2, a.2, q.2, concl. What is of primary importance here is that emotion—which the classical tradition had judged to be *obscuring of being* [*seinsverdunkelnd*]—experiences a positive reevaluation and gains an *elucidating* function. The connection of a positive doctrine of emotions with the usage of metaphors of light also becomes quite clear in (Ps.) Witelo's *Liber de intelligentiis* (ed. Baeumker): *amor* and *delectatio* are the soul's primary "answers" to the luminosity of being; in them, the *appetitus substantiae cognoscentis ad ipsum cognoscibile* emerges, without which the gaze would not be open for phenomena; it would be an *ordinatio huius ad hoc* preceding all spiritual "acts" (prop. 18).

Consistent with this, Duns Scotus, in whose works the Augustinian tradition has to assert itself within the constraints of Aristotelian axioms, carries out an extreme (though stabilizing) *reduction* of *illuminatio*. He lets *illuminatio* be rooted in the *one* original phenomenon, the *primum obiectum* associated with the univocal concept of being.[90] Here, *esse* is not *esse commune*, at the last derivative of abstraction, but rather the first and total anticipation of the meaning of all merely possible phenomena. In this way, with the help of the illuminative representation, the "naturalness" of truth, its antecedence relative to all that is predicatively true, receives a subtle articulation yet again.

This "yet again" is explained by the fact that it is precisely in Duns Scotus that the Augustinian tradition takes a direction in which "natural light" increasingly obscures itself to focus the situation of man (vis-à-vis the absolute) entirely on "hearing the Word." Nominalistic fideism needs the backdrop of a darkening of the world in order, once again, to drive out the *credo quia absurdum*; the doctrine of *Deus absconditus* no longer allows for the "naturalness" of truth. Nor is this tendency halted, in the fifteenth century, by Nicholas of Cusa's development of the "language of light," which he treats in all its richness, yet also in a way that unmistakably and excessively grants metaphor independent stains as metaphysics (for example, in the dualism of *De coniecturis*). His *Magnae potentiae veritas est*[91] remains a historically isolated experience at the close of the Middle Ages.

What is more essential is that the medieval "internalization" of light prevents the worldly dark from fully penetrating and disempowering the subject. To keep with the metaphor, so much transcendent light has "passed over" to the subject that the subject has become "self-luminous." Augustine's principle within the illumination doctrine—*Lumen tibi esse non potes*—emerges weakened by the change in the language of light that begins at this point. In the late medieval experiment, where it is left to itself vis-à-vis *Deus*

---

90. See Etienne Gilson, "Avicenne et le point de départ de Duns Scot," *Archives d'histoire doctrinale et littéraire du moyen-âge* 2 (1927): 116f.

91. *De apice theoriae.*

absconditus, the human mind proves itself to be authentic light. This is shown, purely grammatically, by the fact that in the expressions *lumen rationis*, *lumen intellectus*, and so on, the *genitivus objectivus* becomes the *genitivus subjectivus*.

There are transitional forms that remain indeterminate, such as Francis Bacon's *lumen experientiae*, in which the object of experience as well as the act of experience can be "light."[92] The luminarity of the human mind can be seen precisely in the fact that the analysis and subsequent elimination of the obscurations and misdirections of this light come to be understood as the new task of philosophical "method."[93]

What characterizes the dawn of a new epoch here, indicated in the metaphors of light, is that it can be said of man—at least in his highest realization, *studiosus homo*—that he is *naturalis lux*.[94] Man does not find already in place an objectively fixed world structure that obligingly presents itself and to which he has to adapt himself; rather, he becomes, himself, the principle of a structural formation that emanates from him. And by realizing himself as *sapiens*, he gains that emanative force: self-realization becomes a condition for world-realization. *Sapientes* "realize" the world in that they *quodlibet ad proprium finem ducunt*.[95] Cognizing the world and the *rite uti* of its things is not a relation of *receiving* but of *giving*. In cognizing and in using, man remedies the one great defi-

---

92. *Novum Organum* 1.49; see 1.56, where the difference in kind among intellects is determined according to *admiratio antiquitatis* or *amor novitatis*, and where it is then said, "veritas autem non a felicitate temporis alicuius, quae res varia est, sed a lumine naturae et experientiae, quod aeternum est, petenda est."

93. *Novum Organum* 1.49: "intellectus humanus luminis sicci non est; sed recipit infusionem a voluntate et affectibus."

94. Carolus Bovillus (Charles de Bovelles), *Liber de sapiente* (*Studien der Bibliothek Warburg* 10 [1927], ed. Klibansky), c.51. This statement cannot be put in the same context with the fact that Aristotle represented *nous* in its active–passive double function as *phōs* (*De anima* 3.5.430a14–17). This *nous* is genuinely cosmic and associated with the human soul only "from the outside" in cognitive accomplishment. The "direction" of this light is thus from the inside to the outside; what is crucially new is the inversion of this direction.

95. Bovillus, *Liber de sapiente*, c.19.

ciency of being, namely, that being *is* everything, but is everything *unknowingly.*[96] The physical only becomes "fulfilled" in the mental. Theory and practice are no longer derivatives of an all-binding nature but are rather its integration and its fulfillment of being. *Homo denique fulgor est, scientia, lux et anima mundi.*

Once this turn has been taken, we are not far from the comprehensive historical significance of the concept of "enlightenment," whose descent from the language of light is so tangible in French[97] and English: *siècle des lumières, progrès des lumières,* the *Aufklärer* (enlightenment figure) as an agent of light, *qui propage les lumières,* as well as the English word "enlightenment."

With the emergence of the Enlightenment, "light" moves into the realm of that which is to be accomplished; truth loses the natural *facilitas* with which it asserted itself. Even (or rather, only) in caricature does the now-broken connection between metaphors of light, on the one hand, and trust in the "naturalness" of self-presenting truth, on the other, demonstrate itself. Thus, in the *Dialogo* (*Dialogue on the Two Chief World Systems*), Galileo endowed Simplicio—the figure of the Scholastic, often ironically characterized as "Middle-Aged"[98]—with this trust, now exposed as careless confidence. There is, for example, a discussion of the problem of the cause of the tides, in which Simplicio says that although there can be only *one* cause, there are many opinions about this and that one has to take into account that the true explanation will not be among them; otherwise, it would certainly be most astonishing for

---

96. Bovillus, *Liber de sapiente,* c.19. "Omnia siquidem est mundus: scit tamen novitque nihil. Porro exiguum et fere nihil est homo: scit attamen novitque universa."

97. The transition is, in the simultaneity of its nuances, particularly tangible in Pascal's language, for example, in Fragment 337 (ed. Brunschvicg): "par une nouvelle lumière, par une autre lumière supérieure, selon qu'on a de lumière." In the first fragment of Pascal's study *De l'esprit géométrique, lumière naturelle* is both the limit of the human mind with regard to its aspiration to prove all its premises *and* the foundation of those exacting proofs that are in fact possible for the mind, in spite of its limitations.

98. [The German here (*mittelalterlich*) can mean both "middle-aged" and "medieval."]

the true not to emit so much light as to shine out through the darkness of such mistakes.[99]

As a result of the inversion of metaphors of light during the Enlightenment, it is precisely this conception of truth (as that which is self-luminous and penetrating) that becomes a way of *reproaching* the Middle Ages for its credulity, for not noticing its own darkness. According to d'Alembert, the principles of science and the arts were lost during the twelve centuries of the Middle Ages because the beautiful and the true, which *seem* to reveal themselves to people from all sides, do not actually get through to people until they have them pointed out.[100] The ignorance of the Middle Ages must thus be attributed precisely to the illusion that the truth "reveals itself." The truth does not reveal itself; it must *be revealed.* "Natural" luminosity cannot be relied on; on the contrary, truth is of a constitutionally weak nature and man must help it back on its feet by means of light-supplying therapy, as it were, *parce que rien n'est si dangereux pour le vrai et ne l'expose tant à être méconnu que l'alliage ou le voisinage de l'erreur.* That is the exact, literal opposite of the state that Galileo had Simplicio attribute to the true!

In this characterization of truth as weak and in need of assistance, the background of the late-medieval concept of God is still perceptible: d'Alembert compares the universe to a literary work *d'une obscurité sublime,* whose author tries, again and again, by means of "flashes of hope," to give the reader the illusion of having understood almost everything. As it is found, "natural" light thus acquires virtually the function of misleading: in the labyrinth of the world,

---

99. "Dialogo IV," *Opere,* ed. Albèri, 1:456: "anzi così credo esser veramente perchè gran cosa sarebbe che il vero potesse aver sì poco di luce, che nulla apparisse tra le tenebre di tanti falsi." The connection of *simplicitas*—though in a positive sense!—with this basic view is found, with exceptional expressiveness, in a thirteenth-century tract, *De usuris,* written by Aegidius of Lessines as an exegesis of the first sentence of Aristotle's *Metaphysics:* "Quam (sc. veritatem) si quis concupiscit vero corde, et eam quaesierit in simplicitate cordis sui, ipsa seipsam manifestabit." Cited in Martin Grabmann, *Mittelalterliches Geistesleben II* (Munich, 1936), 522.

100. *Discours Préliminaire de l'Encyclopédie,* ed. Picavet: "Les principes des sciences et des arts étaient perdus, parce que le beau et le vrai semblent se montrer de toutes parts aux hommes, ne les frappent guère à moins qu'ils n'en soient avertis."

once we have left the path, the few *éclairs* can just as well lead us further away from the path as back to it.[101] In such a world, which has become the playing field for a divine game (*où l'Intelligence suprême semble avoir voulu se jouer de la curiosité humaine*), the value of an individual truth is ambiguous—it can be either a beacon or a will-o'-the-wisp—as long as its sporadic character has not been put into a *systematic* context. "Truth," as such, is dubious [*zwielichtig*], as long as it lacks a well-ordered origin in *method* and a well-ordered position in a *system*. The dictionary and the encyclopedia become exemplary instruments of the Enlightenment: d'Alembert wrote not only the introduction but (along with it) the metaphysics of the great *Encyclopédie*.

In the idea of "method," which originates with Bacon and Descartes,[102] "light" is thought of as being at man's disposal. Phenomena no longer stand in the light; rather, they are *subjected to the lights of an examination*[103] from a particular perspective. The

---

101. It would require a separate study (which would be part of the history of the concept of "probability") to demonstrate this ambivalence in the change of meaning of *verisimile* [Blumenberg presents this study in *Paradigms for a Metaphorology*, chap. 8.]. Originally, the "appearance" of the apparently true is entirely appearance as pale reflection of the *proximity* of truth (see footnote 22 above). [The author's use of metaphors of light here cannot be rendered fully in English: "Der 'Schein' des Wahrscheinlichen ist ursprünglich durchaus Schein als Abglanz der Nähe der Wahrheit."] This understanding of the term has, however, metaphysical premises that no longer hold for Descartes. For him, "appearance" means possible deception; the apparently true (or probable) is only something that looks like the true and must therefore be methodologically "bracketed." Until an object can be confirmed by *clare et distince percipere*, it is without significance for truth [*wahrheitsindifferent*]. "Certum etiam est, cum assentimur alicui rationi quam non percipimus, vel nos falli, vel casu tantum incidere in veritatem" (*Principia philosophiae* 1.44). The idea that one could "hit upon" the truth "by chance" is a previously unthought and unthinkable thought, one in which the entire tradition of the metaphorics of light is negated and raised to a higher level [*aufgehoben*]. "Method" then takes this annoying element of chance by the hand and puts it at man's disposal.

102. See Hans Blumenberg, "Philosophischer Ursprung und philosophische Kritik des Begriffs der wissenschaftlichen Methode," *Studium Generale* 5, no. 3 (1952): 133–142.

103. [*Beleuchtet*: the translation here attempts to capture the double meaning that Blumenberg is playing on here: *beleuchten* can mean both "to shine light on something" and "to examine."]

result then depends on the angle from which light falls on the object and the angle from which it is seen. It is the conditionality of *perspective* and the awareness of it, even the free selection of it, that now defines the concept of "seeing." The significance, for the modern age, of perspective and a consciousness of location would require a study of its own. All that can be done here is to indicate the way *technological* figures come to invade the metaphorics of light, the way light turns into an encompassing medium of the focused and measured ray of "direct lighting."

The status of this development as a historical signature is best illustrated in painting. During the sixteenth and seventeenth centuries, the idea of light as the homogeneous, unquestioningly presupposed medium of visibility that ensures the unaccented presence of that which is to be represented, turns into a localized factor which can be "adjusted." Caravaggio and Rembrandt already engage in something like "a staging of lighting," although the "quantity" of light—subject to the law of inverted quadratic proportion—is still limited. Not until the nineteenth century do Drummond's "lime" lights put the *theater* in a position to generate, in combination with concave mirrors, lighting "effects," a development that begins to open up new possibilities for an accentuating approach to vision, an approach that always *takes as its point of departure, the dark as the "natural" state.*

But it is only because these possibilities for *directed* light were discovered at all that the technology for this discovery could ultimately make possible the most violent of methods and devices, and it is significant that the term *lighting*[104] is used to refer to thoughtless accentuation by artificial light, as well as to the technological selection and overemphasis of the work of man, which—as the only things thought to be worth seeing—is to be made impossible to overlook. This manipulation of light is the result of a long process.

In nocturnal spaces, an "optics of prefabrication"[105] is being developed, which eliminates the freedom to look around within a gen-

104. [The German here, *Illumination*, refers primarily to artificial outdoor lighting.]

105. [*Optik des Präparats.* Consistent with his general emphasis on the intimate interrelations between science and *mentalité*, Blumenberg here uses *Optik* (optics) to refer not to a specific science but to a view of light and vision that is

eral medium of visibility and confronts modern man with ever more situations of coerced vision [*Zwangsoptik*].[106] The connection between vision and freedom is being dissociated. Due to the dominance of the prefabricated and technologically precast situations and aspects, the modern extension of sensory spheres has not become a source of freedom.[107] The structure of this world of optical prefabrications and fixations of the gaze is once again approaching that of the "cave." (W. H. Auden portrays the cave situation of modern man in *Age of Anxiety*.) As a paideutic metaphor, "leaving the cave" is regaining real relevance.

Man—on whom the technological light of "lighting" has imposed, in many forms, an "optics" that goes against his will—is the historical antipode of the classical *contemplator caeli* and his freedom to gaze. Today, there are even people who have never seen a star. "Stars? Where?" This is the unbelieving (but now believable) cry of the modem metropolitan lyricist.[108]

Translated by Joel Anderson[109]

---

embedded in a general consciousness. *Präparat* generally refers to a laboratory or pharmaceutical "specimen," but it is rendered as "prefabrication" to convey the central idea that in the world of artificial lighting, visual possibilities are shaped in advance.]

106. Today, one speaks of the "technology of light" in a sense not at all limited to the generation of light or to "lighting" [*Beleuchtung*], but rather one that understands light as a construction unit like steel, concrete, and so forth. See the book by Walter Köhler and Wassili Luckhardt, *Lichtarchitektur* (Berlin, 1956).

107. Whether it has become a source of truth is a question that Werner Wagner has raised: "Versuch zur Kritik der Sinne," *Studium Generale* 4, no. 5 (1951): 256.

108. Gottfried Benn, *Gesammelte Gedichte* (Zürich, 1956), 98.

109. [Minor corrections and additional editorial footnotes by Hannes Bajohr and Florian Fuchs.]

INTRODUCTION TO *PARADIGMS* FOR A *METAPHOROLOGY*

(1960)

Let us try for a moment to imagine that modern philosophy had proceeded according to the methodological program set out for it by Descartes and had arrived at that definitive conclusion that Descartes himself believed to be eminently attainable. This "end state" of philosophy, which historical experience permits us to entertain only as a hypothesis, would be defined according to the criteria set out in the four rules of the Cartesian *Discours de la méthode*, in particular by the clarity and distinctness that the first rule requires of all matters apprehended in judgments. To this ideal of full objectification[1] would correspond the perfection of a terminology de-

---

Originally published as "Einleitung," in "Paradigmen zu einer Metaphorologie," *Archiv für Begriffsgeschichte* 6 (1960): 7–142; from Hans Blumenberg, *Paradigmen zu einer Metaphorologie* (Frankfurt am Main: Suhrkamp, 1998).

1. Descartes defines the characteristics of clarity and distinctness as follows: *Claram voco illam (sc. ideam) quae menti attendenti praesens et aperta est* [I call a perception clear when it is present and accessible to an attentive mind] (Charles

signed to capture the presence and precision of the matter at hand in well-defined concepts. In its terminal state, philosophical language would be purely and strictly "conceptual": everything *can* be defined, therefore everything *must* be defined; there is no longer anything logically "provisional," just as there is no longer any *morale provisoire* [provisional morality]. From this vantage point, all forms and elements of *figurative* speech, in the broadest sense of the term, prove to have been makeshifts destined to be superseded by logic. Their function was exhausted in their transitional significance; in them, the human mind rushed ahead of its responsible, step-by-step fulfillment; they were an expression of the same *précipitation* regarding which Descartes, likewise in the first rule, states that it ought carefully to be avoided.[2]

Having arrived at its final conceptual state, however, philosophy would also have to relinquish any justifiable interest in researching the *history* of its concepts. Seen from the ideal of its definitive terminology, the value of a history of concepts can only be a critical and destructive one, a role it ceases to perform upon reaching its goal: that of demolishing the diverse and opaque burden of tradition, summarized by Descartes under the second of his fundamental critical concepts, *prévention* (corresponding to Francis Bacon's "idols"). History is here nothing other than precipitancy (*précipitation*) and anticipation (*prévention*), a failing of that actual presence whose methodical recuperation renders historicity null and void. That the logic of the first rule eviscerates history was first recognized by Giambattista Vico, who set against it the idea of a "logic of fantasy." Vico proceeded from the assumption that the

---

Adam and Paul Tannery, eds., *Œuvres de Descartes* [Paris: Cerf, 1905], 8:13); *Distinctam autem illam, quae, cum clara sit, ab omnibus aliis ita seiuncta est et praecisa, ut nihil plane aliud, quam quod clarum ist, in se contineat* [I call a perception distinct if, as well as being clear, it is so sharply separated from all other perceptions that it contains within itself only what is clear (8:22); René Descartes, *The Philosophical Writings of Descartes*, trans. John Cottingham (Cambridge: Cambridge University Press, 1985), 1:207–208]. The debt to the Stoic doctrine of knowledge and its ideal of cataleptic presentation is unmistakable, although it has yet to be sufficiently clarified.

2. [René Descartes, *Discourse on Method and the Meditations*, trans. F. E. Sutcliffe (Harmondsworth: Penguin, 1968), 41.]

clarity and distinctness called for by Descartes were reserved solely for the creator in his relationship of insight to his work: *verum ipsum factum* [what is true is precisely what is made]. What remains for us mortals? Not the "clarity" of the given but solely that of whatever we have made for ourselves: the world of our images and artifacts, our conjectures and projections—in short, the universe of our "imagination" in the new, productive sense of the term unknown to antiquity.

In the context of the task of a "logic of fantasy" there falls also, indeed in an exemplary fashion, a discussion of "transferred" speech or metaphor,[3] a subject previously confined to the chapters on figures in handbooks of *rhetoric*. The traditional classification of metaphor among the ornaments of public speech is hardly fortuitous: for antiquity, the logos was fundamentally adequate to the totality of what exists. Cosmos and logos were correlates. Metaphor is here deemed incapable of enriching the capacity of expressive means; it contributes only to the *effect* of a statement, the "punchiness" with which it gets through to its political and forensic addressees. The perfect congruence of cosmos and logos rules out the possibility that figurative language could achieve anything for which common speech (*kúrion ónoma*) could not furnish an equivalent. In principle, the orator and poet can say nothing that could not just as well be presented in a theoretical, conceptual way; only how they say it is specific to them, not what is said. The possibility and potency of persuasive speech had been one of the elemental experiences of life in the polis—so elemental, in fact, that Plato could present the decisive phase of his mythic cosmogony in the "Timaeus" as the rhetorical act by which Necessity (*Ananke*) was swayed. It is difficult for us today to overestimate the importance of rhetoric, an importance that explains just how crucial it was that philosophy interpret persuasive force as a "quality" of truth itself, and oratory, with all its "tools of the trade," as nothing but the fitting implementation and amplification of that quality. The battles fought over the functional classification of rhetoric, the contestation of the Sophis-

---

3. [The Greek verb from which the word "metaphor" is derived literally means "to translate," "to transfer."]

tic claim of autonomy for the technique of persuasion—these were fundamental processes in the ancient history of philosophy that we have barely even begun to investigate. The Platonic subordination of rhetoric, sealed by the church fathers, definitively transformed the objects traditionally assigned to rhetoric into the merely technical armaments of "persuasive means," even if these were now to be found stockpiled in the armory of truth itself. Whether the rhetorical artifice of *translatio* [metaphor] could do anything more than arouse "pleasure" in the truth to be communicated remained undiscussed. Of course, the fact that this question was not asked and could not be asked does not mean that metaphors had not in fact always already yielded such a surplus of expressive achievement. Otherwise, the task of a metaphorology would be doomed from the outset, for we will see, curiously enough, that the *reflective* "discovery" of the authentic potency of metaphorics devalues the metaphors produced in the light of that discovery as objects of a historical metaphorology. Our analysis must be concerned with detecting the logical "perplexity" for which metaphor steps in and an aporia of this kind is most conspicuously evident precisely where it is not "admitted" by theory in the first place.

These historical remarks on the "concealment" of metaphor lead us to the fundamental question of the conditions under which metaphors can claim legitimacy in philosophical language. Metaphors can first of all be *leftover elements*, rudiments on the path *from mythos to logos*; as such, they indicate the Cartesian provisionality of the historical situation in which philosophy finds itself at any given time, measured against the regulative ideality of the pure logos. Metaphorology would here be a critical reflection charged with unmasking and counteracting the inauthenticity of figurative speech. But metaphors can also—hypothetically, for the time being—be *foundational elements* of philosophical language, "translations" that resist being converted back into authenticity and logicality. If it could be shown that such translations, which would have to be called "absolute metaphors," exist, then one of the essential tasks of conceptual history (in the thus expanded sense) would be to ascertain and analyze their conceptually irredeemable expressive function. Furthermore, the evidence of absolute metaphors would make the rudimentary metaphors mentioned above appear in a different light, since the Cartesian teleology of logicization in the context of which they were identified as "leftover elements" in the first place would already have foundered on the existence of absolute translations. Here the presumed equivalence of figurative and "inauthentic" speech proves questionable; Vico had already declared metaphorical language to be no less "proper" than the language commonly held to be such,[4] only lapsing into the Cartesian schema in reserving the language of fantasy for an earlier historical epoch. Evidence of absolute metaphors would force us to reconsider the relationship between logos and the imagination. The realm of the imagination could no longer be regarded solely as the substrate for transformations into conceptuality—on the assumption that each element could be processed and converted in turn, so to speak, until the supply of images was used up—but as a catalytic sphere from which the universe of concepts continually renews itself, without thereby converting and exhausting this founding reserve.

Readers familiar with Kant will at this point recall §59 of the *Critique of the Power of Judgment*, where the procedure of "the transportation of the reflection" is thematized under the heading "symbol," even if the expression "metaphor" does not appear in this context. Kant proceeds from his basic insight that the reality of concepts can be secured only through intuitions. With empirical concepts, this occurs through examples; with pure concepts of understanding, through schemata; with concepts of reason ("ideas"), to which no sensible intuition can ever adequately correspond, it occurs through the provision of a representation that has only the "form of the reflection" in common with the intended referent. Kant has his reasons for not wanting to concede the expression "symbol" to "recent logicians"; we no longer have them, or rather we are only too pleased to be rid of this overfreighted term. Kant gives the name "characterization" to thetic expressions that function as mere "means of reproduction," whereas his "symbols" correspond fairly exactly to metaphors, as the term will continue to be used here. This

---

4. *Opere*, ed. Ferrari[2], V, 186. [Giambattista Vico, *New Science*, trans. David Marsh (London: Penguin, 1999), 162.]

is clearly shown in Kant's paradigms, among which we reencounter Quintilian's *pratum ridet*.[5] Our "absolute metaphor" appears here as "the transportation of the reflection on one object of intuition to another, quite different concept, to which perhaps no intuition can ever directly correspond." Metaphor is clearly characterized as a model invested with a pragmatic function, from which a "rule of the reflection" can be gleaned that may then "be applied" in the use of the idea of reason; it is thus "a principle not of the theoretical determination of what an object is in itself, but the practical determination of what the idea of it ought to be for us and for the purposive use of it." In this sense, "all our cognition of God is merely symbolic" (in the Kantian terminology), an argument intended to skirt the twin perils of anthropomorphism and deism. Or to take another of Kant's examples: the metaphor of the machine, when applied to the state, signifies that "between a despotic state and a hand mill there is, of course, no similarity, but there is one between the rule for reflecting on both and their causality." Immediately following this example there appears the sentence that provided the initial stimulus for the present study: "This business has as yet been little discussed, much as it deserves a deeper investigation."[6]

To be sure, the task of a metaphorological *paradigmatics* can only be to lay the groundwork for that "deeper investigation." It endeavors to stake out the terrain within which absolute metaphors may be supposed to lie and to test criteria by which they may be ascertained. That these metaphors are called "absolute" means only that

---

5. ["The meadow laughs" (*pratum ridet*) is a stock example of metaphor commonly (but erroneously) ascribed to Quintilian, the first-century author of *The Orator's Education*.]

6. ["*Übertragung der Reflexion über einen Gegenstand der Anschauung auf einen ganz andern Begriff, dem vielleicht nie eine Anschauung direkt korrespondieren kann . . . Regel der Reflexion . . . ein Prinzip nicht der theoretischen Bestimmung des Gegenstandes . . . was er an sich, sondern der praktischen, was die Idee von ihm für uns und den zweckmäßigen Gebrauch derselben werden soll . . . alle Erkenntnis von Gott bloß symbolisch . . . zwischen einem despotischen Staate und einer Handmühle . . . zwar keine Ähnlichkeit (ist), wohl aber zwischen der Regel, über beide und ihre Kausalität zu reflektieren . . . Dies Geschäft ist bis jetzt noch wenig auseinander gesetzt worden, so sehr es auch eine tiefere Untersuchung verdient.*" Immanuel Kant, *Critique of the Power of Judgment*, trans. Paul Guyer and Eric Matthews (Cambridge: Cambridge University Press, 2000), 225–227.]

they prove resistant to terminological claims and cannot be dissolved into conceptuality, not that one metaphor could not be replaced or represented by another, or corrected through a more precise one. Even absolute metaphors therefore have a *history*. They have a history in a more radical sense than concepts, for the historical transformation of a metaphor brings to light the metakinetics of the historical horizons of meaning and ways of seeing within which concepts undergo their modifications. Through this implicative connection, the relationship of metaphorology to the history of concepts (in the narrower, terminological sense) is defined as an ancillary one: metaphorology seeks to burrow down to the substructure of thought, the underground, the nutrient solution of systematic crystallizations, but it also aims to show with what "courage" the mind preempts itself in its images and how its history is projected in the courage of its conjectures.

Translated by Robert Savage

8

An Anthropological Approach to the Contemporary Significance of Rhetoric

(1971)

What man is has been formulated as a thesis in countless, more or less formal, attempted definitions. The varieties of what we now call "philosophical anthropology" can be reduced to *one* pair of alternatives: man can be viewed either as a poor or as a rich creature. The fact that man is not fixed, biologically, to a specific environment [*Umwelt*] can be understood either as a fundamental lack of proper equipment for self-preservation or as openness to the fullness of a world that is no longer accentuated only in terms of vital

Originally published as "Approccio antropologico all'attualità della retorica," *Il Verri. Revista di Letteratura*, nos. 35/36 (1971): 49–72; first German printing as "Anthropologische Annäherung an die Aktualität der Rhetorik," in *Wirklichkeiten in denen wir leben: Aufsätze und eine Rede* (Stuttgart: Reclam, 1981), 104–136; from Hans Blumenberg, *Ästhetische und metaphorologische Schriften*, ed. Anselm Haverkamp (Frankfurt am Main: Suhrkamp, 2001), 406–434. English-language version published in *After Philosophy: End or Transformation?*, ed. Kenneth Baynes, James Bohman, and Thomas McCarthy (Cambridge: MIT Press, 1987), 429–458.

necessities. Man is made creative either by the urgency of his needs *or* by playful dealings with his surplus talents. He is the creature that is incapable of doing anything to no purpose *or* he is the only animal that is capable of an *acte gratuit* [gratuitous action, André Gide]. Man is defined by what he lacks *or* by the creative symbolism with which he makes himself at home in worlds of his own. He is the observer of the universe, in the center of the world, *or* he is the "eccentric," exiled from Paradise on an insignificant dust speck called Earth. Man contains in himself the orderly stored-up harvest of all of physical reality, *or* he is a creature of deficiencies [*Mängelwesen*],[1] left in the lurch by nature, plagued by residues of instincts that he does not understand and that have lost their functions. I need not go on enumerating the antitheses; the principle by which the list could be extended is easy to see.

As far as rhetoric is concerned, the traditional basic conceptions of it can likewise be reduced to *one* pair of alternatives: rhetoric has to do either with the consequences of possessing the truth *or* with the perplexities that result from the impossibility of obtaining truth. Plato combatted the rhetoric of the Sophists by suggesting that it was based on the thesis of the impossibility of truth and that it deduced therefrom its right to pass off what people could be persuaded of as what was true. The most influential doctrine of rhetoric in our tradition, on the other hand, that of Cicero, starts from the premise that one can possess the truth and gives the art of speaking the function of beautifying the communication of this truth, making it accessible and impressive—in short, dealing with it in a way that is appropriate to the object. The Christian tradition vacillates between the two possible consequences of the premise that one possesses the truth: on the one hand, that God's truth has no need of human aids of the kind represented by rhetoric and that it should present itself with as little adornment as possible (a pattern that is repeated in every rhetoric of sincerity), and on the other hand, that this same truth is humanized in the housing of the canons of rules of rhetoric. In modern aesthetics, rhetoric's implication that it has

---

1. [A term introduced by Arnold Gehlen in his *Man: His Nature and Place in the World* (New York: Columbia University Press, 1988).]

to do, positively or negatively, with the truth celebrates its final triumph when the connection is reversed: it becomes permissible to infer truth content from rhetorical art, from style, from beauty—or beauty and truth can even become identical. The enmity that Plato postulated between philosophy and rhetoric is decided in philosophy itself, or at least in its languages, as aesthetics against philosophy. Only as aesthetics?

It is easy to see that one can coordinate the two radical pairs of alternatives, in anthropology and in rhetoric, unambiguously with one another. Man as a rich creature exercises his disposition over the truth that he possesses with the effective aid of the rhetorical *ornatus* [ornament]. Man as a poor creature needs rhetoric as the art of appearance, which helps him to deal with his lack of truth. The epistemological situation that Plato imputed to Sophism is radicalized, anthropologically, into the situation of the "creature of deficiencies," for whom everything becomes part of the economy of his means of survival and who consequently cannot afford rhetoric—unless he has to afford it. A consequence of this anthropological intensification of the initial conditions is that the concept of a rhetoric that is associated with those conditions must also be formulated in a more elementary way. Here, the technique of speech appears as a special case of rule-governed modes of behavior that produce something to be understood, set up signs, bring about agreement, or provoke contradiction. Keeping silent, visibly omitting some action in a context of behavior, can become just as rhetorical as the reading aloud of an outcry of popular wrath, and the Platonic dialogue is no less rhetorically inclined than the Sophist's instructional discourse, which it opposed by literary means. Even below the threshold of the spoken or the written word, rhetoric is form as means, obedience to rules as an instrument [*Organ*]. Nietzsche may have erred in his statement that Plato's struggle against rhetoric is to be understood as a product of envy of rhetoric's influence, but he is right when he says in the same place that with rhetoric the Greeks had invented "form in itself."[2]

---

2. Friedrich Nietzsche, *Gesammelte Werke*, ed. Richard Oehler (Munich: Musarion, 1920–1921), 6:105. [Now in Friedrich Nietzsche, *Sämtliche Werke: Kritische*

Plato's two great rejections, the rejection of atomism and the rejection of Sophism, probably had even more important consequences than the positive dogmas of the part of its effectual history that is entitled "Platonism" and has thus become identifiable. Philosophy's preference for language's semantic relation to reality [*Sachverhältnis*] produced a permanent sensitivity vis-à-vis rhetoric's pragmatic conception of language, a sensitivity that took a turn in favor of rhetoric only episodically, when conceptual language, in forms of Scholasticism, deprived its reference to reality of credibility. The Platonic Socrates's principle (now a commonplace that everyone learns in school) that virtue is knowledge makes what is self-evident, instead of what is an "institution," the norm of behavior.[3] No one would want to deny that with this principle Socrates formulated an ideal without the pursuit of which—sometimes confident, sometimes desperate—the European tradition cannot be imagined. But it is equally true that it constituted an excessive demand, and hard on its heels came the resignations—beginning with the catastrophic reverse that the doctrine of the ideas underwent in Plato's own school as a result of the outbreak of Academic Skepticism hardly a century after the death of the school's founder and ending with what Nietzsche called "nihilism." The philosophy of absolute goals did not legitimate the theory of means; instead, it repressed and suffocated it. An ethics that takes the self-evidence of the good as its point of departure leaves no room for rhetoric as the theory and practice of influencing behavior on the assumption that we do not have access to self-evidence of the good. This also affects the "anthropology" that is inherent and embodied in rhe-

---

Studienausgabe, ed. Giorgio Colli and Mazzino Montinari (Berlin: de Gruyter, 1999), 7:757.]

3. ["Institution" is used by Blumenberg in a special sense (introduced by Arnold Gehlen in his *Urmensch und Spätkultur: Philosophische Ergebnisse und Aussagen* [Bonn: Athenäum, 1956]) that stresses the "pre-given," habitual, unquestioned character of certain behavior patterns and modes of thought (as in the Latin *institutio*, "custom")—rather than, and as opposed to, their being intentionally "founded" (as in one of the main senses of *Institution* or "institution" in ordinary usage). Awareness of this special usage should clarify the contrast here between "institutions" and norms that are based on what is "self-evident" (and with which one's compliance is presumably conscious and intentional).]

toric; as a theory of man outside the realm of ideality, forsaken by self-evidence, it has lost the possibility of being "philosophical," and becomes the last, and belated, discipline of philosophy.

Rhetoric's anthropological importance stands out best against the background of the metaphysics that has been dominant since antiquity, a metaphysics that has a cosmological ground plan: the ideas constitute a cosmos that the phenomenal world imitates. Man, however privileged his position may be as an onlooker in the center of the whole, is nevertheless not a pure special case but rather a point of intersection of alien realities, a compound—and, as such, problematic. In the modernized model of levels [*Schichtenmodell*], the idea lives on that in the case of man things have come together that have difficulty harmonizing with each other. In principle, this metaphysics says that man's thoughts could also be those of a god and that what moves him could be what moves a celestial sphere or what moves an animal. Nature, which otherwise only presents itself in pure form and regulates itself without a detour, here confronts us with a complication that can most readily be explained as an accident or a mixture of heterogeneous elements, in which case the problem of conduct was to assign to one of these elements authority over the others—to establish a sort of substantial consistency. In short, the metaphysical tradition at bottom has had nothing special to say about man, with his asserted uniqueness. That is striking, but it is closely related to philosophy's banishment of rhetoric. For rhetoric starts from, and only from, the respect in which man is unique: it is not that language is his specific characteristic but that language, in rhetoric, appears as a function of a specific difficulty of man's. If one wants to express this difficulty in the language of the metaphysical tradition, one will have to say that man does not belong to this cosmos (if, in fact, it exists), and this is not because of a transcendent surplus that he possesses but because of an immanent deficiency, a deficiency of pre-given, prepared adaptive structures and of regulatory processes for a nexus that would deserve to be called a "cosmos" and within which something could properly be called part of the cosmos. In the language of modern biological anthropology, too, man is a creature who has fallen back out of the ordered arrangements that nature has achieved and for whom actions have to take the place of the automatic controls that he lacks or correct those that have acquired an erratic inaccuracy. Action compensates for the "indeterminateness" of the creature man, and rhetoric is the strained effort to produce the accords that have to take the place of the "substantial" stock of regulatory processes in order to make action possible. From this point of view, language is a set of instruments not for communicating information or truths, but rather, primarily, for the production of mutual understanding, agreement, or toleration, on which the actor depends. This is the root of "consensus"[4] as a basis for the concept of what is "real"; "We say that that which everyone thinks really is so," says Aristotle,[5] and always has a teleological argument for this in the background. Only a skeptical destruction of this teleological support makes the pragmatic substratum of consensus visible again.

I know that the term "skepticism" is not popular at present. Too much is once again known too precisely for that to be the case, and in such a situation one does not want to play the part of troublemaker. But in the tradition of skepticism (which is mostly below the surface and only occasionally flares up) the anthropology whose repression by metaphysics I have attempted briefly to locate has become especially urgent when the eternal truths had to be scaled down to what is most immediately reliable, and man no longer appeared as the disguised variant of a pure spirit. The first philosophical anthropology that deserved this name was, at the beginning of the modern age, Montaigne's *Apologie de Raymond Sebond.*[6] In the hands of a skeptic who sees himself as prevented from extending his questioning beyond man, a body of material that is mainly conventional gets into a new overall state

---

4. [Blumenberg has "consensus" in italics throughout this piece, even though the term is used not uncommonly in contemporary German, because he wants to remind us that it is a technical term that was introduced into philosophy and rhetoric by Cicero. I have used quotes for the same purpose.]

5. Aristotle, *Nichomachean Ethics* 1172b 36–37, trans. W. D. Ross (New York: Random House, 1941), 1095.

6. [Michel Montaigne, "Apology for Raymond Sebond," *The Complete Essays*, trans. Donald M. Frame (Stanford, CA: Stanford University Press, 1965), 318–457.]

in which the only possible object of man forces everything to now be only a symptom of this object. This tradition leads, by way of the literature of moralism, to Kant's (explicitly so designated) *Anthropologie.*[7]

The skepticism that is piled up—only for the purpose of definitively disposing of it—in the preparatory phase of theories of knowledge (but also in Husserl's phenomenology) deprives itself of the favorable opportunity to yield dividends for anthropology, dividends that turn on the question of what man is left with if he fails in his attempt to seize pure self-evidence and absolute self-foundation. An illustration of this state of affairs is the way in which Descartes disposed not only of his radicalized theoretical doubt but also of the problem of a *morale par provision* [provisional morality], which was supposed to act as a substitute, until the completion of theoretical knowledge, for the *morale définitive* [definitive morality] that would then become possible. Descartes's illusion, which is still instructive, was not so much that the *morale définitive* would have to come soon, because physics could be completed quickly, but rather that the intervening period could be a static phase of holding fast to what had always been binding. Descartes took no cognizance of the retroactive effect of the process of theory on the supposed interim of the provisional ethics. It is very remarkable to reflect on the consequences of this idea of a *morale par provision* assuming that the eschatology of science does not arrive and to recognize in them much of what the final expectations directed at science, which are disappointed again and again, produce as shared characteristics. The fact that Descartes wanted to stage the preliminary situation as a standstill meant that he was not compelled to think through the anthropological implications of this state. Thus, he could propose as an example of the provisional ethics a person who has lost his way in a forest, who only needs to go resolutely in one direction in order to get out of the forest, because all forests are finite and can be regarded, in the imagined situation, as unchanging. The recommendation of formal resoluteness in favor

---

7. [Immanuel Kant, *Anthropology from a Pragmatic Point of View*, trans. Robert B. Louden (Cambridge: Cambridge University Press, 2006.]

of the provisional ethics means a prohibition against considering all the concrete characteristics of the situation and their changes, including how man is equipped for dealing with situations in which his orientation is uncertain. The "method's" promised final achievement gets in the way of man's process of self-understanding in the present and also gets in the way of rhetoric as a technique for coming to terms in the provisional state prior to all definitive truths and ethics. Rhetoric creates institutions where self-evident truths are lacking.

One could dissolve the dualism of philosophy and rhetoric (which has again and again frustrated attempts at harmonization) in a specific conception of the philosophy of history that reshapes Descartes's model by skeptically modifying the implications of the *morale par provision*. What remains doubtful is not only the possibility of completing scientific knowledge, in whatever area, but also the possible profit of such completion for a *morale definitive*. We have almost forgotten that "progress" is nothing but the form of life, adjusted for the long term, of that Cartesian interim for which the provisional ethics was intended. Where Descartes was right is in his assumption that there is no sort of preliminary participation, granted in advance, in the success of the whole. To put it differently: philosophy's program succeeds or fails, but it does not yield any profit in installments. Everything that remains this side of self-evidence is rhetoric; rhetoric is the instrument of the *morale par provision*. This statement means above all that rhetoric is an aggregate of legitimate means. Rhetoric belongs to a syndrome of skeptical assumptions. We will not be deceived into overlooking this by the fact that it was only able to defend itself against the charge of being a "mere means" by presenting itself as the means employed by the truth. For even in its victories, rhetoric had to proceed "rhetorically": When, in the fourth century BC, rhetoric had in practice eliminated philosophy's claims, Isocrates, using a Sophistical device, called his Sophism "philosophy." For Jacob Burckhardt, the Greeks' feeling for effect [*Wirkung*], as opposed to reality [*Wirklichkeit*], is the basis of rhetoric, which only for "momentary effects" rose to the level of "public oratory" but had been primarily "devoted to achieving results before tribunals."[8] But the Greeks themselves contrasted persuasion to subjugation by force: in the dealings of Greeks with Greeks, Isocrates says, the appropriate means is persuasion, whereas in dealings with barbarians it is the use of force. This difference is understood as one of language and education, because persuasion presupposes the commonality of one horizon, allusions to prototypical material, and the orientation provided by metaphors and similes. The antithesis of truth and effect is superficial because the rhetorical effect is not an alternative that one can choose instead of an insight that one could *also* have but an alternative to a self-evidence that one *cannot* have, or cannot have yet, or at any rate cannot have here and now. Rhetoric is after all not only the technique of producing such an effect; it is always also a means of keeping that effect transparent: it makes us conscious of effective means whose use does not need to be expressly prescribed by making explicit what is already done in any case.

As long as philosophy was inclined to hold out at least the prospect of eternal truths and definitive certainties, then "consensus" as the ideal of rhetoric and agreement subject to later revocation as the result attained by persuasion had to seem contemptible to it. But when it was transformed into a theory of the scientific "method" of the modern age, philosophy too was not spared the renunciation on which all rhetoric is based. To be sure, it seemed at first as though science's hypotheses were always temporary expedients employed by cognition, instructions as to how to bring about their verification and thus their final guarantee; but the history of science showed in detail how verification, too, represents the pattern of agreement subject to later revocation, and how the publication of every theory implies a request that other people should follow the paths by which the theorist claims that it is confirmed and should give it the sanction of objectivity without its ever being possible to exclude, by this process, the possibility that by other paths other things may be discovered and the theory contradicted. What Thomas S. Kuhn

---

8. [Jakob Burckhardt, *History of Greek Culture*, trans. Palmer Hilty (Mineola: Dover, 2002), 83.]

in *The Structure of Scientific Revolutions*[9] called the "paradigm"—the dominant fundamental conception, in a scientific discipline, for a long period of time, which integrates into itself all subsequent refining and extending inquiries—this paradigm is nothing but a "consensus," which is able to stabilize itself not, indeed, exclusively, but at least partly by means of the rhetoric of the academies and the textbooks.

Even if a deficiency of self-evidence defines the situation shared by the process of theory and of rhetoric, nevertheless science has provided itself with the invaluable advantage of being able to put up with the provisional character of its results indefinitely. That is not obvious: Descartes would still have regarded it as intolerable. But his idea of "method" made it possible to understand science, and to organize it, as an overall process that is always "transferable" from one person to another and that integrates individuals and generations into itself as mere functionaries. All action that is based as "application" on this sort of theory has to share the weakness of its provisional character: that it can have its authority revoked at any time. Theories, too, implicitly solicit "agreement," as rhetoric does explicitly. The decisive difference lies in the dimension of time; science can wait, or is subject to the convention of being able to wait, whereas rhetoric—if it can no longer be the *ornatus* of a truth—presupposes, as a constitutive element of its situation, that the "creature of deficiency" is under the compulsion to act [*Handlungszwang*]. Thus it copies the process form of science when discussion, as an instrument of public will formation, is regarded as though it were a mechanism for rationally arriving at results, whereas it cannot in fact afford precisely the endlessness (in principle) of rationality in the form that it takes in science. The restricted time allotted to speakers may be only a paltry substitute for rhetoric's rules of form, but even as a substitute it is an essential underlying arrangement for rhetoric; where it is disregarded or unknown, or indeed where its opposite is institutionalized (as in the "filibuster"), rhetoric's character as an alternative to terror becomes

---

9. [Thomas S. Kuhn, *The Structure of Scientific Revolutions* (Chicago: University of Chicago Press, 1962).]

manifest. To see oneself in the perspective of rhetoric means to be conscious both of being under the compulsion to act and of lacking norms in a finite situation. Everything that is not force here goes over to the side of rhetoric, and rhetoric implies the renunciation of force.

In this connection, the compulsion to act, which determines the rhetorical situation and which demands primarily a physical reaction, can be transformed, rhetorically, in such a way that the enforced action becomes, by "consensus," once again "merely" a rhetorical one. Substituting verbal accomplishments for physical ones is an anthropological "radical";[10] rhetoric systematizes it. In his *Philosophy of Symbolic Forms*, Ernst Cassirer described man as the *animal symbolicum* [symbolic animal], whose original achievement is to reinterpret an external "impression" as the "expression" of something internal, and thus to set up, in place of something alien and inaccessible, something else that is sensuously tangible.[11] Language, myth, art, and science are, according to Cassirer, regions of such "symbolic forms," which in principle only repeat that primary process of the conversion of "impression" into "expression." But this theory of Cassirer's makes no claim to explain why the "symbolic forms" are set up; the fact that they appear as the world of culture allows us to infer the existence of the *animal symbolicum*, which manifests its "nature" [*Wesen*] in its creations. An anthropology of man as "rich" sees the cultural housing of the "symbolic forms" as growing upward, layer upon layer, on the base of a secure, or at least unquestioned, biological existence. The enrichment of naked existence has no functional continuity with what makes that existence possible. But to the extent that philosophy is a process of dismantling instances of obviousness [*Selbstverständlichkeiten*], a "philosophical" anthropology has to address the question whether man's physical existence is not itself only a result that follows from the achievements that are ascribed to him as belonging to his "nature."

---

10. [A "radical" in a sense analogous to that in linguistics, where the term refers to a root word or word clement, a base to which other things are added.]

11. [Ernst Cassirer, *The Philosophy of Symbolic Forms*, 4 vols. (New Haven, CT: Yale University Press, 1955–1996).]

The first proposition of an anthropology would then be: it cannot be taken for granted that man is able to exist. The prototype for such a line of thought can be found in the modern social contract theory that deduces the necessity of establishing man's civil condition from its finding that his "natural" condition contradicts the conditions of the possibility of physical existence. For Hobbes, the state is the first artifact, which does not enrich (in the direction of a world of culture) the sphere in which man lives, but rather eliminates its lethal antagonism. What is philosophical about this theory is not primarily that it explains the appearance of an institution such as the state (and the appearance of the *absolutist* state in particular), but rather that it converts the supposed definition of man's *nature* as that of a *zōon politikon* [political animal] into a functional description. I see no other scientific course for an anthropology except, in an analogous manner, to destroy[12] what is supposedly "natural" and convict it of its "artificiality" in the functional system of the elementary human achievement called "life." A first attempt of this kind was made by Paul Alsberg in 1922 in his book—to which too little attention was paid because of its misleading title and language—*In Quest of Man*.[13] Then in 1940, Arnold Gehlen—with his work *Man*, which, though questionable in its intention, was nevertheless fundamental—developed the beginning of a theory of perception and of language, and since then has carried it further by founding a doctrine of "institutions." With Gehlen's absolutism of "institutions," anthropology returns, in a certain way, to its point of departure in the model of the social contract. The discussion of this anthropology

---

12.   [*Destruieren* here is not the usual German word for "destroy" (which is *zerstören*) but instead the same Latinate term that Heidegger used for what he wanted to do to the history of ontology. It has been rendered, not inappropriately, by the French *déconstruire*, "to deconstruct."]

13.   [Paul Alsberg, *In Quest of Man: A Biological Approach to the Problem of Man's Place in Nature* (Oxford: Pergamon Press, 1970). Blumenberg's remark is aimed at the German title *Das Menschheitsrätsel* (The Riddle of Humanity) (Dresden: Sybillen-Verlag, 1922); the English is not a translation but a rewritten version of the German original.]

has not yet settled the question of whether that fateful return is inevitable.[14]

Man's deficiency in specific dispositions for reactive behavior vis-à-vis reality—that is, his poverty of instincts—is the starting point for the central anthropological question as to how this creature is able to exist in spite of his lack of fixed biological dispositions. The answer can be reduced to the formula: by not dealing with this reality directly. The human relation to reality is indirect, circuitous, delayed, selective, and above all, "metaphorical." How man copes with the excess of demands made on him by his relation to reality was laid out a long time ago in the Nominalists' interpretation of judgment. Predicates are "institutions"; a concrete thing is comprehended by being analyzed into the relationships by which it belongs to these institutions. When it has been absorbed in judgments, it has disappeared as something concrete. But to comprehend something *as* something is radically different from the procedure of comprehending something *by means of* something else. The detour by which, in metaphor, we turn away from the object in question and look at another one, which we imagine may be instructive, takes the given as something alien, the other as something more familiar and more easily at our disposal. If the boundary case of judgment is identity, the boundary case of metaphor is the symbol; here the other is entirely other, which delivers nothing but the pure possibility of putting something that is at our disposal in the place of something that is not. The *animal symbolicum* masters the reality that is originally lethal for him by letting it be represented; he looks away from what is uncanny or uncomfortable for him and toward what is familiar. This becomes clearest where judgment, with its claim to identity, cannot reach its goal at all, either because the demands of

---

14. [Blumenberg makes his own view of this question (and the distinction between his own concept of "institutions" and Gehlen's "absolutism" of them) clear in part 2, chapter 1, of his *Work on Myth* (Cambridge, MA: MIT Press, 1985). See especially page 166: "What the heading of 'institutions' covers is, above all, a distribution of burdens of proof. Where an institution exists, the question of its rational foundation is not, of itself, continually urgent, and the burden of proof always lies on the person who objects to the arrangement that it carries with it."]

its object exceed what its procedure can handle (as in the case of the "world," "life," "history," "consciousness") or because there is insufficient scope for the procedure, as in situations where one is under the compulsion to act, in which rapid orientation and vivid plausibility are needed. Metaphor is not only a chapter in the discussion of rhetorical means; it is a distinctive element of rhetoric in which rhetoric's function can be displayed and expressed in terms of its relation to anthropology.

It would be entirely one-sided and incomplete to present rhetoric only as a "makeshift" solution, in view of the deficiency of self-evidence in situations where one is under the compulsion to act. It is not only a substitute for theoretical orientation in the service of action; more importantly, it can be a substitute for action itself. Man can not only *present* one thing in place of another; he can also *do* one thing in place of another. If history teaches anything at all, it is this, that without this capacity to use substitutes for actions, not much would be left of mankind. The ritualized replacement of a human sacrifice by an animal sacrifice, which is still visible through the story of Abraham and Isaac, may have been a beginning. Christianity, through two millennia, has regarded it as quite obvious that the death of one can compensate for the mischief for which all are responsible. Freud saw in the commemorative funeral feast the sons' agreement to put an end to the killing of the tribal father and instead of that to do—something else.[15] In Bremen, before their journey to America together in 1909, Freud persuaded C. G. Jung, whom he suspected of treachery to his school, to drink wine with his meal (which violated the principles of Jung's first teacher, Bleuler), instead of forcing him to perform an act of submission, the content of which would essentially have been a statement that he did not want to be the father himself. Politically, the rebuke that a verbal or demonstrative act is "pure rhetoric" is regarded as a serious one, but that is itself part of a rhetoric that does not want to admit (nor does it have any need to admit) that a policy is better, the more it can afford to restrict itself to "mere words." In foreign policy, warnings are

---

15. [Sigmund Freud, *Totem and Taboo* (New York: Norton, 1950).]

most productive when they are pronounced at the moment in which the one who is being warned has already abandoned the idea of carrying out the act against which he is being warned. Everything can depend on (as we have become accustomed to saying) "leaving it at declarations," on "talking down" the compulsion to act when the risk involved in the action is able to disqualify all possible gains from acting. Here questions relating to the concept of reality become involved, which cannot be dealt with in this discussion.[16]

The lack of self-evidence [*Evidenzmangel*] and the compulsion to act are the prerequisites of the rhetorical situation. But not only substitutive and metaphorical procedures are rhetorical. The compulsion to act is itself not an utterly "real" circumstance but also depends on the "role" that is ascribed to the actor or with which he seeks to define himself—self-understanding, too, makes use of metaphors, and "to cheer oneself up" is an expression that betrays that the internal use of rhetoric is not a novel discovery. The metaphors of roles that are popular again today are based on a very solid tradition of picturing life and the world as "theater," and it is not equally a matter of course for all of the historical forms of theater that its "roles" are as fixed as we nowadays assume when we use the metaphor. To allow someone, in the course of a conflict, to "save face" comes from a different realm of speech, but it coincides to a large extent with the precept, implied in the metaphors of roles, that one should not force the focal person of a transaction (intended to bring about a change in that person's behavior) to leave the identity of his role, but instead one should offer him the required change of behavior in the guise of a credible logical development of his role. There is no need to give illustrations of the extent to which the policy of great and small powers today can be described with the phraseology of "role definition" and "role expectation" (here the anthropological metaphor is again taken as a metaphor, on a second level), and what pragmatic instructions for treating potentially rhetorical behavior as actually rhetorical behavior are contained in this description. Georg Simmel suggested that the metaphor of roles is

---

16. [See the essay "Concept of Reality and Theory of the State" in this volume.]

so productive only because life is an "early form of the actor's art,"[17] but Simmel, especially, knew when he said this that these metaphors no longer have anything to do with the implication that it is a question of illusion, of a theatrical double life, with and without masks, with and without costume, so that one would only need to expose the stage and the actors in order to catch sight of the reality and put an end to the theatrical intermezzo. The "life" of which Simmel speaks is not incidentally and episodically an "early form" of the dramatic art; rather, being able to live and defining a role for oneself are identical. Now I assert that not only is this talk of "roles" metaphorical, but the process of definition that goes with the role concept—a process upon which the consciousness of identity depends and with which it can be damaged—is itself rooted in metaphor and is asserted and defended, both internally and externally, by metaphor. The case of defense, in particular, makes that clear: Erving Goffman's *Stigma* (1963) substantiates it abundantly. The "agreement" that has to be the goal of all "persuasion" (even of self-persuasion) is the congruence—which is endangered in all situations and always has to be secured afresh—between one's role consciousness and the role expectations that others have of one.[18] Perhaps "agreement" is too strong a term, because approval would always already go beyond what is called for. Fundamentally, what is important is not to encounter contradiction, both in the internal sense, as a problem relating to consistency, and in the external sense, as a problem relating to acceptance. Rhetoric is a system not only of soliciting mandates for action but also of putting into effect and defending, both with oneself and before others, a self-conception that is in the process of formation or has been formed. Viewed in terms of the philosophy of science, the metaphorically conceived "role" performs the function of a hypothesis, which is "verified" by every act that does not falsify it. The residue that still remains of all the rhetoric about the teleological value of "consensus" as some-

---

17. [Georg Simmel, "Zur Philosophie des Schauspielers," in *Gesamtausgabe*, vol. 20, ed. Otthein Rammstedt (Frankfurt am Main: Suhrkamp, 2004), 204.]

18. [Erving Goffman, *Stigma: Notes on the Management of Spoiled Identity* (Englewood Cliffs, NJ: Prentice-Hall, 1963).]

thing guaranteed by nature is the ensuring of the noncontradiction—the nonbreakage of the consistency of what is accepted—which people therefore like to call, in the current political jargon, a "platform." It is understandable, in view of this state of affairs, that a need for a "basis of shared convictions" becomes virulent again and again, and in the form of one new proposal after another. People may go on calling "consensus" an "idea"[19] of the effect aimed at by rhetoric, but in the anthropological analysis of rhetoric's function it is redundant.

Rhetorical substitution in the compulsion to act and the rhetorical shielding of self-presentation as "self-preservation" have in common the fact that while they do indeed presuppose creative acts (the creation of symbols, the conception of roles), nevertheless as pure creativity they remain impotent and without any function. Here the question immediately arises whether the connection, so sought-after today, between the aesthetics of production and the aesthetics of reception does not point to an analogous structure.[20] "Every art has a rhetorical level," Nietzsche wrote in 1874 in a fragment on Cicero.[21] The "invention" of the substitutive symbol, for example, can be the most harmless, the least imaginative act in the world; it has to be brought to the point where it is recognized, and for this—in contrast to the aesthetic work—it contains, materially, not the slightest inducement. But this recognition is, in effect, everything; it alone has consequences. Remember the classical political formula that trade follows the flag; today one can reverse it and say that the flag follows trade: states that do not even maintain diplomatic relations conclude trade agreements in the expectation that everything else will follow. The reversal of the old proposition is at the same time an expression of the complete devaluation of the symbol

---

19. [I.e., an unattainable guiding idea. (This is Kantian terminology.)]

20. [*Rezeptionsästhetik*, the aesthetics of the "reception" of works of art by audiences, critics, and so on, is the central concern of a school of literary theory in Germany of which Hans Robert Jauß and Wolfgang Iser are leading spokesmen. It contrasts, of course, with the traditional focus on the work itself or on the process of its "production" as the key to its meaning and status.]

21. Friedrich Nietzsche, "Cicerofragment," *Gesammelte Werke* (Munich: Musarion, 1923), 7:385. [Now in Nietzsche, *Sämtliche Werke*, 7:757.]

of the "flag," which is finally only able to ornament the realities. When it is said (as it used to be) that the respect shown to substitutions is based on "convention," that is both correct and tautological. The convention is a result. How does it come about? Doubtless by being offered and canvassed for. This holds even for the most abstract case in the history of science, the successful promotion of symbolic systems for formal logic; the canvassing rhetoric goes into details or consists of asserting in public, regarding national forms that one does not like, that one will never comprehend them. The less it is the case that political realities can still be "created" outside the sphere of economics, the more important become "diplomatic recognition," questions about names of countries, treaties in which one relinquishes what is in any case no longer possible, and proceedings in which one struggles mightily about what is in any case already well established. As soon as what was once considered to be "real" no longer exists, the substitutions themselves become "the real." In aesthetics, with the surrender of all kinds and degrees of figuration [*Gegenständlichkeit*], the proposal that something should be accepted as a work of art—or even only as what is "called for" after the end of all art—can only succeed at the cost of a great expenditure of rhetoric. It is not primarily the work's need for commentary that asserts itself in texts that accompany and come after it, but rather its being declared a work of art or a work of what has succeeded art; to that extent, harsh criticism by a competent critic is still acceptance into the nexus of history in which art has again and again been produced against art, with the rhetorical gesture of making an end of what has been and a beginning of what is to come. Even the disavowal of rhetoric here is still rhetorical; even the kick that is administered to the conventional viewer who strives to "understand" demonstrates to him that what he does not understand is legitimate and indeed that it occupies the "position" of what one was once supposed to understand, or what is now understood by competent authorities. The "reoccupations" of which history is composed are carried out rhetorically.[22]

---

22. [The idea of "positions" in a mental space, which are "reoccupied" during changes of epoch, is the central idea of the author's *The Legitimacy of the Modern*

Rhetoric also has to do with the temporal structure of actions. Acceleration and retardation are elements in historical processes that have so far received too little attention. "History" is composed not only of events and the connections between them (however these may be interpreted) but also of what one could call the "overall situation" with regard to time. What has been designated in our tradition as "rationality" has almost always benefited the element of acceleration, of the concentration of processes. Even dialectical theories of history accentuate the factors promoting acceleration, because they propel the process toward the critical point where it makes its sudden turning and thus bring it noticeably closer to its final state (thus confirming the law that is asserted to govern the process). The many-layered phenomenon of technization can be reduced to the intention of saving time.[23] Rhetoric, on the other hand, is, in regard to the temporal texture of actions, a consummate embodiment of retardation. Circuitousness, procedural inventiveness, ritualization imply a doubt as to whether the shortest way of connecting two points is also the humane route from one to the other. In aesthetics, for example in music, we are quite familiar with this type of situation. In the modern world, excessive demands result not only from the complexity of circumstances but also from the increasing divergence between the two spheres of (on the one hand) material exigencies and (on the other) decisions with regard to their temporal texture. A disproportion has arisen between the acceleration of processes and the feasibility of keeping them under control, of intervening in them with decisions, and of coordinating them, through an overview, with other processes. Certain auxiliary functions that technical equipment can perform for human action have an assimilating effect: where all the data are quickly available, a quick decision seems to have a special appropriateness to the case. The desire to keep developments under one's control, or to get them under one's control again, is dominant in critical reflections on

---

Age (Cambridge, MA: MIT Press, 1983). See especially pp. 65–69, where it is introduced.]

23. [See the essay "Phenomenological Aspects on Life-World and Technization" in this volume.]

progress, to the extent that they are not pure romanticism. Operations analyses supply optimal problem solutions, but they never also eliminate doubts as to whether the problem was correctly posed— and such doubts already characterize action as something that precedes its theory and does not follow from it as a mere result. There is a clearly recognizable increased accent on delaying factors in public dealings. It is not an accident that such an outmoded word as "reflection" could be renewed as a catchword. There is a need for an institutionalized catching of breath, which sends even majorities that are competent to make decisions on long rhetorical detours. One wants to make it self-evident that one is not "driven" (by whatever it might be) and that one does not intend merely to sanction what has been decided long since. The acceleration of processes is, after all, only a variant of the "flood of stimulation"[24] [*Reizüberflutung*] that the biologically impoverished creature, man, is constitutionally exposed to and that he deals with by institutionalizing his behavior. Here verbal institutions are by no means an atrophied instance of more massive regulatory processes; their potency must be measured against the ideal of decisionistic theories, which consists in taking up only a point in time.

There is something like the expediency of the nonexpedient. Today we observe an extremely rapid dismantling of "obsolete" forms by critical proceedings in which everything that exists carries the burden of proving that its existence is justified, but at the same time we see at work an exuberant inventiveness in the fresh construction of circuitous procedures, which are only distinguished by soberer titles like "rules of procedure," "supervisory agencies," "functional systems," and the like. Whatever time is saved is always immediately used up.

We must increasingly abandon the idea of a model of education or culture [*Bildung*] that is governed by the norm that man must always know what he is doing. In former times, a doctor was supposed to know not only the conditions of the functioning of the organs, conditions whose failure constitutes illness, and the effects of the therapies

---

24. [Gehlen, *Man*, 28.]

and medications that he prescribed as well, but also the derivation of the foreign words that he continually used to label all of this and the use of which was evidence of his being initiated into the guild. A captain was not only supposed to be able to use the sextant and the trigonometric formulae that went with it but also had to know how the instrument functioned and how the formulae could be derived, so that he would be a potential Robinson Crusoe who could start out *ex nihilo* [from nothing] if the already manufactured auxiliary means were lost. As opposed to this, the idea has for a long time been gaining ground that the technical world needs trained functionaries who react appropriately but do not understand its functional connections in every respect. Fewer and fewer people will know *what* they do by learning *why* they do it. Action shrinks to reaction the more direct is the path from theory to practice that is sought. The cry for the elimination of "useless" curricular material is always a cry for "facilitating" functional implementation. Of course, the circuitousness that goes with the claim to know what one is doing is not in itself a guarantee of humane or moral insight, but as a pattern of delayed reaction it is potentially also a pattern of "conscious" action. I suggest that "education and culture," whatever else they may still be, have something to do with this delaying of the functional connections between signals and reactions to them. The result is that their contents, their "values" and "goods," become secondary. The discussion about these values is usually conducted with an unexamined distribution of the burden of proof: one who defends traditional cultural goods is supposed to prove what they are still worth. If we assume that in themselves they are worth nothing at all, their "rhetorical" character becomes clear: they are figures, required exercises, obligatory detours and formalities, rituals, which impede the immediate utilization of man and obstruct (or perhaps only slow down) the arrival of a world of the shortest possible connection between any two given points. If classical rhetoric essentially aims at a mandate for action, modern rhetoric seeks to promote the delaying of action, or at least the understanding of such delay—and it does this also and especially when it wants to demonstrate its capacity to act, once again by displaying symbolic substitutions.

The axiom of all rhetoric is the principle of insufficient reason (*principium rationis insufficientis*). It is the correlate of an anthropology of a creature who is deficient in essential respects. If the human world accorded with the optimism of Leibniz's metaphysics, who thought that he could assign a sufficient reason even for the fact that anything exists at all rather than nothing ("cur aliquid potius quam nihil"),[25] then there would be no rhetoric, because there would be neither the need nor the possibility of using it effectively. The rhetoric that by its dissemination is the most important in our history, the rhetoric of prayer, already had to rely—contrary to the theological positions associated with rationalistic or voluntaristic concepts of God—on a God who allowed himself to be persuaded, and this problem recurs in the case of anthropology: the man whom it deals with is not characterized by the philosophical overcoming of "opinion" by "knowledge."

But the principle of insufficient reason is not to be confused with a demand that we forgo reasons, just as "opinion" does not denote an attitude for which one has no reasons but rather one for which the reasons are diffuse and not regulated by method. One has to be cautious about making accusations of irrationality in situations where endless, indefinitely extensive procedures have to be excluded; in the realm of reasoning about practical activities in life, it can be more rational to accept something on insufficient grounds than to insist on a procedure modeled on that of science, and it *is* more rational to do this than to disguise decisions that have already been made in arguments that are scientific in form. It is true that euphoria about the provision of scientific advice in public affairs has faded away somewhat, but the disappointments in regard to this alliance are due to a failure to understand that lacking self-evidence of the truth of their findings, committees of scientists themselves cannot proceed differently from the institutions they advise—that is, they must proceed rhetorically, aiming at a factual "consensus," which cannot be the "consensus" of their theoretical norms. It is also a

---

25. [Gottfried Wilhelm Leibniz, "On the Radical Origination of Things," in *Philosophical Papers and Letters*, ed. Leroy E. Loemker (Dordrecht: Kluwer, 1989), 487.]

norm of science that one should clearly indicate the modality of one's statements. If one affirms apodictically, or even merely assertorically, what can only be affirmed problematically, one violates this norm. Anyone who is affected by public actions or who has to agree to them has a right to know what is the dignity of the premises that are presented as the results of scientific consultation. Rhetoric teaches us to recognize rhetoric, but it does not teach us to legitimize it.

What is at stake is not only the relation between science and political authorities but also a realm of statements that have very important practical consequences, consequences that cannot be suspended, although in their theoretical status these statements are based, perhaps forever, on an insufficient rational foundation, or may even be demonstrably incapable of being verified. The positivistic proposal that questions and statements that contain no directions as to how they could be verified should then be extirpated involves bringing any practice that depends on such premises to a standstill, and thus becomes illusionary. A decision in such questions as whether man is by nature good or bad, whether his character is determined by his heredity or by his environment, whether he makes or is made by his history, can indeed be deferred by science, but cannot be deferred in practice and cannot be declared to be meaningless. Thus, every kind of pedagogy is already in the midst of a practical process and cannot wait for the delivery of its theoretical premises, so that it is forced to accept quasi-results from among the theoretical generalizations offered by biology, psychology, sociology, and other disciplines. In this boundary zone, remarkable processes of a rhetorical type take place, processes in which rationality and realism seem to diverge, for here, there is not only a compulsion to act (as before) but also a coercion to make axioms of premises without which a theory dealing with compulsions to act would be paralyzed and condemned to sterility. Nevertheless, I think that these decisions have nothing to do with the cynicism of a *liberum arbitrium indifferentiae* [liberty of indifference], and certainly nothing to do with existentialist self-positing.

In the realm in which the principle of insufficient reason holds, there are rational decision rules that do not resemble science in their form. Pascal provided a model of this in his *argument du pari* [argument of the wager], an argument that we no longer find convincing only because it compares the prospect of a transcendent infinite gain with the risk of a finite stake,[26] but that remains valid in that man has to wager the whole stake of his practice, at whatever risk of error, on the particular prospect, as between two theoretical alternatives, that is favorable to his self-assertion and self-development. No theoretical doubt about the validity of the principle of causality or about the possibility of proving it conclusively can alter in any way the fact that in our conduct we wager on its unrestricted validity. One of the most momentous declarations from the realm of various sciences would be an answer to the question to what extent man's modes of behavior are determined by, and therefore modifiable through, endogenous or exogenous determinants. Although one may regard this complex question as scientifically still largely undecided, still it is easy to see that methodological considerations favor an endogenous determinism—just as, quite independently of empirical findings, they imply, in the theory of evolution, that Darwinism will be preferred to the various kinds of Lamarckism. The theory that restricts itself to a few kinds of factors that, methodically, can be neatly isolated and exhibited has a better chance to become a "paradigm" in Thomas Kuhn's sense than the theory that has to offer a range of factors that cannot be separated out as well and that are diffusely distributed. That science will draw closer to a result of the kind typified by the Darwinistic theories seems to me to be inevitable and theoretically well founded.

This development would have far-reaching effects in many areas of public and private life: in education and jurisdiction, in social prophylaxis, in the penal system, even in people's everyday dealings with each other. In fact, however, the preference that is given to certain practical axioms seems not to be governed by what scientific theories are predominant. This is a fact that Kant discovered when, in the doctrine of the "postulates," in his *Critique of Practical Reason*, he assumed the independence of moral positings from

---

26. [Blumenberg discusses this aspect of Pascal's "wager" argument in *Work on Myth*, 233.]

theoretical proofs. For Kant, it is the classical chief principles of all metaphysics—man's freedom, the existence of God, immortality—that, in the form of postulates, "are inseparably connected" to the practical law.[27] The logic of this inseparability becomes clearer when one sees that only someone who disregards the law has an interest in citing his unfreedom and the futility of law-abiding behavior as far as well-being is concerned. We would count the postulates, entirely apart from metaphysics, as part of the rhetoric of ethics: they sum up what makes up the "consensus" of practical axioms through persuasion and self-persuasion—what produces assent to public and private efforts and gives meaning to improving the conditions for a life that is free of crime and conflict and to trusting in the possibility of repairing backward or misguided lives. We act "as if" we knew that efforts and expenditures of this sort, for the benefit of man, are not in vain and are not called in question by science. In our practice, we turn into an axiom as a "postulate" what provides a motive for taking advantage of the greater humane prospects. Here rhetoric is also the art of persuading ourselves to ignore what speaks against betting on these prospects. The depressing results of genetic research on twins have not been able to discourage the adherents of theories of environmental influence—and properly so. However narrow the zone of the uncertainty for scientific statements may become, it will never disappear entirely, and we will bet on it where theory appears to be more than can be demanded of, and intolerable for, practice. Since Kant, the practical postulate stands against the overwhelming determinism of the world of possible scientific objects.

Rhetoric has to do not with facts but with expectations. That which in its whole tradition it has called "credible" and "verisimilar" has to be clearly distinguished, in its practical valence, from what theory can call "probable" [*wahrscheinlich*].[28] That man "makes" history is a prospect on which, after detours through philosophy of

---

27. [Immanuel Kant, *Critique of Practical Reason*, trans. Mary Gregor (Cambridge: Cambridge University Press, 2015), A 122.]

28. On this, see Hans Blumenberg, *Paradigms for a Metaphorology*, trans. Robert Savage (Ithaca, NY: Cornell University Press, 2010), 81–98.

history, the modern age has wagered. What this proposition means can only be understood if one perceives the "reoccupation" that is accomplished by means of it. I introduced and explained this concept in my *Legitimacy of the Modern Age* (1966),[29] but I did not yet see that it implies a theoretical process. For who is the acting subject of history is not discovered or proven; the subject of history is "appointed." In our tradition's system of the explanation of reality there is a "position" for this historical subject, a position to which vacancy and occupation refer. The accomplishment and establishment of the reoccupation are rhetorical acts; "philosophy of history" only thematizes the structure of this process, it is not the agency responsible for it.[30] Not accidentally, the act by which the subject of history is determined and legitimized has borne the name of a fundamental rhetorical figure, as *translatio imperii* [transfer (or: trope, metaphor) of power]. "Carryings over,"[31] metaphorical functions, again and again play an essential role here. Alexander conceives his historical project as a reversal of Xerxes's march across the Hellespont. The God of the Old Testament transfers his sovereignty in history by means of a covenant. The citizens of the National Convention, in the French Revolution, take metaphors of the Roman Republic literally, in their costume and their speech. "Men make their own history, but they do not make it just as they please; they do not make it under circumstances chosen by themselves, but under circumstances directly encountered, given and transmitted from the past," Marx writes in the *Eighteenth Brumaire*.[32] The deeper the crisis of legitimacy reaches, the more pro-

29.   [Hans Blumenberg, *The Legitimacy of the Modern Age*, trans. Robert M. Wallace (Cambridge, MA: MIT Press, 1983).]

30.   ["Philosophy of history," *Geschichtsphilosophie*, here and earlier in this paragraph refers—as it usually does in contemporary German writing—to the classical philosophies of history of writers like Condorcet, Saint-Simon, Hegel, Marx, and Comte, who all posit an overall necessary progress in history. Blumenberg's point is that abandoning this kind of philosophy of history need not prevent one from accepting the kind of "reoccupation" that he is describing here.]

31.   [Metaphor is, in its Greek etymology, a "carrying over." "Transfer" and *translatio* (translation) are Latin versions of the same thing.]

32.   Karl Marx/Friedrich Engels, *Selected Works* (New York: International Publishers, 1968), 97.

nounced the recourse to rhetorical metaphor becomes—it is not inertia that makes tradition but rather the difficulty of living up to one's designation as the subject of history. So one contents oneself more easily with participating in the role of the subject of history: one *is* not the subject, but one is *part* of it, or one would have to be part of it if only things went *properly*. Rhetorically, both attributions of responsibility and excuses are always equally readily available.

I am not celebrating rhetoric here as an innate creative gift that man possesses. To illuminate it anthropologically is not to demonstrate that it gives man a special "metaphysical" distinction. As a behavioral characteristic of a creature that lives *nevertheless [trotzdem]*, it is literally a "certificate of poverty." I would hesitate to call it a "cunning of reason"; not only because it would then be in even more questionable company but also because I would like to hold to the idea of seeing in it a form of rationality itself—a rational way of coming to terms with the provisionality of reason. It may be that the provisionality of theory that it avails itself of and profits from is only a grace period for it, if it does not prove to be the case that there is no irrevocability in theory. Against all rhetoric that is not "an elegant and clear expression of the conceptions of the mind," Hobbes recommended the use of "right reason." This phrase resembles the one that is going around currently: "critical reason." That is all very well, but what else could judge whether the "right" reason is being employed in each case, except reason once again—that is, "right reason"? For Hobbes, one of the most important objections to democracy is that it cannot manage without rhetoric and consequently arrives at decisions more *impetu animi* [by a certain violence of the mind] than *recta ratione* [by right reason], because its orators are guided not by the "nature of the things" but by the passions of their listeners. "Nor is this fault in the *man*, but in the nature itself of *eloquence*, whose end, as all masters of rhetoric teach us, is not truth (except by chance) but victory, and whose property is not to inform but to allure."[33] A remarkable proposition, which

---

33. Thomas Hobbes, *De Cive*, X, 11 [from Hobbes's own English version (which has also been used for the bracketed translations of quotes from the Latin

explicitly absolves men of responsibility for the effects of an instrument that they invented and use only on account of those very effects. An especially remarkable proposition when one confronts it with the type of rationality that Hobbes's theory of the state represents: self-preservation, as the rational motivation of the contract of submission, risks, in the undetermined and undeterminable will of the absolute ruler, every *impetus animi* that Hobbes disparages as the correlate of rhetoric.

Hobbes's pathology of rhetoric traces the excitement of the passions back to the "metaphorical use of words." For him, too, metaphor is the distinctive element of rhetoric; in his opinion it is "fitted to the passions" and thus "separated from the true knowledge of things."[34] What is the basis of this relationship between metaphor and the passions, which Hobbes suggests to us here as something obvious? For him, metaphor is opposed to concepts; by excluding the instruments of reason, metaphor opens the field to everything that traditionally is curbed and controlled by reason, everything that likes to escape from the exertion of concepts into the ease of orientation by images. In this passage, Hobbes admits an eloquence (*eloquentia*) that abstains from metaphor and arises "from the contemplation of the things themselves," an eloquence that consists only in the elegance with which one expresses what one has grasped. When it is compared to the "nature of the things," as something that one could possess, rhetoric does indeed appear as an eccentric and artificial means. Yet if one considers Hobbes's theory of concepts, one is surprised to find that his rejection of metaphor depends on crediting the human intellect with more than he is able to grant it in this theory. For the concept, too, is only an artificial means, which has nothing in common with that "nature of the things." It is not incidentally, here, that I point out this inconsistency in Hobbes's critique of metaphor as the essential element of rhetoric. It suggests the conjecture that Hobbes's critique of metaphor with reference to its affinity to the passions is based on the contradiction between the

---

original), in *Man and Citizen*, ed. Bernard Gert (Garden City, NY: Doubleday Anchor, 1972), 231].

34. Hobbes, *De Cive*, X, 12; 253–254.

idea of the absolute state and a rhetoric that Hobbes describes, in opposing it, as "necessary to a man born for commotions." Now metaphor is in fact not only a surrogate for concepts that are missing but possible in principle and should therefore be demanded; it is also a projective principle, which both expands and occupies empty space—an imaginative procedure that provides itself with its own durability in similes. As Ahlrich Meyer has recently shown,[35] the absolute state that is rationally deduced from the principle of self-preservation is caught between metaphors of the organic, on the one hand, and of mechanism, on the other. Such key metaphors have their own power of persuasion, which reacts, precisely through its possible extensions, on the metaphorical core: for example, the possibility of an organic philosophy of history reinforces the organic model of the state. Hobbes himself overlooked the contradiction between his organic metaphor of the "state as a person" and the artificiality of the state's origin—and this is especially instructive, because the prohibition of metaphor makes it more difficult to perceive its actual background function.[36] Even the prohibition of rhetoric is a rhetorical occurrence, which, then, only the others perceive as such. The example of Hobbes shows that in the modern age, antirhetoric has become one of the most important expedients of rhetorical art, by means of which to lay claim to the rigor of realism, which alone promises to be a match for the seriousness of man's position (in this case, his position in his "state of nature").

Rhetoric is an "art" because it is an epitome of difficulties with reality, and reality has been preunderstood, in our tradition, primarily as "nature." The reason there is so little perceptible rhetoric in a surrounding reality [*Umweltwirklichkeit*] that is extremely artificial is that it is already omnipresent. The classical antirhetorical figure of speech *res, non verba!* [things, not words!] then points to states of affairs that themselves no longer have any of the sanction of what is natural but instead already have a rhetorical tincture. On the other hand, this easily makes the emphatic recommendation or presentation

---

35. Ahlrich Meyer, "Mechanische und organische Metaphorik politischer Philosophie," *Archiv für Begriffsgeschichte* 13 (1969): 128–199.

36. [On "background metaphors," see Blumenberg, *Paradigms*, 62–76.]

of rhetoric's stylistic means a little (or more than a little) ridiculous. One then ascribes this difficulty to one's higher degree of realism. Rhetoric's modern difficulties with reality consist, in good part, in the fact that this reality no longer has value as something to appeal to, because it is in its turn a product of artificial processes. Thus, one enters the specifically rhetorical situation of securing an exhortatory cry for oneself so as not to let the others have it: "Ad res"; "Zur Sache und zu den Sachen!" [To the matter at hand, to the things themselves!] It is rhetoric when one suggests to others, as a premise, that it is necessary to think and to act once again, or to do so for the first time ever. If reality could be seen and dealt with "realistically," it would have been seen and dealt with that way all along. So, much more than with the reality that it promises, the attitude of the *retour au réel* [return to the real] has to concern itself with the explanation of the illusions, deceptions, and seductions that have to be disposed of in connection with it. Every rhetoric of realism needs the conspiracies that have prevented it until now. Plato's allegory of the cave, in which because of the shadows playing on the wall the captive people never come to know what is truly real unless they are freed from the cave by force, is the model of such unmasking. It is directed against rhetoric because the machinators of the shadow world are the Sophists, as "makers of images"; and it is itself rhetoric, since it is based on an elementary metaphor of "coming into the light" and expands it into a simile for an absolute reality, whose promise of self-evidence cannot be fulfilled. Philosophy's turning from the shadows to reality was usurped by rhetoric and, in its wake, by aesthetics. Jean Paul reflected this, ironically, in two sentences in the *Invisible Lodge*: "Ah! we are only trembling shadows! and yet will one shadow tear another to pieces?"[37]

In the *Critique of Judgment*, Kant declares that rhetoric, as "the art of using the weakness of people for one's own purposes . . . is not worthy of any respect at all." This "deceitful art" deals with moving people, "like machines, to a judgment in important

---

37. [Jean Paul Friedrich Richter, *The Invisible Lodge*, trans. Charles T. Brooks (New York: Lovell, 1883, 203).]

matters."[38] Now it is not at all in dispute here that man's constitutive dependence on rhetorical actions is always also a susceptibility to being influenced by rhetoric; there are enough dangers of and pressures toward his becoming a machine. The theory of rhetoric has always exposed people's intentions of taking advantage of this "weakness of people" at the same time that it served them. In an anthropological localization of rhetoric, the issue is this weakness, not those intentions. Here anthropological approaches to rhetoric converge on a central descriptive statement: man has no immediate, no purely "internal" relation to himself. His self-understanding has the structure of "self-externality" [Selbstäußerlichkeit]. Kant was the first to deny that inner experience has any precedence over outer experience; we are appearance to ourselves, the secondary synthesis of a primary manifold, not the reverse. The substantialism of identity is destroyed; identity must be realized, it becomes a kind of accomplishment, and accordingly there is a pathology of identity. What remains as the subject matter of anthropology is a "human nature" that has never been "nature" and never will be. The fact that it makes its appearance in metaphorical disguise—as animal and as machine, as sedimentary layers and as stream of consciousness, in contrast to and in competition with a god—does not warrant our expecting that at the end of all creeds and all moralizing, it will lie before us revealed. Man comprehends himself only by way of what he is not. It is not only his situation that is potentially metaphorical; his constitution itself already is. Montaigne's formulation of the result of his anthropology as self-experience is that the worst place that we could choose is in ourselves ("la pire place, que nous puissions prendre, c'est en nous").[39] He refers to the Copernican revolution, which as a trauma of man's interiority in the world metaphorically strengthens skepticism about his interiority in himself. Self-persuasion underlies all rhetoric in external relations; it makes use not only of the very general, practically effective

---

38. Immanuel Kant, *Critique of the Power of Judgment*, sec. 53, trans. Paul Guyer and Eric Matthews (Cambridge: Cambridge University Press, 2000), 205 [B 327].

39. Montaigne, "Apology for Raymond Sebond," 427.

propositions of which I spoke earlier but also of self-understanding through self-externality. So the most daring metaphor, which tried to embrace the greatest tension, may have accomplished the most for man's self-conception: trying to think the god absolutely away from himself, as the totally other, he inexorably began the most difficult rhetorical act, namely, the act of comparing himself to this god.[40]

Translated by Robert M. Wallace[41]

---

40. [In the original, this "god" could just as well be read as "God" since all nouns are capitalized in German.]

41. [Minor corrections and additional editorial footnotes by Hannes Bajohr.]

9

OBSERVATIONS DRAWN
FROM METAPHORS

(1971)

Locating the Observer

Since the publication of the first volume of the *Historical Dictionary of Philosophy*[1] [*Historisches Wörterbuch der Philosophie*], the situation for doing research in the history of concepts has changed. Joachim Ritter's preface analyzes not so much the changes that this new dictionary might bring about as the changes that occurred since the last edition of the *Eisler* dictionary appeared, on which the conception of the much larger undertaking just embarked upon is based. In an editor, this reservation is understandable. For the interested

---

Originally published as "Beobachtungen an Metaphern," *Archiv für Begriffsgeschichte* 15, no. 2 (1971): 161–214. Sections 1, 3, 4, 7, 8, and 9 are translated here.

1. [Joachim Ritter, Karlfried Gründer, and Gottfried Gabriel, eds., *Historisches Wörterbuch der Philosophie. Völlig neubearbeitete Ausgabe des 'Wörterbuchs der Philosophischen Begriffe' von Rudolf Eisler*, 13 vols. (Basel: Schwabe, 1971–2007).]

audience, however, it is more exciting to ask what standards are being established by this work. Hopefully, the journal *Archive for the History of Concepts* [*Archiv für Begriffsgeschichte*] can collect and present part of the discussions that will be sparked by the abundance of material, by the conception and the method, by the successes and possible failures, and by what is presented and what is omitted.

I feel personally addressed by the explicit declaration of what the *Historical Dictionary of Philosophy* does not include. Ritter says that the editors decided not to include metaphors and metaphorical phrases in the nomenclature of the dictionary. I would like to state from the outset that the reason for this omission makes sense to me and that there is no point in criticizing it. It is correct that the current state of research would have condemned any attempt in that direction to be an "insufficient improvisation,"[2] as Ritter himself put it.

It is at least revealing that this omission was "not taken lightly."[3] This fact can definitively be related to where Ritter situates the project in his preface and through which he distinguishes his endeavor from the situation in which Rudolf Eisler first conceived of his *Dictionary of Philosophical Concepts* [*Wörterbuch der philosophischen Begriffe*] in 1899. Eisler's regarding the stage of development of philosophy that his dictionary was meant to represent was determined by Auguste Comte's law of three stages, from which Eisler derived the assumption that "all methods, concepts, and questions that do not and cannot merge into science are destined to fall back into the past of merely historical existence."[4] Thus, for Eisler, the systematic definitions that introduced each article were that achievement which could be justified by the remaining material only insofar as its character as a result standing at the end of an overarching development was beyond doubt. History had its product, and it was

---

2. [Joachim Ritter, "Vorwort," *Historisches Wörterbuch der Philosophie*, 1:9.]
3. [Ritter, 1:9.]
4. [Ritter, 1:5.]

simply a matter of identifying it with regard to its status as *ultima ratio.*

Ritter is right not simply to leave behind the Cartesian ideal of a definitive terminology as an outdated moment in some greater schema of stages but rather to voice only such doubts about its ubiquitous possibility in the overall area of the formation of philosophical languages and concepts that, since Eisler's final product in the nineteenth century, had been exaggerated as much as they had been justified. The new work is supposed to withstand the very tension that has arisen between the two poles of, on the one hand, a Cartesianism transformed into a philosophy of science and a new logic and, on the other, "a philosophy that conceives of itself historically."[5] Without this tension, we could understand neither the research into the history of concepts nor any of the expectations held of it. Besides being orientated toward the history of concepts, those expressions are treated whose "function is constituted by their being detached from history."[6] A historical presentation is chosen "where it is necessary or desired in order to understand the concept."[7] Where such necessity or desire is to be found, however, can only be determined through the "experiment" of the historical presentation itself and through the understanding it yields about the matter constituted in the concept. One may call this a pragmatic procedure— which is supposed to sound improper today—but it is, after all, the only procedure that remains possible in the tense field of philosophical positions and at the same time promises conducive results.

But these results carry an unevenly distributed burden of proof, which seems to be unfavorable to the historical aspect. Historical terminology does not have sovereignty over the constructive formation of concepts; its "things" are always already made and the achievements embedded in them can only be deduced. The counterposition to the Cartesian ideal of clear and distinct concept formation will undoubtedly be represented impressively by the *Historical Dictionary*, but will still be put to a tough comparative test by

---

5.   [Ritter, 1:5.]
6.   [Ritter, 1:8.]
7.   [Ritter, 1:8.]

the thetically constructive conceptuality of its articles. This juxta-position is found not only among the attractions but also among the thought-provoking aspects that elevate this project above the function of a mere reference instrument.[8]

Precisely because the burden of proof is so unfavorable for his-torical terminology, it will need to go beyond its own factual repre-sentation in this work and necessitate reference to that which, it was proclaimed, had to be omitted. Only with difficulty was the history of concepts able to free itself from the permanent complication stemming from the fact that most of its historical sources and proofs did not attain the form of clear and distinct determination. In other words, it can barely free itself from the unacknowledged preference for the Cartesian ideal and its successors.

This is the reason expanding research in the history of concepts toward metaphorology can be seen not just as the addition of a spe-cific chapter, whose omission would mean a relief from an addi-tional risky task. Metaphorology renders conceptual history the ser-vice of helping it approach a genetic structure of concept formation that, while it may not meet the requirement of univocity, nonethe-less permits the univocity of the end result, which indicates an im-poverishment of the imaginative background and the threads lead-ing back to the life-world. In the methodical confrontation between Cartesianism and historicism (given that such keywords are even sufficiently differentiated), the dualism of the world model and the life-world, as it has become pressing in our reality, is reflected. Re-garding its subject matter, metaphorology must not simply be con-sidered a preliminary stage or substructure of concept formation; instead, and in the reverse direction, metaphorology opens up the

---

8. It is part of the alphabet's deviousness that a historico-conceptual diction-ary must disrespect its own results by having the article "history of concepts" [*Begriffsgeschichte*] lining up already in the span of its first thousand columns. The apology, which only the completed whole will fully be able to represent, is at least outlined in the pertinent article by Helmut G. Meier, which must almost be called diplomatic due to its thoughtful balance. Between the boundary values of the "sub"(sidiary) and the "inter"(disciplinary)—between incompetence and om-nicompetence—a course is mapped out for which almost every other article will imply a correction.

possibility of tracing back the constructive instruments to the constitution of the life-world, from which they do not actually stem, but back to which they often refer. The life-world not only provides the material that is to be processed but also possesses a complex structure of resistance to such processing, as well as to an acknowledgement of what it has achieved.

Without developing the field of metaphorics in the broadest sense, it is impossible to reach the results in which philosophical or prephilosophical language has resisted being dissolved into conceptuality and in which metaphor can take on that absolute function that makes apparent that it can be neither translated into "literal" speech nor reoccupied by it. Certainly, even absolute metaphors are still lacking this functional determination, which would state that, at any particular time, only *one* given imaginative element could take its position. When Lessing says that metaphorics is a "means to elevate . . . arbitrary signs to the value of natural signs," so that they obtain "the power of natural signs,"[9] then "naturalness" in this context means obvious validity under conditions of unquestioned contingency.

When I first presented the draft for what was to become *Paradigms for a Metaphorology* in Jugenheim in May 1958, during a meeting of the German Research Foundation's senate commission for historico-conceptual research, Bruno Snell inquired about a possible system of absolute metaphors. He who raised the question at that time is under no suspicion of having pedantic systematic needs. But it is immediately clear that there is a very specific heuristic trait to his question, namely, that it aims at starting from the linguistic phenomena of metaphorics to reach the very findings that separate and distinguish themselves by the untranslatability of their metaphorical representatives. Since such a system can claim no intrinsic value, there is no need to rush into drafting it. But it may be seen that here typological work has to lead the way.

---

9. [Gotthold Ephraim Lessing, "Laokoon: Paralipomena," in *Werke 1766–1769*, ed. Wilfried Barner (Frankfurt am Main: Deutscher Klassiker Verlag, 1990), 310–311.]

We currently tend to undervalue typological procedures. To many, they appear—as, for example, Dilthey's typologization of worldviews—to be some kind of display of wares to choose from, that is, as the preliminary stage to a decisionist act. But that is not the primary function of typology. Its primary function is the virtual opposite: it neutralizes decisionist processes that have already occurred by trying to present the complete field of possibilities, that is, confronting prejudice with the judgments that would have been possible in the first place, and by retroactively supplying it with what still is. The decisionist character of preconceived "opinions" becomes transparent with regard to what has not at all been consulted in the life-world and therefore could also not at all have been eliminated. Of course, typology can never be an end product of theory, but it is an essential step of rationalization with its own immanent question: What are the negations implied in a position?

Thus, it is easy to see that every anthropology stands in a metaphoric horizon of an opulence or poverty of the being thematized by it, and that already its point of origin is determined by the makeup of this horizon. Typology seeks to lock in place what historically actualizes itself as a constant search for the latitude of the possible, as a part of those "processes of extension" in which Kant's "Conjectural Beginning of Human History" saw the "tempting" function of reason.[10] Every present wants to reassure itself that it is not the embodiment of necessity but that, and how, it lies within the latitude of the possible. Typology is above all discredited by the role it played in biologism. But it must be grasped more precisely of what this offensiveness consists. Above all, it is caused by the boundary case of physiognomics and race theory, that is, by substituting the external for the internal, the factual for the essential. The resistance to typology—in our tradition perhaps represented most brilliantly by Lichtenberg's great objection to Lavater's physiognomics—consists in the fact that humans cannot and must not accept that they are what they appear to be. If the villains in a work of art also

---

10. [Immanuel Kant, "Conjectural Beginning of Human History," in *Anthropology, History, and Education*, ed. Günter Zöllner and Robert B. Louden (Cambridge: Cambridge University Press, 2007), 160–175.]

look evil, we are bothered not only by the lack of realism but also by the physiognomic presumption of categorizing humans on the grounds of the very thing for which they are not responsible.

This remark seems to me to be necessary to replace the denigration of typological procedures with an insight into their functional limitations.

In looking for clues on how to structure the realm of absolute metaphors, one stumbles upon the historical diagnosis that certain concepts have always been under suspicion of not fulfilling the requirements necessary for their status as concepts and possibly never even being able to fulfill them. I would like to call to mind the dispute over whether there ever could be a concept of time in the strict sense. In the *Critique of Pure Reason*, Kant, for one, says: "Time is no discursive . . . concept."[11] What this means we need only discuss here with regard to how this deficiency of the concept of time in all its attempted determinations apparently finds its expression in the fact that it contains a metaphorics of space that cannot be eliminated. It may be the case that this is connected to circumstances having to do with the brain's development, in which the achievements of spatial representation are genetically older than those of temporal representation.[12] One may dismiss the traditional question of what time is, given the great possibilities to measure it without having to determine it by anything other than the parameters of this measurement—unless I am much mistaken, this old and perhaps all too great question will continue to rear its head, at least as a disruptive factor in measuring time.

It is similar with the concept of "world." World may be everything that is the case, but in no way could a Cartesian be satisfied with this pseudo-definition. Kant discovered that world is an idea and thus a reference to something that *cannot* fulfill the intuition demanded by concepts and that nevertheless contains the claims that intuitions should be interconnected, and that the stock of intuitions reached

---

11.   [Immanuel Kant, *Critique of Pure Reason* (Cambridge: Cambridge University Press, 1998), 162 (B47).]

12.   Georg Schaltenbrand, "Bewußtsein und Zeit," *Studium Generale* 22 (1969): 455–472; 463.

should always be exceeded. Especially as an embodiment of postula-
tions, an idea does not reach the dignity of a concept—not because
it is content with less, but rather because necessity demands more.
It is similar with the totalities that we have grown accustomed to
calling "life" or "history."

In the wake of Cartesianism, it was perhaps believed that the concept of the subject that lies in the "I think" would represent the
purest fulfillment of the demands for determinateness raised by concept formation. The most accurate presence that the subject possesses for itself has to allow for the boundary case of clear conceptuality. Leibniz still thought it evident, in accord with all of tradition,
that the spirit [*Geist*] as the self-aware subject might be problematic in its theoretical approach to anything else, that is, to the world
of physical material objects, but that it possessed immediate knowledge in relation to itself and thus remained entirely unproblematic.
Only Kant's curious *Dreams of a Spirit-Seer* from 1766 broke with
this traditional evidence in a way that at first remained unclear.
"We" do not know what the spirit thinks and how it immediately
thinks about itself, what it may be doing when we are physically
deeply asleep (not dreaming!, since the dream will be discovered
only much later as a substitution for this hidden self). The wakeful
subject has a system of ideas of itself transposed [*übertragen*] by
"symbols." Here, the mechanism of the metaphor itself becomes a
metaphor for the mechanism by which spirits experience themselves:
"For these influences can enter the personal consciousness of man,
not, it is true, directly, but, nonetheless, in such a fashion that they,
in accordance with the law of association of ideas, excite those images which are related to them, and awaken representations which
bear an analogy with our senses. They are not, it is true, the spirit-
concept itself, but they are symbols of it."[13] Kant comprehends the
possibility of such symbolism according to the procedure of metaphorics; its possibility becomes distinct according to "the way in
which the higher concepts of reason, which are fairly close to the
spirit-concepts, normally assume, so to speak, a corporeal cloak in

---

13. Immanuel Kant, "Dreams of a Spirit-Seer," in *Theoretical Philosophy 1755–1770* (Cambridge: Cambridge University Press, 1992), 301–359; 326.

order to present themselves in a clear light."[14] In addition to the moral characteristics of the divinity and the allegorical personifications, Kant mentions the example of the representation of time as a line, "although space and time only agree in their relations; they thus, presumably, only agree with each other analogically, never qualitatively."[15] The emergence of spirit-sensations in consciousness thus receives the character of a transition through the excitement of the imagination, and the appearances of spirits are finally nothing but hypertrophic metaphors in which the mere images of the imagination take on the semblance of real sensations. Here, the available technology of the metaphor turns into an intangible psycho-physical limit case of a sensorium that is symbolic in nature. We need take this matter no further, yet in its "magnification," the boundary case shows the constitution of the absolute metaphor.

Metaphors draw us into imaginative contexts. This is explicitly how the simile arises from a metaphor. If such explicitness is not reached, this orientation can remain in the background. If humans play roles in their human environment, who is their observer? Does a self-conception as being involved in role playing also imply a claim for specific observers, so that the role fails if it misses its addressee? Does the pathology of the failed role consist in providing the failed actor with proof of his observers and to finally therapeutically make such proof available to him, thereby at least hinting at it by offers of reception? What is the function of the therapist in this imaginational nexus? The secret, covert, or even suppressed role—can it finally be played, because the observer has been found, because someone tentatively assumes the function of the addressee, because an infinitely attentive, infinitely curious observer occupies the position that had previously been vacant—one as a placeholder for many or for specific others about whom he will never learn? The sequence of these questions is not supposed to constitute the development of a theory but only to hint at a possible theory. The almost associative character of this sequence demonstrates how much

---

14. Kant, "Dreams of a Spirit-Seer," 326.
15. Kant, 326.

support a background metaphorics, once found, can provide for a field in which one can work only with heterogeneous material.

We know what a narrated story is. But we do not know what it means that we can call the totality of all possibly stories "history" [*Geschichten . . . die Geschichte*], according to a principle of selection that is difficult to define. No reminder is necessary that this collective singular is not old at all.[16] Nor need attention be drawn to the fact that the transferability of this metaphor originally simply consisted in narratability. Here there was no sign of its disposition becoming the great philosophical standard problem, which seems to be following as a matter of necessity from the hypostasizing achievement of the singular. The singular of "history" is itself an absolute metaphor, one of the great words from the world of those nouns that create the great problems for us as well as the metaphysics corresponding to these problems. No critique of language seems equal to the task of avoiding them. There was the philosophy of life [*Lebensphilosophie*]; perhaps it will return under another title, for questions such as "What is life?" are ineradicable, despite the fact that the toughest answers may already have been given—like Nietzsche's: "What is life? . . . Constantly being a murderer?"[17]

The totalities for which only examples are given here seem to form an ordered structure of entanglement with each other, to which the functions of absolute metaphorics might correspond. "Life" as the totality of individual existence; "the self" as this totality's bearer, unknown to itself; "history" [*die Geschichte*] as the overall unity of such totalities of life; and finally, "the world," itself the comprehensive totality of all realities that have an effect on history, or rather of the realities that are characterized as indifferent to history, such as nature or the indifference of the stars—even those stars whose

---

16. [Blumenberg here refers to Reinhart Koselleck's studies of this shift; see Reinhart Koselleck, "Historia Magistra Vitae: The Dissolution of the Topos into the Perspective of a Modernized Historical Process" (1967), in *Futures Past: On the Semantics of Historical Time* (New York: Columbia University Press, 2004), 26–42).]

17. Friedrich Nietzsche, *The Gay Science*, trans. Walter Kaufmann (New York: Vintage, 1974), 100.

light could not yet have reached us. At least one other totality is conceived of beyond the world, which Jaspers, for instance, has called "the encompassing" [*das Umgreifende*], namely, everything that by way of myth has become differentiated into supraworld and underworld, into the antemundane and eschatology.[18] Projection is the means by which the extraworldly spaces of the imagination are populated, transcendence the form in which its boundaries are transgressed. The metaphors and myths of beginnings may be demiurgic or organic, those of the end juridical, catastrophic, or theatrical.

The great conceptions of the whole and of its phrasings conceal their metaphoric orientation. In a sense, Freud's death drive is a metaphor to the same degree that Ernst Haeckel's "biogenetic law" derives its plausibility from the transfer structure: ontogenesis is the metaphor of phylogenesis. Freud basically thought this matter one decisive step further into a total perspective. If one takes the expression "phylogenesis" in a broader sense still, it comes to comprise not only the development of organic life itself but even the step from the anorganic to the organic. Haeckel's basic law can be interpreted as perpetual return of nature to its points of origin, to the beginnings, to the repetition of a constant ritual. In that case, however, the ritual is incomplete; it repeats only part of its history—only the organic episode—and excludes the physical, chemical prehistory. Now one might say that only the conception of the death drive radicalized this repetition, integrated the organic episode into the more encompassing principle of inertia, and finally provided the second law of thermodynamics with its psychoanalytic correlate. The individual is a metaphor of the total history of nature and not merely of the history of organic nature. It seems that Lou Andreas-Salomé was the first to characterize Ferenczi's idea of the "death tendency" and Freud's idea of the "death drive" correctly: "I cannot escape the idea that the tendency to death and rest—which Freud attributes to every living being as its essential being, inborn, and from which

---

18. [Karl Jaspers, *Reason and Existenz: Five Lectures* (New York: Noonday, 1955), 51–76.]

it is reluctant to be disturbed—is itself a rather neurotic estimation of life."[19]

Gottfried Benn spoke of the "boastfulness" [*Aufschneiderei*] of the metaphorical.[20] Indeed, not only poetical but also philosophical metaphorics always have some kind of this having-promised-too-much that evades all demands of redemption. We have "no relationship to the totality of existence,"[21] but we turn "the world" into the subject of statements, just as we do with "history." It may be that metaphorics rhetorically overextends the anticipatory or overarching aspect [*Vorgriff und Übergriff*] of promising-too-much; yet it does not create the structure of anticipation and overarching but rather enters into it. If the life-world did not have the intentionality of anticipating and overarching extensions, which, according to Husserl's description, unanimously persist, but can also experience "cancelings-out,"[22] then negation could not exist. Anyone able truly and insistently to live only in a receptive-immediate manner would not possess this instrument. Even neopositivist falsificationism still makes this very clear: we do not live by confirmations but by the absence of denials, that is, by those very "cancelings-out." The life-world is a world, as it were, on probation. The metaphor offers an exemplary manifestation of this unsurpassable state of affairs, in which this undefined expectation horizon first articulates itself. The constitutive anticipatory aspect easily becomes overarching, potentially even lapsing into Benn's "boastfulness." Realists are always reducing metaphorics, which certainly is fair enough—but is reality what then remains?[23]

---

19. Lou Andreas-Salomé, *The Freud Journal*, trans. Stanley A. Leavey (New York: Basic, 1964), 172.

20. Gottfried Benn, "Zur Problematik des Dichterischen," in *Gesammelte Werke*, ed. Dieter Wellershoff (Wiesbaden: Limes, 1959), 1:73.

21. Georg Simmel, *The Philosophy of Money*, 3rd enlarged edition (London: Routledge, 2004), 78.

22. [Edmund Husserl, *The Crisis of European Sciences and Transcendental Phenomenology: An Introduction to Phenomenological Philosophy* (Evanston, IL: Northwestern University Press, 1970), 145.]

23. No longer to be metaphorical, as an index of maturity and solidity, is apparent in a remark by Goethe recorded in Kestner's papers from May 1772: "Possesses an extraordinarily vivid imagination, and hence generally expresses himself

If one keeps this in mind, significance accrues to a very specific form of metaphorics that I have described as "explosive metaphorics,"[24] because its own futility is always simultaneously expressed in its intentional expansion, the anticipatory aspect is expressed at the same time as the retraction of the overarching aspect. The invention of this configuration of metaphors stands in the tradition of negative theology, the mystical *via negationis* [way of negation], that is, the very self-representation of every theology's elemental conundrum: to be supposed to keep talking about God while not being afforded the confidence to say anything about Him. For his *coincidentia oppositorum* [coincidence of opposites], Nicholas of Cusa devised the explosive metaphorics of the circle whose radius becomes infinite, thereby causing its peripety to have an infinitely small curvature, ultimately coinciding with a straight line. One might not suppose such an eminently medieval pattern of expression could still be useful to illustrate a specific aspect of historical consciousness of the modern age. In one of his journal fragments, Georg Simmel decisively amended Nietzsche's concept of the eternal recurrence of the same with the help of this explosive metaphor: "The world process strikes me as the turning of an enormous wheel, as, however, it is the premise of the eternal recurrence. But the result, the actual repetition at some point of the identical, is not the same—for the wheel has an infinitely large radius; only once an infinite amount of time has elapsed—that is, never—can it reach the same point again. And yet it is a wheel that turns, that, in its ideal, aims at the exhaustion of the qualitative manifoldness without ever exhausting it in reality."[25]

The space of metaphor is the space of concept formation that is impossible, has failed, or is not yet consolidated. The norm of

---

in images and similes. He often says, himself, that he always speaks figuratively, and can never express himself literally; but that when he is older he hopes to think and say the thought itself as it really is." [Quoted in George Henry Lewes, *The Life and Works of Goethe* (Cambridge: Cambridge University Press, 2011), 1:149.]

24. Hans Blumenberg, *Paradigms for a Metaphorology* (Ithaca, NY: Cornell University Press, 2010), 122–126.

25. Georg Simmel, "Aus dem nachgelassenen Tagebuche," *Postume Veröffentlichungen* (Frankfurt am Main: Suhrkamp, 2004), 263.

conceptuality is based on anticipatory orientations, which in turn and by necessity lie outside the normative and its systematicity, yet do not form its mere genetic preliminary stage that consumes itself in the process.

The Sources

The critique of rhetoric and especially that of the use of metaphors tends to give rise to the expectation that "literal" speech [*"eigentliche" Rede*] in the traditional sense would also be univocal. This expectation is not confirmed. Scientific language does indeed tend toward the univocal use of its means, but at the cost of being restricted to a mere technical language, which is then again prone to metaphorical "misuse" outside its realm. The aesthetic use of language is opposed to the process that tends toward univocity; the ambiguity of linguistic means is either being restored or fabricated anew by being bound to contexts hitherto unacceptable. The task of seeking out metaphorics even in the internal language of science does not aim for its possible aesthetic revaluation, that is, at maintaining or awakening equivocity, but rather for a factor of consistency conserved in metaphorics. For a metaphor is orientated a certain way when it homogenizes a context, and it prepares the context's understanding with regard to this orientation. It makes more explicit how things that at first appear different could have come together and how they are related. The function of a metaphorology can therefore be to secure univocity for a hermeneutical conception or to support attempts to correct such a conception that has not yet been secured. Hence, metaphorology has no aesthetical aspect, because, far from tolerating ambiguity, it accepts the tendency toward univocity within scientific language.

In a technical language such as that of philologists and historians, there exists a metaphor, barely perceived as such anymore, of the type of "the sources." When such a metaphor is suddenly "taken at its word," a kind of life-worldly self-evidence is shattered for those who have been using the technical language. Such a moment happened when in August 1957, during a conference at the Fonda-

tion Hardt on the *Sources de Plotin*, Richard Harder, shortly before his death, picked up on the use philologists make of the expression "source" and pointed out that they were dealing with a
metaphor—a fact that of course everybody who was present knew,
but had not been made aware of as long as anyone can remember.[26]
"Were classical studies ever to begin," said Harder, "to think about
their own concepts, such metaphors would surely be in need of examination, the biological ones, like family tree and development,
as much as the physical ones, like cause and effect."[27] Harder acknowledges reservations against the concept of the source and that
such metaphors are not helpful for understanding the issue. What
does he do who draws from a source? He draws, but what comes
of it will later be an "influence," in the language of the historian.
And what has happened to the source from which he drew? "The
water from the source is pure; who draws from it, muddies it."[28]

Harder's remarks on the topic of "Source or Tradition?" were
originally merely the introduction to his presentation, which has not
survived, on "The Whole Before and in Plotinus." But the discussion about this introduction, recorded in the proceedings, still reveals how irritating, if not unsettling, this unexpected metaphorological redirection of attention toward a background that is
no longer perceived can become. It suddenly emerges that a single
metaphor belongs to and indicates a system of orientations, but that
at the same time the latency of the background is also secured and
shielded by the supposed self-evidence of the metaphor. In the discussions, this disruption met with defensiveness. The editor of Plotinus, Hans-Rudolf Schwyzer, whose merits are beyond dispute, indeed acknowledges that "source" is a mythological expression, but
remarks that this does not make it an impermissible concept: "one
has only to agree on what one means by it."[29] Yet there lies the
rub: the plausibility of the metaphor, its pictorial self-evidence, skips

---

26. Richard Harder, "Quelle oder Tradition? (& Discussion)," in *Les Sources de Plotin: Entretiens sur l'Antiquite Classique, Fondation Hardt, Entretiens* (Vandœuvres-Genève: Fondation Hardt, 1960), 5:327–339.
27. [Harder, "Quelle oder Tradition? (& Discussion)," 327.]
28. [Harder, 327.]
29. [Harder, 333.]

the need for agreement and suggests that everyone already knows what is meant by it. "At times," Schwyzer writes, Harder gives the reader the feeling that "he was seeing ghosts from the deep."[30] Does one really know what that is supposed to mean? The metaphor carries a potential for implications and connotations that cannot be exchanged at will, that permanently may offer themselves up, but that can also remain untapped until someone needs them. Above all, let us not forget about the "purity" of sources—as the sources of streams that later become muddied, which does not only imply the methodical postulate of recuperation and development, but which, in the call "to the sources," also becomes a criterion for quality and dignity. There is an aversion to the implications offered by metaphor, such as when Willy Theiler says the following in the discussion at Vandœuvres: "I myself have no recourse to the word source . . . because following through with that image causes linguistic difficulties." Theiler continues that which of the "mythological modes of expression" one happens to be using may be relatively insignificant: "The key point is to work together on the issue." But what is the issue here without the imaginative system of orientation through which its contexts are registered?[31]

We are dealing here with an imagination from the philosophy of history that anticipates how events (in the widest sense) can relate to one another. Johann Gottfried Herder has made use of this system of imagination to differentiate his, one feels almost compelled to say, subterranean, concept of historical progress against skepticism on the one hand and against the rationalist idea of progress on the other: "Should there not be manifest *progress* and *development* but in a higher sense than people have imagined it? Do you see this *river current* swimming along—how it sprang forth from a little source, grows, breaks off there, begins here, ever meanders, and bores further and deeper—but always remains *water!*, *river current!*, drop always only drop, until it plunges into the ocean—what if it

---

30. [Harder, 333.]
31. [Harder, 336.]

were like that with the human species?"[32] Does one arrive at the sources if one traces this schema in the philosophy of history in the opposite direction? Goethe has accused the "philosophers of the intellect" of being unclear because they are too in love with clarity, causing them to end up like the man "who follows a river from its mouth upward, thus always coming across inflowing brooks and creeks, which again divert, so that finally he will completely lose his way and come to rest *in deverticulis* [up a byway]."[33]

Sources are something that one stumbles upon. This is true of the historian's sources because they have entered the stream of history without drowning in it. Against the overrating of tradition, Bacon coined the malicious image of time as a torrent in which the very thing that has the least weight is carried along and endures. What becomes a "source"? Is it a process of canonization when things are conserved, collected, copied, merged in documentations, critically secured, and finally diplomatically edited? Some things only become a source once there exists the respective historical discipline or subdiscipline which expands the original canon, such as the history of economy, the history of science, folklore studies, name studies, the history of concepts. What was a mere relict before now becomes an authentic source. It is in the nature of an epoch shaped by historical consciousness that it begins to archive almost everything as worthy of being passed on. But will it be what future historians will want to know about this epoch? Will their concept of "life-world" and its totality not be more encompassing than what can be fulfilled by some kind of archiving canon as it is currently defined? And above all: Will this legacy still be called "source"? Metaphorology also poses the question of how far a metaphor's coverage extends. At any rate, we are leaving potential future historians other and different materials than those that were left for us. They no longer have in

---

32. Johann Gottfried Herder, "This Too a Philosophy of History for the Formation of Humanity," in *Philosophical Writings* (Cambridge: Cambridge University Press, 2002), 298–299.

33. Johann Wolfgang Goethe to Friedrich Wilhelm Riemer, November 1806, in Goethe, *Gedenkausgabe der Werke und Briefe*, ed. Ernst Beutler (Zurich: Artemis, 1949), 22:421.

common with "sources" that they are stumbled upon. Transmission has rather taken the form of an aqueduct, whose bed is cemented against loss. It carries along all that has been not so much purposely left behind as accidentally left lying around, and all that has by law been destined for preservation. The metaphor of the source only comes to be revealing if one sees through it onto the possible, no longer "source-shaped" modality of materials that were saved only because there no longer were any criteria for distinguishing that which is *not* worthy of being passed on.

From this perspective, the source stops being the original and the final—and thus also that which is pure and to be kept pure, and entrusted to the philologies as such. By interrogating it, it is possible to go beyond the source, toward either the will that left it behind, or the conditions for its appearance. Within the metaphorical guiding system of the "source," Johann Gustav Droysen has illustrated the possibility of inquiring about what feeds the source in his *Outline of the Principles of History*. To begin with, Droysen has a final conception of sources: "Under sources belong past events as human understanding has apprehended them, shaped them to itself and passed them over to the service of memory."[34] Throughout large parts of the text, the metaphorics of the "source" have been so far extended and forgotten in the terminology of the historian that the following mixing of metaphors becomes possible: "Even the very best [sources] give him [the scholar], so to speak, only polarized light."[35]

Independent of the will that leaves the source as such behind, for Droysen the very historical fact to which the source attests is already "a complex of acts of will, often many, helping and hindering acts of will."[36] Source criticism has to determine how the materials relate to those past acts of will. The source therefore is a product that

---

34. Johann Gustav Droysen, *Outline of the Principles of History* (Boston: Ginn, 1893), §24, 19. This edition gives the text of the second edition from 1882. The *Outline* first appeared printed in manuscript form. In the first edition, the sentence quoted does not make use of the concept of "service" [*Zweck*]: "Under sources belong past events as human understanding has apprehended and expressed them, and passed them over shaped as memory."

35. Droysen, *Principles of History*, §25, 20.

36. Droysen, §28, 22.

for us precedes the historical circumstances, it is the emergence of a hitherto shapeless supply system. It is to the very bottom of this wellspring that Droysen now refers in a sentence in which he surprisingly and curiously reveals and enacts the metaphorical reference to the term "source": "The primitive 'source' does not consist in the dreary maze of contemporary opinions, accounts, reports. This is only the daily repeated atmospheric process of ascending and self-precipitating vapors from which the true Sources or springs are replenished."[37]

It is indicative of the function of metaphor that the terminological use of an expression is pivoted to its imaginative horizon in the very moment in which a discipline transgresses, with regard to its foundations, the area of its fixed and methodically defined object. The historian no longer has anything to do with such a drainage basin that feeds his sources beyond their methodical conceivability. The everyday business of opinions and narratives, of news and rumors, of ascending and precipitating vapors is not his topic, but the metaphorical extrapolation at least records what, as a process of objectification, forms the basis of a discipline's achievements, and what in that process was left outside of the horizon of objectivization.

Finally, here are two examples of how the imaginative system of "source" might be resorted to in a polemical manner. In his 1670 introduction to the work of Marius Nizolius, Leibniz said against the pseudo-philosophers that the objects of philosophy were in principle none other than those of common thought, and that its language could be that of the quotidian if one were ready to accept a greater effort than that which scholastic terminology demands. Philosophers only feel what others feel, too, but they attentively perceive what others overlook. Yet even if one acknowledges that, Leibniz writes that those who resort to Aristotle and the classical thinkers, and defy the scholastic mudding of those sources, are not to be despised: "qui ex Aristotelis et veterum fontibus potius quam lacunis scholasticorum sua hauserunt" [those who draw from the

---

37. Droysen, §34, 24.

sources of Aristotle and the ancients rather than from the cisterns of the Scholastics].[38]

The second reference is as historically lighthearted as it is now apt to evoke wistfulness. Christian August Vulpius, Goethe's brother-in-law, published a *Glossary for the Eighteenth Century* in 1788, in the alphabetical order of which only this short formula is to be found under the rubric of "university": "the most pleasant place to suffer thirst at the source."[39]

Paradigm, Grammatically

In his widely discussed book on *The Structure of Scientific Revolutions*, Thomas S. Kuhn introduced the concept of *paradigm* into the theory of the history of science.[40] In the preface, he states how he came to use this concept. He spent the year 1958/59 as a natural scientist at the "Center for Advanced Studies in the Behavioral Sciences" at Stanford, in a research group that largely consisted of social scientists. To the natural scientist, it was surprising how many different opinions on the social sciences' methods and problems existed and how extensively they were debated. Kuhn then did not content himself with assuming that the exact sciences enjoyed greater security and solidity with regard to fundamental questions, but arrived at the assumption that other historical and social structures of scientific practice had favored the solidification of specific premises to eliminate controversies. Kuhn writes: "Achievements that share these two characteristics I shall henceforth refer to as 'paradigms,' a term that relates closely to 'normal science.' By choosing it, I mean to suggest that some accepted examples of actual scientific practice . . . provide models from which spring particular coherent

---

38. Gottfried Wilhelm Leibniz, "Preface to an Edition of Nizolius," in *Philosophical Papers and Letters* (Dordrecht: Springer, 1989), 124; translation slightly altered.

39. Christian August Vulpius, *Glossarium für das achtzehnte Jahrhundert* (Hannover: Wehrhahn, 2003), 107.

40. Thomas S. Kuhn, *The Structure of Scientific Revolutions* (Chicago: University of Chicago Press, 1962).

traditions of scientific research."[41] It is, then, the very validity of the paradigm that finally leads it into a crisis, namely, when at a certain point of theoretical development the refinement and precision of procedures to determine anomalies leads to the expectations that are active and persistent in the paradigm being disturbed. In a certain way, the concept of the paradigm thus represents a moment of discontinuity within the schema of the history of science. "Violations of expectations" are possible and consequential only when a consolidated stock may be endangered. The paradigm is a latent complex of premises which, as implications of scientific practice, need not even be expressly formulated but already have entered into the methods and into the framing of problems. "Scientists work from models acquired through education and through subsequent exposure to the literature often without quite knowing or needing to know what characteristics have given these models the status of community paradigms."[42] Scientific progress must thus not be conceived of as an additive process; rather, the spontaneity that occurs in it resembles a "technique for producing surprises."[43]

One reads this text without perceiving the term "paradigm" to mean anything other than "example." However, it is telling that already Georg Christoph Lichtenberg used the expression "paradigm" as a metaphor with reference to the history of science. In the last volume of the Göttingen edition of Lichtenberg's writings from 1800 to 1806, the following may be found among the texts entitled "Unpublished Fragments": "I believe that among all our heuristic pulleys none is more effective than what I have called 'paradigmata.'"[44] Lichtenberg continues that he believes that "by means of a paradigma chosen from physics . . . one could have discovered Kantian philosophy."[45] The text does not reveal what might have prompted Lichtenberg to use the term paradigm in this context. On this, Gottlieb Gamauf's recollections of Lichtenberg's lectures offer

---

41. Kuhn, *Structure of Scientific Revolutions*, 10.
42. Kuhn, 46.
43. Kuhn, 52.
44. Georg Christoph Lichtenberg, *Philosophical Writings*, trans. Steven Tester (Albany: State University of New York Press, 2012), 160.
45. Lichtenberg, *Philosophical Writings*, 160.

some insight. Here we find the following text by Lichtenberg, which sounds quite authentic: "The finest example of the great usefulness of hypotheses is given by astronomy. Now the Copernican system is almost completely beyond any doubt. It is, as it were, the paradigm according to which all other discoveries are supposed to be declined [*dekliniert*]. Here human understanding has penetrated the furthest and deepest."[46]

The expression "paradigm" is used metaphorically in this text, as the phrase "as it were" makes amply clear. The function of astronomical theory of Copernican rank is that of an example from a grammar textbook, by means of which students learn the declension of all other nouns of the same stem type. Lichtenberg himself demonstrated again and again in what sense the Copernican system is such a paradigm by which other discoveries can be "declined." Out of his affinity for this astronomical paradigm, Lichtenberg finally also composed the most beautiful biography of Copernicus that exists in German.[47]

Another significant example in this context that I would like to adduce can be found in Lichtenberg's *Geological-Metereological Fantasies* in which he uses the expression "paradigm" in the distinct metaphorical meaning of the textbook example. In this passage, Lichtenberg discusses the problems of the possibility of periodical fluctuations of solar radiation and how climate variations might depend on them. The Göttingen astronomer Mayer had made proposals for setting up radiation meters on mountains, as suggested by William Herschel's work. On that topic, Lichtenberg writes the following in the *Göttingisches Taschenbuch*, of which he is also the editor:

> The editor of these pages is boundlessly delighted to see here once more what the astronomical mind or, it is tempting to say, astronomical sen-

---

46. Gottlieb Gamauf, "Erinnerungen aus Lichtenbergs Vorlesungen," in Georg Christoph Lichtenberg, *Vorlesungen zur Naturlehre* (Göttingen: Wallstein, 2008), 2:27.

47. [Georg Christoph Lichtenberg, "Nicolaus Copernicus," in Lichtenberg, *Schriften und Briefe*, ed. Wolfgang Promies (Frankfurt am Main: Zweitausendeins, 1994), 3:138–188.]

sitivity is capable of when it comes to arranging research plans in the sciences. As he has said repeatedly, not all parts of the sciences will do well until the procedure used by astronomers to extend their science is recognized as the paradigm to decline all other parts of sciences accordingly and the history of astronomy in a nutshell is nailed as a chart to walls of the physical and chemical laboratories. Now might also be the time to advise the eager antiphilologists to take to heart the history of the invention of the true world system. Lavoisier has undoubtedly become the Copernicus of chemistry.[48]

Lichtenberg likes to think of the state of the sciences of his time as pre-Copernican. Part of the reason for this is the confusion that had resulted from the hypertrophy of auxiliary constructions and newly discovered elements. Foremost and repeatedly this applies to chemistry, where in Lichtenberg's view far too many "new earths" had been discovered. This indicated to him that a radically simplified approach based on the paradigm of astronomical reform was due in this science. In a note published posthumously, Lichtenberg writes:

> I truly cannot say that I like those discoveries of new earths. These accumulations of new bodies remind me of the epicycles in astronomy. What would those astronomers have done with their epicycles if they had known the aberration of the fixed stars? Much geometrical acuity could have been demonstrated, like Copernicus did, for example, in his errors. But what is that? What I actually meant to say is: If chemistry does not soon receive its Kepler, it will be crushed by the number of epicycles; nobody will study it anymore, and languor will at the end know how to simplify it, which an active intellect could have done better. There need and must be a point of view from which everything looks simpler. As soon as one deems a perceived irregularity in the leaves of a tree to be significant enough to remark on it as a great event in the history of the tree, it is no longer possible to think about discovering the nature of the tree.[49]

---

48. Georg Christoph Lichtenberg, "Geologisch-Meterologische Phantasien," in *Vermischte Schriften, nach dessen Tode gesammelt und herausgegeben von Ludwig Christian Lichtenberg und Friedrich Kries* (Göttingen: Dieterich, 1804), 7:203–204.

49. Georg Christoph Lichtenberg, "Sudelbücher," in *Schriften und Briefe*, 2:533–534.

The scientific paradigm of the Copernican type is preceded by the paradigm that language provides for all thought. Lichtenberg is captivated by this idea, and he did say that the whole of our philosophy is the correction of our use of language and thus also the correction of the most common, always already existing philosophy. This, in turn, is expressed in a grammatical metaphor: "Our false philosophy is incorporated into language in its entirety; we cannot reason, so to speak, without reasoning falsely. One fails to consider that any speech, regardless of its topic, is a philosophy. . . . But only this common philosophy has the advantage of possessing declensions and conjugations. Thus, true philosophy is always taught in the language of false philosophy. Explaining words does not help, for in such explanations we do not yet alter the pronouns and their declensions."[50]

If one considers how frequently the metaphorics of words, syllables, and letters, and that of an open and enciphered semantics occur in the metaphoric complex of the "book of nature," then only Lichtenberg's metaphorics helps us to see—from the vantage point of the end of that tradition—that no metaphors of syntax and morphology had existed for this "book of nature." The perception of that which does not exist is the most difficult.

Critical Masses

It is no rarity to observe that metaphorics are "taken at their word." In the process, the metaphor is seized from the limited intention of its author, made independent, and extended in a direction that often changes the clarification into an explanation. The metaphor of the wax tablet, which was intended to illustrate specific epistemological expressions, for Diderot becomes an explanation of the function of memory. For some of his students, the energetic metaphorics of Freud's psychoanalysis take on the form of hypostatization, most clearly in Wilhelm Reich's "Orgon" mysticism. The traditional theater metaphorics of "life" and "world" have gradually led to "real-

---

50. Lichtenberg, *Philosophical Writings*, 100–101.

istically" formulated anthropological, psychological, and sociological theorems of "role behavior" and "primal scenes" [*Urszenen*], with sceneries, props, masks, and other inventory. The simile not only extends the metaphor but also condenses it, and thus takes away the degree of nonbindingness and of rescindability that it originally possesses and that is demonstrated in retaining the possibility of "coexisting" with other metaphors.

Given this premise, the question arises whether the reverse can also be proved, whereby that which is "to be taken at its word" is, in the end, not taken, but instead localized in another language. This type of unlawful "transfer" [*Übertragung*] is most likely to occur when the technical language that someone speaks is not recognized or understood, that is, it is taken to be a "metaphorics of technical language" inadequate to the speaker's intention.

I would like to offer one revealing example that is relevant for a number of reasons. September 1970 saw the first visit of a West German minister of science to the Soviet Union. The journalist Claus Grossner, who was well known at the time for a recent series of newspaper articles entitled *Philosophie in Deutschland*, accompanied the German delegation and reported very critically about the composition of the West German representatives and their preparation for and attitudes about negotiation.[51] In the report it appears almost naive that the delegation should try to downplay the political dimension of scientific interests when in contact with their Soviet partners. The "theoretical positivism" of the German "experts" does indeed have "dangerous effects when put into practice." As a contemporary, one can discern what language is being spoken. But can we simply assume that the other side also speaks this language? The reporter tries particularly to distinguish the opposite type across the negotiation table to delineate the lost chances that are supposed to rest on the existence of some kind of "Scientists' Internationale." Mikhail Lavrentyev, the president of the Sibirian Academy of Sciences in the scientific metropolis of Akademgorodok, invokes his three thousand-kilometer distance to Moscow and

---

51. Claus Grossner, "Leussinks Mission in Moskau," *Die Zeit* 40 (October 2, 1970).

says, "We have here gathered around us a critical mass of scholars." To which the reporter adds by way of interpretation: "—which
are of course also a political power." The expression "critical mass"
has seized the reporter's choice of language. He continues, "This attitude, which openly articulates what many of the young elite scientists are thinking in this Siberian super-academic city, demonstrates that the plans for a German-Soviet scientific agreement are
not merely concerned with a 'superstructure' treaty [*"Überbau"-
Vertrag*]." Through what attitude is what being demonstrated?

The Siberian president of the academy has been speaking to
people who know what a "critical mass" is and who can easily grasp
its metaphorical application in relation to the effectivity of scientific institutions. In the sphere of nuclear reactions, the expectation
that a "mass" becomes "critical" when it reaches a level that triggers self-perpetuating activity has long been fulfilled, albeit not in a
manner apt to afford us much comfort. In an unintended sense, the
reporter is right: within the technical languages, there is today a
greater possibility for an understanding beyond national borders
than there is, within a national language, between the worlds of
technical languages.

Sensus Communis, Metaphorically

Since the Copernican turn, modern science has been governed by
the self-perception that its results were essentially radical disappointments and corrections of the everyday image that humans
create of the world and of the language that draws on this everyday image. Positivism has expressed this idea of science most starkly
by designating the discovery of scientific research as the solemn refutation of good judgment: "La scienza positiva si stabilisce con
una scoperta. E la scoperta è una smentita solenne del senso commune" [Positive science establishes itself with a discovery. And the
discovery is a solemn denial of common sense].[52] This formulation

---

52. Roberto Ardigò, quoted in Wilhelm Büttemeyer, "Der erkenntnistheoretische
Positivismus Roberto Ardigòs" (dissertation, University of Bochum, 1970), 195.

looks like the counterpoint to a dictum by Goethe, addressed to Riemer on July 24, 1807, in which the metaphorics of the senses and of common sense, as the central organ of sensibility that is traditionally used to unify and harmonize the achievements of the other senses, are being used to represent the relation that all sciences among themselves and as a whole have toward philosophy: "Single sciences are just, as it were, the senses with which we stand face to face to things; the philosophy or science of sciences is the *sensus communis*."[53]

Even when Goethe used this metaphor, it had, in a way, already become anachronistic. This is the case at least since the emergence of a thought that forcefully obtrudes upon the human relation to the world, namely, that human sensibility might only be a random selection of the possibilities for accessing reality. This thought occupied Montaigne, Voltaire, and Lessing; Goethe is not bothered by it. The scientific representation of the world dissects reality into measurable properties and it is characteristic for this dissection in particular that it tries to free itself from the randomness of the data accessible to the sense organs, beginning with the difference between primary and secondary sense qualities. Fritz Mauthner coined the metaphor that with regard to the world, our senses open only "accidental breaches," and furthermore refuses to account for why it remains unknown to us just "what cannot be seen through these breaches."[54]

That the expression *sensus communis* should appear in both quotes ought not to blind us to the fact that it means something different in each case. For this expression has degenerated from the very specific meaning of a mediating and attributing central organ of sensibility to that of a common sensibility as that average of perceptions that may be assumed to apply to all humans, or at least to those we may assume to form a community of understanding. What Goethe has in mind for philosophy's relation to the sciences, however, is not this role of representing the common as an average common to all;

---

53. [Quoted in F. F. Cornish, "Some of Goethe's Views on Education," *Transactions of the Manchester Goethe Society, 1886–1893* (Warrington: Mackie, 1894), 107.]

54. Fritz Mauthner, *Die drei Bilder der Welt* (Erlangen: Weltkreis, 1925), 57–58.

rather, he has in mind the role of enabling communication among the sciences through agreement within a functionally higher organ. This organ's role could be, for example, according to Molyneux's much debated problem, to ascertain the identity between an object only given through sense of touch with an entity that is optically presented only thereafter.

The Background Metaphorics of Cultural Critique

Metaphor falls under the remit of rhetoric. In our tradition, this attribution is deemed as carrying a low status. It lies in the function of metaphor that it has an anticipatory quality, something that goes beyond the area of what has been theoretically vouchsafed and that it connects this orienting, detecting, roving anticipatory quality with the suggestion of safeguards that it cannot obtain. What is merely a matter of configuration appears as an explanation. From this duality of risk and security, it is possible to understand the function of metaphor. Metaphor uses the suggestion of intuitiveness and is therefore not only the preliminary stage or the basis of concept formation, but at the same time prevents it or misleads it in the direction of its suggestion.

This function can be concealed when the metaphor accompanies a highly indeterminate concept (in the sense of a "vague legal concept" [*unbestimmter Rechtsbegriff*]) in an explanatory way. In Hans Freyer's *Theorie des gegenwärtigen Zeitalters* [Theory of the Present Age],[55] the concept of the "secondary system" plays a central role. It is striking how the necessary correlate to a "secondary system"—the "primary system"—does not appear in the text with any terminological explicitness, yet is always presupposed in the imaginatively created complementary notions.

Here the numerous additional metaphors come into play that center around the difference of fertility and sterility as the foundational conditions of the two systems. There is no "primary system" to

55. Hans Freyer, *Theorie des gegenwärtigen Zeitalters* (Stuttgart: DVA, 1955); especially 190–198.

begin with, because what presents itself in the metaphors as the primary cannot have the quality—or more accurately, the disquality—of "system" belonging to the secondary. Between both realities there is therefore a relation of irreversibility. This comes with its own metaphorics of reduction and exhaustion, of the unsound management of capital, of borrowing, of the depletion of reserves. All this explicates the schema of the two systems, makes it comprehensible, but at the same time also provides it with some kind of superficial self-evidence: the organic, solid management, the primary, the stratigraphically foundational has suggestive advantages for argumentation, which are well known and concentrated in the formula of the *terra inviolata* [unplowed earth].

All of this would not be that interesting had the author not warned explicitly against the dangers of this imagery and shown himself to be intimately familiar with them. He claims to be aware of the fact that "sociology has to proceed with extreme caution when using images taken from organic life. Specifically, it is highly dangerous to identify matters of fact concerning historicity and the continuing influence of tradition with the help of such images. This leads one to think of temporalities as spatialities, of processes as organic structures."[56] Cultures and civilizations had not developed through growth, but through achievement, and in history there were incipient decisions that had no full parallel in the area of organic life.

Despite expressing this awareness of the dangers of metaphorics, Freyer falls back into his imaginative system of orientation only a few lines later. The present age has turned the possibility of the *secondary system* into a reality and has reached the point of no return. This modern system must be characterized as a whole and complete world, or at least such a world in the making. "The attempt of laying a concrete foundation to build a construction in the 'suspended' style has now really been undertaken, and as far as it has succeeded, one supposes that the roots have been cut and the capillaries blocked as well."[57] The ground as something that has

---

56. [Freyer, *Theorie des gegenwärtigen Zeitalters*, 190.]
57. [Freyer, 191.]

grown is being consumed by deforestation, karstification, and desertification, and the old metaphor of "groundlessness" [*Bodenlosigkeit*]—as artistic unconcern—returns not only in the senses of mismanagement and desertification but also as the intention to uncover the surrogates of the soil. In this way, it is said of language as a "secondary system" that it is "completely groundless; to supply it with a ground would be in contradiction to its principle of formation."[58] And the dilemma of modern humans to restore the balance of natural powers they have disturbed is described in the following way: "After they have overcultivated the ground in the proper sense of the word, they try to put a new ground underneath their rational cultivation."[59] But here indeed the talk of the ground is supposed to illustrate that what has grown cannot as such be made: "Where we are dealing with the balances of nature, with 'ground' in the proper sense of the word, nature has the last word, and its answer can very much arrive via detours and from a completely different corner than expected."[60]

This brief paradigm serves as a clue for the necessity of a metaphorology of cultural critique [*Kulturkritik*], which, though it may not have its own jargon, at least has its own imaginative background.

Translated by Florian Fuchs

---

58. [Freyer, 195.]
59. [Freyer, 197.]
60. [Freyer, 198.]

10

PROSPECT FOR A THEORY
OF NONCONCEPTUALITY

(1979)

A metaphoris autem abstinendum philosopho.
[But the philosopher should abstain from metaphor.][1]

           —GEORGE BERKELEY, *DE MOTU*

When Erich Rothacker included my "Paradigms for a Metaphorology"
in his *Archive for Conceptual History* [*Archiv für Begriffsgeschichte*],[2]
he had in mind—as did I—a subsidiary methodology for conceptual

    Originally published as "Ausblick auf eine Theorie der Unbegrifflichkeit," *Schiff-
bruch mit Zuschauer* (Frankfurt am Main: Suhrkamp, 1979), 75–93; from Hans
Blumenberg, *Ästhetische und metaphorologische Schriften*, ed. Anselm Haverkamp
(Frankfurt am Main: Suhrkamp, 2001), 193–209.
    1. [George Berkeley, "De Motu," in *De Motu and The Analyst*, ed. Doug-
las M. Jesseph (Dordrecht: Springer, 1992), 74.]
    2. [Hans Blumenberg, *Paradigms for a Metaphorology*, trans. Robert Savage
(Ithaca, NY: Cornell University Press, 2010). The German original, "Paradigmen

history, an enterprise that at the time had only just started its work. Since then, nothing has changed in the function of metaphorology, but much about its reference—especially as metaphorics are now understood as merely a narrow special case of nonconceptuality.

Metaphorics is no longer primarily regarded as the guiding sphere for tentative theoretical conceptions, as the preliminary stage of concept formation, or as a makeshift for situations in which technical languages are not yet consolidated. Instead, it is now conceived of as an authentic way of grasping connections, which cannot be limited to the narrow core of the "absolute metaphor." The absolute metaphor was initially only defined through its indisposition toward being "replaced by literal predicates [*Sachprädikate*]" on the same linguistic level. Another way of putting it would be to say that the line of sight has been reversed: it is no longer directed primarily toward the constitution of conceptuality but also looks back at the connections with the life-world as the constant motivational support of all theory—even if this support cannot be kept in consciousness at all times. If we have to acknowledge that we cannot expect *the* truth from science, we would at least like to know why we wanted to know what knowing is now a matter of disappointment. Metaphors are, in this sense, index fossils for an archaic stratum of the process of theoretical curiosity, a curiosity that does not need to be anachronistic simply because there is no way back to its wealth of stimulation and expectations of truth.

The riddle of metaphor cannot be understood simply from the perplexities surrounding concepts. For what is enigmatic is the question of why metaphors are "tolerated" at all. That they appear in rhetoric as "ornaments of speech" may be attributed to their choiceness; that they are tolerated in objectual [*gegenständlich*] contexts, however, cannot be taken for granted. For in any such context, metaphor is first and foremost a disturbance. If we consider consciousness as it is "affected" by texts—as a structure in which in-

---

zu einer Metaphorologie," appeared first as a special issue of the *Archiv für Begriffsgeschichte* 6 (1960): 7–142.]

tentionality is achieved, as phenomenology has it—then any metaphor endangers its "normal harmony."[3]

In the functional transition from mere intending to fulfilled intuition, metaphor constitutes a heterogeneous element and it refers
to a context that is different from the one at hand. Now, discursive
(that is, not only temporally isolated) consciousness is perhaps nothing but the "repair" of a disturbance, the overcoming of a dysfunc-
tion in the stimulus-response system that has proved so successful
organically. In this way, only the synthetic processing of stimulus
manifolds into "objects"—as complexes that can be determined not
only through signs but through properties—has made object-related
behavior possible. To offset its own disharmonies, to find a way
back to the harmony of data as those of *one* experience remains the
constitutive achievement of consciousness, by which it reassures itself that it is following reality, not illusions.

Metaphor, however, is at first a "conflict in harmony" [*Wider-
stimmigkeit*], to use Husserl's term.[4] This would be fatal for consciousness, which is left to care for its own identity; it has to be the
constantly successful organ of self-restitution. From that follows,
also and especially for metaphor, the rule that Husserl articulated:
"Anomaly, as a break in the originally harmonious unity of appearance, is integrated into a higher normality."[5] The element that is
initially destructive only *becomes* metaphor under the duress of having to repair the imperiled consistency. Metaphor is integrated into
intentionality through the device of reinterpretation. To declare the
exotic foreign body a "mere metaphor" is an act of self-assertion:
the disturbance is qualified as an aid. In experience, this corresponds
to the necessity to incorporate even the most surprising appearance
bordering on a supposed "miracle" into the total causal system.

---

3. [Edmund Husserl, *Die Krisis der europäischen Wissenschaften und die
transzendentale Phänomenologie* (The Hague: Nijhoff, 1976), 464. This addendum is not part of the English translation of Husserl.]

4. [Edmund Husserl, *Formale und transzendenzale Logik* (The Hague: Nijhoff, 1974), 510. This addendum is not part of the English translation.]

5. [Edmund Husserl, *Zur Phänomenologie der Intersubjektivität: Texte aus
dem Nachlass*, vol. 3 (The Hague: Nijhoff, 1973), 438.]

To follow Quintilian's much-belabored example, it is an accident within the smooth processing of information if the intention aimed at a meadow—surprisingly and outside the scope of typical expectations—jumps over to the predicate, so that this meadow now laughs: *pratum ridet.*[6] The text's ability to achieve something seems all over now until the "excuse" arrives that no possible series of the thing's literal predicates that were at first expected could ever be able to convey such information about a meadow that is encapsulated in the expression of its laughter. Such an expression would have no place within any descriptive language. Yet it would also be wrong to say that we are here faced with poetry *in nuce*, no matter how many poets have made meadows laugh.

What does not appear in the properties of a meadow from an objective perspective, but is neither the subjective nor the imaginative addition of a spectator who only for himself could make out the shape of a human face from the meadow's surface (a mandatory game for visits to limestone caves), is arrested by metaphor. It achieves this feat by assigning the meadow to the inventory of a human life-world in which not only words and signs but the things themselves carry "meanings." Its anthropogenetic primal type may be the human face with its unequalled situative meaning. Montaigne provided the metaphor for this meaning-content of metaphor: *le visage du monde* [the face of the world].[7]

It was one of the most laborious reconstructions of theoretical language to retrace what the expression "landscape" denotes.[8] Metaphor reclaims a primordiality in which not only the private and leisurely provinces of our experience are rooted—the worlds of flaneurs or poets—but also the dissecting aspects of the theoretical attitude

---

6. ["The meadow laughs." The example is, in fact, not Quintilian's; Blumenberg may have found it in Ernst Robert Curtius's *European Literature and the Latin Middle Ages* (Princeton, NJ: Princeton University Press, 1953), 128, where it is introduced together with Quintilian as a stand-in for the whole rhetorical tradition.]

7. [Michel de Montaigne, "Of Custom," in *The Complete Essays*, trans. Donald M. Frame (Stanford, CA: Stanford University Press, 1965), 83.]

8. [Blumenberg here likely refers to Joachim Ritter, "Landschaft: Zur Funktion der Ästhetik in der modernen Gesellschaft," in *Subjektivität* (Frankfurt am Main: Suhrkamp, 1974).]

that are alienated through technical language. For this attitude, Quintilian's meadow is no laughing matter. And yet, what laughter means for us was not only once "carried over" [*übertragen*] onto a meadow but as this meaning, "laughing," it has been enriched and "fulfilled" by being able to return in the life-world. In the life-world, there must always have been relationships of retransferring intuition in order that the stress that metaphor puts on consciousness could be borne.

Hence the validity of Wittgenstein's 1929 dictum, "A good simile refreshes the intellect."[9] Refreshment is itself a metaphor here, an antithesis to the equally metaphorical exhaustion: the simile reveals more than what is already in that for which it has been chosen. The parallel case is true for hermeneutics, but in the opposite direction: it is not that the full interpretation enriches the text beyond the knowledge the author has brought to bear on it; rather, the foreign reference unpredictably contributes to the productivity of texts. The imprecision of metaphor, of which the rigorous self-exacerbation of theoretical language has become contemptuous, corresponds in another way to the highest level of abstraction of concepts—like "being," "history," "world"—that do not cease to impress us. Metaphor, however, conserves the richness of its origins, which abstraction must deny.

The more we remove ourselves from the short distance of intentionality that can be fulfilled and instead refer to total horizons that our experience can no longer traverse or delimit, the more impressive the use of metaphor becomes; the "absolute metaphor" is thus a boundary value. "The hushed, black woods are dreaming"[10] is another case of the "laughing meadow," but in the case of the woods, we are already accustomed, once we have entered into it, not to see it for the trees. Here, then, is a "leap" in our intuition. In this respect, the world is a forest that we never perceive except when standing in it—*in hac silva plena* [in this forest full of woe],[11] Marsilio Ficino says—and that we always miss for the trees. The

---

9. [Ludwig Wittgenstein, *Culture and Value: A Selection from the Posthumous Remains*, rev. 2nd ed., ed. Georg Henrik von Wright (Oxford: Blackwell, 1998), 3.]

10. [Matthias Claudius, "Evening Song," *A Harvest of German Verse*, ed. Margarete Münsterberg (New York: Appleton, 1916), 39.]

11. [*The Letters of Marsilio Ficino*, vol. 1 (London: Shepheard-Walwyn, 1975), 181.]

absolute metaphors that have been found for the world do not dissolve into qualities and determinable properties as this superordinate wood does into trees. And yet it is the wood in which one gets lost, according to Descartes's simile, and has to decide to follow a *morale par provision* [provisional morality], precisely *because* one does not possess a total view of it (for which Descartes's theoretic program nevertheless allows).

The world may be everything that is the case, thus vindicating its old definition as a *series rerum* [series of things]; a Cartesian, driven by the demand for clarity and distinctness, could never be satisfied with this. Above all, it would be pretty much what, of all that can be said of the world and as unarguable it may be, is the least interesting—as little to the cosmologist as to the theologian, or even to those who are fed up with interpreting the world and ready to set about changing it. That the world is a book in which one can read or, after some arduous deciphering, will eventually be able to read, is a metaphorical expectation about the type of experience. The life-worldly attitude before any theory and below any theory in our history can hardly be imagined without it, and for this alone one must keep an eye on it, because it reveals the pure use-value of the world that is mediated through the instrument of science as a secondary sense of direction of theoretical conduct. The excitement, with which circumstances are received in which there is once again something to "decipher" in nature, or which even seem to reintroduce the relationship between writing and reader into the process of nature, is atavistic.

The "book of nature" is, after all, not only a collection of references for topos research. It also provides an orientation for inquiring from the factual status of theoretical dealings with the world back toward the life-worldly imbuing with meaning that underlies it. It would be pure romanticism to do this with a view to renewing the position of the reader of the world book. Rather, it is about the pure suspension of the present as obviousness, which to the contemporaries will always seem like the last word to be said on the topic. It is also about the suspension of expectations of meaning that are of a specificity that can only be grasped metaphorically, and whose unsatisfiability, which one does not want to believe, already predetermines disappointment.

One feels that there is something suggestive in all metaphorics, which makes it the preferred element of rhetoric understood as that agreement that is solicited where univocity is not or cannot be reached. Losses are factored into the process of cognition. The definition of time as what is measured with a clock appears sound and is highly pragmatic when it comes to avoiding disputes. But is that what we have deserved since we began to ask what time is?

That time is no discursive concept is part of Kant's defensive move that allows him to make it, by way of Newton's absolute time, the a priori form of the inner sense. But when Kant uses the definition of time as an argument in his "Refutation of Idealism" in the second edition of the *Critique of Pure Reason*,[12] it becomes clear that even with him the metaphorics of space are at the bottom of the intuition of time and cannot be eliminated from it. It may be that this has to do with certain facts about the brain in which genetically the achievements of representing space are older than those of representing time.

Then again: Is even the notion of the *fluxus temporis*, of the stream of time, a necessary metaphorics? Is the commonality of, on the one hand, the absolute metaphor of the stream for consciousness and, on the other, for the constitution of time the guiding thread according to which phenomenology declares time to be the originary structure of consciousness?[13] Does the application of the principle of the inertia of substance onto this figuration allow for the extra step made by Otto Liebman, who "imagines" the "I" as "the resting shore or rather the fixed island past which flows the stream of events, the *fluxus temporis*"?[14]

---

12. [Immanuel Kant, *Critique of Pure Reason*, trans. Paul Guyer and Allen W. Wood (Cambridge: Cambridge University Press, 1998), 326–333 (B 274–9).]

13. [Edmund Husserl, *The Phenomenology of Internal Time Consciousness*, trans. James S. Churchill (Bloomington: Indiana University Press, 1964).]

14. [Otto Liebmann, "Geist der Transcendentalphilosophie," in *Gedanken und Thatsachen: Philosophische Abhandlungen, Aphorismen und Studien* (Strasbourg: Trübner, 1904), 2:15.]

Finally, we need the historical reminder that the metaphor of the stream of time took a destructive turn against Francis Bacon's assurance that truth would be the daughter of time, a belief that allows this stream to transport to our factual standpoint only that which was light enough not to sink into the river—the metaphorical self-evidence for the failure of tradition faced with the burden of truth.

Across the portal of Camille Flammarion's observatory in Juvisy is written *Ad veritatem per scientiam* [To truth through science]. Today, one would hardly write this across the portal of a university or a scientific institution. Why not? It seems the saying assumes that the truth at which one wants to arrive is not identical to the science through which one wants to arrive at it. There is a difference with regard to which our expectations must be called extraordinarily vague and imprecise, and, despite all specifications in the scientific world, almost confused. In other words, we no longer know exactly why we undertook the whole enormous enterprise of science in the first place—regardless of all the services it performs for the viability of our world, which make it almost indispensable for it. This truth apparently is something that cannot be and probably never has been expressed in the language of science through which this truth is supposed to be reachable.

Seen from the topic of the life-world, metaphor is, especially in its rhetorically precisely defined short form, something late and derivative. If it does not want to limit itself to the achievements of metaphor for concept formation but become the guideline for regarding the life-world, a metaphorology cannot do without being integrated into the wider horizon of a theory of nonconceptuality. That one can speak of the "laughing meadow" is a poetic suggestion only because its aesthetic evidence lies in the notion that all saw it without having been able to say it. The homelessness of metaphor in a world determined by disciplined experience can be grasped in the discomfort encountered in everything that does not meet the standard of a language approaching objective univocity—unless it qualifies, according to the countertendency, as "aesthetic." This attribute grants the final, and thus completely uninhibiting, license for ambiguity.

Under the title of nonconceptuality, one has at least to reckon with the expectation that even the class of the unsayable is not empty. Granted, Wittgenstein's *Tractatus*, which begins with the sentence "The world is all that is the case," does end with a prohibition regarding what is not the case or of which it cannot be said unambiguously that it is the case: "What we cannot speak about we must pass over in silence."[15] This is, however, the prohibition of confusing the unsayable and the sayable. All that is the case has an unambiguous degree of linguistic availability, the scope of which does not, however, coincide with what can be experienced. Otherwise he would not have written immediately before the final prohibition: "There are, indeed, things that cannot be put into words. They *make themselves manifest.* They are what is mystical."[16] This is the nonchalant statement of a relic, which, since it does not fall under the definition of reality, is, as it were, homeless. It shares this exoticism with the "meaning of the world" that must be situated outside of this world, and even with the definition of the mystical, which is located in *that*, not *how*, the world is.

The counterposition has been articulated by Paul Valéry, one of the few modern poets of whom it can be said without exaggeration that they also were significant thinkers, in his play *Mon Faust*: "Only the ineffable is of any importance."[17] After all, it holds for Wittgenstein as well that even if all possible questions regarding what is the case could be answered, "the problems of life [would] remain completely untouched."[18] Between the life-world and the world of theoretical states of affairs, there could then be no context of justification. The situation after all scientific questions are answered is peculiarly that of the sentence: "Of course there are then no questions left, and this itself is the answer."[19] The philosopher, Wittgenstein

---

15. [Ludwig Wittgenstein, *Tractatus Logico-Philosophicus* (London: Routledge, 2001), 5; 89.]

16. [Wittgenstein, *Tractatus Logico-Philosophicus*, 89.]

17. [Paul Valéry, "My Faust," *Plays* (Princeton, NJ: Princeton University Press, 1971), 94.]

18. [Wittgenstein, *Tractatus*, 88.]

19. [Wittgenstein, 88.]

later writes in his *Philosophical Investigations*, treats a question like an illness.[20]

The boundary values of sayability and unsayability lie even further apart than those of definitional determinacy and imaginative sketching-out. It is not the existence of correlates of alleged speechlessness that is descriptively at issue, but that of the effort belonging to the history of our consciousness to represent unsayability itself linguistically. I once described this by means of the paradigm of the "explosive metaphorics"[21] that occurs in the tradition of the mystical *via negationis* [way of negation], that is, in those self-portrayals of the elementary perplexity that riddles every theology—having to speak of God incessantly without presuming to dare say anything about him. Nicholas of Cusa made this perplexity a speculative means of representing his *coincidentia oppositorum* [unity of opposites]. He invented the explosive metaphor of the circle whose radius approaches infinity and thus produces a circumference with an infinitely small curvature so that the circle's arc coincides with its tangent. Here, the intentionality of intuition is over-expanded in order that its futility be expressed in itself, so that the anticipation [*Vorgriff*] performs the retraction of the trespass [*Übergriff*].

It may be surprising still to find modern references for this eminently medieval pattern of expression. Georg Simmel elucidated a particular aspect of the modern consciousness of history in one of his journal fragments by amending Nietzsche's concept of the eternal recurrence of the same into an explosive metaphor: "The world process strikes me as the turning of an enormous wheel, but understood as the premise of the eternal recurrence. But the result, the actual repetition at some point of the identical, is not the same—for the wheel has an infinitely large radius; only once an infinite amount of time has elapsed—that is, never—can it reach the same point again. And yet it is a wheel that turns, which, in its ideal, aims at the exhaustion of qualitative manifoldness without ever exhaust-

---

20. [Ludwig Wittgenstein, *Philosophical Investigations*, 4th ed. (Malden: Wiley-Blackwell, 2009), 98.]

21. [Blumenberg, *Paradigms*, 123.]

ing it in reality."[22] Nothing is left of the "sad necessity" of metaphor of which the Enlightenment thinker could speak. Even a desperate effort, something hitherto unspoken and believed to be
unspeakable—not a sentence about a state of affairs, but about the
totality of all states of affairs—can be an incomparable gain, which
the author may have seen under the commandment of silence, although he is no stranger to using paradoxes for the ambiguity of
"life" in his published texts. There is a border zone of language in
which the act of writing something down would be equal to feeling
ashamed before the public, without the claim of having perceived
something being withdrawn. Naturally, a philosophy that discovered the theme of "life" had to make the early linguistic experiences
of Heraclitus all over again.

The boundary value of the mystical in this context is only a *pro
memoria* item [*Erinnerungsposten*] of the fact that the nonconceptual is not congruent with intuitiveness. It is not true that myth was
the home of intuition before the odyssey of abstraction. The mythical sentence that everything is surrounded and descended from the
okeanos is, after all, no more intuitive than the sentence that everything came to be from water. Both sentences have their difficulties
in being executed as instructions to our faculty of imagination. Nevertheless, this "translation" of Thales of Miletus is so momentous
because a sentence appears here that wants to be taken as a response
to a question. This is largely foreign to myth, even if the Enlightenment would have liked to see it as the epitome of naive answers to
the same questions that science had attended to in the meantime
with incomparable success.

To avoid the pitfalls of myth theories at least in this instance, I
shall try to look more closely at one of the most consequential sentences of a mythical quality ever created, that of the Revelation to
John: "The devil . . . knows that his time is short."[23] Since we know
how strong an effect this sentence had until very recently among

---

22. [Georg Simmel, "Aus dem nachgelassenen Tagebuche," *Postume Veröffentlichungen* (Frankfurt am Main: Suhrkamp, 2004), 263.]
23. [Revelation 12:12.]

religiously awakened emigrants, as Ernst Benz has shown,[24] one is tempted to attribute this out of hand to the intuitiveness of mythical sentences. But this assumption does not withstand closer scrutiny. The apocalyptic-visionary author may have had an image of what the devil looks like; the reader has to take it from elsewhere— for instance, from his experiences with the paintings of more than a millennium later. But what it meant for John's contemporaries to learn that time was short for this devil completely eludes intuition: time, what time? That of the clock, of the calendar, of history? Short or long in relationship to what? It is astonishing how little material the exegesis of this sentences has yielded for filling the imaginative void. Nevertheless, it is hardly tied to the cultural conditions of its origin; it could be translated into any language using a different name. At the same time, however, it strikes one that this sentence must have transformed the sense of the world [*Weltgefühl*]. Its warning comes indirectly because it does not tell humans the same old story that their time is short but asserts it of another who can be counted on to summon up the utmost of his abilities to use his time to deprive everybody else of it. It is a one-sentence myth that does not even get our imagination going but is merely a formula for something that could not have been expressed conceptually: the power determined to do harm to mankind is itself under the pressure of time. What comes next was expressed by the evangelist Luke, again in a one-sentence myth, as the vision of the expired reprieve: "I saw Satan fall like lightning from heaven."[25]

In the service of conceptual history, metaphorology has categorized and described the perplexities that arise in the preliminary stage of concept formation, in the vicinity of the hard core of clear and distinct determinateness, and even in complete distance from it. A historical phenomenology, however, must also attend to the degenerate forms that appear after speech has been taken literally as the perplexity in the face of the claim to realism. Theological

---

24.   [Ernst Benz, "Akzeleration der Zeit als geschichtliches und heilsgeschichtliches Problem," *Akademie der Wissenschaften und Literatur in Mainz. Abhandlungen der geistes- und sozialwissenschaftlichen Klasse* 2 (1977): 3–56.]

25.   [Luke 10:18.]

Christology, in its opposition to docetisms of all kinds, invented stringent types of realism that were previously unknown, or at least could not be articulated rigorously, when dealing with myths and their allegoreses, with epiphanies and metamorphoses whose seriousness was variously indeterminate. The realism of the incarnation turned away indignantly from the Gnostic insistence that God in his historical appearance had only passed through human form as water runs through a pipe. The background of the nonbinding handling of mythologemes forced the dogmatic codification of a rigorism of finality for the salvific union of God and man. But the exegetical arts of multiplying scriptural meaning already softened this realism; metaphor is the form of language that eschews realism's strict demands.

Anyone who does not want to observe the crisis symptoms of the late Middle Ages in the increasing metaphorization of theological dogmatics can study this avoidance of difficulties in the repeated metaphorization in our own century after the phase of excessive demands made by dialectical theology. Demythologization is for a good part nothing but remetaphorization: the punctual *kerygma* [proclamation of salvation through Jesus] radiates a corona of linguistic forms that no longer need to be taken at their word. Dogmatic realism had "understood" what resurrection was supposed to mean; as an absolute metaphor for the certainty of salvation, it is something of which one may say that it had better remain nonunderstood.

Reduction to indeterminateness is indeed a peculiarity of sacral texts, which survive by fending off banal literalism because they are credited with something that cannot be examined as to what it may in fact be. To trace church language back to a vernacular delivers every text up to being interrogated defenselessly. In order not to make use of Latin again, I ask what would become of the chorales of Paul Gerhardt if one were to subject them to translation from German into German. It is their art, not their sacral content, that protects them from this.

Metaphor can thus also be late form. In the history of science, a striking example of this is molecularism's loss of reality in the nineteenth century. For it had, since Laplace, been expected to show that the microstructure of matter would prove to be a repetition of the macrostructure of the universe, and thus a field of application for Newton's dynamics. Molecularism emerges at a time that admitted no hope for solving the problem of material microstructure empirically; it is an expression of the economic assumption that the solar system represents the simplest building principle of all physical systems. In the other direction, for clarifying the construction of cosmic supersystems of the type of the Milky Way, this hypothesis had already, as the "Copernican Comparative," proved a successful and empirically justifiable projection.[26] Thus, adopting the identical procedure for the underworld of the ultimately invisible seemed to be the application of a unified world principle. Analogy is the realism of metaphor.

What destroyed this realism of molecular solar systems was, at first, positivism and its reduction of all physical questions to those of pure analysis modeled on the rational mechanics of Euler and Lagrange; what continued this destruction was, absurdly, the generosity of Maxwell, in interpreting Faraday's "lines of force," to allow understanding to make use of any physical analogy. This was his conclusion from the insight that the positivists' demand—the demand that a scientific statement contain nothing but differential equations and reality itself be structured mathematically—had come no nearer to reality than the molecularists' Newtonian systems. These were not antithetical theories but changing occupations of the positions of the "scientific metaphor."[27] Human thought, Maxwell wrote, can move in the sphere of pure positivity only by means of an intermediary; it certainly cannot be satisfied without deploying a metaphor for the symbolism of calculus.

Undoubtedly, this procedure was governed by the principle of insufficient reason.[28] Thus, Wittgenstein would later describe philos-

---

26. [See the fourth part, "The Copernican Comparative," of Hans Blumenberg's *The Genesis of the Copernican World* (Cambridge, MA: MIT Press, 1987).]

27. [James Clerk Maxwell, "Address to the Mathematical and Physical Sections of the British Association," *The Scientific Papers*, vol. 2, ed. W. D. Niven (Cambridge: Cambridge University Press, 1890; reprint, New York: Dover, 1965), 227; English in the original.]

28. [See Hans Blumenberg, "An Anthropological Approach to the Contemporary Significance of Rhetoric," in this volume.]

ophy as based on the preference for similes without adequate justification for their choice. Indeed, he writes, a much greater proportion of the opposition between humans is based on the "preference for certain similes" than one would think.[29]

It seems natural to object that metaphorology and still more a theory of nonconceptuality deals in irrational decisions and reduces man to Buridan's ass. Even if that were the case, it would not produce but only describe this state of affairs. But when this theory goes back to the genesis of that state of affairs and analyzes it with regard to needs and motivations, something comes to pass that I would like to call the rationalization of deficiency. It consists in supplementing the consideration of how much we ought to achieve [*wir . . . leisten sollen*] in fulfilling consciousness' intentionality with the more anthropological consideration of how much fulfillment we can afford [*wir uns . . . leisten können*].

In a fragment first published in 1959 by Helmut Sembdner, Kleist proposed dividing humanity into two classes: "(1) those who are adept at metaphor, and (2) those who are adept at formula."[30] Those who understand both are too few to constitute a class. It looks like there is an exclusive alternative in this typology. But in fact we cannot take recourse to metaphors where formulae are possible. We can afford the abundance of metaphors that our rhetoric produces only because the power of formulae determines our latitude for what goes beyond the bare securing of our existence, and therefore also for what metaphors offer us in going beyond formulae. Above all, formulae ensure that a process's initial state can be linked to arbitrary final states without presupposing any empirical objectivity for the intermediate field or the totality. Nonconceptuality wants more than the "form" of processes or states, it wants their *Gestalt*. But it would be premature to see in this the offer to decide between intuitiveness and abstraction, which are, in any case, not identical with metaphor or formula, symbol or concept. They

---

29. [Ludwig Wittgenstein, *Culture and Value*, ed. G. H. von Wright, trans. Peter Winch (Chicago: University of Chicago Press, 1980), 20e.]

30. [Kleist, *Sämtliche Werke*, vol. 3, ed. Roland Reuß and Peter Staengle (Basel: Stroemfeld, 1999), 555.]

stand in a complex and often contrary relation particularly to intuition.

What unites concepts and symbols is their indifference to the presence of what they enjoin us to imagine. While concepts potentially tend toward intuition and remain dependent on it, symbols, in a reverse motion, detach themselves from what they stand for. It may be that the capacity for making symbols arose from the inability to make an image, as Freud suspects;[31] or from magic with its technical desire to dispose of reality as a whole by investigating a splinter of this reality; or from the disposition to the conditional reflex, in which a concomitant circumstance of the real stimulus assumes and retains the stimulus function itself. What matters is that this elementary organ of the relationship to the world makes it possible to turn away from perception and representation as a free disposition over that which is not present. The operability of the symbol is what distinguishes it from imagination [*Vorstellung*] as well as depiction [*Abbildung*]: not only does the flag represent the state that has chosen its color sequence, but it can, in contrast to the state, be captured or disgraced, shown in the position of mourning or of sporting victory, misused for some ends and held aloft for others.

For a long time, this capacity for intertwining the heterogeneous inhibited understanding what happens in human cognition and that it is not subject to the obvious but also contradictory evidence of the proverb "like through like." It may have been the first absolute metaphor of philosophy when Heraclitus described thought as "fire," not only because to him fire was the divine element but because it has the quality of constantly absorbing the alien and transforming it into itself. Atomism misunderstood this to mean that fire atoms are spherically shaped, and that the sphere contains all other atomic shapes and is therefore the most accurate representation of the soul's properties of motion and cognition. Only the concept of the symbol—partly prefigured by the concept of the symptom in ancient medicine—allows what happens in perception and cognition to be grasped. The secondary qualities of the senses do not depict what, as such, is not

---

31. [Sigmund Freud, *The Interpretation of Dreams*, trans. David Strachey (New York: Basic Books, 1955), chap. 6.]

in the thing, just as the external symptoms do not depict the internal diseases; both only achieve what they do because the connection with what they refer to is stable.

Money, by way of its connection with a rare substance, sought to represent value, with the idea of which, however, it needs only to be linked in a reliable manner, for instance by means of the state's guarantee of its acceptance. But the symbol is powerless to communicate anything about its reference object. It stands for the nonrepresentable without helping to reach it. It maintains this distance to constitute a sphere of nonobjectual correlates of thought—the sphere of what can be symbolically represented—between object and subject. This is the possibility of the effect of mere ideas, of the idea as the epitome of possibilities such as that of value.

Or that of "being." Do we really understand what Heidegger's question of fundamental ontology—the question concerning the "meaning of being"—was supposed to mean? We proceed here as with any other question about "meaning" by using a substitution. When, for example, we ask about the meaning of history, we unconsciously replace what we have asked about with something else by attributing a purpose to the course of history, and by locating this purpose in an ultimate state of the historical process that justifies everything prior to it. For the question of the meaning of being, this does not work, because that which is to be established by asking is clearly not subject to change, at least as long as the "history of being" does not yet exist. The device that helps in this situation is the assertion that the question need not be answered with reference to its subject matter at all. Rather, we already have this answer, and in fact are ourselves nothing but the possession of that answer. This would mean a further increase of the Platonic *anamnesis* [recollection], with the difference that this possession manifests itself not in concepts but in the structure of consciousness itself and the behavior founded on it. The reframing of the question of being by way of concepts avoids the path of the Platonic *anamnesis* by making the understanding of being into the essence of *Dasein* without having to say what logical "form" it has. Nonconceptuality here means that we thoroughly experience what the understanding of being is *not*.

Thus, the answer to the question of being can be seen as the radical of our ways of conduct, as the epitome of its implications and of these implications' implications. This is why *Dasein*'s being is care, the implication of care is time, the implication of time is being. Such an answer does not refer to any of the objects we know, or to their totality as a world like the one in which we live. That *Dasein* is "being-in-the-world" indeed means that the world of this "being-in" does not consist of "objects," but nor can it be grasped in metaphors.

It only takes a small supplementary theory to make us understand why this possession could be hidden from us for so long and with such disastrous consequences. It is the additional theorem of the inauthenticity of our existence; only later did Heidegger remodel it into a component in his concept of a history of being, which wanted to comprehend what he previously called "inauthentic" as an episode of the concealment of being—or rather, the self-concealment of being. As a historical fatality, its consequences are worse than when it was still unredeemed authenticity. It has ordained that scientific reason should be blind to the origin of its possibility in a world-relation.

Heidegger set up his question of being as an enemy of positive science, an enmity supposedly more profound than that between intuition and concepts, between metaphor and formulae. But what is also true for this relation and what the evaluative inclinations in this field cannot overlook is this: the question of the "meaning of being" is able to concern or preoccupy us only because it neither decides nor even affects the question for the conditions of *Dasein*.

At first, the artifice of accepting the answer to the question of being as always already given presupposed a link between *Dasein* and that about which it asks. From this, results a coupling of *Dasein* and being that is so constitutively nonobjectual, both lifelong and life-deep, that one could become the symbol for the other, or rather: the foundation of all symbols. What I called "implication" as the schema of the methodological context of the existential analytic and ontology is at the same time a prohibition of metaphorics, including absolute metaphors. Metaphorically, nothing can be "represented" if all elemental behaviors toward the world have their original wholeness in care, whose ontological meaning lies in temporality, and which, in turn, is probably the unfolded horizon of a final radicalism, the designation of which may be arbitrarily interchangeable. For them, a strict prohibition of metaphors once applied; the language of the "history of being" proves that it could not be upheld.

Likewise, what is expressed by the word "freedom" falls under the verdict of being a metaphor. Because it can only be approached "as a necessary presupposition of reason," Kant says that freedom is an idea. Not only is there no experience of the reality of freedom, but also no possible way of intuiting its idea. For it alone Kant explicitly denies the mere possibility of symbolization—in the sense in which he used the term "symbol" closely to that of absolute metaphor—"because no example of anything analogous can ever be put under it."[32] But the danger of an absolute metaphor for the idea of freedom is perceptible in Kant himself and its serious, necessarily misleading consequences can be discerned in the way he introduces the transcendental concept of action. It suggests understanding as freedom everything that can be represented as a transcendental action of the understanding.

Kant presented the synthesis of the transcendental apperception as a process of the understanding, and the categories as its final regulating instances. Can this, with regard to the concept of action in the theory of practical reason, already or still be called "action"? The theory of practical reason may and must presuppose the identity of a subject that is the condition of all possible responsibility and accountability. The theory of theoretical reason is not capable of doing this; it shows the identity of the subject precisely *in statu nascendi* [in the state of being born]. The understanding is not the subject that makes use of procedures in its actions; instead, it is nothing but the epitome of this regulated procedure. If we take the linguistic distinction of the understanding from such "actions" at its word, then the whole critique of reason, not only that of practical reason (which as such, of course, is theoretical), becomes practical. If,

---

32. [Immanuel Kant, *Groundwork of the Metaphysics of Morals*, trans. Mary Gregor (Cambridge: Cambridge University Press, 1997), 63.]

then, everything is practical and nothing theoretical anymore, this may offer reassurance to all, but leave them none the wiser for it.

Nothing is gained for an understanding of freedom as the conditioning ground of morality if one is told that the synthesis of representations is "already" an action of the understanding. This misunderstanding, however, is older than its later inventors believe. It is already part of Simmel's much-admired interpretation of Kant and his subsequent attempt, in his philosophy of history, to extract from it something against deterministic historism. Humans would then "make" their history in freedom, or in more freedom, because the synthesis of their representations would be an "action" of their understanding. Yet this is just an absolute metaphor taken at its word, leading us astray.

Translated by Hannes Bajohr

11

THEORY OF NONCONCEPTUALITY

(circa 1975, excerpt)

Concepts are thought to be a product of reason, if not its triumph, and they most probably are. This does not permit the reverse, however: that reason is only to be found where reality, life, or being—whatever one wants to call the totality—is articulated conceptually, be it successfully or at least with the intent of succeeding.

There is no identity between reason and concepts, although it would of course be nonsense to say that the intention of reason was completely disconnected from the achievement of concepts. It is possible that the achievement of concepts is only a part of the intention of reason, which always seems to have something to do with totality.

Concepts do have something to do with the absence of their object. This can also mean: they have to do with the lack of the completed representation [*Vorstellung*] of the object. This relationship

Excerpted from Hans Blumenberg, *Theorie der Unbegrifflichkeit*, ed. Anselm Haverkamp (Frankfurt am Main: Suhrkamp, 2007).

has been compared to that between different sense organs: seeing only substitutes for the possibility of touch, of feeling, and thus of possession. Optical presence anticipates tactile presence, even when it forgoes the latter. Visibility is the lack of tangibility due to the distance from the object. If one imagines the distance to be further increased—in space or in time—all that is left is the concept, which in turn substitutes for the entire spectrum of what can sensually be accessed.

One could say that reason is the epitome of such achievements at a distance—the integration of that which already lies within a concept as the substitution of presence and hence also of that which cannot at all become present because it does not have the quality of being an object, such as the world, the ego, time, space (ideas—rules as if they were objects).

Schopenhauer was of the opinion that through reason we had a "a complete view of life independent of time. We always have, so to speak, a reduced, colourless, abstract, mathematical sketch of the entire world."[1]

Concepts may not be surrogates but they are, to the chagrin of the philosophical expectations invested in it, not the fulfillment of the intentions of reason, but merely the transitional stage in which it takes its bearings.

I try to understand this anthropologically and genetically. Man, the creature that raises itself upright and leaves behind the close range of perception, is the creature of *actio per distans* [action at a distance]. He acts on things he does not perceive. In the caves, which are his first shelter, he paints on the wall the objects of his desire and of his struggle for existence. Concepts emerge in the life of creatures who are hunters and nomads. Maybe one could best elucidate what concepts achieve by thinking of the fabrication of a trap: it is in all its aspects prepared with the shape and dimensions, the behavior and way of movement of an object in mind that is only expected, not present, and yet to be brought into one's grasp and

---

1. Arthur Schopenhauer, *Manuscript Remains in Four Volumes* (New York: Berg, 1988), 1:105.

possession. This thing again stands in reference to needs that are not immediate, that possess a temporal aspect. An anthropological theory of concepts is an urgent desideratum, for it alone allows for a functional reflection of both the achievements of concepts as well as its falling behind of demands that do not directly arise from a nomadic lifestyle but require the leisure of sedentarism: we are faced with the strange state of affairs that concepts are indeed a product of the hunter and nomad's form of life but that theory, which appears to be the epitome of concepts' achievements, presupposes urban sedentarism and the division of labor.

Concepts are not capable of everything that reason demands. Not only is there a hiatus between the highest developmental level of concepts and the claims of reason but it needs to be considered whether the consummation of a concept interferes with or even inhibits the claims of reason. Using the Cartesian characterization of concepts, Lichtenberg expressed this as follows: "To tune down distinct concepts to clear ones."[2] What could this mean? The terms "clear" and "distinct" belong, according to Descartes's characterization that was so definitive for the modern age, to the initially representational and then conceptual first rule of the *Discourse on Method*. It is the ideal of complete objectification [*Vergegenständlichung*], and, on this basis, that of the completion of terminology. Attaining this ideal would mean that the final state of a philosophical language as purely conceptual, in the strict sense, had been reached. Just as there would no longer be a provisional morality, nothing provisional would any longer be possible with such concepts. What these two terms signify is what Edmund Husserl, the last Cartesian, called the "universality of the coincidence between speech and thinking."[3]

Concepts developed from the *actio per distans*, from action across spatial *and* temporal distance. As concerns temporal distance, it is easy to see the difference between the determinateness that a story

---

2. [Georg Christoph Lichtenberg, *Schriften und Briefe*, ed. Wolfgang Promies, vol. 1, *Sudelbücher, Fragmente, Fabeln, Verse* (Frankfurt am Main: Zweitausendeins, 1994), 270.]

3. Edmund Husserl, *Formal and Transcendental Logic*, trans. Dorion Cairns (The Hague: Nijhoff, 1969), 24.

about past events can assume (names and the detailed description of occurrences can be sufficient for it) and what kind of intertwining between indeterminacy and the limitation produced by typification is needed to articulate an expectation that refers to approaching and possible events and objects. Concepts must possess enough indeterminacy in order still to grasp these approaching experiences in such a way that expedient attitudes toward them can then be adopted even if—on the level of detailed, full specificity—there are small deviations from past experiences. Concepts require a latitude for all the concrete that is to be subjected to its classification. They admittedly need to have enough distinctness to exclude what is altogether irrelevant, but their exclusivity must not be as narrow as the name needs to be, referring to the individual and its identity, its identifiability. In this respect, concepts are not so much the instruments of a creature that is capable of memory but one that is attuned to preemption [*Prävention*]: it seeks to cope with what is not yet immediately at hand. Understood anthropologically and genetically, the ideal of concepts' distinctness refers to the elasticity of the latitude within which a concretely perceived or imagined creature is still supposed to be admitted to everything that is, with regard to attitudes and precautions, typical of action and that is inherent, prepared, or prefigured in experience.

The ideal of clarity has its origin in spatial distance. This is a question not of determining tolerances within which something can still be recognized and acknowledged as something, but of the premises of this act with regard to the obstacles that are posed by the variations of the view brought about through spatial proximity or distance—particularly, too, by those optical obscurations that are the consequences of leading a life depending on a medium, an atmosphere. Life and optics rely on opposite preconditions: the ideal of optics is empty space that does not allow for any obstruction of light; the precondition of life is a certain density of the medium in which breathing is still possible. The ideal of clarity has in its origin something to do with this antinomy of the optical situation.

The preemptive creature is not necessarily a social creature. Anthropologically, it must be assumed that humans stem from a line of primates in which by the prevalent tendency toward flight behavior all the specializations for close combat body-to-body have been lost; instead, it was gaining space that always bestowed benefits in terms of survival. In preemptive behavior, the advantage of gaining space is connected with the pressures resulting from the loss of the specializations for close physical combat. The pivotal situation of this development can only be one in which flight cannot be continued at will, where the flight animal was confronted with the necessity to hold out against its pursuer despite its lack of physiological equipment for body-to-body combat. The compromise consists of the *actio per distans*, the action of throwing. It is not by accident that human history is dominated by projectiles and throwing devices.

If we imagine preemption not so much as an immediate necessity but as a conception, a project, or a planned order that has at one point been understood in its capacities, then the extension of preemptive behavior leads by necessity to the creation of societies. The flight animal that defends itself across spatial and temporal distances may have not yet become an organic system capable of close combat, but it has become one that itself applies and extends its learned abilities in the hunt for its prey. The trap, too, is an action in the absence of both the prey and, at a temporal remove, the hunter. The trap acts on behalf of the hunter in the moment in which he himself is absent but the prey is present, while constructing the trap displays the inverse relationship. It is expectation turned object. Since one has to return to traps to monitor and enjoy their success, they require a certain degree of sedentarism. The trap also represents the very tolerance between exactness and inexactness of its reference object that can only be created by way of concepts. One need only think of the still current significance of a fishing net's mesh size, on which depend both the quality of the current prey as well as the protection of their numbers for future forays. But a fishing net is much less specifically designed than the trap of a stone age hunter must have been when one thinks of the fact that even mammoths were caught in traps. The fact that the hunt is the reversal of a flight animal's primary behavior means that by necessity it becomes socialized [*vergesellschaftete*] action. It turns the only now linguistically realized concepts into an instrument for organized behavior.

At this point, some might heave a sigh of relief and think that we have now finally arrived at socialization and thus at salvation. But as little as it can be denied that the origin of concepts has something to do with the ways of conduct that impelled to socialization or were made possible through it, as little can it be denied that *concepts* are just as provisional as *socialization*, which in the hunting behavior or in the *preemption* of the struggle for existence is a mere *means*—a means, of course, that carries one from subjectivity to that objectivity which is inevitable in any intersubjectivity, in any socialization. *Objectivity* is not yet a goal; it is initially only a means in order to be able to *act* collectively. Digging pitfalls requires a shared imagination of what they ought to trap. Objectivity is not yet the final state that dissociates humans from animals. Schopenhauer again writes: "Animals bend their heads to the ground because they simply need to see only what affects and concerns them, and they can never arrive at a really objective contemplation of things."[4] I am using an old humanistic formula to make clear that raising gait and gaze, extending the horizon and thus the ability to objectify what is not yet physical proximity, is *not the terminal point of this process*. The old teleological anthropology of the Greeks and Romans agreed that the upright gait and flexibility of the human head were evidence of nature's ultimate intention for man to be the beholder of the heavens. This means that the gaze is not fixed on the spatial and temporal horizon in order to expect and act upon that which is approaching; rather, the gaze that had already been raised by ninety degrees horizontally from looking at the earth, is *again raised by ninety degrees* and directed to the *starry sky*.

Having done so, this gaze then meets with an object whose quality can be characterized as follows:

1. It does not contain any aspect of expectation or preemption as long as the fear of certain signs in the sky and the associated forecast of extraordinary celestial phenomena does not play a role.

---

4. Schopenhauer, *Manuscript Remains*, 1:231.

2. The object is beyond the reach of any kind of action, praxis, or technology; it is a purely theoretical object, released from everyday life and its demands, not related to any professional practice.
3. The object may be given clearly but not distinctly in the sense of the tradition (I will explain the difference in a moment), because this object is a totality or close to the totality of the world; the gaze is directed *toward the whole*—for the Greeks, the words for *sky and world* are synonymous. The gaze directed toward the sky not only changes its object once it leaves the quotidian and life-worldly horizon of individual things and interactions; it also elevates itself above the particularity of objecthood and its differentiability, toward the last whole that can still be reached, even if it is by certain phenomena always kept from this totality.

For the Greeks, contemplating the sky meant not only contemplating a special and divine object of the highest dignity, but the paradigmatic case of what *theory ought to be*, what is at stake for it. The ideal of theory is the contemplation of the sky as an object that cannot be handled, that cannot be conceived of as a means. *What can no longer be a means* is totality itself, which encompasses the means.

Now, this is not a simple and conflict-free ascent of man from earth-boundedness, objectivation, and concept formation, toward totality and ideality. This is an all-too-easy image, developed by traditional metaphysics. In each of these stages, there is the possibility, the danger, and the *conflict* of neglecting what, with a great philosophical contrast term, has been called "life"—reality, realism, praxis, existence. As regards pure theory, I call to mind the anecdote of Thales: the Miletian protophilosopher and astronomer Thales, contemplating the stars at night in an open field, falls into a cistern; his Thracian maid, having witnessed this, laughs at him loudly and reproaches him for occupying himself with the distant things up there in the sky but overlooking what is in front of his feet. Many fine and witty things have been said about this anecdote for more than two thousand years. Plato turned it into the prototype for his

Socrates, whose philosophy made him misjudge the praxis of life and the state in such a way that the conflict came to a deadly ending for him.[5]

What happens at the heart of this anecdote is a multifaceted conflict. Its anthropological aspect is that pure theory, the claim for the totality of the world, cannot be had without an alienation from the realism of the practical world. The laughter of the Thracian maid certainly had originally been mythical: she believes the subterranean gods of her home, Thrace, to be in the right against the worshippers of the stars, the surface gods, the Olympians who are allied with the light. The laughter is, however, also the constant exhortation to realism, to return to the simple bringing-to-mind of what concerns oneself or may do so, to turn away from that which, with respect to the fate of one's life, concerns no one but oneself.

One has to understand that the *tendency* toward this kind of idealized theory is *already inherent in the upright gait*. Preemption, too, is always *a too-much in regard to immediacy*, to coping with whatever needs to be done. Instruments for possibilities must be much more extensive and subtle than instruments for a pressing reality.

By his origin, man is bound to the principle of superfluousness and luxury. The upright gait is, from its first appearance, luxuriating: to see what is not yet present, what *does not yet have any urgent necessity*, to preempt what is only a noncorporeal possibility, potential threat, or temptation—that is always a matter of too much effort and therefore, and not by chance, as much the beginning of as the possibility of the end to all *aggressions*. To arrive at an astronomy by contemplating celestial phenomena that—as in the legend about Thales of Miletus—allows a solar eclipse to be predicted, is a preemption of such an extreme type that it cannot forestall anything else but the bare *fear* of the suddenness with which the event of the solar eclipse irrupts. We believe the liberation from fear to be one of the greatest and most arduous efforts of human history.

---

5. [See Hans Blumenberg, *The Laughter of the Thracian Woman: A Protohistory of Theory*, trans. Spencer Hawkins (London: Bloomsbury, 2015).]

But to a biological-realistic reflection, this must seem like a small return for a great expense.

Two aspects are illustrated here that concern the difference between *concepts and reason*. An anthropological theory of concept formation will be hard pressed to describe liberation from fear as a result of the rational principle of self-preservation as a true purpose of human history. That this is an idea which rises above the level of the economy of self-preservation, one will be prepared to concede only if one acknowledges the right of pure theory to be realized independently of the complex of self-preservation of life as a form of realizing freedom—namely, the freedom from being bound to the means-structure [*Mittelstruktur*] of the objects. *Freedom from fear and freedom from instrumental objectivation* might not be mutually dependent, but are functionally analogous, that is, they are ideas devised by reason for processes that can concern long durations and the whole of history because the minimum of the self-preservation of the species and the individual does *not* depend on them.

[. . .]

In his anthropology, Arnold Gehlen has described the emergence of concepts as an achievement of *unburdening* [*Entlastung*] under the conditions of sensory overload [*Reizüberflutung*].[6] This allows him to exercise the special type of *rationality* that is inherent in the concept of *economy*. Every achievement is here an economizing: the word economizes intuition, intuition economizes touch—one could add: even touch is an economizing of smelling or tasting as the accompanying senses of devouring. The *end of isophagy* may be reached at the moment when, instead of devouring one another, it is enough only to rub each other's noses or to hug at the airport.

I have highlighted the aspect of *preemption* because it corresponds most precisely with the process of raising oneself up as a primal anthropological achievement. But even preemption is an epitome of unburdenings. It relieves future situations from being scattered or

6. [Arnold Gehlen, *Man: His Nature and Place in the World*, trans. Clare McMillan and Karl Pillemer (New York: Columbia University Press, 1988), esp. 1–77. Translation modified.]

suffocated by distracting stimuli. It does so by *processing the possible in advance*. For Gehlen, the epitome of what is the result of unburdening even in its highest forms of symbolic-abstract structures of achievements is nothing but pure self-preservation, the epitome of responses to the question of how this imperiled organic system can *survive* at all. Despite the question's rationality, I tend to see *too little* in this for a philosophical anthropology.

I believe that the basic concept of preemption gets us further. For in addition to mere unburdening, what we get here is the fact that the *having*-to-perceive-*less* is placed in the service of the *being-able*-to-perceive-*more*, which is preemption itself; but at the same time, it is also the root of a farther-reaching engagement with what is now made available in this process. For preemption creates the freedom to interpret what it perceives for the benefit of anticipating the possible also as an offer of active choices that tend toward *pleasure* [*Genuss*]. As important as the liberation from fear as the purpose of history might be, the creature that is liberated from fear and liberates itself from it does not attain contentment in doing so, because in the actions of *neutralization* it has become aware of the relation toward the ability to take pleasure. A textbook case seems to me to be *myth*: in its function, it belongs originally to the nexus of the purpose to liberate from fear; at its end, it is also the inexhaustible reservoir for the basic figures of what can only be enjoyed in obsolete rituals and their aesthetic appeals, in poetry, in tragedy.

If this is the case, then the arsenal of preemption and unburdening is not the pinnacle of human creations. The *achievement of concepts*, too, would not be something final and valuable in itself.

My thesis: The turn away from intuition is wholly at the service of a *return to intuition*. This is of course not the recurrence of the same, the return to the starting point, and certainly not anything at all to do with romanticism. Concepts, the instruments of unburdening, of the easy representation [*Vergegenwärtigung*] of what is absent, are at the same time the instruments of a claim to a new presence, a new intuition—but this time, one that is not coerced but sought. *Pleasure* requires the return to full sensibility [*Sinnlichkeit*] under the conditions of the returning agent. The movement of unburdenment from stimuli is reversed in a movement of looking for stimuli, which is only possible from that basic position that before has been unburdened. *The success of concepts is at the same time the reversal of their function*: it only initiates the process in which a *tremendum*—something unknown and terrible—that has become an object, returns as an object that now can be enjoyed. Already theoretically the achievement of concepts is only to keep the object potentially available and retrievable.

Metaphor is also an aesthetic medium precisely because it is both native to the original sphere of concepts and because it is continually liable and has to vouch for the deficiency of concepts and the limits of what they can achieve. Metaphorology might not be an aesthetic discipline—it regards the relationship between concepts and metaphors as a genetic and functional one—but it is certainly part of its thematic range to describe and explain how metaphor enters into the aesthetic context, or rather, how the aesthetic in its entirety emerges from the metaphoric and mythical substrate.

In the *aesthetic* sphere, the functions of the anthropological development recur, but without the connotation of negative qualities such as anxiety and fear, but hence also without being put to use for preemption. What is unexpected now becomes what is surprising. Even the audacity of a metaphor connecting extremely far-flung spheres is made subservient to pleasure. The unexpected now appears as tamed, in dressage, in domestication. Fear has turned into the pleasant shudder in the face of a beast that is dangerous only for its animal tamer (shipwreck and spectator).

Here, however, the reverse confusion also becomes possible for those who want to have metaphor taken at its word, who confound appearance and reality insofar as they believe that in changing the appearance they have already achieved something in reality. Conversely, there is the reproachful spectator who is not satisfied with the merely aesthetical and resents fiction for just wanting to be fiction.

Aesthetic fiction as the atrophied state of a reality that could only be endured and withstood in the exertion of *preemption* proves to be an irreversible step at least to reclaim reality, perhaps without knowing which reality this would have to be. The relaxed situation of the spectator is not endured or is not supposed to be endured, the confusion of reality and fiction does not become the precondition for its own kind of rhetoric, which demands the end of art because it believes itself able to exchange it *eo ipso* for reality.

To put an end to illusions, however, does not yet mean to begin with realism—otherwise, centuries of working to reduce prejudices would have to have opened up an unclouded view onto an objectivity without presuppositions.

The quality of surprise that belongs to the aesthetic, therefore, is the unburdened comprehension of the early anthropogenetic situation in which all possibilities had to be anticipated. In art, everything has been tried again and again to restore the primordiality of the unexpected, of that which is at its extreme dissimilar to any reality. Surrealism was one of the aesthetic currents that attempted to exploit the confusion between fiction and reality. Anaïs Nin reports an experience with the founder of the school of surrealism, André Breton, in the fall of 1937.[7] Breton had told her a story "which was the opposite of what I had expected." The surrealists had performed something that we today would call a "happening," an unplanned action with the intent of bringing about surprises. They had taken a train to an unknown place and waited there for something to happen, hoping that one day one might encounter a real surprise. It was an attempt to make the unexpected expectable. The story Breton tells Anaïs Nin looks at it from the perspective of this aesthetic disposition of the founder of surrealism. It went as follows: a few days ago, Breton had received a letter from a woman, a beautiful letter that spoke of the importance that Breton attached to aesthetic chance, to surprise. The letter writer then suggested such a surprise: she would like to meet Breton at midnight under the Pont Royal, but she did not wish to reveal her identity. The listener of the story waits for the adequate conclusion. But Breton ends with the sentence: "I did not go, of course." The listener is amazed and asks why this is a matter "of course" to him. Answer: "Because I have many enemies, and it could have been a trap." Breton notices his listener's disappointment and adds to his story: "I went the sec-

---

7. Anaïs Nin, *Diaries, Vol. 2: 1934–1939*, ed. Gunther Stuhlmann (New York: Swallow Press, 1967), 247–248.

ond time, though, after she wrote to me. But I was careful to post two loyal friends on the bridge where I could call out to them in case of danger." For Breton's listener, this is the perfect self-exposure of the aesthetic theorist: instead of grasping the possible aesthetic conception of the situation, he once again opts for preemption by not being able to maintain the readiness for surprise as an aesthetic one, but by taking the fiction at its word—as a risky reality to be approached with regard to its ambiguity. The readiness for surprise proves to be, as Anaïs Nin writes, "conscious, premeditated, and an intellectual technique," a matter for the laboratory. This accusation is naive, psychologically completely unjustified, but it is a consequence of precisely those confusions whose production corresponded to the aesthetic program of surrealism. The listener thus reacted just as she was supposed to if the program had been able to function. She applies the concept of reality that this aesthetic theory presupposes to its founder—which is rightly embarrassing for him but belongs to the unavoidable embarrassments for those who embark on such a theory. The uninvolved spectator to whom this anecdote is offered reacts to it in a completely different way from the two persons involved in it, namely, by laughing. What is ridiculous is the fact that Breton and his listener have different concepts of reality.

[. . .]

The proof that the theoretical need is not exhausted by the achievement of concepts in judgments and combinations of judgments can only be produced by describing the boundary of concepts and whatever must be achieved beyond this boundary.

In principle, a concept must be *definable* even if in a given situation no one is capable of fulfilling the demand for a definition. Rationality does not begin with the *fulfillment* of certain demands, but when they are *acknowledged*.

What is a definition? Linguistically, it appears as a replacement of one expression by another. Logically, it is described as a relationship of equivalence between the one expression and the other. The definition is the rule according to which an expression can become equivalently replaced by another. [. . .]

"World" is an expression for which the attempt to find rules for replacing the word is constitutively doomed to fail. Some people say that this generally voids the right to speak of the world, because, "What we cannot speak about we must pass over in silence."[8] (According to the seventh and last main proposition of Wittgenstein's *Tractatus*—who himself, however, did in no way abide by this proposition but quite unabashedly made the opposite into the epitome of his later philosophy.)

Even if I were inclined to agree that sentences about "the world" should from now on be no longer constructed or used, I would still be very unsure if this ban could ever be successful. Let me confront this last proposition of Wittgenstein's *Tractatus* with another proposition that perhaps explains why an apodictically inclined young philosopher was later not willing to abide by his principle. This sentence is by Paul Valéry, from his work *Mon Faust*: "What can be written down is mere foolishness. Only the ineffable is of any importance."[9]

Perhaps someone might say we can very well dispense with the expression "world." Such remarks as "The world is bad" or "The world is on the brink of the abyss," the argument would go, do not actually say anything and are not worth the trouble of uttering them. The difficulty is how far one is willing to go. One who has dispensed with "the world" might hesitate at being expected also to dispense with the expression "freedom" under the same conditions. Particularly for freedom, Kant emphatically assessed this issue: We have no concept of freedom, because we cannot provide any rule according to which the expression "freedom" might be substituted. It can only be deduced "as a necessary presupposition of reason." Thus, not only its objective reality but also what its concept might contain of that reality cannot be demonstrated. *Kant explicitly states that for freedom, even the method to insert analogies and examples for want of concepts fails.* Kant reasons that this is the fact "because

---

8. [Ludwig Wittgenstein, *Tractatus Logico-Philosophicus* (London: Routledge, 2001), 89.]

9. [Paul Valéry, "My Faust," *Plays* (Princeton, NJ: Princeton University Press, 1960), 94.]

no example of anything analogous can ever be put under it."[10] That the use of the expression "freedom" is still indispensable results from it having to be approached "as a necessary presupposition of reason." Exactly this is meant by saying that freedom is not a concept but an idea. Perhaps "world" is a boundary concept; "freedom," at any rate, is an idea. Nevertheless, I do not want to omit that there is a definition that Goethe expressed toward Chancellor von Müller on June 20, 1827: "Freedom is nothing but the possibility of being able to act reasonably under all circumstances."[11] It corresponds to Kant's understanding.

Reason awakes the expectations of the understanding and at the same time disappoints them.

To assign concepts to the *understanding* and ideas to *reason* is not only a specialty of Kant's philosophy of dividing up the mind into capacities but also has its cause in circumstances that could be described as achievements or as the limits of achievements.

Now, the suspicion arises easily that every concept that cannot clearly be assigned to a complex of intuitions (for example, the concept of the elephant is assigned to one's expectations when booking a safari in a travel agency) is nothing but an invention, a fiction, a construct of the human intellect. For lack of any corresponding reality, the concept of freedom would then be nothing but a label for the human illusion of being not merely an element in the nexus of nature and its determinations.

Yet the issue is more complicated. Concepts are not only based on objects but concepts also constitute objects. If a concept is a rule to represent *representations* in a certain way, that is, a *representation of representations* [*eine Vorstellung der Vorstellungen*], then there are concepts that arrive at their objects in no other way than by the rule itself creating the object. Kant held the view that our mathematical concepts are of this type. This was an objection to any

---

10. Immanuel Kant, *Groundwork of the Metaphysics of Morals*, trans. Mary Gregor (Cambridge: Cambridge University Press, 1997), 63.

11. Johann Wolfgang Goethe, *Gedenkausgabe der Werke, Briefe und Gespräche*, ed. Ernst Beutler (Zurich: Artemis, 1949), 23:481.

kind of Platonism that even claims what is physically not present to be discoverable and given, such as the concepts of ethical norms, the values of goals of action, and so forth.

I am thinking of still another issue, which distinguishes itself from the creation of mathematical concepts in that it opens up access to empirical evidence. Something of this kind is the *concept of the unconscious*. If one thinks about how this concept came to be and what transformations it underwent historically, one cannot stop marveling at how potent such a conceptual coinage can be. It really appears as if we are initially confronted with a word that simply offers no help at all in conceiving of an object, an issue, or a process. (Something similar is currently happening with the concept of "institution.") The unconscious is accessed in a comparable way to what Kant had claimed for freedom. A certain content of consciousness supposedly allows no other explanation than that (1) in the past, with a long temporal gap, an event or an experience happened that initiated a certain reaction that led to the disappearance of this very experience as a conscious content; that (2) the disappeared has not dissolved but has disguised and conserved itself according to a principle of preservation; and that (3) this concealed content affects and becomes noticeable in specific correlates within consciousness. [. . .]

In the strict sense, the concept of the unconscious is a procedural rule about how to behave in the face of a specific content of consciousness, or at least of something that can be phenomenally objectivized: one has to search for, ask about, analyze what experience lies at the foundation of the unknown issue whose effects have outlasted the latency phase and that in itself cannot be objectivized. The unconscious is an *auxiliary concept* for specific technical operations that would certainly be possible but not comprehensible without it. The concept of the unconscious claims a totality of consciousness that is not verifiable in any memory or expectation, that is, in no form of identity's self-consciousness: the energetic history of the subject, governed by the principle of constancy, is in principle without gaps, and it can only be that way because the discontinuity of consciousness is supported and bridged by the energetic latency of the unconscious.

It is not by accident that the unconscious "works" in a codified language: in symbols (if only they are empirically decodable, that is, through contingent attributions), in metaphors (if they are immanently decodable: while the phallus is a symbol of fertility, if one knows that . . . yet this does not mean that the snake is a symbol of the phallus but is metaphorically mediated).

For me, the observation was surprising that for the functions demonstrated above the concept of the unconscious is *strictly analogous* to that of freedom. The unconscious is the thing itself—better still: one of the things themselves. I quoted what Kant said in the 1786 *Groundwork for the Metaphysics of Morals*: that no example can ever be provided for freedom by way of analogy. Yet it is striking that Kant himself infringed against this declaration a year later in his preface to the second edition of the *Critique of Pure Reason*, namely, in the important note in which he puts Copernicus and Newton into the same relation in which theoretical and practical reason stand for him. This completely and exclusively refers to the concept of freedom.

This strange preface was written six years after the first publication of the *Critique of Pure Reason*. Kant had made disappointing experiences with the effects of his work. He had overestimated the possible success of his line of argument. Now, in the preface to the second edition, Kant with great care makes the offer to the reader that, for a start, he may only treat the main thesis of his work as if it were a hypothesis, to test it provisionally and have it prove itself. The most important among the tests that Kant himself had in mind is probably the philosophy of practical reason (1786 *Groundwork for the Metaphysics of Morals*; 1788 *Critique of Practical Reason*; 1794 *Religion within the Boundaries of Mere Reason*). How is it possible that morality can become the confirmation of metaphysics? Kant says that "the experiment providing a checkup on the truth of the result of that first assessment of our rational cognition *a priori*"[12] lies exactly in the fact that it "reaches appearances only, leaving the thing in itself as something actual for itself but uncog-

---

12. [Immanuel Kant, *Critique of Pure Reason*, trans. Paul Guyer and Allen W. Wood (Cambridge: Cambridge University Press, 1998), 112 (B xx).]

nized by us." Of this "thing in itself" no concept exists; it is, in Kant's wording, a "noumenon in the negative sense,"[13] a void left empty, for which seemingly no definiteness can be reached. Every attempt still to find definiteness for this void has to lead to antinomies, paralogisms, and contradictions, as proved by the transcendental dialectic. Now the distinction between appearance and the thing in itself is theoretically no advantage; on the contrary, it is a grave disappointment, because all statements of science can henceforth be only related to appearances, and nothing can be said about the thing itself any longer. The compulsion to concede the decision despite this disappointment was only based on the contradictions that had resulted from the application of our concepts to things in themselves.

But now comes the surprise for Kant's audience, namely, that the disappointment of *theoretical* reason emerges after the fact as the only possibility for *practical* reason, that is, as the only possibility to think freedom despite the absolute determinism of nature and the natural sciences. There is no consciousness of freedom, no experience of freedom, no construction of freedom—and therefore no concept of freedom in the strict sense. But it is the condition of the possibility of our knowing the difference between good and evil, of our ability to be moral beings. Were there the experience of freedom, then there would *eo ipso* be no possibility for experience anymore—because the validity of the determinism of causality is the condition of the possibility of objects of experience. For practical reason, the existence of freedom becomes itself a *postulate* as the condition of its own possibility to give an ought in consciousness. One could say, *whatever it might be, freedom must exist*. And at this point, the "critique of practical reason" uses that space left vacant by theoretical reason to place in the position of the noumenon in the negative sense the very same in the positive sense—one that is only thought and for which no experience could ever provide the intuition. There can be no concept already because what is thought this way must not understand itself as the expectation to be fulfilled by intuition. Kant understands this empty space as if theoretical rea-

---

13. [Kant, *Critique of Pure Reason*, 361 (B 307).]

son had not only admitted but had downright persuaded practical reason to make use of it. Kant writes, "By such procedures speculative reason has at least made room for such an extension" (i.e., with regard to the existence of freedom), "even if it had to leave it empty; and we remain at liberty, indeed we are called upon by reason to fill it if we can through practical data of reason."[14]

The note mentioned earlier now refers to this word, "to fill." In this note, Kant views the relationship between *Copernicus and Newton* in the following way: Copernicus had put forward a new hypothesis about the planetary system that made the sun the central body. To him, it was secondary, if not even unknown, that he put the body with the greatest mass into the center of the system. This circumstance was astronomically of no consequence to him. Now Newton comes along and recognizes under the conditions of the Copernican system that it does mean something for the body with the greatest mass to be the central body of the system; that is, it means something under the condition that the bodies attract each other relative to their mass (and in the opposite relation to their distance). The concept of this *attraction* was inferred in view of this Copernican system, as there is *no possible experience* of forces that reach beyond the empty space between bodies. But only the theory of gravitation that was deduced from the Copernican system fully confirms the accuracy of the Copernican hypothesis.

Now, the same relation is supposed to exist between theoretical and practical reason—the concept of freedom is supposed to have the same function as the concept of gravitation. Newton's central laws about the center had proved "the invisible force that binds the universe," "which would have remained forever undiscovered if Copernicus had not ventured, in a manner contradictory to the senses yet true, to seek for the observed movements not in the objects of the heavens but in their observer."[15] While Newton, then, was afraid that the concept of gravity would introduce a hypothesis into his system that he believed he should not tolerate, Kant exactly reverses this relation: Copernicus is the man of the hypothesis, Newton the

---

14. [Kant, 112–113 (B xxi).]
15. [Kant, 113 (B xxii).]

one who introduces the confirming reality. This is also how the reader is supposed to see the relation between theoretical and practical reason, between determinism and freedom.

If we now take a step back from this example and try to grasp by it the *relation between understanding and reason*, between concepts and ideas, then it follows first and foremost that there is no decline at all from the solidity of concepts to the idea's excessive tension and fictionality. Rather, and conversely, the idea of freedom affirms the procedure, in theoretical reason, of the distinction of appearance and thing in itself even more, and brings it positively to certainty. *Although* the idea (of freedom), taken on its own, would not have been able to arise and persist without the transcendental discovery of theoretical reason—it would have had neither space nor air to exist—*neither can the idea be what is primary*, nor can the solid work of conceptuality be omitted and skipped over. Whatever one may think of Kant's results and systematic classifications, he cannot be easily dispossessed of this accomplishment.

Nor can, at the level of concepts themselves, *solidity stand at the beginning*. Many readers of Kant's *Critique of Pure Reason* see little significance in the fact that the main division of the work does not correspond to the grand outlines that become apparent in its effect: not the analytic and the dialectic are the main parts, nor even do the aesthetic and logic make up the great dichotomy; rather, the laconic main division is that between the doctrine of elements and the doctrine of method. Hardly anyone reads all the way up to the doctrine of method, and those who do so have had to muster such enormous efforts of understanding that there are few reserves left for method, and one is inclined to hold it in low esteem. I cannot remember ever having read or heard of a seminar being conducted on the transcendental doctrine of method. But that is exactly what would have to be wished for.

A doctrine of method describes the steps along a path according to a rule. In this respect, it can proceed strictly conceptually. But the notion of the path is related to a totality that can hardly be addressed other than metaphorically: the path leads through a landscape; it bypasses or bridges obstacles, and in the best case it even has a goal, instead of leading back to the starting point. In the metaphorics of the path, much has been said of what has been assumed about the act of cognition and its chances of success but has also been reluctantly expressed with the directness of an assertion. Kant prefers to communicate the totality of his undertaking to the reader through the *metaphor of building a house*. Much could be said about why Kant preferred this constructive metaphorics, which is detached from the conditions of nature, to that of the path.

Kant writes: "If I regard the sum total of all cognition of pure and speculative reason as an edifice for which we have in ourselves at least the idea, then I can say that in the Transcendental Doctrine of Elements we have made an estimate of the building materials and determined for what sort of edifice, with what height and strength, they would suffice. It turned out, of course, that although we had in mind a tower that would reach the heavens, the supply of materials sufficed only for a dwelling that was just roomy enough for our business on the plane of experience and high enough to survey it; however, that bold undertaking had to fail from lack of material, not to mention the confusion of languages that unavoidably divided the workers over the plan and dispersed them throughout the world, leaving each to build on his own according to his own design."[16]

It is immediately discernible that Kant prefers the metaphorics of construction simply because it allows him to draw a relation between the failure of traditional metaphysics and the biblical story of the confusion of languages during the construction of the Babylonian tower. It is telling, however, that Kant does not explicitly invoke arrogance and blasphemic defiance as cause for the builders' failure; rather, they fail because of technical circumstances, which are not those of the constructive design, but of the deficiency of their materials. *This deficiency, however, is constitutive.* It apparently cannot be remedied. And that is the reason why the alternative of the dwelling as a refuge sufficient (to experience) for doing business on the "plane" is taken up. The confusion of languages appears as the consequence, rather than the cause, of the failed tower construction. It is the emblem of the confusion, of the isolation of systems.

---

16. Kant, 627 (A 707/B 735).

Through this simile, Kant also wants to depict the relation between the doctrine of method and the doctrine of elements. In the strict sense, it is called the doctrine of elements because it provides the elements, that is, the materials for the edifice. Kant continues: "Now we are concerned not so much with the materials as with the plan, and, having been warned not to venture some arbitrary and blind project that might entirely exceed our entire capacity, yet not being able to abstain from the erection of a sturdy dwelling, we have to aim at an edifice in relation to the supplies given to us that is at the same time suited to our needs.—By the transcendental doctrine of method, therefore, I understand the determination of the formal conditions of a complete system of pure reason."[17]

By placing the doctrine of method at the end of his magnum opus, Kant took a clear stand against the obsession in German academic philosophy since Christian Wolff, again present in today's, with not beginning to philosophize before all questions of method have been clarified and all concepts defined. Time and again, the irresistible model of mathematics has not so much corrupted philosophical morals (indeed, nothing would be more urgently desirable than to have clarified all preliminary questions before the main issue is approached), as cut off the air for philosophical thought to breathe.

For Kant, *mathematics cannot be the model of concept formation* for all types of strict thought because in mathematics, although the concepts may stand at the beginning, they can also be freely formed and constructed by intuition. One can therefore easily agree on such concepts, provided that their noncontradiction can be ascertained (such as the concept of the greatest sphere or the longest route). Mathematical concepts, for Kant, are not analytical; until they are realized in intuition, only very little can be concluded from the constructive rule that they indicate: from the concept of the circle, it cannot be inferred that all points equidistant from a given point have to lie on this circle (or, considered three-dimensionally, have to lie on a sphere). In this respect, the mathematical concept is the exact *opposite of the concept of God* of traditional metaphysics from which it was possible to deduce *everything*—not only all

---

17. [Kant, 627 (A 707/B 735).]

attributes, but also existence itself. This paramount achievement of concepts still fascinated Hegel so much that he tried to rescue and restore the ontological proof of God's existence against Kant's criticism: it was for him the purest model of all achievements of concepts and of their history.

For Kant, the concept is building material, a tool. One has to see in the course of one's work how the tool can be modified according to the task and increasingly adapted to it. For this reason, there is no occasion and no possibility to emulate mathematics by providing the definitions of concepts in advance for all matters, unless as a trial and tentatively. "Philosophy is swarming with mistaken definitions, especially those that actually contain elements for definition but are not yet complete. If one would not know what to do with a concept until one had defined it, then all philosophizing would be in a bad way." In philosophy, approximations to definitions of concepts and those in the process of history must be seen as useful. Kant expresses that with the laconic sentence: "In mathematics definitions belong *ad esse* [to the being], in philosophy *ad melius esse* [to the improvement of being]. Attaining them is fine, but often very difficult. Jurists are still searching for a definition of their concept of right."[18]

The result is that "in philosophy the definition, as distinctness made precise, must conclude rather than begin the work."[19] But if that is so, one has to ask by which means—if not yet by those of the clarified concept—the path of this clarification can be covered. One can also put it like this: *for the benefit of concepts, there has to be a preliminary field of nonconceivability [Unbegreiflichkeit]*, even if, under the criteria of the possible perfected concept, one were inclined to cross this field disparagingly and let it be altogether forgotten in the state of perfection.

Nonconceptuality in the service of concepts—that would be an option for taking a generous view of addressing this issue as a mere philosophical auxiliary discipline. Yet a more serious situation remains to be confronted, namely, that the work at the preliminary

---

18. Kant, 639 (A 731/B 759).
19. [Kant, 639 (A 731/B 759).]

stage of concepts *does not arrive at its goal,* be it de facto or even out of the necessity of the subject matter. If the latter were the case, then it would be so in connection with the concept's dependency on intuition and the failure to meet this condition when it comes to the *idea.*

The desire for linguistic definiteness, for the establishment of *ortho-languages* will, as a utopia, no more disappear than Esperanto has. It is defined by the urge to put the unambiguous mapping of concepts and linguistic medium at the beginning of every discursive act and every internal or external consideration. This desire is either bound to the ideal of mathematics to cover, with the use of a constructive set of instruments, all noncontradictory possibilities up to the point that the unordered barrage of experience and the factual situation can be faced calmly. Or it is of the phenomenological type, which considers the rigor of a fundamental science to consist in bringing about pure intuitions of states of affairs as they are in themselves, and in then assigning to them a system of concepts (this, then, is not about antecedent definitions so as to be prepared for everything—no defining into the blue, as it were—but it is about intuiting only so as to bring into conceptual form what has or is "essence" [*Wesen*]). Kant, in any case, must not be associated with the mathematical ideal: "Mathematics is thoroughly grounded on definitions, axioms, and demonstrations. I will content myself with showing that none of these elements, in the sense in which the mathematician takes them, can be achieved or imitated by philosophy."[20]

Almost ten years after the *Critique of Pure Reason,* Kant returned to the problem of the concept's need for substitution in the *Critique of Judgment,* whose §59 bears the title "On beauty as a symbol of morality." Here, as always, Kant proceeds from the assumption that the "reality of our concepts,"[21] which for him means the relatedness of concepts to states of affairs, happens in intuition, or more precisely, in Kant's language: "intuitions are . . . required." The sim-

---

20. Kant, 637 (A 726/B 754).
21. [Kant, *Critique of the Power of Judgement,* trans. Paul Guyer and Eric Matthews (Cambridge: Cambridge University Press, 2000), 225.]

plest case of this realization of concepts is to show it. If I ask someone, What is money? the easiest procedure to answer me is for him to dig into his pocket and to hold in front of me a coin or a banknote.

But one can easily see that this procedure is only a very imprecise reaction to my question. It passes the further work on to me. When a single piece of money is shown to me, I am being reminded that I know more about money than can be conveyed through a single empirical intuition. In a certain respect, this is Socrates' procedure with the slave boy in *Meno*, which is performed there as a proof for the *recollection of ideas*. This procedure can be described as *exemplary method*. A singular exemplar of a certain class of objects is shown not because it itself allows perception of the concept, but because it evokes or refers to the concept. It would be of no help to someone who has not the slightest idea about the function of money to react to his question what the expression "money" actually referred to by holding a coin or a banknote to his face. To someone, however, who knows what money is and how it works, one would do a sufficient service if one answered his question about the meaning of the Latin expression *moneta* by showing him a random coin of a random currency. This coin would work like a trigger for a whole complex of familiar knowledge and modes of reaction, and would fully suffice to regulate the use of this expression henceforth. Just think of the situation when someone who has been instructed in such a way is confronted by a man at night in a dark alley with a threatening gesture and the exclamation *moneta!*—he will know what he has to do if his life or his physical integrity mean something to him.

For this reason, Kant says that the type of intuition that is required for the reality of empirical concepts is called "example." *No empirical object* stands in by itself and sufficiently for the intuition on which its concept is based, but it does so to a sufficient degree to help bring about the reality of the concept, the fabrication of its object relation. In this example, it is very much the question whether intuition is in service of the concept or the concept in service of intuition. Does it suffice to refer to one example to be able to use the concept from then on as one pleases, or is adducing an example to *clarify the concept only the first step*, so as to limit and enrich the sphere of examples from then on in such a way that in this dealing with objects the concept is, as it were, *only an auxiliary organ*, basically already of no further use because one is occupied with the thing itself and is absorbed in its use or enjoyment. The concept would then relate to the object like possibility to reality. But at the same time, the example also demonstrates that *there are no demonstrative definitions* in the strict sense: no pointing at something can ever be the sufficient answer to the question of *what* something is that I am introducing through its concept.

To sustain the correlativity of concepts and intuition in its full rigor, even the *pure* concepts of the understanding have to possess *their* kind of intuition, which is necessarily a nonempirical intuition. This is what in the *Critique of Pure Reason* is called schematizing and *schematism*. For just as there are *pure* concepts (i.e., those that are not formed *from* empirical material), there are also *pure* intuitions that only make it possible to have mathematical objects and synthetic judgments a priori. Since the forms of outer and inner sense—time and space—are a priori and stand in a foundational relation (which takes the greater generality of the inner sense over the outer to indicate a justificatory relation), the obvious thing to do is to turn the form of time into the very intuition through which all pure concepts of the understanding gain their "reality."

This whole problem is much more difficult when it comes to concepts that are created by reason and with the help of which it directs its demands at the understanding as the organ of concepts *for* experience and *from* experience (i.e., the categories and empirical concepts). These concepts of reason are called *ideas* in Kant. To demand a verifiable object relation also for them, that is, to verify their "objective reality" in their theoretical function, would, according to Kant, mean to desire something impossible "since no intuition adequate to them can be given at all."[22] It is impossible to offer an intuition for the concept "world," be it merely that of an example—already because "world" cannot exist in the plural, the hyperbolic use of language notwithstanding, and it is hence impossible to present a world as an example for the intuition signified in

---

22. [Kant, *Critique of the Power of Judgement*, 225.]

the concept of "world." We are dealing here with concepts whose reality can only be grounded in the *process* of reason itself, if they can claim such a thing at all.

Expressions that can neither be defined by showing nor by rules of substitution naturally have a broad range of variations when it comes to their definiteness in individual and social contexts. In the minimum of standardized definiteness and the maximum of additional determinability lies their disposition for attracting imaginative and evaluative material, and only then to specify themselves. This is also the reason for the very special historical capacity of *symbols*, which for themselves and at first mean *nothing*, but, because of this, are able to assume meaning. This is a trait they share with ideas: they cannot be made *exemplarily* sensible by any completed or completable experience. While they attract experience and even set the direction in which this happens, this only increases their ambiguity and thereby puts it in opposition to the urge toward definiteness inherent in every concept formation. The epitome of the achievements of concept formation, that is, of all rules for the unity of representations as represented representations, is denoted by the name "understanding"; a system of rules, which for its part is capable of forming rules for representations, becomes distinguishable through the title "reason" as the epitome of rules that are unsurpassable because they in each case imply the totality. For reason, nothing new can and may appear or be added: the plural "worlds" has always been something threatening to reason, and the young Kant had therefore defused this plural by speaking, in his cosmogonic early work, of a "world of worlds,"[23] thereby restoring the old singularity. It can be easily shown that since classical atomism and medieval nominalism, this restoration has time and again been the most pressing function of reason in its self-preservation and as an organ of self-preservation. The metaphorics that enters into the indeterminate space of the idea of "world" can produce almost every ambiguity, provided that it does not endanger the unity of that

---

23. [Immanuel Kant, "Universal Natural History and Theory of the Heavens," in *Natural Science*, ed. Eric Watkins (Cambridge: Cambridge University Press, 2012), 221.]

which it thereby denotes. As with the concept of time, we are dealing here with the problem of identity, and nothing is more dangerous—in every sense, right up to that of psychopathology—than to make this identity questionable. On this also rests that the *pure* concepts of the understanding for Kant can only be schematized by *one* sensible rendering [*Versinnlichung*], whose own form is that of absolute identity and unity, and which logically cannot be thought in any other way: namely, time.

What is important here: Just as Kant uses the concept of the schema for the correlative intuitiveness of pure concepts of the understanding, he uses the concept of the *symbol* for the intuitiveness of the pure concepts of reason, the ideas. Symbolization is constructed in a manner analogous to schematization because one cannot, according to Kant's premises, analyze the relation between idea and intuition in itself. The representation of a pure concept of reason as rendering sensible is "symbolic, where to a concept which only reason can think, and to which no sensible intuition can be adequate, an intuition is attributed with which the power of judgment proceeds in a way merely analogous to that which it observes in schematization, i.e., it is merely the rule of this procedure, not of the intuition itself, and thus merely the *form of the reflection*, not the *content*, which corresponds to the concept."[24] The symbol is not only a sensible sign for a concept, as Kant imputes about the use that "recent logicians"[25] had made of the expression "symbolical" and that according to him should be called "*mere characterizations*"[26]: words, or signs of an algebraic, even mimetic nature, mere expressions for concepts, that can be inserted instead of their formalisms.

Kant's example is not the world, but the state: "Thus a monarchical state is represented by a body with a soul if it is ruled in accordance with laws internal to the people, but by a mere machine (like a handmill) if it is ruled by a single absolute will, but in both

---

24. [Kant, *Critique of the Power of Judgment*, 225; Blumenberg's emphases.]
25. [Kant, 226.]
26. [Kant, 226; Blumenberg's emphasis.]

cases it is represented only symbolically."[27] One can easily see that the expression "symbolic" for Kant means nothing other than "metaphorical," certainly with an accent in the direction of the *absolute* metaphor. Kant justifies the procedure for the case of the state in the following way: "For between a despotic state and a handmill there is, of course, no similarity, but there is one between the rule for reflecting on both and their causality."[28] The symbolic procedure, as Kant calls it, then consists in introducing an intuition for a concept, which as such cannot serve as an example, but which permits "applying the mere rule of reflection on that intuition to an entirely different object, of which the first is only the symbol."[29]

Our language, says Kant, is full of such "indirect presentations, in accordance with an analogy, where the expression does not contain the actual schema for the concept but only a symbol for reflection."[30] The procedure therefore consists in the "transportation" [*Übertragung*] of a reflection about an object of intuition to another primary concept "to which perhaps no intuition can ever directly correspond."[31] At this point, Kant also says how he would think about the task of a metaphorology, without calling it by such a name: "This business has as yet been little discussed, much as it deserves a deeper investigation; but this is not the place to dwell on it."[32]

The idea provides not a determination of objects but of our behavior toward objects. For this reason, Kant says, "all of our cognition of God is merely symbolic,"[33] which excludes the hypertrophy of all anthropomorphisms as well as the conceptual speculation of all deisms, both of which do not allow any cognition, not even one with practical intent. Hence, an "object" that cannot quite be determined by its concept is still "represented" as the sum of influences for our practical behavior. Finally, Kant says that the "beautiful" is the symbol of the morally good. What does that mean? *The*

---

27. [Kant, 226.]
28. [Kant, 226.]
29. [Kant, 226.]
30. [Kant, 226.]
31. [Kant, 227.]
32. [Kant, 226.]
33. [Kant, 227.]

beautiful as that which pleases seems primarily to be governed by mere subjectivity. But the agreement that it receives this way in turn demands the agreement of all others, and the reason for this is that it is not aware of any *limited interest*—not even the interest in its own pleasure, since aesthetic pleasure in principle is divisible at will without decreasing, but thereby in principle also demands that this be communicated. The naive reaction that has become ready for caricature, namely, to break out in cries of rapture in front of an aesthetic entity, preferably in the interrogative (such as: Isn't this wonderful?)—this quotidian observation confirms that the judgment of taste is *judgment for others* not by chance and incidentally, but is so constitutively, because it is looking for intersubjective agreement. This immediate compulsion of the aesthetic object not to be absorbed in sensible reception, Kant now interprets as expression of a deeper root in which the theoretical and practical faculties are "combined . . . in a mutual and *unknown way*, to form a unity."[34] The immediacy of the agreement, which the aesthetic object demands without an appeal to self-interest, and the nonarbitrary freedom of the imagination [*Einbildungskraft*] that it grants, determine the applicability to practical reason that reflection allows to find. Kant concludes this consideration with the sentence: "Taste as it were makes possible the transition from sensible charm to the habitual moral interest without too violent a leap by representing the imagination even in its freedom as purposively determinable for the understanding and teaching us to find a free satisfaction in the objects of the senses even without any sensible charm."[35]

The justification for finding the traditional metaphor in Kant's symbolical sensible rendering can philologically most easily be found in the fact that at least one of his examples comes from Quintilian's rhetoric, where it is an example for metaphor: when we find "fields smiling and joyful," and according to Kant they "contain something analogical to the consciousness of a mental state produced by moral judgments,"[36] then we can easily recognize Quintilian's *pratum ridet*

---

34. [Kant, 227; Blumenberg's emphasis.]
35. [Kant, 228.]
36. [Kant, 228.]

[the meadow laughs].[37] But the laughter of a meadow or a field is something other than the laughter of the world spirit, and it is not even that easy to describe what the difference is. This attempt, however, has to be made if one intends to show that metaphor can achieve more than the paraphrasing of an issue that could be determined equivalent, as is the case with the laughing meadow.

[. . .]

Perhaps it is no longer perceived that an odium of illegitimacy clings to the very title of a metaphorology. In our tradition, the responsibility for the linguistic institution of the metaphor lies with rhetoric. The relationship of rhetoric to truth—that is, to one of the uncontested values of this tradition—is more than disputed; it is ambiguous, questionable in no good sense of the word. It has never been surprising to find that a philosophical author such as Locke sees the metaphor as one of the basic deceptions of the human mind, whose elimination is among the tasks of philosophy. Rhetoric is the institutionalized antitype of philosophy.

Viewed historically, this is first of all the victory of Plato—and of everything that depends on him, hence also of Socrates—over Sophism. By presenting his enemies accordingly, Plato presented this victory as that of ethics over demagoguery, of logic over aesthetics, and it appeared to the centuries and millennia after him as a great fortune that Sophism had perished through the nonexistence of its literary records, and has only survived as invective, just as Plato allegedly bought the works of Democritus—that is, of atomism, which he had likewise overcome—to burn them and to save posterity from them. But here a more serious problem comes into play than that of historical successes and defeats. Plato gave his work the form of the Socratic dialogue. This form, developed with the authority of Socrates and perhaps indeed by capturing his unmethodical method, is not only supposed to communicate contents of

---

37. [The example is, in fact, not Quintilian's; Blumenberg may have found it in Ernst Robert Curtius's *European Literature and the Latin Middle Ages* (Princeton, NJ: Princeton University Press, 1953), 128, where it is introduced together with Quintilian as a stand-in for the whole rhetorical tradition.]

a specific kind (which probably quickly veered far away from Socrates' self-limitation), but as a form was supposed to bring objections to bear on rhetoric, to bring them to self-evidence. Rhetoric as the art of persuasion appears as the master's one-sided business toward those who only got involved with him through listening, without measuring up to his studied and trained art. From the beginning, rhetoric appears as the constitutive lack of rational reciprocity as it is represented in dialogue. Persuasion seems to gain ground where the argument is missing or believes that it is unable to hold its ground. Framed this way, metaphor becomes a deception with the aim of gentle temptation, and hence is even more effective when the listener is lacking his or her own conceptual overview and can therefore be offered a surrogate of orientation. Dialogue, in contrast, appears as the institution in which everyone can defend themselves, where play of rational powers is opened up and where the power of truth can assert itself. Everyone looking closely at Plato's Socratic dialogue and not deceived by its canonical validity and literary appeal quickly recognizes that dialogue, too, has its perils of temptation—that dialogue quickly turns into dialectics, and that its nooses and pitfalls still always catch the other person, who is left with no other option than to surrender, not because he has seen the truth, but because he cannot proceed in his own manner. Still, dialogue became, through early Aristotle, Cicero, Saint Augustine, and up to Nicholas of Cusa and Giordano Bruno, a literary form of a certain freedom of thought and its tropes. In fact, in all the authors mentioned we find nothing but an overwhelming prevalence of rhetoric in the guise of dialogue, dialogue as rhetoric. I am giving this brief indication only because it can shed light on what is real about the traditional antithesis of philosophy and rhetoric.

Admittedly, rhetoric does not have a clear tradition. It has come to terms with its Sophistic disreputability and established itself as a more or less open technique [*Technik*] of persuasion and temptation, as a technique of speech before the law, before the people's assembly, and finally, before the congregation, which wants to be tempted into its salvation. This tradition culminates in Machiavelli, in the political realism of the attainment, exercise, and maintenance of power, for which the word is but one instrument, albeit the one that implicitly already includes the others. Naturally, there never were many demagogues willing to reveal themselves as such and additionally as teachers of their subject. Voltaire writes about Frederick the Great and his early work *Anti-Machiavel* that Machiavelli himself could have given his disciple no better advice than to write an Anti-Machiavel.

An easier task in the tradition of rhetoric fell to those who sought again to bring it closer to philosophy, believing they could turn the antithesis into a relation of service. To prevail, truth, too, requires a good presentation, an accommodating form, and even the ornamentation of rhetorical figures. It is clear that one and a half millennia in which the most important trivial literary form was the sermon had to be a support for this tradition of rhetoric, affirming it in spite of all sophistic suspicion. I say all this with regard to metaphor and its assessment and classification within our intellectual history.

Undoubtedly, the divergent conceptions of rhetoric in our tradition also contain fundamentally different, implicit conceptions of language and its function. Rhetoric conceived of as the shaping and decorating of expression takes language primarily to be assertion and communication of contents, particularly of knowledge. Such a conception is today widely regarded as naive and as a factor in many misunderstandings of logic and philosophy. The other conception, which in the meantime has also largely supplanted the expressive conception of language, sees it as a vehicle by which humans influence humans, as a starting point for action and the inducement to actions. It is thus quite consistent to understand language neither primarily as expression nor as communication but as a "speech act" [*Sprachhandlung*]. Such shifts should always be seen within an anthropological horizon of preferential assessments. The creature that prefers to act is not only distinguished by this fact from others but is also characterized as a creature that cannot afford the stages of rest prior to actions; it is a creature pressed for action and interaction, for whom nothing is more urgent than to establish communications and solidarities, which themselves can always only be preliminary stages of actions. An aficionado of revolution will be inclined to pass off language itself as action; one will soon be the surrogate of the other. If language is action, then its purpose is not at the same time and already its content (as it is the case for the assertion whose linguistic form only serves a single purpose that at the same time is its content). What is important to the speech act is not what it might have to say. The concept of the speech act displays a high degree of affinity to the sophistic concept of rhetoric (or rather, the concept of rhetoric ascribed to sophism).

This remark regarding the speech act shows what it means that the division of rhetoric's self-conception has preconditions in anthropology. Not by chance was it often the skeptics who had the least confidence in theory and who saw in it no precondition for action, who counted on the indispensability and unpostponability of action as a constitutive aspect of human existence, and who agonized over the question of where, for lack of theoretical orientation, action might find its rules. The lack of truth, from which the skeptic has to proceed for better or for worse, indicates or connotes to him the other shortcomings that compel humans to be acting creatures. But if truth is absent, the whole scale of probabilities has to serve the orientation of action. On this very scale rhetoric resides, if it proceeds from the assumption that persuasion has its place only or especially where rationality is not easily specified, to be found, or practiced. A field opens up to view that is delimited by familiar markings and whose structure is that of a homogeneous anthropological horizon: skepticism, acting creature, probability, persuasion. If science were ever to be completed, there would no longer be any perplexity about what to do and how to do it—that is, there would be a definitive morality that is truly obvious. Then also all rhetoric would be superfluous and ineffective, except maybe as the mere entertainment of demonstrating a skill, just as artistic rhetoric has been all too often when it created the mannerism of postclassical epochs by showing off its means.[38] Cartesianism deprives every rhetoric in the strict sense of its object; rhetoric and the possibility of a definitive morality exclude each other. The institution of provisional morality provides a new latitude for rhetoric, however, especially if its epoch

---

38. On the excess of the *ornatus*, see Curtius, *European Literature and the Latin Middle Ages*, 273.

proves more extensive than supposed or planned. With regard to the imminence of the end, this latitude can be used with a better conscience and hence with more unscrupulous methods. Not only Cartesians enjoy this license of the provisional interim; all eschatologists possess it and use it. Immediately before finality, it must be permitted, if not required, to tempt humans into their happiness. Rhetoric always has something do with this concept of happiness.

Metaphor—as the significant element of rhetoric—points to an anthropological deficiency and in its function corresponds to the anthropology of the "creature of deficiency" [*Mängelwesen*]. But it remedies the deficiency from the stock of a surplus and from the digression beyond the horizon of vital necessities, insofar as this horizon separates possibility and reality. The poverty of our relation to reality (amidst the wealth of our relation to the possible) is not only a poverty of cognition, truth, or theory, but already one of language, which emerges within the life-world horizon of nonmodalized givenness, but has to relate its achievements to the unknown and the possible, which are positioned around this immediacy. Metaphor connects the language areas of the primary relation to reality with those of the secondary relation to possibility. Put even more formally: The metaphor is the instrument of an expansive relation to the world, which has long abandoned those regulations and trigger mechanisms of the biological environment [*Umwelt*] that do not require language, and was only transitionally admitted to the taken-for-granted institutions of the life-world. This centrifugal dynamics is decisive when it comes to a genetic explanation. Cicero compared the genesis of the metaphor to the emergence of human clothing: first and foremost it had been invented for the cold and other weather emergencies, but later it started to also serve as decoration of the body and an indication of dignity—"so the metaphorical employment [*translatio instituta*] of words was begun because of poverty, but was brought into common use for the sake of entertainment."[39] For us, such a statement is no longer productive enough because it states a mere relationship of succession,

---

39. Cicero, *De Oratore*, trans. H. Rackham (Cambridge, MA: Harvard University Press, 1942), 3:122–123.

but does not help us to understand the transition from the situation of deficiency to that of luxury as something that is grounded in and legitimized by the situation of deficiency as such. Anthropologically, this poverty of language—the *egestas verborum* that Cicero sensed while attempting to translate the language of Greek philosophers into Latin—signifies only an aspect of inaccuracy with which humans have been embedded into reality, rather than possibly being fitted to it. If it were the logos of the world expressing itself in human language, having merely obtained an organ other than nature, then it would be impossible for anything to exist besides univocal speech in the Aristotelian sense of the *kyrion onoma*. There would be no need for the courage of metaphor, which always already represents part of the courage to venture conjectures about the nature of reality. Of course, it is a "sad necessity" to require metaphor and to be dependent on its economic effect, but still at the same time this sad necessity reveals to us that we have laid hold of areas of reality that lie beyond our deficiency and neediness, that is, they reflect our freedom to us. In Lambert's exchange of letters with Holland, we find one passage that refers to paragraph 343 of the "Semiotic" in Lambert's *New Organon*: "I wished that you, Sir, had said a few more things about this in the *Organon*. Since we have been placed into the sad necessity of at least making shifts with words of this kind, it would indeed be very much worth the effort to state extensively the way of using them and to determine most exactly the limits of their legitimacy. I think that we owe a large part of our knowledge, and an even larger part of our errors, to the development of metaphors."[40] Here, everything is said with the fewest possible words: the sad necessity of a makeshift solution leads to the ambiguous excess of a guidance for knowledge on the one hand, and to a relegation of deception on the other.

It is the distrust of language that makes metaphor at the same time indispensable and suspect. To escape this dilemma means to trans-

---

40. Letter from Georg Jonathan von Holland to Johann Heinrich Lambert, May 8, 1765, in *Johann Heinrich Lamberts deutscher gelehrter Briefwechsel*, ed. Johann Bernoulli (Berlin: Bernoulli, 1781), 1:39–40.

form the human relation to the world into one that is quintessentially and specifically metaphorical and rhetorical. The philosophy that would result from this could be anticipatorily characterized as a philosophy of rhetoric that in itself becomes rhetorical. Nietzsche comes closest to this type. For him, rhetoric as the epitome of modes of behavior and stylistic means is being formed in a situation of a lack of truth or when scientific knowledge lags behind the great expectation of truth. Plato's hatred of rhetoric is for Nietzsche the starting point to translate his hatred of Plato and Platonism into a rehabilitation of rhetoric. In the winter of 1872/73,[41] Nietzsche gave a lecture course of three hours a week entitled "Description of Ancient Rhetoric." Initially, one is perplexed at how Nietzsche explains the primacy of rhetoric in ancient as opposed to modern education by arguing that there "the feeling for what is true in itself is much more developed."[42] What is contained in this concept of truth, however, becomes clear in the explanation that Nietzsche directly adds: "[R]hetoric arises among a people who still live in mythic images and who have not yet experienced the unqualified need of historical accuracy: they would rather be persuaded than instructed. In addition, the need of men for forensic eloquence must have given rise to the evolution of the liberal art."[43] Nietzsche is likely the first to give a reason for this relation between myth and rhetoric that goes beyond the obvious observation on which it rests: "The mythical and the rhetorical are employed when the brevity of time allows for no scientific instruction."[44] This is a clue that, anthropologically, also goes beyond a mere state of deficiency because it no longer relies on assessing the initial situation and the basic constitution of humans within the antithetics of cognition and rhetoric—whether, for example, one has to proceed from humans' richness of creative endowments or from the poverty of their physiological regression. Nietzsche's clue touches on a constitutive deficiency that puts the availability of time for rational processes in a re-

---

41. [Blumenberg erroneously dates Nietzsche's lecture course to summer 1874.]

42. Friedrich Nietzsche, "Description of Ancient Rhetoric," in *Friedrich Nietzsche on Rhetoric and Language*, ed. Sander L. Gilman et al. (New York: Oxford University Press, 1989), 3.

43. Nietzsche, "Description of Ancient Rhetoric," 3.

44. Nietzsche, 7–9.

lation to their gains: lack of time is a radical of the determinedness of human life, and reason may not demand any price of time. For this circumstance, the answer is rhetoric.

There is a precious passage in Kant's correspondence with Carl Leonhard Reinhold from the year 1789. In the *Allgemeine Literaturzeitung*, Reinhold had refuted Johann August Eberhard's attacks against Kant, published in his "philosophical magazine." Kant adds additional remarks about this in two letters. For part of the disciplines that had fallen prey to Kant's *Critique of Theoretical Reason*, Eberhard had claimed that further progress of the work would perhaps still bring about successes. He had written, "But even regarding the work of the disputed sciences of cosmology and theology, we do not need to let our hands sink; we can always continue working to further them, we can always seek to enrich them with new truths, without beforehand committing ourselves to the transcendental validity of those truths."[45] Kant provides this text with a short allusion to an anecdote: "Here one might ask, as the foreign scholar did when they showed him the Sorbonne lecture hall, 'They have been arguing here for three hundred years; what have they found out?'"[46] At this point, one is tempted to say that rhetoric rests on the fact that one cannot afford to dispute for three hundred years before anything can be agreed upon. But immediately it becomes clear that Kant, in the place of rhetoric, establishes something completely different that nevertheless has the same function of replacing the intolerability of theory's dilatory procedure with quicker self-evidence—practical reason. Precisely because it is dependent only on the self-limitation of theoretical reason, but not at all on the latter's progress and completion (as Descartes had wished), it can achieve autonomously what rhetoric believed to be able to achieve only heteronomously. This would be the perfect displace-

---

45. Johann August Eberhard, "Über logische Wahrheit oder die transzendentale Gültigkeit der menschlichen Erkenntnis," Immanuel Kant, *Der Streit mit Johann August Eberhard*, ed. Marion Lauschke and Manfred Zahn (Hamburg: Meiner, 1998), 16–31; 30.

46. Immanuel Kant to Karl Leonhard Reinhold, May 19, 1789, in Immanuel Kant, *Correspondence*, trans. Arnulf Zweig (Cambridge: Cambridge University Press, 1999), 304.

ment of rhetoric and its function, were it not for the suspicion that the authority of practical reason had previously been restricted to morality in the strict sense in such a way that too large a scope of human behavior and action would have to remain outside of morality and would be abandoned if the relation of displacement between rhetorical and practical reason were to be seen in Kant's sense.

I will frame the issues hinted at here in a hard thesis. There is a contradiction between, on the one hand, the infinity implications of reason and its procedures and, on the other, the anthropological conditions of finitude. If this is the case, there not only has to be a critique of pure reason in the sense of a constitutive limitation of its thematic extension, that is, a self-limitation of reason that for Kant could be captured in a spatial, territorial metaphorics. There also has to be a critique of pure rationality that refers to the temporal structure of the processes of reason and that can only be represented in a one-dimensional metaphorics. Not only an infinite being in the theological sense but already a being of infinite access to time would have to accept the demands of pure rationality without objection. It is temporal finitude that compels dissent and insists on shortened processes that cannot suffice for pure rationality, and would compel assumptions about legality and presumptions regarding the burden of proof; these things are often characterized as conservative because they are not prepared to expose what exists to the theoretical postulate of absolute justification. One does not even have to articulate this conjecture as one about the rationality of what exists, but only about the rationality of that which makes proportioned demands of time. Conversely, there is simulated rationality that very much seeks to identify itself through its consumption of time.

Translated by Florian Fuchs and Hannes Bajohr

PART III

NATURE, TECHNOLOGY, AND AESTHETICS

12

THE RELATIONSHIP BETWEEN NATURE AND TECHNOLOGY AS A PHILOSOPHICAL PROBLEM

(1951)

It is not just before our own eyes but also in our own hands that the world of technology is fashioned and subsists. There is nothing about it that we might first have to accept as given to be able to penetrate it cognitively. Technical reality is such that its translation into actuality is enacted only by reason and virtue of cognition accomplished and calculations made. If this altogether calculable matter in today's world should nonetheless confront us with a problem, and indeed one of the darkest and most urgent problems of these times, it must belong to a different level than the matter of discerning the conditions under which technical contrivances function. Yet even though we are aware of a set of problems aggregating

[Originally published as "Das Verhältnis von Natur und Technik als philosophisches Problem," *Studium Generale* 4, no. 8 (1951): 461–467; from Hans Blumenberg, *Ästhetische und metaphorologische Schriften*, ed. Anselm Haverkamp (Frankfurt am Main: Suhrkamp, 2001), 253–265. English-language version published in *Graduate Faculty Philosophy Journal* 40, no. 1 (2019): 19–30.]

in an ever more foreboding fashion, we are still far from reaching so much as an approximation of a guiding question; indeed, we do not even know in what specific realm of possible questions this particular one might be unfolded and broached.

1. The Problem at Present

Initially, we might expect all possible questions concerning this matter to form a branch of the natural sciences. Technology has historically constituted itself as applied natural science—as a constructive extension of nature—and this structural continuity would seem to determine the character and methodology of its problems once and for all.

The historical reality of human life with technology has failed to confirm this basic assumption, however. Technology, as an objective domain within the modern world, has more and more visibly separated itself from its functional continuity with nature and has entered into new constellations that are sui generis and, indeed, diametrical opposites to natural reality. From the mere *use* of nature for eking out a living through to the increasing *exploitation* of nature as a reservoir of energy and natural resources, the development of technical consciousness and the technical will tend toward making a claim for the radical and total *transformation* of nature as mere *materia prima* for the exercise of human power.

This being so, an examination of this complex will show *man* to be the principle in which the relationship between nature and technology is founded as posited [*Setzung*] by an act of will. As a being whose existence is not vouchsafed by its organic adaptation to the natural environment, and thus as a being that is forced into self-assertion and into producing for itself the conditions of its life as a mode of existence, man brings forth technology in answer to the specific problems of his being. Man *is* a technical being; technical reality corresponds to a deficiency in his natural endowment. Modern technology is thus not a development unique in and to human history but merely the conscious and deliberate implementation of a necessity rooted in human nature.

Yet even this anthropological approach proves unequal to the phenomenon of technology. What is increasingly emerging as the defining trait of the technical sphere is its *autonomy*, its increasing intractability to man, the way his decisions, wishes, and needs come to be overlaid by a dynamic inherent in technology, which imprints on the entire life of an epoch an unmistakable homogeneous *style*. The outward and inward domination that technology has attained over present-day man is reflected in the common metaphor of the "demonism of technology" [*Dämonie der Technik*], which provides the clearest testimony to the unresolved state of the issue. Talk of technology's autonomy and demonism, its inescapable perfection, prepares and justifies an imminent capitulation to a supposed necessity. Such talk solidifies a resigned equanimity in the face of the aporia, the predicament, and it cuts off the properly philosophical path that leads from the aporia to the framing of the problem. If, however, philosophy refuses to let its claims be curtailed by the precipitate positing of absolutes, it might at least be able to preserve awareness of how questionable the commonplace formulations are in which the stupefying poison of resignation is taken.

What estimate to give of the possibilities of philosophy in this situation is a question that is thrown into relief only against a broader historical horizon.

2. Natural and Manufactured Entities in Greek Metaphysics

According to the Greeks' understanding of being, being and nature—*ousia* and *physis*—are concepts of nearly identical meaning. That which constitutes what is [*das Seiende*] as an entity [*Seiendes*] is that which rests on itself, by itself—and not on anything that might interpose or insinuate itself; what is as an entity is that which it is by its essence, its character of subsisting in itself (*ousia*). This basic trait of the entity qua entity, however, is gleaned from the essence of nature: the natural entity contains the principle of its being and becoming (*entelecheia*) in itself.[1] Plants and animals *autonomously* become and are what they are able to become and be, within the genetic nexus of nature. This genetic nexus is self-sufficient, requiring no contribution from the outside: again and again, each entity descends from another entity of the same specific imprint (*eidos*). The unity of nature, as such a genetic nexus of constant basic forms, has no need for questions concerning a beginning; it may be understood by itself, specifically and only as the unity of a temporally infinite nexus: "All things . . . come to be from what is" [*ex ontos gignetai panta*].[2] The concept of "nature" coincides with and fulfills the concept of being.

But how can the character of being of something *manufactured* be related to this basic conception? The origin of a manufactured thing is skill (*technē*); as such, it seems not to reside in nature's self-sufficient and infinite nexus but to *begin* in an act of positing that represents a leap in the continuum of specific formations. Only by a deeper interpretation of the ancient concept of *technē* can it be shown that what is manufactured also depends for its character of being on the inner nexus of nature; what comes into being by *technē* can be called an entity only by virtue of that nexus. Man as bearer of *technē* is not the *radical* principle of technical reality (*technē onta*). He himself is what he essentially is entirely as a link in the genetic unity of nature, so much so that he can constantly be invoked as a paradigm of self-sufficient relatedness: "All things . . . come to be from what is" [*ex ontos gignetai panta*]—"human begets human" [*anthrōpos gar anthrōpon genna*] (*Met.*, 12.3.1070a8). Man is a link in the *kosmos* and nothing above or beside it. The human animal is set apart from other species of this genus by possession of *logos* (*zōon logon echon*).[3] *Logos* epitomizes man's special relationship to the *kosmos*, which consists in his ability to "convene" [*versammeln*] the being of the *kosmos* within himself as understanding and cognition (*legein* originally meaning "to gather" [*sammeln*]). All potentialities of this

1. [Aristotle, *De Anima*, trans. C. D. C. Reeve (Indianapolis, IN: Hackett, 2017), 2.1.412a19–21.]

2. Aristotle, *Metaphysics*, trans. C. D. C. Reeve (Indianapolis, IN: Hackett, 2016), 12.2.1069b19.

3. [Aristotle, *Politics*, trans. C. D. C. Reeve (Indianapolis, IN: Hackett, 2017), 1.1.1253a10.]

"human" are governed by and founded on its possession of *logos*, including *technē*, the skill at manufacturing works. In being related to nature, this skill sheds the appearance of spontaneous, originary radicalism and brute force: *technē* is possible only as the enactment of man's relation to nature—its setting itself to work—which is founded in *logos*. This finds confirmation, for example, in Aristotle, who will admit only to a gradual and not an essential difference between the work (*ergon*) of man and the "work" of plants and animals.[4] *Logos* only allows for additional possibilities but no essential difference in terms of work as action [*Wirken*]. Only by virtue of resting on natural being [*pyhsei on*], then, is technical being [*technē on*] itself an entity (*ousia*), a secondary mode of natural being.[5] For technical being to escape from this secondary mode of natural being would be against *logos* and thus against human nature—futile violence (*bia*) against the entity and theft (*steresis*) of its being.

Upon this interpretation of the relationship between nature and technology, which is guided by a particular understanding of that which is as something founded on itself, rests the ancient view of the hierarchy of human behavior: *theōria* [theory] is placed before and above *praxis*, not only as an instrumental condition but insofar as it is theory that makes praxis possible in the first place. Theory, by having authentic and essential access to being, prepares the ground for any work-like [*werkhaft*] manner in which praxis may depend on or be derived from theory while excluding sheer violence. Accordingly, freedom is also clearly assigned its rank and scope.

3. The Reversal of the Relationship between *Natura* and *Ars* by the Idea of Creation

Man's self-understanding as a link in the homogeneous nexus of nature, freedom's meaning derived from the scope of the given shape

---

4. [Aristotle, *Nicomachean Ethics*, trans. C. D. C. Reeve (Indianapolis, IN: Hackett, 2014), 1.7.1097b24–1098a3.]

5. [Aristotle, *De Partibus Animalium I*, in *De Partibus Animalium I and De Generatione Animalium I*, trans. David M. Balme (Oxford: Clarendon Press, 2003), 1.1.640a28–9.]

of the world, *technē* founded on the *kosmos* as gathered within *logos*—these were the corresponding aspects of the ancient understanding of being, according to which "being," in the precise sense, can only be infinitely self-fashioning nature that manifests its constant creation of form in the genetic nexus, while a work-like entity qua entity can only be understood as being derived from that realm of meaning. A radically new view of the relation between nature and technology, and thus the opening of a much-extended scope for technical freedom, will consequently be able to develop only on the ground of a changed understanding of being.

In what does the radicalism of this transformation, the opening of new possibilities of thought and action, consist? What can be said in a preliminary way is that the *self-sufficiency* of nature and its effective context as the fundamental ontological dimension is ruptured. The clearest expression of this rupture is that the nexus of nature must now be conceived of as a temporal, finite one, and that the question of the principles and structures of its immanent course are superseded by the question concerning a *beginning*. Only from the circumstance that being and the cosmos are no longer congruent, that the *kosmos* no longer itself is or contains the divine being [*theion on*] but can be understood only in terms of, and as having its origin in, an *other* does this question draw its meaning and its urgency. No longer is the being of entities fully absorbed in, and sufficiently founded on, its genetic nexus. Instead, nature as a unity of *physei onta* is now itself a *technē on*. Nature's genesis, traced back by deduction, breaks off amid the nothingness, which is the impossibility of its self-sufficient foundation, from which it was seized by the act of divine force of the *creatio ex nihilo* [creation from nothingness]. The *creatio ex nihilo* is a technical primary act in the most precise sense—the most radical *leap*—which thought can comprehend only as the boundary of its rational possibility. At the same time, here originates the stark inversion of the relationship between nature and technology that must be considered the epitome of the "conversion" (*conversio*) of ancient ontology. *Freedom* no longer receives its meaning from being given as nature; conversely, nature's meaning derives from the divine freedom expressed in the primal, founding act of the creation decision—God's will [*quia voluit*]—which is impervious to further questioning.[6]

But where does *man* stand within this new relationship between nature and technology? Man is no longer to be understood as a link in the genetic nexus of nature; he is no longer simply "nature," and no longer is his essence reliant on the grounding provided by nature. Yet by no means does his singularity—an aspect usually maintained at the expense of others—reside foremost in being chosen and destined for salvation, a destiny that might also draw him out of a primal rootedness in the natural whole. Instead, this uniqueness exists already by virtue of his *origins*, which are not simply coeval with the entirety of creation; rather, each individual human being begins primally as a singular, originary, and unmediated creature of divine power. That the individual human soul should issue forth not in the course of the natural act of conception but from a discrete and particular act of creation by the hand of God means nothing less than the foundation of man's radical autonomy, his having grown independently [*Eigenwüchsigkeit*] within nature as a whole, in which he is nonetheless phenomenally rooted. That man, according to his essence, should be capable of confronting and opposing nature—of relating to it through power and violation—is a possibility that can be understood only against the horizon of Christian ontology. The difference between Christian *creationism* and ancient *generationism* with regard to the origin of the soul is of unforeseeable latent consequence for the manner in which Western man will one day relate to the world. Only a human being, who, by virtue of his being, is *placed* into nature, rather than having emerged from it, and who thus finds no "natural" and hence unquestioned prefiguration of his existence therein, can potentially be a "technical" human being, forced to live in confrontation with nature.

---

6. Augustine, *On Genesis: A Refutation of the Manichees*, in *On Genesis*, trans. Edmund Hill, ed. John E. Rotelle (Hyde Park, NY: New City Press, 2002), bk. 1, chap. 2, §4; *De Genesi contra Manichæos*, ed. Dorothea Weber, vol. 91 of *Corpus Scriptorum Ecclesiasticorum Latinorum*, ed. Kommission zur Herausgabe des Corpus der lateinischen Kirchenväter (Vienna: Verlag der Österreichischen Akademie der Wissenschaften, 1998), bk. 1, chap. 2, §4.

4. The Theological Exacerbation of the Difference between Nature and Human Existence

Now, on the ground of the Christian understanding of being, the heterogeneity between man and nature is exacerbated to the point of a tragic *hiatus* through the consciousness—which suffuses Christian existence—of man's primal decision, by which a failure to measure up to how he ought originally to be became the defining trait of his existence. Man, who set his freedom *against* being as God had intended being, is nonetheless unable to escape the necessity of having to make a life *with* and *from* this being. Original sin makes nature the antagonist of man's self-possession; his life is thus characterized, as is already clear from the third chapter of Genesis, by the effort, severity, and labor of the *and yet* [*Und doch*] of having to live in nature—nature, which, to him, is no longer the ground supporting his existence and the ready wellspring of life, but that into which he is instead thrown like a person banished.[7] The irreconcilable difference between freedom and necessity, the consequence of sin, predestines him to an existence that is largely effort, work, use of force, and violence—that is to say, "technical"—and which sets his will the target, which is as unattainable as it is impossible to relinquish, of nonetheless bringing into effortless harmony existence and nature, compulsion and choice, freedom and necessity. It is no coincidence that the origin of the modern age is marked not just by the ascent of scientific thinking as a means of technical realization but also by the Reformation's deepening of the sense of sinfulness and thus of the hiatus between existence and nature. Modern technology may be the application of modern knowledge of nature, yet such a dynamic transposition of knowledge into reality is not sufficiently justified by this underlying connection between science and technology; rather, it is a consequence of that understanding of the position of existence within nature. These connections have been thoroughly explored with regard to the emergence of the specifically modern form of economy, yet we are still lacking

---

7. [3 Gen. 14–24, Revised Standard Version.]

an analysis of the intellectual-historical background of the origins of technology.

5. The Abrogation of the Medieval Separation of Use and Enjoyment

A formidable objection to this account may now be raised: How, with these fundamental conditions in place, could the Middle Ages— the historical sphere of a Christian ontology—be such an untechnical era, in phenomenal terms? Against this objection, it must be brought to bear not only that the genuinely Christian driving forces in the Middle Ages were decisively hidden and kept latent by the impact of ancient metaphysics, which is hardly to be overestimated, but also that against a dynamic realization of these forces stood a peculiarity of the Middle Ages, which was to curtail the exigencies of the world and secular existence *sub specie æternitatis* [under the aspect of eternity]. Augustine's formulation, according to which relations with the world were restricted to *uti* (use) while reserving *frui* (enjoyment) for the consummation of being in the hereafter as the absolute goal, provides the clearest illustration of this view.[8] The significance of this reservation in *keeping latent* the impulses stimulating technology finds confirmation when viewed from that era's end: among the decisive preconditions for the specific technical and economic development of the modern age is the abrogation of the difference between *uti* and *frui*, between use and enjoyment. The necessary use of nature finds fulfillment in its free and self-sufficient enjoyment.

What emerges ever more clearly is that to define technology as the *application* of modern science is insufficient as an *explanation* of its place in the picture of the modern age. For it is not at all self-evident that understanding should *not* be sufficient unto itself and self-contained, and instead demands application. Classical antiquity found understanding [*Erkenntnis*] and the knowledge [*Wissen*] that

---

8. [See Augustine, *De Doctrina Christiana*, trans. and ed. R. P. H. Green (Oxford: Oxford University Press, 1995), bk. 1, §9.]

came with it to be the highest good and the epitome of human striving, as the beginning of Aristotle's *Metaphysics* testifies [*Met.*, 1.1.980a22]. Why, at the outset of the modern age, knowledge came to be no longer sufficient unto itself can hence not be accounted for by saying it *demanded* to be applied. A more plausible interpretation is that the historical understanding of self and world virtually *challenged* modern science to adopt its instrumental function—indeed, that its own rise was decisively provoked by the advanced state of the technical will. From a philosophical perspective, the commonly assumed precedence of science over technology appears to be inverted.

The consequences of the abrogation of the fundamental medieval difference between use and enjoyment are fathomless. The instrumental use of the world in anticipation of consummation in the hereafter is essentially *finite*, whereas enjoyment of the world, into which mere use becomes absorbed, is *infinite*. The replacement of a finite picture of the world by an infinite one—a process in itself characteristic of the epochal threshold of the modern age—also marks this historical line. Though the consequences will only emerge much later, the decisive transition is, in principle, already made here, leading from the use of nature and the application of its laws to its unremitting exploitation and conquest through which the dynamic of technology furnishes its own meaning. How stark the inner contradiction of a foundation that has *enjoyment* as its goal and *work* for a precondition is will only become apparent at the end of technical development.

6. The Unity of the Origin of Science, Technology, Art, and Power, and the Beginning of the Modern Age

The ontological connections presented here find even stronger confirmation if the largely neglected unity of preconditions through which modern *art* is connected to modern *technology* is taken into account. The Latin word *ars* inherits the meanings that in Greek were denoted by the word *technē*: art [*Kunst*] and technology [*Technik*], in present usage, are expressions of man's primordial *ars*, an art that may be understood as the unity of man's ability to create works. The novelty that modern art and technology hold in common is man's conception of his abilities with respect to the fulfillment of his will to enjoyment [*Genußwillen*]. The factor of enjoyment constitutes one defining trait of modern aesthetics, the other factor being the artist's creative power. The new perspective, in which man becomes aware of his own ability, can only be understood against the backdrop of the intellectual-historical situation of the Late Middle Ages, which is defined by *nominalism*.

Here, essentially theological considerations lead to the confidence of the High Middle Ages in the power of reason to effect understanding being shaken at the very root; access to the essence of being, which was brought forth by the divine creator's infinite freedom, is foreclosed to man's finite reason. Only in the praxis of orientation toward the world and in coming to terms with reality is the totality of our knowledge confirmed and vindicated as "right." Terms [*Begriffe*] are mere "names" [*nomina*] rather than "concepts" [*conceptus*], and "right" and "wrong" now express merely the economic function of making one's arrangements and finding one's way within the world. As such, however, our entire capacity for understanding has assumed, a priori, a character that may safely be called "technical": this capacity does not perceivingly submit [*vernehmend hingegeben*] to what is while remaining unable to access it; instead, it is, by its very origins, creative and productive of a unity of terms and laws arranged with the sole purpose of facilitating man's task in the world. Our *understanding* essentially is art and technology as one already, the very *ars humana*, whose division into the forms of work and expression known as "art" and "technology" in the modern sense is but a secondary development. For the first time, human *autonomy* reveals itself to be the defining trait of the dawning epoch. Its origin, however, lies not in man elevating and aggrandizing himself, but in answering the need imposed by his essential strangeness in this world and his falling short of its truth that is founded in God. What is primary is not the excess and ardor of power but rather an exercise of power that submits to *necessity*. Since the world God created cannot become mankind's property, man is now compelled to build his own world by his own efforts.

As it is given, nature, however, which is concealed in its essence and accessible to the quantifying formulas of science only as *res extensa*—becomes mere *raw material for ars humana*. The style of relating to the world, of which the foundations are described above so profoundly imbues the spirit of the modern age that even today it continues to bridge a world divided into East and West: both here and there, the program—which is stated ever more bluntly—is to bend nature to man's will. What a technician in an American laboratory has to say about the meaning of his work is likewise expressed in the projects propagated by the East: *Here, the world is being created a second time*! How hidden this self-proclamation of the technical will was, until recently, and how explicit it has today become, finds a striking illustration in the history of those surrogate, or *ersatz*, substances, which were originally *imitated* laboriously from nature but now represent an immense branch of technology in which nature is anticipated or improved upon.

The insights thus gained into the historical nexus from which modern technology emerged as an incomparable phenomenon are confirmed when one attempts to understand the wider realm of notions and concepts that mark the beginning of the modern age as forming a unity of meaning. This is the backdrop to the Renaissance argument over whether art was essentially *imitatio* or *inventio*; the concept of *invention*, which later was to define the technical realm, only becomes meaningful in this context. That a key figure of nascent modernity such as Leonardo da Vinci should have been both an artist and a technician is no coincidence but rather confirms the unity of origin. By the same token, the emergence of the concept of political *power* as a claim to a rational, technical means of handling public affairs will have to be based on these same foundations.

Theology tries to keep human autonomy within the province of Christianity by framing it as a divine command. Accordingly, Nicholas of Cusa, who is also one of the founders of the *experiment*—that is to say, the attempt to force nature under the conditions of human understanding—writes: "O Domine . . . posuisti in libertate mea ut sim, si voluero, mei ipsius. Hinc nisi sim mei ipsius, tu non es meus" [O Lord . . . you have placed within my freedom that I be my own if I am willing. Hence, unless I am my own, you are not mine].[9] It is also in this context that the many-layered programmatic term "reformation" ought to be considered. In proclaiming it, Marsilio Ficino would have it be understood in a universal and cosmic sense, and would find its exemplary fulfillment in art: the counterpart to God's formation of nature is human *re-formatio*, which concerns man because he is rooted in the original creation neither self-evidently nor as though it were his own property.[10] The distance between existence and nature always provides the ontological foundation. Descartes demands that we throw away [*jeter par terre*] all that is presupposed [*prévention*] by history and nature,[11] thus cleaning the slate for a *project* for science and nature that is altogether radical and, as it were, ex nihilo in its approach. Framing the unity of science as such a project is an essentially technical stance. Giambattista Vico merely uses another word in attempting to describe all varieties of human work and action as *poietic*; in doing so, he becomes the first to include *history* within the realm of *ars humana*.[12]

Thus emerge the outlines of an interpretation that seeks to understand the signature developments of the modern age—science, technology, art, and power—in terms of the unity of their origin in the historical process whereby meaning is imparted by being. The problem of technology cannot be torn from this unity as something to be formulated or solved on its own.

---

9.   Nicholas of Cusa, *On The Vision of God*, in *Selected Spiritual Writings*, trans. H. Lawrence Bond (Mahwah, NJ: Paulist Press, 1997), chap. 7, §25; *De visione Dei*, ed. Heide Dorothea Riemann, vol. 6 of *Nicolai de Cusa Opera Omnia*, ed. Heidelberger Akademie der Wissenschaften (Hamburg: Meiner, 2000), chap. 7, §25.

10.   Marsilio Ficino, "Quam decens Dei hominis que coniunctio," in *De christiana religione*, in *Opera Omnia*, ed. Paul Oskar Kristeller and Mario Sancipriano (Turin: Bottega D'Erasmo, 1962), vol. 1, chap. 18, lines 1–2, 4–10.

11.   [René Descartes, *Discours de la méthode*, in *Discours de la méthode et essais*, vol. 6 of *Œuvres de Descartes*, ed. Charles Adam and Paul Tannery (Paris: Léopold Cerf, 1902), 13, 18; *Discourse on the Method*, trans. Robert Stoothoff, in vol. 1 of *The Philosophical Writings of Descartes*, trans. John Cottingham, Robert Stoothoff, and Dugald Murdoch (Cambridge: Cambridge University Press, 1985), 117, 120.]

12.   [Giambattista Vico, *The New Science*, trans. Thomas Goddard Bergin and Max Harold Fisch (Ithaca, NY: Cornell University Press, 1948), §367.]

7. The "Second Nature" of the Machine World as a Consequence of the Technical Will

Now, a weighty objection has been leveled against an understanding of the history of modern technology as the relentless unfolding of an inner principle. In his "Thoughts on Technology," which, even though their ontological underpinning leaves much to be desired, remain of considerable descriptive value, Ortega y Gasset points to the essential distinction that must be made within the technical realm itself between a tool and a machine.[13]

Can we continue to explain this ineluctable difference by appealing to an unmodified account of the ontological foundations disclosed so far, or is this the point where something radically new emerges? We have seen that modern man is situated so as to necessarily need technical world-making, a need that was recast as a virtue—that is, as the dignity, pride, and hubris of human autonomy and autarky—only by the consciousness of the strength it took to accept the task. It belongs to the inner dynamic of that task and its fulfillment that what began as makeshift has become elevated to the absolute rank of a "second creation," manifesting itself in creations that are not essentially inferior to those of the first creation. If what was created in the first creation is to be understood as "nature"—that is to say, a creation out-of-itself of fashioning and exertion, which is grounded in itself—then the same tendency toward that very ontological rank must inhere in the second creation—that is to say, the second creation can find its fulfillment only in a "second nature." By this logic, the distinctive property of natural being—to carry within itself the principle of its fashioning and its function—is transposed into the realm of technical work. This is where the impetus for the evolving design of automata, engines, and machines can be found, those devices in the modern world that function "out of themselves," which could seem ever more adequate to "first nature," to the degree that it became plausible to

---

13. [José Ortega y Gasset, "Thoughts on Technology," trans. Helene Weyl, in *Philosophy and Technology: Readings in the Philosophical Problems of Technology,* ed. Carl Mitcham and Robert Mackey (New York: Free Press, 1972), 290–313.]

conceive of first nature itself as a "world apparatus." This schema for the interpretation of nature does not spring primarily from the expansive tendency of technical man's basic notions; rather, this schema is simply what enabled the machine to be conceived of as a technical transposition of the concept of nature.

That the machine should produce, that it might be put to industrial use, is, by comparison, only a late and secondary trait. Accordingly, the defining *caesura* must be sought not in the invention of industrial machines (e.g., the mechanical loom [1825]) but in the baroque "play" world of automata, the dream of the perpetual motion machine, which signifies the absolute technical "out-of-itself." Yet the key word of this essential tendency of the technical stance toward the world is the nonconcept [*Unbegriff*] of "organization," which assumes the organic to be the product of a construction.

But does the concept of a "second nature" really carry the implications of the modern age's understanding of nature to their conclusion, to the end of all its possible consequences? Is the claim to "unconditioned production," as Heidegger has called the technical will,[14] enacted in the "second nature" of a perfected machine-world? Or does such unconditionality imply that it will suffer nothing else alongside it—which is to say that not only has "second nature" provided the potency for the *nullification* of the first nature but that the former's essence also pushes toward the latter's realization? Man's experience of this ultimate stage of possible technical fulfillment is only just beginning.

Translated by Joe Paul Kroll

---

14. Martin Heidegger, "Letter on Humanism," in *Pathmarks*, trans. Frank A. Capuzzi, ed. William McNeill (Cambridge: Cambridge University Press, 1998), 259; "Brief über den 'Humanismus,'" in *Wegmarken*, ed. Friedrich Wilhelm von Herrmann, vol. 9 of *Gesamtausgabe*, ed. Friedrich Wilhelm von Herrmann (Frankfurt am Main: Klostermann, 1976), 340.

13

"IMITATION OF NATURE"

Toward a Prehistory of the Idea of the Creative Being

(1957)

I.

For almost two thousand years, it seemed as if the conclusive and final answer to the question, "What can the human being, using his power and skill, do in the world and with the world?" had been given by Aristotle when he proposed that "art" was the imitation of nature, thereby defining the concept with which the Greeks encompassed all the actual operative abilities of man within reality—the concept of *technē*. With this expression, the Greeks indicated more than what we today call technology [*Technik*]: It gave them an inclusive concept for man's capacity to produce works and form

Originally published as "Nachahmung der Natur: Zur Vorgeschichte der Idee des schöpferischen Menschen," *Studium Generale* 10, no. 5 (1957): 266–283; from Hans Blumenberg, *Ästhetische und metaphorologische Schriften*, ed. Anselm Haverkamp (Frankfurt am Main: Suhrkamp, 2001), 9–46. English-language version published in *Qui Parle* 12, no. 1 (2000): 17–54.

shapes, a concept comprising the "artistic" and the "artificial" (which we so sharply distinguish between today). Only in this broader sense should we use this term we translate as "art." "In general," then, according to Aristotle, "human skill [*technē*] either completes what nature is incapable of completing or imitates nature."[1] This dual definition is closely tied to the double meaning of the concept of "nature" as a productive principle (*natura naturans*) and produced form (*natura naturata*). It is easy to see, however, that the overlapping component lies in the element of "imitation." For the task of picking up where nature leaves off is carried out, after all, by closely following nature's prescription, by starting from the entelechy of the given and carrying it out.[2] This stepping-in of "art" for nature extends so far that Aristotle can say that the builder of a house only does exactly what nature *would do*, if it were able, so to speak, to "grow" houses.[3] Nature and "art" are structurally identical: the immanent characteristics of one sphere can be transposed onto the other. This idea was then established as fact when tradition shortened the Aristotelian formulation to *ars imitatur naturam*, as Aristotle himself had already expressed it.[4]

What contemporary significance can this formulation have that would make its preconditions and historical transformations worth investigating? Has not modern man long been insisting that he is a "creative" being, starkly opposing nature to the manmade [*Konstruktion*]? In 1523, Parmigianino painted his self-portrait from a

---

1. Aristotle, *Physics* 2.8.199a15–17. [The English translation used here is *Physics*, trans. Robin Waterfield (New York: Oxford University Press, 1996).]

2. See the formulation in *Politics* 4.17.1337a1–2: "The purpose of education, like that of art generally, is simply to copy nature by making her deficiencies good." [The English translation used here is *The Politics of Aristotle*, trans. Ernest Barker (New York: Oxford University Press, 1946), 331.]

3. *Physics* 2.8.199a12–15. Nature is, so to speak, "auto-technical," comparable to the physician who heals himself (199b30–32). The inference that such auto-technicality is identical with deliberate intention would be rejected (199b26–28). Aristotle does not demonstrate for us any (at least hypothetically) requisite original situation in which nothing exists yet, or nothing very specific. Since all of his specificity is always already there, for Aristotle there is no moment when something must have been "thought up" and transferred from the imagination into reality. As a rule, thought thinks the existent only *afterward*.

4. *Physics* 2.2.194a21f. *Meteorology* 4.3.381b3–7.

distorted convex mirror—thus not allowing the natural to preserve and increase itself in the artistic, but rather to refract and transform itself.[5] Since then, the mark of the creative human being aware of his power has become ever more clearly evident in works of art. As a personal challenge and a testament to the genuine power of his being, art first became for modern man "the truly metaphysical task of this life."[6] A recognition of the bindingness of this task crystallized around the question, "What is nature's authority over art?" Surveying the latitude for artistic freedom; the discovery of the infinity of the possible beyond the finitude of the factual; the easing of the relationship to nature through the historical self-objectification of the artistic process as art reproduces itself over and over within and through art[7]—these are fundamental processes that appear to have nothing more to do with the Aristotelian formula. It has often been said and demonstrated that the world in which we live is a world of deliberate, even vehement, outperformance, disempowerment, and distortion of nature, a world in which what is given is insufficient. Perhaps it was André Breton who first gave surrealism the ontological formulation that what is not is equally as "real" (*intense*) as what is—and this is the precise expression for possibil-

---

5. See *Exhibition Catalog No. 88*, "The Triumph of European Mannerism" (Amsterdam: Rijksmuseum, 1955).

6. Friedrich Nietzsche, "Preface to Richard Wagner," in *The Birth of Tragedy and the Case of Wagner*, trans. Walter Kaufmann (New York: Vintage, 1967), 31–32.

7. See Werner Hoffman, "'Manier' und 'Stil' in der Kunst des 20. Jahrhunderts," *Studium Generale* 8 (1955): 9. Kant had already transferred the aspect of imitation to the reproduction of one artwork by another. Nature, on the other hand, is the ultimately productive Ur-instance of art, through the medium of "genius," in a sense, however, that implies not imitation but "production through freedom." Immanuel Kant, *Critique of the Power of Judgement*, trans. Paul Guyer and Eric Matthes (Cambridge: Cambridge University Press, 2000), § 46, 182. Genius "is to be entirely opposed to the spirit of imitation" (Kant, *Critique of the Power of Judgement*, § 47, 187). Although genius must be understood as "nature in the subject" (Kant, *Critique of the Power of Judgement*, § 46, 186), an ultimately formal bindingness of nature is presupposed that no longer has any explanatory value. Only the historical process is still obviously imitative by "the product of a genius" becoming exemplary "for emulation by another genius, who is thereby awakened to the feeling of his own originality," so that art "gives rise to a school"—"and for these people, beautiful art is to that extent imitation, to which nature gave the rule through a genius." Kant, *Critique of the Power of Judgement*, § 49, 195–196.

ity of the modern will to create [*Kunstwillen*] overall, for the *terra incognita*, whose untrammeled state entices imaginations. A work does not refer through suggestion or representation to some other, antecedent being; rather, it has an authentic share of being in the human world: "A new picture is a unique event, a birth, which enriches the universe as it is grasped by the human mind, by bringing a new form into it."[8] To see the new and to produce it is no longer merely a question of an instinctive "curiosity," in the sense of the medieval *curiositas*; rather, it has become a metaphysical need: man tries to realize the image he has of himself. It is not because necessity is the mother of invention that "invention" is a significant act in the modern world; nor is it because our reality is so riddled with technological structures that they crop up as subject matter in the artworks of the period. Here, we perceive instead the formative power of a homogeneous impulse that prompts the articulation of a radical human self-understanding. Whence, however, the violence and force with which this self-understanding makes itself known?

Precisely this question we will not be able to answer adequately if we do not keep in mind what the modern concept of man had set itself *against*. The vehement passion with which the attribute of creativity was gained for the subject was marshaled in the face of the overwhelming importance of the axiom of the "imitation of nature." This struggle has not yet come to an end, even as other, new formulations seem to be triumphing. But it is not merely a political commonplace that the enemy becomes a liability for the victor at the moment of defeat. The opposition, against which all powers were necessarily marshaled, disperses, and the forces once mobilized against it easily overshoot the position they once besieged.

II.

I shall first try to describe more precisely the historical setting in which this contest took place. Although the "beginnings" of anything

---

8. Henri Matisse, as cited in Werner Haftmann, *Painting in the Twentieth Century*, 2 vols., trans. Janet Seligman (New York: Frederick A. Praeger, 1965), 1:78.

historical are always elusive, the *terminus a quo* I have selected already represents the striking early development of our problem. I am thinking of the Idiot in the *Three Dialogues* of Nicholas of Cusa of 1450. To characterize this figure in the dialogue, it is not enough to derive a sociological explanation based on the new consciousness of the layman in his conflict with the clergy in the fifteenth century, as it is here reflected. The Cusan confronts his Idiot equally with the Philosopher as a proponent of scholasticism and the Rhetorician as a representative figure of humanism.[9] The Cusan "layman" is, to be sure, partially modeled on the opposition of the mystics and the *devotio moderna* [new piety] to the Scholastic and educational arrogance of the time. But the irony with which this *illiteratus* [unlettered] counters these intellectual luminaries, the, as it were, democratic style he employs in conversation, paying no mind to the dissimilarity of the premises, has a rather different basis—it suggests a new kind of man, who understands himself from the outside and justifies his worth by what he does and what he knows how to do—by his "achievement" [*Leistung*], we would say. The not at all historically obvious connection between achievement and self-consciousness is palpable in the Cusan Idiot, and precisely in the aspect that concerns us.

In the second chapter of the dialogue *On Mind*, the layman demonstrates to his interlocutors, the Philosopher and the Rhetorician, what his own trade, spoon-carving—which provides him with only a modest living and which society regards as lowly—means for his own self-conception and self-worth. This "art," too, is indeed imitation—but not the imitation of nature. Rather, what is imitated is the *ars infinita* [infinite art] of God himself, specifically in the sense that this production is original, generated spontaneously, and creative, but not in the sense that this imitation created the world. "A spoon has no other exemplar except our mind's idea of [the spoon]." The spoon, not exactly a work of high art, is nevertheless something absolutely new, an *eidos* not represented in nature, and the simple

---

9. See the editor's introduction to the *Dialogues* in Nikolaus von Kues, *Die Kunst der Vermutung: Auswahl aus den Schriften*, ed. Hans Blumenberg (Bremen: Schünemann, 1957), 231ff. [The English translation used here is "The Layman on Mind" in *Nicholas of Cusa on Knowledge and Wisdom*, trans. Jasper Hopkins (Minneapolis, MN: Arthur J. Banning Press, 1996).]

"layman" is the one who fashions it: "I do not imitate the visible form of any natural object." The forms of the spoons, jugs, and plates that the layman manufactures are purely technical forms. And there is no leap necessary to get from the pleasure derived from this fact to accentuating it in the product itself—the essential feature of modern industrial design. Humanity no longer looks to nature, to the cosmos, to discern its place in the realm of being; rather, it looks to the world of things, created *sola humana arte* [by human art alone].[10] Also important for our point is that the Idiot explicitly contrasts his own "achievement" to the accomplishments of the painter and the sculptor: after all, they get their *exemplaria a rebus* [models from the things]—*non tamen ego*—"but not I!" It is of immeasurable significance that here the entire pathos of creative, originary human beings breaking with the principle of imitation is expressed by a *technician*—not by an *artist*. This distinction is probably *positively* accentuated here for the first time, and therein lies the value of the testimony, when one looks ahead and sees how almost immediately creative testimonials center on pictorial art and poetry. Part of the development of art from the end of the Middle Ages on is precisely that it becomes the place where the artist begins to discuss himself and his creative spontaneity.

The history of technology is generally poor on such self-revelations by its practitioners. This cannot simply be a typological phenomenon, a case of the sober inventor. Neither is it due merely to the sociological fact that public awareness and esteem for the intellectual

---

10. It is exceedingly characteristic of the "medieval" aspect of Cusa that yet another hidden reference to Aristotle's dual definition of "art" is contained in the statement of the Idiot cited here: "ars mea est magis perfectoria quam imitatoria figurarum creaturum et in hoc infinitae arti similior" [So my artistry involves the perfecting rather than the imitating of created visible forms, and in this respect it is more similar to the Infinite Art]. It is implied that the two parts of the Aristotelian definition refer to a *general* difference (instead of a *specific* one) and that they are to be applied differently. Since the Idiot cannot take his art to be *ars imitatoria* [imitating art], he is left only with the option of referring to the *ars perfectoria* [perfecting art], since there is no possible third term left over for him—although the description of what he does, given just before, offers no specific evidence that he takes up something left uncompleted by nature and "completes" it, unless it be the material that he uses. Here it is evident how the history of the human spirit can be canalized through definition (read: through the claim to definitiveness).

origins of technical innovations only began with the recognition of the *artes mechanicae* [mechanical arts] in the French Encyclopedia. It is above all a phenomenon of "being at a loss for words" [*Sprachlosigkeit*] in the practical arts. For the poet and the artist, there was already an arsenal of ready categories and metaphors in antiquity, from the anecdotal to the more basic, that, at least in their negation, sufficed to express how the creative process would like to reconceptualize itself. No language was at the disposal of the approaching technological world, and the people involved with it could hardly have created such a language. It is not until today—when the technological arena is held in high regard as something "useful to society"—that the very striking situation has arisen in which the people who determine the face of our world most powerfully know the least about, and know the least how to express, what it is they do. Autobiographies of great inventors—in contrast to the refined self-interpretations of modern artists—are often at a touching loss for words for the phenomenon that they would like to explain. Just one example: Orville Wright gave the invention of the airplane a typical stylization, explaining that six years before their first flight at Kitty Hawk, the Wright brothers had gotten hold of a book on ornithology. With the book, they made the breakthrough to understanding why the bird possessed an ability that man could not appropriate for himself by using a scale model of the physical mechanism.[11] But that is exactly the topos that Leonardo da Vinci used four hundred years before.[12] This of course made sense for Leonardo, and even for Lilienthal,[13] since they actually attempted a homomorphic design. The hiatus lies between Lil-

---

11. Orville Wright, "How We Invented the Airplane," *Harper's Magazine*, June 6, 1953.

12. Leonardo da Vinci, *Tagebücher und Aufzeichnungen* [*Diaries and Sketchbook*], ed. and trans. Theodor Lücke (Zürich: Schweizer Druck- und Verlagshaus, 1952), 307. "You must do an anatomical study of the wing of a bird, along with the breast muscles that move the wing. And you must do the same with a human being, in order to determine what possibilities there are for man if he wants to keep himself up in the air by flapping wings." Here, along with the *ars imitatoria*, the *ars perfectoria* comes directly into play—that is, the whole of Aristotle.

13. Otto Lilienthal, *Birdflight as the Basis of Aviation*, trans. A. W. Isenthal (London: Longmans, 1911).

ienthal and Wright: the airplane was an actual *invention* in that it freed itself from the old dream of imitating the flight of birds and solved the problem using a new principle. The invention of the combustion engine (which itself represents an actual invention) is therefore not nearly as essential or unique as the use of the propeller. Rotating elements are of a pure technicity—that is, derivable neither from *imitatio* nor *perfectio*—since rotating organs must be foreign to nature. Is it somewhat too audacious to contend that the airplane is so contained in the immanence of the technical process that it would have come to that day at Kitty Hawk, even if never a bird had flown?

But the reference to what is already available, to the bird with its God-given ability to fly, does not have anything like the function of explaining the genesis of the idea. Its purpose is rather to express the more-or-less defined feeling of *illegitimacy* about what man demands for himself. The topos of imitation of nature is a cover for the incomprehensibility of human primordiality [*Ursprünglichkeit*], which is thought to be metaphysical violence. Such topoi serve a purpose in our world, as when naturalistic titles are placed beneath abstract paintings at modern art exhibitions. What cannot be formulated cannot be represented. Paradise was: knowing the name of everything and familiarizing oneself with it through that name. Where the *logon didonai* (in its double meaning, "to name" and "to give a reason for") fails, we have a tendency to speak of the demonism of the thing—as in the common expression of the "demonism of technology" [*Dämonie der Technik*]. A problematic like modern technology is characterized by the fact that we feel it to be a "problem," but are completely at a loss to formulate it as such. I shall trace back this embarrassment to the validity of the definition of art as the imitation of nature. I am attempting to show that this idea affected and controlled our metaphysical tradition and how it did so in such a way as to leave no room for the conception of *authentic* human creations. The creative self-consciousness that emerged at the border between the Middle Ages and the modern period found itself ontologically inarticulable. As painters began to search for a "theory," they assimilated Aristotelian poetics: the creative "notion" [*Einfall*] was referred to with the metaphor of *enthusiasmo* [enthusiasm] and by using expressions of a secularized *illuminatio* [enlightenment]. The difficulty of articulation in the face of the over-emphasis of the *imitatio* [imitation] tradition *and* the Renaissance gesture of rebellion are all of a piece. The appearance of something that had become ontologically unquestionable constituted a zone of legitimacy in which new ways of understanding could only suc-ceed with force. One thinks as well of the "bursting onto the scene" of the "original genius" in the eighteenth century, who is system-atically absorbed, so to speak, by idealism.

Only in historical retrospect do we understand what Cusanus's experiment could have signified—his formulation of the idea of man as an original creator of being with the irony of his spoon-making Idiot in such a way that it comes out as the unavoidable consequence and legitimate explication of the theological conception of man's being made in the image of God by God's will—as (in the earlier Hermetic formulation) *alter deus* [second god]. Measured by its his-torical effectiveness, this attempt to see the modern period as an immanent product of the Middle Ages—an attempt in which the metaphysical legitimization of ascribing the attributes of the creator to man is only *one* component—did not succeed. We have to con-sider Nicholas of Cusa's Idiot a historical indicator, not a historical force. For the sum of modern intellectual history constitutes the an-tagonism between construction and organism, art and nature, the will to form and the givenness of forms, between labor and con-tinuance. Human creation sees its room for maneuver hemmed in by reality. Nietzsche formulates this fact most sharply, when he says in *Thus Spoke Zarathustra:* "Whoever should like to be a creator for good or ill, he must first be a destroyer and transgress values. Thus the greatest evil belongs to the greatest good: this is the way of creation."[14] Here nihilism is functionally assigned to the human claim to originary creation of being, but it is nonetheless unclear whether what is here expressed as an ontological law instead indi-

---

14. Friedrich Nietzsche, *Thus Spoke Zarathustra.* I quote from the somewhat altered self-reference in *Ecce Homo: Gesammelte Werke* 21 (1928): 111 [*Ecce Homo,* trans. Walter Kaufmann (New York: Vintage, 1967), 327].

cates a historical situation in which man finds his creative freedom hindered by a specific metaphysical tradition (precisely the metaphysical tradition whose specifics we are laying out). The antinaturalism of the nineteenth century is pregnant with this feeling of the narrowing of the possibility of authentic human production by an oppressive horizon of fixed conditions. The new pathos of labor directed itself against nature: Comte coined the term "antinature"; Marx and Engels spoke of "antiphysis." Nature had not only lost its role as authoritative example, reduced to an object whose meaning was exhausted by its theoretical and practical mastery; it became, moreover, something like the opposing term to technical and artistic will. Its effect on the emotional susceptibility of humanity awakened mistrust: the self-sufficiency, the maturing, the returning-onto-itself of nature assumed the character of a temptation for the human will to create works to be unequivocal.[15] Moreover, it has been the case in our century that natural resources, on the one hand, and the physical capacities of humanity, on the other, have been disturbingly unequal to the demands technology has placed on them. A curious inertia has revealed itself as a property of the organic. The conception of overcoming it was first developed in ruthless

---

15. No one could have depicted this more tangibly than Bertolt Brecht, who in one of his *Anecdotes of Mr. Keuner* entitled "Mr. K. and Nature" has one of his characters say: "Now and then I would like to see a few trees coming out of the house." The subjunctive [*Ich würde gern*] is like a hidden man-trap in this quasi-idyll, which reveals itself now, where the "special degree of reality" of natural objects as opposed to the pure relativity of use-objects is celebrated, "something soothingly independent" about the trees, "outside myself." The hope is finally uttered that perhaps there is something unuseable, nonmaterial about these trees. But this sharp-eyed phenomenology of an underground need for nature ends with a call to order. Its casual style—the following sentence is in parentheses and begins "Mr. K *also* said"—is merely a paideutic tactic. "We must also make use of nature sparingly. Spending your time amidst nature without any work, you may easily fall into a diseased condition; you are seized by something like a fever." Brecht, *Tales from the Calendar*, trans. Yvonne Kapp (London: Lion, 1961), 110 [Translation slightly altered]. To abide in nature without work is a horror to the contemporary (and not just to those of Marxist observance, if they exist). The modern working garden shows this just as much as the various ways the allegedly nature-needy are accompanied by technical equipment that neutralizes the impression of nature.

fashion with Ernst Jünger's idea of the "organic construction" in *The Worker*.[16]

This, by way of examples, is an indication of the *terminus ad quem* [the point at which the process terminates] of the historical process, whose metaphysical *terminus a quo* [the point from which the process takes its departure] we would like to consider here. The metaphysical exclusivity of the concept of nature, as will be shown in more detail, eliminated the space for authentic human works, or, more precisely, did not provide for their occurrence. By the end of a violent countermovement, nature itself had its value disputed in the face of the absolute claim of technical and artistic works. And not coincidentally, from Idealism on, on any occasion when one believed one could ask about what "being" was, art took on exactly the same exemplary role in philosophy that nature had held in classical thought and the metaphysics it spawned.

Perhaps it has been made clear to the reader of our essay that one can say—without the presumption of a mental leap—that the modern pathos of the authentic human creation in art and technology springs from the protest against the metaphysical tradition of *the identity of being and nature*, and that the definition of human works as "imitation of nature" was the direct consequence of this identity. A fundamental investigation of the historical background will be necessary here.

III.

It is worth beginning with a look at the tenth book of Plato's *Republic*. As is well known, here Plato issues a polemic against poetry, and representative art in general, and he does so with an argument that does not so much protest against its negative consequences as against its *origins*, by focusing on its ontological foundational context. That art imitates nature is therefore not just an assertion, but in fact the decisive objection. To put this objection into sharp

---

16. [Ernst Jünger, *The Worker: Dominion and Form* (Evanston, IL: Northwestern University Press, 2017).]

relief, Plato takes as paradigms two basic everyday objects (*skeuē*), couch and table. The craftsman (*dēmiurgos*) *produces* them, the painter (*zōgraphos*) only *represents* them. The craftsman, however, is not in addition the "inventor" of the couch or table, since no craftsman begets their *Idea* as such.[17] The negative formulation of Plato's sentence presupposes a particular definition of *invention*: it is the begetting of the Idea itself. But where does the craftsman get the Ideas for couch and table, if he did not beget them himself and did not find basic shapes of this kind in the given reality? The answer runs like this: Just as it contains the Ideas for the things already present at hand in the world, so the world of Ideas also contains the Ideas for couch and table.[18] When the craftsman makes use-objects such as these, their Ideas are somehow pre-given to his mental gaze. The artist, however, gazes not upon the Ideas itself, but upon its already rendered copy. To reproach him for this, and to derive from the reproach a critique of the imitative arts, necessarily implies the premise that *imitation is in some way negative*. Plato, it is true, uses the expressions "to imitate" and "to participate in" indiscriminately and interchangeably—often for one and the same state of affairs. It is nonetheless important to recognize that *methexis* [partaking] has a *positive* connotation that emphasizes the relation of material things to the reality of the Idea, whereas *mimēsis* [imitation] emphasizes the *negative* aspect of the difference between Idea and thing, the defect of phenomenal being as over against Ideal being.[19] Imitation means precisely: *not to be* the imitated itself.[20]

---

17. Plato, *The Republic*, 10.596b: "For presumably none of the craftsmen fabricates the Idea itself." [The English translation used here is *The Republic of Plato*, trans. Allan Bloom (New York: Basic Books, 1968).]

18. Plato, *The Republic*, 10.596b: "There are presumably two, one of couch, one of table."

19. Aristotle admits only a nominal difference: *Metaphysics* 1.6.987b10–13. For him, however, the ambiguous nature of the situation, which Plato was to have corrected, is no longer the case.

20. Explicitly in Democritus: "One must either be good, or imitate a good man." [The English translation used here is Kathleen Freeman, *Ancilla to the Pre-Socratic Philosophers: A Complete Translation of the Fragments in Diels*, Fragmente der Vorsokratiker (New York: Cambridge University Press, 1971), 99.] Even his derivation of human achievements from those of animals (weaving, darning,

Art is therefore only a derivative of being; in the example of a painting of a fabricated object, it is already "third from what is."[21] The craftsman can at least be excused by the need that his work will fill, but how can the painter justify himself?

This negative aspect of the imitation of the Ideas will become so pronounced in the later history of Platonism that eventually even the *first* imitation, the foundation of the visible cosmos by the world Demiurge, cannot help but acquire a negative connotation. One should keep in mind this Neoplatonic one-sidedness if one is to understand why it was precisely the Platonism of the late Middle Ages that participated so vigorously in the overcoming of the mimetic formula for the work of art. The *Aristotelian* tradition—which made the "imitation of nature" formula its own, more than any other—never understood, could never even conceive of the idea, that imitation could be a stricture that would put the *worth* of human works into question.

For Plato himself, of course, priority should probably still be given to the positive aspect connected with the concept of *methexis*. It is easy to understand this when one keeps in mind the original hostility of the Socratic-Platonic doctrine of the Ideas to the Sophists. It is the Sophists who first conceive of an absolute positing, a *thesis* of what does not have its basis in the pre-given.[22] But this concept still lacks almost everything that the concept of the "creative" ought to entail. The state, language, morality are, to be sure, seen here as derived from man, guided by human *technē*; likewise, "history" is first understood as a product of human making in Sophistic rhetoric. But this achievement does not attach to humanity as an honor; rather, its "technical" trait is an indication of human neediness, of a lack of natural endowments and discernible organizing structure. The Sophists also do not have a concept of the thinking subject to whom some sort of metaphysical "distinction" could be ascribed. "Positing" is indeed a contrasting concept to "nature,"

---

building houses, singing; Democritus, fragment 154) clearly implies the superiority of a *natural* attribute over the poverty of an acquired one.

21. Plato, *The Republic*, 10.599a.

22. The inclusion of the Sophists refers back to a discussion of my thesis with Dieter Henrich.

but precisely because of this, positing turns out to be close to mere *tychē* [chance], which is how this contrast is usually expressed. What must have happened for the conception of the complete spontaneity of human activities first developed here to have procured its metaphysical dignity? The answer is easy to give in retrospect: "positing" first acquires metaphysical value because it is discussed as a theological concept, an attribute of the divine. Only the transplantation of a concept onto theological soil makes it flourish so as to be sufficiently attractive in the history of human self-understanding—from the *homoiōsis theōi* [mystical longing for likeness to God] to the defiant usurpation of divine attributes in what has been called the hubris of the Renaissance—to move the will. Thus, the fundamental question here is not at all about where the authenticity of human accomplishments was first conceived but rather about where it achieved the unique metaphysical status that would allow it to be at the center of an entire epoch's thought. Necessity is indeed the mother of invention, as the saying goes, but she is not able to give invention the luster that drives one to confirm incessantly that one is capable of it.

The Sophists' concept of *thesis* justifies appearance [*Schein*], *not being* [*Sein*]: it has no reference to *truth*. *Technē* and *alētheia* are foreign to each other. To bring a *foundation* to this foundationless human activity, to provide a relation to being, a binding authority—that was the motive for the theory of Ideas and its correlative concept of mimesis. The craftsman who produces the couch and table makes something *new* only from the perspective of the phenomenal world, but not from the perspective of the world of Ideas, in which the Ideas of these objects are *always already given*. When Plato now says that these Ideas signify the couch and the table *en tēi physei* [in essence],[23] then the implicit, specifically Platonic meaning of the imitation of nature formula becomes clear: To imitate nature means to copy the Idea. But what then? Can one ask about yet another source behind the Idea, or is it the absolute itself, without origin? Is the concept of a *creative* act foreign to Platonic metaphysics?

---

23. Plato, *The Republic*, 10.597b–c.

Traditional Platonism, in any case, will leave that impression, and it will become evident how this impression arises. In our passage, however, in the tenth book of the *Republic*, it is explicitly stated that it is the god who wanted to be the true begetter of the couch that actually is—not just any couch that any craftsmen can make—and he accomplished this by establishing the couch, in the singularity of its nature, as an Idea.[24] Three times in short succession, Plato insists on this formulation, and he calls the god who creates being "Futurgos" [natural begetter]. It is here that *creation* is first conceived as the act of the originary formation of being and made a divine attribute. One would think that this conception of the creation idea in its radical form would have been recognized and acknowledged at the very latest when the biblical creation idea was being described in terms of ancient metaphysics and adapted to the tradition. But, as has been shown often enough, another element in the Platonic canon succeeded for this purpose: the myth of the Demiurge of the *Timaeus*. The Demiurge was seen to prefigure the biblical creator, God. But the Demiurge is *not creative*. He is—according to his function and not his metaphysical status—just as much a craftsman as the carpenter in book 10 of the *Republic*. The Demiurge of the *Timaeus* functions as the founder of the visible cosmos, not of being. He is supposed to clarify how, along with the cosmos of Ideas, there is its pendant, the phenomenal world. He is thus intended to bridge over a perplexity in Platonic philosophy, at which Aristotle then so persistently took offense. The Demiurge's function is *auxiliary*, subordinate to the absolute being of the Ideas; the metaphysical accent lies not on this "creator" but on his blueprints. He only makes that which actually is (which one must imagine, as the Neoplatonists did, as being induced to announce itself) appear in a recognizable form; he translates it into the language of the senses. Whether or not the original model requires such an "expression" of its being is an unimportant question, at least as long as the Demiurge is not the god who must be justified as the source of good. This identification of the Demiurge with God had already been introduced in the first century BC, and it dominated Christian

---

24. Plato, *The Republic*, 10.597d.

Platonism. Since the Futurgos of the *Republic* met with no interest and the Demiurge of the *Timaeus* was instead the influential model in the historical reception, the concept of "creation" had to be interpreted using the categories of the structural scheme of imitation. Although a conception of *human* spontaneous creation was still of little concern here, it was nonetheless *predetermined* to a considerable degree, when one considers how the concepts that make up the self-consciousness of the subject often incubate in theology. The adaptation of the Demiurge concept to the concept of God implied the decisive sanctioning of the principle of the "imitation of nature."

But the *Timaeus* introduces an important modification to yet another aspect of the position introduced in the tenth book of the *Republic*. Aristotle informs us of the fact—astounding in light of previous explications—that according to the Academy, there were no Ideas for artificial objects, as for a house or a ring.[25] How could Plato or his school have later abandoned the notion of Ideas for artificial objects? The reason is readily apparent in the *Timaeus*. The Demiurge copies pre-given, original designs into pre-given matter, but he does not do this as he pleases, not by making a choice. He is subject to the principle of optimal effect: the cosmos he produces is *kallistos tōn gegonotōn* [the best of things that have become] and his work is qualified by *aristos tōn aitiōn* [the best of causes].[26] The realm of Ideas itself, in its double ontological and ethical function makes obvious that the Ideas are not simply guidelines for *how* this work *can be* fashioned but rather like obligatory norms for *that* it *ought to* be fashioned. In this way, Plato secures not only the unity of the real cosmos but also its *complete compatibility* with the Ideal model.[27] But this means, consequently, that the Demiurge exhausts the potential of the Ideals; the real represents the Ideal exhaustively. Everything that is possible is *already there*, and there are no unrealized Ideas left over for the works of man. This considerable deviation

---

25. Aristotle, *Metaphysics* I, 9; 991b 6ff. Formulated positively: *Metaphysics* XII, 3; 1070a 18–20.

26. Plato, *Timaeus* 29a. [The English translation used here is Francis M. Comford, *Plato's Cosmology* (Indianapolis: Hackett, 1997), 22–23.]

27. Plato, *Timaeus* 30c–d, 31. See also Cornford, *Plato's Cosmology*, 40f.: "The intelligible Living Creature corresponds to it, whole to whole, part to part."

from the tenth book of the *Republic* allows the question of the origin of human works to persist as a problem within Platonism. Aristotle reached the only possible conclusion: Everything "new" that is fashioned recalls what already is. The idea of the complete equivalence of possibility and reality does not allow for man's originary, imaginative creation. That means that man's efforts cannot ontologically "enrich" what is; or put another way, essentially *nothing* is created in the works of man. Human creation has no real intrinsic truth of its own. No wonder, then, that it had no significance for traditional metaphysics.[28]

IV.

The entire system, as Plato has already laid it out, is given in its traditionally accepted version by Aristotle. The eternity of the Ideas becomes the eternity of the real world itself, and the complete correspondence of Ideas to appearances becomes the uniqueness and completeness of the cosmos in relation to the concept of *possibility*. The exemplary aspect is weakened in this Aristotelian reformulation: *Why* nature *ought to be* imitated is easier to understand in Plato, since the real world appears as simply the best endowed creation; it would not make sense to conceive of a different one. The Stoics will pick up this thread again. But what is more explicitly expressed by Aristotle than by Plato is why a work *can only be* a copy of nature. Nature is the embodiment of all that is possible. Thought can be defined only as a faculty concerned with a totality that already is. The possible is only what is already a reality in terms of its Idea: the cosmos is the All of the actual as well as of the pos-

---

28. Ancient Platonism soured on this hypothesis, as Willy Theiler has shown in *Die Vorbereitung des Neuplatonismus* (Berlin: Weidmann, 1930). On the exclusivity of the Ideas for *physei onta* [natural things], it was maintained (e.g., in *Chalcidii Plato Timaeus*, ed. Johann Wrobel [Leipzig: Minerva, 1876]): "ideae sunt exempla naturalium rerum" [Ideas are examples of the natural world]. One can be resourceful, with any kind of "Scholasticism," and use nominal distinctions that lack conceptual cohesiveness, such as the distinction between *idea* and *eidos*, already touched on by Plato. *Eidos* is supposed to be the Idea inherent in the work.

sible. Accordingly, the immanent law of motion (in the broadest sense that this term had for Aristotle, as change) is the eternal *self-perpetuation of being*. This basic structure encompasses entity and thought, nature and "art"; it is, finally, the inner structure of the absolute being of Aristotle's metaphysics: the "Unmoved Mover" is the purely intellectual form of self-perpetuation through *noēsis noēseōs*, thought that thinks itself. This self-enclosed self-sufficiency of the absolute is as little externally creative as it is internally innovative. (How astonishing that Christian theology nonetheless took it as a model!) The self-perpetuation of the absolute in the cosmos works according to imitation: it explains the first, undistorted circular orbit of the spheres simply as the loving assimilation to the highest principle returning to itself. It is mirrored in the circulation of the meteorological waters;[29] it is the fundamental law of all generative processes in which each entity always reproduces its own kind. Expressed as a general rule: What is derives solely from what is.[30] *Technē* is ranked very low in the organization of this cosmic process: the produced does not, after all, perpetuate itself. Only indirectly—precisely through the unavoidable dependence on "imitation"—does the act of *technē* rejoin the basic cosmic structure and avoid being mere *bia* [force] or *tychē* [chance]. Likewise, "art" is "saved" for the cosmos, functionally incorporated into it, a testament to its uniqueness and completeness. The theologizing of the cosmos, which first the Stoics would develop fully, is basically determined here. Where the completeness of being is absolute, it cannot "enhance" being, not even through God. The will has no power to bring into being; it can only will what already is, can only—like the god himself—"keep things in motion." Seen in the context of this completeness of his metaphysics, the homogeneity of the Aristotelian doctrine of knowledge becomes obvious.[31]

---

29. Aristotle, *Meteorology* 1.9.346b16–347a5.

30. Aristotle, *Metaphysics* 11.21069b19; 11.3.1070a8. See Hans Blumenberg, "The Relationship between Nature and Technology as a Philosophical Problem" [in this volume].

31. Samuel H. Butcher, *Aristotle's Theory of Poetry and Fine Art* (London: Macmillan, 1927), 126, points out correctly that one cannot render Aristotle's *fantasia* precisely as "imagination," which would imply "an image-making power."

In the interpretation of Aristotelian mimesis, the significance of the dynamic conception of nature is referred to repeatedly—not as the total, given eidetic constant, but rather as the embodiment of the generative processes producing this constant at any given time: "the creative force, the productive principle of this universe."[32] Here we have the classical distinction between *natura naturans* and *natura naturata*. But I am not able to discern here a significant addition to Plato: even if one emphasizes the *static* character of the world of Ideas—ignoring the final formulation of the Platonic school—there is still an initializing *dynamic* concentrated in the Demiurge. Aristotle must bring all of this—Idea, matter, Demiurge—under the rubric of nature. This leads to the ambiguity that pervades the mimesis idea. "Imitation of nature" thus means not only the reproduction of an eidetic stock, but the mimicking of the productive process of nature: "Art in general imitates the method of nature."[33] I cannot see that any decisive meaning comes out of this distinction for our question, however, since for Aristotle all generative processes of nature are in fact regulated by an unchangeable eidetic constant. Nature duplicates itself eternally by reproducing itself. What, then, makes it possible to ascribe a "creative force" to it? Here, of course,

---

The more direct translation of "fantasy" also allows for a similar inference of an additional meaning, whose ontological possibility is precisely what concerns us here. One should not retroactively attribute this meaning to Aristotle. This makes all the less comprehensible to me Butcher's mysterious remark: "The idea of a creative power in man which transforms the materials supplied by the empirical world is not unknown either to Plato or Aristotle, but it is not a separate faculty or denoted by a distinct name" (Butcher, *Aristotle's Theory of Poetry and Fine Art*, 127n1). It is characteristic of the history of the meaning of the term "fantasy" how late the first, original connotations flood in and no less that it was a representative of the so-called Second Sophistic Movement in the third century AD who gave a new definition to *phantasia* as "creative imagination." *A Greek-English Lexicon*, ed. Henry G. Liddell and Robert Scott (Oxford: Clarendon Press, 1925) lists Philostratus, in his *Apollonius Vita* (*Flavii Philostrati Opera*, 2 vols., ed. Carl Ludwig Kayser [Leipzig: Teubner, 1870/71], VI, 19) where "fantasy" and "imitation" are expressly contrasted, and this in reference to what inheres additionally in the statue of gods by Phidias or Praxiteles, the addition of what is not seen, not pregiven: "Mimesis enacts what has appeared, while *phantasia* enacts what has not appeared."

32. Butcher, *Aristotle's Theory of Poetry and Fine Art*, 116.
33. Butcher, 117.

the implications of the modern concept of nature, defined by evolution, are frequently brought to bear. This consistently leads to the overemphasis of *epitelein* [leading to the goal] in the Aristotelian definition of "art." How can nature require any kind of completion? Here, lack, in any case, does not mean "vacancy" [*Leerstelle*], but rather the *developmental goal* that is factually *not yet* reached. When Aristotle says it is the task of artists to imitate natural objects as they *ought to be*,[34] that does not mean by referring to any transcendental norm of one of these objects, but rather by "extrapolating" from the developmental process to its completion, from *genesis* to *telos* [goal]. The generative quality of the concept of nature is important for mimesis because it does not allow "art" to remain satisfied with a mere factual *state* of being and focuses it on the *developmental goal*, the *entelechia* [final shape] of the artwork. But the concept takes on importance only because once the Ideas are set aside, and despite their being set aside, some "ideal" is still necessary for man to understand what it is in the work—and especially the work of art—that defines him. Should nature ever forfeit its eidetic constancy, the Aristotelian doctrine of "art" would likewise lose its foundation. Where is nature to acquire an exemplar of what ought to be, if the concept of *natura naturans* means not the eternal perpetuation of finite ontogenesis but an infinite phylogenesis induced by selection and mutation? This allusion to what comes later is only intended to indicate that fundamental philosophical concepts cannot just experience a renaissance for no reason.

At the core of the Aristotelian concept of *technē* is the idea that man the maker cannot be assigned an *essential* function. What one would call "the human world" basically does not exist here. The human has his place in the physical teleology as maker and actor: he brings to completion what nature *would have* brought to completion; the "ought to be" is immanent in nature, not in him. *Technē* and *physis* are congruous constituent principles: one affects *from the outside* what the other affects *from within*.[35] Production is tied

---

34. Aristotle, *Poetics* 25.1460b11, 35.
35. Aristotle, *Metaphysics* 12.3.1070a7ff. "Now art is a principle of movement in something other than the thing moved, nature is a principle in the thing

to its counterpart, growth. The aesthetic or technical work therefore only has a *referential* meaning and contains no inherent truth. The possibility of experiencing something unique in a work of art is still unthinkable: the work is not yet a medium for human self-recognition and self-confirmation.

In the Hellenistic period, the pseudo-Aristotelian work, *On the Cosmos* provides a not insignificant variation on the mimesis concept with the addition of a Heraclitan theme.[36] Mimesis does not depend primarily on the eternal eidetic constancy of nature, but rather on its *formal* structure (if one does not understand "formal" in the sense of Aristotelian-Scholastic *forma*). The cosmos is, according to Heraclitus, a network of contradictions that do not cancel each other out, just as a *polis* composed of rich and poor, weak and strong, bad and good, making up a unified whole. Nature realizes itself in contradictions, such as male and female, dry and wet, warm and cold. And it is in this way that art imitates nature, as, for instance, when painting depicts contrasting colors, music harmonizes low and high notes, or the art of writing combines vowels and consonants. To be sure, this formalization of mimesis wins some "latitude" for artistic authenticity, but it is not yet apparent how heterogeneous music or language (writing) is different from any natural process.

The Stoics broadened the metaphysical foundation of mimesis considerably by elevating the completeness and unity of the cosmos to predicates of theological dignity. Man's position was nevertheless strengthened through the universalization of the theological principle that nature is organized to be at man's disposal and that the works of men are an imitation and completion of this relation.

---

itself." [The English translation used here in *A New Aristotle Reader*, ed. J. L. Ackrill (Princeton, NJ: Princeton University Press, 1987), 342.]

36. Pseudo-Aristotle, *De mundo* 5.396a33–b22. It is surely wrong to claim that the mimesis element in this connection is present already in Heraclitus, as Carl Michaelis does, s.v. "mimeomai," *Theologisches Wörterbuch zum Neuen Testament*, ed. Gerhard Kittel et al. (Stuttgart: Kohlhammer, 1943) [available in English as *Theological Dictionary of the New Testament*, ed. and trans. Geoffrey W. Bromiley (Grand Rapids, MI: Eerdmans, 1964)], probably prompted by the complete rendition by Hermann Diels, *Zwei Fragmente Heraklits* (Berlin: Akademie der Wissenschaften, 1901), 22 B 10.

Technē is close to receiving almost religious sanction when, for instance, Posidonius traces the dyer's craft back to the sun, which gives plummage, flowers, and minerals their splendor, while also employing human "art" in its task.[37] There is no longer a definitive boundary between the natural and the man-made, a single *energia* is at work: "Art" is nature by other means. The example of dyeing shows nicely how the boundary between nature as a work of God and "art" as a work of man will be restored by the Christian creation idea: in certain patristic authors a polemic can be found against the processing of textiles with the reasoning that God would have created colored sheep if he had wanted man to have colored clothing. Tertullian generalized this into a very typical polemic against *ars*: "There is nothing that God found pleasing, that he did not himself bring forth. Was he incapable of creating purple or steel blue sheep as well? Even though he was capable of doing so, he did not want to do so; what God does not want to make, man must also refrain from making. . . . What does not come from God, must come from his adversary."[38] Here, then, we have an anticipation of the "demonism of technology," which places nature and "art" in a dichotomous schema. Of course this first required a new general conception of nature as an *expression of the will* of God and the still implicit presupposition of *other entities* as factual possibilities of being, willed as such.

But to demonstrate a fairly typical distinction I have jumped ahead. For Posidonius, imitation of nature represented only an external aspect of the homogeneity of the singular, total process working through both man and nature. "The theory of imitation becomes a theory of the relationship that allows for creation: the invention is an interpretation, a judgment, a deciphering of what is written in nature. Nature is not a model applied at man's discretion, but rather directly, of its own accord, and man is to complete

---

37. "And the arts of mortal men, imitating the working of the sun in the physical world . . . having been instructed in this by nature." Diodorus Siculus, *The Library of History*, vol.1 (Cambridge, MA: Harvard University Press, 1933), 2.52.7.

38. Tertullian, *De cultu feminarum* I, 8.

nature according to its essential, not its accidental, possibilities."[39] "Invention," as the uncovering of nature's blueprint, serves as instruction, so that for the first time the classical theory applies directly to the composition of the work, and philosophy appears as the root of material culture as well. Seneca's polemic against Posidonius is aimed less at this fundamental conception as at the "elevation" to which technical skills, as the highest achievements of nature itself, are transported: the theoretical ideal forfeits its rank as the absolute—as is the case in Cicero. With precisely the same teleological principle, Seneca argues the exact opposite: nature, centered completely on man, provides sufficiently, making technical advancements and work superfluous, having the character of luxury.[40] "Imitation of nature" is unnecessary, since nature provides for every need. There is no legitimate *transition* from nature to "art." Here, "art" and hubris are already fundamentally one, a consequence of insufficient natural-divine *providentia*. The human being himself—his *artificial* needs, his weariness with the *facilis actus vitae* [easy act of life]—drives the development of the *artes*. "The things that are essential are acquired with little bother; it is the luxuries that call for toil and effort. Follow nature and you will feel no need of craftsmen . . . . She equipped us for everything she required us to contend with."[41]

What is instructive about this reversal is that completely opposite conclusions are derived from one and the same metaphysical principle. While Posidonius so exaggerates the mimesis idea beyond its internal premises that it nearly cancels itself out in the cyclical

39. Karl Reinhardt, *Poseidonios* (Munich: Beck, 1921), 400. In this connection, see Cicero's expanded formulation of this relation with reference to the art of rhetoric in *De ratione ad C. Herennium*: "Art imitates nature because what the latter desires the former finds, and what the latter shows the former follows."

40. Seneca, *Epistulae morales ad Lucilium* 90.16; "The things that are indispensable require no elaborate pains for their acquisition; it is only the luxuries that call for labour. Follow nature, and you will need no skilled craftsmen." [The English translation used here is *The Epistles of Seneca*, trans. Frank Justus Miller (Cambridge, MA: Harvard University Press), 4:405.]

41. Seneca, *Epistulae morales ad Lucilium* 90.18. [The English translation used here is *Letters from a Stoic*, trans. Robin Campbell (New York: Penguin, 1969), 166.]

pattern of a self-reproducing nature, Seneca sees for the first time the authentically human in the feeling that the provisions of nature are insufficient—he sees the infinity of self-perpetuating needs, the desire for luxuries (with negative connotations, of course) as the source of the technical drive. Here, "imitation" has basically lost its meaning since the impetus for "art" is precisely seen as the rejection of the strictures and the contesting of the completeness of nature. Here, as is so often the case, a negative formulation has brought what is essential into focus.

V.

The history of the corrosion and deracination of the mimesis idea, however, is not—as the example of Seneca's polemic against Posidonius could lead one to presume—a process of the eruption of its inner contradictions. It is much more a process of the inauguration of new, external, specifically theological ideas. Of course, this is not to say that the biblical story of creation contributes novel premises here. Rather, it will become apparent how this process easily gets caught up in the existing interpretation of being. The two elements that were constitutive of the mimesis idea—the exemplary bindingness of nature and its essential completeness—seem at first to fit well with the concept of creation. Indeed, one must admit that the *bindingness* of pre-given nature was strengthened by the idea that it manifested the *will* of the creator, as the citation from Tertullian shows. It was not at all apparent at first that the justification of nature's bindingness by an act of will would cast doubt on the idea that the actual world was *necessarily* the full realization of the possible. Accordingly, in the quotation we cited, Tertullian must formulate the expression of God's will in the facticity of nature this way: Not only did God *not create what He did not want*, but also *He did not want what He did not create*. But what does this "unwanted and not created" consist of? A possible kind of being not yet represented in nature? This compelling deduction is not yet thinkable. It implies the *facticity* and *incompleteness* of nature—an opening for the possibility of the "artificial." This example makes it possible to demonstrate the ontological consequences of adding will to the process of creation. The shoring up of the bindingness of nature by claiming that God decreed His will through it leads to the inevitable correlate of unwilled possibilities—the sort of thing to immediately arouse interest in an impious, curious mind, fond of splitting hairs, that is yet to come.

This interpretation rules out the usual explanation of the new Christian understanding of being in the context of the creation idea as a conception first explicated fully by Augustine. Rather, it was precisely this thinker who grasped the immanent consequences of the idea of creation in classical ontology. It is certainly correct that with his reduction of *materia prima* [first matter] to the absolute *nihil* [nothing] of the *creatio ex nihilo* [creation from nothingness] he had insured against dualism from all sides. But it is wrong to see this as the central problem. What is decisive here is that the divine spirit of creation is now identified with the Platonic *mundus intelligibilis* [intelligible world]. The Ideas and the power of the Demiurge are indeed now unified in *one* authority, but this does not change the fact that the *mundus intelligibilis* still represents a single unity—Plato's *zōon noēton* [intelligible living being]—which can only be transposed into the *mundus sensibilis* [sensible world] as a whole. Here Augustine is under the spell of the pedantry with which Neoplatonism rehearsed the correspondence of the physical and noetic world.[42] The divine act of will that determines the creation can only refer to the fixed totality of the singular cosmos of Ideas. Therefore, only the "that" of creation and not its "what" becomes a *fact*. In Augustine, the concept of *omnipotence* is not yet joined to the concept of *infinity*. Thus, he remains within the structure of the classical correspondence of being and nature. There is no alter-

---

42. For example, *The Enneads* of Plotinus, where the duplication of the world is executed in such detail that the underlying logical structure of the realm of Ideas is given up in favor of the exactitude of a model of the physical world. The world then seems conceivable only in this *one* particular, binding form. Even the reversal of rank, described by Willy Theiler, between the Demiurge and the Ideas—which, with the aid of logical speculation, Philo subordinated to the *organon* of the creator god—did not alter the absolute exemplarity of the Ideas as an integral stock (Theiler, *Die Vorbereitung des Neuplatonismus*, 30).

native to the given actuality of the creation—not even for the creator. *After* the act of creation, nothing of essential originality can be brought into being. How a finite world and the infinite potential of God's power, the real and the possible, could be related to one another was one of the hardest problems left to the Middle Ages to think through to its conclusions.

My thesis about the *antiquity* of Augustine's ontology (as I presented it in Munich) is contradicted by Henry Deku's shrewd history of the *possibile logicum*[43]—the history of the development of a realm of possibility, which encompasses the Ideal as well as the real cosmos—what we have here considered as the "latitude" for originary creation. Deku, who begins his history with Augustine, refers mainly to *De spiritu et littera* (*On the Spirit and the Letter*), where the concept of *possibilitas* appears most frequently. But here—as is typical of Augustine—this concept appears only in conjunction with the Pelagian controversy, in other words, within the framework of salvation theology. It is a matter of the possibility of man without sin, of a *possibilitas non peccandi* [the possibility to avoid sinning]—that is, of the possibility of a quality inherent in human behavior, a *possibilitas naturalis* [natural possibility], as opposed to salvation through grace alone.[44] God is therefore not the reason for *being*, but the reason for *salvation* in this interpretation, just as the "ability" of humanity arises only in regard to its being worthy of salvation. The treatise is directed against the tribune Marcellinus, who was the target of an earlier work, *De peccatorum meritis et remissione* (*On the Merits and Forgiveness of Sins*). It reacts to an objection made against this earlier treatise that it was inconsistent to claim that humanity can rid itself of sin through good will and with the aid of grace if one must nonetheless admit, "There is nobody who has been, is, or will be of such perfect justice in this life." Put differently, how can one assume as possible what does not really come to pass.[45] Marcellinus, in any case, reasons very much

---

43. Henry Deku, "Possibile Logicum," *Philosophisches Jahrbuch* 64 (1956): 10.

44. Augustine, *De natura et gratia* 44.52.

45. The pervasiveness of the problem is most clearly formulated in *Retractationes* 2.7: "how . . . this could be the case when there is no precedent for it." [The

within the horizon of ancient ontology: What is possible will only be proven by what is real—through the "actual coming into being" of the Ideas. The argumentation is as close as possible to Lucretius, who objected to creation, "how can the gods be creators of nature when they lack the *exemplum* which only an already actualized nature can provide—unless nature itself provided a model of the creation."[46] Marcellinus's objection, which is unavailable to us, must be close to this position, if Augustine can say of it: it appeared absurd to you to say that anything was possible of which no example ever occurred."[47] It is then shown that the biblical revelation offered a new guide to what is "possible with God," since God himself provides a testament of what is possible for him and the "word" takes the place of the "thing" as a proof in its own way: the story of the camel that can go through the eye of a needle, the faith that can move mountains—"although, nevertheless, it was never done, so far as we have ever read or heard."[48] However, these theological renditions of possibilities do not touch on the ontological basis of Augustinian metaphysics, since here the issue is God's ability to *restore* His own work of creation, man, to the originary constitution of his being—in Platonic terms, the realization of the Idea. The horizon of the ideally preformed cosmos is *not broadened* by the question of human salvation, but rather reconstituted. When it is said that "*omnia possibilia sunt Deo*" [all things are possible with God],[49] this *omnia* still does not in any way indicate the possibility of more than what is actually created; rather, the correspondence between *mundus intelligibilis* and *mundus sensibilis* became defective because of the original sin of man, and it is a question of correcting this defect. To hold on to man's *posse non peccare* [being able not to sin] is therefore a logical necessity—without this

English translation used here is *Revisions*, trans. Boniface Ramsey (Hyde Park, NY: New City Press, 2010).]

46. Lucretius, *De rerum natura* 5.181–186 [*On the Nature of the Universe*, trans. R. E. Latham and John Godwin (New York: Penguin, 1994)].

47. Augustine, *De spiritu et littera* 1.1 [*Basic Writings of Saint Augustine*, 2 vols., ed. Whitney J. Oates (New York: Random House, 1948), 461].

48. Augustine, *De spiritu et littera* 25.62.

49. Augustine, *De spiritu et littera* 5.7.

possibility, nothing can reasonably be said about the *posse peccare* [being able to sin]. Man is defined precisely as a being who determines his own conformity to the Idea. But this freedom arose very much *within* the Ideal scheme.

There is no doubt that the idea of *willing*, introduced into cosmogony by the Hellenic period and made thoroughly virulent by Augustine, is a "disruptive concept" of the highest order for the continued validity of ancient ontology and that it exercised a "denecessitating influence on what had become reality."[50] Nevertheless, it was not Augustine whose understanding of being was so fundamentally distorted that he somehow actually broke through the visual horizon. I believe I can even give the reason for this: Manicheanism initiated and brought to the forefront the problem of the elimination of the *materia prima* and the tendency toward dualism inextricably bound up with it. One believes oneself to be in the thick of our theme when one finds Augustine distinguishing between *creatum* and *creabile*, the created and the to-be-created, only to discover with disappointment that the expression *creabile* refers to the material substrate that he wants to be sure is included in his *tu fecisti* [of your (i.e., God's) making].[51] Where the discussion concerns what is *not yet*, but *could be*, it is always about matter, the possibility of being as formal indeterminacy, which is associated with Aristotle.[52] The emphasis on willing in the concept of creation has its limit in the anti-Gnostic position, which attempts to understand

---

50. As formulated by Henry Deku in correspondence.

51. Augustine, *Confessiones* 12.19.28: "It is true that you have not only made whatever has been created and given shape, but also whatever has the capacity to be created and take shape, for all things come from you." [The English translation used here is *Confessions*, trans. Carolyn J.-B. Hammond (Cambridge, MA: Harvard University Press, 2014), 301.] (Günter Gawlick alerted me to this quotation.)

52. Augustine, *De vera religione* 18.36: "Thus everything that is, insofar as it is, and everything that is not yet, insofar as it can be, has its being [or potential being] from God." [The English translation used here is "True Religion," in *On Christian Belief*, trans. Edmund Hill (Hyde Park, NY: New City Press, 2005), 52.] The context of this citation is also illuminating in connection with the previously discussed *De spiritu et litera*. The theological concept of *salus* [salvation] is here identified with that of *bonum* [good] and laid at the foundation of classical assumptions as *integritas naturae* [integrity of nature]—in Platonic terms, as an expression of Ideas.

creation as a rational act: "Who would dare to say that God created everything in an irrational manner?"[53] But here "rational" can
only be interpreted in accordance with Plato's notion of the Demiurge as the guiding corresponding thread between the noetic and
the real world. In this way, the concepts of omnipotence and infinity are necessarily separated since *infinitum* [the infinite] in ancient
understanding is incompatible with rationality; it is the hyletic
apeiron [the boundles]. Infinity does not yet figure as an attribute
of God. Only when God's *potentia* is first understood as *potentia
infinita* [infinite power], does it become logically necessary to stop
defining *potentia* (and the Ideas it implies) on the basis of the possible and to do the inverse—to define the possible on the basis of
potentia.[54] It is only then that the limits of possibility are defined as
its *logical* limits and the cosmos of Ideas is rendered irrelevant for
the question of what *omnia* means as the extension of *omnipotentia*. As a consequence, the concept of rationality will be reduced to
the concept of *noncontradiction*, while even in Augustine the concept of *ratio* is still not separable from the exemplary Idea and
therefore implies a final, objective order. Only *now* for the first
time can the decisive step for our inquiry into the ontological latitude of the creative be taken: The supposedly finite cosmos does
not exhaust the infinite universe of possibilities of being—in other
words, the possibilities of divine omnipotence—and *cannot* exhaust
them. The cosmos is necessarily only a factual portion of this universe, and there remains a space of unrealized being—which of
course will long be the unquestioned preserve of God and will not
come up in connection with humanity's inquiry into its own potential. But the discussion of the concept of omnipotence made this

---

53. Augustine, *De diversis quaestionibus* 83, q. 46.

54. For the derivation of *possible* from *posse*, I quote the versio latina of *De
natura hominis* of Nemesius of Emesa: "tria igitur haec sunt ad invicem se haben-
tia: potens, potestas, possibile, potens quidem essentia, potestas vero a qua habe-
mus posse, possibile autem, quod secundum potestatem natum est fieri." ["So
those three things, as we said, depend on each other—being able, power and possibility: what is able is the substance, power is that from which we are able, the
possible that which is of a nature to come about through power." Nemesius, *On
the Nature of Man*, trans. R. W. Sharples and P. J. Van Der Eijk (Liverpool: Liverpool University Press, 2008), 182.]

space ontologically implicit and comprehensible as part of the background of the reality of the world. This is primarily an eminently *religious* idea, not only insofar as the *that* of the world has lost its obviousness but also insofar as its *what* can now be understood as an act of a specific, divine decree. At the same time, however, it broadens the basis for a *philosophical* critique out of which an abundance of consciousness-shaping questions arise. The world as *factum*: this ontological presupposition makes it possible— practically serves as the inducement and temptation—to fashion something of *human origin*, to render the authentically "new" in the realm of the unrealized by using what has not yet actually been realized, advancing beyond the dependence on "imitation of nature" to a place untouched by nature.

VI.

Of course, there is no temptation here for the Middle Ages: All speculative boldness will focus on investigating to its farthest reaches the possibilities of God, not those of man. It will require yet a further, decisive motivation for humanity to be able to know and grasp the theologically discovered incongruity between being and nature as a possibility for *its own* originary creativity.

The contact between *omnipotence* and *infinity*, which produces the initial spark, apparently occurs around the eleventh century, when it becomes necessary to systematize the doctrine of divine omnipotence in response to the "dialecticians," above all in response to the damage done by Berengar of Tours to the doctrine of transubstantiation. It is, above all, Petrus Damiani who takes the lead here with his *De divina omnipotentia* [Of Divine Omnipotence].[55] I cite here only the typical rhetorical question, found in chapter twelve: "Quid est, quod Deus non valeat nova conditione creare?" [What is there that God would not be able to create under different

---

55. The significance of this author for the history of the concept of possibility is demonstrated by August Faust, *Der Möglichkeitsgedanke* (Heidelberg: Winter, 1931), 1:72–75.

circumstances?] The being of the world acquires a certain peculiar arbitrariness here, a revocability and hypothetical interchangeability that it first receives in the waning Middle Ages, when the period's anxiety about facticity goes from *logical* to *emotional*—that is, is related by humanity to itself. I am not able to give a description of this transformation here. My intent is to present the *growing* incongruity between being and nature, and through it the growing relevance of the space of originary creativity. One ought not imagine this process as organic, nor attribute to it the honorable movement of historical necessity, which it appears to have a posteriori— especially coupled with the selective reading on which every study of this kind must rely. It is easy to see that the role the Scholastics played in this process of the reconceptualization of ontological premises hardly fits the description of "historical necessity." But one should likewise not consider the classical revival brought on by the Aristotle reception as a violent reversion, as is already demonstrated by the insight gained from Augustine that the implications of ancient thought continued to have potency. It is all the more appealing to see precisely in the high Scholastic revival of ancient metaphysics the often unarticulated but nonetheless significant distortions that prove *what could no longer be reversed*.

Ontological premises that seemed valid to Augustine without needing to be explicitly formulated were now "ripe for questioning" in the Scholastic manner. A revealing quotation with reference to our citation from Augustine is the polemic of Albertus Magnus against the *fons vitae* of Avicebron (Ibn Gabirol) with its identification of the metaphysical principle of light and will: "it is not possible for will to be first principle."[56] The function of divine will is

---

56. Albertus Magnus, *De causis et processu universitatis* 1 tr. 3 c. 4: "Primum enim et operi proximum, in quo primi est potentia agendi, est illud, quod dat formam operi, et non illud, quod iubet et praecipit opus fieri; lumen autem intellectus universaliter agentis est forma operis opus determinans ad rationem et formam, voluntas autem non est nisi praecipiens ut fiat" [The first and the most proximate (principle) for action—in which, first, lies the power to act—is that which gives form to the action, and not that which orders and commands that the action be done. The light of the generally acting intellect is the form of the action determining the action according to content and form—will, however, is commanding it to happen].

concerned with the *existence* [*Existenz*] of the world, with the order *ut fiat* [that it be done], not, however, with the *forma operis* [form of the work], the essential stock of being, which here also has the obviousness of the formal, predetermined totality.

Even Thomas Aquinas does not go beyond this conception. There is, however, a broader understanding of the principle of imitation of nature insofar as it is accompanied by the related idea of imitation of God that serves as second foundational context.[57] This relation existed formally in Aristotle, according to whom the precise circular motion of the first sphere was the imitation of the Unmoved Mover. But this exhausts the potential of the relation. Aristotle must therefore explain the genesis of a house, for example, as the architect's rendering of what nature *would have* allowed to result. In other words, the architect must *imagine* the artificial structure as a product of nature to then imitate this hypothetical representation. In this way, the universal validity of mimesis was guaranteed. Aquinas restricted the imitation of *nature* to only what nature indeed can make on its own[58]—a house, however, is a purely artificial object, it always results from artifice, "as every house is a work of art."[59] Here, of course, we do not have a discrepancy but a very great difference in emphasis. This is even more apparent in the commentary on the *Physics*, where he discusses the seminal passage cited at the beginning of this essay (II, 8; 199a 15–17).[60] The Latin version available to Aquinas reads: "ars alia quidem perficit

---

57. Thomas Aquinas, *Summa Theologica* 1, q. 9a. 1 ad 2: "suam similitudinem diffundit [sc. divina sapientia] usque ad ultima rerum: nihil enim esse potest quod non procedat a divina sapientia per quamdam imitationem" [it (i.e., divine wisdom) diffuses its likeness even to the outermost of things; for nothing can exist that does not proceed from the divine wisdom by way of some kind of imitation].

58. Thomas Aquinas, *Summa contra Gentiles* 1.75 ad 3: "In these things that can be done both by art and nature, art imitates nature." [The English translation used here is *Of God and His Creatures* (London: Burnes & Oates, 1905), 191.]

59. [Thomas Aquinas, *Summa contra Gentiles* 2.75 ad 3.]

60. *In octo libros Physicorum Aristotelis exposito* 2, lect. 13 n. 4. [The English translation used here is *Commentary on Aristotle's Physics*, trans. Richard J. Blackwell, Richard J. Spath, and W. Edmund Thirlkel (New Haven, CT: Yale University Press, 1963), 119.] To show how a more authentic rendering of Aristotelian meaning can be achieved, I cite the translation of Johannes Argyropylos (ed. Immanuel Bekker [Berlin 1831], 3.109b): "atque ars omnino alia perficit, quae natura

quae natura non potest operari," to which his commentary reads: "He says that art makes certain things which nature cannot make." This is formulated more radically than it could have been intended by Aristotle, who, after all, always takes for granted what is already on the way to becoming in nature when he discusses the human task of completion. *Why* the imitation of nature has so recognizably lost its invulnerability, *why* "art" *can* be taken out of the context of nature, Aquinas does not make explicit.

Not so his contemporary, Bonaventure, who does not participate in the attempt to interpret the creation idea with the metaphysics of the Prime Mover, since for him the mechanical character of this conception loses the sense of a divine will *desiring to express itself through its works.* "Expression" means, namely, that the limitless power of God does not, as it were, execute itself "automatically," but rather inheres in the finite, which a finite being can conceive of and comprehend.[61] A will to announce itself in the world emerges, which wants to make comprehensible not *everything possible*, but rather *something specific* ("multa non omnia") [many, not all]. God brings out many but not all of the treasures in His chest of possibilities to prove Himself in His greatness to creation.[62] The feeling expressed here, one could say, is that the difference between *omnia* and *multa* is a mere "remainder," perhaps prudently and lovingly withheld from humanity—in any case, not a reason to feel short-

---

nequit perficere, alia imitando naturam facit" [And art makes entirely different things, which nature cannot make, and makes others by imitating nature].

61. Bonaventure, *Breviloquim* 2.1.1: "The entire fabric of the universe was brought into existence in time and out of nothingness, by one first Principle, single and supreme, whose power, though immeasurable, has disposed all things by measure and number and weight." [The English translation used here is *The Works of Bonaventure* (Paterson, NJ: St. Anthony Guild Press, 1963), 2:69.] Deeply rooted ontologically in this factual specificity is the "incentive" to measure, to count, to venture, which opens the empirical route to knowledge.

62. Bonaventure, *II. Sententiarum* 1.2.1.1 concl.: "Propter ergo immensitatis manifestationem multa de suis theauris profert, non omnia, quia effectus non potest aequari virtuti ipsius primae causae." The Aristotelian foundation for the vast heterogeneity of reality is typical. However, Bonaventure was more conscious of the difference between him and Aristotle than Aquinas was; in fact, he believed that he could praise Aristotle as a historical figure who understood the eternity of the world rightly, and in accordance with Bonaventure's own principles.

changed in access to or possession of the store of being. But William of Ockham, who forced the Franciscan tradition through to its conclusions, will reverse Bonaventure's formulation by putting the *multa* on the opposite side, on the side of the unwilled-unrealized: "There is much that God can create which he does not want to create."[63] One can almost sense how an agonizing, gnawing awareness of the arbitrariness of the factual must arise, the growing uncertainty about why *this* and no *other* world was called into being—a question that could only have the stark *Quia voluit* [because he wanted to] of Augustine hurled against it as a nonanswer. Its offensiveness to rationality made palpable the unbearableness of this facticity: all of a sudden, the accent shifted from the divine expression of will contained in the *creation* to the implicit and withheld in the *uncreated*. We can discern this process of accentuating the

---

63. William of Ockham, *Quodlibeta Septem* 6, q. 1: "Deus multa potest facere quae non vult facere" [God can do many things that he does not want to do]. Here the relationship of our problem to Ockham's "nihilism" is apparent: The realism of the *universalia* proves itself to be incompatible with *creatio ex nihilo* in the strict sense of the term. The *universale* as somehow concretely reproduced and reproducible has only one meaning as long as the universe of possible existence is a finite whole (as the *mundus intelligibilis*), for which only existence is, as it were "supplied" (*distinctio realis*). The concept of the *potentia absoluta*, however, implies an *infinite* possible universe; it makes no sense to interpret individual entities as "duplications" of a universal. Creation signifies the ex nihilo of the *essentia* of every creature. In this way, Ockham argues, the notion that God contained his *potentia* through the creation of what is, is ruled out. The establishment of a *universale* only within the bounds of its reproduction of itself would make only imitation possible, and not creation: "creatio est simpliciter de nihilo; ita quod nihil essentiale vel intrinsecum rei simpliciter praecedat in esse real!" [Creation happens simply out of nothingness, and so this essential or intrinsic nothing of a thing simply proceeds into real existence]. The realism of the universe would mean that "per consequens omnia producta post primum productum non crearentur, quia non essent de nihilo" [consequently, all things produced after the first production are not created because they do not come into being out of nothingness] (Bonaventure, *Sententiarum* 1 dist. 2 q. 4 D). How much room the realm of possibility already allowed for is apparent in Ockham's refutation of the claim of his predecessor, Duns Scotus, that God alone possesses creative powers. Ockham, *Quodlibeta Septem* 7.23. This is not yet the investiture of human beings with the attribute of creating, but it releases the potential of this idea from its exclusively theological conception and makes its transfer predictable.

uncreated best in the careful attempts to deal with it, to absorb it—even to give it a positive valence.

The work of Nicholas of Cusa provides the most multifaceted response to the difficulty of this problem. In his early phase, Cusa anticipated Leibniz's attempt to justify the noncreation of the uncreated by finding the actual world to be the highest form of reality, the self-exhaustion of the creative principle as *deus creatus*.[64] But in this Christianized Neoplatonism inheres a contradiction between two elements of speculative theology: on the one hand, the maximal version of the concept of perfection of creator and work makes it necessary to say that nothing more perfect *could have been* made. On the other hand, the maximal version of divine omnipotence makes it necessary to say that no actual creation of the creator comprises the full extent of what He in His greatness and perfection could have achieved. This dilemma cannot be overcome. In *De beryllo*, almost two decades later, Cusa understands the creation with the model of legal statutes: he refers twice to the quotation in the digests, according to which the will of the ruler has the force of law.[65] At the end of his intellectual career, in the text *De ludo globi*, Cusa attempts to harmonize his two previous positions, explaining the difference in terms of perspective: seen from *God's* point of view, there is room for the play of possibility; from the point of view of

---

64. Nicholas of Cusa, *De docta ignorantia* 2.2: "Quoniam ipsa forma infinita non est nisifinite recepta, ut omnis creatura sit quasi infinitas finita aut Deus creatus, ut sit eo modo, quo hoc melius esse possit; ac si dixisset creator: Fiat, et quia Deus fieri non potuit, qui est ipsa aeternitas, hoc factum est, quod fieri potuit Deo similus."

65. "Quodprincipi placuit legis vigorem habet" (*Corpus Iuris Civilis: Iustiniani Digesta* 1.4.1, ed. Theodore Mommsen [Berlin: Weidemann, 1877]), as cited in Nicholas of Cusa, *De beryllo* XXIX. This is explicitly aimed at the inability of classical metaphysics to explicate the act of creation: "Cur autem sic sit et non aliter constitutum, propterea non sciret nisi quod demum resolutus [I] diceret: Quod principi" [But why it was established to be such and not otherwise, [Aristotle] would not thereby know—except in the end he would say without hesitation(!): For what has pleased the Prince] (Nicholas of Cusa, *De beryllo*. See XVI). Ecclesiastes 7:17 is cited for biblical authority: "Omnium operum Dei nulla est ratio" (There is no reason for all the works of God). [The English translation used here is from *On [Intellectual] Eyeglasses (De Beryllo)* in Nicholas of Cusa, *Metaphysical Speculations*, trans. Jasper Hopkins (Minneapolis, MN: Arthur J. Banning Press, 1998), sec. 51.]

the *world*, there is none.[66] This is based on a metaphysics of the concept of possibility; in creating, God not only realized the possible or from among the possible, but also created possibility itself: "et fieri posse ipsum factum est." Certainly, this is meant to wave off and ignore pressing, meddlesome questions. Nicholas of Cusa tries to do this through turning logic metaphysical, Martin Luther will do so by radicalizing the exclusive claim of theology. With a decisive turn against Ockham's formula, he insists that "omnipotence" has no logically comprehensible meaning outside of its Scriptural meaning, and precisely does not indicate the power of God to realize much more than he had realized.[67] God's *potentia absoluta* [absolute power], the inconceivability of which worries the young Luther, as it does the late Middle Ages as a whole, is to be understood as limited by God himself to the *potentia ordinata* [ordered power] through the instrument of the Revelation. Asking about anything beyond God's gracious self-restraint assumes the odium of rejecting this act of grace. Only by not asking about the infinite latitude of possibility does one escape the threatening uncertainty of that which it leaves open.

VII.

But the force of the questions once they have emerged cannot be contained. Where they lead, we can see already expressed almost to the fullest extent in Descartes. With Descartes, philosophy is a systematization of the possible; now what actually is, is understandable from the point of view of what is possible. Hence, the new

---

66. Nicholas of Cusa, *De ludo globi* I: "perfectiorem et rotundiorem mundum atque etiam imperfectiorem et minus rotundum potuit facere Deus, licet factus sit ita perfectus sicut esse potuit" [God could make a more perfect and rounder world, and even one that was more imperfect and less round, although the world that he did make would be as perfect in its own way as it could be].

67. Martin Luther, *The Bondage of the Will*, trans. J. I. Packer and O. R. Johnston (Ada, MI: Baker, 1990), 217: "And by the omnipotence of God I mean, not the power by which He omits to do many things that He could do, but the active power by which He mightily works all in all. It is in this sense that Scripture calls Him omnipotent."

meaning of *hypothesis*, which satisfies the intellectual desire to construct a *possible* nexus of being [*Seinszusammenhang*] and reacts with indifference to the question of the *actual* nexus. For the will to *construction*, it is irrelevant if nature is imitated by chance or if a solution not yet realized in nature results; the normative principle of *economy* is a principle of the human intellect designed for its benefit, not for the workings of nature. The principle of *possible worlds* is so endlessly fruitful that an agreement between their deduced, hypothetical construction and the *actual world* can only be a coincidence.[68] It is already apparent with Descartes how the idea of freedom depends on the independence of rational formulae from the factually given: with the example of an "ingenious machine," he demonstrates the force of the mind as so capable of originality that the inventor is able to conceive of the machine "without having seen anything like it anywhere."[69] Man "chooses" his world, just as God chose a world to create from the possible worlds. Leibniz will one last time attempt to limit these worlds with his notion of preestablished harmony and to balance the weight of endless possibilities with a metaphysical optimism. But when this boundless optimism collapses in the middle of the eighteenth century, the whole trouble of the matter comes to light: The reality of being can only be an arbitrary value in the realm of the possibility of being. What justification then remains for the possible to continue as possible? Nature is the factual result of mechanistic combinations: How can it be binding or serve as a model for the man-made through mimesis? The arbitrariness of natural formations stands in opposition to human creations—aesthetic and technical—with their necessity.

What remains of Leibniz's "best of all possible worlds" ontologically is not the "best world" but rather the infinity of possible worlds, a notion that becomes intellectually attractive precisely as

---

68. "The Principles . . . are so vast and so fertile, that their consequences are far more numerous than the entire observed contents of the visible world." Descartes, *Principles of Philosophy*, "Part Three: The Visible Universe," sec. 4, in *The Philosophical Writings of Descartes*, vol. 1, trans. John Cottingham, Robert Stoothoff, Dugald Murdoch (New York: Cambridge University Press, 1985).

69. Descartes, *Principles of Philosophy*, "Part One: The Principles of Human Knowledge," sec. 17.

the real world no longer plausibly represents the world chosen as best. Without being aware of the metaphysical background, Oskar Walzel traces the mid-eighteenth-century idea of the creative genius back to Leibniz.[70] Walzel makes it especially clear how the comparison of God to the creative artist already contained within it the artist's comparison of himself to God. In terms of *logic*, there will be nothing added here between the Renaissance and the *Sturm und Drang*. It is nonetheless decisively important that *poetry* comes to achieve a particular significance in this comparison. While the comparison of God to the master craftsman and the painter go back to antiquity, now the poet becomes the preeminent "creator," and not coincidentally, but rather—as is now simply obvious—because of the destruction of the mimesis idea. In his *Treatise on Painting*, Leonardo da Vinci established the similarity of the painter to God: by imitating nature, the painter imitates its creator. And the rebellion of Mannerism against mimesis had de facto only managed an ostentatious deformation of nature. In the poetic tradition, the rebellion against *imitatio* was primarily against the stylistic restrictions of the classical canon; it was an insistence on the individuality of the expressive form against Aristotelian poetics and Ciceronianism.[71] Yet Julius C. Scaliger in his *Poetics* of 1561 had already defined the difference between poetry and all other art forms: only the poet's occupation was *condere* [to compose], while that of all other artists was *narrare* [to narrate], a retelling as opposed to the creation of the poet, who as an *alter deus* could found a *natura altera* [second nature].[72] But this idea is still without ontological foundation: it receives a grounding first through Leibniz, who did not himself, however, draw any conclusions from the infinity of possible worlds,[73] and could not because of his metaphysical optimism. It is the "Swiss" who first establish the connection between the imagination of the creative poet and the idea of "possible worlds," which kindled a spark and determined the meaning of art as "metaphysi-

---

70. Oskar Walzel, *Das Prometheussymbol von Shaftsbury zu Goethe* (Munich: Wortkunst, 1932).

71. See August Buck, *Italienische Dichtungslehren* (Tübingen: Niemeyer, 1952).

72. The passage is cited at length in Walzel, *Das Prometheussymbol*, 45ff.

73. Walzel, *Das Prometheussymbol*, 51.

cal activity" for the next era. Johann Jakob Breitlinger's two-volume *Critische Dichtkunst* [*Critical Poetics*] of 1740 is an "aesthetic" application of Leibniz's doctrine of "possible worlds."[74] The poet finds himself in the position of God before the creation of the world, facing the entire infinitude of possible worlds, out of which he may choose; therefore, poetry is—and here comes the most astonishing formulation on our theme that one could wish for!—"an imitation of creation and nature not only in their reality but also in their possibility." So powerful is the foundational formula of "imitation of nature," so deeply rooted in the metaphysical tradition, that its sanction for the significance of human creations cannot be dispensed with, even when it is used to express—even to proclaim!—the exact opposite of its intended meaning! The endlessly possible now takes on the same role of regulative ideal as the Platonic Ideas, if it is possible for the discourse of imitation to take on yet another meaning. Johann Jakob Bodmer in his ca. 1740 *Abhandlung von dem Wunderbaren in der Poesie* [*Treatise on the Wonderful in Poetry*] speaks of poetry in almost the same language: "It is always preferable that the material to be imitated come from the possible rather than from the present world."[75] The example of Milton shows how the poet exceeds the boundaries of the given and is even able, via a "metaphysical exercise," to demonstrate nothingness precisely because he throws out everything that makes the world the world by invoking "the creation before the creation." Here comes the further, astonishing formulation that "through their art and by means of imitation" poets "produce things that are not."

The nineteenth century decisively sharpens the factual character of nature. What lies before us as nature is the result of unregulated mechanical processes, of the condensation of swirling primordial matter, of the interplay between randomly scattered mutations and the brutal fact of the struggle for survival. The result can be anything—only it cannot be an aesthetic object. How can random chance produce such surprising evidence of the beautiful? The previously unthinkable becomes comprehensible: nature becomes *ugly*.

---

74. Walzel, *Das Prometheussymbol*, 39, and the passage following.

75. Walzel, *Das Prometheussymbol*, 43, for this and the following quotations.

As Franz Marc writes, "The trees, the flowers, and the earth showed every year more and more of their ugly and repulsive sides, until suddenly I became fully conscious of the ugliness and uncleanness of nature."[76] The ontological background is more precisely expressed by the French painter Raoul Dufy, when he replies to the criticism that he makes too short work of nature, "Nature, my good Sir, is a hypothesis."[77] In the aesthetic experience of nature, the proviso of an endless number of possible worlds has had sufficient impact so that, since Descartes, we cannot say with scientific certainty which of these possibilities are realized in nature, but rather only with which of these possibilities we can functionally *cope*. This nature has nothing more in common with the ancient concept of nature to which the mimesis idea referred: the unmakable model of all that is made. That all phenomena can be manufactured is instead the universal presupposition of experimental investigations of nature, and hypotheses are outlines of instructions for the manufacture of phenomena. Nature then becomes the embodiment of the possible results of technology. What remains of nature's exemplary bindingness is revoked. For the technician, nature could become more and more of a substrate whose given constitution stands in the way of the realization of its constructive use, rather than promoting it. Only through the reduction of nature to its raw potential as matter and energy is a sphere of pure construction and synthesis possible. This results in a state of affairs that seems paradoxical at first glance: an era of the highest regard for science is at the same time an age of the decreasing significance of the object of scientific study.

VIII.

Only now can the *positive* significance of the dissolution of the identity of being and nature be discerned. The devaluing of nature is

---

76. This and other references from Hans Sedlmayr, *Art in Crisis: The Lost Center*, trans. Brian Battershaw (Chicago: Henry Regnery, 1958), 159.

77. Cited in Maurice Raynal et al., *Geschichte der modernen Malerei: Fauvismus und Expressionismus* (Geneva: Skira, 1950), 69ff.

thus not simply a nihilistic process, because it becomes possible to believe that "what is visible is but a fragment of the whole, there being many more latent realities,"[78] and that this world "is not the only possible world."[79] Thus, art no longer points to another, exemplary being, but rather it is itself this exemplary being for the possibilities of humanity: the work of art no longer wants to *mean* something; rather, it wants to *be* something.

But is not this being, which selects one out of the numberless many possibilities that are left lying *alongside* nature, nonetheless equally limited in its facticity and arbitrary in its selection? All questions arising out of the overcoming of the bindingness of mimesis revolve around this. We are too much in the wake of the agonal process of overcoming mimesis to permit confidence in specific answers. We are dependent on hypotheses where we would like to flee from what is "merely a hypothesis." There are many indications, however, that the phase of violent assertion of the constructed and the authentic, of "work" and "labor," was only a transition. The overcoming of the imitation of nature [*Nachahmung der Natur*] could bring with it an "anticipation of nature" [*Vorahmung der Natur*]. Although humanity seems very much devoted to making certain of its originary power through the "metaphysical task" of art, a sense of the always-already-there comes through in creation, "as if it were a mere product of nature."[80] I am thinking of a life's work as paradigmatic in its deliberate intentions as that of Paul Klee, which demonstrates how unanticipated structures crystallize in the latitude of creation, allowing what is ancient and eternal within the original foundation of nature to reemerge with renewed powers of persuasion. Thus, Klee's titles are not to be interpreted as the usual difficulty of abstract painters to appeal to familiar associations; rather, they are the acts of a bewildered recognition, which almost announces that only *one* world validly realizes the possibilities of

---

78. Paul Klee, cited in Werner Haftmann, *The Mind and Work of Paul Klee*, trans. anon. (New York: Frederick A. Praeger, 1954), 90.

79. Paul Klee, *Über die moderne Kunst* (Bern: Benteli, 1945), 43. [The English translation used here is *On Modern Art*, trans. Raul Findlay (London: Faber and Faber, 1966), 45.]

80. Kant, *Critique of the Power of Judgement*, § 45, 185.

being and that the road to the infinity of the possible was only an escape route from the unfreedom of mimesis. Are the infinite worlds, which Leibniz bequeathed to aesthetics, only endless reflections of *one* foundational character of being? We do not know this, and we also do not know if we will ever know it; but further investigations into this question will be made innumerable times. Could it just be a circle that takes us back exactly where we started? The prospect of such a circle frightens many today, who fear that all these bold acts might have been in vain. But that is indeed mistaken. It makes a crucial difference whether we *put up with* reality as unchangeable or if we rediscover it as the core of what is evident in the latitude of the infinite possibilities and are able to consent freely to *recognize* it—if we are capable, finally, of "making the accidental essential."[81]

Translated by Anna Wertz[82]

---

81.   Klee, cited by Haftmann, *Paul Klee*, 71 [translation altered].
82.   [Minor corrections and additional editorial footnotes by Hannes Bajohr.]

14

Phenomenological Aspects on Life-World and Technization

(1963)

In the second of his three 1919 essays on Leonardo da Vinci, Paul Valéry makes one of his many open, or, even more frequently, hidden, attacks on Pascal. He sets his hero Leonardo off against the dark foil of a thinker who is without any feeling for art, obsessed only by the risky wager on the absolute. For Pascal, nature was nothing but the gaping abyss of infinity on the path to salvation. Valéry characterizes the thinker and technician Leonardo, on the other hand, in the following terms: "No abyss opening on his right. An abyss would make him think of a bridge."[1]

Originally published as "Lebenswelt und Technisierung unter Aspekten der Phänomenologie," *Filosofia* 14, no. 4 (1963): 855–884; from Hans Blumenberg, *Schriften zur Technik*, ed. Alexander Schmitz and Bernd Stiegler (Berlin: Suhrkamp, 2015), 17–29.
1. [Paul Valéry, "Note and Digression," in *Leonardo Poe Mallarmé*, trans. M. Cowley and J. R. Lawler (Princeton, NJ: Princeton University Press, 1972), 79.]

This is to put the whole elementary state of affairs most succinctly: that the commonly used antithesis of nature and technology [*Technik*] is insufficient when it comes to understanding the
modern phenomenon of technization [*Technisierung*]. Rather, already at the level of intuiting what is given, the relationship between modern man and the world is highly nuanced, reflecting the
choice the age has already made in the matter. The image of the
abyss provides its metaphor: An eye like Pascal's is transfixed by
that image's vertical line; the unfathomable dark of the chasm captivates the gaze only to prepare thought resolutely to choose the opposite direction, that of transcendence. An eye like Leonardo's
spontaneously seizes on the image's horizontal line as the chance to
connect both edges of the abyss to vault the obstacle; or it sees in
the void of the chasm the testing ground for a mechanical bird.
There is not only the kind of nature that resists technology and is
destroyed and abused by it—nature that lets the enormous vanity
of man's efforts slide off of itself and that renders it perceptible by
continually shattering his instruments. Instead, there is also the kind
of nature that is like a call for man's reins and bridles, his paths and
bridges, his gripping and clearing machinery, his toys and his appetite for consumption.

The challenge the modern gaze recognizes in nature has no longer
anything to do with the notion that nature is, as it were, prepared for
man, disposed towards his needs, or at least that nature contains the
economic minimum necessary to support his existence. Neither in
Leonardo nor in Pascal is there any room for the astonishment at
the order that takes each and every creature into account, which the
Greeks, under the name of cosmos, designated so explicitly as the
motivation that gave rise to the fundamental questions of philosophy. Neither Giordano Bruno's enthusiasm in the face of the infinite,
nor Pascal's horror at this abyss contain anything of the reassurance
guiding pure theoretical contemplation that the cosmos bestowed
upon the Greeks. If the Leonardo of Valéry's dictum had really
thought of a bridge in the face of the abyss, then he, too, would
have merely leapt over the stage of feeling horror, but he would not
have omitted it. The act of self-assertion, which avoids exposure to the
chasm's pull in the first place, does not make it disappear. Thinking

from one fixed point to another—which includes the leap as much as giving oneself up to transcendence—receives its necessity and energy precisely from the anxiety about its ineliminable discontinuities. Insofar as the modern age finds itself confronted with philosophical problems of its own making at all, they arise not from astonishment, but discontent, from the "uneasiness" of Locke.[2] This is why the problem of technology is such a characteristic element of modern, contemporary thought, even though the *problem* of technology has not yet been clearly distinguished from the *problems* of technology (spoken once in the *genitivus obiectivus*, and once in the *genitivus subiectivus*). We are richly blessed with ontologies, theologies, and especially demonologies of technology— but this abundance is the very reason for the tedium that makes one hope to hear the word "technology" only from the mouth of a technician. In this way, the productivity of professionalized philosophy contributes to the continuous renewal of this uneasiness, which in turn today nourishes philosophy.

The problem of technology may have concealed itself under the mass of spoken and printed words among which nothing appears to remain unsaid—for in what is interrogated excessively, the questionable withdraws much more thoroughly than in that which is still uninterrogated, a state in which the Greeks found the world to be. Whenever philosophy was too willing to believe itself close to solving its problems, it had to deal with the fruitful disappointment of learning that it had not even discovered these problems themselves, or rather, had thought them to be posed too crudely. To that which is supposedly already on its course, calls to order have always sounded trivial, annoying, foolish, and disruptive in this situation. This was the case at the beginning of our century, when Edmund Husserl's call to order—"to the things themselves!"—rang out. Philosophy, fully immersed in criticizing everything else, was once again called back upon criticizing its own relationship to its objects. The century or so of what called itself philosophy of technology that has passed since the appearance of Ernst Kapp's *Elements of a Phi-*

---

2. [John Locke, *An Essay Concerning Human Understanding*, ed. Peter H. Nidditch (Oxford: Oxford University Press, 1975), esp. chaps. 7 and 20.]

losophy of Technology: On the Evolutionary History of Culture (1877) has produced a sense of obviousness of what in the case of technology was "the thing itself"—a sense that is already highly suspicious. The definition of this thing itself Kapp presented by consistently developing the motto that he gave to his book: "All of human history, upon close scrutiny, ultimately resolves into the history of the invention of better tools."[3]

Correspondingly, the term "technology" evokes in us a colorful series of images: devices, vehicles, propulsion motors, storage units, manual and automatic instruments, conductors, switches, signals, and so forth—in short, a universe of things that are at work all around us, whose complete classification has often been attempted to little success, whose unifying factor, which the concept "technology" signifies, seems impossible to grasp, and which is therefore rendered unquestionable in a nominalistic way. With the appropriate conceptual frugality, "technization" is then to be understood as the constant multiplication and condensation of this thing-world.

I.

But where exactly is the "problem" of technology located? Where can it be located, since each and every one of these technical things, whose existence is based on being constructed, poses no problem other than that of its technological improvement or obsolescence, and which is generally devoid of any problem insofar as one can, in principle, understand its construction? Anyone who sees a tree is confronted with an impenetrable and, as we have to believe today, inexhaustible theoretical dimension; the observer of a locomotive has a thing at hand all of whose data are stored in a factory's construction office.

The problem of technology seems to result from the combined problems having to do with the *side effects* of technological

---

3. [Ernst Kapp, *Elements of a Philosophy of Technology: On the Evolutionary History of Culture*, ed. Jeffrey West Kirkwood and Leif Weatherby (Minneapolis: University of Minnesota Press, 2018). The motto is by Edmund Reitlinger.]

achievements: the traffic accidents, the noise of machinery, the exhaust fumes, the garbage, the waste water of industrial plants, the speed that is imposed on our work by machines, and the deviation from the natural rhythms of life, including the monotonization of industrial work, and so forth. If technology is defined in this way, optimists have an easy time, for all these are problems immanent to technology, which are often already technologically solved, even if these solutions are not profitable or unattractive in terms of social prestige and are thus not realized. It is not this kind of problematic that the problem of technology yields, because in the end it amounts to the realization that the sphere of technological things and achievements is not technological enough, lagging behind its own principles. When in 1936 Chaplin's cruel satire *Modern Times* supplied the uneasiness with technology with the most drastic images of men subservient to mechanisms, every technological expert had already known for a long time that the worker chasing the assembly line with his wrench was, from a technological point of view, by then a fossilized phenomenon, whose continued existence had other than technological reasons. Any kind of thinking that believes itself to be reacting to or against technology in this direction will very quickly find itself confronted with the consequence of having to demand not the limitation or overcoming but the *full execution* of the principle of technicity. It was Rousseau, who, in a significant passage, first connected his critique of the conditions of the society of his time with the postulate fully to execute the principle at work in this state, because he understood that history was irreversible.[4] Against his critic Diderot, he demanded not a

---

4. See "The General Society of the Human Race," the first version of the second chapter of the *Social Contract* (from the "Geneva Manuscript"), which was not included in the definitive version. In this context, Kant adopted the term "perfected art" (*art perfectionné*) from Rousseau and reshaped it in such a way that "perfect art once more becomes nature." Immanuel Kant, *Handschriftlicher Nachlaß: Anthropologie* (Berlin: de Gruyter, 1923), 2.1:887, 896. "Art" here is the totality of the form of life made possible by freedom: "Morality is a matter of art and not of nature" (Kant, "Reflexion 1454," in *Handschriftlicher Nachlaß: Anthropologie*, 636). Of course, through artificiality the passage leads "once more" to nature only in a *formal* sense, that is, to the *materially* perfectly heterogeneous correlate of a, in turn, "purposive establishment" as a "system of happiness" (Kant,

return to nature but the consistent and thorough carrying out of artificiality in the structure of human socialization: "Let us show him in perfected nature the redress of the evils which beginning art caused to nature."[5]

Here we can see how historicism, with its insight into the irreversibility of history, together with cultural and social criticism, increased the dynamism of the modern age's inner tendencies and still continues to do so—also with regard to the consciousness that supports technization.

But this criticism of a misguided approach does not give us any more insight into our "thing itself." It is the rule of the above-mentioned antithesis of technology and nature that still stands in the way of our getting a clear view of the thing itself, or, put more tentatively, what does so is the association of these concepts in our tradition since the Greeks.[6] In this coupling, the concept of technology was subject to a transformation in the history of the concept that turned "nature" from a concept for the generative principle of objects into the epitome of the generated objects itself—in other words, from the focus on the *natura naturans* [creating nature] to a focus on the *natura naturata* [created nature]. To the Greeks, their *technē* [art; technology] had primarily meant those skills and abilities that were apt to create specific achievements and products, and which could be learned through looking and imitating,

---

"Reflexion 1454," 869). The goal of constituting such a formal congruence is the regulative meaning of considering the state of nature, which is Rousseau's "life-world": "Rousseau does not want that one returns [*zurückgehen*] to the state of nature but only that one looks back [*zurücksehen*] at it" (Kant, "Reflexion 1454," 890). It may be this difference between a single letter that kindles the greatest number of misunderstandings and the fiercest fallings-out in the political and intellectual situation issuing from Rousseau in the following two centuries.

5. Jean-Jacques Rousseau, "The Geneva Manuscript," in "*The Social Contract" and Other Later Political Writings* (Cambridge: Cambridge University Press, 1997), 153–161; 159.

6. My first work on the problem of technology still adopted the traditional antithesis naturally as a topic: "The Relation between Nature and Technology as Philosophical Problem" [in this volume]. A different approach then came with the Brussels conference paper "Technology and Truth" ("Technik und Wahrheit," in *Actes du XIème Congrès International de Philosophie (Bruxelles, 20–26 août 1953): Epistémologie* [Louvain: Nauwelaerts, 1952], 2:113–120).

just in the same way one can learn a "technique" in sports, for instance. That it was possible to learn a technique in this way—that one could understand doing a thing without having to understand the thing itself and tying back the necessity of its execution to the essence of that thing—distinguished technical knowing-how from the theoretical-scientific relation toward the object. But in the end, the tradition of learning and imitating had to begin with someone who had, once and for all, deduced skill from insight, who had been able to develop what is appropriate to the thing from understanding the thing, so that, after all, technology and knowledge, skill and insight, converged at their root and were, at bottom, one and the same.

The separation of understanding a thing and mastering a thing was presented to the Greeks as a grand opportunity, both as a chance and an experiment, through the attitude represented by the *Sophists*. In the second half of the fifth century, the type of a released and isolated "technology" was presented for the first time in the realms of politics and law. The sophists offered an education that only required to know *how* something was done, which taught the steps and skills of the art that led to any chosen goal without any insight into law, grounding, and the objective necessity of the formulae handed down. Our whole tradition has been marked by the effective resistance with which Socrates—emerging himself from the bosom of Sophism—opposed it and demanded that all ability always be kept within the horizon of understanding, that no skill be released from the insight that constitutes it, that all correctness [*Richtigkeit*] be based on the question of its rightfulness [*Rechtlichkeit*]. Philosophy reached its classical heights in antiquity not only by setting itself apart from rhetoric, but in so doing, it also incorporated into its foundations the conceptual standards with which rhetoric—a technology that had no reference to being, truth, and the good—could henceforth be put in the wrong. It was not only the priority of theoretical intuition as an attitude appropriate to human reason, but even more so the priority of an objective realm untouched and untouchable by man, which opposed anything technical and artificial to the natural and would concede the former any meaning only through its origin in the latter—that is, through mimesis. The separation of philosophy from rhetoric, of theory from technology, of *scientia* from *ars* was, however, unsuccessful precisely at the point where philosophy appeared to have reached a deadlock in pursuing its self-posed absolute aspirations, as in late antiquity and at the end of the Middle Ages. At these moments, the *artes* became autonomous, acquired the title of philosophy and demonstrated what man is capable of without ever knowing to the last detail why. Philosophy had, at each end of each epoch, reached its end in skepticism and mysticism respectively, and gave way to skill unconcerned about its justification. In both cases, we find proof that the engineer as much as the geometer were given the title *philosophus*.[7] It had become philosophy's fate that it could achieve the self-assertion of its substance only *against* "technology" in the broadest sense.

On these historical presuppositions rests the mutual conditionality of the traditional questions for nature as well as culture and technology (both of which are derived from their common conceptual root of the "artificial"). In this way, the question for "natural nature" can be posed, in search for a normative orientation for the original determination and classification of human existence in the world. The artificial appears here as a superimposition onto the fundamental stratum of the natural and can be uncovered by a process of "subtraction." In the fifth book of his didactic poem *De rerum natura* [*On the Nature of Things*], Lucretius developed the notion—which had a long-lasting effect on all modern forms of cultural criticism—of a pretechnical human state of existence, which, through spontaneous inventions by man, had been distorted and deformed into the state of culture. In the following tradition and in variations of this scheme, the authentic series of the *inventiones* [inventions]—from the primal achievement of humans, kindling and taming fire, all the way to the invention of the plough, agriculture, clothing and housing, forms of socialization, mores and laws, marriage, language, property, and religion—was reshaped again and again in characteristic fashion. Once this cultural stratum is cleared away, Lucretius's

---

7. Ernst R. Curtius, *European Literature and the Latin Middle Ages*, trans. Willard R. Trask (Princeton: Princeton University Press, 2013), 203–207.

prehistorical man comes to the fore. He is human from the start—not yet thought to have emerged from the animal world—but a human who nevertheless shares the animals' way of life: "vitam tractabant more ferarum" ["they passed their lives after the wide-wandering fashion of wild beasts"].[8] This meant that man was, according to his original and binding nature, an atechnical being, completely immersed in the dumb consumption of what the natural environment offered and thus a being without any unmet needs, without wonder and fear, without questions. According to this schema, a deviation must have occurred, that original sin through which man sought to uncouple the self-creation of his existence from the pre-givenness of nature and elevate himself to the rank of a sophisticated and questioning counterpart of the given. Lucretius at once sees this as an act of self-empowerment of man against nature: "homines voluerunt se . . . potentes" [men desired to be . . . powerful].[9] As man began to fill his world with the *novae res* [new things], the innovations of his inventive power, he did not also begin to fulfill and actualize his natural predisposition, but ceased to be the essentially mature and world-competent natural being in his original equilibrium. One can see at once the potential for cultural criticism hidden in this schema, and it was Rousseau who fully exhausted it, probably specifically because he associated the incomprehensible fact of the human will to superfluity with the ideas of the fall and the lost paradise, which through Christianity had become a part of consciousness. This highly virulent amalgamation has had a lasting effect on the ambivalent relation of modern man toward his cultural world. But it served to orient his moral assessments more than his understanding. For despite the obvious familiarity with the motif of the fall, the transition from self-sufficiency in the state of nature toward the luxuriating of inventiveness remained especially difficult to understand or was only imagined to have been understood—that is, in other words, Lucretius's *fortuna* [chance], which made the world emerge from the swerve of falling

---

8. Lucretius, *On the Nature of Things*, trans. W. H. D. Rouse (Cambridge, MA: Harvard University Press, 1924), 451 (V, 932).
9. Lucretius, *On the Nature of Things*, 467 (V, 1120).

atoms.[10] That the problem of this *transition* is, however, the main point, we hope to indicate by speaking of "technization" as a process, and not of technology as a sphere of things.

This problem, of course, remains concealed, if one accepts as an unquestioned result of biological or philosophical anthropology that man—as a creature occurring in nature and testified to in his products—could only be recognizably defined by his use of fire and tools and the traces he leaves through them, that is, that man could from the start and by virtue of his definition only be a *homo faber*. Neither the antithesis of nature and technology—"nature" being the remaining difference once the strata of culture have been subtracted—nor the presupposition of the "natural" technicity of man leads toward the problem that is technization as a process. This process begins spontaneously in history and seems to stand in no comprehensible relation to human nature but, on the contrary, ruthlessly impels the adaptation of this nature, which is so inadequate to his needs.

II.

One methodically obvious way to circumvent the old questions so influenced by the assumptions of metaphysical anthropology is to yield to the demands of a phenomenological approach; with the problem at hand, too, this approach seeks to initiate a philosophy of unbiased new beginnings. Since Descartes, we may have been very much aware that a pure and ahistorical beginning never existed and cannot be performed. The commitment of that aspiration, however, remains as an idea that is constantly making claims on us.

We would have to ask, then, whether phenomenology as it is, in the methodological shape given to it by Edmund Husserl, can offer an approach to the problem of technization—an approach that, as befits the radicalism of this problem, may lie in the scope of the most fundamental phenomenological analysis. Husserl has provided us with unmistakable hints in his late work, *The Crisis of European*

---

10. Lucretius, 453 (V, 960).

Sciences and Transcendental Phenomenology, written between 1934 and 1937, that at least he himself regarded the achievements of his method to be fruitful for this problem by, for the first time, projecting the insights of phenomenology's eidetic and transcendental method onto the level of the historical genesis of our intellectual world. In this undertaking, the sphere of historical facts served only as a symptomatic layer that allowed hidden complexes of meaning to be disclosed which, to Husserl, would in the end form an idea of European history's purposefulness. Not for a moment do I deny that such a *teleology* transcends the competence of strict phenomenological description and analysis, and that it claims the right of conjecture, which is, of course, open to all sorts of doubts. But speculation is not the caprice typical of fiction; it has its own type of justification and its own specific prudence of utilization. I shall begin by elucidating the nexus of consequences in which this late speculation stood to Husserl's early deployment of phenomenology.[11]

Phenomenology strives to *describe* what is given to us and how it is given to us. In so doing, it comes upon the most fundamental fact, as something that is given to us most directly, that our consciousness only ever exists insofar as something is given to it—it is conscious of something. For this trivial-seeming fact, Husserl adopted Franz Brentano's concept of *intentionality.* Phenomenology had used this term to oppose the atomistic view of consciousness, which interpreted objects as associations of data in the stream of consciousness. Against this, Husserl emphasized as essential that every consciousness does not simply "have" its objects, but that it, wherever possible, always stands in intention toward the full givenness of its objects. Consciousness is a meaningfully directed productive structure, interlaced with an unceasing directed purposefulness, which—extending from the empty negation contained in the mere appellation of a name toward the fulfilled *intuition*—leaves no possibility for any further determination. Mundane and practical life may interrupt the performance of such fulfillments of ob-

<hr />

11. Edmund Husserl, *The Crisis of European Sciences and Transcendental Phenomenology: An Introduction to Phenomenological Philosophy,* trans. David Carr (Evanston, IL: Northwestern University Press, 1970).

jecthood, and out of necessity content itself with fragments of intuitions, with indications and intimations, with formulae and signs; but the theoretical stance, once it is left to its own devices and set into motion unwaveringly, passes through the wealth of perspectives that can be taken in regard to the object. Consciousness is never satisfied with intuiting the object statically; instead, it always has a direction, predetermined by the object's internal contexts that can be deduced from it. Objects are not accumulations of the contents of consciousness but consist in their "possibility of . . . original identification" and their allocation to one "identical pole."[12]

It is plain to see that Husserl opposed the mechanistic notion of consciousness in late nineteenth-century psychology with an interpretation of the phenomena of consciousness that by its very design implies a teleology of consciousness. This consequence Husserl realized himself only late in life, but a reader whose view is sharpened through the late work may already discern it when Husserl extends the problem of the object toward the problem of the object horizon [*Gegenstandshorizont*]. This object *horizon* repeats the structure of original relations and of internal contexts of reference Husserl initially had uncovered in the structure of the intuitions of objects in the process of being fulfilled. The "internal reference" that the process of experiencing an object follows finds its counterpart in the "external reference," grounded in a typology of the continuation of experience that is always part of the actual givenness. Now, this structure of reference does presuppose the unbroken and noncontradictory harmoniousness of the given, which Husserl also calls the "universal normal harmony" [*universale Normalstimmigkeit*][13] of experience and in which this harmoniousness is founded; its effect is that we judge the given to be reality and accept it as such for us. But the horizon structure is more than the unity of this negative determination; it is something like a morphological determination.[14] In the

---

12. Edmund Husserl, *Formal and Transcendental Logic*, trans. Dorion Cairns (The Hague: Nijhoff, 1969), 156, 164.

13. [Edmund Husserl, "Beilage XVIII," *Die Krisis der europäischen Wissenschaften und die transzendentale Phänomenologie* (The Hague: Nijhoff, 1976), 464. This supplementary text is not part of the English translation.]

14. Husserl, "Beilage XVIII," 464.

last instance, the intentionality of consciousness is fulfilled in the most comprehensive horizon of horizons—in the "world" as the regulative pole-idea of all possible experience, the system that keeps all possibilities of experience in a final harmony, and in which alone what is given to experience can prove itself to be real.[15] Husserl had described in his earliest analyses the sense data of sensualism to be characteristics that cannot be isolated from their objectual base, and that have been objectified only through an act he called "emphasis,"[16] and similarly, in the "world" as the horizon of all horizons, objecthood is likewise isolated and stressed in an act analogous to emphasis. "Nature," too—and this is essential for our topic—is the result of such emphasis. It is thus not equiprimordial to *world* but a derivative, already constricted objective horizon. *Nature*, so much can already be seen, cannot be the counterconcept to technology, for already in the concept of nature itself we find a deformation—an emphasis—of the original world-structure.

Now, what is crucial is that in his late work Husserl extends the approach he had found in the intentionality of consciousness onto *history*. Only here does the horizon-structure attain its full meaning: that which is co-present in all experience can now be the memory of a whole cultural community and its tradition, but also its

---

15. Husserl, *Crisis*, 305–306.

16. Edmund Husserl, *Logical Investigations*, 2 vols., trans. J. N. Findlay (London: Routledge, 2001), 2:253. In retrospect, Husserl recognized the starting point for further developing the problem of the world and the horizon in his *Logical Investigations* in the fact that he "could not finish with occasional judgments and their signification." (Husserl, *Formal and Transcendental Logic*, 199). Indeed, everything leads toward "transferring" [*Übertragung*] the structure of intentionality from the objective immanence onto the objective transcendence, that is, onto the intentionality of "situational horizons" (Husserl, *Formal and Transcendental Logic*, 199), and so forth. What for the eidetic ideal is bothersome—the occasionality of meanings—reveals itself to be conditioned by the irresolvable fact that every experience has its "horizon of unregarded mental processes" (Edmund Husserl, *Ideas Pertaining to a Pure Phenomenology and to a Phenomenological Philosophy*, 2 vols., trans. Fred Kersten [The Hague: Nijhoff, 1983], 1:197). That the absent is co-given has the function of "an idea in the Kantian sense" (Husserl, *Ideas*, 197). Husserl calls it an "eidetically valid and evidential statement that no concrete mental process can be accepted as self-sufficient in the full sense" (Husserl, *Ideas*, 198; translation altered).

expectations of the future that depend on a very specifically pre-formed consciousness of possibilities. The Husserl of the *Philosophical Investigations* had already shown how in the perception of objects from "partial intentions" a "total intention" arises that integrates them and that is already inherent in them.[17] Yet this schema gains its full illuminating power only with history as its subject. Before the phenomenologist's eye, history loses the illusion of facticity: That man has history can mean for him only that, even in the course of generations and epochs, he stays with what is already irrefutably inherent in the basic structure of consciousness, that is, with the fulfillment of intentionality. In a manuscript from 1936 that Eugen Fink published only three years later,[18] Husserl highlighted the difference between a mere history of facts and *his* form of contemplating history as an "inner structure of meaning" via the example of geometry, which, of course, suited his purposes rather well: "All factual history remains incomprehensible because, always merely drawing its conclusions naively and straightforwardly from facts, it never makes thematic the general ground of meaning on which all such conclusions rest, has never investigated the immense structural a priori which is proper to it."[19]

The "internal history" Husserl demands here not only can but indeed must gravitate toward the "highest question of a universal teleology of reason."[20] The subject of "history" is defined in the last consequence of phenomenology thus: "[H]istory is from the start nothing other than the vital movement of the coexistence and the interweaving of original formations and sedimentations of meaning."[21]

But this definition of history does not simply address the question of coping with it scientifically and theoretically. It also defines the self-determination and self-responsibility that is assigned as a task to all subjects who live and participate in history, that is, the self-determination toward those subjects' function in history. As will

---

17. [Husserl, *Logical Investigations*, 2:247, 212.]
18. Edmund Husserl, "The Origin of Geometry," in *Crisis*, 353–378.
19. Husserl, "The Origin of Geometry," 371.
20. Husserl, 378.
21. Husserl, 371.

be shown in the following, the problem of technology essentially has to do with the manner in which man is *responsible* for history; this was in fact true long before it could be perceived and become vivid that technology actually determines man's existence, and indeed, decides his possibilities.

III.

A peculiar piece of Cartesian heritage is embedded in Husserl's understanding of history: history, which Husserl saw as a process of founding and developing meaning, has a *beginning*. This is by no means obvious if we keep in mind that any individual finds himself always already "enclosed" in history and that we therefore can have no experience of any such beginning. For those familiar with Descartes, of course, a model is available in his decision—who for so long counted as the founder of modernity—once in his life and thus once and for all to start from scratch and from the ground up with the business of knowledge. We need not discuss the question of how Cartesian Husserl has been to see without any doubt how lasting an impression this decision of Descartes's made on Husserl's own enterprise.[22] This is why for him the Cartesian decision for a radical beginning can exist as the "primal establishment" [*Urstiftung*] of the whole of European intellectual history, namely, in the first adoption of the theoretical attitude by the Greeks. That here Husserl can speak of a "reorientation" presupposes a primary state that had not been theoretically structured but by a "natural primordial attitude, . . . the attitude of original natural life," and this state corresponds to "the first originally natural form of cultures."[23] European history unfolded from a decision for a "fixed style of willing life" of European humanity.[24] This image of the historical beginning is certainly in accordance with the ethos of philosophizing and the

---

22. See Ludwig Landgrebe, "Husserl's Departure from Cartesianism," in *The Phenomenology of Edmund Husserl: Six Essays*, ed. Donn Welton (Ithaca, NY: Cornell University Press, 1981), 6–121.

23. Husserl, *Crisis*, 281.

24. Husserl, 280.

conception of man that was authoritative for Husserl—but in the development of the phenomenological approach and its concept of consciousness' intentionality, it is inconsistent to posit such a "beginning" for the theoretical attitude and have it be preceded by a heterogeneous phase of original naturalness in the human attitude toward the world. If, according to its intentional makeup, consciousness is predisposed toward fulfilled intuition, then the "telos of intentionality"[25] may be unfulfilled or even unknown in its final aspirations, displaced by other claims and necessities of life, but it cannot be, as it were, invented as something new, but can only proceed from its intentional implications and break through toward formulating and recognizing itself as "idea-as-a-task."[26] If consciousness is intentionality, and if the possibility of fulfilled intuition and self-evidence determine the unity of what is given to it, then the notion of a natural, pretheoretical primordiality is a mythic fiction.[27]

The double meaning of Husserl's "life-world"—as, on the one hand, a historical starting point of theoretical reorientation, and, on the other, a still co-present fundamental stratum of life as it is differentiated into tiered interests—burdens this concept with the danger that it be put on par with the always futile attempts to find something like a "natural nature" and to present this nature as a norm of the primordial life of which one is actually deserving. Against this interpretation stands Husserl's definition of *life-world* as a "universe of what is pre-given as obvious."[28] Obviousness

---

25. [Husserl, *Krisis*, 533; not part of the English translation.]

26. ["*Aufgabenidee*," Husserl, *Krisis*, 442; not part of the English translation.]

27. In all of phenomenology, the "continuity" between the natural life of consciousness and its fulfillment in self-evidence is so obvious that one could speak of "science in the historically oldest sense" as of a "naively straightforwardly effected work of theoretical reason" (Husserl, *Formal and Transcendental Logic*, 1). And self-evidence could be determined as "an all-pervasive teleological structure, a pointedness toward 'reason' and even a pervasive tendency toward it" (Husserl, *Formal and Transcendental Logic*, 160). But the great ethical claim of the *Crisis* project demanded something like a responsible and binding act of will at the beginning of our "actual" history.

28. Husserl, *Crisis*, 180.

[*Selbstverständlichkeit*], however, is by no means a positive value, no expression of existence's security within the stable and unquestionable. Quite the contrary, the obvious is the mirror concept to the "self-understanding" [*Selbstverständigung*] that for Husserl must be the real task of any phenomenological philosophy.[29] After all, essential to the obvious is not simply that no one thinks it capable even of not being understood [*Unverstandensein*], but, further, that it constitutes a guarding sanction that disavows all questions that penetrate into this sphere as impudence and curiosity. Understood this way, the life-world—no matter whether it is understood as pre-world or common world—is the always inexhaustible reserve of the unquestionably available, familiar and, precisely due to this familiarity, unknown. Everything that is real in the life-world has an influence on life, is used and consumed, sought after and fled from, but it also remains hidden in its *contingency*, that is, it is not experienced as something that could also be different. If Husserl sees the meaning of European intellectual history in "transforming the universal obviousness [*Selbstverständlichkeit*] of the being of the world . . . into something intelligible [*Verständlichkeit*]"[30] and presents his phenomenology as the realization of this historical meaning, particularly resolving "the obviousness . . . into its transcendental questions,"[31] then for him, the life-world as the universe of self-asserting obviousness cannot, after all, have a salvific or salutary meaning. The dismantling of the life-world as such could not have led European history into its modern-age crisis. It does Husserl more justice to assume that it was rather the form of this dismantling, its illegitimacy as exploitation, that has led to the crisis. It was not the theoretical reorientation that prompted the decision to step out of the life-world, but the *inconsistency* with which this step was executed that rendered the overall process critical. Likewise, technization is not the alternative to the life-world, but the self-realization of theoretical reorientation's inconsistency. If we consider this analysis more closely, some light is shed on technology as "applied" sci-

---

29. [Husserl, 88.]
30. Husserl, 180.
31. Husserl, 183.

ence, a notion that seems perfectly self-evident. For Husserl, as will be shown, technization is the manifestation of a science to which itself and its process of understanding is not yet or no longer clear. In this case, the recourse to the life-world obtains its function through the fact that it tries to find, precisely in the concealment of the obvious, a preliminary approach for the mode of access that is appropriate to discovery. For Husserl, there is no innocence in what he calls "natural experience."[32] Rather, the task is to recognize its debt [*Schuld*] and to shoulder it so that one can fulfill the obligations imposed on us. In this way, all natural experience carries out "a kind of abstraction" that then "tempts philosophical thought into absolutizing mere abstractions."[33]

If Husserl sees the essence of the modern age's natural science in a specific *abstraction* underlying it, then this is not a late lapse in European intellectual history, but only the late consequence of a contraction of intuition that is already inherent in natural experience. The life-world, then, by no means has the fullness and opulence of a mythical paradise nor the innocence that goes with it. When Husserl saw himself confronted with "the great task of a pure theory of essence of the life-world,"[34] he was not concerned with an ideal object but with the attainment of a boundary notion able to do justice to the construction of an ahistorical beginning of history, an atheoretical "prehistory," and which in this way had to legitimize the possibility of "repeating" a radical beginning in thought—but in the end, he ended up doing the opposite and could not have done any better. For Descartes and Bacon, the problem of the "beginning" had been simpler, that is, postscholastical: for them, the whole of history that had preceded them had only led to a tremendous burden of prejudice that could easily be thrown off and left them with the task of reconstruction without any presuppositions. Husserl, too, had adopted this pathos of a radical beginning and connected it with the methodical demand of "free variation,"

---

32. [Husserl, 86.]

33. Edmund Husserl, *Erste Philosophie: Kritische Ideengeschichte*, ed. Rudolf Boehm (The Hague: Nijhoff, 1956), 1:184.

34. Husserl, *Crisis*, 141.

for which the complex of intuitions that can be had in a world makes up a stock that can be handled arbitrarily in manifold ways. The limit concept of the life-world reduces the boundlessness of the eidetic *variation* to the methodology of *description* and the "imaginative variation"[35] into a "systematic survey."[36] The life-world was discovered by constantly refining the main methodological instrument of phenomenology, the so-called phenomenological reduction. With this *reduction*, every assertion was to be suspended that could not be traced back to the immediate givenness of consciousness—above all, the "general thesis" of the transcendent existence of a world independent of consciousness. While constantly increasing the precision of this instrument of reduction, it became clear that it was not enough to "switch off" such assertions, but to "understand" them as rooted in the structures of consciousness. The concept of the "general thesis" still contains the early phenomenological notion of the possible initial position of consciousness, which, as we find it, has chosen the *doxa* of the real external world prematurely and without any foundation, but which might as well have relinquished this assertion or could have chosen another one altogether. What was initially supposed to be set aside in the brackets of phenomenological reduction in order to release the field of eidetic investigations independently of the factual assertion of the quotidian performance of life now is infused more and more with meaning, increasingly attracts the attention of phenomenology, and, above all, puts an end to the primacy of possibility before reality—as it originally existed in phenomenology—since the *fact* of a particular state of consciousness, that is, the life-world, begins to draw a unique interest. Phenomenology must return to its original task of description as soon as it has encountered this fact, although this fact too is completely assigned to the transcendental question. Fiction no longer "makes up the vital element of phenomenology,"[37] and it is no longer true that "the freedom of eidetic research also necessarily de-

---

35. Husserl, 49.
36. Husserl, 147.
37. Husserl, *Ideas*, 169 [the word *Fiktion* is translated as "feigning" there].

mands operating in phantasy."[38] The talk of the intentionality of consciousness has itself made it necessary to explain why the consciousness does not, as it were, automatically follow its eidetic tendency until its fulfillment but must always be "brought to reason." The "universe of obviousnesses"[39] [*Universum der Selbstverständlichkeiten*] of which Husserl now speaks is no longer merely the contrasting concept to the "universe of conceivability"[40] originally intended as the epitome of phenomenological goals. The life-world is precisely that universe which has not been chosen and cannot be chosen freely, but which one can exit only by way of a reorientation, as happened at the beginning of European intellectual history through Husserl's "theoretical reorientation." This world is the only worldly facticity of which one cannot also say: "I stand *above* the world."[41] Its validity can—precisely because the sanction of self-evidentness is part of its definition—not be suspended at will. In this, it is radically different in Husserl from the factual historical world, which may be regarded as "one of the conceptual possibilities"[42] not only through free imaginative variation but with regard to whose factual process phenomenology raises the hope of revising the direction of its meaning.

IV.

At this point, it seems that we have hopelessly lost sight of our topic. For we are still and only speaking of the life-world as a stock presupposed for theoretical dismantling. What does this have to do with technization? But it is exactly here that we encounter the possibility of analyzing the problem from aspects that are unique to Husserl's phenomenology. To be sure, the life-world is a fact that essentially conceals and hides its own facticity by pretending to be

---

38. Husserl, 168.
39. [Husserl, "Beilage XV," *Krisis*, 451. This supplementary text is not part of the English translation.]
40. Husserl, *Formal and Transcendental Logic*, 249.
41. Husserl, *Crisis*, 152.
42. Husserl, 375.

the universe of obviousnesses. At the same time, however, this means that every reorientation that steps out of this life-world—above all and in a unique way the reorientation toward the theoretical attitude—must make conspicuously apparent the very facticity of the immediately pre-given reality. Theorizing drives out the contingency of the life-world and makes it the immediate impulse of the question of why the given is just as it is, which arises for our thinking about the world no later than at the end of antiquity. Husserl did not see or no longer saw the problem of technization under this viewpoint, although his investigations suggested it. In this question, he remains bound to the naturally quite correct historical observation that modern technology would be unthinkable without the ascent of modern *natural science*. This relation of mutually effective conditions has long been interpreted in such a way that technology, in resorting to the purely theoretically intended result of natural science, develops its constructive possibilities autonomously, so that technology can be defined as the embodiment of theoretical results. Historically, it has become unquestionable today that the specific approach of scientific questioning at the beginning of the modern age already contains a technical element. Scientific hypotheses, according to their inherent ideal, were and are instructions for the production of the phenomena they want to explain, and the identity of the phenomenon realized in experiment is the ideal verification of the hypothesis. From this point of view, it was possible to set aside deliberately the question of whether nature took an identical or different path for realizing the phenomenon.

Husserl has taken a significant step beyond this historically well-founded conception of the genetic relationship between modern science and technology. His thesis can be formulated as follows: technization is primarily an immanently theoretical process, representing a consequence of the dismantling of the life-world, but it is not the only and legitimate one. To confirm this, Husserl wants to show something like the "inner history" of the modern age's *idea of science*. For it is by no means self-evident to him that this idea had to be exemplarily realized as *natural* science. Rather, this process is based on a factual preliminary decision, which Husserl describes as follows: "The natural science of the modern period, establishing itself as physics, has its roots in the consistent abstraction through which it *wants* to see, in the life-world, only corporeity. . . . Through such an abstraction, carried out with universal consistency, the world is reduced to an abstract-universal nature, the subject matter of pure natural science. It is here alone that geometrical idealization, first of all, and then all further mathematizing theorization, has found its possible meaning."[43]

Once again, we encounter the peculiarly voluntaristic element in the midst of Husserl's rationalism: the selection among the life-world's richness of meaning, the reduction of "things" to physical objects, reveals no driving motive. To be sure, Husserl speaks of the "purposive reshaping" of prescientific knowledge that happens on the foundation of the life-world, but he does not say what the purpose of such purposefulness could have been.[44] Such voluntarism easily gives the impression that the fact it "founded" can again be revoked, and this factor may play a role here. But the sentence "Straightforward experience, in which the life-world is given, is the ultimate foundation of all objective knowledge"[45] articulates the principled demand to understand the transformation of the life-world into an object world from impulses stemming from the life-world itself, instead of introducing something like an "original sin" in the form of an act of will that cannot be investigated. At any rate, there is nothing in Husserl's analysis to suggest that this primary act of volition was already geared toward technization as the last in a series of steps, but it looks as though constructive availability is merely what will be the unexpected "output" of an increasing sequence of modifications and achievements. The blindness that prevails here must be recognized in its contrasting function for the idea of a teleology of European intellectual history. Man in the modern age has hurried into his technological fate with open eyes—this premise allows Husserl to seize the opportunity of making this man see again through phenomenology. It is part of that blindness of the actual wrong way modern science has taken that it has "forgotten"

---

43. Husserl, 227.
44. Husserl, 226.
45. Husserl, 226.

its own origin from the described transformation of the life-world and had to keep it in oblivion to avoid uncertainty about its claim of realizing the ultimate form of humanity's striving for knowledge. To conceal this historical condition allows modern consciousness to believe that exact science, with the help of mathematics, could discover and present the world, usually hidden behind the phenomena, "as it truly is in itself." *Concealing* the genesis of this exact world of objects through abstracting from the life-world justifies the *unquestionable* naturalness of this nature. In this way, the *critical* meaning of the life-world sought by Husserl can be seen: if it were disclosed as the universe of obviousnesses, the derivative that is "nature" would at once be discovered as only supposedly and questionably obvious. It can be seen how the whole efficacy of this complex depends on the fact that the life-world remains not responsible for the abstraction to which it has been subjected.

For Husserl, forgetting the origin of the abstract world of objects—objects that are exactly accessible in their corporeality—manifests itself in the immanent consequence of further developing their mathematical means of representation. This development has the general tendency of *formalization*, that is, it implies a rejection of any descriptive elements. Among the many expressions that Husserl uses for this process, it is best to use that of "the process of becoming method":[46] after all, for Husserl, "method" epitomizes tradition and the possibility of passing down achievements whose origins are now concealed.[47] As soon as knowledge surpasses the capacity of a human lifetime to acquire it genuinely, the prerequisites for the acquisition of knowledge are handed down as a ready-made toolkit, and soon it becomes questionable whether the original founding achievements can be *reactivated* by anyone who deals with and uses them. Ancient geometry, Husserl believes, was conscious of its origin in the idealization of the physical world, but in the reception of this geometry in the beginning of the modern age, the underlying idealization was forgotten, and this circumstance gave way to the purely technical handling of the inherited tool. In

---

46. Husserl, 67.
47. Husserl, 367.

the first stage of stripping away meaning, this leads to the "arithmetization of geometry."[48] In the second step, it leads to turning geometry into algebra. The final outcome is a purely formal "theory of manifolds" and the construction of a "world-in-general."[49]

The takeaway of what I have just presented is that technization is a process that takes place in the *theoretical* substrate itself. After all, geometry has become "a mere art of achieving, through a calculating technique according to technical rules, results."[50] Novalis, for example, had already complained that true mathematics had "degenerated into mere technique [*Technik*] in Europe."[51] Taking recourse to a metaphor from specialized language, one could formulate this thesis as follows: the "phenotypically" quite different worlds of nature and technology represented by exact science "genotypically" have an identical structure—they are worlds made up of formulae. But this means that they share a fundamental *loss of meaning*, a depletion of the theoretical and constructive achievements from the acts of intuition that support and enable them. Technization is the "transformation of a formation of meaning which was originally vital" into method, which then can be passed on without carrying along the "meaning of [its] primal establishment" that has shed its "development of meaning" and does not want to acknowledge it any longer in the sufficiency of mere function.[52] Primarily, technology is not a sphere of certain objects resulting from human activity. In its primordiality [*Ursprünglichkeit*], it is a state of human world relation itself. The dominance of the "sense of method," however, does not only mean a functional transformation of the theoretical process, which has become detachable from its intuitive substrate and, as detached schema, can be applied to arbitrary substrates. Rather, the given state of the world for humans is adjusted and levelled. Here, Husserl uses the metaphor of the

---

48. Husserl, 45.

49. Husserl, 45–46.

50. Husserl, 46.

51. Novalis, *Schriften*, ed. Paul Kluckhohn and Richard Samuel (Stuttgart: Kohlhammer, 1969), 3:295. [*Technik* could equally be translated with "technology" or "technics."]

52. Husserl, *Crisis*, 56–58.

"garb of ideas," which ensures "that we take for true being what is actually a method."[53] That technization leads to very specific objective realities—"machines" in the broadest sense—has, as a secondary phenomenon, already been decided and anticipated in that science and its method itself have become "like a machine, reliable in accomplishing obviously very useful things."[54] The real mechanism may not represent the phenomenon of technology by mere accident, but nor does it do so directly. It is no coincidence that the calculating machine belongs to the earliest dreams and attempts at realizing the modern age's world of machines, nor is it a coincidence that the development of computers has led to a stage of perfection in which their efficiency is practically beyond the reach of the human brain. In the end, the world—which has resigned itself to dealing with what is already finished and to being monitored in the handling of the finished concepts and sentences according to the rigor of a mostly inscrutable methodology only by the success of this handling—finds itself standing helplessly before this level of production; all it does is struggle to create the space this world's products require.

Now, it looks as if Husserl—a mathematician by origin and disposition—was intent on vilifying the feats and achievements of mathematics and the natural sciences that it made possible, as if it was only a logical step for him to hope for these achievements to be reversed. But Husserl is only concerned with making visible in exemplary fashion how disastrous in the broadest sense human action can be where it no longer knows what it is doing, and with exposing what one might call active ignorance as the root of all those disoriented activities that have produced human helplessness in the technical world. This has nothing to do with demonizing technology or assigning it the character of fate. But the irresponsibility of the purely theoretical disciplines, which accept that, by chance,

53. Husserl, 51. I discuss the "garb of ideas" metaphor in Hans Blumenberg, *Paradigms for a Metaphorology*, trans. Robert Savage (Ithaca, NY: Cornell University Press, 2010), 75.

54. Husserl, *Crisis*, 52.

they happen also to be apt to be applied, as a more or less welcome addition, is seriously challenged by a standpoint for which practice is not a form of recourse to the reservoir of theory, but that speaks of "*the* practice that is called theory."[55] But it is, of course, one thing to say that the line of history leading from the beginning of the modern age to technization was not fateful and inescapable, and another to say that in the present situation technization in the precise meaning Husserl gave it was a deviation of history that could still be rectified. For Husserl, both statements are closely connected: the process of the constitution of the modern age is not clearly determined; it contains an ambivalence.

Husserl identifies the decisive figure of the early modern period in Galileo, with whom "the surreptitious substitution of idealized nature for prescientifically intuited nature" begins.[56] Galileo is characterized as "at once a discovering and a concealing genius."[57] This formulation seems to me to hold a very deep insight. Discovery and concealment are inseparable in the history of the modern age's achievements. Is it, however, something of a law of modern intellectual history that each of its discoveries was won only at the price of concealing something else? Husserl would have answered in the negative; he only sees a coupling in fact, not principle, only the actual succumbing to temptation—the temptation of the shortest path, of the perfect function. But for him, appealing to the origin remains possible and the demand of reactivating the sense continuum can still be fulfilled. Even his language shows this: it is about concealment, not destruction, and it is a gentle image for the lost context of meaning when Husserl says that science "hovers as if in empty space above the life-world."[58] The position of phenomenological analysis cannot be pushed until it reaches its antithesis.

---

55. Husserl, "Beilage XIV," *Krisis*, 449. [This supplementary text is not part of the English translation.]

56. Husserl, *Crisis*, 49–50.

57. Husserl, 52.

58. Husserl, "Beilage XIV," *Krisis*, 448.

V.

This brings us back to our starting point: in the work of Husserl, technology is no longer understood as an antithesis to nature. Now we can say: it is understood from the perspective of a relationship to history. In technization, as Husserl understands it, man evades the integrity of the intelligible, that is, originally intuitive, performance of his praxis in the broad sense that includes theory as well. He wants to move ahead, so to speak, "in leaps." He omits history. This can also be framed more rigorously in phenomenological terms: in technization, man limits himself to the possibilities of the *understanding* and eludes the claim of *reason*. This Kantian conceptual difference Husserl applied onto the intentionality of consciousness: reason is fulfilled intention, perfect possession of the object in the abundance of its aspects, or at least the keeping-oneself-open for this abundance. The understanding is dealing with empty intentions, with beliefs that are taken to be the things themselves, or, in a banking metaphor popular with Husserl, a "method of exchange and conversion, which is based upon mere treasury bonds."[59] The essential inner disposition of consciousness, by virtue of its intentionality, is "bringing the discursive understanding to reason" at all times so as to exchange the treasury bonds for the assets that they cover.[60] History executes and actualizes this disposition, but technization disrupts this process, constantly increasing the "sign values," the nominal representations, the uncovered bonds; it is, to stay with this metaphor, the bringing-about of ownership rather than the justification of property, or exercising domination without any regard to its legitimacy.

I would like to give an example of what this actually recognizes and reveals about the issue at hand. I shall choose the primitive example of a doorbell. There are the old mechanical models operated by pulling a cord or turning a knob: when using such a bell, I still have the immediate feeling of producing the intended effect in its

---

59. Husserl, *The Idea of Phenomenology*, trans. Lee Hardy (Dordrecht: Springer, 1999), 46.

60. Husserl, *The Idea of Phenomenology*, 46.

specificity, since there is an adequate nexus between the hand that activates it and the sound that rings. That means that if I am standing in front of such a mechanism, I know not just what I am to do, but also why I am to do it. The case is different for the electrical bell, which is activated by a push button: the action of the hand is assigned to the effect heteromorphically and without any specificity—we no longer produce the effect, but only trigger it. The desired effect is kept ready for our use, available for us, as it were, within the design of the apparatus; indeed, it carefully hides its conditionality and the complexity of its realization from us in order to suggest itself to us as something effortlessly available. For the sake of this suggestion of the always-ready, the technical world, regardless of all its functional requirements, is a sphere of casings, disguises, nonspecific façades, and blinds. The functional part that is still human is homogenized and reduced to the ideal minimum of pushing a button. Technization makes human practices increasingly unspecific. To be sure, I am not saying anything about the simple physical fact that the difference between a mechanical and an electric doorbell objectively lies in that, in the one case, we have to supply the energy for the process itself, while in the other, we are tapping into available external energy. What is crucial in the present context is the phenomenological aspect: how does what is given to immediate experience present itself to us. In the ideal of "at the touch of a button," the withdrawal of insight (in the most literal sense of looking inside!) celebrates itself: direction and effect, command and product, will and deed have been moved together at the shortest distance, coupled as effortlessly as in the secret ideal of all post-Christian productivity, the divine "Let there be . . . !" of the beginning of the Bible. In a world that is increasingly characterized by triggering functions, not only the interchangeability of the people needed for nonspecific actions increases, but also the likelihood of confusing the triggers. To abide by our door bell: How often don't you press the bell button in a stairwell when you in fact had "meant" the light switch? Behind each such trigger lies a long history of human discovery, a whole complex of inventive achievements, but the trigger is "packaged" in a way that it conceals this history and deprives it from us in its abstract uniformity—a "product" that offers up its inner workings for all to see is a poor product indeed. The self-presentation of the technical object not only rejects all curious questions by treating them as possible investigations by someone who does not want to pay the price for the secret function or wants to profit from it himself; moreover, it seems to do everything in its power not to let questions arise in the first place—and not just questions concerning the secrets of its design and its functional principle, but above all, questions concerning its right to exist. The ever-ready that can be triggered and retrieved at the touch of a button does not justify its existence either by reference to its theoretical origin or to the needs and impulses of life, which it purports to serve. It is legitimized by being ordered, accepted, transferred, and put into operation. The fact of availability, however, does not presuppose the existence of meaningful needs—rather, it itself demands and coerces the existence of new needs and meanings. For this purpose, a whole layer of motivations and fictions of validity must then be created artificially and with technical effort. The ideal of such manipulation is to shroud the artificial product with obviousness; it silences all questions regarding necessity, meaning, humaneness, and justifiability. The artificial reality, the foreigner among the encountered things of nature, sinks back into the "universe of what is pre-given as obvious," the life-world.[61]

The connection between life-world and technization is more complicated than Husserl believed it to be. The process of concealing what has been discovered, as analyzed by Husserl, reaches its telos only when what has become unconscious through theoretical inquiry returns to being unquestionable. The technical as such becomes incomparably more invisible by being implanted into the life-world than through the mimicry of casings and covers. Technization not only ruptures the foundational context of theoretical behavior emerging from the life-world, but it in turn begins to control the life-world by making the sphere in which we do not *yet* ask questions identical with that in which we no *longer* ask questions, and by regulating and motivating the occupation of this sphere of things through the immanent dynamics of the technically always-ready,

---

61. [Husserl, *Crisis*, 180.]

that is, through the irrevocability of production which puts itself on equal footing with the forces of nature. The process of technization discloses its own "teleology" in that it makes life its own dependent quantity not only by producing things and achievements but also by making producible the unproducible, that is, obviousness.

Here I shall suspend the analysis that was to demonstrate the contribution of phenomenology to the question of the "thing itself" and instead follow Husserl's real interest in this problem in the *Crisis* essay—an interest that is, at first glance, directed at therapy rather than diagnosis. In a situation in which Husserl himself was condemned to silence in Germany, and in which his phenomenology had already been drowned by the wave of existential ontology, he is full of faith in this philosophy's secular mission. For Husserl, the therapy for the crisis that had come to fruition in technization cannot lie in reversing or even just stopping a development on whose respective final results the possibility of human existence has become more and more dependent. But to Husserl, therapy quite indubitably means that something needs to be "caught up on." This idea to repeat or catch up on a genesis—which, in the end, is always the intentionality of consciousness itself—is essentially connected with the project of phenomenology. If the analysis of technization revealed that in its process the authentic justification of all its steps had been missed, omitted, and skipped, then the attitude of phenomenology almost automatically offers itself as a therapeutic countermove, in which the inquiries into the foundations, into the meaning of the primal establishment and the resulting explication of meaning can be caught up on, for they were forgotten and glossed over in technization. Phenomenology wants to restore history—history in an absolute sense. Its basic demand is to "repeat the entire history ... of the subjective activities."[62] Phenomenological knowledge is the radical remedy to a radical crisis, and it is so by itself, by the sheer presence of its late realization in European intellectual history—that's how Husserl sees it. It counteracts the immanent

---

62. Edmund Husserl, *Experience and Judgment: Investigations in a Genealogy of Logic*, ed. Ludwig Landgrebe, trans. Spencer Churchill (Evanston, IL: Northwestern University Press, 1973) 49.

structure and the growth of the critical process like an antibiotic, as it were. It constitutes a resistance against the formalization of theoretical achievements that grounds the essence of technization, so that it can "never undergo the unnoticed transformation into a mere *technē*,"[63] but is able to accomplish "reactivating the original activities"[64] that can retrieve science, which has been "lowered to the status of art or *technē*"[65] into the bindingness of theoretical responsibility—if we indulge Husserl's faith for a moment. Phenomenology itself, as "intuitive knowledge," is "that form of reason that sets itself the task of bringing the discursive understanding to reason."[66]

In the midst of the technical age and the technized world, it is a testament to the great, indeed magnificent, confidence of the aged Husserl to have extracted—in the forty thousand pages of his self-reflective protocols—the antitoxin of the technization that terrifies him. He contrasts the always-ready with the always-beginning of philosophical thought, which alone "takes up a new will to life,"[67] and opposes a world that demonstrates itself to be meaningful only by hinting at the facticity of its enormous presence with the call to remain faithful to oneself in the teleological consistency of an identical, once-grasped meaning.[68]

VI.

An *engagement* with the ideas Husserl develops in his *Crisis* should not mean again to abandon what phenomenological investigation has without a doubt achieved here, and what could most fruitfully be presented as an immanent critique. It seems to be a lasting insight to me that technization—in the sense of a loss of self-understanding

---

63. [Husserl, *Crisis*, 199.]
64. [Husserl, 366.]
65. [Husserl, 197.]
66. [Husserl, *The Idea of Phenomenology*, 46.]
67. Husserl, "Beilage XX," *Krisis*, 472. [This supplementary text is not part of the English translation.]
68. Husserl, "Beilage XXIV," *Krisis*, 486. [This supplementary text is not part of the English translation.]

and self-responsibility—is a transformation originating in the bosom of the total process of theory. What seems less certain to me is that this transformation should, with Husserl, be seen as a *pathological* phenomenon, as a modification deliberately posited or factually erupting in consciousness, as an aberration in the self-actualization of consciousness' intentionality. This assumption alone made it possible for Husserl alone to offer his phenomenology as a therapy. But is this assumption correct? I shall answer this question from Husserl's own premises.

In Husserl's view of history, the teleology "immanent in the history of Europe"[69] begins with the Greeks as a new "interest in the All."[70] This new interest contained "intentional infinities,"[71] which could become effective and real only in a humanity "which, living in finitude, lives toward poles of infinity."[72] In this formula, Husserl has articulated a decisive *antinomy* that dominates his own phenomenology as well without being noticed. As early as 1913, Husserl writes that in the intentionality of consciousness every given property of a thing "draws us into infinities of experience: that every experiential multiplicity, no matter how extensive, still leaves open more precise and novel determinations of the physical thing, and it does so in infinitum."[73] By necessity, however, this being-draw-in eludes fulfillment; the talk of an "infinite work" and "infinite tasks" runs through the whole work of the founder of phenomenology. What he sees before him are "veritable infinities of facts . . . never explored prior to phenomenology";[74] when he speaks of the "infinity of executing work,"[75] one does not perceive any terror; in general, "work" is one of the characteristic words of Husserl's language.[76]

---

69. Husserl, *Crisis*, 274.

70. Husserl, 276.

71. Husserl, 277.

72. Husserl, 277.

73. Husserl, *Ideas*, 9.

74. Edmund Husserl, *Cartesian Meditations: An Introduction to Phenomenology*, trans. Dorion Cairns (The Hague: Nijhoff, 1982), 41.

75. Husserl, *Cartesian Meditations*, 88.

76. One could extract a whole world of workshops and workplaces from Husserl's vocabulary, often in dense accumulation, for instance: Husserl, *Erste Philosophie*, 142, 144, 146, 147, 150, 191, 204. The almost ecstatic plural of the

The idea that underlay the early promise of a *Philosophy as a Rigorous Science* (1910) was a final self-evidence that can be attained in all areas; it now has split into a complicated plurality of self-evidences, and it "may be left open" whether the adequate evidence "does not necessarily lie at infinity."[77] If it is true that the modern age has brought to light the consequence of the "idea of an infinity of tasks"[78] that was latent in the ancient concept of science, then Husserl's phenomenology is an extreme escalation of this *infinite* claim imposed on a *finite* existence. The pathos of the idea of infinity obscures this contradiction: the demand for the absolute self-evidence and radicalism of justifications and genetic analyses of meaning puts itself in the wrong before the idea of the demanded infinite theoretical work. Self-evidence and radicalism of justifications require that thought return to the absolute beginning—and that it do so for every existence wishing to become transparent to itself, just as Descartes had demanded with his *semel in vita funditus denuo* [once in the course of my life, to demolish everything completely and start again right from the foundations].[79] Against this, the infinity of work to be done requires that what has historically been achieved can be made the precondition for what remains to be achieved—that is to say, it requires its functionalization as a possession of knowledge that merely needs to be learned and can be adopted as a methodology. Only thus can the starting point of progress be pushed ever further into the untrodden. Thus, *formalization* is nothing but the most handy, most serviceable kind of *functionalization* of what has already been achieved; but in this, it is potentially technization, for what can be formalized—that is: what gains its applicability independently of any insight into its actual

---

"veritable infinities of descriptive work" is also telling (Husserl, *Erste Philosophie*, 110). Helmuth Plessner was right in characterizing phenomenology as a "way to integrate philosophy into the modern world of work." Helmuth Plessner, *Husserl in Göttingen: Rede zur Feier des 100. Geburtstages Edmund Husserls* (Göttingen: Vandenhoeck & Ruprecht, 1959), 9.

77. Husserl, *Cartesian Meditations*, 15.

78. [Husserl, *Crisis*, 278.]

79. [René Descartes, *Meditations on First Philosophy*, trans. John Cottingham (Cambridge: Cambridge University Press, 2017), 15; Blumenberg gives a condensed version of Descartes's sentence.]

execution—that is at bottom already mechanized, even if no actual mechanisms for its preservation and regulated association have been available. All methodology seeks to create *unreflected repeatability*, a growing foundation of presuppositions that may always be involved but is not always actualized. There is no escape from this antinomy between philosophy and science: philosophy's ideal of knowledge defies methodization, science as a finite being's infinite claim impels it. The last time philosophy and science appeared to be in harmony with each other was in the scholastic illusion of reason disavowing itself because of its curiosity. The separation of philosophy and science—brought about by the philosophical idea of science itself—marked the transition to technization in the modern sense that is heterogeneous to all previous human technology. But this separation was necessary and legitimate. Here, the critique of Husserl's position takes shape. The *loss* of meaning of which Husserl spoke is in truth *renunciation* of meaning imposed by the consequence of the theoretical pretension itself. One cannot rhapsodize about "mankind's development as it becomes mankind with infinite tasks"[80] and at the same time deny the price for this becoming.

Husserl might have already studied this problem in his great hero, Descartes, who had initially believed that the realization of his scientific program could be a matter of *one* lifetime, his own. The treaty on method is already the result of thorough resignation, for it primarily indicates the process by which one can make available to other members of a human race engaged in research over a succession of generations what has been achieved in such a way as not to recreate the philosophical original situation of the radical beginning anew each time. Against this implication of the idea of method, the thought that preparing the chain of deductions for increasingly faster processing that is increasingly less dependent on a deceptive memory—analogous to the number series—is an episodic if quite telling element, for here we can sense the hesitation before the step into formalization. Leibniz was probably the first to develop this

---

80. Husserl, *Crisis*, 279.

whole problem in his argument with Descartes.[81] He confronts Descartes's ideal of knowledge—supposedly derived from mathematics and according to which no further step of deduction may be made without the full rigor of proof—with the actual procedure of geometry since Euclid, which had accepted many renunciations of proof and thus became an *ars progrediendi* [technique of progress]. If it had postponed the elaboration of its theorems and problems until all axioms and postulates had been proved, perhaps there would still be no geometry today—foregoing proof and postponing the strictest demands serve as conditions of possibility of the progress of knowledge.

In Husserl's own phenomenological analyses, too, there is no lack of elements of unsatisfiability that arise from the antinomy of infinity and intuition. In the syntheses of empirical intuition, a selection of the thing's aspects happens always and necessarily; in the continuum of adumbrations [*Abschattungen*] leaps are made, as it were, because the ideal equivalent to pure intuition in the empirical ideal of going through all possible perspectives cannot be fulfilled. "The pure intuition that corresponds to an empirical thing is denied to us, it lies hidden after a fashion in the complete synthetic intuition itself, but as it were dispersedly, with a perpetual admixture of signitive representation."[82]

But that means that at the lowest elemental level of its achievements, the human intellect is always already engaged in formalization. It is almost inevitable that Husserl could not, even with the

---

81. Gottfried Wilhelm Leibniz, "Critical Thoughts on the General Part of the Principles of Descartes," in *Philosophical Papers and Letters*, ed. Leroy E. Loemker (Dordrecht: Kluwer, 1989), 383–412; 384. Against Descartes, Leibniz presents the paradigm provided by the mathematicians: "If they had tried to put off the discovery of theorems and problems until all the axioms and postulates had been proved, we should perhaps have no geometry today" (Leibniz, "Critical Thoughts," 384).

82. Husserl, *Logical Investigations*, 2:248. The talk of the intuition of the empirical thing that is "denied to us" appears here still to hint at Husserl leaving open the possibility of an originary intellect in the Kantian sense. His later eidetic description of the physical object posits its discursive constitution as absolute (see Husserl, *Ideas*, 1:363); this does not change anything about the fact that for the finite intellect, discourse is by necessity deficient and its "gaps" are signitive bridges.

pathos of the *Crisis* treatise, conceal the conflicting nature of intentionality between progress and fulfilled intuition. The solution that he hints at amounts to a kind of vicarious function of philosophy for science: what science, in its impetuous progression, omits and skips over, philosophy catches up on and harvests. At least this is how the following text, both important and obscure, can be understood: "Actually the process whereby material mathematics is put into formal-logical form, where expanded formal logic is made self-sufficient as pure analysis or theory of manifolds, is perfectly *legitimate*, indeed necessary; the same is true of the technization that from time to time completely loses itself in merely technical thinking. But all this can and must be a method which is understood and practiced in a *fully conscious* way. It can be this, however, only if care is taken to avoid dangerous *shifts of meaning* by keeping always immediately in mind the *original bestowal of meaning upon the method*, through which it has the sense of achieving knowledge about the world. Even more, it must be freed of the character of an *unquestioned tradition* that, from the first invention of the new idea and method, allowed elements of obscurity to flow into its meaning."[83]

This arguably means, or at least could mean, that the legitimacy technization is granted here establishes a historically new role of philosophy that is no longer preceptory (for it now is catching up on the consequences of its own anticipation): it is supposed vicariously to administer the treasure of the structures of meaning that technization has skipped.

I would like to place the complex of the phenomenological interpretation of technology in a larger historical context. The *implication of infinity* within phenomenology belongs to the well-established tradition of our intellectual history that can be called *Platonism*. A self-evidence attainable only in infinity has a meaning that touches on human existence only in a mental structure in which *truth is* not only recognized as absolute value, but also stands in a conditional relation to the *fulfillment of human existence*. Adequate self-evidence as the goal of every intellectual journey—historically

---

83. Husserl, *Crisis*, 47. [The original emphases have been restored.]

speaking, the unmediated intuition of ideas—is the core of any Platonism. But this also explains why Plato's rejection of Sophism implied the *exclusion of technology from the intellectual legitimacy of the European tradition.* For sophism had developed the idea of a formal ability, of an unspecific intellectual potency—that is, the mastery of a thing detached from understanding the thing—and, at bottom, made omnipotence the ideal of its educational practice, to which it assigned everything theoretical in advance. What had manifested itself in Sophist rhetoric and dialectic (tellingly, it was in the tradition of these disciplines that the terminology of technical behavior and technical achievements has been developed) was the most arbitrary transferability of a formal skill applicable to any concrete end—pure "method," that is. The Socratic-Platonic objection not only rejected this primacy of pure skill but has not even left any ground on which purely formal powers might be included in the image of a fulfilled human existence. This has determined our tradition, right down to the formation of the Christian idea of eternal bliss as *visio beatifica* [beatific vision] in the perfect identity of theory and happiness. Husserl's "infinite task" provides the same answer to the question of the ultimate meaning of human existence, with the admittedly decisive difference that in view of the infinite task, the individual, concrete human being can neither be necessarily fulfilling nor fulfilled, but can enter into a context that overarches him only as a functionary. The infinity of theory as "research" [*Forschung*] requires transferability, methodization, formalization, and technization. The Sophist position reappears at a certain point on Platonic ground: the concrete human being is not at all the subject of an infinite task; this subject must be artificially constituted in the form of society, nation, humanity, science—and as a principle of ruthlessness against the individual's claim to happiness at that. Before technized industrial society had functionalized man, the modern idea of science had already carried out this elementary act of modern history by way of example. The transcendental self-investigation of subjectivity initiated by Husserl is one of the attempts—and perhaps the most important—to restitute the lost substance. But the fate of phenomenology itself is marked not only by what has happened to it from the outside, but also by the awareness it raised to a significant extent that the philosophical subject stands lost before its own pretension to radical self-foundation and infinite self-justification.

VII.

Phenomenology, as has been shown, cannot escape the consequences whose premises it has itself brought to light so clearly. The emergence from the life-world, that is, from the "universe of obviousnesses," was not only the beginning of the European intellectual process which Husserl saw culminating in his own phenomenology; it was also the reversal of all of reality's characteristics of self-evidence into contingency. *Contingency* means the appraisal of reality from the standpoint of necessity and possibility. The awareness of reality's contingency is, however, the foundation of a technical attitude toward what is given: if the given world is only an arbitrary segment from the infinite scope of the possible, if the sphere of natural facts no longer exerts a higher justification and sanction, then the world's facticity becomes the nagging impulse not only to judge and criticize the real from the perspective of the possible, but also to augment merely factual reality by way of realizing the possible, of exhausting the latitude of invention and construction, to form a cultural world that is in itself consistent and can be justified through necessity. Thus, if we have to consider contingency as a stimulant to the realization of the demiurgical potency of man, then it becomes clear how the technical pathos of the modern age could arise in correspondence to the extreme increase of the consciousness of contingency in the late Middle Ages.[84] This statement makes even clearer the critical function that the concept of the "life-world" assumed in

---

84. I have substantiated this thesis in: "'Imitation of Nature': Toward a Prehistory of the Idea of the Creative Being" [in this volume]; "Ordnungsschwund und Selbstbehauptung: Über Weltverstehen und Weltverhalten im Werden der technischen Epoche," *Das Problem der Ordnung: Verhandlungen des Siebten Deutschen Kongresses für Philosophie, Münster 1962*, ed. Helmut Kuhn and Fritz Wiedmann (Meisenheim: Hain, 1962), 37–57; "Kontingenz," *Religion in Geschichte und Gegenwart* (Tübingen: Mohr, 1959), 3:1793–1794.

Husserl's engagement with modern technization. This concept of the life-world is formed as the virtual embodiment of all opposing characteristics to a world of contingency, but also to a world whose inner necessity has become possible only in the assertion against the consciousness of the facticity of the world—and that is, against a technical world. That Husserl should have investigated this life-world in the late phase of his thinking, even before the problem of technization had become acute for him, was an urgency that arose out of the immanent development of phenomenology itself. The phenomenological method—and this is now decisive for our train of thought—is, after all, itself a paradigm of the consciousness of contingency, of that basic process in the spiritual substratum of the technical world one could describe as "dismantling of obviousness" [*Entselbstverständlichung*]. To call into question even the last and most hidden self-evidences could almost be stated as the program of phenomenology. To make the life-world itself an object of theoretical description means, after all, not saving and preserving this sphere, but, in the process of disclosing it, the inevitable destruction of its essential attribute of obviousness. The term that is critically needed and searched for cannot be found without undoing the thing. For the phenomenologist, the task is "transforming the universal obviousness of the being of the world—for him, the greatest of all enigmas—into something intelligible."[85]

Thus, to determine the theoretical location of phenomenology—according to which "we place ourselves above this whole life and all this cultural tradition and, by radical sense-investigations, seek for ourselves singly and in common the ultimate possibilities and necessities, on the basis of which we can take our position toward actualities in judging, valuing, and acting"—means nothing but to intensify contingency.[86]

A philosophy of "absolute universality within which there must be no unasked questions, nothing taken for granted that is not understood,"[87] fulfills with its pretension the "telos of

---

85. Husserl, *Crisis*, 180.
86. Husserl, *Formal and Transcendental Logic*, 5–6.
87. Husserl, *Crisis*, 265.

intentionality,"[88] but in doing so, it renders those questions virulent that cannot be put off for answers residing in unattainable infinities, which by their nature do not tolerate the delay of theory but provoke man's anticipating-beyond-himself that cannot be caught up with by philosophy, which is precisely what Husserl has shown to be the nature of technology.

Husserl has been said to have been "totally devoid of any sense of history."[89] But while it was believed that this lack could be recognized in the fact that Husserl was only able to project the historical figures of philosophy to the level of his own needs, this lack rather reveals itself in the fact that he misjudged the historical role and position of his own phenomenology: he sought what is essentially invariable with the methodological instruments of reduction and free variation, "the example . . . freed of all its factualness," "the indissolubly identical in the different and ever-again different, the essence common to all,"[90] and in so doing he articulated the freedom of the means rather than the necessity of the end, executing the spirit of the modern age while believing to turn it against the modern age, as that variation, which is "carried on with the freedom of pure phantasy and with the consciousness of its purely optional character," so that "the variation extends into an open horizon of endlessly manifold free possibilities of more and more variants."[91]

Already on the level of language, this talk of the "fully free variation, released from all restrictions to facts accepted beforehand,"[92] resembles the modern age's solemn formulae of emancipation, which all share in the illusion of freeing oneself from the factual in order to arrive at the essential; in effect, they always only accentuated the insuperable obtrusiveness of the factual. We may thus regard the idealized "life-world" in Husserl's thinking as the correlate to and

---

88. Husserl, "Textkritische Anmerkungen zum Haupttext," *Krisis*, 533. [These editorial notes are not part of the English translation.]

89. Arendt, "What Is Existential Philosophy?," *Essays in Understanding*, ed. Jerome Kohn (New York: Schocken, 1994), 166.

90. Husserl, *Formal and Transcendental Logic*, 248.

91. Husserl, 247–248.

92. Husserl, 248.

corrective for the increase in contingency unnoticed in technization.[93]

The *contemporary significance* of the phenomenological analysis of technology has become immensely increased in a very current
problem that Husserl had not yet noticed and which is almost something like an experimental isolation of the whole complex: the glo-
balized grafting of European science and technology onto peoples
and cultural worlds once considered exotic. Here, technization does
not appear as a leap out of the continuum of theoretical performance, which stands in a foundational context with the life-world;
rather, it is an exogenous superimposition of often almost untouched
life-worlds, of codifications of understanding and behavior that are
enclosed in obviousness. The motivation that has been called "civila-
tory impatience"[94] has in this case not *grown* from the consciousness of the "infinite task" but was *induced* by what has been called
"international demonstration effect."[95] The tremendous accelera-
tions that have become technically necessary in the syndrome called
"underdevelopment" create tensions which are rendered understandable precisely through Husserl's idea of the process of meaning catching up on history, but which at the same time make comprehensible an affinity to an ideology which has demonstrated
spectacularly, and continues to do so, how suited it is as a justification for the kind of industrialization eager to make up for lost time.
From the perspective of our immanent critique of Husserl's position, the problem of *catch-up development* does not lie so much in
the exogenous supply of technical means and civilizatory behaviors,
but rather in the absence of the inherent motivations to accept and
assimilate this supply: the *motivations* themselves are supplied ex-

---

93. For the concept of the life-world, see Aron Gurwitsch, "The Last Work of
Edmund Husserl II: The Lebenswelt," *Philosophy and Phenomenological Research*
17 (1957): 370–398. Analogies to Ludwig Wittgenstein's "natural worldview" and
the problem of natural languages in neopositivism are drawn in Hermann Lübbe,
"'Sprachspiele' und 'Geschichten': Neopositivismus und Phänomenologie im Spät-
stadium," *Kant-Studien* 52 (1960/61): 220–243.

94. [Hans Raupach, "Die Sowjetwirtschaft als historisches Phänomen," *Vier-
teljahrshefte für Zeitgeschichte* 10, no. 1 (1962): 15.]

95. [Ragnar Nurkse, *Problems of Capital Formation in Underdeveloped
Countries* (Oxford: Blackwell, 1957), 65.]

ternally, but they would have to be developed *endogenously*. The result our study was unable to produce for the European modern age—an approach that would allow one to speak of a "pathology of technology"—may still turn out to be a severe desideratum on a global scale in the late phase of technization.

Technology is, phenomenally speaking, a realm of mechanisms. To understand it as the "thing itself" it is not enough to classify this realm, to investigate its effects and side effects, and to trace its enabling conditions back to the knowledge of the laws of nature. All mechanisms are ultimately designed to enhance a finite given capacity, that of human existence; they extend, if one may say so, the scope of each existence spatially and temporally, they allow us to take leaps instead of steps. The radicalism of the question, up to the threshold of which Husserl advanced his analysis, lies in the fact that it asks for the historical emergence of the motivation for and the will to this increase in finitude. Technization arises from the tension between the theoretical task, which has revealed itself as infinite, and the capacity of existence found in man that is given as a constant. The antinomy of technology consists in the tension between *achievement* and *insight*. Phenomenology—in the form Husserl gave it—has not resolved this antinomy but has exacerbated it and made it more perceptible and effective for our intellectual situation.

Translated by Hannes Bajohr

SOCRATES AND THE *OBJET AMBIGU*

Paul Valéry's Discussion of the Ontology of the Aesthetic Object and Its Tradition

(1964)

In a letter to Paul Souday dated May 1, 1923, Paul Valéry recounts the circumstances under which his dialogue *Eupalinos* came into being.[1] He had been commissioned to write a text for an album of architectural ground plans and layouts but the length and the layout had already been set and the typeface selected so that the remaining space for Valéry's contribution could be determined exactly, down to the number of characters—that is, 115,800—to which,

Originally published as "Sokrates und das *objet ambigu*: Paul Valérys Auseinandersetzung mit der Tradition der Ontologie des ästhetischen Gegenstandes," in *EPIMELEIA: Die Sorge der Philosophie um den Menschen. Festschrift für Helmut Kuhn*, ed. Franz Wiedmann (Munich: Pustet), 285–323; from Hans Blumenberg, *Ästhetische und metaphorologische Schriften*, ed. Anselm Haverkamp (Frankfurt am Main: Suhrkamp, 2001), 74–111.

1. I quote Valéry's works according to the two-volume *Pléiade* edition with volume and page number; the general correspondence, *Lettres à quelques-uns* (Paris: Gallimard, 1952) is abbreviated as *L*, and the correspondence with André Gide (André Gide/Paul Valéry, *Correspondance 1890–1943* (Paris: Gallimard, 1955) as GV.

however, he also had to adhere. Valéry mentions this, as he writes, "à titre de curiosité" [as a matter of curiosity] (*L* 147). But it can easily be inferred from these and other statements that he did not consider the genesis of *Eupalinos* as atypical of his own mode of working or of the conditions under which works of art arose. Not only did he accept, but, as he admits, he ultimately found the narrowness of necessity, the "bizarre contrainte" [bizarre constraint], to be interesting. Choosing the form of the dialogue made it easier to meet the exact length, he explains, and he ironically leaves open whether the text might not have suffered a little under these circumstances, before finally invoking the great example of the ancient sculptors who had to accommodate their Olympian cast of characters to the obtuse triangles of temple pediments.

Now, this was a commissioned work, a *prose* piece, which could be wrested from Valéry only from time to time and through external incentives.[2] This might not hold for *poetry*—of it one is inclined to believe that it emanates from the manner of spontaneous excitation and conception. But in a letter to George Duhamel from 1929 (*L* 178ff.), Valéry relates the formation of his first poetic work after the self-imposed pause of a quarter-century, the *Jeune Parque* (*The Young Fate*), during World War I. This great poem of crystalline serenity admittedly did not come about under conditions of external coercion but through the experience of the loss of inner freedom. He had wanted to force himself at a set hour of the day to work under the self-imposed strictures of formal requirements, and let the poem emerge from the most extreme pressure: "Je m'imposai de faire des vers, de ceux qui sont chargés de chaînes" [I forced myself to make verses, of the kind that are weighed down by chains]. There had not been, he writes, any *sérénité* in him whatsoever and the poem attested to the fallacy of inferring from the mood of the work the mood of the author, who had reacted to deep disturbances

---

2. Valéry writes the statement that he only produces prose by commission and request in a letter to Jean de la Tour, July 28, 1933, where he adds, illuminating the circumstances of such commissions: "sujet imposé et parfois conditions fort bizarres" [imposed topics and sometimes perfectly bizarre conditions] (*L* 207).

and catastrophic foreboding with fearful resistance, but indeed by *not* reflecting these feelings.

Back to the origin story of *Eupalinos*. More than ten years after the letter to Paul Souday, Valéry returns to this prehistory (Letter to Dontenville, January 20, 1934, *L* 214–215) and confirms once again that he had chosen the form of the dialogue for its elasticity and malleability. And there can be no doubt that it is this form that led to Socrates carrying the dialogue. All this, including the choice of the name "Eupalinos"—an ancient architect Valéry found in an encyclopedia—is of paramount facticity, which, if not labored, was certainly perceived as adequate. But this facticity, which *befell* the poet, was at the same time *provoked* by the needs of his poetic self-understanding—and was, of course, stylized in retrospect.

I.

It is in this arbitrary manner, then, that Socrates ended up in this text. It is a conversation in Hades, a subject that can no longer claim any originality.[3] But this Hades is not the place of a higher perspective on things; rather, one could say that it is the position from which the world presents itself from its "reverse." The Hades of Valéry's *Eupalinos* is different from the afterlife discussed by the Platonic Socrates in one crucial respect: it does not possess the same finality as the judgment of the court of the dead, nor the finality of the last possible intuition of truth in and of itself, seen from an unsurpassable standpoint; instead, this Hades is again only *one* perspective on things, possibly a privileged one, but if so, then only because not everyone can occupy it at any given time. For the position Valéry wants his Socrates to take, Hades is above any suspicion of the "naturalness" that gives truth no chance. In the notes that are published as *Cahier B 1910*, Valéry formulated this princi-

---

3. As early as 1893, Gide had hinted to Valéry that nevertheless the genre of the dialogues of the dead contained untapped possibilities: "Mais le dialogue des Morts est peut-être possible entre autre chose que des poncifs" [But, among other clichés, the dialogue of the dead is maybe possible] (GV 187).

ple of the non-natural aspect as follows: "La vérité, la découverte du nouveau, est presque toujours le prix de quelque attitude anti-naturelle. La profonde réflexion est forcée. . . . Il faut faire ou subir violence pour voir mieux ou autrement" [The truth, the discovery of the new is almost always the price of some antinatural attitude. The deep reflection is forced. . . . We must do or suffer violence to see better or differently] (II 580).

But something else characterizes Valéry's Hades: the inexhaust-ibility of time and a form of thought appropriate to it—a thought that does not know the termination of its immanent intentionality, which in all things can carry itself out up until the final consequences, and which is, precisely because of this lack of any material resis-tance, condemned never to be distracted: "We are now too much simplified not to undergo to its very end the motion of some idea."[4] Giving up interest is chained to the most agile form of mental self-realization. What is deemed so bothersome in life, thinking's finitude and potential for confusion, is shed, but at the same time thought has lost its living relevance. The dialogue does not wait for a more fortunate hour; it has become an atmospheric omnipresence: "They speak aimlessly, and their shades drone on."[5] Socrates and Phaedrus stand at the shores of Ilissus, the river of time, in which all things lose their contour and substance—even *anamnesis* [recollec-tion] cannot be conjured up in the face of the shapelessness of what floats by. The sensual no longer aids thought.

One could title this Hades situation "the disappointment of fini-tude." Truth has become apparent, but no one is interested in it anymore—nor, however, does it evade being present and consid-ered, as if closing one's eyes had become impossible: "Here every-thing is negligible, yet everything counts."[6] The unfurling of the sit-uation in Hades commences the critique of Platonism that pervades the dialogue. The dead Socrates and his interlocutors have left everything behind that once was corporeality, temporality, and

---

4. Paul Valéry, *Eupalinos, or The Architect*, in *Dialogues*, trans. William M. Stewart (Princeton, NJ: Princeton University Press, 1956), 65.

5. Valéry, *Eupalinos, or The Architect*, 66.

6. Valéry, 67.

appearance, and still they have not achieved what the Platonic Socrates had attached to these conditions: fulfilled immediacy of the true and the beautiful, finality in the face of the ideas,[7] pure intuition as the epitome of happiness. The noncorporeal position that was defined as the final goal of all striving for knowledge turns out to be the place in which the exposed truth can no longer be "grasped." "But from here all is unrecognizable. Truth is before us, and we no longer understand anything at all."[8]

The initial circumstances of the dialogue must be kept in mind in order not to abandon the ironic abeyance that they give to Socrates's progressive insight into his own intellectual development. But at the same time, this insight receives its dignity from being set in Hades; for as Socrates turns more and more toward his memory by recurring to the decisive situations of his intellectual biography, he frees himself from the awkwardness of the "Platonic" disappointment Hades had caused him. Memory here does not mean to conjure up image-like reproductions, but to carry out once more the life decisions that are irrevocably made. Already in the very first phase of the dialogue, the great self-correction of Socrates is initiated, namely, in the instant in which Phaedrus asks him for the origin and the meaning of that *goût de l'éternel* [taste for the eternal] that can be observed in the living and which Socrates himself had shown in his striving for knowledge, just like those who build temples and tombs with the effort of making them indestructible. Socrates replies that this is folly, but it is a senselessness indispensable to man's existence that was assigned to him by fate. Without it, there would be neither love nor science, nor the energies from which human culture emerges. Thus, immortality exists, but it compromises itself as the motive of all the monstrous efforts of which in this dialogue the architect is the thematic figure.

Phaedrus's memories steer the conversation toward the figure of the master builder Eupalinos. He radiates a fascination to which Phaedrus testifies, and it unfolds from the antithesis between the resistance of the material and the circumstances—between the disobedi-

---

7. Valéry, 67.
8. Valéry, 67.

ence of what is given on the one hand, and the ease of the mastered form, the reality that complies with the word on the other. This architect, to whom Phaedrus imputes the power of Orpheus, seems to build only with language; everything he does comes to fulfillment in the word: to the untoward chaos of the material he foretells its future as being realized in a building, and the things seem to follow his voice to the place appointed to them. His speeches to the workers act as forces within his master plan, and Phaedrus expressly reports that from the difficulties of his nightly considerations nothing emerges but the pure shape of command and number. What can Socrates reply to this evocation other than, "That is the very way of God."[9]

The very way of God? Let us consider where the accent is placed in this highest of distinctions an idea can receive in our intellectual history. The demiurge in the myth of Plato's *Timaeus* runs into difficulties in the execution of his work of making the world as soon as he is faced with *anankē* [necessity], and the way he masters this difficulty is tied to the word: it is persuasion. The biblical creator does not seem to hit on any difficulty, unless he does not achieve the totality of his work at once but gains, in the first access of creation, only the formless void. The ease with which he demonstrates his power over things lies in the immediate succession of the command and its realization; only once command becomes commandment, that is, in relation to the obedience of man, does it meet with resistance. What the Platonic Demiurge and the biblical creator have in common—and what tends to be overlooked in highlighting the difference that in one case matter is given and in the other there is only nothingness—is that the origin of their concept of the world remains unquestioned. This question is, in the case of the demiurge, answered right from the start by the forms that are given to him, and, in the case of the biblical creator, by the seeming obviousness of the fact that the words of his commands had a "meaning" before the things they referred to came into existence, that is, through some kind of implicit Platonism. Eupalinos's divine way, on the other hand, lies wholly between the nightly meditations and the word that eventually transpires from them as a command, encouragement,

---

9. Valéry, 70.

formula. Everything that follows and lies between the word and the temple's stony reality is only a transposition, an illustration of what was achieved in that first phase. Of course, this word is not only the command that orders to transform a given and presupposed intuition into reality, that is, to re-create an idea; instead, it is the instruction to bring this reality itself into being. The Platonic idea is no longer an image but a *rule* whose execution alone makes visible what was wanted. Only at this point is the systematic or hidden Platonism rejected that is common to the Bible as well as to the *Timaeus*. It is a rejection that Socrates, in this phase of the dialogue, does not yet recognize but which Phaedrus puts into words by saying that the idea and the technique of the work's realization have become identical to him: "I no longer separate the idea of a temple from that of its edification."[10] That, of course, is the exact opposite of what "wretched nature"[11] does, which, by constantly repeating itself and bringing forth the new always as a re-creation of what has already been, provides the Platonic model; it is a pitiful process that may know the eternity of form but not the uniqueness of surprise, and thus, seen from the perspective of Hades, has a desperate similarity to what is not or no longer living.

At this point, Socrates does not yet understand what Phaedrus finds so fascinating about the figure of Eupalinos. For him, it is simply the enthusiasm of a shadow for a phantom. Only the automatism of all conversations in Hades taking their course appears to let him continue in the business of asking questions and of listening to Eupalinos's rules that his interlocutor praises so highly. These sentences immediately grow from the definition of the idea as having a genetic law-structure. The unity of becoming, which, despite its temporal expansion, cannot be divided or atomized, takes the place of the shape-like [*gestaltartig*] unity of the idea—"There are no details in execution."[12] In the dialogue, the ambiguity of the

---

10. Valéry, 70. In 1906, Valéry had written to Gide: "But the final *shape* of *constructed* things no longer attracts me. I am too concerned with things *under construction*." André Gide/Paul Valéry, *Self-Portraits: The Gide/Valéry Letters 1890–1942* (Chicago: University of Chicago Press, 1966), 252.

11. Valéry, *Eupalinos*, 70.

12. Valéry, 71.

French word *détail* plays a role: Socrates understands it to mean *particulars*; Phaedrus interprets it as *trifles*. The one possibility yields a proposition about the homogeneous continuity of a work's becoming, the other a proposition about the equal value of the states of this becoming that may, after all, be discrete. That in becoming there are no *trivialities* appeals to the attention of the practitioner; that there are no "particulars" in it justifies the mystery of the productive process and the impossibility of transferring it.

The second statement of Eupalinos deals with the relationship between the work of art and its viewer. "'My temple,' this man from Megara would say, 'must move men as they are moved by their beloved.'"[13] Socrates again replies by dealing out the highest accolade: "That is divine."[14] Valéry, who admittedly loved to play down, in favor of formal difficulties, the intellectual presuppositions of his works and especially his knowledge of their ancient background, cannot have overlooked the fact that between Eupalinos's proposition and Socrates's predication there exists a more precise relationship than any superficial hearing of the phrase would reveal. What Eupalinos says about the effectiveness of his temple corresponds exactly to what Aristotle had said about the mode of action of his god, the Unmoved Mover: he moves the world, himself resting, simply as an object of love. The temple, too, this seemingly purely static structure, is and shall be, according to the second sentence of Eupalinos: an *unmoved mover*. By picking out the Aristotelian formula of the divine here, he initiates the dialogue's second counter-Platonic evolution. Socrates recalls an expression he heard about Alcibiades and his beauty, an expression of quite a similar type and yet a reverse tendency in meaning: "Looking at him, one feels oneself becoming an architect!"[15] An ambiguous sentence yet again, and we do not learn which interpretation Socrates choses. For, read closely, this sentence goes one step further into the counter-Platonic direction than Eupalinos's second sentence—not only by giving up the ideal of relaxed contemplation, of lingering in the presence of the

---

13. Valéry, 75.
14. Valéry, 75.
15. Valéry, 75.

beautiful, the true, and the good, and by demanding movement as the true correspondence of the viewer onto the presence of the beautiful. In addition, he specifies the type of the viewer's corresponding movement: it is the movement that has as its aim the *production* of the object seen, that is, a conduct that parallels that replacement of the Platonic idea through the unity of the process of becoming. The aesthetic object mobilizes its viewer, always also letting him potentially become the creator of the object. Socrates at this point does not yet know the difference between the theoretical and the aesthetic object; he accuses Phaedrus of having to be much unhappier than himself, who has never sought and loved the sensual presence of beauty but only set his life into the pursuit of truth, of which he could in Hades at least hold onto the idea of continuing the progress of its gaining: "I gladly seek among the shades, the shade of some truth."[16] What an anti-Platonic irony that Socrates freed from his body should now be all the more bound to the cave that Plato had him make into the allegory of the earthly situation of the minds! But he who seeks the shadow of truth in the shadowy realm seems to be better off than he who is fulfilled wholly by the wish for beauty—he from whom, now that bodies are nothing but memories, everything has been taken. It is only in this moment that Socrates is reminded of Plato. When Phaedrus is forced to confess how beauty is bound to finite and mortal life: "What is most beautiful finds no place in the eternal!" it occurs to Socrates to ask: "Is Plato not in these parts?" And this in turn compels Phaedrus to confess: "I am speaking against him."[17] He opposes the idea of immortal beauty that has its home in those models outside nature and viewed by noble souls as binding norms of its plans and the secret example of its efforts. The idea behind Plato's ideas seems too simple to him now and just as if it were too pure in its conception to make conceivable the difference between types of beauty and the change of their hierarchies in human appreciation, that is, its historicity, its possibility to connect with the radically new and creative— its power for recurrence that cannot be put into any law. Every-

16. Valéry, 75.
17. Valéry, 75.

thing converges toward the antinomy between the idea and the facticity of the aesthetic as creation and as history.

If there is something that we believe to be an essential part of the historical figure [*historische Gestalt*] of Socrates, it is that he insists on the definition of concepts. Valéry's Socrates in Hades thus acts in a manner "consistent" with his intellectual biography in now insisting to know what indeed truly is beautiful and thus proper to man, by astonishing without confusing him, by gripping without inuring him. He thus wants to see the characteristics of an objecthood be determined that would be capable of such appropriateness and effect. But Phaedrus evades the question's precision by defining the topic only from the perspective of its effect, which is that which, without effort, elevates man beyond his nature. Phaedrus palpably does not dare to force Socrates across the decisive threshold and uses the recourse to Eupalinos as a detour to lead Socrates toward an experience of which he believes that he had missed it in his lifetime. This inhibition toward Socrates and what was unquestionably valid to him and still seems to be, must appear as the dialogue's device by which the whole difference between the tradition that springs from Socrates, in which the beautiful as a matter of course participates in the eternal substantiality of the true and the good, and the basic idea of the constitutive finitude of the beautiful, its participation in man's mortality. The object of aesthetic enjoyment is not an autonomous world of appearances, characteristics, and qualities. The object of aesthetic enjoyment is, through the mediation of a sphere of objectivations [*Objektivationen*], man himself. Phaedrus has Eupalinos say not only that he had exercised his art the more he thought about it, and that he experienced himself in happiness and suffering to the extent to which he thought and executed as a master builder—and so experienced himself with a pleasure and clarity that became ever more secure. Instead, the artist's self-experience is heightened by another degree, from self-enjoyment to self-creation. The architect becomes his own building: "By dint of constructing . . . I truly believe that I have constructed myself."[18] One can feel how Eupalinos's statement about himself is geared toward a provocation of Socrates's

---

18. Valéry, 81.

maxim of self-knowledge. And so the interjection comes (with a shadow's resigned indulgence) whether or not these are two different things: to construct oneself and to know oneself. It is as if in horror at this question's scale that Phaedrus evades it and proceeds with his report, which continues to deal with the artwork's unsolvable unity of conception and execution, with the exclusion of the priority of the form [*Gestalt*] over becoming.

By an inner consistency, the conversation with Eupalinos that Phaedrus reports reaches the topic of music. Music offers an exemplary counterweight against architecture, which became a topic through the external occasion. An aesthetic interpretation of architecture was, due to its object, initially very close to the ontological position of the Platonic Socrates: the artistic building does not fit into the category of representational arts [*darstellende Künste*] that Plato had criticized as a copy of imitations and it is, moreover, closest to the pure intuition of the static *eidos* that is free of any illusions. But this approximation to the stasis of the archetype was already called into question by the first proposition of Eupalinos, which considers the conception of the work not as seizing the image of an already finished object,[19] but as the anticipation of a process, whose last phase is the finished work. This shows that the "completion" of the work in its thingliness is only an arbitrary break, and that the work, having stepped out of the process of its becoming, immediately enters into a new process, namely, that of communication with its natural and human environment. The scale of resulting possibilities—from sterility to the highest level of intensity—is denoted through the metaphor of the silent, the speaking, and finally, the singing buildings, as Eupalinos was said to have distinguished between them. The metaphorics of music has an anti-Platonic implication: the pure idea has no relation to time whatsoever, and music stands in this relation not simply by chance, but by necessity. It is the projection of figure onto time or even time as a

---

19. Granted, the temple of Eupalinos is an image, too, for it is the memory of a Corinthian girl put into stone, but it is expressly this lover's "mathematical image," Valéry, 82. The concept of image is used almost ironically here.

figure.[20] The "divine analogy" between temple and music that Phaedrus had felt when he first beheld the temple of Eupalinos, the
latter had called an arbitrary association of remote things, which
nonetheless reveal an admirable necessity of the inner unity of form
and time: "that strange parallel of visible forms with the ephemeral
combinations of successive sounds."[21] What the spectator feels as
the musicality of the building is, already in the creative potential of
the architect, a mysterious mixture, a form of the highest self-
possession and an ambiguity—"this state of divine ambiguity"[22]—
which is all the more productive for being yet undecided of that
which, as a unity of analysis and ecstasy, may not remain a dream,
but must become knowledge and technical sovereignty. Isolated ecstasy must be transformed into discursive analysis, the profuse opportunity of the moment must be "stopped," the undivisible must
nonetheless be divided. Phaedrus had suggested that Eupalinos tried
to slow down the ideas—again and again, that is, the assemblage
of ideality and temporality that linguistically is already so resistant.
As the aesthetic problem of the timeless idea emerges and unfolds,
the problem of the soul, supposedly imprisoned in the body and to
be freed, approaches as well—the very metaphysical commonplace
that Socrates had only just mentioned in an interjection when he
spoke of his death and his imprisonment, which segued into the dictum that in reality the only prison he had ever known was that of
his body.[23] And now, Phaedrus has Eupalinos explain that in the
process of creating his works, his own body seems always to have
played a role: this admirable instrument, of whose services the living

---

20. The Pythagorean element in Platonism has somewhat mitigated the sharp-
ness of the difference that must have existed between an ontology, for which authentic being excludes the element of time, and an art, which includes it so essentially and necessarily that of it no nontemporal reality can be thought. It is not by
accident that music first found an adequate foundation in its own reality in that
epoch, which for the first time granted time an absolute reality. Even late Scholasticism still found it difficult to bring to systematic congruence the singing of the
blessed in heaven and its necessary temporality (that is as the transience of each of
its elements) with the eternal *physis* of heaven.

21. Valéry, *Eupalinos*, 86.

22. Valéry, 86.

23. Valéry, 84.

fail to make the fullest use.[24] This turn against Socrates's body-soul dualism is artfully prepared through the steering and inner teleology of the dialogue. The passage culminates in the invocation of the body through the soul, the "unexampled prayer,"[25] as Socrates will call it disconcertedly, in which the body is praised as the transformer and moderator of the soul's dreams, as the anthropocentric reference point of the universe, which the quasi-heterocentrically attuned soul does not dare to or cannot proclaim for itself—a thought that, ascribed to the historical Eupalinos, seems anachronistic and, ironically, is supposed to appear this way, because the anthropocentric world that is thought of here as artistic fiction, was still a reality to ancient thought, or at least could have been. And it, too, is an anti-Platonic intention when the body is evoked, by altering Protagoras's saying, as "the measure of the world."[26] One might say these were trivialities that had been expressed often enough, but here they have the very precise function of undermining the position on which Valéry's Socrates still believes himself to be standing. The disappointment of the metaphysical liberation from the body, the reversal of the direction of the longing from the hereafter toward the here and now, is the punch line of the whole passage; Socrates immediately grasps it: it seems strange to sing the body's praises in Hades, and lamenting the loss of the body is curious in those who longed to be freed from their bodies. He is captured by the excitement of the problem of the arts, and one can easily see that the exemplary rank of architecture and music as similar when compared to all other arts fascinates Socrates because the criterion of this rank has been put in anti-Socratic (and, here, that always means anti-Platonic) terms. It is only these two arts, as Socrates now surprisingly picks up the thought, that create more than a mere sight, more than a form around which one can move, but a *space* into which one can enter, an exclusively human, self-sufficient reality that is not derived from nature, finite and close universes into which we can step away completely from our ordinary

---

24. Valéry, 90.
25. Valéry, 92.
26. Valéry, 91.

reality. To enter fully into the human work, to be spellbound by it, to live and breathe in it—Socrates describes all this as a type of ecstasy, yet it is an ecstasy into immanence and thus it is no longer Platonic, but directed against Platonic transcendence. To be in the universe that is constituted of pillars or of sounds likewise means both to be beyond oneself and at the same time to remain within the human, but in a way that not only leaves man the freedom to enter and leave it, but realizes the consciousness of his freedom precisely in this act of entering and leaving. The result, as Socrates puts it, is: "There are then two arts which enclose man in man."[27] Architecture and music are nonrepresentational [*gegenstandslos*] arts. They do not require mediating signs and representatives in the way the painter does when he uses the color green in one spot of his painting, and paints a tree as the vehicle of this green, as it were, that carries and leads it, and allows him to bring it to this spot. The relationship of the actual tree to the essential green is compared with the concrete and fabulous idea that allows an abstract connection to be made visible: Zeno's paradox of Achilles and the tortoise, which illustrates the problem of the continuum. The topic of art is not a factual objecthood [*Gegenständlichkeit*], but "that hidden power which makes all fables."[28] This hidden power interprets and produces itself in an inexhaustible abundance of possible images and factual transformations, in thousands of transient lives and forms, in an infinity of imaginations. Painting and poetry are, he says, always only these factual correlates; music and architecture realize the ground of their source themselves. Music and architecture restore the soul into its pure potentiality from which everything object-like [*alles Gegenständliche*] springs, but as an already determined givenness, whereas it has already lost this freedom to what in each case has been realized in its formations. One can immediately grasp the proximity to the way the modern age has regarded nature, which does not make forms its object but the laws from which the abundance of formations becomes possible, and which themselves are the epitomes of these possibilities. It would be easy

---

27. Valéry, 96.
28. Valéry, 97.

to show in greater detail that we are confronted with a theory of art here that uses the basic concepts of Platonism by turning them against their systematic origins and roots. Socrates speaks the language of Platonism when he says that in this world, music and architecture are like the monuments of another world, to which to draw attention is their function. But this other world of laws is so different and incomparable that it does not allow the bridge of imitation. Its difference would be that between noise and pure sound. Pure sound is a human creation, while nature "has only noises."[29] But the law the symphony recalls to the mind if it makes its listener forget its own sensual presence, is, as a law of nature, not nature itself, but that which only intellect can formulate, that which was not yet there before man put it into words, "true creatures of man."[30] The intelligibility of the law no longer points to the fact that there is an autonomous object world of pure forms, but rather to the fact that man, and man alone, could have created it. Socrates returns to his great topic, the geometric shapes, whose essence now is no longer that they always have existed and can be gathered from recollection but rather that they are constructed on the basis of a coherent command, a formula—that they emerge from the movement that adheres to this law. The formula that entails the law of the shape entails nothing yet of the shape and is nevertheless the spiritual energy from which the concrete shapes spring in arbitrary variety. Between the law of the action and the product of the action lies the decisive difference. By having the geometric object emerge, by dint of the definitional command, from movement and action, Socrates has found his own way to Eupalinos's dictum that becoming brings forth the object without containing it in a preformed way from the very start. We can find or create this command without already having its result eidetically before us; the word is the potency of the figure: "No geometry without the word."[31]

Socrates rightly admits now that Eupalinos's words had awakened something in him that was similar to those maxims. Phaedrus imme-

29. Valéry, 100.
30. Valéry, 100.
31. Valéry, 95.

diately misunderstands him, however, by confusing potentiality and preformation and by taking Socrates's insight for the expression of something already existing: that Socrates contained an architect in himself. Socrates does not correct Phaedrus; it may remind him too much of his own idea of maieutics, so he takes up the thought: yes, there was an architect in him whom circumstances had not brought to maturity. Between birth and death, he says, an existence's potentiality actualizes itself by discarding its possibilities and deciding for its realities. "I told you that I was born *several* and that I died *one*."[32] The possibilities that do become reality act as doubts, create contradictions, and push toward the crossroads of existence.[33] And it is at

---

32. Valéry, 109.

33. At this point, it is necessary to recall how Valéry treated another central figure of his chosen ancestry, namely, Leonardo da Vinci. Especially in the second of the three great essays on Leonardo, the "Note and Digression" of 1919, he described his method of penetrating into the presence of a historical figure [*historische Gestalt*]. The true task of historical understanding is, according to Valéry, to go back to the possibility of the figure and to understand the historical and real Leonardo, who is attested to in his works and the sources, from the "*potential* Leonardo." Paul Valéry, "Note and Digression," *Leonardo Poe Mallarmé*, 70. Just as the Socrates of *Eupalinos*, Leonardo, too—of whom we know much more historically—is the expression of an "inner law" conditioned by factual circumstances and decisions, a *Gestalt* formula in which we grasp the latitude of the freedom of an existence's self-expression. What is at issue in historical understanding is the relation of potentiality and decision, that is, the freedom from which history becomes fact, and not this fact as such. Here, also, the root of Valéry's opposition against any Platonizing ontology becomes recognizable: the preformation of appearance in ideality leaves, systematically, no place for freedom. The dialogue *Eupalinos* thus again takes up the theme and method of the Leonardo essays in a more audacious and poetic conception, in which the historical figure is, as it were, given the "opportunity" to find its way back to its own potentiality in a kind of *anamnesis* of that "inner law" that resides in the "force that has no object" (ibid., 70, 95). This is closely connected with the theory of pure consciousness as a formal system that can be occupied variably (see below), which is developed in the essays on Leonardo. This theory also determines what, if anything, can "mean something" and thus can occupy a position, and it determines what must remain excluded as an incomprehensibility. The mutual illustrative relation of the essay on Leonardo and the *Eupalinos* cannot be exhausted here; only the function of music in the second Leonardo essay must be pointed out, which metaphorically represents the "pure I" as the "power of the corresponding universe" ("Note and Digression," 102; translation modified). [Such an exhaustive account can be found in Hans Blumenberg, "Paul Valérys möglicher Leonardo da Vinci: Vortrag in der Akademie der Künste in Berlin

this point that Socrates introduces that strange thing which he calls "the most ambiguous object imaginable."[34]

II.

What is this ambiguous object, this *objet ambigu* all about? This is the key question of interpreting the dialogue and, moreover, the aesthetics of Valéry. To being with, it is obvious that the *objet ambigu* is meant as the exact correlate of young Socrates's potentiality prior to his decision in favor of philosophy. He reports that the discovery was bestowed on him by chance when he was still at the point of departure of different possible ways of existence, and that he realized this situation by means of that strange entity as an inner hesitation, so that the ambiguity of the discovered object exactly corresponded to the indecision of his self-image. But if this situation was characterized as the alternative between philosophy and art, then the ambiguity of that strange object must have consisted in its indeterminacy with regard to its theoretical or aesthetic objecthood [*Gegenständlichkeit*] or objectification [*Vergegenständlichung*]. The endless considerations to which this discovery gave rise played between the possibilities "to construct" [*construire*] and "to know" [*connaître*].[35]

Phaedrus is eager to hear a description of this object, but the very possibility of such a portrayal would be in contradiction to the potentiality of the object, in which alone its meaning rested. Instead, Socrates tells of his discovery at the shore and of youth's drunkenness with a life still indeterminate. This narration is one of the most beautiful pieces of prose that I know. Each move of this description, its indissoluble unity of outer scene and inner assessment of life, runs concentrically toward the mysterious discovery, in which this situation finds its most straightforward representation. In his

---

am 21. 4. 1966," *Forschungen zu Paul Valéry/Recherches Valéryennes* 25 (2012): 193–227.]

34. Valéry, *Eupalinos*, 110.
35. [Valéry, 81.]

memory, the Socrates in Hades—who had just been irked by the praise of the body and its sensuous self-enjoyment—discovers himself as having once in his life been absorbed in the sensuous totality of a unique experience. Valéry lets him find a language that the living Socrates would never have spoken, and on whose almost imperceptible appearance he comments with the words: "I have let my talk run on."[36] It is a language of which Phaedrus declares, in awe and admiration, that it lets him come to life again. The thing—that *objet ambigu*—lay on the edge of the sea, embedded in a spectacle of nature that is "alienated" by its being recalled from memory in Hades as something that is irretrievably lost, even though it has been most ordinary and most accessible to everyone, and therefore also most easily lost to everyone. The *objet ambigu*, however, is not just embedded in this setting but is also the product of the forces that are effective in it. Again, Socrates goes far afield to describe the contention between and intertwining of these powers on the border where land and sea, earth and air, meet. It is one of the things the sea flings onto the beach, "a white thing,"[37] hard, delicate and lightweight, polished, of the purest white. Socrates picks it up, cleanses it of sand, rubs it on his cloak, and immediately all his thoughts are ensnared by the uniqueness of this form. We already know whence stems the excitement this object causes: it is a condition lacking interpretability within a Platonic ontology. Socrates recognizes this immediately—it is an object that is not reminiscent of anything and yet is not without a shape. Immediately, one thinks of the discussions of the Platonic dialogues on the question of how far down the exemplary nature of the ideas reaches into the value order of things, and whether one has to assume them to exist even where the canon of a nature self-reproducing in its forms no longer applies.[38] Who could have made this object? is the first question Socrates asks himself. Doubtful is the origin, doubtful the matter of which the thing consists—"matter for doubt."[39] The object that

---

36. Valéry, 113.
37. Valéry, 114.
38. See, for instance, *Parmenides* 130a–e.
39. Valéry, *Eupalinos*, 114.

defies definition, that is, gives no answer to the stereotypical Socratic questions, does not enter the ultimate classification of ancient metaphysics either, the duality of naturalness and artificiality. But it is precisely that the *objet ambigu* is "nothing" and means "nothing," its nonobjecthood in any traditional sense of the word, that increases its meaning to an incalculable level: it poses all questions and leaves them open. This doubtful object repeats as a form what we have already noted in Eupalinos's dictums—dictums that meant nothing or something altogether trivial, which were, so to speak, mere incentives for the self-expression of thought by those who heard them.

The *objet ambigu* is produced by the multiplicity of the natural forces active in this zone in time,[40] and what infinite time produces looks as if it had sprung from an artist's intention guided by the idea, or has its place somewhere in the series of experiments of nature, which tests organs with regard to their functional expediency, and selects or discards them. A thought, which the classic Socrates could not possibly have had, looms large here from the perspective of the modern age's natural science: the long durations' responsibility for the evolution of organisms and the diversity of forms of erosion, sediments, drifts, and cuts, for the innumerable "patterns" that inorganic as well as organic nature produce. In the background, there is always the permission to calculate with tremendously long periods of time and the accumulation of tremendously small forces

---

40. The border zone between land and sea as a region in which purely quantitative units of force become images—that is, characteristic evidence of the link between formula and *Gestalt*—already appeared in 1893 in a letter to Gide. In it, Valéry articulates the writer's admiration for the mathematician, whose ability to make reality comprehensible he had stumbled upon by randomly opening Laplace's work: He was able to grasp in formulas "la déglution de la mer" [the swallowing of the sea] in the calculable action of the tides, and could nevertheless—or rather, precisely because of this—summon the spectacle without any image: "le glouglou et le déhanchement m'en vint, le ton d'acier, le gonflement et les fuites précipitées à l'Ouest. Le mot: syzygie! l'odeur de ce machin qui bouge et luit entre azimuths, coordonnées, parallaxes, etc., la hauteur du soleil,—tout" [the gurgle and the sway came to me, the tone of steel, the swelling, the sudden leakage to the West. The word: syzygy!—the smell of that gadget that moves and shines between azimuths, coordinates, parallaxes, etc., the height of the sun—everything]. Paul Valéry, "Letter to André Gide, August 26, 1893," *Moi* (Princeton, NJ: Princeton University Press, 1975), 143.

of action within them; Socrates himself says what hardly any thinker could have said before Bacon: that the centuries cost nothing, and that whoever knows how to put them into his calculations can transform what he wants, into what he wants.[41] It is significant for the subtlety with which this dialogue is wrought that the same Phaedrus, who had at first inspired and excited Socrates with his report on Eupalinos, now hardly can follow. His clumsiness is shown, for instance, in a minute difference—Socrates speaks of "infinite time,"[42] while Phaedrus takes up this idea under the title of "indefinite time."[43] But Phaedrus, in his own way, pushes forward this thought by contrasting the work of the artist with the efficacy of nature precisely with regard to the dimension of time: the work of the artist must create the objects, for which nature has reserved the infinity of chance and time, within time's finitude. More than once, Valéry expressly denied being influenced by Bergson and even having known him only before he had been elected to the Academy (see, for instance, *L* 163–164). As credible as that may be, it does not really touch on the essence of a statement whose truth does not depend on the fact of literary influence; even in opposition to the zeitgeist, the commonality of spiritual and historical prerequisites leads to deeply related structures. The poet, who has imposed on himself as law the strictness and exactness of form, shrinks from the infinitism of the *évolution créatrice* [creative evolution], just as he wants to assess the relation between philosophy and poetry by the criterion of form. But the figure of Socrates—in whom he wishes to trace the philosopher's self-actualization back to the point at which the potentiality of being an artist was laid out equally ready and was ignored—compels him to leave the relationship between philosophical intention and poetic form not simply unchallenged as a factual opposition, but to explain it from the starting point of their compatibility.[44] The encounter with the *objet ambigu* is supposed

---

41. [Valéry, *Eupalinos*, 115–116.]

42. [Valéry, 115. Translation modified.]

43. [Valéry, 116.]

44. In the letter to Souday (May 1, 1923, *L* 146) already quoted above, Valéry describes this theme as the *véritable pensée* [true thought] in the intention of the *Eupalinos*: "J'aurais essayé de faire voir que la pensée pure et la recherche de la

to designate precisely this point: despite the infinite complication of factors and the infinite time of its impact, the product of nature is, after all, the *finite* and, at every moment, perfect form; for it is apparent to Socrates that the instant of this object's discovery is an accidental point in time, and the state in which the object is found is thus an arbitrary fixation of the process. The artist's work stands in contrast to "infinite time," but in such a way that the predicate of infinity shifts from time to work. An artist makes up for a thou-

---

vérité en soi ne peuvent jamais aspirer qu'à la découverte ou à la construction de quelque forme. Je n'oppose pas tout philosophe à l'artiste, mais seulement m'oppose à celui-ci le philosophe qui ne parvient pas à cette forme finie, ou qui ne se doute pas qu'elle seule peut être l'objet d'une recherche rationnelle et consciente" [I tried to show that pure thought and the search for truth in itself can only aspire to the discovery or construction of forms. I do not set the philosopher against the artist, but only set against him the philosopher who does not reach this finished form, or who does not doubt that it alone can be the object of rational and conscious study]. The finitude of form as an infinite task—that is, a fundamental idea that strikes Valéry repeatedly, especially in relation to his own philosophical notes, in which *The System* once seemed to announce itself (Paul Valéry, "Letter to André Gide, February 22, 1897," *Moi*, 188). A quarter of a century later, he writes about *tout ce fatras* [all this junk], about his own inertia in the face of the hopeless demand for ordering and forming this *hylē*: "et enfin songer à la forme, terrible affaire, et infinie!" [and finally, to contemplate form, a terrible affair, and infinite!] (*L* 150). One's own philosophy, "ma philosophie," in quotation marks, that is, what ought to have become "mon œuvre véritable" [my own true work], is now "exactement le contraire d'une philosophie" [exactly the opposite of a philosophy]. Another ten years later, the antithesis of philosophy and art has resolved in the slogan "philosophy as art." "Le philosophe ne veut pas avouer qu'il fait et ne peut faire qu'œuvre d'art et se refuse à centrer cette œuvre sur soi-même, tel qu'il est. Je crois que prétendre a quelque chose de plus est une absurdité" [The philosopher does not want to admit that he makes, and can only make, a work of art, and he refuses to center that work in himself, such as he is. I think that to pretend to anything more is an absurdity] (*L* 208, July 28, 1933). Another decade later, Valéry confesses to someone who inquires into the word "nothingness" in his works, "que je ne suis point philosophe le moins du monde, peut-être même quelque chose comme un anti-philosophe" [that I am not a philosopher in the least, perhaps even something like an anti-philosopher]. This is grounded on the relation to language, its formal rather than material use, so that also the one *Néant* [nothingness] that was inquired after is only used "comme un peintre emploie une certaine couleur: il a besoin d'un noir, il met un noir" [as a painter uses a certain color: he needs some black, he applies some black] (*L* 242f., November 23, 1943). The inclusion of Hades-Socrates in the process that becomes visible and its immanent finality is easy to carry out according to this.

sand, or even a hundred thousand, centuries, if not more, by replacing nature's blindness and randomness with thought. Art is the finite equivalent of infinite creative development, but as such, it is "un labeur infini" [an infinite labor], as Valéry writes in a letter to Albert Mockel in 1917 about the creation of his poem *The Young Fate*, and this infinite effort is enforced by the self-chosen "jeu difficile" [difficult game], the strictness of his self-imposed conditions (*L* 123). Into this context belongs the fact that for Valéry there is no such thing as the entirely successful work, perfect in form, since the infinite task is precisely that which can never be solved. He therefore stresses the failure of this claim again and again as the artist's experience of the poetic structure's nature that succeeds in self-observation. Valéry's poetics is empirical, both a result of the despair he observes in himself and which all poets experience, as he writes (*L* 161), and of the "idée de l'impuissance consciente" [idea of conscious helplessness] (*L* 141). To the charge of the obscurity of his poems, which Valéry had to face constantly, he replies that this *obscurité* was not deliberate but rather the expression of the powerlessness to be clear (Letter to Aimé Lafont, 1922; *L* 144). But this inadequacy in the face of the poetic claim is indeed not judged negatively, but positively endorsed as the stigma of the pure aesthetic imperative, as the source of the poet's conscious consciousness, his *conscience consciente*.[45] In poetry, the infinite is justified only as a deficiency, as a sign within form, as formlessness shining through form that is nevertheless banished and not admitted. I believe that the meaning of Valéry's self-testimonies about the conditions under which Eupalinos originated, which I quoted at the beginning, can be grasped in the following way: the limited latitude, created by the narrow confines of the task or the poet's self-imposed rules, has the function of spawning the indications of the absolute claim and the infinite work— indications that let the form, wrested from chaos, remain recognizable as "wrested" form and do not allow the submission of language to fully dissolve in the illusion of a total availability. Valéry never understood the aesthetic stock phrase of the "creative" in analogy

---

45. [Valéry, *L* 144.]

to biblical creation as the command to emerge from nothingness, but demiurgically as overpowering the *apeiron* and *anankē* [the infinite and necessity]. What interested him most about the un-bounded activity of the artist who needs to create the goal, the means, and even the resistances for the work, Valéry once wrote (1942, *L* 237), was the latter condition, for it is the real condition of the artist's self-experience: "en créant, je me suis recréé sur un point" [in creating, I re-created myself at one point].

Young Socrates, at the water's edge, the *objet ambigu* in hand, contemplating it from all sides, stood like this for some time, ques-tioning it without accepting any of its answers—and threw it back into the sea.[46] But Socrates remained the prisoner of the thoughts stirred up by this thing, whose direction was determined by the pre-ponderance of one of the possible questions and which either had to point toward a comprehensive conception of nature or an aes-thetic behavior, be it enjoyment or creativity. This unknown object serves only to make clear how close these possibilities were to each other originally and how apt to be confused they were at this ini-tial point. The alternative to become either philosopher or artist, then, is concentrated in the *objet ambigu* as the plurality of its aspects and the consequence of choosing a particular point of view. The situation as a whole defies the ancient ontology, which had to con-sider the problem of the natural or artificial origin of an object to be an always decidable question, and which regarded the artificial—and not only according to time or the material substratum—as second-ary to the natural from the start. The relevance of the *objet ambigu* lies precisely in the fact that it cannot occur in a world conceived of as Platonic. To admit its ambiguity—let alone describe it—Socrates in Hades must step out of the tradition of his own ontol-ogy and add to his conception of nature the modern component of evolution and a state that can factually only be grasped when viewed across time. Only thus does he arrive at a possible relation-ship between nature and art in which the products are equivalent while their genesis is radically different. Just as there exists the es-sentially unprecedented in art, in this nature, too, the surprise of

---

46. [Valéry, *Eupalinos*, 116.]

novelty and improbability exists, without the possibility that any anamnesis of the ideal cosmos could be prompted. Invention and construction—terms around which Valéry's thought revolves, and which he made key terms in his essays on Leonardo—allow man to compensate entirely for the evolution of nature, to wait for which or in which to set his hopes his existence is too short.

The next step in this consideration is the insight that the difference between an unknown object of the *objet ambigu*'s type and the sphere of known objects is not objectively relevant, but that the same perplexity toward the object is also conceivable for the known if we were only able to reach the same attitude of being unbiased and not already in the know. But in the face of the familiar, our vision is always fixed on one aspect—for example, by knowing that and how nature produced such an object.[47] Since we are already in possession of the answers, or believe ourselves to be so, we no longer ask the questions. Our "first education" stands in the way of our "deeper education," as Valéry put it in the first essay on Leonardo.[48] We keep the "obvious standpoints"[49] and "beautiful views"[50] always ready for the things and thus the perspective from which we are able to and wish to see them as that which is already familiar and with which one has come to terms. The painterly technique of the central perspective, which assigns the observer his preferred and standardized place as a spectator, is an expression of this defense against the infinite variety of possible aspects.[51] The anthropocentric tradition—which understood man as a *contemplator caeli* [observer of the heavens] and, ordained by nature and according to his essence, placed him at the center of the world—has, with metaphysical legitimacy, equated the familiarity with the things and the understanding of the world. It is here that Valéry sees the function of the artist, who regains the freedom of intuition, "pure

---

47. Valéry, *Eupalinos*, 118.
48. Paul Valéry, "Introduction to the Method of Leonardo," in *Leonardo Poe Mallarmé*, 20.
49. Valéry, "Introduction to the Method of Leonardo," 20.
50. Valéry, 19.
51. Valéry, 22.

observation,"[52] and does not presuppose the cosmos as the guaranteed given, but turns it—as an achievement that man always has to perform, as a constant transition from disorder to order—into a task. To consider a house, a door, or a jug in such a way that one does not already have all the answers to possible questions, and thus does not actualize the questions in the first place, requires, as Socrates takes up the thread of this idea, that I distance myself from this object in such a way that I see it as a savage who has never seen such things and, therefore, does not know that they are human products. The artist accomplishes the same feat by disturbing the mind of the beholder with a new view of things. Even thought has its own inertia, which can be broken only under the influence of new forces: "One stops, and then one is off again; that is what thinking is!"[53]

The moment at which Socrates throws the *objet ambigu* back into the sea contains, as it were, the decision about the direction of his existence, the decision in favor of philosophy. Socrates lingers on the last question he addressed to the subject: ought it to be classified as a natural product or as an artifact? But by ridding himself of the object provoking this question, he has at the same time lost the other possibility of behaving immediately aesthetically toward it, of letting it stand in its very indeterminacy, and enjoy it. Valéry has, under the heading of "Art," given a definition of beauty: "The beautiful demands perhaps the slavish imitation of what is undefinable in things."[54] This characterization is strangely contradictory, for it takes up the traditional concept of imitation, but defines the objecthood of this imitation in a quite untraditional way by making indeterminacy, the inability to be determined, the essential feature of the beautiful. The aesthetic attitude here differs from the theoretical attitude in that it does not take indeterminacy to be the provocative stimulus to posing questions, searching for features and specific differences, but lets it be and takes pleasure in it. Socrates,

---

52. Valéry, 27.
53. Valéry, *Eupalinos,*" 119.
54. Paul Valéry, "Rhumbs," in *Analects* (Princeton, NJ: Princeton University Press, 1970), 240.

however, turns away from the seashore and its indeterminacies and heads inland, carrying with him the burden of the question concerning the determinability of the indeterminate. From here on, it no longer matters to think carefully about the answer that Socrates finds to this question: the farther one theoretically penetrates into its details and subtleties, nature incrementally adds to the complexity of its parts, the wealth of its structures increases; man reduces nature, by taking from it the materials for his works, to abstract materiality, and he does not care about the found structure, but rather gambles for a new whole, which is less complex than the substrates that were taken from nature and are absorbed into this whole. The formative principle of human works is thus the destruction of a found order: "Their structure is . . . a disorder!"[55] Man is only ever interested in the material taken from nature with regard to a small selection of its properties. The strength of man as a demiurge lies in forgoing the complete insight into nature, in being able to neglect irrelevant quantities. Even his most exact procedures are possible only through tolerated inaccuracy: "Man . . . fabricates by abstraction."[56] As an aesthetic, technical being, man does not require integral nature. The finality of *homo faber* ruthlessly thwarts the finality of nature, constructing and knowing are antinomies, and vis-à-vis nature artificial and artistic work is based on renunciation: man can act and create only because he is able to "ignore."[57] In frustrating the intrinsic structure of the natural, art is fundamentally violence; the order it posits rests on the disorder it causes, just as the art of the strategist, Phaedrus reminds us, is based on the training of individuals whose individuality he disregards: "whereas each element of those figures was the most complex object in the world, a man."[58] The creations of man, then, are founded in the conflict of his order with the order of nature and in the economy that is the condition for man's ability to enforce his thought against that of nature. But the resistance that nature pits against the creative will

---

55. Valéry, *Eupalinos*, 120.
56. Valéry, 121.
57. [Valéry, 124.]
58. Valéry, 122–123.

of man is not overcome and reduced to zero by the human form, but enters into the form; the figure of the Phoenician shipbuilder, Tridon, who is soon introduced to the dialogue, illustrates that in the highest elegance of form, the tension of the resistance that it had to master is still preserved.

The eighteen-year-old Socrates, who had flung the *objet ambigu* back into the sea, became a philosopher the moment he went inland and began to raise questions *about* the object, which could no longer be questions *to* the object. This means that he was not ready for the acts of renunciation that precede aesthetic attitudes. The philosopher cannot renounce: "The philosopher is one who has a greater idea, and wishes to have need of everything."[59] He is the one who always lays claim to a little more knowledge than is necessary. Phaedrus reproaches Socrates for killing the artist in him by immersing himself all too much in the problem of a seashell fragment; in doing so, he had accepted his share in the manifold efforts of men to fill or shatter the eternal silence of the infinite spaces that they find so frightening.[60]

---

59. Valéry, 123. [Translation modified.]

60. Valéry, 125. Pascal apostrophes, like these, are innumerable in Valéry. Only their careful interpretation could provide elucidation about the inner connection between anti-Platonisms and anti-Pascalisms. In 1923, on the occasion of Pascal's 300th birthday, Valéry published the complete paraphrasing of the *pensée* "Le silence éternel." Paul Valéry, "Variations on a *Pensée*," *Masters and Friends* (Princeton, NJ: Princeton University Press, 1970), 86–107. In a letter to Pierre Louÿs (May 21, 1917, *L* 121), he announces a "éreintement sauvage" [savage roasting] of the *Pensées*, but with the balancing addition "au bénéfice du 'Traité de l'équilibre des liqueurs'" [with the benefit of the doubt granted the "Treatise on the Equilibrium of Liquids"]. The biggest annoyance to him is the argument of the wager (*L* 165; alluding to it, with the finest irony, in the letter on the clothing of a nun: *L* 202–203); the conciliatory discovery that Pascal had discarded the sheet from the preparatory work for the apology was made only after Valéry's death. Regarding these materials as a whole, I would limit myself here to the pithy formula in which Valéry expressed his own opposition to Pascal as that of Leonardo to Pascal: "An abyss would make him think of a bridge" (Valéry, "Note and Digression," 79). Faust, too, on the hermit's ridge in *My Faust*, is an anti-Pascal when he says: "Looking into the pit of an abyss, I feel curiosity. More often, indifference." Paul Valéry, "My Faust," in *Plays* (Princeton, NJ: Princeton University Press, 1960), 151.

Almost naturally, Phaedrus, in his architect Eupalinos's stead, now has the adventurous and versatile shipbuilder Tridon enter the scene, whose works are incomparable to Eupalinos's temple in that they realize beauty only secondarily, but primarily serve man's conflict with nature and that of the ship with the powers and the resistance of the sea. Mastering the formula allows this enterprising man not simply to follow tradition in his constructions—not once more to copy the ship of Odysseus—but to exercise his skill from the ground up, that is, to replace the complex of circumstances by analysis of the factors, to imagine the ship as a body on which certain effects are exerted. The formula he eventually finds contains the form that can be opposed to the circumstances and resistances. When Phaedrus tells Socrates about the studies the Sidonian conducts with the fastest fish of the sea, Socrates quite artlessly asks if it is not enough to exploit nature's treasures directly and simply imitate such a fish. Again, the antithesis of imitation and construction appears: imitation takes the forms of nature as such, adheres to their presuppositions, as it were, from the outside, and believes that it can emulate its achievements through repetition; construction is the development of a form [*Gestalt*], as it were, from within, its production from the formula of the law that regulates the relations between the forces and the forms, between the circumstances and the achievements. Phaedrus describes the launching of one of these purest forms of a ship and in that moment elicits from Socrates the longing cry for the lost life. In contrast, the memory of that holy ship's black sails arise instantly, whose return from Delos signaled his death knell—a death that no longer seems to him to be the attestation of his wisdom, and which to see turned into a kind of masterpiece now appears highly dubious to him: "Life cannot defend herself against those undying death scenes. . . . Man's deepest glances are those that go out to the void."[61] The pain of the life unlived conquers the memory of the life lived in fact.

With horror, Phaedrus attends the judgment in which "Anti-Socrates" sits over Socrates.[62] This self-judgment is as unjust as

---

61. Valéry, *Eupalinos*, 141.
62. [Valéry, 144.]

only the judgment can be that is passed over reality by the measure of possibility. Anti-Socrates admits to the most ruthless self-realization, even at the price of breaking through and reversing the cosmic order; he forgets that the living Socrates had not turned the universe upside down precisely because he already considered it anthropocentric; and because the cosmos had an inviolable binding force, art could not appear to him as an absolute reality. But Phaedrus also sees that this shadow, who wants to start his life over again, is, for this very reason, Socrates, the philosopher, to whom the mere fact of a life that has not found its decisiveness from complete insight is an annoyance—as his own life now appears retrospectively from Hades. "You must not wish to begin again,"[63] Phaedrus objects. Socrates, however, has discovered the purpose of Hades in the use of this immeasurable leisure so as to judge himself again and again, to give ever different answers to the questionability of the lost life, to defend himself with the illusion against dissolving in nonexistence, as the living do against the recognition of their existence. The image of Anti-Socrates, who must be a "builder" [*constructeur*],[64] is yet again—and this is the irony that accompanies every step of Hades-Socrates' self-correction—the image of a seeker of truth. He, admittedly, now has a different and new concept of truth that does not conceive of truth as the prerequisite of correct action and identifies virtue with knowledge, but lets truth emerge from action, suspecting knowledge of the universe to be possible only by means of action, by putting oneself in the place of the very God who made the universe through action. In this "great act of constructing,"[65] which in its perfection comes close to the master builder himself, the demiurge is understood solely through his engagement with chaos. Anti-Socrates sees the essential relation determining his work from the beginning not between the demiurge and the cosmos of ideas but in the confrontation of the will to order with the shapelessness and impurity of matter.[66] The master

---

63. Valéry, 143.
64. [Valéry, 83.]
65. [Valéry, 146.]
66. Valéry, 146–147.

builder, whom Anti-Socrates imagines himself to be, comes upon the already finished work of that demiurge, but for his part he sees it as so much chaos and raw material, as an unfinished work that is not sufficient for man and on which he again must set to work. Where the god stopped acting, the artist's action begins. And the necessity of the architect and his action, which encounter nature as the given, but not as the binding, rests in the fact that the demiurge created the world only for himself, for his distraction or out of boredom; art draws its necessity precisely from the fact that it competes with nature's disregard for man, that art imposes on nature consideration for and a focus on man: "The Demiurge was pursuing his own designs, which do not concern his creatures. The converse of this must come to pass."[67] Art is a teleology that is opposed to the ateleology of nature, has to overcome it, and force it into art's order.[68] Socrates's train of thought—when viewed from its emergence in the *objet ambigu*, which seems to contain in itself the connection of nature and art as mere perspectives that are easily confused—has reached the extreme opposite, the antithetical alienation of nature and art. This makes it understandable that the enthusiasm of Anti-Socrates, who still carries in himself so much of Socrates in an ironic way, at the end of the dialogue turns into the melancholy of someone who, as a shadow in Hades, finally no longer trusts his own reality and who, through the rupture in the identity of his intellectual history, begins to doubt the authenticity of all of his thoughts, which appear to him as alienated from himself

---

67. Valéry, 148.

68. In Valéry's Socrates, two motivational strands of the technical-artistic interpretation of the world are formulated: first, the idea of an as-yet-unfinished universe, either predisposed to the definition of man as a "creative" being, or presenting itself as a bare fact in need of his "work"; second, self-assertion against a nature that is no longer thought capable of being the cosmos, or in which man can no longer believe that he is provided for and equipped with a sufficient fund of existence. I refer here to two other works of mine: the section "Incomplete Universe" in Hans Blumenberg, *Paradigms for a Metaphorology* (Ithaca, NY: Cornell University Press, 2010), 55–61, and "Ordnungsschwund und Selbstbehauptung: Über Weltverstehen und Weltverhalten im Werden der technischen Epoche," in *Das Problem der Ordnung: VI. Deutscher Kongreß für Philosophie, München 1960*, ed. Helmut Kuhn and Franz Wiedmann (Meisenheim: Hain, 1962), 37–57.

as if they had sprung from the imagination of someone still alive—and in this way, Socrates seems to restitute these thoughts to their author. In the end, then, and on the whole, it is a futile immortality.

III.

The dialogue *Eupalinos* is central to Valéry's work in that it contains and deploys almost the complete toolkit of the art theorist's concepts. In addition, it suggests a confrontation with the metaphysical tradition that is hidden in or stands behind these concepts. But the meaning of the dialogue and its Socrates character goes a little further: an attempt is made not only to accept as a fact the reversal of the basic aesthetic concepts' tradition, but to make it intelligible through its projection into the history of an identical person—identical beyond death—that of Socrates, who sees the conclusion of the whole tradition conceived as originating in him, compressed in his own life. This leads or misleads to positing analogies between the process of intellectual history and the fictional biography of Socrates. While the reader is nowhere encouraged to make this transfer, he is nowhere warned not to do so. The schema that would be obvious here could almost be described as a piece of biologism, that is, the basic biogenetic law according to which phylogenesis is repeated in ontogenesis, so that conclusions from the later to the former are admissible. For instance, if Valéry's concept of nature proves to be extremely empty and unproductive, as the epitome of misleading and distracting orientations of the artist and of aesthetic theory, and if his Socrates turns out to be the one disappointed by this very nature, then this indeed creates a motivation for conversion in Hades, which centers the dialogue—but an interpretation that would attempt to use or transfer this as a schema of the historical process would be very close to an illusion if not already ensnared in it. The sufficient interpretation of the *objet ambigu* so central in the *Eupalinos* requires that we return once more to Valéry's concept of nature. The figures of Socrates and Anti-Socrates possess a certain symmetry to one another, whose axis, as it were, is represented by the *objet ambigu*. It seemed that the result of the *objet ambigu* lay in the fact that the decision falls either on nature as this object's horizon of origin—and then the theoretical consideration is the appropriate attitude—or that artificiality dominates the impression and the presumption of the object's origin, and then the admiration of the object immediately continues into the will to attain the power to such creation as an artist. The antimetaphysical background of this Socrates has the effect that even the interrogation of the object already leads toward the alternative between nature or art, and this insoluble question as such implies Socrates's philosophical turning inland. But this function of the *objet ambigu*, leading to the original alternative of ancient, traditional metaphysics, does not quite stand out as the solution that Valéry would have sought or found for himself. His concept of nature is, at bottom, not suited to constituting the alternative to art, and his concept of art is no longer essentially dependent on drawing its meaning from the opposition to a nature that is understood as unfinished, ugly, or poor. The bracket of the conceptual antithesis of nature and art remained effective in the whole process of intellectual history in that valuing the one side was possible always only at the expense of the other, that is, that nature's primacy in being could only be stabilized by reducing all artificiality and artifice to the imitation of the ultimately binding exemplarity of nature; else, the accumulation of human self-valuation in art seemed to be feasible only through depriving nature of its essence [*Entwesentlichung*]. Valéry's position, taken as a whole, is indicative of a neutralization of this antithesis and thus of an aesthetics beyond the traditional metaphysical fixation of expressive possibilities. The Socrates of the dialogue *Eupalinos* would then already have taken the wrong path by wanting to remove the *objet ambigu* from its indeterminacy; likewise, he would have taken a wrong—which in this context always means "philosophical"—approach even if he had decided to regard this object as a work of art and to retain it in enjoyment. The defining preliminary decision was the question, and not one of the possible answers. In fact, Hades-Socrates need not reproach himself: there was nothing in his younger self that would have enabled him to absorb the object's indeterminacy and inability to be determined as such. Valéry's aesthetic presuppositions, his concept of nature as well as his concept of art, are still beyond the last verdict that Anti-Socrates passes about himself in self-judgment. In this, above all, I see the significance of the peculiar resignation with which he, as it were, gives the floor back to his author.

In a note from *Cahier B 1910*, Valéry writes: "La 'nature,' c'est-à-dire la Donnée. Et c'est tout. Tout ce qui est initial. Tout commencement; l'éternelle donnée de toute transaction mentale, quelles que soient donnée et transaction, c'est nature—et rien d'autre ne l'est" ["Nature," that is, the Given. And that's all. All that is initial. All beginning; the eternal givenness of every mental transaction, whatever the given and the transaction may be, is nature—and nothing else is] (II 572). This definition of nature starts from its temporal relation to human action; nature is not a certain range of objects or processes, but what is present to man when he begins to be intellectually active and what in the "transaction" cannot and does not remain what it has been. Such action is by no means bound to the field of art; the essays on Leonardo are suffused by the basic idea that the theoretical hypothesis of the natural scientist is essentially nothing else but the inventor's technical construction or the artist's aesthetic constitution. Only the beginning is nature, and in this sense Socrates would have been right if he had considered the *objet ambigu* as "nature." But for the ancient thinker, this would have meant something quite different, namely, to leave the object be in theoretical contemplation [*Anschauung*]. Man, as Valéry sees him, is not opposed to nature, he does not rival her, he does not build his cultural world into or beside the natural world, in competition with it; rather, as soon as he moves away from his beginning, as soon as he becomes involved in his "transaction," nature ceases to be nature and dissolves in the transformations of the human mind. The most absurd program that humans can prepare for themselves is therefore the demand to go "back to nature." In the *Rhumbs*, Valéry writes that there can be no more naive striving than that which wants to discover "nature" every thirty years. Nature, he writes, does not exist at all, or rather: what one considers to be the given is always already an "invention" [*une fabrication*].[69] The

---

69. Valéry, *Rhumbs*, 186.

idea of gaining a relation to the original state of things admittedly possesses an exhilarating power, but its presupposition—that there must be something that virginal—is a groundless imagination, for the sea, the trees, the suns, and, above all, the human eye itself, all that already is art, he writes, and art presupposes that what was initial and original has been forgotten.

In this way, we can understand that in Valéry there is no aesthetic antithesis between object-like figurativeness and nonfigurativeness [*Gegenständlichkeit und Ungegenständlichkeit*]. Valéry's idea of painting, which he develops by the example of Leonardo, is certainly bound up with the object-like figurativeness of the painting, but this figurativeness is secondary and instrumental in relation to a nonfigurativeness, which in the artist is primarily present as the colors' disposition on the surface. Only secondarily does he use objects as a vehicle of this disposition, so that the "induction"[70] of the object-like thing leads back to the elementary structure of color that is restored in the viewer, just as—as Valéry puts it in a marginal note in the same passage—a piece of poetry finally finds its denouement in being read "musically."[71] Although the ateleology of nature justifies the artist in not adhering to the bindingness of its stock, and instead to make use of it for a new order, Valéry seems to assume a teleology of a different type, which conceives of the world as not only disposed to this servitude but, according to Mallarmé, whom Valéry quotes, also as urging toward being expressed. This has nothing to do with the statement that nature tends toward being imitated or represented. Valéry tellingly uses this Mallarmé quote in a passage in which he speaks of Leonardo's excessive notion of painting, which he sees as the "the final goal" of a universal spirit's efforts.[72] The idea of an original nature more or less amounts to subtracting man and his creations from the total stock of reality, to think him away from this total stock and to afford the contradiction of a "view" of things without the eye. But "nature" is as much

---

70. Valéry, "Method of Leonardo," 46.

71. Valéry, 47.

72. Paul Valéry, "Leonardo and the Philosophers," in *Leonardo Poe Mallarmé*, 143.

a linguistic hypostatization as "the world." In this instance, thought has already freed itself from the autonomous powers of language and has paralyzed the immanently linguistic "realities." The expression "nature" is of just this kind, Valéry believes: "It's becoming a mere sound with no thought behind it. All these words seem more and more to be—just words."[73] He, the opponent of infinitism, joins ancient metaphysics in understanding the infinite as the indeterminate and nonexistent, and thus ascribes pure nominality to a universe that is "no longer any whole or center."[74] According to another note by Valéry in the *Choses Tues*, the fact that we nevertheless have the experience of reality of a natural world with which we are confronted—which endures alongside us and against us—is due to the resistance the things put up to our cognition. If no remnant of the enigmatic were ever left to be deciphered, then a completely illuminated universe would have no more permanence than an unveiled swindle (*une escroquerie dévoilée*) or the trick of a magician (*un tour prestidigitateur*) whose secret has been found out (II 506). The reality of the world is based on the resistance man meets, and the correlate of this resistance is the effort in which he measures himself. To this general concept of the relation of man and world belongs, as the outstanding special case, the work of the artist. This basic schema dominates the aesthetics of Valéry, it makes itself felt everywhere in his linguistic preferences, especially in his decisive rejection of the idea of inspiration that places the ease and obviousness of the artwork, which has been developed but not perfected, back at the origin of his conception, and thus before the conscious and accomplished part of the author. In the ease of what has become, the burden of its becoming pays off. Here, further light shines on the *objet ambigu*: its reality lies in the insurmountability of its ambiguity, in the unanswered questions that it takes back into the sea and that yet remain urgently close to Socrates going inland. But at the same time, this is also the description of the aesthetic work's character of reality; it condenses the enigma the world sets against man anyway, but its impenetrability is no longer in any re-

---

73. Valéry, *Rhumbs*, 190.
74. Paul Valéry, "Bad Thoughts and Not So Bad," *Analects*, 376.

lation to man's necessities of life. His reality does not need to be dissolved as a foreign and thus dangerous quantity; rather, one can let this reality be, resting in itself, because this is the mystery that man presents and assigns to himself. Unlike the scientist's hypothesis, the work of art seeks not to dissolve the riddle of the given, but to substitute the human for foreign indissolubility, to put the pleasing, enjoyable indissolubility of the human work—whose character of reality as resistance is thus equivalent to the given but lacks the sting of theoretical unrest—in place of the agonizing indeterminacy of what is encountered from an inscrutable source. The interpretation of the work of art will therefore always be satisfied with a solution that is not the dissolution of the given but may leave conscious the indeterminacy of other possibilities, while the scientist's theoretical hypothesis is burdened with the possibility of other, surpassing solutions, of which none can, however, definitively rule out that their verification may fail. The specific difference between aesthetic work and theoretical achievement is located in this aspect, while both have their generic identity in the structure of the "transaction." The thematically fixed objecthood therefore is the work of art's weakness; the thought must be hidden in the poem as the nutrients in the fruit that may be nourishing but only offers itself as enjoyment, so that one only feels pleasure while in fact taking in substance.[75]

Here, too, we can recognize the reason why in the letter to Duhamel cited above Valéry considers it necessary to correct traditional literary criticism by means of the principle that it is inadmissible to make conclusions from the mood of the work to its situation of origin. Valéry summarizes his self-observation that took place in the creation of *The Young Fate*: "Il n'y avait aucune sérénité en moi. Je pense donc que la sérénité de l'œuvre ne démontre pas la sérénité de l'être. . . . Sur ces questions, toute la critique littéraire me semble à réformer" [There was no serenity in me. I therefore think that the serenity of the work does not demonstrate the serenity of being. . . . On these questions, all of literary criticism seems to me to be in need of reform] (*L* 181). The poem's formal weightlessness is an aesthetic

---

75. Paul Valéry, "Literature," *Hudson Review* 2, no. 4 (1950): 539.

effect that is valid for the reader's perspective and produces the essential illusion of completion, but it is not normative for the author's self-observation, who experiences his work as unfinished and the resistance as unbroken, and for whom no work can complete the challenging and affirmation of the self. Again, on the creation of *The Young Fate*, Valéry writes to Albert Mockel (1917, *L* 122–125) that the real benefit he had gained from this work was the "observations sur moi-même prises pendant le travail" [observations about myself made during the work]. A poetics of aesthetic production will therefore have to look very different from a poetics of aesthetic reception, without one excluding the other or invalidating it by contradiction; one will, in any case, have to ask about every statement to which of the two poetics it belongs. It is, then, not true that the viewer, spectator, or reader would have to repeat the very actions the author has taken, or should feel put into his situation and mood. The reader cannot share the author's experiences; the author's self-observation may gain more from the unsuccessful attempt to cope with the conditions of the work than from mastering them successfully—the reader obtains no immediate gain from such shipwrecks of the poet. In the draft of a letter to a friend intended for publication (1926; *L* 160f.), Valéry deliberately confronts the standpoint of the admiring reader of his verses with what these verses mean to him. Once again rejecting the mythology of inspiration, he goes back to the self-observation of the laboring poet, to "ces efforts de poète contre les étroites conditions que je m'étais données" [these poetic efforts against the narrow conditions that I had given myself], to the "problèmes sans issue" [dead-end problems], and describes the poet's brain as a seabed on which lies the wreckage of many a poem that was shipwrecked by a trifle. Precisely these are the affairs of the spirit, he writes, and the observer learns more about them in defeat than in success, because consciousness and the experience of resistance are inseparable: "Ce qui se fait facilement se fait sans nous" [What is easily done can be done without us].

That which has objecthood appears as an aesthetic temptation that tends to set the conditions for its realization by itself; against this, the "narrow conditions" of form should keep the object from reaching the full presentation of its determinateness, but should push it back into that indeterminacy that allows the ambiguity of the merely aesthetic "object" to persist.[76] The rhyme most clearly demonstrates the indifference between object and form; it pushes the object out of the poem's dominant foreground, precisely by making its externality palpable: "Rhyme constitutes a law independent of the subject and is comparable to an external clockwork."[77] It is, Valéry says, the great benefit of the rhyme that it offends the simpleminded who, in their naïveté, believe that there is something more important under the sun than a convention, and who, just as naively, believe a thought could have greater depth and duration than any convention—and for that very reason, rhyme offers aesthetic enjoyment.[78] Elsewhere, Valéry does not hesitate to explain this fact through a probability statement: if one starts from a fixed notion, it is much less probable to find a rhyme that fits it than if one starts from the rhyme and seeks a fitting literary "idea"—all poetry is founded on this fact, and in particular the poetry of the period between 1860 and 1880 (II 582). After all, this is the theory that underlies the aesthetic meaning of the *objet ambigu*. The aesthetic object

---

76. Valéry brought the whole complex described into contact with formulas for the indeterminacy of that which has objecthood long before the *Eupalinos*, such as "une étrange substance" [a strange substance] in the important note of the *Cahier B 1910* (II 592), the "objet vague" [vague object], which is the presupposition of invention and its self-experience ("j'invente, donc je suis" [I invent, therefore I am]) (II 594). The emphasis on the hyletic aspect and the "travail contre ce hasard" [the work against chance] is directed against the "unbearable idea" of poetic inspiration (II 681), which implies that what costs nothing is the most valuable (II 550), that is, against the acheiropoieton as the boundary notion of the aesthetic conception. That the indeterminate and formless—as opposed to the human and authentic language estranged from things—could be, so to speak, the language of things themselves, things not yet "objectified," comes to light in a nice passage in a letter to Madame Gide, in which he reports on his son Claude's first experiments at producing sounds: "Il commence à tenir des discours informes. Mais cela me connaît. L'informe est ma partie. Lui, l'enfant, profère tout d'abord ce que je cherche si souvent, tuant la phrase, cassant le mot, évoquant le babil même des organes, c'est-à-dire des . . . choses!" [He begins to give shapeless speeches. But that I know. The shapeless is my subject. He, the child, first utters what I am looking for so often, killing the sentence, breaking the word, evoking the very babbling of organs, that is to say . . . things!] (December 26, 1903; GV 402).

77. Valéry, "Literature," 543.

78. Valéry, 543.

does not possess the determinateness of a point, but rather the potentiality of a horizon. As poetic language relinquishes its firm attachment to objects and frees its intentionality from the full determination of these objects, indeed, as language in the final analysis contradicts itself and shatters its referential function, it becomes thing-like itself—even the *objet ambigu* that does not push man away from itself and to other, more authentic things. In *The Nature of Things*, Francis Ponge imagined language as a shell-like casing excreted by man. He thus took up the image of the *objet ambigu* by envisioning that after the extinction of our species, these empty shells would end up in the hands of other beings who look at them just as we look at shells on the seashore. We, however, are denied the chance to regard the linguistic shells as things unknown in their meaning—as Socrates considered the *objet ambigu*; to let ourselves encounter our speech shells as unknown things, we need to destroy the words' use function, their objective meaning-value [*Bedeutungswert*], so that the words—still according to Ponge— become things: produced by us but not comprehensible to us. This ontology of the aesthetic object, which surrenders the criterion of the appropriateness of form to content and of language to that which is signified thereby, in doing so also forfeits its ability to rule on the question of the completion of the aesthetic work. "Instability" [*Unbeständigkeit*] essentially belongs to the aesthetic judgment, which, qua judgment, is constantly resisting the legitimate aesthetic illusion of perfection and compares the factual (as the in each case latest) state of the work with its possible final state. The statement that a work is completed fails because of its essential indeterminacy [*Unbestimmtheit*].[79] This is related to the fact that the author is no more competent to evaluate and judge his work than the reader; the author judges, observes and controls only the process in which the work is produced, but not that work itself, as if it is only the telos of the process (this reminds us again of the architect Eupalinos). "When the work has appeared, its interpretation by the author has no more validity than any other by anyone else."[80]

---

79. Valéry, 544.
80. Valéry, 547.

IV.

I would now like to try one final approach to the *objet ambigu*, taking as a cue a remark found in the second Leonardo essay of 1919.[81] Here, Valéry speaks of a substantial difference between the artist and the philosopher; the artist's sense of wonder related not to the fact that anything exists at all, but that the things are as they are and not different. It should be noted that these sentences are preceded by a discussion of the necessary incomprehensibility of death for consciousness.[82] The consideration of *absolute* contingency, of the possible nonexistence of the world, appears here as an alternative without any meaning and from which nothing can be inferred. But the *relative* contingency that the world might be different than it is, implies, as Valéry puts it, "the secret of inventors,"[83] and that means that the "pattern [*figure*] of this world"[84] can be regarded as arbitrary and surpassable. The metaphysical radicalism of Leibniz's question: *cur aliquid potius quam nihil* [why something should come to exist rather than nothing][85] is pushed aside; but similarly, the question of why this and no other world exists is not asked to prove its sufficient reason, but in the sole interest of legitimizing the claim of art to leave the factual world aside and turn to the unrealized. Amazed by the facticity of the world, consciousness perceives its own freedom. What, for philosophy, must negatively tend toward the rational annoyance at its limitation in asking for grounds becomes, for aesthetics, a positive impulse and justification of its will to regard nature as that which is merely given. This freedom is based on the nature of consciousness as a formalism, as a system of variables that can factually be occupied; consciousness assures itself that things might be different from what they are, without

---

81. Valéry, "Note and Digression," 93.
82. Valéry, 91.
83. Valéry, 93.
84. Valéry, 93.
85. [Gottfried Wilhelm Leibniz, "On the Radical Origination of Things," in *Philosophical Papers and Letters*, ed. Leroy E. Loemker (Dordrecht: Kluwer, 1989), 487.]

itself having to be otherwise than it is.[86] The body and the world appear to it therefore as almost arbitrary restrictions on its function. Art and technology are based on the fact that the event "world" is essentially material, and the event "consciousness," essentially formal. Consciousness represents a "surplus" over the needs of the factually given world, a surplus that as such can be, and actually is, formulated and represented in art. Art is the reflection of consciousness in its transcendence of the world and its autonomy from it. Therein lies the precedence of the formal in art; it does not vary facticity but reflects possibility itself. The *objet ambigu* now is an object that cannot be accommodated in the factual world, and that eludes classifiability and identifiability. It is potentially aesthetic because it does not represent a "restriction,"[87] but already appears to be in the process of breaking it. Socrates, who has not yet converted to Anti-Socrates, throws this doubtful object into the sea, because he does not and cannot know anything of the world's facticity, since for him there can only be the world that actually exists; because of that, he has to reject the *objet ambigu*'s transcendent character, which he cannot bring to language. At the same time, it becomes clear what is actually enjoyable in aesthetic enjoyment. The aesthetic-receptive subject does not enjoy the object as such and no specific aspect of it; rather, the subject enjoys, through the object or by way of it, its own not-being-constrained by the factual world, its freedom toward the "given." The aesthetic object, considered from the perspective of the world, is the improbable; considered from the perspective of consciousness, it is (given the possible's indeterminacy compared to reality's finitude) pure probability, whose absence always puts the factual under the unbearable suspicion of being necessary.[88]

Translated by Hannes Bajohr

---

86. Valéry, "Note and Digression," 94.

87. [Valéry, 94.]

88. The present work is the first of a four-part study of Valéry, which will also consist of the chapters "Leonardo," "Faust," and "Monsieur Teste." I owe essential insights to a seminar on Valéry's poetics that was held in the summer of 1962 together with my colleague at Gießen, Hans Robert Jauß.

16

THE ESSENTIAL AMBIGUITY
OF THE AESTHETIC OBJECT

(1966)

The predicament of any theory of art is captured in the truism that there is no accounting for taste. But why not? Because it is always assumed that a dispute over definite—that is, definable—objects can only be meaningful when its outcome can take the form of that object's univocal determination. Aesthetics, therefore, always seeks to escape its dilemma by setting theoretical objectivation as a model—a model that, even if unreachable, may still be approximated. This is what Kant did when he saw the subjective universality of aesthetic judgment as the only way to save the reference to the aesthetic object from becoming a completely nonbinding relation of absolute

---

Originally published as "Die essentielle Vieldeutigkeit des ästhetischen Gegenstands," in *Kritik und Metaphysik. Heinz Heimsoeth zum achtzigsten Geburtstag*, ed. Friedrich Kaulbach and Joachim Ritter (Berlin: de Gruyter, 1966), 174–179; from Hans Blumenberg, *Ästhetische und metaphorologische Schriften*, ed. Anselm Haverkamp (Frankfurt am Main: Suhrkamp, 2001), 112–119.

individuality. Every philosophy of art must share this basic intention; the question is only whether Kant's is the only possible way.

Is it really the case that aesthetic subjectivity only and primarily belongs to the subject? Or is the aesthetic object itself essentially ambiguous, in the sense that this ambiguity makes its aesthetic function possible, rather than deficient in comparison to the theoretical object? In fact, ambiguity is the indicator through which the objecthood [*Gegenständlichkeit*] of the aesthetic proves itself. It is by no means obvious that a work created by a poet or artist must possess its own aesthetic objecthood. This is of course not meant to denote the kind of physical, spatial-temporal objectivity [*Objektivität*] that allows me to grab hold of a painting and carry it away, to analyze chemically the primer and the paints, or to check its measurements. In fact, such a work can also have a purely mediating or referential meaning, a meaning that is not itself immediately object-like [*gegenständlich*]. For example, it can recall certain situations that may be encountered in nature or within one's inner world of experience, or, as has often been said, make visible or highlight something that, while visible in principle, is still unseen; or the function of the work can consist of communicating thoughts, to convey them more clearly or impressively by supplying them with an intuitive model.

But it is an entirely different matter when a modern author claims that the poet must never utter a thought, but rather an object; that is to say, he must let the thought itself take on the stance of an object. This does not mean, however, that the thought is simply translated into a medium that is suitably intuitive, from which it can be extracted again at any time and returned to its original identity—that is, by another subject. Rather, it means that the thought has definitively and irreversibly become an object, that it will mean something different and personal to each recipient, and that it has fallen from the univocity of its origin into the ambiguity of a history that is immanent to it.

It is precisely by neutralizing everything that is cognitive, semantic, and intentional that the aesthetic object stakes its absolute claim to focus the subject's referential attention onto itself and to contain it for good, so that it does not refer to anything further. Perhaps the example of allegory demonstrates this best. A contemporary playwright jots down the following idea: "Guests sit in a pension, and then a group of bricklayers appears and gradually walls up the windows and finally the doors. None of the guests . . . will leave the room. At first they ignore what is happening, then they grow uncomfortable, then they try to find it funny, then they panic, and in the end they seem to be paralyzed. I imagined the bricklayers as harmless and jovial, but unswerving. They would tell the guests that they are on assignment from the absent landlord."[1] At first glance, one is inclined to call this an allegory, but upon examination it turns out to be missing a feature of the classic allegory, namely, that it always knows what it represents, that its referential nexus claims to be univocal by way of this prior knowledge, and that the process of understanding may not rest until this univocal reference has been uncovered or apprehended. The modern allegory of the type I have cited neither presumes the abstract formulation of any specific content nor does it tend toward being comprehended in such a way. There must always remain the possibility of its being deciphered, but it cannot be realized; or rather, any interpretation may—indeed, must—allow for ambiguity, that is, the fact that it cannot be corrected through another, more self-evident one. The modern playwright continues: "I could be confident that there were a number of answers to the question: 'Who or what are the bricklayers?' Once you have found such a model situation, you don't need to think too hard about it. Others will do that. . . . It wouldn't be any different even if I had decided upon a certain interpretation."[2] This type of allegory is therefore not a fiction that stands in for a predetermined or underlying meaning for which it serves as a vehicle, making it more accessible, profound, legible, portable. Instead, this allegory claims for itself the characteristics of an ultimate givenness, which, though it always provokes interpretations, also deflates them, because they can interfere with and supersede each other—it leaves them in abeyance, neutralizes them, does not allow them to become definitive. The givenness of the object, an object that was originally

---

1. [Dieter Wellershoff, *Anni Nabels Boxschau* (Cologne: Kiepenheuer und Witsch, 1962), 34.]
2. [Wellershoff, *Anni Nabels Boxschau*, 35.]

a sign for something other than itself, changes into that other thing's mode of givenness. It becomes reified and gains an inner consistency that allows it to be apprehended from different perspectives; it offers aspects that indicate a pole of givenness. The realization of these aspects, that is to say, their execution, could in any case be called "commentary." They possess meaning of the kind that generates the consciousness of reality only and specifically in their plurality, in the potentiality of their implications. This abundance's copresence immediately disappears once one of these possibilities is no longer realized aesthetically but theoretically, and carried out to the degree of complete explication. From that emerges the paradoxical state of affairs of modern art—not only in the visual arts but also in, for example, poetry (Eliot, *The Waste Land*; Ezra Pound, *Cantos*)—that its products practically cry out for commentary, but that any commentary has a destructive effect on these products' mode of reality. This paradox is symptomatic of how essential the aesthetic object's ambiguity is.

Since Balzac, the novel has been able to incorporate perspectivism into its narrative arsenal, in its system of representation—limiting the reader, however, to whatever perspective is brought into play. In poetry or in a work of visual art, this kind of perspectivism is, as it were, projected into the space around the work as a web of assignable variables.

If we go another step back from our example of allegory, we hit upon a theory of imagination [*Phantasie*] that is no longer at its core creative, but rather moves as an organ in the space of the encounterable—a space that is neither identical to the space of empirical reality nor connected to the domain of what is called the ideal, which is traditionally quite foreign to the imagination. The products of imagination themselves acquire the character of objectivity, of a solidity that strikes even the subject imagining them as surprising. This gives the ambiguity of the aesthetic object the very sanction necessary to keep ambiguity from being taken for a lack of commitment and clarity on the part of someone who has looked too little, seen too little, and has done a poor job of describing what was created. Thus, even though imagination, specifically in the modern age, has been discovered and defined as creative and inventive, it seems to experience something presenting itself to it as soon as it takes on a certain attitude. It is easy to see that we will not get very far with the classic difference between the subjective and the objective. Instead, that which would have to be called subjective to the highest degree takes on the characteristics of objectivity because it is no longer under the control and the willful determination of its very producer.

This objective facticity in the space of imagination at least allows for the convention that this space is intersubjectively accessible, and that the identity of the subject—which has entered and had experiences in it—is arbitrary. A modern poet addresses the reader in the foreword to his selected poems: "If in the following pages there is some successful verse or other, may the reader forgive me the audacity of having written it before him. We are all one; our inconsequential minds are much alike, and circumstances so influence us that it is something of an accident that you are the reader and I the writer—the unsure, ardent writer—of my verses."[3] The coincidence of the allocation of writer and reader rests precisely on the alleged independence of the work from the subjectivity of its author: they are not invented, but rather found; they have the inner necessity of their being-this-and-nothing-else. They lie, as it were, by the wayside, and it is a matter of pure contingency who finds them there. They are just as foreign or familiar to the subject of the reader as to that of the author. This convention, that is to say, fiction, offers the possibility of the recipient's relation to the aesthetic object being just as authentic and having just as much hope of successful interpretation, as the author's. Their places are interchangeable. The author apologizes for appropriating these objects and claiming them as his own. He is not rhetorically professing modesty, but makes a well-considered attempt to heighten his aesthetic products' degree of reality through the fiction of intersubjectivity, the fiction that their positions can be interchanged. The difference between the aesthetics of production and the aesthetics of reception shall be discarded. Aesthetic interpretation abandons not only the psychological question of what the author intended with his work;

---

3. [Jorge Luis Borges, *Selected Poems, 1923–1967* (London: Penguin, 1972), 291.]

it also departs from the historically objectified approach. The latter would put the author's will in relation to the horizon of what could have been expected from a recipient of his work—in other words, what the author *could have* intended with it. The will of the author, understood as univocally determined, is from the very start inadequate to the essential ambiguity and indeterminacy of that which exists as an aesthetically appealing object. Even the romantic idea of the artwork's self-sublation [*Selbstaufhebung*] (through the implication that only a critic congenial to it ultimately realizes the artwork) inevitably highlights, even mystifies the aesthetics of reception in the strictest sense. For here, the critic becomes the naturally chosen exponent of a public whose ability to be universal is no longer credible, because the special aesthetic status of the genius has been transposed from the sphere of production into that of reception. But the genius of reception brings about the contradiction of multiple absolute integrations, each of which can claim legitimacy through its genius. The ambiguity of the aesthetic object runs counter to this system.

One could argue that such a notion is contradicted by the phenomenon that linear perspective has been neutralized in modern painting. Quite the contrary: this process confirms precisely that the technical determination of the spectator's point of view, chosen by the artist, is a nuisance to be eliminated. The inclusion of a plurality as the simultaneity of aspects into the picture itself (Picasso), and likewise the ruptured structure of anticipation in sculpture (Archipenko, Moore), confirm that the aesthetic object should no longer force the viewer's choice of interpretive standpoint, but should rather leave it open, and that it, exactly because of this, condenses into a new degree of reality. The disdain for generating illusion, which was connected to the technique of linear perspective and with satisfying typical anticipations of space, rests on a dismissal of the sacrifice made when the aesthetic work becomes the terminus, the absolute point of reference of the aesthetic relation. Modern painting and modern sculpture do not wish to be instruction manuals for illusions, making something else visible; they want to be that, and nothing but that, which they present themselves to be.

To return to where we started: the plurality of aesthetic interpretations is not a form of failure of the envisaged attitude and reception; rather, it seems to be the only form in which an expression of "taste" makes any sense at all. One could only believe that "taste" exists as an aesthetic relation to the object that develops in isolation—as a sphere, enclosed within a particular individuality, in which aesthetic judgments can be formulated—if one presumed that a person's individuality is a set of properties independent from whether he enters into exchange, comparison, and opposition with other people. Yet strictly speaking, there is no such thing as an aesthetic "judgment" in the sense of the isolated finality of this logical category. One formulates aesthetic experience indeed only in order to compete with others, to assert oneself against others—not primarily to claim the "correctness" of one's own position, but rather to forge a pluralistic assurance of the object's relevance. That taste can be communicated is really the basic form of its "universality." Discussion of taste seems futile if one understands its ideal and goal to be the objective identity of a result, as in the practice of theory. The "possible exchange" (Valéry) is the meaning of any aesthetic claim.[4] The moment this claim becomes an opinion shared by all possible partners in this exchange, it not only loses its intersubjective meaning but also deflates its object into a "settled matter."

Today we have an aesthetic pluralism in the dimension of time—aesthetic historicism—through which it is self-evident to us that taste undergoes historical transformations, and that each transformed judgment is founded on and legitimized within its respective horizon of meaning. However, we have no system to account for the simultaneous plurality of the relation to the aesthetic object. That is, there is no justification of this condition, which is for the most part tolerated with a "guilty conscience." The aesthetic object cannot be overlooked, and this is its actual "quality." Aesthetic experience cannot sidestep it, just as certain experiences cannot be elided in empirical reality. One might call that acute urgency, ineluctable relevance, or however one might like to call it. In any case, the compulsion to enter into the horizon of potential aesthetic responses is the essential criterion of aesthetic objectuality.

---

4. [Paul Valéry, *Rhumbs*, in *Analects* (Princeton, NJ: Princeton University Press, 1971), 185. Translation modified.]

In his dialogue *Eupalinos*, Paul Valéry illustrates this point through the fateful role of the *objet ambigu* [ambiguous object] that Socrates finds at the seashore.[5] Pondering this memory in Hades as he reflects on his life, Socrates becomes aware of an ambiguity, and he now realizes that his inattention to it rendered his choice of a philosopher's life disagreeably contingent. This "most ambiguous object imaginable"[6] is indeed a product of Nature. However, subjected to an obvious variety of influencing factors over an endless amount of time in the zone between sea and land, its form achieved the paradoxical status of a perfect indeterminacy—something that an artist, even at the height of an enormous effort, struggles to approach. This givenness resists traditional ontology, which since antiquity has had to assume that an object's origin can always be determined as natural or artificial, and from the start regarded the artificial as secondary to the natural. Only in a nature whose fundamental forces were able to be determined as evolution and erosion, the paradox of expected surprise in the face of the never-before-seen determines one's attitude. It finds its complement on the side of art through the fundamental concepts of invention and construction. The Socrates of Valéry's dialogue does not arrive at an aesthetic attitude toward the *objet ambigu* because he insists on the question, definition, and classification of the object—thereby deciding to become a philosopher. The aesthetic attitude lets the indeterminacy stand, it achieves the pleasure specific to it by relinquishing theoretical curiosity, which in the end demands and must demand univocity in the determination of its objects. The aesthetic attitude accomplishes less because it tolerates more and lets the object be strong on its own rather than letting it be absorbed by the questions posed to it in its objectivation.

Translated by Hannes Bajohr and Julia Pelta Feldman

---

5. [See Hans Blumenberg, "Socrates and the *objet ambigu*: Paul Valéry's Discussion of the Ontology of the Aesthetic Object and its Tradition," in this volume.]

6. [Paul Valéry, *Eupalinos*, in *Dialogues* (Princeton, NJ: Princeton University Press, 1971), 110.]

17

SPEECH SITUATION AND IMMANENT POETICS

(1966)

Literary superstitions. I give this name to all beliefs having the common trait that they overlook the *verbal* condition of literature.[1]

— PAUL VALÉRY

Semper mens est potentior quam sint verba [The mind is always more powerful than words] (Matteo Mattesilano).[2] This core tenet

---

Originally published as "Sprachsituation und immanente Poetik," in *Immanente Ästhetik—Ästhetische Reflexion: Lyrik als Paradigma der Moderne (Poetik und Hermeneutik II)*, ed. Wolfgang Iser (Munich: Fink, 1966); from Hans Blumenberg, *Ästhetische und metaphorologische Schriften*, ed. Anselm Haverkamp (Frankfurt am Main: Suhrkamp, 2001), 120–135.

1. [Paul Valéry, *Analects* (vol. 14, *Collected Works*), trans. Stuart Gilbert (Princeton, NJ: Princeton University Press, 1970), 124.]

2. [The source for the quoted expression is unclear; it can, however, be found in another work, not by Mattesilano but by Constantius Rogerius, *Tractatus de juris interpretatione* (Lyon: Frères Roxio, 1549), 14.]

of any extensive interpretation of the law could also be put forward as the condition of the possibility of any hermeneutics. The claim that thought is richer in its possibilities than language protects the legal exegete from the charge of analogy by leaving wide open the identity frame of the rule *eadem ratio, eadem lex* [the same reason, the same law]. For a concept of hermeneutics more broadly conceived, the claim that there is an essential surplus of thought beyond language retains the option at least to believe in the vitality of historical processes—unattainable though they may be—despite the historical inertia of the means of expression. The fundamental experience of a "poverty of language" demands that it be interpreted. Cicero felt the *egestas verborum* [poverty of words] of his own—compared to the Greek, philosophically indisposed—language and was probably the first to articulate that at the very least not every language is capable of capturing to the same extent what thought may be able to achieve. But could not the same be said for the situation of language vis-à-vis thought in general? Mystics of all epochs desperately suffered from the scarcity of linguistic means in relation to what they believed they saw. But it was also emerging historical experience that became aware of the poverty of language and of its own failure to capture those "total impressions" that presented themselves or were demanded, and that language could at best approximate by "tangents" (Justus Möser).[3] This lagging of language behind perception has been a persistent topos in rhetoric and poetics ever since. It has been employed often but almost never believed. Hermeneutics takes as its starting point this basic experience, tries to overcome the difference that has become noticeable in it, and attempts "to feel oneself outward toward the author."[4] This operation intends to uncover the web of references in which the thought that can be formulated in language is connected to other thoughts,

---

3. [Justus Möser, "Also soll der handelnde Teil der Menschen nicht wie der spekulierende erzogen werden," in *Sämtliche Werke*, ed. Ludwig Schirmeyer (Oldenburg: Stalling, 1954), 7:27; Justus Möser, "Über das Kunstgefühl: Von einem Weinhändler," in *Sämtliche Werke*, 7:18.]

4. [Justus Möser, "Wie man zu einem guten Vortrage seiner Empfindungen gelange," in *Sämtliche Werke*, 11.]

premises, and consequences, which cannot possibly enter the linguistic expression but can be partially inferred from it.

This conception of "language" with its implicit incongruence of thinking and speaking—for which, however, thought is always mightier than speech—meets its firmest contradiction in the idea of an exact language, whose criteria were laid down no later than in the prescriptions of clarity and distinctness canonized by Descartes. Their teleology of complete objectification ushered in a new and emphatic revival in phenomenology. According to this phenomenological faith in language, there is a "universality of the coincidence between speech and thinking,"[5] and the "faithful expression of clear data" does not even require an artificial or formal language. There is a transition from common to phenomenological language: "The words used may derive from the common language; they may be ambiguous and their changing senses may be vague," but they can be "furnished with distinct and single significations."[6]

However, to the two concepts of "language" just outlined we can add a third, which downright reverses the juridical principle of interpretation quoted at the beginning by declaring language mightier than thought. In the modern philosophy of language, the complaint that the word is insufficient when faced with the claims of thought seems to have been retracted in favor of the opposite conclusion: that thought can only follow the anticipation [*Vorgriff*] of language, doing so always inappropriately vis-à-vis a depth of meaning that is unfathomable.[7] Language appears as the untranscendable background phenomenon par excellence and its grammar as the imperceptible as well as tyrannical canalization of all processes, in the broadest sense, by which we engage with reality; at the same time, however, we harbor the illusion that we are equipped with a plastic medium for the measurement of the given, which, while not

---

5. Edmund Husserl, *Formal and Transcendental Logic*, trans. Dorion Cairns (The Hague: Nijhoff, 1969), 24.

6. Edmund Husserl, *Ideas Pertaining to a Pure Phenomenology and to a Phenomenological Philosophy*, trans. Fred Kersten, (The Hague: Nijhoff, 1983), 1:§66, 151–152.

7. See, for example, Louis Lavelle, *La parole et l'écriture* (Paris: L'Artisan du Livre, 1942).

perfect, is perpetually getting closer to perfection. Benjamin Lee Whorf spoke of a "linguistic relativity principle" and saw the basic achievement of any language in facilitating certain factual conceptual systems, to which others can be added on equal footing, although not always ones of comparable capability. The implication is, "'Talk' ought to be a more noble and dignified word than 'think.'"[8] If, however, language in this way preforms the latitude of what is possible and impossible for thought, the critical task of philosophy must be methodically to reveal and dismantle the excess of language beyond real, verifiable, and justifiable thought—that is, to practice the kind of linguistic analysis and linguistic critique that continues to shape the face of contemporary philosophy.

These three basic ideas of the relationship between language and thought should help us gain a certain orientation to determine the function of poetic language. After all, an immanent poetics will by necessity depend on examining the function of a work's language. The explication of the immanent poetics of a work will therefore depend on asking the "right" questions with regard to this work's language. Of course, hints can be derived from the author's exogenous poetics, from his self-testimony and self-observation, if this is indeed what they are and not simply the "offshoot" of a normative theory of art. This methodical preliminary question deserves not to be passed over. Already the classification of a text by its author as "self-observation" during the process of aesthetic production expresses a certain aesthetic position. This position permits experience to provide relevant information about the process of a work's emergence; it does not know beforehand, as if by a preliminary decision, that this process happens in a certain manner that is empirically inaccessible. Someone struck by lightning—and be it merely the lightning of inspiration—cannot simultaneously take the minutes of this event or, rather, he is quite certain that he cannot do so without necessarily contradicting his own presumption. To disclose self-observations thus presupposes that it is possible in the first place to occupy the observation position at the same time as the produc-

---

8. Benjamin Lee Whorf, *Language, Thought, Reality* (Cambridge, MA: MIT Press, 1956), 214, 220.

tion position; this is a presupposition of aesthetic objectification incompatible with the expectation of inspiring factors, from the muses up to narcotics. The mere presence of texts their author would like to have classified as self-observations independent of questions of their credibility and exactitude is therefore already a fact of an immanent poetics related to an oeuvre [*Gesamtwerk*]. This does not, of course, preclude that the self-observing authors who believe themselves to be capable of empiricism have their own exogenous poetics, and it is not unimportant to search their poetic works and poetic texts for any inconsistencies between their normative and effective elements. A text's ability to be corrected—at first regardless of whether this question can be historically solved by looking at the manuscript materials or even at the printing history of a work—is a guiding thread to an immanent poetics, which can differ starkly from the position the very same author has taken regarding the alternative of inspiration or perspiration, that is, regarding what I want to call metaphysical poetics.

Among the primary observations (and self-observations) that need to be stated explicitly counts what is addressed by the question of how "language speaks itself" [*wie sich die Sprache spricht*]. Differentiations like that between a language type that is strongly associative or strongly constructive belong here. But even association, for example, which without a doubt is one of the motoric factors of poetic language formation is not homogenous. It can act from the background, conducting the process of language formation from the kernel of a concealed notion, or it can keep this process moving from the foreground, from word to word, in the realm of sound, most palpable in the leading schema of the rhyme. This last distinction is not unimportant, for it determines what the language is thought "to be capable of," whether one abandons oneself to it as the leading constitutive ground or whether one sees oneself confronted with it as material to be overcome, as resistance to be overpowered. There are many different degrees of and reasons for trust in language. Trust in language need not be connected with the preliminary decision for inspiration; it need not mean that one has to listen to the appeal of "being" that acts not *within* language but itself *is* language. This is only the shape and premise of the modern critique of language that has been reversed positively, which none-theless assumes the supremacy of language over thought, only with the difference that it, as it were, prohibits "listening" and strives to exorcise its appeal as a type of bedevilment, that is, to "enlighten" it. No, confidence in a language that speaks itself can dedicate itself to the pure musicality of the ever-continuing procreation of linguistic formation, whereby the language that speaks itself all too easily evades the question about what is thought or imagined in it; thus, even the author's "authentic" interpretation is worth as much and as little as that of anybody else. There are strokes of luck: the titles of Paul Klee's paintings are almost always, even if they come after the image construction or the pictorial association, inventively placed viewpoints, despite the obvious danger of treating them as authentic interpretations. I deliberately chose something outside of the realm of language to show that there are structural analogies to how a work of art can be interrogated immanently.

The question, extracted above, for a text's implicit concept of language must certainly not amount to a static classification. Linguistic implementations have an immanent tendency that cannot be grasped within a framework that captures the relationships of congruence between thought and speech. I would like to describe this tendency by naming the two directions, "univocity" [*Eindeutigkeit*] and "equivocity" [*Vieldeutigkeit*]. This does not require us to ask for an expressly stated program. The language of science, independent of any presumptive considerations, tends toward the univocal designation of concepts, and this tendency can be captured no matter whether one can attest a text such univocity or not. It is also unessential whether scientific language is formed from ordinary language or whether a new nomenclature is invented and introduced by way of convention. The maxim of univocity is already in place through the peculiar mode of scientific communication, which barely allows inquiries or requests for clarification as would be the case in dialogue. The dialogue in ordinary language is able to waive the tendency toward the univocity of its linguistic means; indeed, it achieves clarity precisely by the interference of unclarities. But the tendency of scientific language comes at the cost of its breadth and universality: scientific language only ever exists as a plurality, as the embodiment of technical languages that are exclusive regional idioms, strongly isolated by a sociological factor that makes any translation into ordinary language be felt as a "disciplinary transgression." The linguistic situation of the present is largely determined by its tendency toward univocity within its regionalization, or rather, at the cost of regionalization and thus being reduced to the mere function of transmission. The belief that through logical idealization—which proceeds from the existence of such technical languages—the tendency toward univocity may be converted into a rational common language of at least all the sciences amongst each other, will turn out to be an illusion.

Philosophical language takes a special position in this consideration. I would like to refer to its tendency as being aimed at a "controlled ambiguity" [*kontrollierte Mehrdeutigkeit*]. I cannot elaborate this further here, but this tendency is based on taking into service mundane language for the designation of transcendental concepts, for a specifically transcendental language can obviously not exist, just as the illusion of a language proper to philosophy has melted away since the late Wittgenstein. This phenomenon has a prehistory in the language problems of negative theology and mysticism, with an interesting transition in Nicholas of Cusa and his linguistic efforts that were as authentic as they were in vain. It is first clearly present in the two registers of Leibniz's *Nouveaux Essais*, which speak of the monad by keeping silent about it for the sake of the linguistic community with Locke. In the present, albeit on an even higher level of reflection, there seems to be a repetition of what had characterized the late Middle Ages: the seemingly paradoxical coincidence of two intellectual currents that in the medieval case are called "nominalism" and "mysticism." What they have in common may be described as a certain type of cognitive attention, which at first wants to submit itself to the economy of the sayable, but subsequently becomes aware of how narrow the realm of such precision is and then seeks to evade this disappointment by escaping into the paradoxes of the unsayable. But it is only within this space—between the idealized programming of language to contain the sayable, and the explosion of the linguistic structure in favor of the unsayable—that the actual breadth of the achievements of speech unfolds as an interpretive community's perpetually recalibrating, highly unstable regulatory system.

Where in this space can we place poetic language? Once it was possible to believe that it was the actual *Ursprache* [primordial language] of an early age that expressed itself in "poetic characters" and "fantastic speech."[9] Then, poetry appeared as the laboriously salvaged leftover element of a decay into prose that was only occasionally stalled or made transparent. The premise is not radically different if poetry is portrayed as the selection and collection of specific elements dispersed in language that want to be understood and gleaned. The linguistic situation I described as unfolding between univocity and equivocity allows a different view of the poetic possibilities of language. Suppose language is a potential of equivocity that requires an effort to keep it in service in narrow spheres of necessary informative univocity and that already in dialogue only works by way of the vagueness of idioms that have to become attuned to each other and are "indicative" precisely in mutually going wide off the mark. In this case, poetic language would mean precisely to set free language's immanent tendency toward the multiplicity of meaning. But this eruption of equivocity salvages neither a remainder of that mysterious *Ursprache* nor that alleged wealth of quotidian language that in reality is vague rather than actualizing equivocity and that has a certain "tolerance" with regard to its function. In this question, mistakes are plentiful. Valéry, in his notes from 1928, gave a kind of substantialist interpretation of poetic language under the title of "Pure Poetry."[10] Purity here is understood as the selection of specific poetic elements that, in different combinations and transpositions, are contained in all other linguistic works. This "noble and living substance" can be enriched, developed, and cultivated.[11] Poetry's purity then means that linguistic state in which the originally dominant medium of the common language is no longer traceable, not even as an irritating impurity—a

---

9. [Giambattista Vico, *The New Science*, trans. Thomas G. Bergin and Max H. Fisch (Ithaca, NY: Cornell University Press, 1948) 19, 115.]

10. Paul Valéry, "Pure Poetry," in *The Art of Poetry* (vol. 7, *Collected Works*), trans. Denise Folliot (Princeton, NJ: Princeton University Press, 1958), 184–192.

11. [Valéry, "Pure Poetry," 185.]

goal that is admittedly unattainable, and which, according to Valéry, the art of poetry can only approximate. The basic notion applies regardless of this concession that pure poetry is a fiction, albeit an empirically obtained fiction, that emerges from an observation of language. This basic notion is expressed in the sentence that what is called a poem "is in practice composed of fragments of pure poetry."[12] It is unlikely that poetic elements occur in language since language is "a common and practical element,"[13] a crude set of instruments adapted to quotidian and individual needs. To poeticize language is thus to accumulate a rare material within it: "So the poet's problem must be to draw from this practical instrument the means to realize an essentially nonpractical work."[14] We do not follow here this thought of a specific difference between poetic and nonpoetic elements in language, and thus reject conceiving of poetry as the extraction of a given, rare substance from language. By describing poeticization as a tendency of language, we do not comprehend the poetic moment as an inherent quality, as the result of a possible selection, but as a gain of language that is only possible and only realizes itself within the functional nexus of the poetic entity. The tendency toward poeticization is not aimed at the discovery of given meanings, no matter how root-like, the understanding of which would be the job of a poetic quasi-linguistics; rather, it is aimed at the production of new tendencies of meaning. This is very neatly illustrated in the fact that the expressive assets of specialized regional languages are imported into modern poetic texts, or that historically and philologically indexed and sedimented material can be dispersed within it. The most banal word from everyday language joins the most hallowed metaphysical term, and it is impossible to say to which the actual poetic effect can be attributed (for example, Gottfried Benn's "großer Run der Äonen" [the eons' great run]).[15] This, too, would be a question that can be posed meaningfully

---

12. [Valéry, 185.]
13. [Valéry, 188.]
14. [Valéry, 189. Emphasis removed.]
15. [Gottfried Benn, "Chaos," in *Sämtliche Gedichte* (Stuttgart: Klett-Cotta, 1998), 78.—The substantive "run" as a stock trading term is a relatively recent import into the German language.]

only within the framework of the substantialist theory of poetic language.

The aesthetic effect of language's tendency toward equivocity is, initially, the surprise at the familiar, the bare means gaining a value in itself, the obvious stepping outside the sphere of the "life-world" that as such goes unnoticed. In other words, nothing is "regained" that in some process of decay was historically lost but, at a specific time, could have existed in a primordial presence as a mythical elementary experience that might be restored. Rather, poeticization indeed entails novelty; it has a first-time aspect. The process of poeticization to which language is subjected can therefore be compared to the process of theoretical objectification [*Vergegenständlichung*], which likewise takes place in an elemental way—that what is obvious becomes problematic, and here, too, something steps out of the horizon of the "life-world." Whether this commonality of the theoretical and aesthetic attitude can be assigned to a more comprehensive theory of consciousness is not at issue here. What is, however, certain is that the aesthetic function of language as such constitutes a new degree of the awareness of its quotidian performance and its possibilities.

But the process of dismantling common language's obviousness [*Entselbstverständlichung der Gemeinsprache*] that happens in all poetry and has, as it were, become programmatic in modern poetry (and is free to be utilized toward the pretentious as much as the magical), is not yet a complete description of the aesthetic function of language. In the tendency toward equivocity something happens that could be called a "boundary event" [*Grenzereignis*]. The point is reached at which language fails to serve its semantic function. I will not claim that this boundary event constitutes the pinnacle of language's aesthetic possibilities, but how close to peril this boundary event brings language essentially determines the aesthetic appeal of poetic speech. In this state of imperilment, the attention devoted to language—its attempts to exhaust the latitude of meaning and to interrogate the multiplicity of the possible as to whether it harmonizes with its context—threatens to become meaningless. Poetic language guides coperformance [*Mitvollzug*] down a similar path as mysticism did by means of "explosive metaphorics"[16]: the horizon of information, communication [*Mitteilung*], and instruction is shattered, and it is no longer designation and meaning that language is primarily expected to accomplish. If one were to take a typologizing and classifying approach, one would not be far from making imperilment itself the norm and seeing the goal of the poetic tendency of language in pure nonsense, in Dada. But here, as everywhere, the aesthetic allure lies in the approximation to the turning point toward impossibility and self-negation—in the *approximation*, I say, not in the identification with this extreme. To put it another way: hermeneutic belief and credibility remain aesthetic enjoyment's conditions of possibility. To perform the aesthetic requires going along, following the guideline of the semantic context to certain points of irritation and bifurcation of meaning. And here, too, aesthetic meaning is not exploded into transcendence or left to nothingness, as in all kinds of mysticisms, but, on the contrary, this meaning-expectation is diverted from the referencing function of the word and reoriented toward the objecthood of the linguistic-pictorial presence itself. But I must stress here that "objecthood" does not mean the word's mere phonetic materiality.

In the process of poeticization, then, language is not restored to a supposed primordial state, selected for its secret treasures, or revirginized. Instead, we start from language's constantly critical functional status. Without a doubt, the conscious seizing and escalating of this possibility is something entirely modern that may be connected to a crisis of language, which, in turn, is itself merely a depiction of the acute state of a chronic set of problems that might be linked to the great and exhausted concept of "historicity" [*Geschichtlichkeit*]. History as an ominous, oppressive experience is a modern phenomenon. Connected to it is the circumstance that language is experienced indirectly (that is, by way of the semantic claims it is confronted with) as a contingent fact. Thus, early modernity has for the first time made obvious the indifference of the information toward the word: from the seventeenth century onward, the natural

---

16. [See Hans Blumenberg, *Paradigms for a Metaphorology*, trans. Robert Savage (Ithaca, NY: Cornell University Press, 2010), 122–126.]

sciences retreated from representational words into numbers and formulae; likewise, music retreated from vocality into pure instrumentality. The autonomy obtained by these two formal, paralinguistic spheres has had a strong effect on the understanding of language's possibilities. It also played a substantial role for the postulated ideal notion of a "purity" of language—not only and not primarily in aesthetic matters. Since the middle of the nineteenth century, the notion of an absoluteness of music as idea and as fascination hovers constantly over the attempts at a self-definition of poetry and the poets: music appears as that which is not a medium, but is in itself fully engaging; it does not channel attention through itself toward something else; it is not a "theme-indicator" but a "thematic end" (Husserl).[17] The ideality of music can be such a great temptation because its analogical value is easily forgotten, and this regulative notion is prone to misinterpretation as the demand to transform the poetic word into pure sound. In fact, however, the poetic word remains but word and does not dissolve into sound in a linear fashion; it stays behind the threshold of rescinding its semantic function, which lies between equivocity and the meaninglessly undecipherable. Pure obscurity would also be the end of "obscure" poetry as poetry.

The high degree of language's imperilment in the process of its poeticization is unmistakable especially in the exemplary problem of the relationship between poetry and music. By approximating music, language ceases to be a reference to anything else and begins to signify only itself. But such substantializing can also mean that language changes into the most banal tintinnabulation, into homespun sound patterns or clichés, that is, as pure surface it not so much "condenses" as closes itself off. The poet's attitude, as again Valéry has it, is a kind of *matérialisme verbal* [verbal materialism]; he can look down on philosophers and novelists who are subjected to language since for them, it achieves any reference to reality only through its content. For the poet, on the other hand, it is true that "the reality of a discourse is only the words and the forms."[18] But

---

17.   [Husserl, *Formal and Transcendental Logic*, 27, 250.]
18.   [Paul Valéry, "A Poet's Notebook," in *The Art of Poetry*, 183.]

why, indeed, is language's reference to reality so irritating, and of what does the new "reality" consist that language itself achieves in poetry? The acceptance of reducing the referential characteristics to pure linguistic materiality, writes Valéry, no longer provides any criterion by which to distinguish self-meaning from meaninglessness. In contrast to this, what I have attempted here was to describe this process not as a reduction to the pure phenomenality of language but as an intensification of the equivocity that is its inner tendency. In "Memoirs of a Poem" from 1937, Valéry explained his preference for ornament in the broadest sense and pure music—in other words, the freedom from having meaning—by the fact that here the bond to the factual was undone.[19] In music, in the invention of the musical work, an entirety of possibilities is present at any moment, and this not only without a depicting and reproductive relation to a pre-given reality but also and primarily without limiting what is still possible by what has already been realized. With good reason, Valéry has called this attitude, which revolves around the programmatic term *possibilité*, an antihistorical state of mind.[20] It is not by chance that the common thread running through his thinking about "pure poetry" is the irritation at the *factum*: not just the fact of nature and the pre-given world but also the fact of the pre-given language—that is, pre-given with a distinct arsenal of meaning—and the irreversibility of any mental process enacted through language, in which every presence finds its possibilities limited through that which has already been spoken. Musical formations do not create any such irreversibilities; they are, at every moment, in possession of all their possibilities. This is why "construction" is one of Valéry's favorite words, and not so much as a notion aimed against the organic but rather pointed against the historical. What is fascinating about music for the poet is the purity of the constant presence of an unbounded horizon of possibilities. In one passage, in which Valéry expressly engages in polemics against Proust's *In Search of Lost Time*, rejecting memory as the organ of the factual and thus the epic, he imagines the plan for a work that

---

19. [Paul Valéry, "Memoirs of a Poem," in *The Art of Poetry*, 100–132.]
20. [Valéry, "Memoirs of a Poem," 110.]

would have as its object the nodal points of the possible, the "possible at each moment"—and exactly at this point Valéry adds the remark that he had published different texts of the same poem, including some which had been contradictory.[21] Valéry describes as the epitome of poetic self-experience a mental state of unfettered freedom, which has, vis-à-vis some fascinating object, gained the feeling of a latitude in which the object has returned from its current and completely determined reality into the state of possibility. Pre-given, historically developed language appears to Valéry again and again as a web of bonds and limitations for pure thought; thus, the relationship of the poet to language must for him be determined by the fact that he also restores language into a state of pure possibility and thus makes it into a medium of poetic freedom. From here, setting free language's tendency toward equivocity is revealed as the correlate of the aesthetic restoration of the real into the horizon of its possibilities. The equivocity of poetic language conveys an awareness of aesthetic freedom itself. Language provides the "starting point" for intentional acts—in poetic language, however, such starting points are, as it were, compressed and can thus not initiate specific directions of understanding, but only create a certain sensitivity. Gottfried Benn speaks of a "latent existence" of words in poetry, only to add immediately the banality of "magic" and "last mystery." Why "magic," why "mystery"? It would be easier to say why "Phaiakians, megaliths, Lernaean domains, Astarte, Geta, Heraclitus"—examples Benn gives himself, "admittedly names, admittedly in part created by myself; but when they approach, they multiply"—have their effect even without, no, especially without, this commentary that is meant to add a historical pseudoreassurance. Elsewhere, Benn says, "Words convey more than the message or the content; they are on the one hand spirit, but on the other have the essence and ambiguity of things in nature."[22] This analogy with objecthood is important: where the word fails as an instruction for intuition; where it dispatches onto more than one path of a vaguely

---

21. [Valéry, 104.]

22. Gottfried Benn, "Probleme der Lyrik," in *Gesammelte Werke*, ed. Dieter Wellershoff (Wiesbaden: Limes, 1960), 1:513–514.

developing beginning of an intuition; where it shows many paths that cannot at the same time be taken—there it becomes charged with an anticipation that cannot be executed and brought to fulfillment. Precisely as such, however, as the horizon of unfulfilled intentions, it makes the experiencing subject aware of itself, turning it away from the quotidian speech situation of the objectivated and yet-to-be objectivated word and toward its own omnipotence of imagination.

An immanent poetics will not be able to avoid understanding the poetic quality of the available language from the opposition against the normalization tendency of language today. The frustration of the normal or standardized anticipation is itself a poetic means. It expels the recipient from his attitude of the fluid understanding of language, which always assumes, demands, and deems possible to claim univocity, and which is not bothered by the constant disappointment of this claim in everyday communication, and indeed does not need to be. The resistance of aesthetic language must therefore be all the more massive the more the public language consciousness finds its true or a supposed confirmation in its claim to univocity. It would be difficult to deny that the tendency of language in a world that is becoming increasingly scientific has at least the appearance of confirming the claim to univocity. This is not only true for the world in which science and technology are pursued but also, and especially, for the world in which philology and aesthetics have their place and business. The tendencies of objectivizing and poeticizing language, which point at essentially and immanently opposite directions, will therefore, as one may assume even before perusing concrete evidence, become exacerbated in this sphere. One may expect a poetic language that is vehemently obstinate against any function of reference; a language whose metaphors disturb and negate each other; in which the imagery employed does not resolve itself; which does not allow for any reassuring interpretation of its syntax; in which the original horizons of mythical allusions change constantly and without any aid; in which even a public accustomed to reading rather than speaking is forced to see printed language-images for which it lacks the phonetic equivalents; and where the educated reader all too often does not know, and cannot even guess, from where an "ingredient" might have been taken (I am thinking, for instance, of Ezra Pound); where, in other words, the most fully equipped arsenal of erudition cannot yield any reassurance. It is nearly impossible to define the limits of what the aesthetically receptive consciousness can be expected to put up with. Many examples of such poetry will retain their meaning only as fossils of a specific aesthetic and linguistic situation.

The oppositional quality of poetic language, which can be understood from the speech situation, is, however, not enough to constitute poetry—as if what is elementary only needed to be turned into a presentable form secondarily. Quite the contrary: equivocity is an atomizing, destructive determination; it is a condition but not a constructive factor of poetry. The necessary connection between any oppositional quality and a positive formal determination has been articulated most felicitously, I believe, again by Valéry, who was always flirting with mathematical categories in "A Poet's Notebook" from 1928: a poem's content of pure poetry consists, in the end, in the "apparent and convincing probability in the production of the improbable."[23] The "probability of the improbable" is the logical structural formula of the aesthetic object. Even though for language, too, disorder is the statistically most probable state, as such the tendency toward equivocity does not mean increasing probability and disorder, but rather that kind of loss of linguistic meaning in which univocity is simply that which remains in the end. Poetic language's wealth of meaning is the *improbable*. But as such this is not yet an aesthetic quality; quite to the contrary: in isolation, it reverts to a pure signaling quality. The composition [*Gestaltung*] within which it appears as an element binds it to a *probability* that is unexpected from the perspective of the elementary—in the most fortuitous case, it binds it to self-evidence. What has been taken out of the lifeworld's obviousness and is brought to surprising novelty in its constellation still integrates a context that constantly justifies itself through a new and compelling obviousness. The formal means for such consistency of the inconsistent, *the probability from the improbable*, are well known. Valéry has drawn particular attention to

---

23. Paul Valéry, "A Poet's Notebook," 180.

the much-derided rhyme and, in a note in the *Cahier B* (1924), connected it to his ideas about probability by saying that one had a better chance of finding an idea to match a given rhyme than to find a rhyme for an idea—and it is on this state of affairs that all poetry rests, especially the poetry of the epoch from 1860 to 1880. This is a highly characteristic remark that recurs in different variations, as in the depiction of how a poem originated during a walk from the automatically appearing rhythms of walking, which Valéry took to be an empty form asking to be filled.[24] If one wanted to renew the schema of form and content, one now would have to start from the appropriateness of the content for the form, but this is quite unnecessary, since the equivocity of poetic language itself is a "formal" characteristic. There are formal determinations of different levels; by them alone, the "probability of the improbable" makes possible the criterion of the aesthetic object in its totality. What an "aesthetic stimulus" is—as the countervalue to aesthetic sensitivity—remains a reliable question of immanent poetics, but it does not allow the further premise that the aesthetic object as such is constituted by a summation of aesthetic stimuli. The aesthetic stimulus depends on increasing the elementary equivocity by way of the complexity of constellations and inductions of meaning; but for the constitution of the aesthetic object, this improbability is countered in the substructure by a contrastive "and yet" of formal integration, coping with what is close to being semantically excluded. The poem is spoken on a different linguistic level than its constitutive linguistic elements, each of which has to satisfy the maxim of linguistic poeticization: "We wait for the unexpected word."[25] But the poem is then still realized only as the unexpected fulfillment of an expectation that is, in its process, doubting [*zweifelnd*], but not desperate [*verzweifelt*].

Translated by Hannes Bajohr

---

24. Paul Valéry, "Poetry and Abstract Thought," in *The Art of Poetry*, 61.
25. Valéry, "A Poet's Notebook," 174.

PART IV

FABLES, ANECDOTES, AND THE NOVEL

18

THE ABSOLUTE FATHER

(1952/1953)

Only seldom do the intimate relics of a significant personality meet the expectations invested in them. All too often, what they finally reveal is the immense consumption of substance by which the great work, the lasting achievement, fed on the human substrate. Just as often, what emerges is how slight—at times banal, at times macabre— was the occasion that provided the spark to ignite the great blaze. What a disappointment, for instance, for the high-minded interpreters of Rilke now to learn from the recollections of his erstwhile lover that the poems to God in the *Book of Hours* originally were invocations of earthly love in which only the name was substituted!

Such experiences make us wary when trace upon trace of Franz Kafka's life is now brought to light—be it in its original form or as

Originally published as "Der absolute Vater," *Hochland* 45 (1952/53): 282–284; from Hans Blumenberg, *Schriften zur Literatur 1945–1958*, ed. Alexander Schmitz and Bernd Stiegler (Berlin: Suhrkamp, 2017), 109–114.

a replica cast in a friend's remembrance. But the consuming fire of this so quickly expired existence appears to have destroyed everything in and around itself that was not substantive and worthy of preservation—even though Max Brod, his friend and literary executor, could not fulfill the poet's last will to burn what had nonetheless remained.

Already in his biography of Franz Kafka, which first appeared in 1937, Brod prepared us, by means of hints and individual quotations, for a key document from that estate, the "Letter to My Father," written in November 1919, in which the thirty-six-year-old Kafka unfolds the central conflict of his life. In the years that have passed since Max Brod's first hints, the author of the novels *The Trial* and *The Castle* has become one of the focal points of the world's literary interest. Yet the pressure of curiosity about the background to this bewildering and disturbing oeuvre was unable to overcome the reticence of the estate's guardian, Max Brod; only now has he deemed the time right for the great document to be set before the public: S. Fischer's *Neue Rundschau* (in its second issue of 1952) has printed it in its entirety, and it will also be included in the forthcoming volume of Kafka's collected works.

This is indeed one of the essential documents of human existence as such! The postponement of its publication has as its fortuitous consequence that it can no longer fall victim to the by now receded wave of psychoanalytic fashion. How much has been stripped of its human validity and lowered into the shadowy realm of the abnormal by being all too rashly tagged with that school's vocabulary! However, the temptation remains to declare the overwhelmingly strong experience of his father that finds expression in this letter of Kafka's to be the nucleus around which his work condensed, even if Sigmund Freud's psychic underworld is not brought into play.

Let us try to recreate this relationship between father and son by means of a brief scene. A boyhood friend of Kafka's, Gustav Janouch, reports how after a walk with Franz the father is already standing at the door waiting: a colossal man, his very physical appearance oppressive, irresistible in his claim to dominance. "Franz.

Go home. The air is damp." The order, which brooks no objection, is issued in a booming voice. Franz whispers to his friend shyly: "My father. He is anxious about me. Love often wears the face of violence,"[1] and disappears into the house behind his father.

This father has all the properties assigned to anonymous powers in Kafka's novels and stories—the labyrinthine instances of the court in *The Trial*, the shady bureaucracy of *The Castle*. He is an "absolute" father, inaccessible in his distance, inescapable in his presence. Under his power, one can feel all otherwise reliable realities, as it were, "melt into air"; what remains is the awareness of an unfathomable nothingness. The son's efforts to assert himself against this father, indeed merely to be able to exist beside him, are as futile and hopeless as they are necessary. The "Letter to My Father" is the last of these attempts and at the same time the summary and account of all earlier ones. Kafka never delivered this quite respectful attempt at a reckoning to his father. That is almost symbolic: against this father there was no appeal.

But now a question arises that gives the letter a significance going beyond the personal, indeed beyond literary history: Is this image of his father, which the thirty-six-year-old Kafka sees before him in writing the letter, a faithful recollection of the real father of a childhood long past, or is it the father made larger than life, raised to the mythical realm? Does not this "huge man," "the measure of all things," he who does everything "almost for no reason at all," epitomize an awareness of the absolute and of being subjected to it in a way that can never emerge from the sphere of human realities? Can Kafka's oft-cited sense of transcendence be traced back to his experience of his father? In that case, it is a psychic phenomenon by which modern depth psychology may be troubled before compartmentalizing it. Or is not the reverse the case: that the experience of the father is possible and can be understood only on the basis of a deep-rooted awareness of transcendence? In that case, it is for us to ask how this transfiguration of the absolute can come

---

1. [Gustav Janouch, *Conversations with Kafka*, trans. Goronwy Rees (New York: New Directions, 1971), 24.]

about and what validity it is to be accorded with regard to our intellectual and spiritual situation.

Kafka originated from Prague's German Jewry, which, on the boundary between Western secularization and the ardent faith of the East, made the vain attempt to go along with the former while retaining the latter. He did not succeed in filling his primal awareness of the absolute with that world's religious ideas; it remained faceless, lacking a center, anonymous, spread like a leaden atmosphere over the landscape of this life. From an inner necessity, from the suffering caused by such anonymity, Kafka "occupied" the void of this godless religiosity, at first and then time and again with his father—who may of course have been eminently fit for that purpose—but later also with the images and symbols of his writings.

How little his father was the source and origin, how much he was only the embodiment and function of this outlook, is demonstrated by a little childhood episode to which the "Letter to My Father" alludes. A relatively harmless and, what is more, justified nocturnal punishment of the child is reflected thus: "Even years afterward I suffered from the tormenting fancy that the huge man, my father, the ultimate authority, would come almost for no reason at all and take me out of bed in the night and carry me out onto the *pavlatche* [balcony], and that consequently I meant absolutely nothing as far as he was concerned." The father, with his colossal stature, both represents and obstructs the center of a sense of life and the world, where once had stood the terrible majesty of the Old Testament God and which now was abandoned.

"Ever since I could think, I have had such profound anxieties about asserting my spiritual and intellectual existence that I was indifferent to everything else," Kafka writes to his father. In a world that is subject, without mercy or certainty, to nameless freedom, to the most playful omnipotence knowing neither law nor rule, the care for self-assertion permeates existence into its roots and substance. "But since there was nothing at all I was certain of, since I needed to be provided at every instant with a new confirmation of my existence, since nothing was in my very own, undoubted, sole possession, determined unequivocally only by me—in sober truth a disinherited son—naturally I became unsure even to the thing nearest to me, my own body." This confession suddenly casts a bright light on an elementary motif in Kafka's writing, finding its clearest expression in the famous story *The Metamorphosis*: the unsecuredness of the body, which in this grotesque vision alienates itself into an animal state, into a repulsive insect to which the human ego nevertheless remains bound.

Divisions such as this, between the ego and the body, recur throughout the world of Kafka's writing; they are but the consequences of a primal division that tears man and the absolute asunder unbridgeably—for Kafka: the son and the father. To him, the world is torn into three parts, as he argues against his father: "one in which I, the slave, lived under laws that had been invented only for me and which I could, I did not know why, never completely comply with; then a second world, which was infinitely remote from mine, in which you lived, concerned with government, with the issuing of orders and with the annoyance about their not being obeyed; and finally a third world where everybody else lived happily and free from orders and from having to obey." What is this "third world" that seems to stand outside the drama of transcendence and yet does so much to exacerbate that drama by adding an ideal image, illusory and unattainable of an indifferent absolute? This third world is that which is clearly detached from the process of salvation and damnation, the secularized sphere of the modern age's mere immanence, of one-dimensional temporality. It causes the pain of him who finds himself—by accident, arbitrarily, uncomprehended—exposed to the absolute. It creates the strangeness, the shamefulness of all that is implicated in the "process"[2] of transcendence, the loneliness and ridiculousness of the "select,"[3]

---

2. [*Prozess*, meaning both "process" and "trial."]

3. [*Die Herausgegriffenen*, literally "those picked out," a term that was not to be found in any of the German Bible translations I consulted. It may be that Blumenberg meant *die Herausgerufenen*, "those called forth," in the sense of the people called forth from Egypt by God, or of the lonely prophets. In the New Testament, the Greek ἐκκαλέω, "to call forth, summon," became ἐκκλησία, the gathering or congregation of those called and thus the Church. I am grateful to Judith Becker, Berlin, for suggesting this explanation.]

as the Old Testament calls the chosen and favored. This third world claims alone to be "the" world, "real" reality, and the shame, by which Kafka's figures are gripped, is nothing but the extreme of isolation within this "third world," that which is generally and for them, too, the only one that is recognized and taken seriously. But in the midst of this world of solid reality, which continues around them unperturbed, they are apprehended by the absolute, "arrested," become entangled in the trial, and are judged.

Kafka does not describe a religious world, but nor does he describe its exact opposite; he describes what is new and singular about a world that entirely fulfills itself in its immanence and sets itself as absolute, yet in which persists, in awful solitude, bearing the stigma of exclusion, the drama of being "chosen," of being "selected"—yet the dignity of these terms has become inverted, they signify torment, shame, guilt, humiliation. And this is what confronts Kafka, embodied in his father.

Kafka attempted two forms of self-assertion against this fate, against his father: writing and marriage—attempts at nonetheless taking root in that "third world." On his attempt to create a body of literary work, he himself passed judgment by ordering its destruction. His attempts at marriage—"the most grandiose and hopeful attempts at escape"—he believes to have failed due to the overweening power of his father, who, in this, his "very own domain," as head of the family and simply father, would have suffered no one beside him. Under often grotesque difficulties and misunderstandings of the kind found everywhere in Kafka's writing, he thus failed at what to him was "the utmost a human being can succeed in doing at all." Before the absolute in this transfiguration, his father, the effort "to crawl to a clean little spot on Earth where the sun sometimes shines and one can warm oneself a little" was hopeless. The paternal colossus covers the entire habitable earth, leaving his son only the realm of the uncanny[4] in which to exist. That is more than a real father can ever "mean"; it is the sphere of Prometheus, Sisyphus, Atlas, and Tantalus. In the son's consciousness, from an unsatisfied longing for the absolute, this father grows to be balefully

---

4. [*Das Unheimliche*, literally "the unhomely."]

larger than life, lending his name the anonymous, his face to that which lacks a countenance.

What is happening here is not accidental. The fate of an epoch whose relation with the absolute seems no longer able to find fulfillment in its traditional forms has here found exemplary human expression. Where otherwise the void of the absolute is "occupied" with political, aesthetic, erotic symbols, here the "huge man" acts as a placeholder for transcendence. And it is surely no coincidence that, after all, the name of the "father," which already in the remotest past was fused with the name of God to form the epitome of trust in the absolute, should now, amid the crisis of that trust, fall to the terrible anonymity of nothingness.

Translated by Joe Paul Kroll[5]

5. Quotations from "Letter to My Father": Translated by Ernst Kaiser and Eithne Wilkins; revised by Arthur S. Wensinger. Copyright Schocken Books Inc.

19

THE *MYTHOS* AND *ETHOS* OF AMERICA
IN THE WORK OF WILLIAM FAULKNER

(1958)

In his novel *L'Adultera*, Theodor Fontane introduces young Ebene-zer Rubehn, who will go on to destroy the marriage of Melanie van der Straaten, with the remark: "There is an *American* self-confidence about him."[1] The significant undertone this description carries to the reader of today can hardly have been intended by the author in the year 1882: what we hear is something more than the carefree bra-zenness and self-assurance of the visitor from the New World; we have a sense of the encroaching inevitability and destiny that "Amer-icanness" has taken on for us. The future that has already begun

Originally published as "Mythos und Ethos Amerikas im Werk William Faulkners," *Hochland* 50 (1957/58): 234–250; from Hans Blumenberg, *Schriften zur Literatur 1945–1958*, ed. Alexander Schmitz and Bernd Stiegler (Berlin: Suhrkamp, 2017), 265–286.
    1. ["Er hat etwas *amerikanisch* Sicheres." Theodor Fontane, *L'Adultera* (1882), in *Werke in fünf Bänden* (Berlin/Weimar: Aufbau, 1986), 2:209. Blumenberg's em-phasis.]

there confronts us with the presumption of being *our* future, too. "America lives as we shall live tomorrow" (Thielicke)[2]—that is the unanimous tenor of our emissaries returning from beyond the Atlantic, that is the formula of the fascination which attracts all those to America who believe they have a part to play in our future. How the New World, *terra nova*, Europe's colony, became the "new world," the real utopia, the model for our future, would make one of the most important chapters in a history of contemporary European consciousness. May the individual, depending on his particular valuations, perceive more enticing or more threatening aspects— this difference only confirms the underlying sense of imminence and necessity that images of America evoke within us. Europe has yet to catch up on the inevitable, it is trailing behind in its politics, economy, technology, science, and way of life, which is to say, in the required course of history as a whole. It is in this mythical Americanism that the Old World's mixture of love and hatred for the New World is founded. The imaginations tied to the name of America are elements of a destiny [*fatum*], they are the future [*das Kommende*], just as Ebenezer Rubehn is the "man of the future" [*der kommende Mann*] in Fontane's novel. This mythical immensity stands in the way of our recognizing that America too has a history, whereas a rather more familiar idea is that it is the burden of *our* history and tradition that has left us "trailing behind" America. In this mythical force field, overcome by the very image of desires both splendid and fearsome, the European gaze is blind to the ethical and religious substratum of American history, indeed to its yet unfulfilled decisions. The manner in which the epic oeuvre of William Faulkner[3] is read and understood by us is but a paradigm

---

2. [Helmut Thielicke, "Amerika lebt, wie wir morgen leben," *Die Zeit*, no. 25, June 21, 1956.]

3. German translations are currently available for the following works: *The Sound and the Fury* (*Schall und Wahn*), *The Unvanquished* (*Die Unbesiegten*), *Go Down, Moses* (*Das verworfene Erbe*), *The Wild Palms* [*If I Forget Thee, Jerusalem*] (*Wilde Palmen und Der Strom*), *A Fable* (*Eine Legende*), *Requiem for a Nun* (*Requiem für eine Nonne*), all published by Scherz & Goverts, Stuttgart; *Pylon* (*Wendemarke*), *Absalom, Absalom!*, *Light in August* (*Licht im August*), published by Rowohlt, Hamburg; *Abendsonne* (Stories), published by Piper, Munich; *Spotted Horses* (story taken from *The Hamlet*), published as part of the Insel Library.

for such an obscured view of the freedom underlying history. Is his prose not full of descriptions of overwhelming and intractable fates, entangled and impenetrable, which make it all but inevitable to conclude freedom's meaninglessness from its futility? Is this America of Faulkner not altogether of the mythical kind, of the stuff of fate?

Greatness and Fate of the Pioneer Era

The destinies of Faulkner's characters are tightly interwoven with the primal stirrings from which the American world emerges, with the cosmogony of the continent. But the national glory of the pioneer generations conceals the guilt inherent in their foundational achievements: taking land and carving out property, establishing legislation and ordering society. As they advanced the frontiers of the human realm with tools and guns, with trains and sawmills, the wilderness—mythically embodied in the ruler figure of the old bear—was condemned to death; the free land was put up for purchase and the native reduced to a walk-on part in a sham trade, which laid a deceptive foundation of legitimacy. To master the oft-invoked "unlimited possibilities,"[4] they made everything capable of being put to service, realized, accounted. The reverse of the great founding deeds is the suffering of the innocent. Tragic, irredeemable debts were incurred, and Faulkner's basic idea is that they inevitably come due. Nobody can disclaim this inheritance to avoid the concomitant liabilities, but only few have the courage to assume the debt, to honor and repay it. Faulkner loves the figure of the boy who is the first to see and take on the burden of his fathers, who goes into the wilderness leaving his shotgun behind and ultimately sheds his watch and compass, too—the symbols of occupation by humans—in order once more to feel pure with regard to enslaved nature ("The Bear," 1942); the boy who is the first to break the

---

4. [*Das Land der unbegrenzten Möglichkeiten*—"the land of unlimited possibilities" (in distinction, perhaps, to the more businesslike "unlimited opportunity")—is a phrase used frequently in German as a synonym for the United States. It was coined by the writer Ludwig Max Goldberger in 1903 in a book of that title.]

blood-law of the mythic world (*The Unvanquished*, 1938); the boy who stands up in defense of the wrongly accused black man and fearlessly obtains the proof that saves him (*Intruder in the Dust*, 1948). As long, however, as the inherited debt is not recognized and assumed, it transforms itself into inexorable fate, the nemesis of immanent human self-destruction. It takes neither the fire from heaven nor the earth to open, only man himself, to fell man. "No wonder the ruined woods I used to know don't cry for retribution! he thought: The people who have destroyed it will accomplish its revenge" (*Go Down, Moses*, 1942).[5] Thomas Sutpen in *Absalom, Absalom!* (1936), a Faust of Faulkner's creation, in a frenzy of force wrests his plantation from nature, raises up a colossal building as a mark of his hubris, confronts nothingness as if to measure himself against the *creatio ex nihilo* [creation from nothingness]—but at the end, once again stands nothingness, not irrupted from outside, but burst forth from the innermost being of man himself.

It is from this perspective that Faulkner views the history of his country, the tragic rupture between North and South, supposedly mended in 1865, seeing above all the burning relevance of the "Negro problem," which forms the basso ostinato of all his novels. It is not true, as it is claimed again and again, that Faulkner's America is only that of the South, only a partial, not to say provincial, aspect of this many-faced continent. On the contrary, the central event of the Civil War, which secured the Union *politically*, to Faulkner is also the historical act by which *moral* integration was founded. This was accomplished by the Union of the North forcing upon the Confederacy of the South the political solution to a problem that could be resolved only in the realm of the human and the ethical, and in doing so accepted shared responsibility for its unredeemed continuation. This idea underlies Faulkner's much misunderstood position on the Negro problem, his objection to the juridical formalism by which the central authority tries to discharge its historically assumed responsibility. In *Intruder in the Dust*, this is expressed in what is an almost too theoretical clarity in the little lecture that the

---

5. [William Faulkner, *Go Down, Moses*, in *Novels 1942–1954* (New York: The Library of America, 1994), 269.]

uncle delivers to the young hero after the rescue of the black man accused of murder:

> I'm defending Lucas Beauchamp. I'm defending Sambo from the North and East and West—the outlanders who will fling him decades back not merely into injustice but into grief and agony and violence too by forcing on us the idea that man's injustice to man can be abolished overnight by police. Sambo will suffer it of course. . . . [H]e will even beat us there because he has the capacity to endure and survive but he will be thrown back decades and what he survives may not be worth having because by that time divided we may have lost America. . . . I only say that the injustice is ours, the South's. We must expiate and abolish it ourselves, alone and without help nor even (with thanks) advice. . . . Some things you must never stop refusing to bear. . . . Not for kudos and not for cash; your picture in the paper nor money in the bank either. Just to refuse to bear them. That it?[6]

There is a story of Faulkner's that allows the structure of his works to be seen as if in a model. "Dry September" is set in Faulkner's typical milieu of a small town in the American South. After two rainless months, an unbearable atmosphere weighs on the people. Pent-up rancor and leaden swelter form a fatefully combustible amalgam. An old maid's sexual jitters provide the spark, and a fatal rumor spreads like a fire in dry grass, "Something about Miss Minnie Cooper and a Negro." Nobody knows anything specific. Amid the close atmosphere, a suspicion condenses "in the vitiated air";[7] from a barbershop, a silent yet hasty band sets out to deliver justice, without any grounding in reality. "Facts, hell! . . . Happen? What the hell difference does it make?"[8] Ultimately, the death of an innocent man is the only "fact." The world in which this happens and can happen is a thoroughly deterministic one. Human beings are only the tools of an all-encompassing mechanical operation. It is a mythical event, pure fate, *evil* without *evil men*. Humans are particles of a natural process.

---

6. [William Faulkner, *Intruder in the Dust*, in *Novels 1942–1954* (New York: The Library of America, 1994), 437–439. Omissions by Blumenberg.]

7. [William Faulkner, "Dry September," in *Selected Short Stories of William Faulkner* (New York: Modern Library, 1993), 60.]

8. [Faulkner, "Dry September," 61, 63.]

Only one man is at hand to say the most improbable thing: "I cant let—."[9] Not an exceptional man, destined to offer resistance, no, "a man of middle age; a thin, sand-colored man with a mild face."[10] (Physiognomic remarks are rare accents in Faulkner.) This slight barber forces his way into the gang of men gone to get the black man and drag him out into the night, and it is him of all people whom the victim, putting up a ferocious fight, strikes in the face— and then he, too, joins in the beating of the bound man. Thus, only the victim remains free of guilt. For a moment, the anonymous frenzy has possessed itself of the barber, too. He too gets into the car that leaves for the execution. But then he comes to his senses. He throws himself out of the speeding car and returns, battered and resigned, to the town. The black man vanishes without a trace in the bottomless pits of an abandoned brick kiln. For a day, aging Minnie Cooper relished being the focus of a macabre curiosity. The men return to their petty bourgeois houses, where nobody can imagine them dealing with anything but realities. The waves of the quotidian wash over a death as if nothing had happened. Nothing *has* happened. Nothing *can* have happened.

All of Faulkner is contained in this novella: the implacable density of a sphere of mythic predicament, the way outward aggression cannot be distinguished from an inner ascendancy of fate, the role of the sexual impulse as the motor of catastrophe, and finally, the singularity and solitude of freedom in the tangle of deterministic processes. Faulkner's black characters stand in the midst of events like silent catalysts; once brought from beyond the seas by their masters for mute service, they have now entirely and in every sense become a "question" that is to be endured and answered, and be it with the futility of a mere "I cant let—." Thus, without pathos does Faulkner's America express itself, as the imperiled spark, as the effort, onerous to itself, to stem the tide. Faulkner's entire epic might, however, seem directed at forestalling the conclusion that the futility of this ethos should spell its senselessness and insignificance.

---

9. [Faulkner, 64. Original spelling retained.]
10. [Faulkner, 60.]

The Limit of the Novel as a Subject for the Novel

From the novel *The Sound and the Fury*, published in 1929, to *A Fable*, which appeared in 1954, Faulkner's oeuvre, its formal variety notwithstanding, is remarkably unified in its radical themes. The 1929 novel describes a family falling apart. Three Compson sons bear witness, as it were, on the reader's behalf. But they do not narrate; instead, the reader, as with James Joyce, whose *Ulysses* appeared in 1922, enters into the witnesses' stream of consciousness. This gives the reader access to something akin to a record of their inner experience, the way experience and remembrance are interwoven. It is thus with dismay that the reader perceives, after a few pages, that the "I" which unfolds before him resembles a mirror into which a stone has been thrown: the hundredfold splintering describes the dissolution of epic reality into atoms, admitting only of tentative and conjectural recombinations on the reader's part. It is as though the warp of time had been torn and the experiences strung upon it jumbled about. Seen through the inner world of a madman as a medium, the Compsons' son Ben, the disintegration of the family appears disintegrated in turn. The reader has no choice but to leave incomprehensible ciphers of horrific events standing. Any meaningful reading seeking to make sense of it must, upon the book's conclusion, return to its first part—what then takes place is a true miracle of the recreation of what seemed irreparably shattered, not just through the knowledge of actual events and the meaning of ciphers gained in the meantime, but through a deeper understanding of the figure of poor Ben, which upon first reading seems to present little more than an irritating technical complication in which the author may indeed fashionably have intended to outdo Joyce.

The second part takes us back to 1918, back by eighteen years, to the last day in the life of Quentin Compson, whose suicide in the evening of that day will put an end to all the hopes the family had placed in this heir. Quentin is broken by the fate of his all too beloved sister Caddy who, on account of a child she is expecting, is forced to marry a man to whom she is indifferent and is banished from the family. With cold rigor, the Compsons cleave to their code of honor, which has long lost its foundation in reality. How the Compsons are faring today (1928) emerges from the cynical frankness of the third witness, Jason Compson. Jason is a specimen of the perfect arranger of human affairs; with a speculator's quick wits he stands in the way of disaster. Again and again, his illusions confront the erratic reality of his mad brother, Ben. But he is dealt the final blow by the fate of the seventeen-year-old girl Quentin, banished Caddy's now grown-up daughter, raised by the Comptons. This last chance of the family, at least, Jason believes to be "in his hands." But Quentin, cursed with her mother's sensuality, throws herself away at an itinerant musician. Grotesquely tilting at the void, Jason chases after the runaway, not to save anything human, but because he knows that this is where his resistance to fate will be determined. On Easter morning, 1928, everything is at an end, as the law of tragedy demands. What is left to happen? Why does Faulkner not conclude the story here?

In the fourth part, Faulkner changes his descriptive technique and returns to the conventional narrative perspective, which sees figures and events "from outside." Only in demonstrating the significance of this change of style is it possible to comprehend the many-layered meaning of this mighty work of literature. Up to this point, the reader has been given no visual impression of the novel's characters; after all, he has been seeing *with* them, through their eyes, as it is were. Now the gaze takes a more distant perspective. From there, all of mad Ben's pathetic, emasculated bulk becomes visible, the family's *désastre* [disaster] made flesh, which perfect Jason wants out of the way. Nobody sees that this whimpering nuisance might just be *the* question and task that the Compsons have been set, a demand that can be met only with love. Was it not banished Caddy who had known this? When mad Ben stands at the fence of the nearby golf course and the players shout "Here, caddie" before hitting the ball, he whimpers, jolted by the aching memory of his sister. And yet there is someone else to whom all the Compsons' hollow pride means nothing, a figure who shoulders the misguided pretensions and who, even in the midst of disaster, carries on doing as usual what is needful: the old black woman Dilsey, the Compsons' housemaid. This Easter morning, she takes mad Ben by the hand and leads the white family's son to the black church. In the midst of the mythic tragedy, which all the others execute to the finish like puppets on strings, these two battered creatures represent the "left-over elements," the merest inkling of innocence and freedom. They constitute all the difference there is between the House of Atreus and the House of the Compsons, and it is far from incidental that the author should let this different manifest itself on *Easter morning*. That is when the mute fool sits in the black people's church: "In the midst of the voices and the hands Ben sat, rapt in [the preacher's] sweet blue gaze. Dilsey sat bolt upright beside, crying rigidly in the annealment and the blood of the remembered Lamb."[11] And when on the way home, with the lunatic by her hand, she keeps crying and is admonished by her daughter that people were already staring and they would soon pass by the white people, she replies: "I've seed de first en de last. . . . Never you mind me."[12]

Eighteen years earlier, this maid Dilsey had evoked in young Quentin, on the last day of his life, the following reflection: "They come into white people's lives like that in sudden sharp black trickles that isolate white facts for an instant in unarguable truth like under microscope; the rest of the time just voices that laugh when you see nothing to laugh at, tears when no reason for tears."[13] That is a keenly registering perception, but it is only the outward face of the truth that emerges at the story's end. Dilsey has seen the first and the last; she has seen more than the reader to whom is denied penetrating this person's innermost mysteries, becoming a participant in her seeing, as was the case with the other characters. Only now does the change in narrative technique become meaningful: in its resistance to the revealing clasp of description, it lets it be known that this one has remained whole, unharmed by the mythic twilight of the whites. In admitting to being excluded from this figure's interior, the narrator raises her above the function of a *witness* and makes her the *keeper* of the truth of what has happened. Faulkner has thus, seven years after *Ulysses*, given James Joyce's stylistic revolution a meaning that reveals and that its originator had barely seen: the epic technique of

---

11. [William Faulkner, *The Sound and the Fury* (New York: Vintage, 1990), 297.]
12. [Faulkner, *The Sound and the Fury*, 297.]
13. [Faulkner, 170.]

penetrating an experiencing subject is premised on the condition of that subject itself; it is not the author who breaks it open, but it is open to recording introspection because it is secretly already damaged, because the seal of its sovereignty has already been broken. In realizing his material, the writer comes up against a limit to his subtle analyzing. This limit is objectified in the shift in narrative technique. It is thus that form gives a voice to substance. The old black woman's "never you mind me" is a reprimand to the author as much as to the reader—a tough demand in the age of the dissecting psychological novel. Faulkner demonstrates that Joyce represents not just the radical culmination of this kind of novel, but also its peripeteia.

Directly after *The Sound and the Fury*, Faulkner wrote his most harrowing book, *Sanctuary*, which, however, could be published only in 1932 in a revised version. I shall try to recount what happens. Temple Drake, all but a child, inexperienced and credulous, goes for a drive with a feckless lad. The youth wrecks the car and cowardly abandons the girl in a remote saloon of doubtful repute. Here she falls victim to a man of virtually consummate malice and perversion. That grim night, this man—Popeye—shoots a fellow drinker who gets between him and the girl. The next day, he takes Temple to town, lodging the girl, who is mutely in thrall to him, in a brothel. For the murder in the bootleggers' house, the police arrest Lee Goodwin, an innocent man who is condemned to death because Temple, the only witness, found after a long search by the defending counsel Horace Benbow, perjures herself to protect her demon, Popeye. That villain, in turn, on the way to see his mother is arrested for a murder he did not commit and is sent to the gallows.

This book offers the most support to those interpreters of Faulkner who seek to prove his commitment to a gnostic dualism and find mysticism at each turn. Indeed, Popeye seems to lack nothing to *be* evil hypostasized. His macabre origin is revealed to us only in the final chapter. His mother had conceived him at the same time as she contracted an infection. From the beginning, he was deformed and retarded, sickly and impotent, a monster inside and out, the sheer mechanism of perverted compensations. Popeye is not a person; he is merely the product of biological and social circumstances. There is no spark of freedom within him. "His face just went away, like the face of a wax doll set too near a hot fire and forgotten."[14] His misdeeds are as brilliant as his knack for lighting matches with his thumbnail. That he should perish at the gallows not for the crimes he committed but for the one he did not is an irony apt to puzzle the reader. What does it mean? Is it meant to indicate that this spawn of evil is beyond the measure of earthly justice? Or is it not rather the sign of an immanent justice that Popeye should be made to die instead of another, just as Lee Goodwin was executed in his place? If, however, one brings to bear the fact that to Faulkner, innocent suffering contains man's most unfathomable truth and potential, indeed, signifies a stigma of its relation to the absolute, something like a metaphysical sacrament, then here too another surmise may be added to the interpretation: even this villain is not evil *as such*, for he proved innocent in one respect and suffered a death that he did not deserve uncomplainingly, in enigmatic silence—the sign of innocent suffering in a final, most distorted analogy, at the outermost fringe of hope, which even a poet would not dare to pronounce, let alone this one, who permits himself no cheap effects at the expense of mercy.

Horace Benbow, the attorney, lacks the stature to serve as Popeye's adversary. The mythic monster will not stand a figure to enter into play. Faulkner made this quite clear in the novel's composition: Benbow and Popeye meet just once, right at the beginning, at a spring in the woods close to the bootleggers' house, where Temple is soon to meet her fate. Benbow, drinking at the spring, catches the reflection of Popeye, who is watching him, and instantly grasps what is so inhuman, mechanical, and lacking in depth about the other: "His face had a queer, bloodless color, as though seen by electric light; against the sunny silence . . . he had that vicious depthless quality of stamped tin."[15] For two hours, the men abide there, each taking the other's measure across the spring. It is an afternoon in May, a bird calls. That is when Benbow says something that exposes the other: "And of course you dont know the name of it. . . . I dont

14. [William Faulkner, *Sanctuary*, in *Novels 1930–1935* (New York: The Library of America, 1985), 182.]
15. [Faulkner, *Sanctuary*, 181.]

suppose you'd know a bird at all, without it was sitting in a cage in a hotel lounge, or cost four dollars on a plate."[16] When an owl swoops close to the two of them, the unnatural one is grabbed by fear, he clings to Benbow (who now can literally smell him: "He smells black"[17]). Never again will such insecurity in Popeye be seen. But this scene lays him bare. After their encounter at the spring, the two men never meet again. They are not adversaries, but antipodes. The distance between them is such that no dialectic can emerge, not even physical struggle. To Popeye, the phenomenal shot, the gutless little man at his heels is not worth a bullet. And yet Benbow is the book's "hero," standing in for the human; he has no motto under which to place his deeds, he lacks the shine of the ideal. Only this dogged resistance he puts up against the world closest to him in order to do what he thinks to be right, though petty-bourgeois "society" may treat it with disapproval and suspicion, tells of the power of the ethical norm within him. Alas, he is not understood even by those he defends. Lee Goodwin's wife offers him what everybody has yet accepted if she had no other means of payment. "But cant you see," Goodwin replies, "that perhaps a man might do something just because he knew it was right . . . ?"[18] No, freedom is that which has always been misunderstood, that which is revealed to no experience. Everyone tries to muster commonplace motives to cover up the nuisance that is the exceptional. The free man cannot acquire faith, because one must believe in freedom *before* experiencing it. Anyone shattering what all believe to be certain is ground down until he returns to the commonplace. In the end, Horace Benbow is once again tired and resigned in his daily life to forget and make forgotten his dreadful excursion into the endeavor of freedom.

Twenty years later, Faulkner returned to the subject matter in his closet drama *Requiem for a Nun* (1951). The terrible destiny of *Sanctuary* has not yet been played out. "The past is never dead. It's not even past."[19] That is the very formula of myth! Although Stevens,

---

16. [Faulkner, 182. Original spelling retained.]

17. [Faulkner, 184.]

18. [Faulkner, 370.]

19. [William Faulkner, *Requiem for a Nun*, in *Novels 1942–1954* (New York: The Library of America, 1994), 535.]

the feckless lad who, years earlier, left Temple Drake to her doom, has meanwhile married the girl, this has only set the scene anew for fate. With grim determination, it sets about repeating itself; nothing and nobody seems able to put a stop to the mythic recurrence of the same—were it not for the black woman Nancy, the Stevens's nursery maid, who becomes an infanticide in order to make loud enough the scream that is supposed to bring Temple, sleepwalking into the abyss, back to her senses. She goes to scaffold herself, mute and steadfast. I must confess to bristling at this version of the idea of innocent suffering and the role of black people; I find it misguided and unfeasible. But its exaggerated speculativeness is only an overdyed specimen of Faulkner's central theme. More still than in *A Fable*, Faulkner here pits mysticism against myth. Also close to being mystical is the subliminal relation that Faulkner establishes between the dramatic episodes about Temple and Nancy, and the interspersed pieces of a history of the courthouse and jail of Jefferson, the (fictitious) capital of (fictitious) Yoknapatawpha County: by making Jefferson's jail and law court the site of Nancy's sacrifice, the turbulent prehistory of these buildings, which appear as representative institutions of the American world's formation, "fulfills itself" in a manner no longer accessible to reason. Only Faulkner's oeuvre in its entirety renders this communication comprehensible, but at the same time, a possible, indeed looming consequence becomes visible to which Faulkner seems to be drawn: the troubling consequence of an American mysticism as a means of overcoming the antagonism between *mythos* and *ethos*, as an attempt to give the "high . . . destiny of the United States"[20] an absolute sanction.

The Saga of the Technical Vampires

When an America in which our future has already begun is discussed, what is meant is a world whose aspect is determined by *technology*. It is almost to be expected that Faulkner should have

---

20. [William Faulkner, *Absalom, Absalom!* (New York: Vintage, 1990), 94. The omission of "(and impossible)" is not indicated by Blumenberg.]

given space in his work to this element of the American myth. The novel *Pylon* (1935) is set among stunt pilots and journalists. These two worlds interlock most precisely: the barnstormers provide the newspaper with headlines, often at the cost of a life, and the newspaper transforms mechanical data into stimulating matter for the consciousness of the masses who make the pilgrimage to the air shows. This is symbiosis of cold precision, which chills to the bone that which is natural in man. The only reaction a deadly crash evokes in the photographer is: "Jesus. . . . Why wasn't I standing right here[?]"[21] More than anything else, however, it is a warped Eros that Faulkner identifies as the distinctive phenomenon: it is as though it, too, had become a mechanical function in the sphere of the mechanisms. The barnstormer Roger Shuman and the parachutist Jack share a woman, a being of wordless camaraderie, who like them is in thrall to the machine and anxiously denies any traits of feminine nature like some irritating rudiment. This woman does not know which of the two men is the father of her child, as if this question were just so much ballast to be dropped. To be able to fly, human beings must make themselves "light" in every sense, as empty as their machines, whose streamlined, elegant shells contain only an illusion of "substance": "Unbonneted [the airplane] appeared more profoundly derelict than the halfeaten [*sic*] carcass of a deer come suddenly upon in a forest."[22] So too has the human figure become an illusion, its interiority and substance consumed. "They aint human, you see,"[23] thinks the reporter who joins the pilot group, he too under pressure to perform functionalized tasks, but with the melancholy of a man who has forgotten something crucial and seeks to find it in himself again.

The reporter helps Shuman to find a new airplane after a crash landing, but the machine is of doubtful reliability. Shuman nonetheless takes part in the race, because everything for him depends on the cash prize. The gamble costs him his life. The reporter finds

---

21. [William Faulkner, *Pylon*, in *Novels 1930–1935* (New York: The Library of America, 1985), 938.]

22. [Faulkner, *Pylon*, 787.]

23. [Faulkner, 805. Original spelling retained.]

himself suspected of having procured an unsafe machine for Shuman in order to free the woman for himself. The reporter senses the ambiguity of the situation and retreats. He borrows quite a large sum of money and hides the bills in a toy airplane, which he has someone give the child. The woman takes the child to the dead pilot's parents; she wants to stay with the parachutist, but the child is in their way. The old Shumans are kindly people, who want only their peace after having given their last for their son's to them incomprehensible technological passion and having ultimately lost him, too. Now, the unanswerable question breaks into their lives in the form of the child: "If I just knew that he is Roger's! If I just knew! Cant you give me some sign, some little sign? Any little sign?"[24] But the woman gives no answer; she stands dumbfounded by the eruptive force of a question that has become an irrelevance for her.

Now there follows a scene that is among Faulkner's most powerful. When the woman has left for good, the old man leans over the sleeping child's bed. He is looking for the sign, for certainty. He shakes the child, rouses him. Now the toy airplane falls to the ground. "Where's my new job? . . . Where's my ship?"[25] the child asks blithely in the jargon of the world in which he learned to talk. The old man is filled with blind rage, he grabs the toy, hurls it against the wall, stamps on it in manic fury, tries to tear it into pieces. The boy looks on silent, astonished, almost curious about the old man's act of impotent revenge, which strikes only at the image, the mere symbol of the world that took everything from him, that he regards as the mythical demonism over his life. Here, at this child's bedside, is suffered and endured the humanity that the perfect world of mechanisms has pushed aside. Once again, innocent suffering bears the burden that the others have cast off. The old man and the child, together they must—and without understanding each other—deal with the remnant they have been left with, the not yet germinated remnant of a world of progress. But if that were not enough: the destruction of the phantom inadvertently brings to light the money

---

24. [Faulkner, 988.]
25. [Faulkner, 989.]

that the reporter sent the child. Might this, as a token of the humane from the zone of the mechanical vampires, not bring the old man to his senses? But it leads only to the hatred being increased; the old Shumans end up persuading themselves that the concealed money was the ultimate proof of the depravity of the woman whose child fell to them: the fruits of her indiscriminate venality, kept secret from both men. When the bills have burned up in the fireplace, the old man cries out once more in despair: "It's our boy,"[26] and collapses.

Such is the futility of the heart's labors in the mythic sphere. The reporter has spent himself into the void, his aid stands defamed as a whore's hire. Yet this melancholy reporter in his desolate existence is *the* character in this novel in which Faulkner invests himself, indeed it is precisely this futility of his inept and secretive attempts at doing good that is the stigma, sought time and again, of a truth denied in the inevitability of reality. The reader feels the author's regard fixed upon him to see if he can withstand the crashing down of blind futility over the stirrings of the ethical and humane, or if he capitulates to the seamless appearance of senselessness. The works of Faulkner draw the reader into the experiment. They give him nothing, no solution, no decision, no hope. They only instill in him the question, Do you even now, even after all this, hold on to man? Do you still believe in that little spark of majesty that could neither ignite a fire nor shine a light?

Notwithstanding this conception's undeniable greatness, I have my doubts as to whether this novel's effect has been able to survive unchallenged the twenty years that have lapsed since it was written. To be sure, the "demonism of technology" is still *spoken of* in mythical terms. But does this not seem ever more rhetorical set against the experience of increasing familiarity with the mechanical processes and structures? Chaplin's famous film *Modern Times* was made around the same time as Faulkner's novel—now it looks like a historic document of an ill-conceived utopia, for the dreadful vision of the poor robot at the assembly line has not come true (except to such critics of our times who have not yet found the time

---

26. [Faulkner, 990.]

actually to look at a modern factory). What is seen in Chaplin is not the entelechy of technology, but a caricature of a new formation's early stage, and this is true also of Faulkner: his mechanical vampires are the larval stages of development. I am not taking the part of technological optimism—the dangers threatening us from the sphere of machines certainly have not diminished, but they are more subtle than the carnivalesque atmosphere of the air shows depicted in *Pylon* would have us know. Deaths are died more secretly than in poorly built planes breaking up in the air, and deeper conflicts unbound than that between mechanical servitude and volcanic sensuality. The bourgeois is no longer gazing at the tin dinosaurs from the stands, he is at the wheel himself or enjoys the power that bears him along, and all without having to mutate into some kind of callused species. At bottom, Faulkner still treats the problem of technology in a biologistic manner, as a matter of adaptation, a deindividuating symbiosis (as, around the same time here in Germany, Ernst Jünger's idea of "organic construction" took to a far more rigorous conclusion).[27] This is already historic; the problem of technology is just as "human" as man's problems have always been.

The Demystification of Blood

In *The Unvanquished* (1938), Faulkner leads his American theme to its peak; his powers of depiction and the clarity of his foundational idea converge here to the most felicitous effect. In doing so, Faulkner's language is at its most lucid, attaining even scherzo and burlesque. Young Bayard is growing up in the midst of the Civil War alongside his black milk-brother Ringo [they were nursed by the same woman], on the indistinct boundary between play and bloody seriousness, adventure and doom. They adopt killing and vengeance as the unquestioned rules of the world into which they grow. When the grandmother, sharp and adept at staying on top of

---

27. [Ernst Jünger, *The Worker: Dominion and Form* (1932) (Evanston, IL: Northwestern University Press, 2017).]

any situation, falls victim to the marauding underworld of the Civil War, the two boys will not rest until they have hunted down the murderer. This—and much else—Faulkner renders into episodes that seem almost to be of a merry, carefree adventurousness; not until the last fifth of the book does the reader notice that Faulkner thus tries to capture the reflection in the *boys'* consciousness, in order to show in clearer profile the reevaluation of the past in the *man*'s decision.

The Civil War is over. Among the defeated Confederates, Bayard's father, Colonel Sartoris, returns home. The burned-down house is rebuilt. But the old order of things has collapsed. The looming fate of having killed will not be banished; instead it procreates. The women in particular are left hardened by the futility of their sacrifices. Bayard's cousin Drusilla stands for this mythic relentlessness: although the men may have surrendered, she will not. She lost her father and her betrothed, and dressed as a soldier she sought revenge on the battlefield at the colonel's side. Now at home, Drusilla will once again wear women's clothes only under duress, and when her mother arranges for her to be married to the colonel, she simply forgets to attend the wedding because of her political machinations. For the colonel, too, political struggle or building railways are but forms of war: what still counts is to be the first to pull the trigger. If no enemies can be found, he will make himself some. Resistance stirs within the son against these metastases of war that have turned inward. The colonel senses his son's estrangement, and one evening— another enemy is to be confronted the next day—confesses to him: "I am tired of killing men, no matter what the necessity nor the end. Tomorrow, when I go to town and meet Ben Redmond, I shall be unarmed."[28] Sartoris dies for this decision: this time, the other man pulls the trigger first. This incident brings events to their crisis. Drusilla fails to grasp that this death is unlike the many deaths that have been died before her eyes, that the colonel had to die because he wanted to kill no more. And what she particularly fails to grasp is that this is a legacy to be preserved and executed. In this woman, the spirit of vengeance, the mythical will to the recurrence of the same,

---

28. [William Faulkner, *The Unvanquished* (New York: Vintage, 1991), 232.]

grows to entreating power, assuming the form of Eros to bring young Bayard back under the rule of the archaic, primal law. It is an act of ancient initiation by which Drusilla presses the pistols into the hand of the youth who has fallen for her: "her hand lying light on my wrist yet discharging into me with a shock like electricity that dark and passionate voracity. . . . 'Take them. I have kept them for you. I give them to you. Oh you will thank me, you will remember me who put into your hands what they say is an attribute only of God's, who took what belongs to heaven and gave it to you.'"[29] But these entreaties are dashed against the freedom that young Bayard finds in himself when he hears the news of his father's death: "At least this will be my chance to find out if I am what I think I am or if I just hope; if I am going to do what I have taught myself is right or if I am just going to wish I were."[30] Now the decision has come: when an enraged Drusilla leans over Bayard's hand, in which he holds the gun, to seal the compact of vengeance with a kiss, she is suddenly overcome by uncomprehending horror—with an animal immediacy, she feels her failure in the face of the baffling strangeness of the "no" confronting her. "Then her eyes filled with an expression of bitter and passionate betrayal. 'Why, he's not—'she said."[31]

That day, Bayard goes to see the man who shot his father. He must make public what this death truly means. His father's old companions are standing outside Redmond's house. Once more, Bayard refuses a hand proffering a gun, walking past the question, "Who are you? Is your name Sartoris?"[32] and enters unarmed into the room where Redmond is expecting him with a pistol in his hand. Not a word is spoken—"It was as if we both knew what the passage of words would be and the futility of it."[33] Twice the other man shoots, twice he misses (improbable that he should have been unable to hit his target!); then he picks up his hat, leaves the room, the house, walks past the colonel's retinue and toward the station,

---

29. [Faulkner, *The Unvanquished*, 235, 237.]
30. [Faulkner, 215.]
31. [Faulkner, 239.]
32. [Faulkner, 247.]
33. [Faulkner, 248.]

boards the next train and is never seen again. When Bayard returns home that evening, Drusilla too has gone forever.

With this work, Faulkner has done something unique for his country: he realized the anonymous instant, impossible to pin down in any document or on any historic date, in which after two wars fought for freedom America truly began to be free, when one man made a beginning by casting off the self-perpetuating compulsion of mythical reactions, deciding to forego killing as a last resort. No historical method can ever grasp what yet holds a more elementary sway over human history than facts or records. This is a matter in which poets need fear no competition; it is all theirs. But it is also a matter to which national attributes are no longer essential. Where form is given to those instants in which man is able to justify his creation, the human dimension is included. It was thus only to be expected that Faulkner should seek an expression for the universal validity of his basic theme. He devoted nine years to this highest of tasks.

The Subject of America Becomes an Allegory for All of Humanity

A Fable (1954) is the sheer culmination of all that preceded it. Therein lie both its greatness and its fault. In the spring of 1918, in the last year of the war, against the backdrop of the French eastern front, where Germans, English, French, and Americans have reached a stalemate, Faulkner unfolds the miraculous episode of a cease-fire forced by a mutiny in the French lines. An illiterate French corporal, aged thirty-three (like Ben Compson!), sets in motion events that spread across the entire front: a company climbs from the trenches, and even the enemy respects this act. Then, the front line suddenly moves: the generals of both sides get together to force, against the front, a continuation of the war; they have the "outbreak" of peace shot down by artillery and put the mutiny's leaders to the firing squad. It was not this tendentious plot that fed the controversy over this book, but its consistent parallel in form and content to the biblical passion story. The corporal is marked with distinctive signs, he has his twelve apostles, his Peter, and his Judas with his thirty pieces of silver, his two thieves, and, at the end, his empty tomb. So, a "life of Jesus elsewhere"?

It must not be omitted to set this catalog of references against a catalog of points with no such reference. This corporal has no message, no mission, no claim to power. In doing what to him is the most obvious thing to do, he reveals, as it were, to the others what to them was equally obvious: to climb from their trench and call it a day. The figure of the corporal is not a distillation of all that is good, sacred, humane, and superhuman; on the contrary, it is of startling poverty, with neither face nor soul. It is this very inner void, this figure's stubborn lack of motive, that makes the step out of the trench appear as the nakedly elemental, the radically reduced form in which man becomes aware of what is needful to him: "that all we ever needed to do was just to say, Enough of this."[34] By contrast, the military leaders are those whose gaze ranges far: they are caught up in grand designs whose reach extends in time and space beyond man; they believe themselves to be in charge of the destinies of generations, from which they deduce the right to sacrifice the present one. Faulkner's allegories, which proliferate and tangle to the point of impenetrability, may tempt to dualistic readings, but wrongly so. In the scene between the general and the mutinying corporal, which exceeds all others, the reference to the temptation of Jesus is unmistakable, yet Faulkner's art, fearless in dealing in the improbable, will have the general recognize his own son in the corporal, leaving him helplessly facing the decision either to "tempt him" or to sacrifice him for a "higher purpose." Faulkner has this cleft emerge from the root of one blood, as in his great family epics. The confrontation here is not between good and evil, God and Satan, but at bottom only between different units for measuring the real and necessary, between political and human coordinates. The father-general's grand phrase, "take the earth"—how else could he speak, thinking as he does in terms of the great and global of armies and generations!—is pitted against the son-corporal's "little" objec-

---

34. [William Faulkner, *A Fable*, in *Novels 1942–1954* (New York: The Library of America, 1994), 727.]

tion: "There are still that ten."[35] Those are the stakes in this game: the ten who remain faithful against the power over the earth, the little life against the jurisdiction over centuries, the human against the political.

Faulkner does not make it easy for the reader to bring things back to these proportions. The formal aspects of the novel obscure its substance, the means run wild with the ends. The urge to connect this allegorical drama of humanity, for the first time not set in America, by an umbilical cord to its fount, the mysticism of America, has convoluted the novel's outline to a barely decipherable hieroglyph. Added to this are the analogies with the passion, which tempt the reader to look for relations where all that was intended was, as it were, to stigmatize the plot and its characters: he who ever does the one thing that is needful shares in both the splendor and the scars of the event that came, for humanity, to epitomize the single necessity. But since this comes with a surfeit of grandiloquence and is weighed down by a cargo of encrypted meaning, it seems hard to believe that Faulkner should not have wanted to say *more*. The book thus leaves us conflicted. Amid unexpected demands on our following, untangling, understanding, it appeals to our approval of the simplicity of the corporal, who reduces the hypertrophied commandment to love thy neighbor [*den Nächsten*] to the formula that our task was to do the closest thing [*das Nächste*] at hand—the instrumental effort prevents us from believing that this could really be the simple thing that anyone beside us might also do any moment (for that trench from which one can simply climb with a single step and the words "enough of this" are, of course, to be found everywhere, and we are always already inside it). To dispense with motivation may turn out to be Faulkner's strongest stylistic device: what use, the reader is supposed to think, are motives when what is at stake is that closest thing that requires no intermediate steps? But it is precisely this effect that falls flat here, whereas it is unforgettable, for instance, in the figure of the convict in "Old Man" (1939), where the empty infinity of the flooding Mississippi really does allow for the ultimate simplicity of situations: any next moment

---

35. [Faulkner, *A Fable*, 988.]

leaves only *one* option to this man in a tiny boat with a strange woman just now giving birth—and yet everything he does before returning to jail is full of a hidden freedom. In this, it differs from *A Fable*, in which it seems that ever more screens and props were put up to provide events with a backdrop of the untold, perhaps ineffable. Innocent suffering, Faulkner's great subject, is untied from its human rootedness and significance and set free as a drama for all humanity. The temptation, which can be resisted only at the cost of grasping suffering and death, is far too "great" for this corporal to understand just what it is that he is overcoming. Overcoming? Is it not rather someone walking blindly past an offer for which he has no organ? "Take the earth"—is there even an addressee for this, or is it not a quotation floating freely in space?

To confront, on this point, Faulkner with Faulkner: in the novel *The Wild Palms [If I Forget Thee, Jerusalem]* (1939), Harry Wilborne, in the grasp of demonic Eros, is thrown off course and driven into the utmost hopelessness, and when the maelstrom of fate and guilt releases him, he finds himself in a prison cell faced with the decision between using the proffered poison to evade his liabilities or recognizing and suffering for it—and here it really does take the whole book and all of Faulkner to give credible reality to the one last sentence, at the very boundary of what this figure can still attain, that last sentence upon which is laden the burden of the book's entire meaning: "*Yes* he thought *Between grief and nothing I will take grief.*"[36]

Translated by Joe Paul Kroll

---

36. [William Faulkner, *The Wild Palms [If I Forget Thee, Jerusalem]*, in *Novels 1936–1940* (New York: The Library of America, 1990), 715. Italicization in the original.]

THE CONCEPT OF REALITY AND THE POSSIBILITY OF THE NOVEL

(1964)

The history of Western literary theory can be summed up as a continuous debate on the classical dictum that poets are liars.[1] Even

---

Originally published as "Wirklichkeitsbegriff und Möglichkeit des Romans," in *Nachahmung und Illusion: Kolloquium Gießen, Juni 1963. Vorlagen und Verhandlungen (Poetik und Hermeneutik I)*, ed. Hans Robert Jauß (Munich: Eidos), 9–27; from Hans Blumenberg, *Ästhetische und metaphorologische Schriften*, ed. Anselm Haverkamp (Frankfurt am Main: Suhrkamp, 2001), 47–73. English-language version published in *New Perspectives in German Literary Criticism: A Collection of Essays*, ed. Richard E. Amacher and Victor Lange (Princeton, NJ: Princeton University Press, 1979), 29–48.

1.   For the history of its influence, the origin of this dictum is scarcely relevant, but for a proper understanding of the matter, it is worth noting that at first there was no general devaluation but a critical reminder that the epic is obliged to be truthful—it should not bring up the unprofitable writings of earlier times, but ought to reveal noble deeds through the power of memory (*esthlà anaphaínei*) (Xenophanes, fr. B i, 19–23, Diels). The reproach of untruthfulness is therefore based on the premise that the epic should communicate truth. As Bruno Snell has shown in *The Discovery of the Mind: The Greek Origins of European Thought*

Nietzsche was still under the influence of this assertion, when, claiming a metaphysical dignity for art, he had to invert it, contrasting the *truthfulness of art* to the *falseness of nature*.[2] Halfway between the classical topos and the modern antithesis stands the scholastic concession to literature of a *minimum veritatis* [the least truth].

If we are to consider the pros and cons of the classical dictum, we must first decide what is meant by its antithesis—i.e., that poets "tell the truth." There are, I believe, two sorts of truth involved: first, when it is claimed that literature refers to a given outside reality—whatever that reality may be; second, when literature is said to create a reality of its own. We must also bear in mind the purely logi-

---

(Cambridge, MA: Harvard University Press, 1953), 90–112, the reproach takes on a general significance only through problems connected with dramatic illusion in the theater; here the technique of actualization, arising from the mythical significance of the lyric and tragic chorus, no longer coincides with the consciousness of reality underlying the epic. The transition from ecstatic identification in the cult of Dionysos to technical accomplishments of *representation* tears open the differences between reality and art, a split which, typically, is thought out to its ultimate theoretical consequences by the Greeks: even for Aeschylus, Agatharchos not only painted a decor in perspective but also left behind a treatise on it (Diels, 59 A, 39; 1:14 et seq.). There has also survived a piece by Gorgias (fr. B 23, Diels), with a moralizing justification of illusion in tragedy which is apparently excused by its effect on the spectator. And so in classical times, as in the eighteenth century with Diderot, the starting point for these reflections on poetic illusion was provided by the drama. But in both eras, this starting point was soon abandoned. For the tradition of this saying—that poets are liars—two points became significant: Plato's critique of the truth content of art in general and the Stoic-Christian habit of allegorizing, which depended on defending a *relic of truth* in literature in order to be able to *rescue* it from dispersal or concealment.

2. *Der Philosoph: Betrachtungen über den Kampf von Kunst und Erkenntnis* (Entwürfe von 1872) (WW, Musarion-Ausg., vi, 31). Now the concept of *nature* is completely oriented toward scientific objectification and its command over the concept of truth, which fulfills itself in the destruction of anthropomorphic immanence. But the "taming of science" offers a questionable justification for "the need for illusion" (WW, vi, 12); ultimately, this kind of truth cannot escape from the tradition of *imitation* but is committed only to a world interpreted as an *appearance* that liberates the desire for cognition: "Art therefore treats appearance as appearance, and so does not seek to deceive at all, but is true" (WW, vi, 98). This interpretation of "art as a true appearance" remains bound to the metaphysical tradition of art theory, for it pins art down to the character of given reality, even if this is called *incognizability*. As regards the function intended for art in this reversal of history, it cannot be anything different: such efforts always assume the premises of that which they set out to *repeat*.

cal possibility that both thesis and antithesis may be ignored, and art may be regarded as totally divorced from such considerations as truth and falseness or any criterion connected with "reality." However, this logical scheme does not necessarily coincide with the historical possibilities.

At no time in the history of Western aesthetic theory has there been any serious departure from the tendency to legitimize the work of art in terms of its relation to reality, and so any critical assessment of the foundation of traditional aesthetics must begin with a clarification of what is meant by "reality." This is difficult, for generally in our dealings with what we regard as real, we never get down to the predicative stage of defining exactly what it is that constitutes the reality. And yet the moment a doubt is cast on the reality of an action or a proposition, our attention is drawn to the specific conditions which have led us to regard it as real. The very fact that the "truth" of literature has always been contested has made literary theory a focus for the critical assessment of concepts of reality and for the unmasking of implicit preconceptions. Ultimately, we shall have to recognize what at a given time has been taken for granted as most obvious and trivial, i.e., not even worth stating— and hence never specifically formulated. Our immediate task, then, must be to define the *various* historical concepts of reality.

The first historical concept that I should like to discuss here is what we might call the "reality of *instantaneous evidence*." This concept is not explicitly propounded but is presupposed when, for instance, Plato unhesitatingly proceeds from the assumption that at the first sight of ideas the human mind immediately and with total confidence realizes that it is confronted with the ultimate and unsurpassable reality and, at the same time, is aware that the sphere of the empirical and the sensual is not and could never be such a reality. However, it is by no means taken for granted that anyone could view the duality of the empirical world and the ideal world without risking a corresponding split in his own consciousness of reality—a risk we should certainly apprehend the moment we tried to imagine our minds transferred from the world around us to one that was completely different. The classical concept of reality that gave rise to Plato's doctrine of ideas—though not identical to it—

presumes that reality presented itself as such and of its own accord, and that at the moment of its presence it was there and totally incontrollertible.[3] For these formal characteristics, the metaphor of light is particularly apt. This concept of reality also gave sustenance to a way of thinking that saw nothing problematic in biblical and other accounts of the appearance of God or of a god, who could present himself as such in a moment of direct revelation, leaving absolutely no room for the suspicion or the fear that he was illusory.[4] "Instantaneous evidence" is a concept that involves the instant rec-

---

3. Although I should not maintain that the Platonic world of ideas is representative of the classical concept of reality, I do believe that it would be virtually unthinkable without the implication of that concept. It has been said often enough that the Greeks' access to their world was not just through their eyes but also through their thoughts. This may need elaborating: the Greeks preferred *seeing in repose* and the seeing of *given realities in repose—horan* [to see] is leaving the eyes at rest on the outside appearance of something, on a shape or a picture, as I have learned from Bruno Snell's lectures "Homerische Bedeutungslehre." Aristotle referred to the momentariness of sight as an analogy to pleasure (*Eth. Nic.*, x, 3; 1174 a, 13 et seq.): *horasis* [the act of seeing] is at all moments complete and has no need of additional integration in time, like *hēdonē* [enjoyment]. Reality for sight does not constitute itself within time; although of course objects accumulate, the course of experience does not endow them with anything that could increase their given character. In the here and now, seeing, without any reference to *genesis* [creation], is a whole (1174 b, 9–13). The direct consequence of this is the concept of any *aisthēsis* [perception] (x, 4; 1174 b, 14–17). The fact that sight takes place in a series of aspects, that it is a process which essentially takes in *events*, relations, and representations, causes no difficulties and has no bearing on the formation of concepts.

4. A late, ironic reflection of such instantaneous evidence is to be found in a novel whose theme is the interweaving of fiction and reality, their equivalence as far as human destiny is concerned, and the consequent irrelevance of their identity. This novel is Andre Gide's *Caves du Vatican*. After the funeral of the poor crusader Amadeus, who had failed in his attempt to prove the alleged exchange of popes, there is a conversation in the coach between Count Julius Baraghoul and Anthimos, who is told by the count that the present pope in fact is not the real one. Anthimos, the one-time atheist, who has been as totally converted as he has been totally cured of lameness, thinks over this revelation and returns instantly to his atheism; who can reassure him now that Amadeus Fleunssoire, as he enters Paradise, will not have to recognize that his God is also not "the real one"? The count's answer implies an unclouded faith, for in such a case there can be nothing but momentary evidence: for him, it is a bizarre idea that there could be a false presentation of God, a mix-up "as if one could imagine another God being there." But, typically, this argument makes not the slightest impression on Anthimos. Undoubtedly, he no longer shares this concept of reality, stops the coach, gets out, and—limps again.

ognition of ultimate reality and can be identified precisely through this implication.

A second concept of reality, basic to the Middle Ages and after, may be called *guaranteed reality*. The length of time philosophy took to grasp and express the implications behind man's understanding of an attitude to the world may be gauged from the fact that the history of modern philosophy had its starting point in the systematic formulation of this particular concept. For Descartes, there is no instantaneous evidence of the ultimate reality, either for the self comprehending itself in a quasi-syllogism (*cogito, ergo sum* [I think therefore I am]), or for God, whose existence is deduced from the concept of God. The given reality becomes certain only by virtue of a guarantee which has to be secured by thought in a complex metaphysical process, because only by means of this process can the suspicion of a world as gigantic hoax be eliminated. The idea of God as the guarantor of the reliability of human knowledge—the schema of the third instance—of the absolute witness, had been emerging throughout the history of the medieval concept of the human mind ever since Augustine. This schema precludes the possibility of any one characteristic that might pinpoint the total reality of a given object. The characteristic of clarity and distinctness which Descartes attributes to evidence can only be explained in terms of the metaphysical assumptions arising from his philosophical doubts; otherwise, as has rightly been observed, there would be no difference between this sort of clarity and that found in a state of paranoia. The schema of guaranteed reality, with a third instance mediating in the relationship between subject and object, has had a considerable impact on modern theory of art. It is still to be seen in the attempt to guarantee the truth of the artistic product by referring to the underlying experiences of the artist and the psychological integrity with which he has transformed these experiences.

A third concept of reality may be defined as the *actualization of a context in itself*.[5] This concept differs from the others through

---

5. It has rightly been pointed out that this is the concept of reality of Husserl's phenomenology. Perhaps I should have insisted on being more precise—it is the concept of reality *presented* [*expliziert*] by phenomenology. But I doubt whether

its time component: reality as "evidence" makes itself felt in the present moment; guaranteed reality refers back to the instance that creates and mediates between the world and human reason—in other words, to what scholasticism called *veritas ontologica* [ontological truth] that has its place in the past. The third concept takes reality as the result of an actualization, a progressive certainty which can never reach a total, final consistency, as it always looks forward to a future that might contain elements which could shatter previous consistency and so render previous "realities" unreal. Even when a person's life-space is complete, we can only say that *his* reality has been continuous, and that such and such constituted *his* illusions, delusions, and imaginings—in other words, "his" reality. It is typical of this particular concept that the possessive adjective is linked with the word *reality*. The transcendency of time either invalidates the self's concept of "its" reality, or, at best, allows it the quasi-justification that it is nothing but a single perspectivistic topographical view. Reality as a self-constituting context is a *boundary concept* of the *ideal totality* of all selves—it is a confirmative value for the experience and interpretation of the world that take place in *intersubjectivity*. Obviously, this concept of reality has a sort of "epic" structure, relating to the totality of a world that can never be completed or grasped in its entirety—a world that can be only partially experienced and so can never exclude different contexts of experience which in themselves constitute different *worlds*.[6]

---

this description of the constitution of reality could have been possible at any time; this is why it was important for me to determine what such a phenomenological thematization presupposes, and since when it could have been written and understood. Precisely in this context, it becomes clear that concepts of reality do not simply *take over* from one another, but that the exhaustion of their implications and the excessive strain on their capacity to answer questions inspire a search for a new basis. The fact that *here* I am confining myself to an enumeration of concept-types is due to the thematic interest in the *vertical* foundation structure. More *recent* discussion on the connection of the concepts of reality is contained in my "Preliminary Remarks on the Concept of Reality" [in this volume].

6. The concept of reality of the "open" context legitimizes the aesthetic quality of the *novitas* [novelty], the element of surprise and unfamiliarity, whereas "guaranteed" reality does not allow anything new or unfamiliar to become *real*, ascribes to tradition and authority a world that is already mastered and rounded off as the sum total of all that is knowable, and so leads inevitably to the postulate

The last concept of reality that we shall discuss here is based on the experience of *resistance*. Here illusion is understood as the desires entertained by the self: unreality as the threat to and seduction of the self through the projection of its own wishes; the consequent antithesis is *reality as that which cannot be mastered by the self*, i.e., which resists it not merely as an experience of contact with an inert mass but also—most radically—in the logical form of the *paradox*. This would explain why paradox has become the favorite form of testimony in theology, which in the very frustrations and vexations of its logically inconsistent contents sees the proof of an

---

of *nihil novum dicere* [to say nothing new] (e.g., Petrarch, *Epist. fam.*, vi, 2; cf. x, 1). The change in the concept of reality removes the dubiousness from what is new, and so *terra incognita* [unknown soil], or the *mundus novus* [new world], becomes possible and effective as a *stimulus* to human activity; if one might phrase the process as a paradox, surprise is something to be expected. This is also relevant to the history of the "falseness" of poetry: aesthetic pleasure in *falseness* becomes legitimate so long as it can be regarded as *newness* as well (i.e., as something possible, a reality lying just beyond the horizon). Julius Caesar Scaliger, author of an oft-quoted poetics (1561), discusses in his even more interesting work *De subtilitate ad Hieronymum Cardanum* (1557; I use the edition of 1582), Cardanum's dictum: "Falsa delectant quia admirabilia" [fictions delight because they are marvellous] (*Exerc.* 307, 11; p. 936 et seq.). Scaliger protests against his commentary that it is only children and fools that could have such pleasure in the untrue, because they assume that there is *plus veritatis* [more truth] in it, so that ultimately it would actually *be* a (supposed) form of truth, which gives rise to pleasure. However, art can give far more satisfaction than nature to a naturally infinite, reasoning mind; those falsehoods in which even *sapientes* [the wise] find pleasure (e.g., the *Homerica phasmata* [Homeric inventions]) are revealed as the rich overflow by which art exceeds the (still) constant quantity of nature. "At quare delectant admirabilia? Quia movent. Cur movent? Quoniam nova. Nova sane sunt, quae nunquam fuere neque dum existunt. . . . Mentem nostram esse natura sua infinitam. Quamobrem et quod ad potentiam attinet aliena appetere, et quod spectat ad intellectionem, etiam e falsis ac monstrorum picturis capere voluptatem. Propterea quod exsuperant vulgares limites veritatis. . . . Mavultque pulchram imaginem, quam naturali similem designatae. Naturam enim in eo superat ars" [And why do marvellous fictions delight? Because they are moving. Why are they moving? Because they are new. Indeed, new things are things that have never been done and that do not yet exist. . . . Our mind is infinite in nature. That is why it can, in accordance with its ability, strive for strange things, and, insofar as knowledge is concerned, gain pleasure from the depiction of false and even monstrous things. And this is so because these things transcend the ordinary boundaries of truth. . . . (The wise man) prefers a beautiful picture to one that resembles a natural thing. For art surpasses nature in this respect].

ultimate reality that overwhelms the self and demands that it sub-
jugate itself. Reality here is that which is totally unavailable, which
cannot be relegated simply to the level of material for manipulation, but can only occasionally appear to be processed by one technique or another, then to reveal itself in the full potency of its overwhelming autonomy as a *factum brutum* [brute fact] of which it
may afterwards be said, though not conceived, that it might have
emanated from a free and constructive process of creative thinking.
The significant feature of this concept is that which cannot be further analyzed—the basic constant, the "atomic fact"; it is typified
by such claims as Heisenberg's, that playing off two mutually exclusive images against each other can ultimately convey the correct
impression of a particular reality—or George Thomson's, that a
"complicated section of mathematics is just as representative of
reality as 'mass,' 'energy,' etc." The beginnings of this concept are
perhaps to be found where awareness of reality is supposed to in-
volve an *instinct*, the practical workings of which need not necessarily exclude or remove theoretical doubts but make them irrelevant to our assertions concerning our existence or that of the
self in general. D'Alembert suggests this in the introduction to
the *Encyclopédie*. One might perhaps also cite Lessing's letter to
Mendelssohn—written more or less at the same time—in which he
states, "with every violent desire or detestation, we are aware to a
larger extent of our reality"[7]—an idea that separates awareness of
reality from thought and removes this awareness of reality to the
sphere of experiences unavailable to the mind with itself. Clearly,
then, we must face the possibility that the modern era is one in
which there is no longer any one homogeneous concept of reality,
or that if one particular form of awareness predominates, it does
so through confrontation with another fully developed or developing experience of reality.

   This historical sequence of concepts of reality and the different ways of understanding works of art are dependent on each

---

7. Lessing, *Gesammelte Werke* (Berlin: Aufbau, 1957), ix, 105 (letter of February 2, 1757).

other. Without doubt, the theory of imitation[8]—the concept that is dominant in our aesthetic tradition—is based on the notion of *instantaneous evidence*. The theory of imitation depends upon two ontological premises:

1. a realm of actual, self-evident *exemplary* reality that is given or may be assumed;
2. the *completeness* of this realm as regards all possible contents and forms of reality.

It follows from these premises that an artist can only *repeat* nature, because there is no scope for him to transcend it. Furthermore, it is a fundamental feature of this exemplary given reality that not only *can* it be repeated, but indeed it *should* be repeated: it demands imitation of itself because if, in its exemplariness, it failed to instigate such images of itself, it would remain totally sterile. Thus, Platonic idealism demonstrates why there are such things as works of artifice and art, but also why nothing essential can be "achieved" by them. Herein lies the peculiar *ambivalence of Platonism* in the history of aesthetics: it has always been at one and the same time a justification and a devaluation of artistic activity. Plato himself verifies this in the tenth book of his *Republic*, where he attacks literature and the pictorial arts in general, arguing that in depicting given objects the artist is already creating something secondhand, insofar as whatever he is basing his work on is not itself the true and ultimate reality, but merely an imitation of it by nature or by a craftsman. The work of art, then, is an imitation of an imitation. The fact that the image of an image demands a completely different

---

8. The following description of the origin and historical role of the mimesis theory not only refers to but also partly corrects the corresponding section of my study "'Imitation of Nature': Toward a Prehistory of the Idea of the Creative Being" [in this volume]. Above all, I am no longer satisfied with establishing the ambivalence of the Platonic schema but would like to show that positive and negative evaluation, and emphasis on participation or deficiency, belong to different levels of reference, which might be labelled real and merely relational imitation. This will clarify what takes place in the Aristotelian theory of art, which cannot make this difference and is open only to the positive evaluation of mimesis, and also what Neoplatonism and Platonic Gnosis have "left out."

evaluation from that of the image of the original is also based on
the concept of instantaneous evidence: in the unsurpassable evidence of the "original," reality can be experienced as something
reliable, and the image of this original is legitimized by the *fact* that
it has to be, and not by *what* it has to be (a definition applicable
only to the original). This is confirmed by Plato's example of artistic representation of elementary household objects through the art
of painting. There is no such thing in nature as a table or a bed;
also, for Plato there can be no question of the craftsman's having
invented such objects for a particular practical purpose, for this
would mean that the craftsman was the originator of the idea. According to Plato, for every meaningful human design there must
already be "originals" in the world of ideas, and it is upon these
that the craftsman bases his work. And so the copy of the original
is accomplished by the man who manufactures the table or bed.
The painter, however, who in turn reproduces such objects, bases
his work on something that has already been produced—in other
words, he creates a copy of what is already a copy.

But why does Plato not concede that the painter—just like the
craftsman—may himself see the idea, when depicting such objects,
thus fulfilling the requirements for producing a copy of the original? The tenth book of the *Republic* offers no answer to this question. But the problem is not unimportant if one wishes to understand the ambivalence of Platonism in aesthetic theory. It also plays
a significant role in justifying the thesis that the Platonic residue
within our aesthetic tradition is what denies the *novel* a legitimate
place in the traditional system of aesthetics, making it a *genre of
the bad aesthetic conscience* that has constantly had to be tran-
scended or assimilated into other legitimate genres.

Platonic ideas fix a canon of what is both demanded of and permitted to the copier. They were, first of all, the basis of our abstract
concepts, not yet themselves the primal images of forms, but norms
for the accomplishments of reason, say, for establishing relations between objects, for comprehending geometrical proportions, and,
finally, for evaluating actions. In all these spheres, ideas had the prescriptive character of rules; they were representative not of reality
as it ought to be, but of the actual obligation. The fact that the orig-

inal, preexistent experience of the ideas had to be visualized in the imagination led to their eidetic character's becoming more and more clearly defined, so that they formed primal images of all the vague copies we see in the visible world around us. But these ideas were not only images of pure essences—they were primal images with the true exemplary character that demands and compels imitation. The terms "primal image" and "copy" are not just relational concepts arising out of the completed imitation but they themselves have an ideal quality, corresponding to the origin of the doctrine of ideas: i.e., the primal image is independent of the actual imitation and preceded it as a norm that could be substantiated only through the actuality and the faithfulness of the copy. This consequence of the doctrine of ideas, which had already come to the fore in the *Republic* through the singling out of goodness as an idea of ideas, is revealed in its full significance in the dialogue *Timaeus*: here the fact *of* the creation of the world is shown to need no further motivation than that of a mere glimpse of the ideas by a craftsman who is considered capable of performing this task, and who only requires affirmation of the truthfulness of his work, but not of any particular disposition of his will to take on and execute such a work. The visible world is, accordingly, a fulfillment of the compulsive implications of the primal images, which demand imitation as the correlative that completes their meaning. However, it is clear that in this system only the first, direct copy can be the legitimate fulfillment of the demands of the original, and this first copy therefore represents the end of the process of imitation; its imitative nature, though accepted itself as real predication, precludes the possibility of its becoming a binding model in its own right. The artist therefore only copies something which itself is *already* a copy and can be nothing but a copy, and he thereby raises it to the level of an original—a level which intrinsically it is not qualified to occupy. It is not every copy, or copies as such, that Plato derogates, but only those that did not directly imitate the original—i.e., the "unreal" copies, the indirect secondhand imitations that are based on what is already an imitation. One of the misunderstandings of Neoplatonism is that it gives a totally negative evaluation to all imitations, so that even the creating of the world itself, and not just that of the copies worked by the artist, becomes a dubious event. However, this Neoplatonic misconception of Plato's criticism of imitation at the same time clarifies the curious fact that Platonic elements had a part in a development which led eventually to the liquidation of imitation as a basis for the artistic creativity.

We must not forget that the aesthetic theory of imitation is part of the *Aristotelian* tradition.[9] With Aristotle, ideas became formal principles of nature itself, so that actuality and necessity merged in the world to such an extent that the artist's function was to extract from the external world what ought to be and the way it ought to be. Artistic representation therefore became a direct copy, and was not, so to speak, a copy once removed. The dignity of imitation as the essence of artistic activity was thus established, not by revaluing mimesis itself, but simply by reducing the number of levels of reference: art now took over the position which in Plato had been occupied by nature itself or by the demiurge that created it, a position in which artistic activity had been essentially superfluous and even inconsistent with the system.

It is true that this is but a residue of Platonism in Aristotelism, explaining why a work of art may be possible, but endowing it with neither justification nor necessity. This is why the Aristotelian tradition in aesthetics, even though it sets out to define artistic activity as an imitation of nature, accounts for it and evaluates it almost exclusively in terms of man's emotional needs and its effect on these needs. In Aristotelian aesthetics, the basic concept of *man* is more important than that of reality; it is a system conceived from the standpoint of the viewer or listener. Against such a background, the original, angry dictum that artists, and particularly poets, are liars is deprived of its negatively critical substance, insofar as the Aristotelian definition of art as imitation does not concern what *ought* to be done, but only what *can* be done.

---

9. We must also bear in mind that in this tradition the general metaphysical interpretation of *art* (*technē*) in the broadest sense was predominant, before what we would call Aristotelian *aesthetics* could take effect with the rediscovery of his *Poetics*. Medieval criticism resulted in Aristotelianism minus the *Poetics* (which only follows Arabic lines of tradition); the consequences of this are something that urgently require closer study.

The revival of Platonism during the Renaissance[10] did not signify a reversal of the original derivation—Aristotelian concept arising from Platonian; the critique of the ideal of imitation was now based on a shift in metaphysical interest. In the late Middle Ages, man's interest in himself and in his position in the world became the overriding consideration, and the answer to his questions lay first and foremost in man's own works and achievements. Together with the dignity of man's works, the dignity of art itself became the central theme of the Renaissance. An aesthetic system concerned principally with the observer's reactions scarcely fitted in with such an approach. The comparability of man's creations with those of God was implicit or even explicit in this newly developing concept of the artist; this meant returning directly to the question of art's relationship to reality, and the extent to which this relationship was inevitable or contingent, necessary or dispensable. If this reinterpretation of the early symptoms of the modern view of art is correct, then the result of such an approach is not only a new definition of the difference between physical and aesthetic objects but also an inherent rivalry between the artist and the outside world as a

---

10. It is difficult to define in detail what is really "Platonic" about this revival. In studying the history of concepts, we must not forget that the "Platonism" of the Renaissance after Petrarch originated from Cicero criticism and its capacity for comprehension was determined by this. As a result, a guideline such as the *idea* is unsuited to the discovery of Platonisms, as can be seen from Erwin Panofsky's "Idea" (*Studien der Bibl. Warburg*, 1924; 2nd ed., 1960); by choosing *species* as the Latin equivalent, Cicero had removed all precision from the term (even though he also left it in Greek), out of which humanism made an all-round word. When Panofsky refers, for instance, to Melanchthon's express equation of *idea* with *notitia* [knowledge; notion] for the "pulcherrima imago humani corporis" [most beautiful image of the human body] included in the *in animo* [in the mind] of Apelles, in order to demonstrate the immanence of Platonism, he is contradicted by Melanchthon's own embarrassment, who, when compelled, at one stage, to reproduce an authentic Platonic idea, uses, for instance, *imitatio*, which is scarcely compatible with *notitia*, and so the *statuarius* [sculptor] has in himself a *certa notitia* [certain notion] of his work, which guides his hand: "donec efficiatur similitudo eius archetypi quem imitatur" [until it becomes a likeness of the archetype he imitates] (*Corp. Ref.*, XIII, 305). If *idea* were really taken here "almost as a specifically aesthetic" concept, *archetypus* would not need to be smuggled in in this way, but *idea* is, of course, the nice academic term which in fact can be used for anything except something Platonic.

whole—in other words, the artist offers not only a transformation, idealization, or variation of the world, but works that are, so to speak, of *equal rank* to it. Both in terms of the classical concept of instantaneous evidence and the medieval concept of reality guaranteed by God, this idea of the artist's competing with given reality would have been senseless and groundless. Only a new concept, bestowing upon the intersubjective consistency of the given in space and time the sole right to recognition through a mind conscious of reality, could give substance, and even intelligibility, to the artist's claim to totality as against the claim of the factual world.

The same concept of creation, now involving the possibility of totality in a single work—without this possibility's being systematically made explicit—removed the very foundations of the Aristotelian concept of the artificial and the artistic. While nature appeared as the expression of an omnipotent, divine will, idealization as the task of the artist had become something not only dubious but demonic by the implication that nature was perhaps not what it ought to be; the artist had, as it were, to "catch up" with its possibilities and make up for its deficiencies in relation to what it ought to be. What, according to the Aristotelian definition, could it mean that art and technology completed what nature could not finish? For the medieval view of the world, nature had lost its specific, authentic evidence as reality. The fact, now constituted and guaranteed by an absolute will, was a great new element of ambiguity: it allowed the reassurance of not having to ask questions, and at the same time gave rise to the annoyance that anything factual is bound to arouse in man's reason. The fact that no aesthetics came forth from the premises and postulates of Cartesian philosophy was clearly due to this philosophy's being—in respect of its concept of reality—"medieval," clinging to the guaranteed schema of reality. Cartesian aesthetics could not have been anything but, at best, a theory of medieval art. We should not be surprised or misled by this historical phenomenon; it is quite natural that the most deeply hidden implication of an era—namely, its concept of reality—should become explicit only when the awareness of that reality has already been broken.

If the question of the *possibility* of the novel is put as an ontological one, searching out the foundations of the concept of reality, this means that one is also inquiring into the origin of a new claim of art—its claim, not merely to represent *objects* of the world, or even to imitate *the* world, but to actualize *a* world. A world—nothing less—is the theme and postulate of the novel.[11] It is odd that the premise underlying this approach was created by the renewal of Platonism, for, in this context, Platonism took on a historical function that was quite extraneous to it. Its inherent negative evaluation of imitation was, at the beginning of the modern age, more or less the "desired" effect, whose genuine *premises* certainly were not to be renewed: the difference between what is and what ought to be, as the scope of art, was a possibility that had in the meantime been excluded. Art was rather to concern itself with that sphere which had not been actualized by God or by nature, and so there was no longer any duality of existent reality and formative art. Instead, every work, measured against the new concept of reality, was the *reality of the possible*, whose unreality had to be the premise for the relevance of its actualization.

If our original thesis is correct—namely, that the history of aesthetics is one long debate on the classical dictum that poets are liars—this history must always be intimately related to concepts of the human capacity to "tell the truth." It is *the change in the concept of truth*

---

11. There is a certain affinity between Georg Lukács's comment that "The novel is the epic of a world that has been abandoned by God" (*The Theory of the Novel* [Cambridge, MA: MIT Press, 1971], 88), that is to say, the epic under the conditions of the modern view of the world—and the arguments developed here. The longed-for revival of the Greek epic, and the claim that it set the absolute standard, foundered against a view of reality that took the world for *a* world, the *cosmos* for a *universe*. The ultimate failure of Leibniz and Wolff to ensure the *ratio sufficiens* [sufficient reason] of the factual world opened the gates for a critique of the factual from the standpoint of the rational and the possible—a critique which was bound to work on the imagination and stimulate it into testing out the meaning of its own "worlds." The uniqueness of the cosmos and the Greeks' commitment to the epic as an interpretation of the world were just two aspects of the reality given by *instantaneous evidence*. The novel could not be a "secularization" of the epic after the world's loss of religion; on the contrary, the contingency, the factualness of the indefinite article, the inrush of *possibilia* all go back to the theologizing of the world. The "worlds" which the aesthetically minded self is willing to belong to only provisionally, in the accessible finiteness of a context, are the quintessence of the novel's thematization of reality and the irony essential to it.

which opens up new possibilities for art to be "true." The classical concept of truth, valid throughout most of the Middle Ages, maintained that in cognition, ontologically, there were present and effective the same constituent factors that made objects themselves what they were—in Aristotelian terms, their essential form. Between the object and the act of perception there exists a causal link of clearly *imitative* representation. Connected with the medieval concept of a *transcendently guaranteed reality*, there arose a new possibility of abandoning this direct causal link and, instead, viewing the sphere of cognition as a heterogeneous, individual world of mere *signs for objects*—a world whose internal order needed only to correspond precisely to the internal order of the elements of things for truth to be attained. The concept of *nonimitative cognition*, in which words and figures and their correlations can stand for objects and their correlations, has its metaphysical foundation in the premise of a *third instance*, which guarantees the strict coherence even of that which is totally heterogeneous. The Aristotelian claim that the soul is everything of the possible—a view that gave the most abstract definition to the age-old principle of cognition through similarity and affinity—takes on a new meaning: the cognitive mind, with its capacity for putting symbols in place of things and their correlations, is capable of *every* formulation of objective facts. The late Middle Ages had to abandon the concept of cognition through similarity and imitation mainly because it seemed to set the human spirit up too close to the divine. The new *concept of cognition*, however, radically separates the divine spirit, which sees all things directly and in their essence, from the human spirit, which can only represent them symbolically; the human spirit thus loses its receptive openness to things, and becomes instead a creative principle employing its own symbolic tools.[12] The enhanced *transcendency* of the divine rule over things forcibly gives rise to the *immanence* of the new concept of human mastery over these things. The correspondence between cognition and its ob-

---

12. For the *similitudo divini intellectus in creando* [the similarity of the human intellect to the divine lies in its creative activity], see my book *The Legitimacy of the Modern Age*, trans. Robert M. Wallace (Cambridge, MA: MIT Press, 1983), 530.

jects is no longer *material* but *functional*. The immanent consistency of the symbolic system of concepts remains the only—though adequate—approximation to the given reality. The *concept of the image* is released from its hitherto inescapable confinement between the original and the copy.[13] Truth, in the strict sense of *adaequatio*, remains possible only for what man himself has created and of which he can therefore be completely aware without any symbolic mediation: this includes the structural laws governing his symbolic tools of cognition—laws that are formulated by logic—mathematics, history, language, and, last but not least, art. No longer is absolute truth to be seen somewhere in the relation between the representational work of art and nature; it now lies between the subjective mind perceiving the work and the product which is viewed as a possible piece of reality created by the artist. It is no longer through his relationship to nature, as a form of creation from which he is alienated, but through his cultural works, that man can match God's direct contact with his own works both as creator and as observer. This hitherto unknown metaphysical dignity of the work of art has its foundation in what is, at one and the same time, a limiting and an intensifying transformation and dissolution of the concept of truth. The consequences of this new view of man's spiritual achievements are far-reaching. Reality can no longer be considered an inherent quality of an object but is the embodiment of a consistently applied *syntax of elements*. Reality presents itself now as ever before as a sort of text which takes on its particular form by obeying certain rules of internal consistency. Reality is for modern times a context; even such an important phenomenon in the history of ideas as criticism of the theological interpretation of miracles as testifying to the divine, is totally compelled to maintain this concept of reality. Now, if aesthetic objects can have

---

13. Already in the (disputed) Platonic 7th letter, *eídōlon* [image] and *ónoma* [word] are put on a level as regards their distance from truth (342 et seq.), but in a derogatory sense, as provisional measures for what is then an unsurpassable immediacy. The modern levelling out of the difference between *image* and *concepts* as suppositions which are free of any similarity relation to reality knows no greater approximation or immediate access to reality *as such*. It is, in fact, one of the features of the modern concept of reality that it excludes the "ontological comparative" (Walter Bröcker).

such a thing as a specific reality, they, too, are not only bound by the criterion of context as proof of their reality but are also constrained, as regards their scope and the wealth of elements they incorporate, to compete with the context of *nature*, i.e., to become *secondary worlds*: they no longer extract, by imitation, realities from the one reality, but imitate the fact of being real.

Ultimately, art claims as its subject matter the formal proof of reality and not the material content that presents itself with this proof. Without doubt, the *nonpossible* would represent the fulfill-ment of this claim—namely, the infinite context, which alone could be counted as the normal equivalent to the open-endedness of phys-ical experience. This is the starting point from which modern liter-ature—and the aesthetics appropriate to it—proceeded toward the novel as the most comprehensively "realistic" genre, representing a context which, though finite in itself, presumes and indicates infin-ity. The *potential infinity* of the novel represents its *ideality*, arising out of the concept of reality, as well as the aesthetic *irritation* in-evitable in view of the fact that its task of representing an infinite context can be fulfilled only by aesthetically binding principles of form. Perhaps the clearest embodiment of the problems of the genre is to be seen in the humorous novel: already in Sterne's *Tristram Shandy*, the subject is the possibility as well as the impossibility of the novel. The increasing incongruity between the real and the rep-resented existence brings out the novel's implication of infinity, and shows the dilemma created when a finite text tries to evoke an infi-nite context. As a finite and discontinuous work, the novel thwarts the reader's expectations of the "et cetera," and so focuses his at-tention on its true theme: that it is ultimately not concerned with proving its own validity as a work of art through a sequence of ed-ited events, but with the conflict between the imaginary reality of a context and the reality of the existing world. Another such humor-ous novel that is not only in fact incomplete but also incompletable, and that has reality itself as its subject matter, is Jean Paul's *Der Komet* [*The Comet*].[14] Here the theme is the "experimental" pre-

---

14. Jean Paul himself, in his introductory *investiture* of the reader with the story, points out this thematization by so projecting history and novel onto one

sentation of the illusory world of the supposed crown prince Nikolaus Marggraf, interwoven with the real, or supposedly real, world of the German petty principality; as the two worlds act upon each other, the predicates of illusion and reality appear to be interchangeable. This very fact shows that what we tend to call "representation" in a novel is in fact "asemantic"—i.e., it represents nothing but itself; it removes the boundaries between being and meaning, matter and symbol, object and sign, destroying the correspondences that had been integral to our whole tradition of truth concepts. This destruction, nevertheless, involves continuing dependence on the tradition it negates, indirectly creating the uncreatable by removing the hitherto unchallenged function: the sign no longer purports to represent a "thing," and so itself takes on the substantiality of a thing. This, of course, is an approach that ranges beyond the novel and its basic concept of reality, to an awareness of reality that is determined by resistance, and to a corresponding and confirmatory art form that is made up of means of expression that annihilate themselves, and use their own inconsistencies to demonstrate their own lack of meaning.[15] Once more the novel takes itself as its own

---

another that to convey this *given historical* subject he wishes for himself the capacity of the novelist, so that with "one mighty stroke" he could complete the creation of his hero: "and I shall reach my *goal if I can set out the historical truths* of this story in such a way that they seem to the reader like successful fictions, with the result that, raised above the juridical law of *fictio sequitur naturam* (fiction, or appearance, follows nature), here conversely nature or history follows fiction—or, to put it in Latin, natura fictionem sequatur."

15. Such a *substantialization* through annihilating the function of "means of meaning" has not been discovered in the immanent history of the novel; the reality that occurs in *resistance* is, from the viewpoint of the aesthetics of genre, basic to *lyric poetry*. Late nineteenth-century aesthetic experiences gained from poetry in its strictest and narrowest sense, have become prototypical—among other things, for the changing of novel aesthetics into the thematization of the "impossibility" of the novel. Perhaps I can best define this prototypical discovery of lyric poetry through the passage in Paul Valéry's letter to J.-M. Carré, February 23, 1943 (*Lettres à quelques-uns* [Paris: Gallimard, 1952], 240), in which he tries to systematize the experience of shock caused fifty years back by Rimbaud's *Illuminations*: "le système, conscient ou non, que supposent les passages les plus virulents de ces poèmes. Il me souvient d'avoir résumé ces observations—et, en somme, mes défenses—par ces termes: R. a inventé ou découvert la puissance de l'incohérence harmonique. Arrivé à ce point extrême, paroxystique de l'irritation volontaire de

subject matter; by demonstrating the impossibility of the novel, a novel becomes possible. I should like to go into rather more detail concerning this problem of form. The idea of reality as context imposes on the novel the form of linear consistency within a given system of space and time. But, as I have pointed out, this concept of reality becomes valid only through an agreement among subjects that are capable of understanding one another—i.e., through *inter-subjectivity* and its various possible perspectives. So far as I am aware, the novel first took on a *perspective pattern* with Balzac, whose cycle of novels creates the illusory reality of a whole human society through the recurrence of identical characters viewed from changing perspectives. As far as the question of reality is concerned, there is a big difference between the epic-linear and the perspective recurrence of characters—the spatial consciousness is different, and the world created is far subtler. Balzac's perspective system enables a linear series of episodes to be translated into simultaneous events. But it demands more than mere consistency with elements already dealt with, for perspective consistency allows a transformation of those elements as the emphasis shifts, for instance, from one character to another, or from one aspect of character to another. The result is a highly complex process of reconciling individual aspects to one another and to the overall identity of the object to which they belong. This is basically quite different from the traditional introduction of individual characters drawn in preparation for their ultimate meeting at the climax of the plot. It is no longer merely the characters in the novel that move through the various events

---

la fonction du langage, il ne pouvait que faire ce qu'il a fait—fuir" [the system, conscious or not, that underlay the most virulent passages of these poems. I remember having summed up these observations—and, in short, my defenses—in the following terms: R. has invented or discovered the power of harmonic incoherence. At this extreme, paroxysmal point of voluntary irritation of the function of language, he could only do what he did—flee]. The anticlimax of the "actualization," the exhaustibility of the ontological basis of this concept of reality, are preconditions for the transposition of the principle to other genres and arts (e.g., the abandonment of tonality), but the novel (in a different way from the drama) has shown itself to be particularly resistant to the "paroxysmal" consequence of the principle, and so, as extremely flexible and productive as far as experiments are concerned.

contained in the plot; the reader now moves around the body of imaginary reality, passing through all the different aspects from which it can be viewed. Balzac himself believed, and expressly indicated as one of his most daring intentions, that the recurrence of individual characters in his *Comédie Humaine* [*The Human Comedy*] would endow this fictitious cosmos with more life and movement,[16] but in fact it is not the world of the novel that is set in motion so much as the reader himself as he experiences the various changes of perspective. The world of the novel itself takes on a greater degree of stability and substance, which seems both to the author and the reader more and more to defy total mastery, compelling them to ever greater efforts, by which the imaginative reality itself remains quite unaffected. The more the novel's reality depends on the *standpoint* of the mediating self, the less it seems to depend on that *self* and his imagination, and in fact the more he seems to depend on it.

Clearly, then, the idea of reality as an intersubjective context can lead to an idea of it as the experience of the resistance of any given object. In the novel, this transition is marked as a breaking up of connections between aspects resulting from different perspectives. The beginnings of this process are to be seen in Jean Paul's humorous novel *Der Komet*;[17] and it came beyond all humorous implica-

---

16. "The result is what one might call a novelistic mobile, a whole formed by a certain number of parts which we can approach in almost any order we please.... Evidently, the recurrence of characters or their persistence from one novel to another has in Balzac a much greater importance than in what is called the *roman fleuve*." Michel Butor, "Balzac and Reality," in *Inventory* (New York: Simon and Schuster, 1968), 104. "But Balzac's definitive victory over his great predecessor (Walter Scott), his liberation from him, finds its expression in an extraordinary invention which will utterly transform the structure of his work ... the recurrence of characters" (Butor, 103).

17. It is worth noting how the dialogues in Jean Paul's *Der Komet* always "function" only through misunderstandings and never allow the fictional context to be exploded. But as the structure of intersubjective communication is shown to be strong enough to reify even unreality into quasi-reality, the concept of reality is not only thematized but also used as an aesthetic element—one might almost say it is instrumentalized. Inevitably, the aesthetic instrumentalization creates, indeed even presupposes, critical awareness: suspicion as regards the malleability of reality for specific purposes is here implied; this suspicion is also contained in the unexpected,

tions to full fruition, for instance, in Robert Musil's novel *Der Mann ohne Eigenschaften* [*The Man without Qualities*]. In this immense fragment, even the (existing) conclusion does not begin to bring together the different threads of the plot or to lead them toward any common end; epic perspectivism is here virtually exploded, wrecked on the consequences of its own precision. In 1932, Musil wrote of his *Mann ohne Eigenschaften*: "This book has a passion for something which nowadays is to a certain extent out of place in the field of literature: namely, correctness and precision. What the story of this novel amounts to is the fact that the story which is to be told is not told."[18] The increasing specificity of the narrative leads to a demonstration of the impossibility of narrative itself. But this impossibility in turn is felt to indicate the unbreakable resistance of the imaginary reality to being described, and in this sense the aesthetic principle inherent in the concept of reality of immanent consistency leads at a certain point of transition to a different concept of reality altogether. Herein lies the reason why the constantly anticipated "liquidation" of the novel has never been achieved. It also explains why irony seems to have become the authentic mode of reflection as far as the aesthetic claims of the modern novel are concerned: the novel becomes ironic through the connections with reality that it is unable to dispense with and yet incapable of forming. Thomas Mann once spoke of the *seeming accuracy* of scientific discourse used as a stylistic means of irony: in his 1942 lecture on *Josef und seine Brüder* [*Joseph and His Brothers*], he calls this the application of the scientific to the totally unscientific—and this precisely is for him the purest expression of irony.

I should like to deal with just one more facet of the basic connection between the concept of reality and the feasibility of the

---

socially critical virulence of the novel, in the ceaseless *probing*, for instance, of the deformability of elements of reality, up to the discovery of the breaking point as in the solipsistic dialogues of Kafka or Beckett. The triumph (as yet not properly understood) of finally having hit upon something stable, is what marks the phrasing of this development: the functional collapse of intersubjectivity releases a new concept of reality.

18. [Robert Musil, *Tagebücher*, ed. Adolf Frisé (Reinbek: Rowohlt, 1983), 1598.]

novel. I have tried to show that the concept of reality as a phenomenal and immanent consistency lies at the root of the autonomous reality of the work of art. What I have not mentioned, but what actually brings together man's created works in competition with the existing reality of nature, is the strange fact that, on the one hand, man asserts himself in the actualization of his creative potential, while, on the other, he must seek to conceal the dependence of his art on his own abilities and will; he must do this, because only then can his works take on the unquestionable autonomy and individuality that will make them indistinguishable from the products of nature. It may therefore be taken as a characteristic feature of modern art and literature that they have undergone a sort of dereification; the more familiar *alienation* is only a partial phenomenon within this trend. Human art presents itself neither as an imitation of nature nor as a "piece of nature," but it is to have the same rank and dignity as natural objects; it is to be the work of man, but it is not to be characterized by the contingency of the individual will, or the actuality of the mere idea. In other words, it must be, at one and the same time, both novelty and fossil. We want to be able to disregard ourselves as the condition of the possibility of these works, because we do not want them to be a part of our conditional or our historical nature, of which we are proud despite the afflictions they cause us; we do not want our works to be *objects* dependent on subjects, but to be *things* in themselves. And these works for their part should not *represent* aspects but should *offer* us aspects of themselves. From the perspective structure systematically prepared and laid out in the novel, there can emerge a perspective potential that is stimulated by the work and yet at the same time is not fulfilled by it; we recognize this potential when we realize the essential openness of modern art to commentary and varied interpretation which is apparent from Romanticism onward. This *hermeneutic ambiguity* is integral to the "reality" of the work of art, insofar as it is this which proves its independence of our own subjectivity. This is why we tend artificially to *historicize* the work of art, in order to strip it of its dependence on ourselves and to "reify" it. Just as archaic sculpture exists in the landscape, such as the *things* tossed on to the green grass of Otterloo, there is also the novel distanced by language or by the artifice of a narrative framework—the type of novel of which we "know too much" for it to have its desired effect of alienation on us. In the same way that we can artificially historicize, we can also artificially *naturalize*, but no longer can we do this by representing or imitating nature; we must instead claim "naturalness" for our works, erecting things which resemble the products of eruptions or erosions, like the *objet ambigu* in Paul Valery's *Eupalinos*. Corresponding to these in the novel is the artificially artless transcript of streams of consciousness and interior monologues— the "writing-the-minutes" type of novel [*Protokollroman*], which claims to create, and at the same time renounces, the creation of a whole world.

The concept of reality of the phenomena's context presents a reality that can never be assured, is constantly in the process of being actualized, and continually requires some new kind of confirmation. This idea of reality, even when transformed into the reality of an aesthetic object, remains a sort of consistency which is, so to speak, open at both ends and dependent on continuous proofs and accomplishments, without ever achieving the finality of evidence that characterized the classical concept of reality. This is one reason for the uneasiness and dissatisfaction that have been a constant critical undercurrent throughout the history of the novel. One way out of this dissatisfaction is to resist the need for an endless actualization by deliberately breaking through set patterns of formal consistency—a breaking through which shows by the way it is handled that it does not spring from any failure or exhaustion of creative powers but, on the contrary, represents a conscious effort which can afford to disregard the quasi-objective principle of formal consistency. The idea that poets are liars can be completely invalidated only if they no longer set out to prove its antithesis— namely, that poets tell the truth—but concentrate on deliberately breaking the bonds of this antithesis and indeed all the rules of the reality game itself. Commitment to reality is rejected as an unwanted limitation on form, an aesthetic heteronomy wearing the mask of authenticity. Herein lie the roots of an aesthetic concept that can now present as "true" what all previous concepts of reality would have designated as unreal: paradox, the inconsistency of dreams, deliberate nonsense, centaurian hybrids, objects placed in the most unlikely positions, the reversal of natural entropy, in which refuse can be used to make *objets d'art*, newspaper cuttings be made into novels, or the noises of technology into a musical composition.

Modern art, however, has not freed itself from the compulsion to refute its dependence on the given realities of nature; its anti-physicism is not even directed against a constant *nature* whose dimensions are known or defined. The liberation of the imagination always being proclaimed, for instance by Breton, goes so far as to dissolve even the (now merely formal) connection between the concept of reality of immanent consistency and its commitment to the reality value of *nature*, and so it is again and again compelled to make desperate efforts to actualize itself despite its extreme improbability, in what remains, when all is said and done, a type of *instantaneous evidence*. The fact that the novel still adheres to the concept of reality of immanent consistency can be gauged from the problems that accrue to it from any heterogeneous concept of reality. It cannot actualize itself simply by contradicting whatever has hitherto been regarded as significant evidence of reality. The ideal of the *perfetta deformità* [perfect deformation] cannot be fulfilled by the novel. But it is characteristic of the novel that at this point it takes its own possibility as its subject matter, thus demonstrating its dependence on the concept of reality. I need only point to the technique of uncommunicative dialogue to explain what I mean: the failure of conversation, its hypertrophy in meaningless chatter, misunderstanding as a constituent product of language—all this remains essential to the novel, embedded in a world that is still presumed and produced with too much imagination for it ever to be said that pure absurdity can really become the subject matter. The novel has its own "realism," which has evolved from its own particular laws, and this has nothing to do with the ideal of imitation but is linked precisely to the aesthetic illusion which is essential to the genre. Fixing (or causing) a world [*Welthaftigkeit*] as a formal, overriding structure is what constitutes the novel. When the absurd was proclaimed the program of art, its function was defined as "transcending the foundations," and ultimately even architecture showed itself suited to this function of the absurd. But the novel had advanced much earlier and much more spontaneously to this transcending of the foundations—i.e., to the resolution of the conflict between reality and fiction—and, as I have shown, it had taken as its theme its own possibility, not as a fiction of reality, but as a *fiction of the reality of realities.* The novel's preeminence in the actualization of basic modern ideas of aesthetics is comprehensible only if one realizes that it has not adopted absurdity, that new criterion of absolute poetry, because it has no need of such a stigma. The novel fulfills the aesthetic norm which, according to Boswell's diary, was first formulated by Samuel Johnson during the famous conversation in the Literary Club about the excessive price of an antique marble dog: the extension of the sphere of the *humanly* possible (April 3, 1778),[19] whereas even the broadest interpretation of the Aristotelian ideal of imitation—perhaps Johann Jakob Breitinger's— is concerned with the sphere of the *naturally* possible.[20]

Translated by David H. Wilson[21]

---

19. [Blumenberg paraphrases Boswell's account, which has: "Everything that enlarges the sphere of human powers, that shows man he can do what he thought he could not do, is valuable." James Boswell, *The Life of Samuel Johnson, LL.D* (Ware, Hertfordshire, UK: Wordsworth Editions, 1999), 636.]

20. The notes added subsequently to this paper have been written, with grateful acknowledgments, as a result of suggestions, doubts, and objections raised during the discussion.

21. [Minor corrections by Hannes Bajohr.]

Pensiveness

(1980)

When confronted by a question, every form of life strives to supply an answer without delay or deliberation. The model of stimulus/response is a drastic simplification of things and events, yet it is the latent ideal for the behavior of organisms.

Man alone demonstrates the opposite tendency. He is the creature who hesitates. Life would not forgive that flaw if the resulting loss were not compensated for by an expanded range of activities, the outcome of which we call experience [*Erfahrung*]. Man perceives not only signals but things; this means that he has learned to wait—to wait in expectation of that which is yet to happen. To risk indecision before the alternatives of fleeing or attacking is to renounce quick solutions, the shortest ways. Although never detectable in any

Originally published as "Nachdenklichkeit," from *Neue Zürcher Zeitung* (November 22, 1980): 65–66. English-language version published in *Caliban* 6 (1989): 51–55.

archeological excavation, this indecision may have been the first step toward culture.

Hesitation, measured against the norm of brisk, efficient behavior, might be understood as the result of a disturbance. A change in the biosphere—a change, say, in vegetation after climatic variation—could have darkened, distorted, and deformed the clarity and familiarity of the environmental data for our behavior. This lack of distinctness, this estrangement from the environment [*Umwelt*] could have encouraged the process that cognitive theorists call the synthesis of a manifold of sensations.

The pleasure of functioning is missing in hesitation, but in recompense, hesitation—the forced deferment of action—might itself have become a new source of pleasure. And each newly won sense of security would have enhanced the possibility of such pleasure. Life demands purposefulness, but to its favorites it grants the experience of purposelessness. Every culture grows out of this gift. The most primitive displays of culture—the decoration, the ornament on the tool—already embody the gesture of the winning of purposelessness, of suspended economy. Hesitation, as momentary helplessness, as the mere utilization of a delay, can become a competence that has a different value for life than has the weighing of options.

The linguistic terms for this life-value appear to be worn out, degraded. Witness: we used to speak of the "contemplativeness" of old age that was not supposed to depend on contemplating something in order to overcome it. Nor does "pensiveness" enjoy a good name; contemporaries demand decisiveness. Pensiveness is considered an unseemly, idle use of time. Thought and thought about thought may bestow competence in a field; pensiveness is not claimed as a part of any profession or discipline.

Our notion of thought is that it produces the shortest connection between two points—between a problem and its solution, between a need and its satisfaction, between various interests and their consensus. By tracing the thread of discourse connecting these points, even children capable of critical thought are expected to come to quick conclusions and to find their independence.

Yet at least we are ready to grant indulgence to the pensive person. Results are not expected from him when he gets out of his chair. No one gets worked up by what he does, or rather doesn't do, least of all he himself. One of the descriptions of pensiveness is that whatever comes to mind is allowed to pass through one's head unaltered.

Pensiveness is an experience of freedom, especially the freedom of digression. The reactions of bystanders faced with the digression of the pensive man range from the high points of humor to the exasperation of those whose point is to reach a goal.

But no intersubjectivity can allow its members to break the bond of function. Excursuses demand a degree of freedom that cannot be tolerated in the discourse of rational thought. Dialogue strategies do not allow for pensiveness. For in pensiveness, one can let this pass for that, can loosen the strict reins of control and apply no measure to the questions' importance. It is doubtful whether thought about the meaning of life according to the rules of a discipline is possible; but still one may be pensive about the meaning of life without ever coming closer to an answer—not even to one among many that may be possible. And these possible answers are finally indeed not possible.

Philosophy is seen as the methodical disciplining of such questions, and in the extreme case it bans such questions because the answers have proven inaccessible by reliable means. Regulated thought appears far removed from mere pensiveness. But many philosophers defy this separation. Was Socrates a thinker in this strict sense?

As thinker, his results would have been the most paltry of all possible results: what could be achieved by knowing that one knows nothing? And what was achieved by ironically pushing or pulling others into helplessness when they believed themselves in the possession of knowledge? Unless this is understood as leading thought back to its origin and base in pensiveness, the terrain from which it took leave but to which it must also always return. This terrain may be called the base of the life-world.

On that base, philosophy has survived all doubts about its right to exist, to the wonder of those who have pronounced it dead. I do not equate philosophy with pensiveness, but also do not deny its origin in and service to pensiveness. The ideal philosopher is not only the "thinker" who adheres to all the rules of the discipline and is hindered from proceeding by pure reflection on method. Otherwise, would Socrates, Diogenes, Kierkegaard, or Nietzsche have become a part of philosophy's history?

In his prison, before his death, Socrates turned to the fables of Aesop, which were familiar to the Greeks from early childhood. This small gesture is a hint that I should like to pursue for a moment.

The Aesopian fable is a creation of great yet artful simplicity. I offer an example:

> An old man, who had travelled a long way with a bundle of sticks, found himself so weary that he cast it down and called for Death. Death came straightway at his call and asked him what he wanted. The old man answered, "Help in loading my burden on my back again."

One notices that the short—the shortest possible story—if one surrenders to it, makes one pensive. Nothing other and nothing more than pensive.

Now the fables handed down under the name of Aesop do not end with the narration. They also include sayings for what they are supposed to teach, or were supposed to teach: their *Epimyth*, the moral of the story.

Humanists and philologists have always been struck by the inadequate or nonexistent proportion between these maxims and the stories to which they are assigned. If one has surrendered to the pensiveness that the story induces, then its "moral," the result that is supposedly to be derived from it, is often not only sobering, but dismaying and annoying in its nonunderstanding [*Unverstand*]. Although almost none of the teachings can be declared completely wrong, they are in themselves somewhat peculiar and inexplicably inappropriate.

Since ancient times, but perhaps not the most ancient, the fable I have chosen, "The Old Man and Death," has included the explanation that the story (*logos*) shows that every person is a lover of life (*philozōos*), even when things are going badly for him.

Certainly not wrong, and yet disappointing. Not only a regrettable reduction of the meaning of the fable, but a disruption of the pensiveness that has just been aroused. For pensiveness is now abruptly called on to measure the significance of the brief event against the banality of the moral; one is forced to doubt whether such a wonderful work could really have been thought down into this quintessence.

If we then try to extract the supposed message of the fable ourselves, we soon notice that *any* sentence would flatten out the depths of that which can be apprehended, but not comprehended, in pensiveness. As correct as it may be that no degree of misery can completely devalue life, this excludes too much to be acceptable.

I should like now to go a small step further by saying that the pensiveness that the fable provokes has something to do with the pensiveness that is exhibited *within* the fable. The old man in the story is certainly no "thinker" who, between the throwing down of the burden and the arrival of Death, has changed his conclusion about the valuelessness of life. But he is one who experiences the profit in delay that delay first allows. He has thrown down the unbearable burden because he is determined to end it all and wait for Death. But throwing down the burden provides him the respite to catch his breath, to look around, to see once again the world that had gone unobserved while he was weighed down by his load; now he can see what price must be paid for the finality of being freed from his burden. Death, when called upon, descends upon his pensiveness, and it seems that the old man obtains from Death an extension of the very respite that he had first received through a disgust with life. The fable tells nothing about what passed through the head of the old man; we do not know what made him urge Death to help carry his burden farther—as if his call to Death had been for this purpose. Precisely through that which the fable forgoes, it provides us with the space for play [*Spielraum*] of pensiveness.

But pensiveness is also exhibited in the incongruity between the fable and its moral. One would almost like to believe that the *Epimythia* are invented only to demonstrate to listeners and readers how little would be accomplished by drawing a lesson out of the story, by reducing it to a concluding and easily transportable sentence. Instead, everything would depend on producing a condition, an attitude, a circumspection that guards against such sentences. Pensiveness is also a respite from the banal results that thought provides for us as soon as we ask about life and death, meaning and meaninglessness, being and nothingness.

My conclusion—since I must present one because of my profession—is that philosophy has something to preserve, if not revive, from its life-world origin in pensiveness. Philosophy must not be bound, therefore, to particular expectations about the nature of its product. The connection back to the life-world would be destroyed if philosophy's right to question were limited through the normalization of answers, or even through the obligation of disciplining the questions by beginning with the question of their answerability.

Philosophy represents only a more general condition in each culture: that of the irrepressibility of its elemental needs and questions despite attempts to overcome them. Culture also means respecting the questions that we cannot answer, the questions that only make us pensive and let us stay pensive. Heine freely expressed his scorn for Kant when he suggested that Kant wrote the second critique—the one on practical reason, with the topics of pensiveness: freedom, the existence of God, immortality—only for the benefit of his old servant Lampe.[1] After the scorner's audacity has faded away, one becomes pensive: could not that in fact be true?

But we do not need to call up the venerable names. In the life-world, we wanted and want to know where we stand. By now we must be certain that for this question there will be no answers to formulate, and formulated answers will not prevail. Yet we are not easily moved to renounce them—we do this only temporarily, only in the assurance of a substitute answer. We think about where we stand because we were disturbed in not thinking about it.

Pensiveness means: everything is not as obvious as it was. That is all.

Translated by David Adams[2]

---

1. [Heinrich Heine, "On the History of Religion and Philosophy in Germany," in *On the History of Religion and Philosophy in Germany and Other Writings* (Cambridge: Cambridge University Press), 87.]

2. [Minor corrections and additional editorial footnotes by Hannes Bajohr.]

Moments of Goethe

(1982)

Revisions to Seizing the Moment of Birth

Nobody can remember the first moment of their life. One who none-theless wants to write about it will not wish to stick to the most common aspects of the genre: I came, I saw nothing, I screamed. Much rather it has to be something exceptional, and not always are the reports by witnesses, the mother, the midwife, or the doctor full of exceptionalities. What appeared exceptional enough to humans, on account of their repetition over long periods of time, were the constellations of stars at the time of their birth. The literary pro-totype of this introduction to an autobiography was created by Girolamo Cardano, and Goethe was his most successful follower: "My horoscope was propitious: the sun stood in the sign of the virgin,

Originally published as "Momente Goethes," from *Akzente* 29, no. 1 (1982): 43–55.

and had culminated for the day; Jupiter and Venus looked on him with a friendly eye, and Mercury not adversely; while Saturn and Mars kept themselves indifferent; the moon alone, just full, exerted the power of her reflection all the more, as she had then reached her planetary hour. She opposed herself, therefore, to my birth, which could not be accomplished until this hour was passed."[1]

Such appeal to the constellation at the hour of birth is ambiguous: humility regarding the submission to fate and pride regarding the cosmic circumstances of one's own origin; both are possible, and they are not easily distinguished. Karl Friedrich Zelter, Goethe's friend in old age, clearly and with a rare distance, corrected his friend's attitude when, at Goethe's encouragement, he began to keep a record of his own life: "What star or unlucky star [*Unstern*] might have resisted my arrival in this world, I could not say. My mother lay dead to the world and I screamed on."[2] Apparently, Zelter had never bothered with his constellation.

But for Goethe, this almost perfect favor of the stellar conditions that the horoscope revealed did not yet suffice. There was the opposition of sun and moon, or, put more plainly: the full moon. Such a conflict marred the image for him, and it is a matter of no small consequence that in his most important aspiration of his existence he found a means by which to change if not the constellation, at least its interpretation, time-honored though it was.

The *Theory of Colours* unexpectedly offered this opportunity. In 1810, he had completed the work of two decades. At the time, he knew nothing about the discovery that the French physicist Louis Malus had made in 1808; since 1812, Thomas Johann Seebeck had shown him experiments in Jena, which he reproduced for some part from Malus and expanded with his own ideas for other parts, and by which he was able to show the polarization of light. For one of these experiments, the opposition of the sun and the moon is reconstructed in such a way that one has the sun at the back and is looking at a glass pane that is brought to polarization by heating

---

1. [Johann Wolfgang Goethe, *The Autobiography of Goethe: Truth and Poetry Relating to My Life*, trans. John Oxenford (Portland, OR: Floating Press, 2008), 60.]
2. [Carl Friedrich Zelter, *Selbstdarstellung* (Zurich: Manesse, 1955), 9.]

and cooling, causing black circles to form on its corners that make the space between them appear as a bright cross. However, if one is positioned in the astrologically favorable direction of the two half-moons, the waxing and the waning, that is, to the north or the south, then the relationalities reverse: the circles in the corners of the pane turn bright and the cross between them turns black. Goethe was delighted at this phenomenon, not merely because of the transitional colors between light and dark that play such an important role in his color theory and further substantiated it, but because this appeared like an experiment regarding the astrological interpretability of the opposite positioning: it was impossible that it might be negative given that it produced the most sublime phenomenon. Merely ten years after the horoscopic beginning of *Poetry and Truth*, Goethe writes down its correction: a birth during full moon, which is actually a "friendly response" to sunlight, moreover, "must be considered as highly fortunate."[3]

Once more, the readability of nature seemed to have increased for him; not only did it seem to provide encouragement for his most beloved life's work, but now also appeared to emphasize the true findings about his origin as the shadowless favor of the universe itself. Such evidence is of a kind needed only after one has already begun doubting.

First Infinity, then Clarity

Dictionaries instruct us in an all too discreet manner. We learn something about the variants and nuances of the meaning of a word and find each one of them documented. But was that all we wanted to know? Do we not also want to learn what we encounter and are confronted with most and in our present, what fashionable "role" the word played among contemporaries, whether it contributed to

---

3. [Johann Wolfgang Goethe, "Entoptische Farben," *Sämtliche Werke: Briefe, Tagebücher, Gespräche*, ed. Dieter Borchmeyer et al. (Frankfurt am Main: Deutscher Klassiker Verlag, 1989), 25:682–728; 716.]

conversational chic with the swift ephemerality to which those successful in that career are condemned?

When reading the literary texts, the letters and conversation accounts from the time of the *Storm and Stress*, the first of a wave of youth movements, one certainly encounters the metaphysically highly charged gestural word "infinite," which passes that charge on to everything it touches. One need not consider how little it was worth when the Greeks invented it and through it conceived of the misshapenness of shapelessness. But through Plotinus it had already entered into the treasure of attributes of the divine and there infected everything to which it connected, from power to goodness. It ultimately even infected the work of that power, to render it as appropriate to itself: the universe became infinite.

What the world was able to attract to itself could not remain foreign to the subject equal to it in birth; at least as aesthetic creativity within the horizon of its unlimited possibilities it became equally infinite, as a power whose reach was no longer restricted by any rule. Everything that it touched and everything that it required was pulled into this vortex. And that was simply not only literature, not only a poem, but jargon, the identification mark of everyday language among initiates. In the genius period of Weimar, between Goethe's arrival and his clandestine departure for Italy, many things were possible, and "infinite" was a "universally recurring keyword," as Karl August Böttiger reported. When Goethe wanted to invite himself for dinner at Wieland's, he sent his servant and had him ask for "an infinite bowl of infinite Borsdorf apples (steamed)."[4] In general, he who held the attributes once limited to higher entities seemed to have made this knowable particularly through his needs. The duke, patron and fellow traveler of the genius business, pestered his environment every now and then with bratwursts, "which had to be made in infinite amounts."[5]

Such insights into the jargon, into the contagiousness of the language of the avant-garde at the time, are granted to us only through

---

4. [Karl August Böttiger, *Literarische Zustände und Zeitgenossen* (Leipzig: Brockhaus, 1838), 221–222.]

5. [Böttiger, *Literarische Zustände und Zeitgenossen*, 222.]

rare and incidental sources. The phenomenon did not yet attract the observers in a comparable manner, because they could not apprehend what the multipliers of modeled and prescriptive language could achieve in terms of spreading such originally innocent inventions.

What came after *infinity*? Böttiger, who heard all this from Wieland, records the latter's remark from July 15, 1798: "Clarity is now Goethe's favorite word. The genius has now sat aground and clear water floats to the top . . ."[6]

It is odd how little Goethe noticed in his old age that the activities of the Romantics around him, which he observed with contempt, were so similar to what he himself had practiced and spread during the genius period. He did not understand that "clarity" could not become the word of the youth because the surprising experience that "clarity" is necessary and exists presupposes an emergence from confusion and perplexity, and not the other way around.

Unexpected Confirmation

Bernhard Rudolf Abeken was home tutor to Schiller's children. But in everything that remains of him, the name of Goethe dominates, culminating in the title *Goethe in My Life*, the kind of title that can only be awarded once.

In the house of Friedrich Schiller's friend Wilhelm von Wolzogen in January 1809, he heard Goethe utter a strange prediction. The sun, he said, would one day gain a ring like Saturn already has. "This prediction should be engraved into an iron tablet, which then should be buried in the ground, so that the people who found it in later times might recognize how wise we were."[7] Statements of this kind, which strive to draw into history the starry sky that is equipped with metaphysical invariability, are familiar from the Romantics. They held nothing to be impossible—that was the sting of their imagination.

In this year of 1809, Goethe, distracting himself from the adversities of the earth's soil, must have indulged in cosmological speculation.

---

6. [Böttiger, 221.]
7. [Bernhard Abeken, *Goethe in meinem Leben* (Weimar: Böhlau, 1904), 80.]

Like Hegel later with Heine, he is standing at the window with Johannes Daniel Falk and is looking at the night sky. This is another favorite idea of Romanticism: that of the incompletion of creation, which he utters and which makes the prediction about the ring of the sun more comprehensible. "Everything is so enormous that it is unthinkable that any side might ever stop." This is true especially for "the sun, which after all provides everything." Should it have run out of "the power to form earths and moons" or remain passive? He did not believe at all that "it already had fully finished the creation of its own planetary system." Mercury anyway had turned out small enough and thus it seemed highly likely to him that behind the planet closest to the sun "one day an even smaller star will appear." To be sure, the positioning of the planets and the disposal of their masses indicated that the sun's power to design its system by itself, which Goethe calls its "power of projection," was weakened. From that the conclusion had to be drawn that some day "an attempted casting of a planet" could fail. Then the ejection and detachment of the last and innermost planet would no longer succeed and the latter would, incomplete, lay itself as a ring around the sun.[8]

There is an eschatological aspect to this. The shadow effect of this ring might "cause evil effects" for the earth-dwellers: darkening and coldness would come over the solar system. Goethe seems already to have put the sunspots in relation to this "unease for the future."[9]

These two accounts from the same year of 1809 affirm one another, and Falk, who is always under suspicion of dreaming things up, appears quite plausible in this context.

After they were derided for a long time as epitomes of unscientificity, we tend at least "methodically" to rehabilitate such imaginations as images, as metaphoric projections of a state of mind, of time, of fear and hope. It no longer presents us with quite such difficulty to view gross "unscientificity" as preparations for possibilities as soon as perhaps not the real history of our solar system but the rapid history of our discoveries brings something to light that

---

comes close to the theoretical vision of a mind hard pressed by variants of images.

In March 1979, one of the few great surprises from the exploration of the solar system with astronautical technology emerged. The American space probe *Voyager 1* sent images of the moons of Jupiter to Earth, moons that have been so consequential in the history of science. From these images taken in close proximity to the planet, it could be discerned for the first time that Jupiter, too, is surrounded by a ring. *Voyager 2*, the probe that soon followed, was set in such a way to take better advantage of the reflection of the sunlight by the particles of the ring and transmitted extremely clear images of what at first had only been a blurred appearance. The ring has a radius of 128,000 kilometers and a width of 6,000 kilometers, with a diameter of only 0.5 to 30 kilometers. As with Saturn, future space probes will perhaps produce evidence that further rings follow until close to the surface of Jupiter.

Of course, Goethe did not end up being right. The sun has no ring, or not yet. But Jupiter, which is by far the planet most similar to the sun and also by far surpasses the other planets in mass, eventually had to reveal its own. The story of the "power of projection" may transform into a theory of destruction of a former planet through the immense influence of Jupiter's mass, as it may have exerted itself onto the external body like a tidal force, tearing it apart and grinding it into dust. Then the vivid image of Romanticism's nature with its inexhaustible productive power would have been supplanted by an image that strikes us as more timely at the end of the millennium, but which to future retrospection will only appear as our own projection into space, namely, the image of nature as a monstrous apparatus of destruction, in which everything is bound to result in deformation, atomization, agglomeration of mass, deterioration of energy, and the spreading of a blackness without light.

Goethe would not have ended up being proved right, or only partly so, but from his case we would have better understood what the matter is with the interpenetration of theoretical perception and the projection of images into reality. We have to be concerned about saving the statements of imaginatively versed intelligent beings from accusations of being senseless and too remote even to be considered, because though they may seem significant, they do not stand up to the rules of science since they are out of reach of any method of proof. We should contemplate refining the means as to how such statements could be assigned to a broader spectrum of meaning— be it nevertheless, still, or barely meaningful.

Hairstyles of the Zeitgeist

For February 3, 1830, at table, Eckermann recorded only that the topic of conversation was Mozart. Goethe saw the seven-year-old during a concert when he himself was fourteen. What did he re- member after almost seven decades? The sword and the hairstyle. Little though it might seem, Eckermann's eyes widened; he took it to be a small miracle "that Goethe was old enough to have seen Mozart when a child."[10]

This is how things look in the *Conversations*. Since we have gained insight into Eckermann's original notes in a few diaries, the Mozart conversation turns out to be a cut left after its lowly occasion was redacted. There was no talk at all about Mozart, but about the masquerade ball on the occasion of the grand ducal birthday at the castle the previous day. Goethe's son, August, with his wife, Ottilie, and the beloved grandson, Wolf, attended; Eckermann, too, had, according to his account, looked on "from all corners and sides," and even received a blue ribbon that made him happier than all the court's princely splendor. This prompted him to the diaristic moralism that nature had furnished man in such a way "that the littlest things suffice him and that it is in very little in which he finds his true happiness."[11]

What remained of the ball was the magnificent head of ironed curls of the boy Wolf. The grandfather delights in them and would like to see the grandson like this more often; it would do no dam- age at all to the hair, since he himself had had his own curled for

---

10. [Johann Peter Eckermann, *Conversations of Goethe with Eckermann and Soret*, trans. John Oxenford (Cambridge: Cambridge University Press, 2012), 2:223.]

11. [Heinrich Hubert Houben, *J. P. Eckermann: Sein Leben für Goethe. Nach seinen neuaufgefundenen Tagebüchern und Briefen* (Leipzig: H. Haessel, 1925), 1:463.]

seventy years and it was still good. The grandson revolts against such an imposition: the others would make fun of him if he were to walk around with ironed hair. The grandfather does not accept this; let the others laugh, as long as he looks better than them. Even Eckermann has to object here and touch quite brusquely on the old man's trauma about lifetime: "All younger people, I said, that are born after the French Revolution have very strange prejudices in this regard. They think it is some kind of dishonesty if one appears more agreeable than what nature has made."[12] Goethe takes the rebuke lightly; after all, it is given indirectly. Yet his rejoinder strikes at the attempt to invoke nothing less than reason itself against the habit of flaunting victories of nature as reason: "It is an odd generation, said Goethe, but it should become reasonable little by little."[13]

Now Eckermann backs down. The exterior view of that youth to which Goethe belonged must not have been without effect for the interior; hairstyle, shoes, hat, sword surely made for good posture and decency. Only at this point can a nice concession be attached to a great example. Unlike in the final editing of the *Conversations*, the transition has solely this one function: "That is how I saw Mozart as a six-year-old boy."[14] There was no talk about Mozart; Goethe had him appear only fleetingly as the lovely silhouette of the prerevolutionary zeitgeist.

This path, however, from the conversation topic of the masquerade ball via the outmoded curls to Mozart did not appear to Eckermann as quite worthy of him who had in the meantime passed away. But since there was nothing else to say about the two genius children—whose age was raised a bit on each side, incidentally, to make the confrontation appear less like a childish amusement—Eckermann's complete amazement about this primordial miracle of an encounter had to fill in the gap.

In this editorial infringement of the original substance, the latter-day observer recognizes a loss. More manifold experiences with mutability make the coiffure appear to him as one of the more enig-

---

12. [Heinrich Hubert Houben, *J. P. Eckermann*, 1:463–464.]
13. [Houben, 1:464.]
14. [Houben, 1:464.]

matic, but all the more effective means of demonstrating the zeitgeist. Even in view of the scene at Goethe's luncheon table, it is a
phenomenon that does not suppress the suspicion that at the phys-
iologically determined point of greatest deformability of the human
body, a mutability is demonstrated that is intended to conceal the
immutability at the core.

The Sealing of "Faust"

In July 1831, Goethe completes the fourth act of the second part of
Faust after the fifth act. In mid-August, he places the manuscript of
the second part under seal.

This has been memorialized as a biographical date because it
symbolizes in an incomparable way the identity of the time allotted and the moment of completion granted to this life. The definitive edition of his works had been completed in spring and already
thereby the completion of *Faust* took on the aspect of something of
an unplanned and unplannable transgression of what might reasonably be demanded. Undoubtedly, this would have not been possible
without the trust in the absolute reliability of his estate's [*Nachlass*]
administration. Here lies implied that this life moment could not
have been Goethe's alone.

We would have learned more about Eckermann's investiture with
the most important office in delivering the second *Faust* if the fourth
volume of the *Conversations* had been completed. But a fragment
from it has survived that refers precisely to that incomparable act
by which the work passed into the hands of Goethe's most loyal
friend: "Today Goethe passed the manuscript of the second part of
his Faust on to me, so that someday it will be edited together with
the rest of his literary estate."[15] This must have been before July 22,
when Goethe noted in his diary: "Last version."[16] For he instructs

---

15. [Houben, 588.]

16. [Johann Wolfgang Goethe, *Sämtliche Werke: Briefe, Tagebücher, Gespräche*,
ed. Dieter Borchmeyer et al. (Frankfurt am Main: Deutscher Klassiker Verlag, 1993),
38:431.]

Eckermann to read everything again and to make a note of anything conspicuous, "so that we can bring it into a clean version step by step."[17] Then there is, above all, the constraint not to let anyone else read it after only Zelter and Ottilie had been allowed to be involved. This reminder is followed by a message about screening: "I led other good friends who revealed some curiousness about the manuscript to believe that I had put seven seals on it and locked it tightly. We will leave it at that so that I am not bothered any further."[18]

Was the sealing of "Faust" only a mystification against intrusive curiosity? To this day, we don't know. All evidence from sources can be related to a reservation for pure defense: hence also the alleged unsealing in January 1832 in order to read for a month from the manuscript to the daughter-in-law.

By whatever last word scholars will see fit to close this question, the difference between the harmless mystification and the loftiness of the last act's gesture with regard to the work's reception history will be offensive only to those who want to locate a historical fact exclusively in the consciousness of those taking part in it.

It fits well into the evaluation of Eckermann's part in the completion of *Faust* that it almost always allowed what was, at least until Nietzsche, his underestimated subservience—honored by being bestowed with the task of edition—to recede behind the ritual of sealing; generally, the evaluation of Eckermann sought to ascribe his part, especially in this work, to the hubris of the man who recorded the *Conversations*. But Eckermann overestimated Goethe rather than himself, and should he have overestimated himself by means of Goethe, that did not make him an inventor of things Goethean. It was not to Eckermann, but to chancellor Müller, that Goethe said on June 8, 1830, that Eckermann was skilled at "extorting" literary products from him. Thus, he was "the principal cause that I continued *Faust* and that the first two acts of the second part are nearly ready."[19] *Helena* had been the first and surprising product of this influence. Goethe completed it when Eckermann

---

17. [Houben, *Eckermann*, 589.]
18. [Houben, 589.]
19. [Houben, 257.]

returned to Weimar from a visit to his bride Johanne Bertram and gave it to him with the words, "After all, I owe it to your participation that the piece is now completed."[20]

No, Eckermann did not invent his driving and eventually successful share in the completion of *Faust* in order to provide his bride, who waited for him for more than a decade, with a human and world-literary consolation. This second part is indeed no longer the work of a stormy inspiration but rather of calculated balancing and considered worldliness. Eckermann included a remark in the *Conversations* that seems quite bold with respect to the relationship to Schiller, but which need not be hyperbolic from Goethe's mouth since he had not yet reached his goal—for it is only March 7, 1830, and Goethe himself will at the time hardly have believed in the completion that Eckermann would eventually bring about: "It is not good for man to be alone . . . and especially to work alone. On the contrary, he needs sympathy and suggestion to do anything well. I owe to Schiller the *Achilleis* and many of my ballads, to which he urged me; and you may take the credit to yourself, if I complete the second part of *Faust*. I have often told you so before, but I must repeat it, that you may know it." Eckermann eventually added that he was delighted by these words, "for I felt that there might be much truth in what he said."[21] All this on a day on which Goethe had disclosed to him that he had had to put aside the "Classical Walpurgis Night" to finish the last installment of the definitive edition. But since he had been on a good streak, it should be easier to build on the stock of what he had already invented than if he continued writing until his workflow stagnated.

When Eckermann published this exchange and appealed to Goethe's oft-repeated statement, too many of the inner circle of the table talk and other occasions were still alive, so that he could not risk exaggerating in this sensitive matter. In addition, we have the original diary entry for that day, and the sole considerable devia-

---

20. [Houben, 268.]

21. [Johann Peter Eckermann, *Conversations of Goethe with Eckermann and Soret*, trans. John Oxenford (Cambridge: Cambridge University Press, 2012), 1:449.]

tion is to be found in a nuance, when it comes to the rapporteur's own reaction: "I was pleased with Goethe's words and received them happily with the feeling that there might be much truth in them."[22]

Eckermann writes four letters about Goethe's death to persons close to him. In the letter to the Prussian council of state Christoph Ludwig Friedrich Schultz, who belongs to the most astute of Goethe's correspondents in the last two decades, Eckermann also reports about the completion of *Faust*. Fortunately, Goethe had finished it the summer before and "nothing fragmentary remains in this immortal work."[23] Then Eckermann does something that reveals how he identified Goethe with the late Faust: He relates the admittedly illusory completion of the land reclamation work of the blind Faust, the awareness of which—independently of the realism of his perceptions—provides him with the greatest moment, to the completion of Goethe himself: "It is remarkable [*merkwürdig*] that *Faust* ends with the words 'The trace of my days on earth / Cannot perish for aeons,' which might indeed now be rightly applied to the deceased himself."[24] Goethe is dead, and now Eckermann speaks like Goethe; for this would also have appeared "remarkable" to him, with that very word, that he had applied with a preference to ominously significant things.

Immortality only in the trace, only in the work—that was still too little for Eckermann. To him, Goethe did not die, but he had the decency to say so only in the description of the death itself—a death, as if it were no death: "He sat in his armchair in the most comfortable position like a slumberer and lay in the sarcophagus four days later stretched out like a sleeper, whom one would be afraid to wake up by the slightest noise. Death had respect for him. Not with a forceful hand had he separated the spiritual from the terrestrial, he seemed barely to have touched him with a finger, indeed he seemed only to have waved at him from afar."[25]

---

22. [Houben, *Eckermann*, 473.]
23. [Houben, 628.]
24. [Houben, 628.]
25. [Houben, 631–632.]

The demonic, for which Goethe had found the most valid of his formulas only a few months earlier in the conclusion of the fourth part of *Poetry and Truth*—he had never laid claim to it for himself. But now Eckermann saw him as someone for whom even death had respect, whom he had let depart his life in the pagan, gentle manner, with a mere wave. It was no act of violence, but of consenting renunciation, of nature accomplishing itself. It was the last thing that was contained in the resigning way to read the "prodigious saying" [*ungeheurer Spruch*], which Goethe had just quoted once more in the last book of *Poetry and Truth*.

Once to Have Seen Him Weep

Upon the news of Goethe's death, Karl Friedrich Zelter wrote one last letter to Weimar, thus concluding the great correspondence that was kept up with an earnest intensity on his part. He confessed the relentlessness of his tears to Chancellor von Müller, and added: "I did, however, see him weeping once; that must vindicate me."[26]

This is not just a phrase. When Zelter followed his friend hardly two months later, as he had desired, Lea Mendelssohn-Bartholdy, the mother of his student Felix, wrote: "Indisputably he died from not being able to survive Goethe. . . . He really perished from a broken heart."[27]

We know of nobody else who saw Goethe weeping. Eckermann could barely believe the dispassion of the father who had to accept the news of his son's death in Rome. Repeatedly, there were rumors of his coldness, most bitterly by Jean Paul, for whom tearfulness was a way of life.

When and about what might Goethe have wept? We do not know, and never will with certainty. Nevertheless, it is not futile to ask about the moment that Zelter had witnessed. It forces the observer to take a stand.

---

26. [Karl Friedrich Zelter, *Selbstdarstellung* (Zurich: Manesse, 1955), 417.]
27. [Zelter, *Selbstdarstellung*, 422.]

Zelter visited Goethe in Weimar many times. The encounter with the most intensely unsettling background is that of November and December 1823. Goethe had been gravely ill and for two weeks could ward off convulsive coughing only by sitting up day and night. It was the physical crisis that caused the definite renunciation of "youth" as an aspiration of his life, one last time embodied by Ulrike von Levetzow.

When Zelter arrives at the desolate house on Weimar's Frauenplan, his first impression is, "He is dead!" But then, in view of the convalescent, he finds: "One who looks as if he had love, all of love with all of the agony of youth in his body."[28] He helps the friend to sit upright, consoles him—with what? With the testimony of that very crisis, the Marienbad "Elegy." This is the scene: Not Goethe reads to Zelter, but he to Goethe, knowing that "he will feed on it all his life."[29] We can think of no greater intimacy in this closeness of friends, and to it Zelter, who is usually averse to pathos, applies the words: "A god lives in us. Man must grow old, the god gets younger."[30] If one thinks what it is that Goethe had spoken from the mouth of his friend, it is dismay at no longer enjoying the favor of the gods.

Now he has no longer just written it—from posting house to posting house on the return journey from Marienbad—now he hears it from the friend who had made so many things audible to him, who set "At Midnight" to music for him: "I have lost the whole world, I have lost myself / I who but lately was the darling of the gods." It is the last farewell to Promethean thought, because once more he thinks about Pandora, now seeing her become one with Ulrike: "They put me to the test, they gave me Pandora / With her abundant store of blessing and greater abundance of danger."[31]

Emerged from the darkness of this turning point in his life, Goethe in early January 1824 thanks him who has returned to Berlin for having rendered the poem "so faithfully by heartfelt devotion to the

---

28. [Zelter, 317.]

29. [Zelter, 322.]

30. [Zelter, 322.]

31. [Johann Wolfgang Goethe, "Elegy," *Selected Verse*, ed. David Luke (London: Penguin, 1964), 316.]

reading"[32] and then reaches for the nearest comparison with what the composer did for so many of his poems. This had been a repetition of sorts, albeit peculiar in "that you wanted to read and read again, that you let me hear with your sensitive and gentle voice what pleases me to a degree I do not care to confess to myself."[33]

Now the sentimental involution of these readings is ensured, but at what point, one may ask, is Goethe supposed to have wept?

Here, for once, everything must be staked on reversing the question: How else could he have heard the lines of the "Elegy" that fail to leave untested even a reader remote in time: "I am far from you now. This present minute / what does it demand? . . . / unending tears are my only counsel."[34] If ever at all, then here.

Translated by Florian Fuchs

---

32. [Johann Wolfgang Goethe, *Die letzten Jahre*, ed. Dieter Borchmeyer (Frankfurt am Main: Deutscher Klassiker Verlag, 1993), 1:137.]

33. [Goethe, *Die letzten Jahre*, 137–138.]

34. [Goethe, "Elegy," 315.]

Beyond the Edge of Reality

Three Short Essays

(1983)

Gestures of a Loss of Reality[1]

Philosophers have readers and listeners. They are not seen by their readers, who are, what is more, confronted with final products, from which all is deleted that might be taken as an involuntary trace of subjectivity. Although listeners perceive what is strange and curious about the speaker in front of them, they are subject to the expectation that what is important for them will be something audible—a fact that makes many not even look up just so as to be able quietly to take their notes. To others, only in memory does the association of this or that gesture to what was said appear meaningful: perhaps a

---

Originally published as "Über den Rand der Wirklichkeit hinaus: Drei Kurzessays," from *Akzente* 30, no. 1 (1983): 16–27.

1. [This section exists in a much more extensive version in *Care Crosses the River*, trans. Paul Fleming (Stanford, CA: Stanford University Press, 2010), 33–39.]

gesture that gave the secret desire to communicate something yet
unspoken—the last will, maybe, to express it—its almost unnotice-
able place. Memory supplants what Nietzsche claimed to be able
to do even as a reader: that he "cannot read a single word without
seeing gestures."[2]

The philosopher of life, remembered as lecturing, promises to
show something of the tension inherent in the very concept of such
a philosophy that goes all out. Ludwig Marcuse recalled two unforgettable gestures of his teacher Georg Simmel, which relate to
one another in a manner that needs to be brought before the mind's
eye. The first: "He, while bobbing on the very edge of the lectern,
stabbed the sharpened pencil into the air—into an invisible matter,
as it were." Marcuse immediately adds his interpretation: this is to
be understood as the gesture of the passionate analyst. The first gesture is followed by a second, which, although more essential, had
been less noticed: "He left the exposed edge of the lectern, and the
outstretched pencil sank between his fingers, and with his head lowered he went silently across the lectern until he had composed himself sufficiently to continue the lecture." Here, too, memory helps
in the understanding of this turning away from the gesture of stabbing that which offers no resistance: "In this silent second of self-
forgetfulness, he inwardly annulled what he had just found by his
stabbing."[3] Each of Simmel's readers, who have been increasing
in numbers ever since, recognizes this turning point of so many of
his arguments, when he goes beyond what seemed to be the final
formulation attainable, and considers and relativizes his barely won
result from the opposite pole of possibilities. It was no different in
the live performance of the teacher, who left behind what he had
just seen, but was able to give only a tacit promise to go beyond it.

---

2. [Friedrich Nietzsche, *The Anti-Christ*, in *The Anti-Christ, Ecce Homo, Twilight of the Idols, and Other Writings* (Cambridge: Cambridge University Press,
2005), 41.]

3. [Ludwig Marcuse, "Erinnerungen an Simmel," in *Buch des Dankes an Georg
Simmel*, ed. Kurt Gassen and Michael Landmann (Berlin: Duncker und Humblot,
1958), 191.]

To memory, the scene presents itself as a moment of utter per-plexity—as the "immeasurable tragedy"[4] of philosophical thought becoming tangible, not only in the present thinker and his thought. He seems doomed to prevent himself from exhausting his rigor. Sim-mel's thought process seemed apt to become optically perceptible when his pleasure in analysis was still in the thin airspace of the most subtle reality, or rather, no-longer-reality, which could be ruth-lessly and cruelly tugged back down to the ground of empirical facts. That is why Simmel, before becoming a "philosopher of life," had tried his hand at one of the objects most resistant to thought: the philosophy of money.

When Ludwig Marcuse made his observation on Simmel's teach-ing *Gestus* [bearing, manner], the latter had already philosophi-cally found "life" and appointed it the placeholder of metaphysics, whereas Husserl had not yet made the "life-world" the subject of phenomenology. His students in Göttingen considered him a realist and put all their expectations in the promised return "to the things themselves." The confusion was great when in 1913 the master of the school published his program in the form of his *Ideas*.[5] Helmuth Plessner, whose life's work we can now appreciate in full,[6] reports his observation of Husserl's wishing gesture.

Plessner had submitted a treatise on Fichte's *Wissenschaftslehre* [*Science of Knowledge*] to Husserl, in order that the latter's appraisal might clarify how his new conception of the power of conscious-ness was distinct from Fichte's concept of the creative ego. One day on his way home from the seminar at his garden gate, Husserl ad-mits he had always disliked all that German idealism. He had been looking for reality his whole life: "And saying this, he brandished his thin silver-topped cane and, leaning forward, braced it against the doorpost."[7] To Plessner, the emphasis placed in this gesture of

---

4. [Marcuse, "Erinnerungen an Simmel," 191.]

5. [Edmund Husserl, *Ideas Pertaining to a Pure Phenomenology and to a Phe-nomenological Philosophy*, 3 vols. (The Hague: Nijhoff, 1983).]

6. [Helmuth Plessner's collected works were published between 1980 and 1985 with Suhrkamp Verlag.]

7. [Helmuth Plessner, "Husserl in Göttingen," *Schriften zur Philosophie* (Suhrkamp: Frankfurt am Main, 1985), 367.]

a lifelong search for reality appears to embody phenomenology's basic theme: "In an unsurpassably palpable manner the walking stick represented the intentional act and the post its fulfillment."[8] This was written in 1959 to mark the celebration of Husserl's centenary at Göttingen.

The stick as an instrument of contact with reality that has become foreign to us had of course already belonged to Wilhelm Dilthey, and Max Scheler referred to it when, in 1926, he demonstrated the contrast between idealism and realism in the experience of resistance. But he refined Plessner's image by saying, "When we brace a stick against the wall, the resistance is experienced at the end of the stick, but the tactile sensation, in the hand."[9] However, in Dilthey's treatise of 1890, "The Origin of Our Belief in the Reality of the External World and Its Justification,"[10] the instrument had been, more properly scientific, a probe, which one would hardly brace against a wall. Since Scheler, too, had had contact with Göttingen phenomenology, it is reasonable to assume that the tidings of Husserl's use of the walking stick might have had an effect on the distortion of the Dilthey quotation.

From Husserl's time in Freiburg a decade later, Hans-Georg Gadamer gives us a report of his teaching *Gestus*. During his lectures, Husserl often looked at his hands, which were kept busy "with the fingers of the right hand circling the flat palm of the left hand in a slow, turning movement."[11] Initially, Gadamer interprets this as a movement of focusing, but this does not quite meet the standard of his hermeneutical vigilance. At the same time, he adds, this gesture "brings 'close to hand' [*handgreiflich*] the hand-worked [*handwerklich*] ideal of precision in the Husserlian art of description."[12]

---

8. [Plessner, "Husserl in Göttingen," 367.]

9. [Max Scheler, *Späte Schriften* (Bern: Francke, 1976), 211.]

10. [Wilhelm Dilthey, "The Origin of Our Belief in the Reality of the External World and Its Justification," *Selected Works*, vol. 1, *Understanding the Human World*, ed. Rudolf A. Makkreel and Frithjof Rodi (Princeton, NJ: Princeton University Press, 2010), 8–57.]

11. [Hans-Georg Gadamer, *Philosophical Apprenticeships*, trans. Robert R. Sullivan (Cambridge, MA: MIT Press, 1985), 35.]

12. [Gadamer, *Philosophical Apprenticeships*, 35–36. Translation altered.]

The eyewitness always has the primacy of authentic transmission. But for him who comes another two decades later, such metaphorical "handiness" [*Handgreiflichkeit*] also appears as a helpless gesture of fear of that which Husserl called by the dreaded word "solipsism" and which for him denoted the catastrophe of the loss of reality. If one looks back at the Göttingen walking stick, it certainly must have been of contemporary elegance and, therefore, pliable thinness, so that it could appear to the observer as an arc of intentionality rather than a tool for testing the solidity of the robust gatepost. A problem had not yet reached the severity that would find its solution only in the concept of intersubjectivity.

But the circling of one hand on the inner surface of the other has something of a desperate reassurance, which takes place only in the system of one's own lived body and gives the oldest sense of reality, touch, and something of a demonstrative satisfaction without going beyond the boundary of immanence. However remote the answers to questions may have been, the intensity of the experienced lack of reference to reality signifies belonging to the great epoch-making idiom of philosophy.

Contemplating a Sentence by Nietzsche

Immortality, which Plato was the first to proclaim as provable, has become a rather irritating as opposed to exhilarating piece of metaphysics. It could contribute little to the general happiness of humanity simply because the requirements for reaching and spending an "eternal life" undisturbed had been set very high, at times unattainably so, during the bloom of its undoubted validity. It no longer amounted to any loss or sacrifice when immortality was finally removed from metaphysics by Kant and degraded to the alleged harmlessness of a postulate. This initiated a century that perceived a dangerous distraction from intensive this-worldliness in such kinds of expectations: Just stand firmly and take a look around. . . . Promises that were to be fulfilled only after death could be but blandishments to fend off any insistence on a share of that which is of this world.

Did Nietzsche not also have to follow this tendency of the century? Could the *superhuman* [*Übermensch*] turn out right if the contenders to that title had other prospects than just earthly thoroughness?

And then we come across—surprisingly, unexpectedly—something written in the phase of the incipient *Zarathustra*: "That we could *bear* our immortality—this would be supreme."[13] Yet before one can arrive closer at the contents of the sentence, at its oddly hypothetical subjunctive, it stimulates curiosity because it seems so little to befit the necrologist of the "dead god" and other metaphysical decompositions. For the hesitant reader, assistance is readily at hand, of which earlier editors too made use when incorporating the sentence into all kinds of other writings about the eternal recurrence of the same, and about the *superhuman* as a repeat offender distinguished by the fact that he cannot and does not want to let it be: "And then finally: to want this entire sequence once again!"[14]

But it is permissible to refuse to tolerate that these two sentences are on the same page and that one should only be the complement of the other. For everything about the eternal recurrence is pure boasting, a metaphysical surrogate to balance out that expired God and to make the human fill his vacancy as someone who can deal with the most outrageous imposition. In contrast, the sentence about immortality is of the highest order. According to which criterion? According to none other than that of causing pure pensiveness and of not letting anyone wrest himself from it.

When Nietzsche, during the time of *Zarathustra*, jotted down the sentence about being able to bear immortality, the *Philosophy of 'As-If'* had already been written—assuming one follows Hans Vaihinger's own account in this respect, as the work could only appear in 1911—and had formulated a compelling central question: "How is it possible that we can reach correct results through knowingly

---

13. [Friedrich Nietzsche, *Unpublished Fragments from the Period of Thus Spoke Zarathustra (Summer 1881–Winter 1883/84)*, trans. Paul S. Loeb and David F. Tinsley, vol. 14, *The Complete Works of Friedrich Nietzsche*, ed. Alan D. Schrift and Duncan Large (Stanford, CA: Stanford University Press, 2019), 531.]

14. [Nietzsche, *Unpublished Fragments*, 190.]

false ideas?"[15] Vaihinger had studied this problem in Kant's doctrine of postulates, among others, which he of course tore from the context in which Kant had placed it by insinuating conscious falsehoods: That which is unprovable, that which does not require proof, even more, that on which a ban on proof has been imposed, could not and should not be what is known to be false. And exactly that still applies to Nietzsche's handling of immortality.

The way he believed he could think and allow it, as eternal recurrence, it was meant to be imposed as a threat on the human determination to surpass himself, that is, as a challenge that was to have nothing to do with the rewards and punishments of old. Undoubtedly, this quest for superlatives, by which humans could work their way up to becoming superhuman, also applies to the brief apophthegm that does not release the one pondering it all too easily: a hypothetical subjunctive, indeed, but one that is thrillingly apodictic. Averted from the abstract generality of what should be fit to become law, each man is considered to stand at the limit of his own moral capacity. He is compelled to look beyond it onto the unlimited witness he bears of himself, as which immortality alone could be the autonomous tribunal.

For humans die before they have the chance to see what becomes of the aggregate of their actions that have constituted their life. What this means is revealed by magnification: Luther died before the Thirty Years' War, Rousseau before the French Revolution, Bismarck before the two World Wars of his short-lived empire, Freud before the collapse of all resistances to his general thesis during the sexual revolution. As an argument of immortality, this only means that one must be allowed to imagine everyone was obliged to watch their own consequences unfold. Whether they would enjoy or be troubled by it must not interest us—there may be something in humans that one can rely on once they have come to rest, in every sense.

Thus, there is no longer any talk of happiness, of which modern humans will scarcely think themselves any longer capable, even if they were still to desire it. They have become too complicated for

---

15. [Hans Vaihinger, *Philosophie des Als-Ob* (Leipzig: Meiner, 1922), xii (quote from the preliminary remarks not included in the English translation).]

the Christian heaven. Nietzsche's talk moves from bearability—self-bearability—as an infinite test all the way to the finite. No court threatens him who would have to think of himself as immortal, except the sole authority that could make his continued existence harder than anything that the Valley of Jehoshaphat might have had in store: he himself, with his burden of memory, with the shame of identity.

Nietzsche turns the postulate of immortality into a thought experiment about one's own moral subsistence, about the validity of one's own actions, which would be capable of withstanding any future retrospection. The moral of an attitude that is wholly committed to the world corresponds to the imperative to act as if one's actions would have to withstand, for all eternity, the scrutiny of him who had ordained that it should be so. Put into a formula: Live in such a way that you can be in agreement with yourself at any time about having wanted to live that way and wanting to live that way again! The moral subject, finite in its proportions, possesses himself of the dimension of infinity as that of a self-judgment that will never be final.

This particular equipping of immortality with the ritual of eternal recurrence can also be considered an exaggeration, a piece of postmetaphysical rhetoric: in going beyond immortality as mere catamnesis of the unique conduct of one's life toward the supposedly greater mercilessness of being compelled to live again, Nietzsche risks the refutation that the current course of the world and all responsibilities therein might already be a cycle of the eternal recurrence. Thus, however, contrary to the intention of maximizing the burden of accountability, an excuse would be provided in the form of the justness of that which stands decided by eternity.

Certainly, the idea of return had its own allure of ancient paganism for Nietzsche: not only are we supposed to be able to bear surviving but bear having to exist, in turn, as those and only as those as whom we had, one single time, the liberty to constitute ourselves. What Nietzsche does not tell us, however, is that it must remain unknown to us whether it is this time and this life that the fate of the world has entrusted to us. Like many things in Nietzsche, this thought is a bit too magnificent not to be thought over people's heads—including those of the aspirants to superhumanity: the rotating cosmos is not supposed to release its true demiurge from its clutches and imbue his consciousness with an almost unbearable accountability.

"Permanence does not concern him,"[16] Rilke's sixth Duino Elegy says of the "Hero." Nietzsche wanted to prevent this heroic type of uniqueness that appears as the self-sufficiency of a deed's magnitude by confronting it with his own type, who is concerned with nothing but permanence. The proof of having been equal to one cycle of the world would thus lie only in proving equal to all of them and, having passed that test, in whether one was subject to the compulsive desire to keep providing this force with opportunities for its enactment. "My doctrine states: to live in such a way that you must wish to live again, that is the task—you will anyway!"[17]

To put the discretum of living-once-again in place of the continuum of merely continuing-to-live appears to Nietzsche as the decisive step beyond classic versions of immortality. Above all, the having-to-desire in place of the being-able-to-bear—this is the very gaiety of self-excess that arose with *Zarathustra*. Yet because of the attached threat—"you will anyway!"—the implication of freedom is eliminated from the description of the task of getting through life to the wanting-to-live-again. From the level of the *as-if*, this is the relapse to metaphysics.

It marks a return to the calculation of Pascal's wager that if further things are unavoidable, one should decide to optimize them. In the repetition of the same, there is still something from Dante's principle of correspondence. But the relapse goes further, because— it needs to be reiterated—the current presence of a decision could already be for all time Dante's Inferno of futility, with no possibility of thinking of any sign that might provide clarity in the matter.

Anybody able to desire what he must desire would be aware of the remorselessness about the world that bears his trace. None of

---

16. [Rainer Maria Rilke, *Duino Elegies*, trans. Stephen Mitchell (New York: Vintage, 2009), 37.]

17. [Friedrich Nietzsche, *Nachgelassene Fragmente: 1880–1882*, vol. 9, *Kritische Gesamtausgabe*, ed. Giorgio Colli and Mazzino Montinari (Berlin: de Gruyter, 1977), 505.]

the worlds to come could fill him with shame. It is tangible: this *would* be the superhuman. But he will not be. His chance has already passed, if it ever was. It went under in the fear of that which will arrive anyway *because* it will come anyway. That is why one can fall back onto Nietzsche's other dictum: to bear immortality. This would be something that might not fully require the superhuman, as long as it meant to bear the consequences of one's own existence within its proportions.

The talk of enduring immortality is an abbreviation; what is supposed to be the highest that can be borne is the idea, neither blurred nor distorted by any calculation of reward or punishment, of remembrance beyond the boundary of physical existence. What would compel the imagined survivor to bear himself continuously, and to be before himself only the one that he was, the one as whom he lived in this way and no other, that would be his *memoria* [memory], released from the protection of oblivion and from repression. Should a philosophical eschatology to succeed the theological one have to speak of a "court" to occupy the position in the economy of consciousness whose vacancy is apparently hard to bear, *memoria* would be the court that alone could complete the autonomy of the ethical subject.

It was a peculiar deficiency of the theological eschatologies that in encircling the otherworldly fates of humans they could not help everybody to attain their own fulfillment. That would have rendered unrecognizable the burdens as well as the reliefs of the divine order of salvation, their unforgivable sins as much as their sovereign offers of mercy. Even in Schopenhauer's metempsychosis there was too much of a regulation of salvific fate; there it was necessary to take care of general justice as an external observer of the world would have seen it for the whole of world time. Being and justice coincide only once it is no longer required that everyone must make do with himself and his memory. As far as being able to bear immortality is concerned, it is still a boundary value in the wake of Kant's critique regarding the substantiality of the soul, guaranteed by no ontological security, a fragile instability. To perish from shame [*vor Scham vergehen zu können*], this idiomatic turn of phrase, if it were translated into the eschatological, could be the form in which immortalities wither away, revert into finitude—in the paradox of their unbearability.

Might Nietzsche's sentence contain, or even represent, the ethics that would satisfy the "principle of responsibility"?[18] For the latter, it may be necessary to specify what the one who survives himself would have to bear. What remains present to him might be not only the *memoria* of his actions and maxims, but also the sight of his own consequences in the world, to be witness to which would mean immortality as long as they remain: the trace of his days on earth. Not wanting to perish *or* wishing never to have existed defines the extremes of what might arise from extending Nietzsche's basic idea with regard to a novel, radically threatening condition of the world.

Nietzsche's belief in the practical effectiveness of a theoretical thought—for what else was eternal recurrence and could it be—is baffling; the reality of the superhuman was to consist in the ability of being equal to the burden of this thought. Undoubtedly, only rigorisms have a chance to find their type and leave their stamp on it in the wide field of ethics. Only the Stoa and the categorical imperative have left such a stamp. Nietzsche was sure that his ideas had the power to impress because he shared the suspicion of all creators of thoughts that the thoughts shaped hitherto must have been simply too weak to assert their claim. Every subsequent thinker must surely account for the disappointment in the effect of ideas by the indecisiveness of his predecessors. To what is achieved must be added the consciousness of the utmost that is achievable, in order finally to put the capabilities of thought to the test. Because no author himself can ever attest to the outcome of this trial—hence his need for immortality!—he takes the consolation of the extremist to his grave that he has risked the utmost. One need not participate in this consolation—need not have expectations for the ultimate after the penultimate—in order still to find it inevitable that the attempt will continue to be made to find the point where the idea is content

---

18. [Hans Jonas, *The Imperative of Responsibility: In Search of an Ethic for the Technological Age* (Chicago: University of Chicago Press, 1985). The German original was titled *Das Prinzip Verantwortung* (The Principle of Responsibility).]

enough with itself at least no longer to allow excuses for its ineffec-
tiveness to be found. This is part of the indefatigability of all philosophical efforts. In this they have their experimental character within
the laboratory of history.

For the contemplation of Nietzsche's sentence, this would mean:
if any one idea should at all be powerful enough to change the tenor
of human existence, it might as well or indeed would have to be
this one. It should succeed in connecting itself with the concept of
memoria in such a way that humans would not just be subject to
the intimacy of their identity—not only in the candor of their memory about the I that they had been—but would also have to become witnesses of their posterity [*Nachwelt*], as the epitome of the
history of their world [*Welt*].

At this point, contemplation of Nietzsche's sentence may converge with the primal question about what the human can be
thought of as capable of doing. Is he content with what has been
demanded from him since the dictum of the Delphic Apollo: essentially to know himself through the thought of being able to bear
immortality, in order *to be as he would be able to bear himself*?

The Dreamed

Ernst Wilhelm von Brücke, neurophysiologist and Freud's teacher,
was made immortal by the fact that the student dreamed of the
teacher. Brücke had been dead for almost a decade when the *The
Interpretation of Dreams* appeared, which demonstrated its primal
instituting meaning [*urstiftende Bedeutung*] for psychonanalysis
precisely with the dream that introduces Brücke as its initiator: "Old
Brücke must have set me some task; strangely enough, it related to
a dissection [*Präparation*] of the lower part of my own body."[19]
Only the superficial reader of Freud can be puzzled by the fact that
while expertly disemboweling his own pelvis, he does not take the
shortest path to the cardinal issue, but rather relates the reflexivity

---

19. [Sigmund Freud, *The Interpretation of Dreams: The Complete and Definitive Text*, ed. James Strachey (New York: Basic, 2010), 459.]

of the dreamer about his own body completely to the oddity that inevitably had to stand at the beginning of the new procedure: "The task which was imposed on me in the dream of carrying out a dissection of my own body was thus my self-analysis which was linked up with my giving an account of my dreams."[20] Freud is sober minded and careful enough to treat this dream with the understatement of not ascribing to it any legitimizing meaning for what, according to the theory, is an altogether impossible endeavor.

In the old teacher's command itself lies the metaphor for the impossible: self-dissection. It is more important that during his lifetime the teacher did what he would do again by way of the dream: preventing the discovery from being discouraged and left half done. Old Brücke, writes Freud, rightly appears in the dream, since it had already occurred in the first years of his scientific work "that I allowed a discovery of mine to lie fallow until an energetic remonstrance on his part drove me into publishing it."[21] It is not hard for the reader as interpreter of the interpretation to recognize in the figure of Brücke the source of energy that could no longer be represented by any divine or demonic inspiration.

Three years before Freud was born, on November 8, 1853, Ernst Wilhelm Brücke led a friend through the newly built insane asylum of the city of Vienna. The friend made the following note: "Terrible: To see the masses of insane people, for it makes the abnormal seem normal again."[22] With astonishment, the visitor in the corridor of the asylum observes one inmate shaving another; he is stunned by the banal remark of the doctor that he too availed himself of the man's service.

The friend of the young psychiatrist Brücke deserves our attention because of a duplicity that once more deserves to be called "strange enough" in Freud's words: he, too, dreamed about Brücke and portrays him as a man about whom it was apparently fit to dream. Friedrich Hebbel, who was this friend and whose diaries tell

---

20. [Freud, *The Interpretation of Dreams*, 461.]
21. [Freud, 461.]
22. [Friedrich Hebbel, *Tagebücher: Neue historisch-kritische Ausgabe*, ed. Monika Ritzer (Berlin: de Gruyter), 1:673.]

us about this relationship, also provides a clear hint about what made Brücke so disposed for dreams and particularly for those with a grade of absurdity like that about the order for self-dissection: he was an admirer of paranoid punch lines. Once he told a story, reports Hebbel, of an argument about whether the moon was populated; a Croatian doctor had heckled, "What populated, when moon wanes, what would happen to population?"[23]

One will have to take notice of the difference between the intention with which this might have been related and the one with which it was recorded. The doctor, with little sense for the "sense" of the phenomena that appeared on his objects, will have brought forward the anecdote as a "case" of unenlightened Balkan backwardness in the midst of an at least slightly scientific discussion of a problem contemporaries took quite seriously: How could one still be so behind the times [*hinter dem Mond*] about the nature of the moon in this century!

Hebbel did not write this down as a joke about a lunatic. His sympathy is on the side of the heckler. For his interjection is of an indubitable aesthetic grace. One can feel the jealousy of ignorance's freedom still to use an idea of such vivid force to reduce a claim to absurdity: imaginary peoples at the edge of the melting moon, fleeing from its depletion and huddled in the ever tighter space of the crescent-like remainder, finally to disappear into nothingness—which is indeed why nothingness is where they belong. What so regularly would be prevented from surviving cannot exist. Not a good argument?

It is strange that in his *Vienna Letters* to the *Augsburger Allgemeine Zeitung*, Hebbel reports a similar story about a Hungarian astronomer, which was supposed to have circulated in Vienna—where one liked to poke fun at the backward peoples of the empire. During an educated disputation about the phases of the moon, this astronomer believed it necessary seriously to prove their merely illusory nature and for this purpose referred to inhabitants of the moon. If the changes of the moon were not just semblance, but the real disappearance and return of substance, this would result in

---

23. [Hebbel, *Tagebücher: Neue historisch-kritische Ausgabe*, 1:673.]

the inhabitants of the moon "not knowing whereto they should retreat."[24]

Of course, there are many variations of such stories that produce the laughable from the collision of progress and backwardness. Nevertheless, it is worth thinking about why the Hungarian variation is so much worse than the Croatian. For an aesthetic component is added here. The Hungarian astronomer assumes the population of the moon and takes as the condition for their existence the mere "seemingness" of the phases of the moon, of which his science assures him anyhow; the Croatian doctor, on the contrary, refutes the population on the moon with the interjection that it would be rendered impossible by the reality of the changes of the moon. To take the illusiveness as the real is the aesthetically more pleasing option, instead of requiring a hypothetical reality to defend the illusiveness. The Croatian doctor sees a monthly lunar tragedy before his eyes, the paradox of which is that it itself repeals the premise that makes its repetition possible.

This referentiality of the idea about the conditions of its implementation must have given greater pleasure to the man about whom it was possible to dream that he had ordered Freud to dissect his own pelvis and thus metaphorically provided the justification of psychoanalysis through self-analysis.

Translated by Florian Fuchs and Hannes Bajohr

---

24. [Friedrich Hebbel, *Vermischte Schriften II* (Berlin: Behr, 1903), 259.]

24

OF NONUNDERSTANDING

Glosses on Three Fables

(1984)

The Pauper's Coin

An impudent man threw a stone at the inventor of the fable. He struck him, and Aesop praised him: "Pretty good already," he said and presented him with a small coin. "I'm afraid that's all I have, but I want to show you where you can get it." A rich and powerful man came along, and Aesop advised the impudent man to claim his prize from him. He did as he was told. He was arrested and made to suffer on the cross.

Phaedrus put this into verse in the third book of his fables. The Phrygian slave's ruse of connecting the punishment of his abuser to an attack on a powerful man has been understood as a tribute to the spirit of the fable.

Originally published as "Vom Unverstand: Glossen zu drei Fabeln," from *Neue Zürcher Zeitung*, March 24, 1984, 67.

This is a far-ranging thought, one that well befits the spirit of the times. I read the fable as a hint about how important it is for the poor man, too, to carry at least a small coin about him. For the clever idea that the tiny initial success could be repeated and extended if only one were to pitch at a more wisely chosen target could, after all, not be made convincingly without having demonstrated in cash how it might work; what was left to show was only how more could be made. Nothing could have been bought with this sou, but it was exactly the right symbolic means to put the good face of him who could not fight back on the matter.

Now one might want to ask why Aesop himself had to appear in this fable and why it is not staged with the costumes of his bestiary. Unfortunately, the answer would have to be that animals cannot throw, at least not on target. But nor can they speak, and do they not do just that in the Aesopic corpus? It is for exactly this reason they must remain what they are in all other respects.

Inconsiderate Improvements

The later it is in antiquity, the more variable the roles of the gods become. In a lyric fable of Babrios from the second century, Zeus, Poseidon, and Athena engage in an art competition. Zeus makes the human, the most sublime creature of all. Athena, being helpful to the father, builds a house for the human; Poseidon, always idiosyncratic, creates a bull. Momos is appointed the judge, as he is said to be a reliable critic. He finds that the horns are incorrectly placed on the bull, that the human lacks a window to look into his soul, and he complains that the house lacks the wheels that would allow for a change of abode.

Those are not very deep insights, one might think—had not a commentator acquainted with the modern world added that the critic's last complaint was recently addressed by the invention of the motor home.

It is thus worth reconsidering whether Momos would have approved of the achievement. Though in possession of many motor homes, the residential mobility of humans has thoroughly decreased. Their wheeled dwellings bring them so much pleasure because they are the very exception to sedentarism. It is not the house of Athena that has been put on wheels, but only its miniature, in order to leave behind one's permanent residence for a matter of days or weeks yet also to come home to it. Coming home to a stable normality is what is required for the episode of wandering to have experiential value.

As for the complaint about the windowlessness of the human, the commentator unexpectedly provides proof that Momos must have missed something about the nature of humans. A window in the chest would only lead to the application of a procedure that every motor home demonstrates in some variety: curtains would have been put up. Humans still exercise their right to opacity when they put the reduction of their residential castle onto wheels. Leibniz was right against Momos; his creature, the monad, is windowless.

Aspects of a Donkey Deserving to Die

The Spanish humanist Juan Luis Vives recorded the fable of the peasant who killed a donkey because it swallowed the moon while drinking from a bucket, and because the world could sooner do without a donkey than without heaven's lamp.

This fable can be read in different ways.

The peasant certainly lacked enlightenment. Otherwise he would have known that the moon would not be affected by a donkey making its reflection disappear from the water's surface.

But did the donkey—and for that reason, it had to be a donkey—not simply deserve to die because it did not pause in awe before the reflection of heaven's light, which would have allowed a piece of beauty to remain in the world?

The peasant was right: When in doubt, one has to treat the world so carefully as to prevent the slightest possibility of damaging it. Could there not be a secret spell that causes the moon to wane and disappear, because peasants let their donkeys guzzle away its reflection?

And then there is the type of reader who always knows best: the peasant killed the donkey because he felt like some donkey meat, but because he was a peasant, he was also looking for an excuse that would lay on the donkey the complete blame for being slaughtered.

No, says one last reader, that is not yet the whole truth. The peasant kills the donkey because more money was offered to him for the donkey's meat than the donkey was worth to him. He tells the buyer the story about the moonlight only to prevent him from realizing that it had been about the money all along.

Translated by Florian Fuchs

25

UNKNOWN AESOPICA

From Newly Found Fables

(1985)

Preliminary Remark

Aesop was—if he ever really existed—a slave. Based on his origin, he is referred to as a Phrygian, in some sources as Lydian, in better ones as Thracian. Testimony in favor of this origin is given by Wieland's detailed proof in the *History of the Abderites*,[1] according to which there had been a cultic worship of all kinds of animals in the Thracian capital of Abdera. To come thence would be plausible for the inventor of speaking animals. Recently, more has become known.

From Thrace, too, came the slave whom Socrates introduced into world history in recounting the nocturnal accident that befell the

---

Originally published as "Unbekanntes von Äsop: Aus neuen Fabelfunden," from *Neue Zürcher Zeitung*, October 5, 1985, 47–48.

1. [Christoph Martin Wieland, *History of the Abderites*, trans. Max Dufner (Bethlehem, PA: Lehigh University Press, 1993), cf. esp. third book, chapter eleven.]

forefather of philosophers. This man, Thales of Miletus, left the town to observe the stars but overlooked a well and fell into it. The Thracian woman who also dwelt there at the same time—albeit for no such reason—laughed at the fallen man. Socrates, of whom it is said that he brought down philosophy from the heavens to earth and into the homes of humans, was not without sympathy for the mocking Thracian. He simply called her pretty.

There was also some marveling—as philologists are wont to marvel: by athetesis [rejection]—that the protohistory of philosophy told by Socrates should be included in a collection of fables that from time immemorial had been ascribed to *Aesop*—there, however, without naming the philosopher and without identifying the know-it-all. In the Aesopic corpus with its talking animals, the anecdote cuts an unfortunate figure. How did it end up there?

Now there is an answer to that. Aesop smuggled an encrypted history of his own origin into the vehicle of his literary immortality.

The Thracian woman was not a chance witness to the philosopher's accident. Nor was her laughter motivated by spiteful schadenfreude. She must have had a soft spot for philosophers. Every night, she secretly followed the stargazer. Her intuition that during such nonsensical activities there would be no lack of situations where help might be needed was faultless. So it came to pass that by her wit and throaty laughter, she was able to help the man who had fallen into the well get over his embarrassment in order to encourage him to return to realism: he ought to stick to what was comprehensible down here.

By betraying the secret of Aesop, Socrates subtly implied how the fable—which he was the first to put into verse while in prison awaiting his death—arrived at the inexhaustibility of its wisdoms: the forefather of all philosophy was also that of all fables.

Thus, the disconcerting problem that Aesop placed himself on rare occasions in his stories (which were therefore suspected to be apocryphal) is finally solved. The new findings, three of which are presented here, prove that intermediate forms between animal fable and anecdote belong to the original stock [*Urbestand*]: Aesop with his talking animals.

Perhaps they are attempts that he discarded, in which case they would be further evidence for the fact that discarded matter from all ages has good prospects one day to be pulled from the scrapheap and into the light of imperishability.

The Fish's Complaint

> . . . the mute, phlegmatic stock of fishes . . . [2]
>
> —RILKE, "DOLPHINS"

A large fish was brought to the house in which Aesop served as a slave. The fish was supposed to be prepared for the master's table, but it was not forbidden for Aesop to have an appetite for the leftovers.

When the fish noticed who he was dealing with, he said to Aesop: "In your fables you let all animals speak, except the fishes. You seem not to be as much in favor of equality as your interpreters claim."

"Fishes are mute," Aesop responded briefly and succinctly.

"But the other animals that you allow to speak," the fish insisted, "have no language, either."

"You see," Aesop concluded reluctantly and turned away, "now the fish had one opportunity to say something—and what does he make of it? He talks about other animals. Thus, there is a truth in the expression 'mute as a fish,' namely that fishes are mute because they have nothing to say."

The Wolf's Complaint

One day, the inventor of the fable encountered the wolf for whom he had tailor-made some of the most beautiful of his pieces. Yet he greeted him sullenly.

"You seem bad-tempered," said Aesop.

---

2. [Rainer Maria Rilke, "Dolphins," trans. Edward Snow, in Rilke, *New Poems: The Other Part* (San Francisco: North Point Press, 1987), 10.]

"I am angry with you," the Wolf replied.

"You have no reason for that. I have always made the mistake with you to let you look for causes, where you had none. What is there to complain about?"

"You've distorted my nature," the Wolf answered.

"And how so?" Aesop wanted to know.

"You let me talk too much. No talking while eating is even what humans tell their children. We, too, enjoy the finest of upbringings. We don't talk while we eat. Our mouth is already dripping with greed and it would sound outrageously un-wolfish if we were to say something. But you, Aesop, are letting me gas on incessantly, which is why in a moment I will enjoy my meal."

"You are right," Aesop admitted. "But had I let you be as you claim to be, you would have never ended up in the fable. We would have heard nothing from you except your nighttime howling."

The Fox's Complaint

The Fox, too, complained to Aesop. He made him look ridiculous with all the cleverness he imputed to him. "I am not smarter," the Fox said, "than I need to be in order to survive."

"In return you are preventing others from surviving," Aesop pointed out to him. "Think about the chickens you are stealing."

"They have their own art of survival," the Fox protested. "They have invented the easiest procedure to reproduce—they pursue it while seated."

Aesop did not want to let the Fox get away with that. "You are confusing two things there. The chickens that you feed on can no longer make their kind by sitting. But you live on each time, and even better, meal by meal."

The Fox did not relent. "But were it not for my devouring chickens, the world would be full of chickens, as easy as it is for them to become many."

Aesop took the objection in good grace. "That wouldn't be bad. Then even we slaves would have our daily egg and our chicken on Sundays."

"But," the Fox triumphed, "you could no longer invent fables, because the interpreters and exegetes think they have recognized that your little stories are cryptic outcries of a slave's misery."

From Aesop's own hand, we find the addition: Here Aesop was silent. He never told of just how clever he had to find the Fox to be.

Postscript

The Frankfurt publisher to whom I offered these unknown Aesopica declined on the grounds that Aesop was not a German classic.

Translated by Florian Fuchs

26

ADVANCING INTO ETERNAL SILENCE

A Century after the Sailing of the Fram

(1993)

When the Norwegian Arctic explorer and Nobel Peace Prize laureate Fridtjof Nansen died in 1930, he was president of the International Society for the Exploration of the Arctic Regions by Means of the Airship (Aeroarctic). There is a certain irony to this. Already four years earlier, a member of the society had used a semirigid construction named *Norge* to prove that the society's ultimate goal—reaching the North Pole—was indeed feasible. Two years later, the Italian general Umberto Nobile, who had been in charge of this enterprise, made a second attempt to reach the North Pole from Spitzbergen in the *Italia* but crashed in the fog. Only some of the crew could be saved after they had retrieved their emergency gear, radio, and batteries and dragged them on an ice floe, along with the "Red Tent" that has since become proverbial. They were rescued

Originally published as "Vorstoss ins ewige Schweigen: Ein Jahrhundert nach der Ausfahrt der 'Fram,'" from *Neue Zürcher Zeitung*, December 24, 1993, 53–54.

only thanks to the emergency signals they sent via radio, which set off a multitude of flights and rides of ice-breakers and which allowed the rescuers systematically to zero in on the red tent.

Nansen, who by then was almost seventy, must have been reminded of his own helplessness during his east–west drift on board the *Fram*, clenched and crushed by the pack ice for three winters. Contrary to his theory, the *Fram* had missed the pole and failed to give a grand finale to the century of polar expeditions when, in the third year of the expedition, Nansen tried to conquer the last stretch of the way on dog sleds, with the ship as the base camp close to the pole. But now, when Nobile made his attempt, the blocked passages and pack ice, and the unspeakable hardship of overcoming or bypassing them, were surmounted by air, as if by sleight of hand. In fact, a means of rescue that Nansen could not have anticipated in 1893/95 was at hand even in the disastrous second attempt to reach the pole by plane: the radio device on the drifting ice floe. The Italian Guglielmo Marconi had put a valuable precautionary measure in the hands of his compatriot Nobile by equipping him with a radio. The advance into eternal silence, which for Nansen had still meant disappearing, as it were, into the oblivion of incertitude, was thus mitigated by the constant ability to broadcast coordinates and, ultimately, a call for rescue. While Nansen had already generated electricity on the *Fram*—as long as the ship was still under steam, there were no limitations to illuminating the crew's games and reading—once the engines came to a halt in the bed of ice, the wind turbine soon froze up along with everything else. Yet even had that not been the case, nobody would have known then that electricity could be used to send or receive radio signals. One and the same decade had produced the problem and its solution—without, alas, introducing them *to each other*.

This situation fit neatly into the greater set of problems at the end of the century: it was the uneasy question of how long the vital condition of the sun would last, a question that for Nansen, as for others, fell under the apocalyptic rubric of "heat death." Eternal silence was therefore only a sort of rehearsal for the final destiny of the solidification of everything.

In the year of Nansen's death, the barricade around the earth's poles had long been breached, the dark threats hanging over his adventure lifted, and the routes opened for transpolar air traffic. Yet a murky emotional reservation continued to hover unresolved over humanity's self-image: the sun's grace would not be bestowed for as long as the unbroken promise of "progress" demanded and apparently deserved. By its very radiation, the central star was burning itself up, diminishing in mass, and in doing so, depleting the "fuel" that produced the warmth and light on which life on earth depended. No escape was yet known from the shortage of time imposed by the only accepted scientific explanations for the processes of energy generation in the sun's core and its resources.

In the decade after Nansen's death, the "chemical" solution to this problem was supplanted by a "physical" solution: Hans Bethe and Carl Friedrich von Weizsäcker found the formula of the nuclear fusion cycle at solar temperatures, which suddenly extended both life's past and future to new dimensions. For just a few moments in the history of science, the frontier of the apocalypse receded into a distance out of mind, though thermodynamics could not be tricked into supporting absolute promises of any kind. Yet the moment of time between this brilliant consolation and the dawning of an era of the new apocalyptic implications of uranium fission passed as quickly as the advances in nuclear technology would move henceforth.

We can no longer look back triumphantly on Nansen's melancholy in the midst of "night and ice," nor on the fin de siècle of "heat death," no more so than on the breaking of the silence at the ends of the world. Soon, they would be crisscrossed by the incessant noise of "radio traffic," a suitably ambiguous term. For Nietzsche, it was still a grand metaphorical gesture to write: "Beyond the North, beyond the ice, beyond death—*our* life, *our* happiness ... We have discovered happiness, we know the road, we have found the exit out of whole millennia of labyrinth."[1] It was with no lesser degree of pathos, if still with the laconism of a frozen hand, that Nansen then during the last winter of his expedition, on Christmas Eve 1895,

---

1. [Friedrich Nietzsche, *The Anti-Christ*, trans. R. J. Hollingdale (London: Penguin, 1990), 127.]

wrote in his diary: "Oh, the road to the stars is both long and difficult!"[2] Too long, it would turn out, and too costly.

Humans are *risky* beings, and not just because they seek frontier-pushing adventures like the voyage adrift of the *Fram*. They are risky for the very reason that their biological origins lie in the narrow span of the last interglacial period, when they learned the ability to cope with life caught between the advancing and receding glaciers; the natural being was now pitted *against* nature. To make itself independent of uncertain living conditions, this being even gained access to the fossil hoard of solar energy accrued in earliest times— were it not for the finitude of this hoard, which soon began to frighten this being like "heat death" did a century before. All its survivors retain a legacy from this prehistory: the need to test their resilience against nature, even to the point of enduring zero gravity. Once that was achieved, however, the natural being was spared the challenge of holding out in soundlessness, in the "eternal silence" of the outer spaces that still horrified Pascal, thanks to the very "medium" that had not connected Nansen to the "world."

Without having lost the acoustic umbilical cord to the well-nurtured sphere of culture, it might never have occurred to him that his expedition had led him to the "intuition" [*Anschauung*] of what had been called "heat death" since the middle of the nineteenth century. Yet experiencing his first winter in the icy camp of the *Fram* coincided with the shocking vision of what seemed to be the inevitable fate of the planet, in a time frame measurable only by "masses of centuries": "The world that shall be! Again and again this thought comes back to my mind. I gaze far on through the ages. Slowly and imperceptibly the heat of the sun declines, and the temperature of the earth sinks by equally slow degrees. Thousands, hundreds of thousands, millions of years pass away, glacial epochs come and go, but the heat still grows ever less; little by little these drifting masses

---

2. [Fridtjof Nansen, *Farthest North: Being a Record of a Voyage of Exploration of the Ship* Fram, *1893–96, and of a Fifteen Months' Sleigh Journey by Dr. Nansen and Lieut. Johansen*, 2 vols. (New York: Harper & Brothers, 1897), 2:453.]

of ice extend far and wide, ever towards more southern shores, and no one notices it; but at last all the seas of earth become one unbroken mass of ice. Life has vanished from its surface, and is to be found in the ocean depths alone."[3] The expedition gave itself some consolation in this last refuge when its probings below the ice sheet brought all manner of little creatures to the surface.

But the extrapolation into the future was not over yet, the generosity of reckoning with time not yet exhausted. The temperature had to sink even further: "But the temperature continues to fall, the ice grows thicker and ever thicker; life's domain vanishes. Millions of years roll on, and the ice reaches the bottom. The last trace of life has disappeared; the earth is covered with snow. All that we lived for is no longer; the fruit of all our toil and sufferings has been blotted out millions and millions of years ago, buried beneath a pall of snow."[4] Only now has the earth become a "star among stars," against all expectations implied in its name, having fully surrendered to the cosmic rule of torpor and silence. Nansen, the wayfarer upon the ice, shows no signs of longing for such silence, for his habitual world has not yet become loud enough.

"A stiffened, lifeless mass of ice, this earth rolls on in her path through eternity. Like a faintly growing disk the sun crosses the sky; the moon shines no more, and is scarcely visible." All of this is in no way original for its decade, yet it differs in one aspect from the descriptions usually composed with didactic intentions. Nansen's writing doesn't simply result from the nineteenth-century epistemological habit of expanding science into knowledge, but from the *intuition* of the first polar winter that he just survived aboard or inside the *Fram*. For this very reason, the play of color of the Aurora borealis remains a powerful experience each time. Although its correlation with the solar cycle had already been recognized, its nature was only explained the year after Nansen's return. These northern lights troubled him, because they appeared as an "aesthetic" event removed from human sight and thus like a demonstration against the human entitlement to "enjoy" them. It thus

---

3. [Nansen, *Farthest North*, 1:439–440.]
4. [Nansen, 440.]

seems like a "counterdemonstration" to this rather distressing event
that the 1897 publication of the expedition saga included what at
the time were costly reproductions of a large number of water-
color and pastel sketches.

Since Nansen could not have known that the northern lights require solar energy, he took them as illustrations of the ice deserts
that would outlast the "heat death" of life, albeit in diminished gran-
deur: "Yet still, perhaps, the northern lights flicker over the desert,
icy plain, and still the stars twinkle in silence, peacefully as of yore.
Some have burnt out, but new ones usurp their place; and round
them revolve new spheres, full of new life-worlds [*Lebenswelten*],
new sufferings, without any aim. Such is the infinite cycle of eternity; such are nature's everlasting rhythms."[5] "Heat death" appears
as a universal event, against which the only consolation is the fact
that such futility of life will occur over and over again somewhere.
No one, it turns out, will have been alone in the extreme solitude
of the polar winter. This appeared like a delusory comfort after the
waning century had started to destroy the sense of cosmic "socia-
bility" that the Enlightenment of the prior century had dreamed of
by making the masses of space and time explode—the worlds had
nothing but silence to gain from their plurality.

Except for the "life-worlds" presented in them, Nansen's eschatological banalities belong to contemporary history rather than to the
history of science. They also resound with biblical notions, causing
the premundane *tohubohu* to echo in that of posterity, in the normal state of things from which the glory of the world had risen by
divine command as a mere episode, only to sink back at the fading
of that order: "I have never been able to grasp the fact that this earth
will some day be spent and desolate and empty. To what end, in that
case, all this beauty, with not a creature to rejoice in it?"[6] asks the
Stoic, to whom Copernicus could have been but the theoretical cor-
rector of an excess of self-importance. But now there is only the
prospect of the wild ice and the droning of its senseless compres-

---

5. [Nansen, translation altered.]
6. [Nansen, 253.]

sions and fractures: "Now I begin to divine it. *This* is the coming earth—here are beauty and death. But to what purpose? Ah, what is the purpose of all these spheres? Read the answer, if you can, in the starry blue firmament."[7]

The deflection of our gaze toward the starry sky is a late nineteenth-century figure of thought that is hard for us to retrace. The countless repetitions of the same, or better yet: of the same futility in different *life-worlds* intend to reflect a semblance of meaning onto this experiment, which Nansen had compressed into an "expedition": an experiment in torpor, in nautical passivity, of giving oneself over to the dubious ice drift. This experiment is, in brief, a simulation of how to make sense of "heat death." It takes place in a future in which the earth is nakedness, when even snow will no longer fall onto the vastness of glacial upheavals and rupture lines: "Why will it not snow? ... This snowless ice plain is like a life without love—nothing to soften it. The marks of all the battles and pressures of the ice stand forth just as when they were made, rugged and difficult to move among."[8]

Even though this is a diary entry, it anticipates the conditions under which advancing on the pole by sleds would fail later on. Without the intangible and imperviously drifting vessel that was the *Fram*, nothing was possible in this world—unless one had fallen prey to anachronism and thought of flying over the pole. This was the idea of the Swede Salomon August Andrée, who would pay the ultimate price in 1897, when he refused to submit to nature's obstructions.

In the thick of the third polar winter, during his march back and at an undetermined position, Nansen, from the crude hut in which he spends the winter with Johansen, catches sight of the moon over the unknown land. "A weird beauty, without feeling, as though of a dead planet, built of shining white marble. . . . And everything so still, so awfully still, with the silence that shall one day reign when

---

7. [Nansen, 253–254.]
8. [Nansen, 335–337.]

the earth again becomes desolate and empty."[9] Not enough to conjure up the beginning of the Bible; also, what hovered over the waters on the first day of creation is now back again, in what becomes the final scene of all things ever formed: "In the flaming Aurora Borealis the spirit of space hovers over the frozen waters. The soul bows down before the majesty of night and death."[10]

All of a sudden, the reflection via the detour through the universe fails to yield up meaning:

> As we walk up and down here shivering we gaze into the boundless starry space, and all our privations and sorrows shrink into nothingness. Starlit night, thou art sublimely beautiful! But dost thou not lend our spirit too mighty wings, greater than we can control? Couldst thou but solve the riddle of existence! We feel ourselves the centre of the universe, and struggle for life, for immortality—one seeking it here, another hereafter—while thy silent splendor proclaims: At the command of the Eternal, you came into existence on a paltry planet, as diminutive links in the endless chain of transformations; at another command, you will be wiped out again. . . . Is, then, the whole thing but the meteor of a moment? Will the whole history of the world evaporate like a dark, gold-edged cloud in the glow of evening—achieving nothing, leaving no trace, passing like a caprice?[11]

When Nansen notes in his diary that he read Darwin's *On the Origin of Species* while lying in bed, this feels like a mise-en-scène that neatly corresponds to the *Fram*'s ice-bound predicament. Nansen is a zoologist, not an engineer like Andrée or Nobile; it does not occur to him to "overfly" the three-year-long hardship in ice and darkness, for his ideas never deviate from the basic pattern of the struggle for survival. The ship's construction was designed to "endure" the forces of nature, not to override them. Departing the icy stronghold on dog sleds to storm the target point of the absolute north is thus very much the consequence of viewing humans as caught in the ultimate test to which they might submit themselves. The probability was zero that the two groups—the *Fram* group and

---

9. [Nansen, 2:440.]
10. [Nansen, 441.]
11. [Nansen, 441–442.]

Nansen and Johansen on their sleds—would ever make it back home, across the frontier of silence, anywhere close to the same time. But that is precisely what happened, endowing their endeavor with the aura of an almost mythical validation.

And now, as if by an explosion, the silence was shattered by means of a technology that might have been designed for the geographical location and shape of Norway: telegraphy. Virtually in a single moment, the message spread that ended the long uncertainty about the expedition; that it still relied on wires to achieve this end was insignificant. However, it makes us aware how shortly before the ubiquity of connections the venture of advancing into eternal silence was made. The era of unreachability was hastening toward its end.

Translated by Florian Fuchs

Glossary

Anschaulichkeit/anschaulich	intuitiveness/intuitive
Anschauung (*Kantian term*)	intuition
Bedeutsamkeit/bedeutsam	significance/significant
Begriff/begrifflich	concept/conceptual
Begriffsgeschichte/begriffsgeschichtlich	conceptual history (also: history of concepts)/ historico-conceptual
Distanz/distanziert	distance/distanced
Eindeutigkeit/eindeutig	univocity/univocal
Mehrdeutigkeit/mehrdeutig	ambiguity/ambiguous
Vieldeutigkeit/vieldeutig	equivocity/equivocal
Epochenschwelle	epochal threshold
Evidenz (*phenomenological term*)	self-evidence (not: evidence)
faktisch	factual
Faktizität (*phenomenological term*)	facticity
Gegenständlichkeit/gegenständlich	objecthood/objectual (also: object-like)
Objektivität/objektiv	objectivity/objective
Vergegenständlichung/vergegenständlichen	objectification/objectify

Geschichtlichkeit	historicity
Gestalt	form (also: *Gestalt*)
Grenzbegriff (*Kantian term*)	boundary concept
Grenzfall	boundary case
Grenzwert	boundary value
Idee (*Platonic term*)	idea/Idea (not: form)
Lebenswelt/lebensweltlich	life-world/life-wordly
(*phenomenological term*)	
Leistung (sometimes:	achievement (also: capability)
phenomenological term)	
Mensch/menschlich	the human (also: man)/human
Metakinese	metakinetics
Metaphorik	metaphorics
Mitvollzug	coperformance
Nachdenklichkeit	pensiveness
Neuzeit/neuzeitlich	modern age/of the modern age
	(also: modern)
Präparat	specimen
Prävention/präventiv	preemption/preemptive
	(not: prevention/preventive)
Sagbarkeit/sagbar	sayability/sayable
Unsagbarkeit/unsagbar	unsayability/unsayable
Sein/Seiendes (*Heideggerian terms*)	being/entities (also: what is)
Selbstbehauptung	self-assertion
Selbsterhaltung	self-preservation
Selbstverständlichkeit/selbstverständlich	obviousness/obvious (not:
	self-evidence/self-evident)
Entselbstverständlichung	dismantling of obviousness
Spielraum	latitude
Stelle	position
Stellensystem	system of positions
Technik	technology
Technisierung (*phenomenological term*)	technization
Umbesetzung	reoccupation
Unbegrifflichkeit/unbegrifflich	nonconceptuality/nonconceptual
Vorbegrifflichkeit/vorbegrifflich	preconceptuality/
	preconceptual
Unverstand	nonunderstanding
Ursprünglichkeit/ursprünglich	primordiality/primordial
Vorgriff	anticipation
Wirklichkeitsbegriff	concept of reality

BIBLIOGRAPHY

This bibliography lists the main publications of Hans Blumenberg, with an emphasis on essays and monographs. Due to space constraints, newspaper articles are only given for translated pieces. English translations are listed with the original publication. Entries marked with three asterisks (***) are part of this Reader. For a full bibliography, see Hans-Blumenberg-Handbuch, *edited by Oliver Müller and Rüdiger Zill (Stuttgart: Metzler, 2020).*

A. Qualifying Theses

1. "Beiträge zum Problem der Ursprünglichkeit der mittelalterlich-scholastischen Ontologie." Dissertation, Kiel, 1947.
2. "Die ontologische Distanz: Eine Untersuchung über die Krisis der Phänomenologie Husserls." Habilitation, Kiel, 1950.

B. Monographs

1. *Die kopernikanische Wende.* Frankfurt am Main: Suhrkamp, 1965.
2. *Die Legitimität der Neuzeit.* Frankfurt am Main: Suhrkamp, 1966.
   2.1. Second edition in three volumes: Part 3: *Der Prozess der theoretischen Neugierde.* Frankfurt am Main: Suhrkamp, 1973; Part 1 and 2: *Säkularisierung und Selbstbehauptung.* Frankfurt am Main: Suhrkamp, 1974; Part 4: *Aspekte der Epochenschwelle: Cusaner und Nolaner.* Frankfurt am Main: Suhrkamp, 1976.
      2.1.1. English as: *The Legitimacy of the Modern Age.* Translated by Robert M. Wallace. Cambridge, MA: MIT Press, 1983.
   2.2. Second edition in one volume: *Die Legitimität der Neuzeit. Erneuerte Ausgabe.* Frankfurt am Main: Suhrkamp, 1988.
3. *Die Genesis der kopernikanischen Welt.* Frankfurt am Main: Suhrkamp, 1975.
   3.1. English as: *The Genesis of the Copernican World.* Translated by Robert M. Wallace. Cambridge, MA: MIT Press, 1987.
4. *Arbeit am Mythos.* Frankfurt am Main: Suhrkamp, 1979.
   4.1. English as: *Work on Myth.* Translated by Robert M. Wallace. Cambridge, MA: MIT Press, 1985.
5. *Schiffbruch mit Zuschauer: Paradigma einer Daseinsmetapher.* Frankfurt am Main: Suhrkamp, 1979.
   5.1. English as: *Shipwreck with Spectator: Paradigm of a Metaphor for Existence.* Translated by Steven Rendall. Cambridge, MA: MIT Press, 1997.
6. *Die Lesbarkeit der Welt.* Frankfurt am Main: Suhrkamp, 1981.
7. *Wirklichkeiten in denen wir leben: Aufsätze und eine Rede.* Stuttgart: Reclam, 1981.
8. *Lebenszeit und Weltzeit.* Frankfurt am Main: Suhrkamp, 1986.
9. *Das Lachen der Thrakerin: Eine Urgeschichte der Theorie.* Frankfurt am Main: Suhrkamp, 1987.
   9.1. English as: *The Laughter of the Thracian Woman: A Protohistory of Theory.* Translated by Spencer Hawkins. New York: Bloomsbury, 2015.
10. *Die Sorge geht über den Fluß.* Frankfurt am Main: Suhrkamp, 1987.
    10.1. English as: *Care Crosses the River.* Translated by Paul Fleming. Stanford, CA: Stanford University Press, 2010.
11. *Matthäuspassion.* Frankfurt am Main: Suhrkamp, 1988.
    11.1. English as: *St. Matthew Passion.* Translated by Paul Fleming and Helmut Müller-Sievers. Ithaca, NY: Cornell University Press, 2020.
12. *Höhlenausgänge.* Frankfurt am Main: Suhrkamp, 1989.
13. *Die Vollzähligkeit der Sterne.* Frankfurt am Main: Suhrkamp, 1997.
14. *Ein mögliches Selbstverständnis.* Stuttgart: Reclam, 1997.
15. Reprint of C 32: *Paradigmen zu einer Metaphorologie.* Frankfurt am Main: Suhrkamp, 1998.

15.1. English as: *Paradigms for a Metaphorology*. Translated by Robert Savage. Ithaca, NY: Cornell University Press, 2010.

15.2. Reprinted with commentary as: *Paradigmen zu einer Metaphorologie: Kommentar von Anselm Haverkamp*. Berlin: Suhrkamp, 2013.

16. *Gerade noch Klassiker: Glossen zu Fontane*. Munich: Hanser, 1998.

17. *Begriffe in Geschichten*. Frankfurt am Main: Suhrkamp, 1998.

18. *Lebensthemen: Aus dem Nachlaß*. Stuttgart: Reclam, 1998.

19. *Goethe zum Beispiel*. Frankfurt am Main: Insel, 1999.

20. *Die Verführbarkeit des Philosophen*. Frankfurt am Main: Suhrkamp, 2000.

21. *Löwen*. Frankfurt am Main: Suhrkamp, 2001.

21.1. English as: *Lions*. Translated by Kári Driscoll. London: Seagull, 2018.

22. *Ästhetische und metaphorologische Schriften*. Edited by Anselm Haverkamp. Frankfurt am Main: Suhrkamp, 2001.

23. *Zu den Sachen und zurück*. Edited by Manfred Sommer. Frankfurt am Main: Suhrkamp, 2002.

24. *Beschreibung des Menschen*. Edited by Manfred Sommer. Frankfurt am Main: Suhrkamp, 2006.

25. *Theorie der Unbegrifflichkeit*. Edited by Anselm Haverkamp. Frankfurt am Main: Suhrkamp, 2007.

26. Blumenberg, Hans, and Carl Schmitt. *Briefwechsel 1971–1978 und weitere Materialien*. Edited by Alexander Schmitz and Marcel Lepper. Frankfurt am Main: Suhrkamp, 2007.

27. *Der Mann vom Mond: Über Ernst Jünger*. Edited by Alexander Schmitz and Marcel Lepper. Frankfurt am Main: Suhrkamp, 2007.

28. *Geistesgeschichte der Technik: Mit einem Radiovortrag auf CD*. Edited by Alexander Schmitz and Bernd Stiegler. Frankfurt am Main: Suhrkamp, 2009.

29. *Theorie der Lebenswelt*. Edited by Manfred Sommer. Berlin: Suhrkamp, 2010.

30. *Quellen, Ströme, Eisberge: Beobachtungen an Metaphern*. Edited by Dorit Krusche and Ulrich von Bülow. Berlin: Suhrkamp, 2012.

31. Blumenberg, Hans, and Jacob Taubes. *Briefwechsel 1961–1981*. Edited by Herbert Kopp-Oberstebrink and Martin Treml. Berlin: Suhrkamp, 2013.

32. *Präfiguration: Arbeit am politischen Mythos*. Edited by Felix Heidenreich and Angus Nicholls. Berlin: Suhrkamp, 2014.

33. *Schriften zur Technik*. Edited by Alexander Schmitz and Bernd Stiegler. Berlin: Suhrkamp, 2015.

34. *Rigorismus der Wahrheit: "Moses der Ägypter" und weitere Texte zu Freud und Arendt*. Edited by Ahlrich Meyer. Berlin: Suhrkamp, 2015.

34.1. English as: *Rigorism of Truth: "Moses the Egyptian" and Other Writings on Freud and Arendt*. Translated by Joe Paul Kroll. Ithaca, NY: Cornell University Press, 2018.

35. *Schriften zur Literatur 1945–1958*. Edited by Alexander Schmitz and Bernd Stiegler. Berlin: Suhrkamp, 2017.

36. *Phänomenologische Schriften 1981–1988.* Edited by Nicola Zambon. Berlin: Suhrkamp, 2018.
37. *Hans Blumenberg alias Axel Colly: Frühe Feuilletons (1952–1955).* Edited by Alexander Schmitz and Bernd Stiegler. *Neue Rundschau* 129, no. 4 (2018): 5–123.
38. *Die nackte Wahrheit.* Edited by Rüdiger Zill. Berlin: Suhrkamp, 2019.

C. Essays

1. ***"Die sprachliche Wirklichkeit der Philosophie." *Hamburger Akademische Rundschau* 1, no. 10 (1946/47): 428–431.
2. "Das Recht des Scheins in den menschlichen Ordnungen bei Pascal." *Philosophisches Jahrbuch* 57 (1947): 413–430.
3. ***"Das Verhältnis von Natur und Technik als philosophisches Problem." *Studium Generale* 4, no. 8 (1951): 461–467.
4. "Philosophischer Ursprung und philosophische Kritik des Begriffs der wissenschaftlichen Methode." *Studium Generale* 5, no. 3 (1952): 133–142.
5. ***"Der absolute Vater." *Hochland* 45 (1952/53): 282–284.
6. "Technik und Wahrheit. In *Actes du XIème Congrès International de Philosophie (Bruxelles, 20–26 août 1953)*, vol. 2, *Épistémologie*, 113–120. Amsterdam: Nauwelaerts, 1953.
7. "Ist eine philosophische Ethik gegenwärtig möglich?" *Studium Generale* 6, no. 3 (1953): 174–184.
8. "Eschatologische Ironie: Über die Romane Evelyn Waughs." *Hochland* 46 (1953/54): 241–251.
9. Review of *Die Entwicklung zum Menschen als geistig-sittlichem Wesen*, by Pierre Lecomte du Noüy. *Deutsche Universitätszeitung* 9, no. 21 (1954): 19.
10. "Kant und die Frage nach dem 'gnädigen Gott.'" *Studium Generale* 7, no. 9 (1954): 554–570.
11. "Marginalien zur theologischen Logik Rudolf Bultmanns." *Philosophische Rundschau* 2, no. 3/4 (1954/55): 121–140.
12. Review of *Kausalität im Verständnis des Theologen und der Begründer neuzeitlicher Physik*, by Heimo Dolch. *Philosophische Rundschau* 3, no. 3/4 (1955): 198–208.
13. "Der kopernikanische Umsturz und die Weltstellung des Menschen: Eine Studie zum Zusammenhang von Naturwissenschaft und Geistesgeschichte." *Studium Generale* 8, no. 10 (1955): 637–648.
14. "Die Peripetie des Mannes: Über das Werk Ernest Hemingways." *Hochland* 48 (1955/56): 220–233.
15. "Rose und Feuer: Lyrik, Kritik und Drama T. S. Eliots." *Hochland* 49 (1956/57): 109–126.
16. "Einleitung." In Nikolaus von Cues: *Die Kunst der Vermutung. Auswahl aus den Schriften*, edited by Hans Blumenberg, 7–69. Bremen: Schünemann, 1957.

17. "Autonomie und Theonomie." In *Religion in Geschichte und Gegenwart*, 1:788–792. Tübingen: Mohr Siebeck, 1957.
18. "Kosmos und System: Aus der Genesis der kopernikanischen Welt." *Studium Generale* 10, no. 2 (1957): 61–80.
19. ***"'Nachahmung der Natur': Zur Vorgeschichte der Idee des schöpferischen Menschen." *Studium Generale* 10, no. 5 (1957): 266–283.
  19.1. English as: "'Imitation of Nature': Toward a Prehistory of the Idea of the Creative Being." Translated by Anna Wertz. *Qui Parle* 12, no. 1 (2000): 17–54.
20. ***"Licht als Metapher der Wahrheit: Im Vorfeld der philosophischen Begriffsbildung." *Studium Generale* 10, no. 7 (1957): 432–447.
  20.1. English as: "Light as a Metaphor for Truth: At the Preliminary Stage of Philosophical Concept Formation." In *Modernity and the Hegemony of Vision*, edited by David Michael Levin, 30–86. Berkeley: University of California Press, 1993.
21. ***"Mythos und Ethos Amerikas im Werk William Faulkners." *Hochland* 50 (1957/58): 234–250.
22. "Epochenschwelle und Rezeption." *Philosophische Rundschau* 6 (1958): 94–120.
23. "Kritik und Rezeption antiker Philosophie in der Patristik: Strukturanalysen zu einer Morphologie der Tradition." *Studium Generale* 12, no. 8 (1959): 485–497.
24. "Hylemorphismus." In *Religion in Geschichte und Gegenwart*, 3:499–500. Tübingen: Mohr Siebeck, 1959.
25. "Individuation und Individualität." In *Religion in Geschichte und Gegenwart*, 3:720–722. Tübingen: Mohr Siebeck, 1959.
26. "Kontingenz." In *Religion in Geschichte und Gegenwart*, 3:1793–1794. Tübingen: Mohr Siebeck, 1959.
27. Review of *Geschichte und Eschatologie*, by Rudolf Bultmann." *Gnomon* 31, no. 2 (1959): 163–166.
28. "Das dritte Höhlengleichnis." *Filosofia* 11 (1960): 705–722.
29. "Melanchtons Einspruch gegen Kopernikus: Zur Geschiche der Dissoziaton von Theologie und Naturwissenschaft." *Studium Generale* 13, no. 3 (1960): 174–112.
30. "Naturalismus. I. Naturalismus und Supranaturalismus." In *Religion in Geschichte und Gegenwart*, 4:1332–1336. Tübingen: Mohr Siebeck, 1960.
31. "Optimismus und Pessimismus." In *Religion in Geschichte und Gegenwart*, 4:1661–1664. Tübingen: Mohr Siebeck, 1960.
32. "Paradigmen zu einer Metaphorologie." *Archiv für Begriffsgeschichte* 6 (1960): 7–142.
33. ***"Weltbilder und Weltmodelle." *Nachrichten der Gießener Hochschulgesellschaft* 30 (1961): 67–75.
34. "Die Bedeutung der Philosophie für unsere Zukunft." In *Europa-Gespräch 1961: Die voraussehbare Zukunft*, edited by Amt für Kultur Volksbildung und Schulverwaltung der Stadt Wien, 127–140. Vienna: Verlag für Jugend und Volk, 1961.

35. "Augustins Anteil an der Geschichte des Begriffs der theoretischen Neugierde." *Revue des Études Augustiniennes* 7 (1961): 35–70.
36. "'Curiositas' und 'veritas': Zur Ideengeschichte von Augustin, *Confessiones* X 35." In *Studia Patristica: Papers Presented at the Third International Conference on Patristic Studies Held at Christ Church, Oxford, 1959*, edited by F. L. Cross, 6:294–302. Berlin: Akademie, 1962.
37. "Ordnungsschwund und Selbstbehauptung: Über Weltverstehen und Weltverhalten im Werden der technischen Epoche." In *Das Problem der Ordnung: VI. Deutscher Kongreß für Philosophie, München 1960*, edited by Helmut Kuhn and Franz Wiedmann, 37–57. Meisenheim am Glan: Hain, 1962.
38. "Die Vorbereitung der Neuzeit." *Philosophische Rundschau* 9, no. 2/3 (1962): 81–133.
39. "Substanz." In *Religion in Geschichte und Gegenwart*, 6: 674–677. Tübingen: Mohr Siebeck, 1962.
40. "Transzendenz und Immanenz." In *Religion in Geschichte und Gegenwart*, 6: 989–997. Tübingen: Mohr Siebeck, 1962.
41. ***"Wirklichkeitsbegriff und Möglichkeit des Romans." In *Nachahmung und Illusion: Kolloquium Giessen, Juni 1963. Vorlagen und Verhandlungen*, edited by Hans Robert Jauß, Poetik und Hermeneutik I, 9–27. Munich: Eidos, 1964.
    41.1. English as: "The Concept of Reality and the Possibility of the Novel." In *New Perspectives in German Literary Criticism: A Collection of Essays*, edited by Richard E. Amacher and Victor Lange, 29–48. Princeton, NJ: Princeton University Press, 1979.
42. ***"Lebenswelt und Technisierung unter Aspekten der Phänomenologie." *Filosofia* 14, no. 4 (1963): 855–884.
43. ***"'Säkularisation': Kritik einer Kategorie historischer Illegitimität." In *Die Philosophie und die Frage nach dem Fortschritt: Verhandlungen des Siebten Deutschen Kongresses für Philosophie, Münster 1962*, edited by Helmut Kuhn and Franz Wiedmann, 240–265. Munich: Pustet, 1964.
44. ***"Sokrates und das *objet ambigu*: Paul Valérys Auseinandersetzung mit der Tradition der Ontologie des ästhetischen Gegenstandes." In *EPIMELEIA: Die Sorge der Philosophie um den Menschen. Festschrift für Helmut Kuhn*, edited by Franz Wiedemann, 285–323. Munich: Pustet, 1964.
45. "Kopernikus im Selbstverständnis der Neuzeit." *Akademie der Wissenschaften und Literatur in Mainz: Abhandlungen der geistes- und sozialwissenschaftlichen Klasse* 14, no. 5 (1964): 339–368.
46. "Das Fernrohr und die Ohnmacht der Wahrheit." In Galileo Galilei, *Siderius Nuncius: Nachricht von neuen Sternen*, 5–73. Frankfurt am Main: Insel, 1965.
47. ***"Sprachsituation und immanente Poetik." In *Immanente Ästhetik—Ästhetische Reflexion: Lyrik als Paradigma der Moderne*, edited by Wolfgang Iser, Poetik und Hermeneutik II, 145–155. Munich: Fink, 1966.

48. * * * "Die essentielle Vieldeutigkeit des ästhetischen Gegenstandes." In *Kritik und Metaphysik: Heinz Heimsoeth zum achtzigsten Geburtstag*, edited by Friedrich Kaulbach and Joachim Ritter, 174–179. Berlin: de Gruyter, 1966.

49. "Contemplator Caeli." In *Orbis Scriptus: Festschrift für Dmitrij Tschizewskij zum 70. Geburtstag*, edited by Dietrich Gerhardt, Wiktor Weintraub, and Hans-Jürgen zum Winkel, 113–124. Munich: Fink, 1966.

50. "Nachruf auf Erich Rothacker. Gehalten am 29. April 1966 in der öffentlichen Sitzung der Akademie der Wissenschaften und der Literatur in Mainz." *Jahrbuch der Akademie der Wissenschaften und der Literatur in Mainz* 16 (1966): 70–76.

51. "Die Vorbereitung der Aufklärung als Rechtfertigung der theoretischen Neugierde." In *Europäische Aufklärung: Herbert Dieckmann zum 60. Geburtstag*, edited by Hugo Friedrich and Fritz Schalk, 23–45. Munich: Fink, 1967.

52. "Nachbemerkung zum Bericht über das Archiv für Begriffsgeschichte." *Jahrbuch der Akademie der Wissenschaften und der Literatur in Mainz* 17 (1967): 79–78.

53. * * * "Wirklichkeitsbegriff und Staatstheorie." *Schweizer Monatshefte* 48, no. 2 (1968/69): 121–146.

54. "Das Universum eines Ketzers." In Giordano Bruno, *Das Aschermittwochsmahl*, edited by Hans Blumenberg, 7–51. Frankfurt am Main: Insel, 1969.

55. "Selbsterhaltung und Beharrung: Zur Konstitution der neuzeitlichen Rationalität." *Akademie der Wissenschaften und Literatur in Mainz: Abhandlungen der geistes- und sozialwissenschaftlichen Klasse* 19, no. 11 (1969): 335–383.

   55.1. English as: "Self-Preservation and Inertia: On the Constitution of Modern Rationality." In *Contemporary German Philosophy*, edited by Darrell E. Christensen, Manfred Riedel, Robert Spaemann, Reiner Wiehl, and Wolfgang Wieland, 3:209–256. University Park: Pennsylvania State University Press, 1983.

56. "Neugierde und Wissenstrieb: Supplemente zur Curiositas." *Archiv für Begriffsgeschichte* 14, no. 1 (1970): 7–40.

57. * * * "Approccio antropologico all'attualità della retorica." *Il Verri. Rivista di Letteratura* no. 35/36 (1971): 49–72.

   57.1. German as: "Anthropologische Annäherung an die Aktualität der Rhetorik." In B 8, 105–136.

   57.2. English as: "An Anthropological Approach to the Contemporary Significance of Rhetoric." In *After Philosophy: End or Transformation?*, edited by Kenneth Baynes, James Bohman, and Thomas McCarthy, 429–458. Cambridge, MA: MIT Press, 1987.

58. "Wirklichkeitsbegriff und Wirkungspotential des Mythos." In *Terror und Spiel: Probleme der Mythenrezeption*, edited by Manfred Fuhrmann, Poetik und Hermeneutik IV, 11–66. Munich: Fink, 1971.

59. "Neoplatonismen und Pseudoplatonismen in der Kosmologie und Mechanik der frühen Neuzeit." In *Le Néoplatonisme*, edited by Pierre Maxime Schuhl and Pierre Hadot, 447–471. Paris: Éditions du Centre national de la recherche scientifique, 1971.

60. "Pseudoplatonismen in der Naturwissenschaft der frühen Neuzeit." In *Akademie der Wissenschaften und der Literatur in Mainz: Abhandlungen der geistes- und sozialwissenschaftlichen Klasse* 21, no. 1 (1971): 3–34.

61. ***"Beobachtungen an Metaphern." *Archiv für Begriffsgeschichte* 15, no. 2 (1971): 161–214.

62. "Die kopernikanische Konsequenz für den Zeitbegriff." In *Colloquia Copernicana I: Études sur l'audience de la théorie héliocentrique*, 57–77. Wrocław: Ossolineum, 1972.

63. "The Life-World and the Concept of Reality." In *Life-World and Consciousness: Essays for Aron Gurwitsch*, edited by Lester E. Embree, 425–444. Evanston, IL: Northwestern University Press, 1972.
    63.1. German as "Lebenswelt und Wirklichkeitsbegriff." In B 29, 157–180.

64. "Der archimedische Punkt des Celio Calcagnini." In *Studia Humanitatis: Ernesto Grassi zum 70. Geburtstag*, edited by Eginhard Horsa and Eckhard Keßler, 103–112. Munich: Fink, 1973.

65. "Kopernikus und das Pathos der Vernunft: Das Denken der Neuzeit im Zeichen der kopernikanischen Wende." *Evangelische Kommentare* 6, no. 8 (1973): 460–465.

66. "On a Lineage of the Idea of Progress." Translated by E. B. Ashton. *Social Research* 41, no. 1 (1974): 5–27.

67. ***"Vorbemerkungen zum Wirklichkeitsbegriff." *Akademie der Wissenschaften und Literatur in Mainz: Abhandlungen der geistes- und sozialwissenschaftlichen Klasse* 24, no. 4 (1974): 3–10.

68. "Ernst Cassirers gedenkend: Rede bei der Entgegennahme des Kuno-Fischer-Preises der Universität Heidelberg im Juli 1974." *Revue Internationale de Philosophie* 28 (1974): 456–463.

69. "Der Sturz des Protophilosophen: Zur Komik der reinen Theorie—anhand einer Rezeptionsgeschichte der Thales-Anekdote." In *Das Komische*, edited by Wolfgang Preisendanz and Rainer Warning, Poetik und Hermeneutik VII, 11–64. Munich: Fink, 1976.

70. "Komik in der diachronen Perspektive." In *Das Komische*, 408–409.

71. "Wer sollte vom Lachen der Magd betroffen sein? Eine Duplik." In *Das Komische*, 437–44.

72. "Unernst als geschichtliche Qualität." In *Das Komische*, 441–444.

73. "Geld oder Leben: Eine metaphorologische Studie zur Konsistenz der Philosophie Georg Simmels." In *Ästhetik und Soziologie um die Jahrhundertwende: Georg Simmel*, edited by Hannes Böhringer and Karlfried Gründer, 121–134. Frankfurt am Main: Klostermann, 1976.
    73.1. English as: "Money or Life: Metaphors of Georg Simmel's Philosophy." Translated by Robert Savage. *Theory, Culture & Society* 29, no. 7/8 (2013): 249–262.

74. "Versuch zu einer immanenten Geschichte der copernicanischen Theorie." In *Science and History: Studies in Honor of Edward Rosen*, 473–486. Wrocław: Ossolineum, 1978.

75. ***"Ausblick auf eine Theorie der Unbegrifflichkeit." In B 5, 75–93.

   75.1. English as: "Prospect for a Theory of Nonconceptuality." In *Shipwreck with Spectator*, translated by Steven Rendall, 81–102. Cambridge, MA: MIT Press, 1997.

76. "Irdische und himmlische Bücher." *Akzente* 26, no. 6 (1979): 619–631.

77. "Rechtfertigung der Neugierde als Vorbereitung der Aufklärung." In *Erforschung der deutschen Aufklärung*, edited by Peter Pütz, 81–100. Königstein/Taunus: Athenäum, 1980.

78. ***"Nachdenklichkeit." *Neue Zürcher Zeitung*, November 22, 1980.

   78.1. English as: "Pensiveness." Translated by David Adams. *Caliban* 6 (1989): 51–55.

79. "Eine imaginäre Universalbibliothek." *Akzente* 28, no. 1 (1981): 27–40.

80. "Glossen zu Fabeln." *Akzente* 28, no. 4 (1981): 340–344.

81. "An Georg Rosenthal erinnernd." In *Katharineum zu Lübeck: Festschrift zum 450jährigen Bestehen, 19. März 1981*, edited by Bund der Freunde des Katharineums, 55–57. Lübeck: Bund der Freunde des Katharineums, 1981.

82. ***"Momente Goethes." *Akzente* 29, no. 1 (1982): 43–55.

83. "*Mon Faust* in Erfurt." *Akzente* 30, no. 1 (1983): 42–57.

84. ***"Über den Rand der Wirklichkeit hinaus: Drei Kurzessays." *Akzente* 30, no. 1 (1983): 16–27.

85. "Glossen zu Anekdoten." *Akzente* 30, no. 1 (1983): 28–41.

86. "Wolf und Lamm: Vier Glossen zur Fabel." *Akzente* 30, no. 5 (1983): 389–392.

87. "Verfehlungen: Glossen zu Anekdoten." *Akzente* 31, no. 5 (1984): 390–396.

88. ***"Vom Unverstand: Glossen zu drei Fabeln." *Neue Zürcher Zeitung*, March 24, 1984.

89. ***"Unbekanntes von Äsop: Aus neuen Fabelfunden." *Neue Zürcher Zeitung*, October 5/6, 1985.

90. "Religionsgespräche." *Akzente* 33 no. 6 (1986): 502–520.

91. "Das Sein—ein MacGuffin: Wie man sich Lust am Denken erhält." *Frankfurter Allgemeine Zeitung*, May 27, 1987.

   91.1. English as: "Being—A MacGuffin: How to Preserve the Desire to Think." Translated by David Adams. *Salmagundi* no. 90/91 (1991): 191–193.

92. "Gleichgültig wann? Über Zeitindifferenz." *Frankfurter Allgemeine Zeitung*, December 30, 1987.

   92.1. English as: "Does It Matter When? On Time Indifference." Translated by David Adams. *Philosophy and Literature* 22, no. 1 (1998): 212–218.

93. "Nächtlicher Anstand: Glossen zu Anekdoten." *Akzente* 35, no. 1 (1988): 42–55.

94. "Die Tötung des Zeugen." In *Die Blinden: Oper von Beat Furrer*, n.p. Vienna: Wiener Staatsoper, 1989.

95. "Wolf und Lamm und mehr als ein Ende." *Akzente* 36, no. 1 (1989): 18–27.

96. "Epigonenwallfahrt." *Akzente* 37, no. 3 (1990): 272–282.

97. "Lebensgedichte: Einiges aus Theodor Fontanes Vielem." *Akzente* 38, no. 1 (1991): 7–28.

98. "Lichtenbergs Paradox." *Akzente* 39, no. 1 (1992): 4–18.

99. "Religionspädagogik." *Arbeitshilfe für den evangelischen Religionsunterricht an Gymnasien* 50 (1992): 9–13.

100. " 'Nichts ist kürzer als Dank': Über ein Wort Theodor Fontanes." *Park: Zeitschrift für neue Literatur* 16, no. 43/44 (1992): 18–19.

101. "Gegenwart, vergiftet zwischen Vergangenheit und Zukunft: Arthur Schnitzlers Pathologie der Eifersucht." *Park: Zeitschrift für neue Literatur* 17, no. 45/46 (1993): 22–27.

102. *** "Vorstoss ins ewige Schweigen: Ein Jahrhundert nach der Ausfahrt der *Fram*." *Neue Zürcher Zeitung*, December 24, 1993.

103. "Egestas: Dem Sprachzauber auf die Schliche kommen." In *Wörterbuch des Friedens*, edited by Karl Dedecius, 41–42. Mannheim: Dudenverlag, 1993.

104. "Glossen zu Gedichten." *Akzente* 44, no. 3 (1997): 245–262.

105. "Repräsentant mit Sinn fürs Mythische: Texte aus dem Nachlaß. Thomas Mann in seinen Tagebüchern." *Neue Rundschau* 109, no. 1 (1998): 9–29.

106. "Das Gewand des Traums: Zur Metaphorik von Verhüllung und Enthüllung bei Freud." *Neue Rundschau* 117, no. 1 (2006): 67–80.

107. "Atommoral: Ein Gegenstück zur Atomstrategie." *Marbacher Magazin*, no. 123/124 (2008): 125–141.

108. "Technik und Wahrheit." *Zeitschrift für Kulturphilosophie* 2, no. 1 (2008): 137–143.

109. "Thesen zu einer Metaphorologie." *Archiv für Begriffsgeschichte* 53 (2011): 186–189.

110. "Paul Valérys möglicher Leonardo da Vinci: Vortrag in der Akademie der Künste in Berlin am 21. 4. 1966." *Forschungen zu Paul Valéry/ Recherches Valéryennes* 25 (2012): 193–227.

111. "Dogmatische und rationale Analyse von Motivationen des technischen Fortschritts." *Zeitschrift für Kulturphilosophie* 7, no. 2 (2013): 407–422.

112. " 'Und das ist mir von der Liebe zur Kirche geblieben': Hans Blumenbergs letzter Brief." *Internationale Katholische Zeitschrift Communio* 43, no. 3 (2014): 173–181.

113. "Automation." In *Metaphorologie, Anthropologie, Phänomenologie: Neue Forschungen zum Nachlass Hans Blumenbergs*, edited by Alberto Fragio, Martina Philippi, and Josefa Ros Velasco. Freiburg: Alber, 2019.

Compiled by Hannes Bajohr

INDEX

Abeken, Bernhard Rudolf, 535
absolute metaphors, 173–76, 213, 215, 218, 240, 243, 287
action, in anthropological perspective, 260–63
actio per distans, 18, 260–63
Adorno, Theodor W., 12, 16, 109n32
Aesop, 528–29, 562–63, 566–70
aesthetics: ambiguity as feature of, 14, 125, 246, 437–38, 441–48, 521–23; anthropological approach to, 269–71; Blumenberg's scholarly contributions to, 13–14; enjoyment as feature of, 311, 440, 459; human creativity as feature of, 311; inapplicable to nature, 354–55; and interpretation, 443, 445–47, 454; Kantian conception of, 288, 441; metaphor and, 246, 269; of poetic language, 456–65; reality in relation

to, 269–70; rhetoric and, 178–79, 194; and subjectivity, 441, 442, 445, 447; surprise as feature of, 269–71; theory compared to, 125, 458; truth and, 499–501; Valéry's, 408–13, 421–24, 431–37, 439, 447, 449, 456–57, 460–62, 464–65. *See also* art
airplanes, 322–23
Akzente (journal), 21
Albertus Magnus, 161, 346
d'Alembert, Jean le Rond, 166–67, 506
allegory, 442–44. *See also* cave imagery
Alsberg, Paul, 188
ambiguity: aesthetics/art characterized by, 14, 125, 246, 437–38, 441–48, 521–23; as feature of metaphor, 246; and objecthood, 416, 418, 424, 442; phenomenological analysis and, 38–39; philosophical language and,

CPSIA information can be obtained
at www.ICGtesting.com
Printed in the USA
LVHW092117230220
647811LV00009BA/30